AMERICA IN THE TWENTIETH CENTURY

COMING OF AGE

DAVID R. CONTOSTA
Chestnut Hill College

ROBERT MUCCIGROSSO
Brooklyn College of the
City University of New York

HARPER & ROW, PUBLISHERS, New York
Cambridge, Philadelphia, San Francisco, Washington,
London, Mexico City, São Paulo, Singapore, Sydney

Sponsoring Editor: Robert Miller
Project Editor: Jo-Ann Goldfarb
Text Design Adaptation: Mina Greenstein
Cover Design: José R. Fanfrias
Cover Photos: National Archives (top and bottom left); Library of Congress
 (top right); NASA (bottom right)
Text Art: Fineline Illustrations, Inc.
Photo Research: Mira Schachne
Production Manager: Willie Lane
Compositor: Waldman Graphics, Inc.
Printer and Binder: R. R. Donnelley & Sons Company
Cover Printer: N.E.B.C.

America in the Twentieth Century: Coming of Age

Copyright © 1988 by Harper & Row, Publishers, Inc.

All rights reserved. Printed in the United States of America. No part of this
book may be used or reproduced in any manner whatsoever without written
permission, except in the case of brief quotations embodied in critical articles
and reviews. For information address Harper & Row, Publishers, Inc.,
10 East 53d Street, New York, NY 10022.

Library of Congress Cataloging-in-Publication Data

Contosta, David R.
 America in the twentieth century.

 Includes index.
 1. United States—Civilization—20th century.
I. Muccigrosso, Robert. II. Title.
E169.1.C717 1988   973.92   87-19659
ISBN 0-06-044636-6

87 88 89 90 9 8 7 6 5 4 3 2 1

Photo Credits

The photos are reproduced by courtesy of the sources listed alphabetically as follows (the numbers refer to the pages on which the photos appear): **AP/Wide World Photos** 353, 362, 375, 397, 441. **Geraldine Ferraro (photo by Rocco Galatioto)** 435. **Jeane Kirkpatrick** 442. **Lee Iacocca** 423. **Library of Congress** 12, 13, 28, 35, 46, 56, 61, 67, 69, 89, 113, 121, 141, 153, 165, 180, 182, 189, 208, 228, 261, 262, 308, 365, 380, 387, 401, 428. **NASA** 325. **National Archives** 18, 19, 21, 26, 39, 40, 43, 50, 54, 55, 57, 73, 77, 80, 82, 88, 102, 106, 109, 112, 116, 124, 128, 131, 136, 139, 145, 148, 152, 156, 159, 161, 170, 174, 186, 194, 199, 203, 212, 213, 217, 219, 223, 226, 233, 235, 242, 249, 256, 263, 271, 274, 276, 279, 280, 283, 290, 293, 301, 303, 313, 314, 315, 321, 332, 334, 335, 337, 339, 346, 361, 369, 384, 389, 405, 414, 415. **Navy Department** 432.

The photos accompanying the Oral Histories are used with the permission of the speakers: Mary W. Bond 6; Joseph Galante 126; Ruth H. Rinehart 172; Ralph Shuping 224; Philip Hazelton 298; Fran Boyce 358; Meri Jiménez (photo by David R. Contosta) 413.

To Meri Contosta and
To the memory of
Henry and Egidia Muccigrosso

Contents

Preface   *xiii*

Prologue: An Age of Transformation   *1*

1   THE SOCIAL FABRIC IN A NEW CENTURY   5

American Society   5

**ORAL HISTORY: Growing Up in the Twentieth Century
     Mary W. Bond   6**

American Culture   17

BIOGRAPHICAL SKETCH: Scott Joplin   28

2   THE PROGRESSIVE IMPULSE   31

The Progressive Temperament   32
The Progressive Agenda   36

BIOGRAPHICAL SKETCH: Margaret Sanger   46

3   THE POLITICS OF REFORM   49

Reforming the Cities   49
State Reform   52

viii CONTENTS

Theodore Roosevelt and the Modern Presidency 55
The Trials of William Howard Taft 61
Election of 1912 64
Wilsonian Democracy 66
BIOGRAPHICAL SKETCH: Louis D. Brandeis 69

4 FOREIGN POLICY COMES OF AGE 72

Governing the New Empire 72
The Open Door and the Far East 75
Reforming the Army and Navy 76
Roosevelt: The Responsibilties of Power 77
Taft's Dollar Diplomacy 83
Wilson and Missionary Diplomacy 85
BIOGRAPHICAL SKETCH: Elihu Root 89

5 MAKING THE WORLD SAFE FOR DEMOCRACY 92

From Neutrality to Involvement 93
HISTORIANS DEBATE: American Intervention in World War I 99
The Nation at War 100
The Search for Peace 110
BIOGRAPHICAL SKETCH: John J. Pershing 116

6 LIFE IN THE NEW ERA 119

The New Prosperity 119
Cultural Conflicts in the New Era 122
**ORAL HISTORY: Growing Up in the Twentieth Century
Joseph Galante 126**
Popular Amusements and the Arts 133
BIOGRAPHICAL SKETCH: Rudolph Valentino 141

7 FROM NORMALCY TO DEPRESSION 144

The Harding Years 144
Calvin Coolidge and the Politics of Restraint 147
Hoover and the Politics of Depression 153
BIOGRAPHICAL SKETCH: Andrew Mellon 161

CONTENTS ix

8 NEW DEAL AMERICA 164

Launching the New Deal 165

ORAL HISTORY: Growing Up in the Twentieth Century Ruth H. Rinehart 172

The Second Administration 178
Life and Culture of the Thirties 184

HISTORIANS DEBATE: The New Deal 185

BIOGRAPHICAL SKETCH: Charles E. Coughlin 189

9 FOREIGN AFFAIRS BETWEEN THE WORLD WARS 192

Postwar Diplomacy 192
The Great Depression and Foreign Policy 198

HISTORIANS DEBATE: Pearl Harbor 210

BIOGRAPHICAL SKETCH: Charles A. Lindbergh, Jr. 213

10 AMERICA IN A WORLD AT WAR 216

Defeating the Third Reich 216
Turnabout in the East 222

ORAL HISTORY: Growing Up in the Twentieth Century Ralph Shuping 224

Big Three Diplomacy 227
Fighting the War at Home 229
Politics as Usual 238
Planning for Peace 240

BIOGRAPHICAL SKETCH: George S. Patton 242

11 WAR TO COLD WAR 245

HISTORIANS DEBATE: The Origins of the Cold War 246

The Roots of Enmity 247
Getting Tough with the Soviets 248
The Lines Harden 251
An Anti-Communist Bloc 253
A Not-So-Cold War in Asia 257

BIOGRAPHICAL SKETCH: J. Robert Oppenheimer 263

x   CONTENTS

12 FROM THE FAIR DEAL TO THE MIDDLE WAY   266

Truman Takes Charge   267
Truman's Second Term   272
Anticommunism and Cold War Spies   273
Victorious Republicans   277
Eisenhower's Middle Way   280
Eisenhower and the World   285
Confronting the Soviets   288

HISTORIANS DEBATE: Dwight D. Eisenhower   290

BIOGRAPHICAL SKETCH: John Foster Dulles   292

13 A CONTENTED SOCIETY   296

The Contours of Prosperity   297

**ORAL HISTORY: Growing Up in the Twentieth Century
     Philip Hazelton   298**

Social Critics   306
Popular Culture   307
Literature and the Arts   311

BIOGRAPHICAL SKETCH: Norman Vincent Peale   315

14 NEW FRONTIERS—AT HOME AND ABROAD   318

Nixon versus Kennedy   318
Glamour in the White House   320
Facing a Hostile World   322
The New Frontier at Home   328
Lyndon Johnson Takes the Helm   331
The Vietnam Quagmire   341
Nixon's Narrow Victory   344

BIOGRAPHICAL SKETCH: Martin Luther King, Jr.   346

15 REVOLT AND REACTION   349

Power in Many Colors and Forms   350
The Sexual Revolution   354
Youth Rebellion and Counterculture   356

**ORAL HISTORY: Growing Up in the Twentieth Century
     Fran Boyce   358**

CONTENTS   xi

The Nixon White House   364
The Imperial Presidency   370

BIOGRAPHICAL SKETCH: Joan Baez   375

16   CRISIS OF CONFIDENCE   379

The Trials of Gerald Ford   379
The Nation's Bicentennial   384
The Bicentennial Election   385
Challenges at Home   387
The Burger Court   390
Ford and Carter Foreign Policy   392
Enter Ronald Reagan   398

BIOGRAPHICAL SKETCH: Nelson A. Rockefeller   401

17   A CHANGING SOCIETY   404

Science and Technology   405
Economic and Demographic Shifts   408

**ORAL HISTORY: Growing Up in the Twentieth Century
          Meri Jiménez   413**

Religious Trends   414
The New Conservatism   417
Life Styles   419
Education   421

BIOGRAPHICAL SKETCH: Lee Iacocca   422

18   THE REAGAN YEARS   425

Domestic Affairs   425
Foreign Policy   429
The Election of 1984   434
Second Term   436

BIOGRAPHICAL SKETCH: Jeane J. Kirkpatrick   442

Epilogue: Coming of Age   445
Index   447

Preface

We offer this textbook in the belief that history has as much to say about the present as it does about the past, for the present has been fashioned by the past, literally molded by thousands of prior ideas and actions from all over the world. This inescapable connection between past and present applies to individuals and groups alike. Physicians compile medical histories for patients because they know that current maladies may have their roots in past illnesses or even in the genes of remote ancestors. The psychotherapist likewise probes into earlier experiences in search of clues to present conditions. Even the process of getting to know a fellow human being is a sort of historical reconstruction, as one gradually exchanges information about ethnic, religious, familial, geographic, educational, and professional backgrounds with a would-be friend.

Churches, schools, neighborhoods, business establishments, and fraternal organizations also have histories that have made them what they are. Nations, too, are delineated by their pasts, and the United States is no exception. Unemployment, oil shortages, racial strife, rising divorce rates, demographic shifts, and changing architectural styles—along with terrorism, war, and disarmament talks—can only be understood through their historical antecedents. And before tackling any problem, nations as well as individuals must begin by uncovering their causes in the near or distant past.

Even the ability to plan ahead depends on a knowledge of history, whether personal, regional, or international. Career expectations, for example, are largely projections from others' experiences in the field. In the same way, weather forecasters suppose that similar meteorological patterns in the future will produce pretty much the same results as they have in the past.

This is not to say that history will repeat itself exactly, or that humankind is a prisoner of prior behavior or trends. Each generation retains some freedom to forge its own future. But without a knowledge of the past, both individuals and communities will be helpless to grasp just how they arrived at the present moment or to project the consequences of present and future actions. To this extent all men and women possess a historical sense. Without it, they would be much like victims of severe amnesia—disoriented, bewildered, and largely helpless to cope with the world around them.

Present-day Americans have been shaped directly by the ideas and experiences of the twentieth century, some of them monumental and terrifying, others unheralded or subtle in their effects. However they have arrived or affected the American people, we

xiv   PREFACE

have tried to present these movements and events in a way that will give students a better sense of their own lives. We have written about the nation's emergence as a global power, the rapid growth of presidential authority, a widespread but uneven prosperity, the continuance of ethnic and religious pluralism, the ongoing struggle for liberation among women and minorities, debates over manners and morals, and the maturation of arts and letters. And although we have nowhere slighted political subjects, we have not assumed that politics have been the primary force in molding recent America. Instead, we have tried to achieve a balance among social, cultural, intellectual, economic, and political factors.

Since most of our readers will be college students, we have devoted considerable space to issues that will interest them: the evolution of popular music, the growth of spectator sports, the impact of journalism and the mass media, the sexual revolution, and the cinema as an expression of national life. For the same reason, we have included seven oral interviews of men and women who describe what it was like to grow up at various periods during the twentieth century. The biographical sketches at the end of each chapter should remind students further that history is made by real people whose lives are similarly shaped by its course. We have also tried to show through our "Historians Debate" boxes just how historians themselves have helped to form the ongoing dialogue between past and present.

Finally, the authors would like to acknowledge the many individuals who have helped them along the way. We wish to thank the following historians who have read part or all of the manuscript and whose criticisms have provided much benefit: John Bodnar, Indiana University; David Burton, St. Joseph's University; Richard Crepeau, University of Central Florida; Charles M. Dobbs, Metropolitan State College; Gary Fink, Georgia State University; Joseph P. Hobbs, North Carolina State University; Thomas Kessner, Kingsborough Community College; Robert La Forte, North Texas State University; Robert Levine, University of Miami; Robert F. Maddox, Marshall University; Samuel McSeveney, Vanderbilt University; William L. O'Neill, Rutgers University; Robert Pierce, Foothill College; Jerry Rodnitzky, University of Texas-Arlington; Richard B. Sherman, The College of William and Mary; Sara Lee Silberman, Connecticut College.

John Lukacs and Head Librarian Helen Hayes of Chestnut Hill College deserve recognition for their assistance. So, too, do the staffs of our respective college libraries, the Prints and Photographic Division of the Library of Congress, the Music Division of the Library of Congress, and the National Archives.

Finally, we owe a special debt of gratitude to various persons at Harper & Row. Marianne Russell, our executive editor, and Robert Miller, our sponsoring editor, have generously given of their time, patience, and knowledge to encourage us and to see the project through to completion. Warm thanks are additionally due to Jo-Ann Goldfarb, our fine project editor, and to Robert Brainerd, our copyeditor. Marie O'Sullivan has also provided useful support.

David R. Contosta
Chestnut Hill College

Robert Muccigrosso
Brooklyn College of the
City University of New York

AMERICA IN THE TWENTIETH CENTURY

COMING OF AGE

Prologue: An Age of Transformation

When did the twentieth century begin? Most will answer, "January 1, 1900," but in fact 1900 was the last year of the nineteenth century. Round numbers are impressive and the confusion is therefore understandable, but for historians the question of beginnings is more difficult, as historical movements have shown scant regard for convenient dates on a calendar. Diplomatic historians might well conclude that the twentieth century began in 1898 with the Spanish-American War, or even three years earlier over the Venezuelan crisis of 1895. Political historians will doubtless choose the crucial election of 1896, while the economic historian will want to focus on the financial panic of 1893 and the ensuing depression.

In truth, many of the forces that have shaped the twentieth century had their origins in the latter decades of the nineteenth century and particularly in the 1890s. Chief among them was industrialization. It was industry that attracted natives and immigrants alike to the cities, that undermined the personal element in economic exchange, and that prompted most of the cries for social, economic, and political reform. It was industry that gave the United States the potential to become a great world power within the space of a single generation.

With rapid industrialization and urbanization had come numerous "growing pains" and the need for large-scale readjustment. While a handful of daring entrepreneurs had reaped undreamed-of fortunes, others were left behind in the wake or became hostages to the new machinery and industrial organization. And as more and more Americans came to depend on factories for jobs, economic depressions became increasingly severe and widespread. Loud protests and demands for governmental action understandably arose. Workers tried to organize and struck for better pay and safer working conditions; farmers formed granges, alliances, and finally the Populist party. Consumers and smaller

1

businessmen demanded curbs on big business, while midwestern farmers and others dependent upon the railroads pushed for regulation of freight rates. Congress created an Interstate Commerce Commission in 1887 and three years later passed the Sherman Antitrust Act. Both were disappointing in many respects, but the way had been opened for more effective regulation in the future.

Politics were also in need of reform as the century came to a close. Most of the larger cities were in the grip of corrupt bosses and their attendant "machines." Although they often assisted the poor with jobs, patronage, and even gifts of food and fuel, they were unwilling and unable to provide systematic solutions for urban problems like crime, public health, or routine maintenance. And on the national level the country had seen a series of relatively weak presidents whose power had been sapped by Congressional patronage, political fragmentation, and the widely held belief that the federal government should remain neutral on economic matters. The election of William McKinley to the presidency in 1896 signaled a shift toward Republican predominance and the beginnings of a more effective executive branch, but few could appreciate the change.

The decision to annex an island empire following the Spanish-American War also proved difficult and controversial. Some believed that taking the Philippines in particular would provide a stepping stone to large markets in Asia, while others welcomed a chance to join the other colonial powers in uplifting the more benighted peoples of the earth. Yet many Americans feared that their presence in the Far East would only stir up friction and possibly war with the great powers, and there were those who saw the new imperialism as a betrayal of the nation's own revolutionary heritage.

In ideas and the arts the United States was likewise awash with change. The painter Thomas Eakins had been scandalizing the public for several decades with his controversial teaching methods and highly realistic canvases. Daring architects such as Louis Sullivan were beginning to create tall buildings with structural steel supports and permitting the interior skeleton to dictate exterior design. And while the skyscraper was being born, William James, John Dewey, and other philosophers questioned the existence of scientific and moral absolutes, setting off an intellectual revolution that would challenge some of the most basic tenets of Western life and thought.

For Henry Adams, a brilliant critic and descendent of two American presidents, the cultural and economic upheaval of the late nineteenth century was profoundly unsettling. Mankind confronted "a far vaster universe," he wrote, "where all the old roads ran about in every direction, overrunning, dividing, subdividing, stopping abruptly, vanishing slowly, with side-paths that led nowhere, and sequences that could not be proved."

Adams clearly believed that the twentieth century would be filled with unparalleled problems and anxieties. Coincidentally or not, these new difficulties arose as the United States settled its vast interior and began functioning as a mature member of the world community. At the same time, fast steamships, oceanic telegraph cables, and growing international trade were making all nations more interdependent, whether they liked it or not. Traditional American desires to stay out of foreign entanglements would not die easily, nor would the old idea that the United States was under a new and perhaps divine dispensation, but Americans were soon to find that they were not exempt from the common burdens of humanity. In this sense the United States would emerge from a kind of national adolescence and "come of age" as the twentieth century unfolded.

Yet most Americans greeted the twentieth century with great expectations. The depression of the 1890s had ended, business was booming, and the country had acquired an island empire at comparatively little cost in money and men. Admittedly, there were a number of outstanding problems, but most citizens thought they could overcome them without too much difficulty. Few could imagine the enormous challenges and responsibilities that lay ahead.

1

The Social Fabric in a New Century

History represents more than a chronicle of great leaders and wars, royal edicts or constitutions. It also concerns itself, as the writer Leo Tolstoy observed, with "the life of peoples and of humanity." One cannot detail the lives of all 76 million Americans as they stood on the threshold of the twentieth century. Yet historians, by sifting through records of the past, have been able to learn much about who these people were, what kinds of lives they led, what sorts of values they cherished or despised. In sum, they have been able to portray a cross section of Americans and the fabric of their society as they struggled to come of age in the modern world.

AMERICAN SOCIETY

Class   The divisions in American society at the turn of the century were varied and complex. No one actually assigned class membership, but the outward marks of social status included such things as family name, date of arrival on American soil, ethnic background, religious affiliation, place and type of residence, leisure activities, educational achievement, yearly income, and occupation. These manifestations of social standing applied primarily to men; women, whose activities outside the home were still very restricted, generally shared the status of their fathers or husbands.

The American Upper Class   By European standards—in the sense of having a hereditary nobility—there was no real upper class in America. Social systems are relative, however, and in comparison to the way most people lived in the United States, there was unquestionably an upper class with unique privileges and characteristics. In every large city this segment was made up of several dozen families who could trace their

5

ORAL HISTORY
Growing Up in the Twentieth Century

MARY W. BOND · *born 1898*

We all went to dancing class, which the boys hated and the girls loved. We'd walk over to the Cricket Club in every-day shoes carrying a pretty little silk bag which had our dancing slippers, and when we got there we'd put on our patent leather slippers and have a wonderful time. Miss Flora Lockwood was one of our dancing teachers. I was crazy about Miss Flora—I guess a lot of us were. She had one of the most beautiful accordion-pleated gray chiffon dresses you have ever seen, and when she made a curtsy she would spread this thing out like a peacock's tail. I remember that we all had to march around the ballroom and curtsy to her and the boys had to bow.

I made my début in 1916, the last coming-out before the war. Believe it or not, we would put on our ball gowns and, again, carry our satin dancing slippers in a little bag, take trains into town, walk over to the Bellevue or the Ritz and go to a ball or party. There were also tea dances in those days, besides the dinner dances and the balls. Sometimes the mothers would come in and take a room at the Bellevue so that the dear, sweet little débutante wouldn't have to come home late and would be properly taken care of.

The tea dances were about five o'clock in the afternoon and lasted about two hours. We would return home, change into evening dresses, and go on to a dinner party or something. Some of those balls were unbelievable. I especially remember one on the roof garden of the Bellevue Hotel. The scene was a hunt, and all the waiters had to dress up in hunt clothes—"pink coat," shiny black boots, and white gloves. And they had live horses up there! They had stalls with straw in them, and we could lean over a fence as if you were at a horse race and pat the horses. I've always wondered how they got the horses up there in the hotel elevators! There was another ball where everybody had to come dressed in old-fashioned clothes. I don't remember, fortunately, whose ball that was, but the girl was a very plain and unattractive débutante. I feel sorry for her now. She was all dressed up and had to stand at the door with her parents, and we had to go through the line and curtsy.

We did waltzes and two-steps. I think that's about all. One time the orchestra leader, Meyer Davis, had all the lights turned low in the ballroom and told all the dancers to take off their shoes. We all danced in our stocking feet while the orchestra played no music, only the drums, very softly. You could hear the swishing of skirts and little shuffling noises. It was simply thrilling!

There was always plenty to eat and drink at these dinner dances and balls. At the Assembly there were scrambled eggs and champagne. When the champagne showed up the fights began. The boys would run from one table to another trying to snatch a champagne bottle away and then there'd be a fight. And I think that as time went on, there were always a few girls who belonged to a "fast" crowd. There was a room in the Bellevue where they served drinks, and some of the boys and girls used to go up there. I don't know what they did. I never got into that "set."

We didn't use the word "dating" in those days. And we didn't "go steady," as girls and boys have been doing for a couple of generations. Girls gathered as many boys around us as they could. We had different kinds of beaux, as we called them. It didn't mean that we wanted to marry them—or they us! These boys were friends: I had a horseback riding friend, a sleighing friend, a musical friend who would take me to the opera. I had a couple of older friends who had more money

than the younger ones. They would take me to the Ritz for dinner. Maybe you had your favorite boy friends, but to be considered popular you had to have a lot of them. You didn't stick to the first boy that interested you—nor he to you!

I met boys at the parties and balls, at the Cricket Club, and at friends' houses. Then they would call at the house. Sometimes when you didn't have a boy to take you to a ball, your mother would take you. Of course, my parents didn't like all the boys I saw in those days. They never really forbade me to see someone, but they gave me some good advice now and then.

The war—World War I—changed a lot of that. Once we got into the fighting, I joined the Emergency Aides. We made bandages and manned Liberty Bond booths. I also trained to be a nurse's aid at Episcopal Hospital. They sent wounded officers from England, Canada, Australia, and France to talk up the Liberty Loans. We aides had a whirl because they were marvelous men; they were utterly decent men—at least most of the ones I knew were. I was proud of my Emergency Aide uniform and of being a sergeant with chevron stripes on my sleeve. The whole war business was a thrilling experience for us.

American ancestors back to the eighteenth century or earlier. They were overwhelmingly British in background and Protestant in religion, with the Episcopal Church the preferred denomination among most of the well-to-do.

Various occupations might be pursued by individuals of these so-called old families, but at some point (and preferably before the Civil War) at least one family member had to acquire a substantial fortune that was then passed down to future generations through carefully guarded trust funds. And while the source of this money might have been a ruthless entrepreneur, it was more acceptable for his heirs to take up banking, law, or a series of corporate directorships than to engage in risky ventures themselves. Careers in medicine or the church were also quite common for gentlemen of inherited wealth and high social standing. The Lowells of Boston, the Biddles of Philadelphia, and the Astors of New York all represent this sort of passage from adventurous family founder to genteel descendant.

American upper-class suburban house, c. 1900.

By 1900 many such families had begun to leave their elite city neighborhoods in favor of prestigious railroad suburbs like Philadelphia's famous Main Line. Out of a renewed interest in their own ethnic roots—and to some extent in reaction to the millions of new immigrants from southern and eastern Europe—many of these upper-class suburbanites built houses in recognizably English or American-colonial styles. Many of their leisure activities further reflected this growing Anglo-American identity, including such English imports as polo, rowing, field hockey, fox hunting, and metropolitan gentlemen's clubs. The ancestral societies that they had founded over the past decade or so, like the Daughters of the American Revolution or the Mayflower Society, were yet another side to their self-conscious associations with the Anglo-colonial past.

Such organizations tended to make class lines more rigid than ever, effectively excluding anyone whose forebears had come to America since the Revolution. Yet another mark of high status was inclusion in the newly created *Social Register*s, which listed members of "polite society" in all the larger cities. But some in the upper strata looked to even narrower definitions of acceptability. In Philadelphia it was an invitation to the almost hereditary Assembly Balls that assured true upper-class ascription, while being among "the 400" select guests at one of Mrs. Astor's lavish parties was the most coveted badge of distinction in New York City.

These families and others of large financial means were likely to spend their summers far from sweltering city streets in the cooling sea breezes of Cape May, New Jersey, Newport, Rhode Island, or Bar Harbor, Maine. And for those who preferred the mountains, there were the not-so-simple "camps" of New York's Adirondack range.

For their children there were exclusive day schools or, for boys in particular, New England boarding schools such as St. Paul's, Exeter, Groton, and Choate. From these, sons went off to Ivy League colleges, with Princeton, Yale, and Harvard in the forefront.

AMERICAN SOCIETY

And to insure that their daughters married within proper society, there was the year-long round of debutante parties where young men and women from ''nice'' families were supposed to meet and fall in love.

Conspicuous Opulence   Often wealthier than this inner circle were the newly rich businessmen and industrialists of the period. Although they were also likely to be white Anglo-Saxon Protestants of ''colonial stock,'' the older families sometimes resented their wealth or found them crude in manners and taste. Particularly shocking was the conspicuous opulence of newly rich families like the Vanderbilts, who had made a fortune in railroads. William K. Vanderbilt engaged architect Richard Morris Hunt to design a huge limestone mansion on New York's fashionable Fifth Avenue that looked much like the château at Blois. Not to be overshadowed, his brother George W. Vanderbilt commissioned Hunt to create an even larger château at Asheville, North Carolina. Called Biltmore, the residence boasted of 40 master bedrooms, a tapestry hall, and a library of a quarter million volumes. Surrounding Biltmore were over 200 square miles of rolling forest and fields. Though upstarts by old-family standards, men like the Vanderbilts could not be ignored in the long run, and their heirs were soon absorbed into proper society.

A Burgeoning Middle Class   Beneath these upper echelons was an increasingly large middle class, its ranks swelled by the thousands of engineers, managers, accountants, and lawyers that were necessary for an expanding industrial economy. Growth in education and in other service fields like insurance, transportation, and medicine further enlarged middle-class ranks.

The middle class itself was subdivided into differing income levels and accompanying modes of living. Upper-middle-class managers, along with more successful lawyers, stock brokers, and physicians, enjoyed large and attractive residences that might be tended by four or five servants. Such families earned at least $5,000 to $10,000 yearly. They could easily afford a month or so at their own summer cottage or in one of the better resort hotels. Their children likely attended private schools, enrolled in dancing classes, and were strongly encouraged to marry within their own class or higher.

At the lower end of the middle class were school teachers, clerical workers, and others whose claim to social respectability derived from the fact that they did not perform manual labor. Incomes might range from $800 to $1,500 a year. Home was a small and often painfully neat house in one of the new ''streetcar'' suburbs or in the modest tree-lined neighborhoods of smaller towns and villages. A high school education (or less) from a public institution was typical for this group. The most they could generally hope for during the summer was a week in an economical boardinghouse at some nearby resort. Otherwise their social life might revolve around church socials, family gatherings, or memberships in fraternal organizations like the Odd Fellows and Knights of Pythias.

Other organizations arose in response to perceived threats to middle-class status. Established communities, with their local markets and culture, dwindled in importance as technology and corporate growth created national markets, an urban culture, and sharper class divisions. Middle-class individuals began to organize for protection. If the individual was weak, the group was stronger, and between 1880 and 1905 a large array of associations sprang up. Professional groups—doctors, lawyers, scientists, engineers, businessmen, teachers, clergymen—organized along national lines. Organization provided two major benefits. First, it brought greater efficiency and higher standards. Second, it permitted individuals to compensate for the cultural and economic dislocations surrounding them. Negatively, these new associations, through their jargon and specialized techniques, tended to become elitist and excluded those outside the group.

Working-Class Ways   Among those excluded were skilled workers who were not considered members of the middle class in 1900, as their manual labor confined them to a working-class status. Fourteen to twenty dollars a week was a typical wage, enough for an urban row house or a small and cheaply built single-family dwelling in smaller cities and towns. A day's railroad excursion to the beach marked the limits of their usual leisure travel, while the music hall, the corner saloon, and later the local movie house provided entertainment outside the home.

Unskilled workers commanded even less respect and comparatively lower incomes, earning as little as $9.00 per week. Many of the unskilled were recent immigrants of Jewish, Roman Catholic, or Greek Orthodox faith, who had to face the added burden of ethnic and religious discrimination. Hundreds of thousands of them lived in cramped and unsanitary tenement houses with little or no money for outside diversions. Some immigrants, having come from countries with no tradition of mass schooling, placed little value on formal education. And in the absence of compulsory education laws even in the United States, their children could easily escape with a minimum of time in the classroom. Others, however, saw free public education as a ladder to social and economic mobility for their youngsters.

Minorities, Farmers, and Domestic Servants   Even worse off for the most part were the former slaves and their children, the majority of whom continued to live in the South as servants, common laborers, or tenant farmers. In addition to their low economic status, they suffered from increasing racial hatred. Similarly at the bottom of the socioeconomic heap were the remnants of once flourishing Indian tribes who endured grinding poverty and racial prejudice. Relegated to some of the poorest lands in America, most eked out a living from the soil or remained on desolate reservations as wards of the nation.

White farmers belonged to yet another social order. At the top were prosperous southern planters and large landholders on the great plains. Of middling status were successful family farmers who produced for the commercial market. On the bottom were sharecroppers, tenant farmers, and landless day laborers. In the South such unfortunate men and women had often been scorned as "poor white trash" by their social betters. The relative isolation of these rural dwellers confined most leisure activities to such things as family reunions, neighborly visits, Grange meetings, church services, and programs of various kinds at the local schoolhouse.

Yet another "pecking order" existed among the million or so domestic servants, most of them recent immigrants, whose low wages released the middle and upper classes from the most distasteful chores of everyday life. First in rank came the butlers and cooks, with parlor maids and coachmen next. Further down the scale were laundresses and kitchen maids, while stablemen and furnace tenders brought up the rear. Ethnic mixtures among household staffs could cause much internal friction, and the fact that many servants continued to be Irish Catholics created additional tension between largely Protestant, Anglophile employers and their staffs.

AMERICAN SOCIETY

The Limits of Mobility Among all these classes and grades, perhaps 20 to 25 percent of the population suffered from some degree of poverty. The contrasts among life styles were thus quite sharp as the twentieth century commenced. While unskilled workers earned as little as $400 a year, steel magnate Andrew Carnegie reaped an average of $10 million annually. Some took comfort from believing that rapid social mobility was the rule rather than the exception in America. The possibilities of such success were celebrated in a series of books for adolescents by Horatio Alger, Jr. And one could point to Carnegie himself, who had begun as a poor Scottish immigrant and became one of the richest men in the world. But studies of social mobility during the period demonstrate that Carnegie's experience was quite unusual. Most citizens remained in the same social niche all their lives. And if their children managed to rise, they typically moved into the nearest social rank rather than climbing all the way to the top. At the other end of the scale, research has shown that over 90 percent of the wealthiest industrialists were of upper- or middle-class background to start with.

The unlikelihood that an unskilled worker or his children would soar into the upper ranks of society is not surprising. It took large amounts of capital to become wealthy, and those with inherited funds had a definite advantage over those who were born poor. Family connections and "old-school ties" were likewise important when it came to obtaining a high-paying or powerful position. Nor could working-class children afford the private schools and university degrees that were increasingly important to success. They also lacked appropriate manners and habits of speech, personal characteristics that did not come easily to those who had not grown up with them.

Those Americans who comprised the nation in 1900 thus lived very different lives, with varied experiences and expectations. Anyone seeking to understand the United States in the early twentieth century must keep such differences firmly in mind.

Ethnicity and Religion Few differences were more significant than ethnic background and religion. Many millions of Europeans emigrated to the United States between 1880 and World War I. These New Immigrants, mostly Italians, Jews, and Poles, uprooted themselves from southern and eastern Europe, unlike the earlier Old Immigrants, who had come largely from northern and western Europe to flee worsening economic conditions or, in the case of Jews, vicious outbursts of anti-Semitism. The yearly number of immigrants accelerated at this time, reaching over a million annually on six occasions between 1905 and 1914. A similar acceleration marked the shift from the Old Immigration to the New. In 1890 more than 40 percent of that year's 455,000 immigrants came from northwestern Europe; in 1914 only 130,000 of the more than 1.2 million did so.

FOREIGN-BORN POPULATION, BY AREA OF BIRTH

	All countries	Northwestern Europe	Central and eastern Europe	Southern Europe
1880	6,679,943	3,494,484	2,187,776	58,265
1890	9,249,560	4,380,752	3,420,629	206,648
1900	10,341,276	4,202,683	4,136,646	530,200
1910	13,515,886	4,239,067	6,014,028	1,525,875
1920	13,920,692	3,830,094	6,134,845	1,911,213

CHAPTER 1: THE SOCIAL FABRIC IN A NEW CENTURY

Americans, faced with a swelling tide of newcomers with strange names and dress, speaking different languages, and practicing different religions, debated whether their country could maintain its tradition as the land of refuge for the oppressed and economic opportunity for the ambitious. Workers worried about so many foreign competitors, skilled and unskilled alike. Businessmen, while pleased to have a reservoir of cheap labor, fretted over the radical ideas that some immigrant workers brought with them. Some simply disliked the characteristics or life styles of these newcomers. Still others, like the journalist Jacob Riis, himself an immigrant from Denmark, expressed great ambivalence. Riis's *How the Other Half Lives* (1890) was filled with stark photographs that documented the pathos of tenement life on New York's Lower East Side, which housed, he estimated, three-fourths of the city's population. Yet he still spoke of the Italian as a "born gambler," who was always ready to wield his knife. The Chinese, he asserted, were "in no sense a desirable element of the population," and as for Jews, "money is their God." Tenement conditions must be improved, concluded Riis, but he also insisted that immigrants must learn English, shed their "greenhorn" ways, and adopt native values.

Was the United States then to be a "melting pot," to use the title of a play written by the English-Jewish immigrant Israel Zangwill? Could immigrants be stripped of their cultural heritage and transformed into unalloyed Americans who might improve both

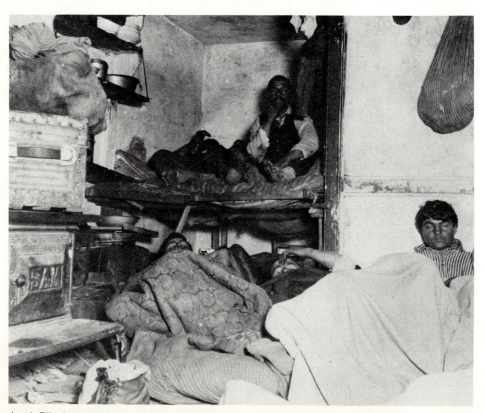

Jacob Riis documented the squalor of tenement life on New York's Lower East Side.

AMERICAN SOCIETY

Class of immigrants studying for American citizenship.

themselves and their new land? Riis and many others thought so. Yet many believed that assimilation was impossible or undesirable, agreeing with the writer Thomas Bailey Aldrich that the immigrants were "human gorillas." Some of these joined exclusionist organizations such as the Immigration Restriction League and the American Protective Association. A few turned to violence, as when an angry mob in New Orleans in 1891 lynched 11 Italian immigrants, assumed to be criminals, while city officials stood by.

Immigrants themselves viewed the melting-pot solution with mixed feelings. Some felt overwhelming joy on reaching America and hastened to adopt its ways. Yet others, like the Chinese immigrants of the mid-nineteenth century, came to the United States with the hope of making their fortunes and returning home. Most of these "birds of passage" ultimately remained, but more than a million of them, particularly Italians, did recross the Atlantic for good in the years before World War I. The typical immigrant experience ranged between these extremes. The newcomers, grateful to their host country and yet resentful at its prejudices and scorn, puzzled over assimilation, not knowing what blend of the old and the new to adopt for themselves and their families. Meanwhile most lived in their ghettos, Little Italys, and Little Polands, and worked to make a materially successful life. Historian Thomas Kessner has shown that New York's Jewish and Italian immigrants achieved upward mobility between 1880 and 1915, underscoring that the United States, at least for some, was still a land of opportunity.

The New Immigrants altered the nation's religious composition. The Old Immigrants, except for the massive influx of Irish Catholics during the potato famines of the 1840s, had been largely Protestant and had established Protestantism as the unofficial religion of the United States. But thanks to the new arrivals the number of Catholics soared from 8.2 million in 1890 to 10.1 million in 1900 and to 14.3 million in 1910.

Yet a united Catholic community failed to emerge because immigrant Catholics perceived the Irish-dominated church hierarchy as insensitive to their needs. Cahenslyism, a movement of the 1890s named for its German-immigrant founder, Peter Cahensly, called for each ethnic group to have its own priests and churches, foreign-language schools, and a proportionate share of high church officials. James Cardinal Gibbons of Baltimore, only the second American to be named a cardinal, successfully defused Cahenslyism, noting that it would fragment Catholicism and weaken it in the face of its enemies. Gibbons also defused some Protestant hostility by insisting that one could be both a good Catholic and a good American.

Differences also divided Jews. German Jews who had immigrated during the mid-nineteenth century established Reform Judaism, which included such innovations as prayers in English. Reform Jews, led by Rabbi Isaac Mayer Wise, readily assimilated into the larger gentile society. Many conservative Jews, however, fought to uphold traditional practices. American Judaism became even more divided with the coming of two million orthodox Jews, primarily from Russia and Poland. Only the rising tide of prejudice and persecution seemed to hold together what theological and ritual differences threatened to tear asunder.

In 1900 American Protestantism also witnessed continued rifts that historically had divided it into numerous sects. The census revealed that Methodists, with their 4,226,000 members, constituted the largest Protestant group, but other denominations—mainly Episcopalian and Presbyterian—attracted a disproportionately larger number with higher incomes and social status. Theology further sharpened differences. By 1900 some Protestants had accepted Darwinism, which had cast doubt on traditional Christian beliefs. For these liberal Protestants, evolution now seemed divinely planned, while the Bible, if not literally true and free of contradiction, was at least divinely inspired. Reaction against this accommodation with science and modernism permitted countless Protestants (as well as Catholics and Jews) to reaffirm accepted beliefs. Conservative Protestants, led by fundamentalist organizations like the Moody Bible Institute of Chicago and fiery evangelists such as the former baseball player, Billy Sunday, battled liberal Protestants over theological matters. They also quarreled over the role of religion in secular affairs (see Chapter 2).

Dislike for non-Protestants united many Protestants who were otherwise divided. A White-Anglo-Saxon-Protestant (WASP) establishment, for example, acted to prevent Catholics and, more especially, Jews from entering the finest hotels and country clubs, private schools and colleges, professional and business firms, and neighborhoods. As the patrician Henry Adams snarled: "We are still in power, after a fashion. Our sway over what we call society is undisputed. We keep the Jew far away. . . ." Sometimes blatant, sometimes insidious, this discrimination remained a dark, little changed aspect of American life well into the twentieth century.

Frustrations of Sex and Race Serious problems affecting sex and race flawed the nation's social fabric. Women and nonwhites, as groups, had never shared equally in the American dream of success. Frustrated, they entered the twentieth century with both hopes and fears.

Men outnumbered women by more than a million, according to the census of 1900, but women, with a life expectancy of 48.3 years, could anticipate outliving men by fully two years. Whether the quality of their lives was better than that of men was debatable and ultimately unanswerable. The American woman continued to suffer from culturally and historically induced liabilities. More than 5 million women were employed in 1900, but probably most worked out of necessity, not for personal liberation, and still remained responsible for the chores of domestic life. Moreover, persistent job discrimination and substandard wages and working conditions continued. Women were attending college in larger numbers. Still, the difficulty they faced if they sought professional careers is implied by the fact of male physicians outnumbering female physicians 124,600 to 7,400 and male lawyers outnumbering their female counterparts 113,500 to 1,000.

The nineteenth century did bring married women increased legal rights, especially property rights. Newer western states tended to be more liberal than eastern and southern states in granting or safeguarding these rights. By 1900, for instance, a married woman still needed her husband's consent to enter into a business contract in Pennsylvania, while in Florida she had no control at all over her earnings. But women's legal rights, all in all, were advancing strongly. This was not true of women's suffrage. Only a handful of states had granted women the vote as the new century began.

Social rights loomed as important as economic, legal, and political rights for many women. Written and unwritten codes of public and private behavior existed for women, both married and unmarried and of all classes. These codes applied to matters such as dress and cosmetics, social customs, and sexuality. Inspired by men, they had secured acceptance by most women, who could expect to pay a steep price for breaking the rules. In Edith Wharton's *The House of Mirth* (1905), the innocent Lily Bart, charming upper-class heroine, becomes the object of rumored scandal. She is then ruined by her moral inferiors and dies pitifully. Carrie Meeber, lower-class heroine of Theodore Dreiser's *Sister Carrie* (1900), provides a reenforcing example, though from an opposite point of view. Carrie, a naïve farm girl from Wisconsin, goes to Chicago, gets involved with a married man, and becomes a successful, admired actress. Since Dreiser did not punish his heroine, he received terrible abuse from the reading public. How many real-life Lily Barts and Carrie Meebers existed will never be known. But the double standard of sexual conduct was a reality in custom and in law, as evidenced by statutes in Pennsylvania and Minnesota that provided penalties for adulterous women but none for men.

Blacks also were suffering. George Washington Cable, a white southern writer, observed in 1885 that "the greatest social problem before the American people today is, as it has been for a hundred years, the presence among us of the Negro." He added: "The ex-slave is a free Negro; he is not a free man." When Cable wrote this, blacks still maintained some civil rights in the southern states where most of them lived, but their situation deteriorated drastically during the remainder of the century. In *Williams* v. *Mississippi* (1898), the Supreme Court validated literacy tests and poll taxes. By the early 1900s these devices, along with grandfather clauses and sheer intimidation, had prevented most blacks from voting. A rigid system of racial segregation accompanied disfranchisement, forcing blacks to use separate public facilities. The Court upheld these practices, particularly in the landmark decision *Plessy* v. *Ferguson* (1896), which ruled that segregation in railway coaches (and implicitly in other public places) was constitutional as long as "separate but equal" facilities were provided. Racial segregation was also a common feature in the North at this time, though it seemed less evident since fewer blacks resided there. Even more appalling, lynchings, mainly in the South, were taking an average of more than 100 black lives each year.

Blacks, humiliated and reeling under the loss of their lives and liberties, looked for leadership. The fiery abolitionist Frederick Douglass, who had outspokenly demanded equal rights, died in 1895. That same year a young black leader, one holding different views and speaking in softer tones, rose to national prominence.

Booker T. Washington was born into slavery in 1856. He toiled at menial jobs after emancipation but managed to secure an education at Hampton Institute, a Virginia school established during Reconstruction to educate former slaves. The Alabama state legislature in 1881 voted funds to set up a similar school and chose Washington to head it. The Tuskegee Institute prospered under Washington and in the next decade became a symbol of successful black self-help. The ''Wizard of Tuskegee'' won widespread recognition and an invitation in 1895 to address businessmen meeting in Atlanta.

In this Atlanta Exposition speech, Washington advocated vocational training and practical education, similar to what he was offering at Tuskegee. He urged blacks to begin life at the bottom and ''cast down your buckets where you are.'' His hope that they would gain white acceptance and respect by making themselves economically needed was misguided since technology was already rendering his educational goals obsolete. Washington further advocated accommodation in social matters, warning that the ''wisest among my race understand that the agitation of questions of social equality is the extremest folly.'' He added, ''in all things that are purely social we can be as separate as the fingers, yet one as the hand in all things essential to mutual progress. . . .'' Thus his policy attempted to meet the worsening situation for blacks by stressing self-reliance and moderation as responses to discrimination and hostility. His ''Atlanta Compromise'' pleased many. Yet others—both black and white—soon questioned whether this approach would help the nine million black Americans entering the new century.

Other nonwhites fared little if any better. Prejudice against Chinese workers began with their arrival during the Gold Rush of the late 1840s. It worsened as native American laborers protested the ''coolie wages'' that the Chinese accepted while helping to build railroads after the Civil War. Congress in 1882 singled out Chinese workers for exclusion, but by 1900 there were still 90,000 foreign-born Chinese and their American-born descendants. A small minority became involved with drugs, gambling, and prostitution. Their behavior caused many to view all Chinese with added suspicion and dislike. Japanese began migrating to the United States in the 1890s. They too received a chilly welcome, culminating in a decision by the San Francisco Board of Education in 1906 to segregate Oriental school children. The twentieth century witnessed a changed attitude toward another Oriental group. Filipinos, warmly regarded as ''our little brown brothers'' during the Spanish-American War, were reviled as uncivilized ingrates during the rebellion that followed the nation's decision to acquire the Philippines. Prejudice came in other colors as well. Mexican-Americans encountered local animosity and discrimination in the areas where most lived, California and the Southwest. As for the Indians, or Native Americans, by the late nineteenth century the government had finally broken their power after a series of wars and had begun the process of pacification. The Dawes Severalty Act of 1887, intended as a reform measure, actually provided Native Americans with two painful alternatives: either to continue their tribal ways on reservations as wards of the government or to leave their tribes, receive a land grant and citizenship, and take their chances in a largely hostile or indifferent society. In either case their once proud and independent lives would be diminished.

AMERICAN CULTURE

Racial prejudice was not limited to the United States. A minority of white Europeans at this time were dominating large numbers of nonwhite, non-European colonials, whom they deemed racially and culturally inferior. One should remember, moreover, that many white Americans were not racists and did their best to help victims of prejudice. Yet it was evident that the nation at large had to solve its race problems before it could truly come of age.

The Family Cutting across other lines of social structure was an all-pervasive unit: the family. In 1900 nearly 28 million Americans were married, with the median age of marriage being 25.9 years. (Significant numbers of women who remained single while working help to account for this relatively late age for marriage.) The extended family, consisting of assorted relatives in addition to parents and children, was more common to immigrants than to natives, who favored nuclear units of parents and children only. Lower-class families, not surprisingly, had more children than upper- and middle-class families. Nonetheless, the overall birthrate had slowed considerably from 39.8 per thousand persons in 1880 to 32.3 per thousand persons in 1900. This decrease troubled those who believed that the nation's well-being rested on a high birthrate, at least among the "fit." Worries about divorce were also growing. The rate, while low (only 198,000 persons were cited as divorced in 1900), was increasing.

The quality or style of family life varied widely. The average annual wage for an unskilled worker in 1900, as noted previously, totaled less than $500. This was considerably less than the $800 needed to maintain a reasonable standard of living for an average family, thus making it necessary for many women and children to work. Other families lived moderately well or even opulently. Wealth or its lack determined a host of everyday basics: food, shelter, health care, education, dress, and tastes. Yet some family considerations depended more on cultural background and individual temperament than on economic status. The patriarchal family may still have reigned, especially among immigrants, but wives of all classes often could and did rule. It is also difficult to generalize about bringing up children. Some parents overindulged their offspring; others beat theirs into submission. Some children were docile; others were troublesome. The fictional Little Lord Fauntleroy provided a model of decorous behavior for some parents to inflict upon their sons. The Fauntleroy costume of black velvet suit and white collar was accompanied by masses of long curls that sometimes made it difficult to distinguish the child's gender. The fictional Peck's Bad Boy, in contrast, was forever playing practical jokes on his unfortunate father; he offered a very different role model. What seems safe to conclude is only that the generation gap operated (though not as strongly as later). Parents misunderstood their children—who fully reciprocated.

AMERICAN CULTURE

Culture, defined in its broadest sense as the sum total of the ways a people experience life, presented a blend of the old and the new. It still reflected the values of some 46 million rural inhabitants, who constituted roughly 60 percent of the population. Yet in other ways it derived from the new: technological changes, rapid urbanization, shifting life styles. Nostalgia for the past battled anticipation of future trends to produce a present as richly diverse and unsettled as the people who lived it.

Popular Amusements Increased leisure time permitted play to become a larger part of national life at the turn of the century. But play was more than recreation and amusement, since it also satisfied the need to adjust to a changing culture, more specifically to the new restraints imposed by urban and industrial life. People left rural areas but brought with them memories of outdoor life. Hemmed in by the city, both they and native urbanites turned to open-air athletics and recreation for compensation. Physicians widely prescribed exercise, as did spokesmen such as Theodore Roosevelt and the health faddist Bernarr Macfadden, who announced that ''Weakness is a Crime.'' The ideal ''New Woman,'' captured by Charles Dana Gibson's popular sketches, was tall and athletic in physique. Changing styles of female dress correspondingly permitted her greater freedom of movement.

Hiking and camping increased in popularity, but bicycling was the greatest craze by 1900. The bicycle, having first been introduced to large numbers of people at the Philadelphia Centennial, changed radically from a bizarre model with a five-foot wheel to one with smaller, even-sized wheels. The introduction of a model for women (one without a top bar) and scheduled races enhanced its appeal, as did lower prices for the vehicle. The young Wright brothers, Wilbur and Orville, were selling a no-frills model for approximately $18 in their Dayton, Ohio store.

Automobiles furnished less exercise but greater thrills and frequent frustration. At first only the well-to-do could afford any of the hundred different models that cost from $500 to $7,000 and were expensive to maintain. Dreadful roads, dust and noise, com-

Automobiles provided a form of amusement for a growing number of Americans.

plaints from irate nonowners, the need to master the complexities of the machine, and its high cost contributed to its narrow popularity. Yet the awe inspired by this powerful contraption promised future approval. Sensing this, Henry Ford began in 1909 to manufacture his revolutionary Model T car, which was simple but sturdy and cost only $950. That year he sold 18,000 of them. In 1917 sales leapt to nearly 800,000, a figure well in excess of his principal rival, General Motors.

Sports provided amusement as well. Croquet, tennis, and golf had their enthusiasts, but organized team sports engaged enormous spectator interest. Baseball and football, as one foreign visitor noted in 1905, generated more excitement than any other public event except possibly presidential elections. Baseball, organized shortly after the Civil War, was more celebrated than ever by 1900. That year saw the formation of an American League to rival the National League. The first modern world series played between the two in 1903 added interest to the game. So too did legendary players like Ty Cobb and Walter Johnson. Salaries were good—too good, some complained. A successful young southpaw for the Boston Red Sox named George Herman ("Babe") Ruth was earning $3,500 a season in 1915. Fine skills and intense team rivalries helped to make baseball the "national pastime." The moderate pace of a game played on grass by people frequently born in rural areas and watched by others of a similar background enhanced its attraction by looking to a vanishing past.

Many considered Jim Thorpe, an American Indian who attended Carlisle College, the greatest football player of the early twentieth century.

If baseball was the game of the masses, football seemed the sport of the elite. Ivy League college teams dominated at first. In 1889, for example, Walter Camp selected his All-American team exclusively from players at Harvard, Princeton, and his own Yale. A popular slogan at Yale around 1900 was: ''We toil not, neither do we agitate, but we play football.'' This bruising sport, however, was beginning to achieve popularity in non-Ivy League schools as well.

Athletics also had its darker side. Gambling and throwing games had marred baseball in the late nineteenth century, while violence disfigured other sports. For example, 44 persons had been killed playing football by 1903 and many had been seriously injured. The brutality of boxing, along with its attraction for gamblers, threatened the popularity earned for it by notable boxers like ''Gentleman'' Jim Corbett and Jim Jeffries. Yet the figure of black Jack Johnson, who held the heavyweight championship from 1908 to 1915 and married a white woman, rekindled enthusiasm as the sport searched for a ''white hope'' to dethrone this controversial athlete.

Amusement parks provided yet another source of popular outdoor enjoyment for the masses. No other feature of the World's Columbian Exposition, held in Chicago in 1893, proved as enticing as the Midway with its games, exotic attractions like the belly dancer Little Egypt, and the giant Ferris Wheel that permitted riders to see the sights from on high. Soon similar parks, including Coney Island in Brooklyn, appeared, offering rides, dance halls, freak shows, and arcade games. They incurred the wrath of some moralists since they were frequented by thieves and prostitutes and afforded young men and women the chance to meet. They also may have helped to preserve disciplined work habits in daily life by allowing people an enjoyable but controlled outlet for their energies.

Music, both serious and lighthearted, also brought enjoyment to millions. Boston, Philadelphia, Chicago, and New York all had first-rate symphony orchestras by 1914, by which time the New York Metropolitan Opera had achieved an international reputation. No towering composer of classical music graced the nation, but the European-trained Edward MacDowell and Charles Tomlinson Griffes won recognition as gifted minor talents. Less heralded but immensely more innovative was Charles Ives, who consistently violated accepted norms and tastes. A successful businessman and the son of a bandmaster, he created works that combined complex modern techniques with traditional American themes. Ives, influenced by the ideas of Ralph Waldo Emerson, tried both to elevate and entertain the masses with assorted compositions that included six symphonies and more than a hundred songs.

In a lighter vein, people applauded the operettas of the Irish-born Victor Herbert and the works of the ''March King'' John Philip Sousa, whose rousing pieces such as ''Semper Fidelis'' and ''Stars and Stripes Forever'' trumpeted national pride and the martial spirit so recently exhibited during the Spanish-American War. Early twentieth-century audiences also acclaimed vaudeville, which offered them variety acts, broad humor, dazzlingly clad or semiclad dance girls, and the latest in popular tunes. There were numerous gifted vaudevillians. These included entire families such as the Foys, but none overshadowed Florenz Ziegfeld and his legendary Ziegfeld Follies. Also capturing popular attention were musical shows, notably those of the Irish-American George M. Cohan, whose patriotic ''You're a Grand Old Flag'' and ''Yankee Doodle Boy,'' as well as ''Give My Regards to Broadway,'' brought him immense theatrical fame.

AMERICAN CULTURE 21

John Philip Sousa, the "March King."

But Americans were not only listening or marching to music, they were dancing to it as well. Ragtime, their favorite dance music, derived from the rhythms of southern blacks, and in the late 1890s Scott Joplin and other musicians were bringing it to the nation's attention. Soon ragtime became a craze as people did the turkey trot, bunny hug, kangaroo dip, and grizzly bear to tunes like Irving Berlin's "Alexander's Ragtime Band." One critic complained that ragtime suffered from St. Vitus's dance, but on the dance floor, in homes with phonographs, and in the corridors of Tin Pan Alley ragtime reigned.

Rumors to the contrary, Americans could sit still, and what they were sitting for in the first five years of the century were the movies. Thomas Alva Edison, who also invented the electric light bulb and the phonograph, created the kinetoscope, which permitted viewing of moving pictures by one person at a time. Subsequent refinements by others made it possible to project pictures onto a screen for viewing by many people at once. Nickelodeons, so called because they charged five cents admission, sprang up throughout the nation after 1905 and enabled all but the poorest to enjoy themselves. Movies like the serialized *Perils of Pauline* (1914), filled with thrills and stunts, riveted people's attention. So did the technically advanced *Birth of a Nation* (1915), which cost more than $100,000 to produce. This controversial film divided people by portraying the

Ku Klux Klan as saviors of the prostrate South after the Civil War. People even in those years worshiped a galaxy of movie stars, including "America's Sweetheart," Mary Pickford, and the British-born comedian Charlie Chaplin.

Science and Education   Americans liked playing, but they also appreciated learning, for its own sake and for the mastery that accompanied knowledge. The list of scientific and technological breakthroughs that allowed the generation of 1900 to enjoy comforts and amenities of life unimagined by their parents seemed endless. Edison's many achievements, as well as Alexander Graham Bell's telephone, were the most famous. But other changes that radically transformed daily life—canned foods, iceboxes, improved indoor plumbing, ready-made clothing, to name a few—were hardly less impressive. The achievements were all the more noteworthy since greater efficiency and the advent of mass retailing stores and mail-order catalogs improved availability and brought the cost of these goods within the range of the average person's pocketbook.

American scientists traditionally had exhibited a practical bent of mind, and they still did, as evidenced by the many uses for the peanut discovered by George Washington Carver, famed chemist and instructor at Tuskegee Institute. But pure research and science were also coming of age. Josiah Willard Gibbs, neglected in his own lifetime, discovered the "rule of phase," which proved a boon to metallurgy. Albert A. Michelson devoted years to measuring the speed of light. Major contributions to biology included Jacques Loeb's study of tropisms, Thomas Hunt Morgan's discoveries in genetics through experiments with fruit flies, and Hermann J. Muller's demonstrations of how radium and x-rays can produce mutations. The human mind itself provided a largely unexplored area for investigation. William James's *Principles of Psychology* (1890) became an internationally celebrated text. James's subsequent fame, however, did not eclipse that of his fellow psychologist, G. Stanley Hall, who as president of Clark University hosted Sigmund Freud in 1909 on his only visit to the United States.

Medicine, though fairly primitive judged by today's standards, scored major achievements in both research and application. Dr. Walter Reed and his team of physicians learned about the transmission of deadly yellow fever in American-occupied Cuba after the war with Spain. At the same time, Major William Gorgas successfully controlled both yellow fever and malaria during the construction of the Panama Canal. Physicians at home also made significant advances against such diseases as hookworm and Rocky Mountain spotted fever. Yet no innovation in medicine ultimately proved more important than the growth of professionalized training. Medical students before the Civil War rarely needed to pass exams in order to receive their degrees. Sporadic attendance at lectures and training for a few years with an established physician usually sufficed. After the war Charles W. Eliot, president of Harvard, suggested reforms, including written exams. This agitated one of the university's professors of surgery, who pleaded that more than half the medical students could barely write. Eliot had his way, however, and by the 1890s the Harvard Medical School offered education of high quality, as did several other schools of medicine, notably Johns Hopkins.

New directions also characterized nonmedical education. Nearly 17 million children were enrolled in primary and secondary schools in 1900, and nearly 90 percent of the population enjoyed literacy. Yet the statistics also revealed upsetting facts. School attendance by white children almost doubled that of nonwhites. While only 4.6 percent of

AMERICAN CULTURE

native-born whites were illiterate, the rate shot up to 12.9 percent for foreign whites and, more alarmingly, to 44.5 percent for nonwhites. Educators responded in various ways. First, they continued to stress the three Rs, with the result that by 1910 the illiteracy rate for whites and nonwhites had dropped to 7.7 and 30.4 percent, respectively. Second, they adopted innovations to improve the quality of education. For example, they began to employ methods for teaching youngsters designed by the Italian pedagogue Dr. Maria Montessori. (Remarkably, her *Montessori Method* ranked second on the list of best-selling nonfiction for 1912.)

Even more compelling seemed the prescriptions of John Dewey, who was convinced that education had become too conservative in its techniques and subject matter to meet the changing needs of an industrial, democratic America. He began a series of experiments at the University of Chicago in the 1890s to solve these problems. Progressive education, as originated and described by Dewey in such works as *The School and Society* (1899) and *Democracy and Education* (1916), called for students to develop their potential within a loosely—critics said too loosely—structured academic environment. Curricula, for example, would offer courses that were more germane to the contemporary world in which students lived. Dewey also emphasized peer interchange and self-government practices as means to experience the democratic process firsthand. Dewey's ideas were popular with many, but traditionalists railed against them.

Critics also challenged changes in higher education. Educators, determined to preserve a fixed, traditional curriculum, predicted disaster when Harvard's President Eliot introduced the elective system there. They were mistaken. American colleges and universities soon achieved striking advances by adopting more flexible curricula, hiring better qualified professors, and profiting from the guidance of such presidents as Eliot at Harvard, Nicholas Murray Butler at Columbia, Daniel Coit Gilman at Johns Hopkins, William Rainey Harper at Chicago, and David Starr Jordan at Stanford.

Professionalization of studies presented one of the most important transformations in American education at this time. The last quarter of the nineteenth century witnessed the establishment of nearly 300 professional schools of law, medicine, dentistry, theology, pharmacy, and veterinary medicine. These schools underscored the democratic commitment to advancement through merit rather than privilege. Ironically, they also created an elite based on professionalism.

Yet a college education for Americans in 1900 was the exception rather than the rule. Fewer than 5 percent of them at that time possessed any college training. Many sought to learn in less formal ways. In 1874, for example, a program was held at Lake Chautauqua in western New York to bring knowledge to audiences through a series of lectures. The Chautauqua idea spread to other locales, and by 1914 hundreds of thousands had heard addresses by politicians, business and labor leaders, clergy, and artists. The written word complemented the spoken word as newer, larger, and finer libraries dotted the land. Philanthropists like Enoch Pratt of Baltimore and William Newberry of Chicago generously contributed to their city's libraries; however, none could match the passion of Andrew Carnegie, who helped to establish 2,500 of them.

Literature Reading was popular among a largely literate people living before radio and television. Tastes varied, ranging from what later critics would call ''highbrow'' to ''lowbrow.'' As always there were those that spanned the two.

Journalism broadened its appeal to mass-market dimensions in the 1890s. New and elaborate methods of advertising captured the attention of readers, as did photographs and reproductions in color. Comic-strip characters such as the Yellow Kid and the Katzenjammer Kids became regular features. The ''funnies,'' as they were known, helped to create an avid readership for the daily and Sunday papers.

More serious questions also influenced and were influenced by the rise of mass journalism. The leading journals of the Gilded Age—*Harper's, Scribner's, Century, Atlantic*—presented important issues in a manner calculated to appeal to well-informed middle- and upper-class audiences. By the 1890s such issues were linked more closely to the profit motive, which, in turn, was tied to winning a mass readership. The battle for increased newspaper circulation between Joseph Pulitzer's *New York World* and William Randolph Hearst's *New York Journal* signaled the rise of Yellow Journalism (named for the color of its illustrations). Both men vied shamelessly for the allegiance of readers by filling their papers with lurid sensationalism. For instance, they printed stories of Spanish atrocities during the Cuban rebellion that were exaggerated or sometimes altogether false. Other American newspapers followed suit. Yet, for all its faults, the new journalism, through investigative reporting and editorial guidance, would provide a useful model in the next century.

Newspapers and magazines kept Americans abreast of current events. Novels—at least many of the best sellers—fulfilled their needs for nostalgia and escape. Historical novels, for example, were constant favorites. Winston Churchill (no relation to the British Winston Churchill) had nine separate works on the best-seller lists between 1900 and 1915. These included *Richard Carvel* (1899) and *The Crisis* (1900), set in the Revolutionary and Civil War periods respectively. The Reverend Thomas Dixon, Jr.'s *The Clansman* (1905) focused on the agonies of Reconstruction and inspired the movie *Birth of a Nation*. Americans also favored historical works set outside their country, such as the Graustark novels of George Barr McCutcheon, who made the best-seller lists during eight separate years between 1901 and 1915.

The popularity of westerns pointed to the nostalgia of an increasingly urbanized people for the fading experience of the frontier. The census of 1890 revealed that the frontier, which had played such a pivotal role in the nation's history, no longer existed. Literature now enshrined it as legend. In *The Virginian,* a best seller of 1902, Owen Wister, Philadelphia-born writer and good friend of Theodore Roosevelt, set the standard for future westerns. His hero acted tough among men but tender toward women; he suffered wrongs but ultimately triumphed over evil. Not a man to be trifled with, he warned: ''When you call me that, *smile.*'' *The Virginian* later became a movie of the same name, starring Gary Cooper, and a popular television series in the 1960s. Yet the popularity of Wister's hero would never approach that of the hero created by a younger writer of westerns, Zane Grey, in *The Lone Star Ranger* (1914).

More serious fiction also found an audience. Late nineteenth-century regionalism—the Deep South of Joel Chandler Harris, the Virginia of Ellen Glasgow, the Maine of Sarah Orne Jewett, the Indiana of Edward Eggleston—continued to appeal to many, as did the diverse works of the nation's favorite humorist, Mark Twain. Increasingly, however, the most significant literature depicted serious problems and admitted that life does not always, or even usually, include happy endings.

AMERICAN CULTURE

Here William Dean Howells was the pioneer. Through his literary realism he maintained qualities that bound him to the genteel tradition of moral propriety—he once said he would write nothing he would be ashamed for his daughter to read. But his many novels treated contemporary themes in a believable manner. A failed marriage provided the focus for *A Modern Instance* (1882); the foibles and pathos of a crude *nouveau riche* businessman filled *The Rise of Silas Lapham* (1885); and the vitality of urban life and labor strife found notable expression in *A Hazard of New Fortunes* (1890). He also wrote the utopian socialist novel, *A Traveler from Altruria* (1894), and furthered the careers of several young writers, including the realist Hamlin Garland, whose *Main-Travelled Roads* (1891) and other works did much to dispel the myth of farm life as idyllic and rewarding.

Naturalism, according to one critic, was merely realism on all fours. The description was somewhat apt since naturalism, in turning to Darwinism and science, frequently stressed the primacy of determinism and predatory instincts in human behavior. Naturalists dissected characters and conditions much—so they imagined—as scientists did in a laboratory. Examining society, they found it brutal and brutalizing. Stephen Crane's *Maggie: A Girl of the Streets* (1893) dealt depressingly with the hitherto taboo subject of prostitution. His *The Red Badge of Courage* (1895) painted not the glory and chivalry of war, but its carnage and cowardice. Frank Norris's *McTeague* (1899) analyzed the steady loss of his protagonist's humanity. In *The Octopus* (1901) and *The Pit* (1903) Norris chronicled the losing battle waged by California wheat growers against entrenched economic interests. Another powerful naturalist writer was the socialist and Darwinist Jack London, who narrated the struggle for survival against nature and human greed in a host of adventure stories and novels. Among these are *The Call of the Wild* (1903), *The Sea Wolf* (1904), and *Martin Eden* (1909). His anti-utopian novel, *The Iron Heel* (1907), remains one of the bloodiest tales of class warfare ever penned. Theodore Dreiser, having recovered from the savage reception accorded his *Sister Carrie,* pursued a similar theme in *Jennie Gerhardt* (1912). His Frank Cowperwood novels, *The Financier* (1912) and *The Titan* (1914), found him fictionalizing the career of the ruthless Chicago traction magnate, Charles T. Yerkes.

A quite different kind of fictionist was Henry James, sometimes considered the greatest writer of the age. His many novels and short stories reflected the artist's concern for understanding psychological motivation, as well as the nuances of social behavior. James, an expatriate who spent most of his adult years in England, was fascinated by the meeting of Americans and Europeans and the cultural conflicts that ensued. His last three major novels, *The Wings of the Dove* (1902), *The Ambassadors* (1903), and *The Golden Bowl* (1904), dealt with these concerns to the satisfaction of his dedicated admirers. His difficult prose style led others to concur with one critic who complained that James wrote novels "as if it were a painful duty."

Nathaniel Hawthorne in the mid-nineteenth century felt that it was his duty to complain about that "damned mob of scribbling women." No fair-minded person could launch a similar complaint in the early twentieth century. Henry James's good friend Edith Wharton skillfully explored the effects of wealth, love, and tradition on the upper class and those who wished to enter it. *The House of Mirth* (1905), *The Custom of the Country* (1913), and *The Age of Innocence* (1920) are her best novels of this type. Her novella *Ethan Frome* (1911), a stark portrayal of a doomed love affair in the backwaters of New England, also gained strong critical and popular acceptance. Among other prominent women writers were Ellen Glasgow, whose three best sellers published between 1904 and 1916 anticipated her achievements of the 1920s, and Willa Cather, author of *O Pioneer!* (1913) and *My Ántonia* (1918).

Art and Architecture The ferment that marked American society in the new century similarly characterized its art and architecture. Fresh ideas, both foreign and native, competed with old ones for favor, as various painters and architects in both Europe and the United States rejected accepted tastes and conventions in search of newer modes of expression. From their quest emerged the sensibilities of artistic modernism.

The rise of realism in painting in the late nineteenth century, exemplified by the work of Thomas Eakins, paralleled that movement in literature. A group of early twentieth-century artists collectively termed the Ash Can School owed much to Eakin's style but not his subject matter. These social realists, led by Robert Henri and including such painters as George Bellows, John Sloan, Everett Shinn, George Luks, and William J. Glackens, rebelled against the artistic traditionalism championed by the National Acad-

John Sloan's *Sixth Avenue Elevated at Third Avenue* is representative of the Ash Can School of painting.

AMERICAN CULTURE

emy of Design. Instead, they preached and practiced an art that captured the humanity of daily life. Whether it was the brutal prizefighting canvases of Bellows or the grimy street scenes of Sloan, nothing seemed too raw or plebeian to escape the brush strokes of these New York-based painters.

Artistic rebels, finding it difficult to exhibit in the nation's foremost galleries and museums, called for a massive presentation of new art. The resulting Armory Show held in New York in 1913 proved a watershed in the history of American art. More than a thousand works by more than 300 American artists went on view, as did representative European art done in the current styles of post-impressionism, cubism, fauvism, and expressionism. It was these latter works, avant-garde in the extreme and included almost as an afterthought, that captured the most attention from the thousands who attended the exhibit either in New York or on its subsequent national tour. Of the 174 works sold, 120 were by Europeans. The Armory Show fascinated, outraged, but rarely bored. Police, for example, had to keep protesters from hurling projectiles at Marcel Duchamps' *Nude Descending a Staircase*. A bemused Theodore Roosevelt claimed that his Navajo rug was better art, and students attending Chicago's Art Institute protested by burning a Matisse painting in effigy. Yet modernism, however objectionable to some, had arrived and would not soon depart.

Architects also fought over questions of tradition versus innovation, of continued imitation of foreign styles versus development of national ones. The late nineteenth century produced many strikingly handsome buildings, but most were derived from European models. Trained at the prestigious École des Beaux-Arts in Paris, Richard Morris Hunt, for example, designed magnificent French châteaux-like residences for the wealthy along New York's Fifth Avenue, in Newport, and elsewhere, as well as stately public buildings in the classical mode like the Metropolitan Museum of Art. Inspired but derivative creations likewise came from the drawing boards of McKim, Mead and White, a distinguished firm that also specialized in homes for the wealthy and massive neo-Roman edifices like New York's Pennsylvania Station. In the years before World War I Ralph Adams Cram gained repute for his architectural feats at West Point and Princeton as well as for a commission to complete the Cathedral of St. John the Divine in New York. Yet he too embraced an entrenched style from the past: Gothic.

Significant changes were taking place, despite the reverence accorded the past by architects and public alike. Skyscrapers appeared in the 1890s. Buildings that originally were limited to a few stories could now soar skyward, thanks to elevators and steel-frame construction. Chicago, symbol of a powerful, industrial America, fittingly assumed a leading role. The partners Daniel H. Burnham and John W. Root were the principal builders in this growing metropolis. Far more significant, though less appreciated, was another Chicago-based architect, Louis H. Sullivan. Sullivan's Carson, Pirie, Scott department store (originally Schlesinger and Mayer) and also his Auditorium, among other buildings, enhanced the Windy City's reputation for appealing structures. More important for its effect on modern architecture was his principle that "form follows function." The design of a building, he argued, should reflect its needs and purposes, not the dead hand of tradition or the whims of its builder. A bank, for example, should be designed to provide efficiency rather than a replication of a Greek or Roman temple, as so many banks at that time did. Yet the graceful flowing lines and ornamentation of his buildings

BIOGRAPHICAL SKETCH

SCOTT JOPLIN · *1868–1917*

Born in Texarkana, Texas, the son of a former slave, Joplin taught himself to play the piano at an early age and left home as a teenager to roam the South as an itinerant musician. In 1885 Joplin settled in St. Louis, where he earned a livelihood playing chiefly in honky-tonks. In 1893, like numerous other musicians, he went to Chicago and entertained at the Midway of the Columbian Exposition.

Ragtime may have been heard at the Exposition, but it became a national craze only after the publication of the first rags in 1897. Between that year and 1920 several thousand rags were published in the form of sheet music and piano rolls. The music of black Americans—plantation songs and dances, for example—provided the chief inspiration for ragtime, whose unusual syncopation captured the public's fancy. Joplin won immediate recognition for his "Maple Leaf Rag" (1899) and soon became known as the "king of ragtime." Adhering to high standards rather than pandering to commercialism, the quiet, retiring Joplin mastered the technical complexities of this new type of music and passed his knowledge on to others. "Never play ragtime fast at any time," he cautioned, while also insisting that "each note will be played as it is written" without improvisation.

Success permitted Joplin to spend less time as a performer and more as a composer. Yet disappointment and tragedy increasingly took their toll. In 1903 his ragtime opera *A Guest of Honor* received only one performance in St. Louis and went unpublished. The following year his child died. The distraught composer broke with his wife, who died shortly after. Joplin then moved to New York, remarried, and became active as a teacher. Meanwhile he composed *Tremonisha*

(1911), an opera portraying black life in Arkansas in the 1880s. An amalgam of ragtime and folk music, the work conveyed his hope that blacks could better their lives through education. It premiered in 1915 in Harlem, which was already becoming a mecca for black artists. Devoid of scenery and with the composer performing all the parts at the piano, *Tremonisha* met with indifference. His bitter disappointment contributed to Joplin's mental breakdown and, in all likelihood, to his death a few years later.

But jazz, another musical form that derived from black culture, had been dethroning ragtime even before Joplin's death. The work of this composer of some 50 piano rags subsequently faded into obscurity. Some interest revived in the 1950s and the 1960s; however, it was the great popularity of the movie *The Sting* (1973), featuring several of his works in its score (most notably "The Entertainer") that restored the reputation of the "king of ragtime." A later film, *Scott Joplin* (1977), starring Billy Dee Williams, portrayed his life for moviegoers.

demonstrated that functionalism did not preclude beauty. Sullivan died a defeated and embittered man, largely unappreciated during his own lifetime. But while he lived he powerfully influenced at least one major talent: Frank Lloyd Wright. During the prewar years this disciple of Sullivan designed such functional structures as the Larkin factory in Buffalo, New York, and also conceived several private residences that blended strikingly with the midwestern prairies on which they were built.

In Sullivan and Wright the nation had found artists who promised to fuse the elements of modernism with a native style. But Americans vacillated, unsure as to whether they should cling to the past or scrap it in favor of a commitment to modernism, uncertain as to whether they preferred foreign tastes to their own. Cass Gilbert's highly praised Woolworth Building in New York, completed in 1912, reflected these ambivalences: Gothic ornament surmounted its 57 stories of structural steel.

Questions pertaining to art and architecture were not the only ones that perplexed thoughtful Americans. What to do about problems of wealth and poverty, immigrants and urban life, business and labor, political corruption and reform, also vexed them. These problems and the answers sought were to constitute one of the nation's most vigorous reform efforts: progressivism.

SUGGESTED READINGS

The literature on the nation's social fabric is immense and varies widely in methodology from highly impressionistic to strongly quantitative. Chapters 2 and 3 suggest some sources that can also serve for this chapter.

Readable accounts of the lives and mores of the upper classes are found in Cleveland Amory, *The Proper Bostonians* (1947) and *The Last Resorts* (1952), as well as Lloyd Morris, *Incredible New York* (1951). The aspirations of the middle class provide the focus for two provocative studies: Burton J. Bledstein, *The Culture of Professionalism* (1976), and Thomas Haskell, *The Emergence of Professional Social Science* (1977). Both Melvyn Dubofsky, *Industrialism and the American Worker, 1865–1920* (1975), and Herbert G. Gutman, *Work, Culture, and Society in Industrializing America* (1976), skillfully analyze working-class life. For studies of social mobility, see Irwin G. Wyllie, *The Self-Made Man in America* (1954); John W. Tebbel, *From Rags to Riches: Horatio Alger, Jr. and the American Dream* (1963); Moses Rischin, ed., *The American Gospel of Success* (1965); and Stephan Thernstrom, *Poverty and Progress* (1964).

Select chapters of Maldwyn A. Jones, *American Immigration* (1960), offer a broad introduction to the New Immigrants, while John Higham, *Strangers in the Land* (1955), provides the best account of nativism. Thomas Kessner, *The Golden Door: Italian and Jewish Immigrant Mobility in New York City, 1880–1915* (1977), aptly combines narrative and quantification. Italian and Jewish immigrants receive further attention in Humbert Nelli's *The Italians of Chicago* (1970) and Irving Howe's richly detailed *World of Our Fathers* (1976).

An overview of religious life appears in pertinent chapters of Winthrop S. Hudson, *American Protestantism* (1961); John Tracy Ellis, *American Catholicism* (2d ed. rev., 1969); and Nathan Glazer, *American Judaism* (2d ed., 1972). E. Digby Baltzell's *The Protestant Establishment* (1964) offers an incisive but unrelenting tirade against upper-class WASPs.

Many works deal with the status of women around 1900. Portions of Eleanor Flexner, *Century of Struggle* (rev. ed., 1975), and Aileen S. Kraditor, ed., *Up from the Pedestal* (1968), provide appropriate reading, as does David M. Katzman, *Seven Days a Week: Women and Domestic Service in Industrializing America* (1978). Two fascinating approaches to the subject are Ann Douglas, *The Feminization of American Culture* (1977), and Lois Banner, *American Beauty* (1983).

For studies of the family, see Michael Gordon, ed., *The American Family in Social-Historical Perspective* (2d ed., 1978), and Carl Degler, *At Odds: Women and the Family in America* (1980).

The literature dealing with race keeps increasing. John Hope Franklin, *From Slavery to Freedom* (3d ed., 1967), provides a balanced and scholarly general history of American blacks. Louis R. Harlan's *Booker T. Washington* (2 vols., 1972, 1983) is an exemplary biography. Gunther Barth, *Bitter Strength* (1964), and Maxine Hong Kingston, *China Men* (1982), deal effectively with the experience of Chinese. For the American Indians, see Helen Hunt Jackson, *A Century of Dishonor* (1881), and Wilcomb E. Washburn, *The Indians in America* (1975).

Several highly informative general works of social history exist. Among them are Nelson Manfred Blake, *A Short History of American Life* (1952), and Foster Rhea Dulles, *America Learns to Play* (1940), as well as the more recent J. C. Furnas, *The Americans* (vol. 2, 1969), and Daniel J. Boorstin, *The Americans: The Democratic Experience* (1973). Athletics and urban amusements are treated in John A. Lucas and Ronald Smith, *Saga of American Sport* (1978); John F. Kasson, *Amusing the Million: Coney Island at the Turn of the Century* (1978); and Gunther Barth, *City People* (1980). Robert Sklar, *Movie-Made America* (1976), presents insights into the early years of the cinema. John Tasker Howard, *Our American Music* (4th ed., 1965), offers a standard survey, but see also Eileen Southern, *The Music of Black Americans* (2d ed., 1983), for neglected figures.

In the area of science Bernard Jaffe's *Men of Science in America* (1944) is helpful. More specific useful studies include Wyn Wachhorst, *Thomas Alva Edison* (1981), Linda O. McMurry, *George Washington Carver* (1981); Muriel Rukeyser, *Willard Gibbs* (1942); Ralph Barton Perry, *The Thought and Character of William James* (2 vols., 1935); and Dorothy Ross, *G. Stanley Hall* (1972). Nathan G. Hale, Jr., *Freud and the Americans* (1971), is a pioneering work on the early years of psychology and psychoanalysis in the United States.

Lawrence A. Cremin, *The Transformation of the School* (1961), gives keen insights into American education, while Sidney Hook, *John Dewey* (1939), looks at one of its most famous figures. Higher education is the subject of Richard Hofstadter and Walter P. Metzger, *The Development of Academic Freedom in the United States* (1955), and Lawrence R. Veysey, *The Emergence of the American University* (1965). Hugh Hawkins, *Between Harvard and America: The Educational Leadership of Charles W. Eliot* (1977), is a study of, arguably, the nation's most important nineteenth-century university president. For the popular appreciation of learning, see Robert O. Case and Victoria Case, *We Called It Culture: The Story of Chautauqua* (1958).

Detailed histories of newspapers and journals are presented in Frank L. Mott, *American Journalism* (3d ed., 1962) and *A History of American Magazines* (5 vols., 1930–1968). Excellent biographies of newspaper giants are W. A. Swanberg, *Citizen Hearst* (1961), and George Juergens, *Joseph Pulitzer and the New York World* (1966). Frank L. Mott's *Golden Multitudes: The Story of Best Sellers in the United States* (1947) looks at changing tastes in popular reading. There are a number of fine studies of the serious literature of the period, including Larzer Ziff, *The American 1890s* (1966); Alfred Kazin, *On Native Grounds* (1942); and Van Wyck Brooks, *New England: Indian Summer, 1865–1915* (1940) and *The Confident Years: 1885–1915* (1952). For specific writers, see Justin Kaplan, *Mr. Clemens and Mark Twain* (1966); Everett Carter, *Howells and the Age of Realism* (1954); and the monumental Leon Edel, *Henry James* (5 vols., 1953–1972).

The most complete survey of art and architecture is Oliver W. Larkin, *Art and Life in America* (rev. and enl. ed., 1960). For architecture only, see John E. Burchard and Albert Bush-Brown, *The Architecture of America* (1961), as well as the lively and highly opinionated Wayne Andrews, *Architecture, Ambition and Americans* (1955). A few useful studies of artists and architects include Lloyd Goodrich, *Thomas Eakins* (2 vols., 1983); Paul R. Baker, *Richard Morris Hunt* (1980); and Robert C. Twombly, *Frank Lloyd Wright* (1973) and *Louis Sullivan* (1986).

2

The Progressive Impulse

Unlike specific events, broad historical movements provide no exact dates of origin or completion. Progressivism is no exception. Yet most historians do agree that this reform movement began around the time of the Spanish-American War and continued until the nation entered World War I. Most further agree that it emerged out of the unsettling developments of the 1890s and flourished during years of general prosperity. Its fundamental meaning, however, remains elusive.

Historians, differing sharply from one another in their interpretations, have demonstrated the enormous difficulties of defining progressivism to everyone's satisfaction (see Suggested Readings at the end of this chapter). Most at first viewed the progressive movement as an urban, middle-class attempt to curb the worst excesses of industrialism, achieve humanitarian reforms, and democratize politics. In the 1950s historians continued to accept the middle-class nature of the movement, but argued that this had resulted from middle-class fears of being crushed between the forces of extreme wealth and giant corporations on one side and extreme poverty and an increasingly radicalized labor movement on the other. Anxious progressives thus sought reform to preserve their threatened status as leaders within their respective communities.

Other historians disagreed that progressivism was an overwhelmingly middle-class movement. Some stressed upper-class leadership; others pointed to the importance of the working class and immigrants in achieving reforms. Meanwhile scholars also began to question the long-held belief that progressivism was antibusiness. Diverse historians now agreed that businessmen greatly influenced progressive efforts, though they disagreed as to how and why. Some, for instance, posited the clash between business groups as an important element of progressivism, while others interpreted the movement as "the triumph of conservatism" in which major industrial and financial concerns subverted reform to their own interests. Additional interpretations focused on progressivism as ''the search for order'' in a fragmented society, or as a loose coalition of disgruntled individuals and groups combining to fight public corruption and inefficiency. Given the welter of conflicting views it is small wonder that one historian, Peter Filene, wrote ''An Obituary for the 'Progressive Movement','' arguing that the term has now lost any significant meaning.

The obituary seems premature. Granted that progressivism lacks a consensus as to its definition and that each interpretation may possess limited validity at best, it can remain a useful concept. Rather than distort its meaning by seeking to impute to it a single cause or direction, one can look at it as a series of different reform impulses held by varying groups who hoped to achieve different goals at a particular time in the nation's history. The progressives—politicians, publicists, intellectuals, clergy, businessmen, workers, ethnics, women, blacks, average citizens—were tied together by their determination to tackle one or more of the manifold problems of American life. Something, they knew, was seriously wrong, but they disagreed with one another over precisely what that trouble was and what to do about it.

THE PROGRESSIVE TEMPERAMENT

The public generally senses a need for reform, but frequently only when publicists articulate the need and offer concrete proposals or new ways of looking at problems does change take place. In all likelihood progressivism might never have emerged as a full-scale reform movement without the efforts of popular writers and crusading editors, intellectuals, and other concerned citizens.

Muckrakers President Theodore Roosevelt coined the term *muckraker* in 1906. Alluding to John Bunyan's famous allegory, *Pilgrim's Progress* (1678), he cited the character ''who was offered a celestial crown for his muck-rake, but would neither look up nor regard the crown he was offered, but continued to rake himself the filth of the floor.'' Roosevelt insisted that these sharp words were meant only for irresponsible critics of American life, but unwittingly he had provided the name for all who offered exposés of early twentieth-century life.

Periodicals, most of them recently established, took the lead in the muckraking movement. Like the yellow journals of the 1890s they reduced the price of individual issues and featured articles that would appeal to large numbers of readers. Beginning around 1902, *Collier's, Cosmopolitan, Munsey's,* and *McClure's* became the most prominent of this group. In the next decade these magazines enjoyed large average monthly circulations. *McClure's* became preeminent thanks to its astute publisher, Samuel S. McClure, and to such outstanding reporters as Lincoln Steffens, Ray Stannard Baker, and Ida Tarbell. Tarbell, for example, captured national attention with her serialized study of the oil monopoly possessed by Standard Oil, causing John D. Rockefeller to explode that ''not a word about that misguided woman'' should be spoken. Yet an important reason for the success of *McClure's* was the careful researching of articles in order to avoid libel suits.

The subjects for muckraking seemed endless: urban corruption, economic monopoly, dubious financial fortunes, depleted natural resources, and harmful food and med-

THE PROGRESSIVE TEMPERAMENT

33

icines, to cite the more conspicuous. One historian has estimated that approximately 2,000 articles appeared in the leading muckraking journals between 1903 and 1912. In addition, a number of muckraking novels dealt with serious social and moral problems. These included Upton Sinclair, *The Jungle* (1906); Winston Churchill, *Coniston* (1906); Brand Whitlock, *The Turn of the Balance* (1907); and David Graham Phillips, *The Cost* (1904).

By 1912 the movement had lost its appeal, in part because of its own success. Problems that it had uncovered and campaigned against had been solved or at least alleviated; further reform efforts either seemed futile or focused on less important matters. Readers also had grown tired of too much sensationalism. What had muckraking accomplished? Muckrakers, with the exception of certain impure food exposures (see Chapter 3), may not have been responsible for any legislation enacted to remedy the ills they had publicized. Yet they did undoubtedly help to focus attention upon the evils of the day and galvanized desires for reform.

Progressive Intellectuals   Other figures, who defy simple categorization, offered more subtle changes than the muckrakers in the manner of looking at values and institutions. These individuals, as social scientists, social engineers, humanists, educators, and jurists, engaged in a revolt against traditional ways of thinking and cultural judgments cherished in the late nineteenth century. Not all of these individuals subscribed to the progressive movement, but collectively, by attacking established values and norms, they provided progressives with useful, coherent arguments as well as new ways of looking at difficult problems. Broadly described, what they attacked included a strong belief in the individual's responsibility for his own fortune or misfortune, in only limited government activity, and in a capitalist system based on the laws of supply and demand. Darwinism colored this thinking and validated the "survival of the fittest" and a glacially slow pace for change as natural conditions. Those who accepted these views probably agreed with the eminent Social Darwinist sociologist William Graham Sumner when he wrote "The Absurd Effort to Make the World Over."

But not everyone thought that such an effort was absurd or that laissez-faire economics had a monopoly on truth. During the late nineteenth century, at Johns Hopkins University, Richard T. Ely trained a group of young economists to believe that "while we recognize the necessity of individual initiative in industrial life, we hold that the doctrine of laissez faire is unsafe in politics and unsound in morals." Government, Ely added, provided that aid which was "an indispensable condition of human progress." One of his students, John R. Commons, fully agreed. His ten-volume *Documentary History of American Industrial Society* (1910–1911) and four-volume *History of Labor in the United States* (1918–1935) called attention to the plight of the working classes and the need for state remediation.

Thorstein Veblen, a son of Norwegian immigrants, also studied with Ely at Johns Hopkins, but unlike his mentor he claimed to divorce ethics from economics. A convinced evolutionist, he has remained one of America's most original thinkers. Veblen considered economic institutions and the market place as ever changing, not fixed, as had the traditional economists against whom he rebelled. For all his disclaimers to moralizing, in *The Theory of the Leisure Class* (1899) he bitingly satirized the "higher barbarian" customs of "conspicuous consumption" and "conspicuous emulation" practiced by the rich. The wealthy, he argued, flaunted their affluence by adorning their wives and children in expensive clothing and jewels, having liveried servants, collecting useless pets and objects, and playing costly sports like polo—all basically to impress others. Worse, other classes felt compelled to imitate the rich as much as possible. In later works Veblen examined the change from industrial to finance capitalism and depicted engineers as the unsung heroes of American society and hope for the future.

Engineers found another champion in Frederick Winslow Taylor, father of time-and-motion studies. Abandoning a career in law for one in industry, Taylor developed and publicized a program of scientific management geared to producing greater efficiency. Since businessmen were too traditional in their thinking, he argued, it fell to engineers to teach both owners and workers the value of rational industrial planning. Taylor, fully as committed to moral and social results as to economic ones, also believed his system would help to build character by inculcating the virtues of hard work and self-discipline. His ideas appealed to a substantial number of progressive businessmen and their growing concern for efficiency, order, and organization.

Sociologists also joined in the revolt against accepted beliefs. Among these was Lester Frank Ward, who claimed that Social Darwinists, bent on stressing competition, had failed to note the importance of cooperation in nature. Viewed from this perspective, government had both the right and duty to restore the balance and harmony among social forces. Ward's disciple Edward A. Ross, in *Sin and Society* (1907), also emphasized the need for active government intervention to secure social progress.

Nobody did as much to attack the narrow framework and traditional precepts of the law as Oliver Wendell Holmes, Jr., the distinguished jurist who served as a U.S. Supreme Court justice from 1902 until 1932. Unlike most progressive reformers, Holmes was not a liberal in most of his personal convictions. He reveled in the memory of his Civil War experiences, admired the drive to power of the businessman James J. Hill, and thought it was his duty as a judge to let people make serious mistakes if they so chose. Nonetheless, he deplored the law's rigidity. ''The life of the law has not been logic but experience,'' he declared in arguing for legal realism. Holmes acidly dissented in *Lochner* v. *New York* (1905), in which the Supreme Court invalidated a maximum-hour law intended to protect bakers on the narrow constitutional grounds that the law abridged the individual's right of contract. ''The Fourteenth Amendment,'' he concluded, ''does not enact Mr. Herbert Spencer's *Social Statics*.''

Though not active as a progressive reformer, William James provided a useful conceptual framework for rejecting rigid thought and institutions. After winning renown as both physiologist and psychologist—he was the first professional psychologist in the United States—James turned his immense talents and energies to philosophy. He rejected the notion that we live in a closed universe where truth already exists and awaits our discovery. Instead, he called for an open universe in which we ''make'' truth. This Harvard University professor and brother of the fictionist Henry James developed his ideas into a philosophy sometimes termed radical empiricism and sometimes pragmatism. This philosophy advocated the testing of ideas from the point of view of their consequences rather than from some preordained criteria.

Much more concerned than James with restructuring American life and society was John Dewey. This younger philosopher, having at one point held to a more rigid pattern of philosophical tenets, came to believe that ideas, far from being eternal truths, were

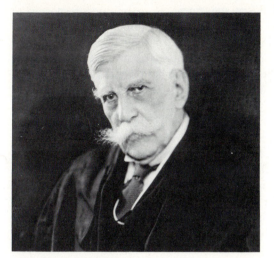
Oliver Wendell Holmes, Jr.

Charles Beard

instruments which people could accept or reject in their quest for progress. While James spoke basically to the needs of the individual, Dewey hoped that his instrumentalism would prove useful in the search for political and economic democracy. Toward this end, as noted in Chapter 1, he suggested major changes for the nation's schools.

Progressive historians also adopted new approaches and points of view. They were not interested in writing the narrative or scientific history that was popular in the nineteenth century, nor were they interested in writing in a detached manner. Rather, they called for a "new history," one which would ally itself with the social sciences and strive for a more just society. In *The New History* (1912), James Harvey Robinson of Columbia University looked for a usable past. Scorning the traditional study of the past as a pageant of royalty and battles, he called for a history that would meet contemporary needs by informing and enlightening the average citizen.

Charles Beard, another progressive historian and Robinson's colleague at Columbia, also subscribed to these ideas. Adopting the tool of class conflict to explain early American history and to show that the past was not, and should not be, sacrosanct, he debunked the Founding Fathers in his *An Economic Interpretation of the Constitution* (1913). Far from acting as disinterested, high-minded patriots, these "Funding Fathers," as he called them, drew up the Constitution in conformity with their own selfish economic interests. That Beard drew upon James Madison rather than Karl Marx for his version of class conflict—which he believed to be healthy for society—mattered not to offended readers. As one newspaper bellowed: "Scavengers hyena-like desecrate the graves of the dead patriots we revere." While later critics were to find his scholarship faulty, his book provided progressives with intellectual ammunition in their battle against the judicial tendency to construe the Constitution more often than not in favor of business interests and against those of labor.

The Social Gospel While muckrakers and intellectuals provided secular dimensions to the progressive temperament, clergymen—mainly but not entirely Protestants—added religious ones in the form of the Social Gospel movement. Many ministers responded to the accelerating industrial strife, growth of cities, and massive influx of immigrants that characterized the post-Civil War years. In part this reflected their fears that American Protestantism was losing touch with contemporary realities. But also they decided that as caring Christians they could not accept the status quo and limit themselves to preaching the salvation of individual souls for the hereafter. The Gospel must be socialized, they agreed, and Christianity made an effective force in daily life.

During the 1880s a few ministers, such as Washington Gladden and Josiah Strong, urged the adoption of Christian principles to combat unreformed capitalism, as well as socialism. By the century's end the Social Gospel had become more radical, particularly as urban conditions and the plight of the lower classes remained deplorable. Among others, Walter Rauschenbusch, a Baptist minister who taught at the Rochester Theological Seminary, preached Christian Socialism and called for government assistance in social and economic matters. Unlike the Marxists who stressed class warfare, Rauschenbusch was convinced that the Kingdom of God could be brought to this world by accepting the simple precepts of primitive Christianity.

The achievements of the Social Gospel are debatable. Certainly a number of clergymen remained conservative in their views or simply spurned an active role in secular affairs. Yet such important progressive reformers as Tom Johnson, ''Golden Rule'' Jones, and even Theodore Roosevelt acknowledged that the movement had influenced them. What does seem clear is that the Social Gospel helped to provide a setting for change.

THE PROGRESSIVE AGENDA

During the Progressive era the reforming impulse belonged to no one group. Rather, it stemmed from diverse elements: business, labor, humanitarians, victims of racial and sexual injustice. Sometimes their aims meshed, and sometimes not. Sometimes they directly conflicted with one another. Taken together, they illustrate that progressivism was an enormously complex movement.

Business   Earlier historians tended to view progressivism as antibusiness, almost by definition. The regulation of business, they argued, formed a key ingredient of the entire movement. Yet later historians have demonstrated that some businessmen themselves stood in the vanguard of regulation, perceiving that such action would redound, one way or another, to their benefit.

The impetus for regulation stemmed from the cutthroat competition that followed the Civil War. Many businesses failed as a result, and industrial prices sagged between the depression of 1873 and the election of 1896. The answer seemed to lay in restricting competition. Between 1895 and 1904 a merger mania occurred. More than 230 trusts capitalized at $6 billion developed between 1898 and 1904 alone. During this period some 300 firms merged yearly, mostly in basic industries. The steel industry, for example, gave rise to the nation's first billion-dollar trust as the powerful financier J. P. Morgan put together the holdings of Andrew Carnegie and others to form United States Steel. Despite hopes to the contrary, mergers did not essentially lessen competition. U.S.

Steel controlled nearly 62 percent of the market when it was organized in 1901, but by 1920 its share of the market had diminished to 40 percent. A similar story could be told for other industrial giants such as International Harvester. Stymied in their efforts, some business groups turned to the government to regulate industrial activity and thereby achieve stability and greater efficiency while not diminishing profits.

Yet it is important to remember that the business community was not monolithic. Businesses varied according to a variety of factors: type of urban or rural setting, region of the country, and size of enterprise. Then, too, there was the nature of the particular business. A railroad owner, for example, would want the highest possible rates to transport goods, while a shipper, who was also a businessman, would want the lowest rates. High-tariff advocates similarly separated themselves from low-tariff advocates, as eastern bankers did from western bankers. Staunchly antiunion individuals and groups such as the National Association of Manufacturers parted from the more conciliatory National Civic Federation and the U.S. Chamber of Commerce, which desired an end to the worst strife between capital and labor.

For all their substantial differences, most businessmen remained committed to certain traditionally shared beliefs. Profit was the legitimate goal of and reward for enterprise; workers' wages should not seriously erode capitalist wealth. In calling for government regulation through legislation and various commissions, they stretched without breaking their customary bias against such action. Still, in their overall search for an orderly economy, they constituted a progressive impulse fully as much as those identified with more obvious reform efforts.

Labor and Socialism Workers both gained and lost during these years. Unemployment, which had reached an alarming high of 18 percent during the depression of 1893–1896, became manageable, rising above 6 percent only three times in the years from 1900 to 1914. The average workweek declined to just under 50 hours, and wages generally increased. On the debit side, inflation seriously eroded these wage increases. The cost of living rose approximately 40 percent between 1897 and 1917. Wages of skilled workers more than kept pace (those for building tradesmen, for instance, advanced 140 percent). But unskilled workers, who comprised the distinct majority of the nation's nonagricultural work force, enjoyed gains of only 25–30 percent and thus suffered diminished real wages.

In their attempts to improve their lot, workers increasingly turned to unions. In 1900 some 791,000 men and women, representing slightly less than 3 percent of the nation's total labor force of 28.5 million, belonged to unions. A decade later union membership had increased to 2.1 million, almost 6 percent of the nearly 37 million Americans employed. The chief beneficiary of this development was the American Federation of Labor (AFL) whose membership between 1900 and 1910 grew from 548,000 to 1,494,000, and by 1915 rose to 1,946,000. At the head of this growing organization was Samuel Gompers. Apprenticed as a cigarmaker in his native London before emigrating to the United States during the Civil War, he headed the AFL from its establishment in 1886 to his death in 1924, with the exception of one year. Gompers advocated bread-and-butter unionism and was opposed to radicals, to third-party politics, and to utopian schemes for restructuring society. Under his tutelage, the AFL, which was composed of skilled workers organized along craft lines, concentrated on the fundamentals of higher wages, lower hours, and better conditions.

Gompers accepted the importance of the strike as a legitimate weapon of labor, though he collaborated with flexible employers to abate capital-labor differences. During the Progressive years there were never fewer than a thousand work stoppages each year, involving hundreds of thousands of workers. Some of these strikes erupted in violence. The Ludlow Massacre of April 29, 1914, for example, ended in tragedy when members of the Colorado state militia killed eleven children and two women while breaking a miners' strike.

Labor problems facing women and children shocked consciences of many Americans. Substandard wages, long hours, and dangerous working conditions provided the focus for progressive agitation, and efforts to improve the situation met with a genuine measure of success. By the time the nation entered World War I, nearly every state had banned labor for young children and had limited the hours older children could work. Similarly, most states enacted general maximum-hour legislation, while several passed minimum-wage laws. Stricter inspection laws improved sweatshop conditions, but by no means eradicated them. Attempts to secure federal laws to protect women and children fared less well. When Congress did act, the Supreme Court could and sometimes did invalidate its legislation. In 1918 *Hammer* v. *Dagenhart* struck down a child labor act. In 1923 *Adkins* v. *Children's Hospital* declared unconstitutional a minimum wage law for women in Washington, D.C.

Socialists rejected the belief of Gompers and the AFL that workers should settle for improved conditions and a greater part of the economic pie. They argued that workers deserved the whole pie, or at least most of it, and that capitalism must be destroyed, not reformed. They disagreed, however, on how to achieve their goals.

The central figure in American socialism at this time was Eugene Victor Debs. As leader of the American Railway Union, Debs had been jailed during the Pullman Strike of 1894 for disobeying a federal injunction. Socialists brought him works by Karl Marx to read while serving a six-month prison term, but he preferred other critiques of capitalism, like Henry Demarest Lloyd's *Wealth Against Commonwealth* (1894). Still, he did embrace socialism afterward, and in 1901 he became a founder of the Socialist Party of America (SPA). As a socialist, Debs was to run for president in every election between 1900 and 1920, except for that of 1916.

From its beginnings the SPA suffered from internal dissension between moderates and extremists. Prominent among the former were such men as Victor Berger, the mayor of Milwaukee, and the New York labor leader Morris Hillquit. Both of them staunchly opposed violence and revolution, placing their faith in elections and cooperation with middle-class liberals to achieve democratic socialism. Other right-wing socialists went no further than advocating public ownership of utilities. Opposed to these moderates were left-wing socialists, notably the Industrial Workers of the World (IWW), or "Wobblies" as they were more familiarly known, and their colorful, pugnacious leader, William ("Big Bill") Haywood. Established in 1905, the IWW pitched its appeal to workers in industries such as mining and lumber, where unionism previously had not made inroads. Unlike the AFL, the IWW also courted immigrant laborers. (The AFL had been wary of foreign workers since many were willing to toil for lower wages or act as strikebreakers.)

Yet what most set the Wobblies' leaders apart was their syndicalism, which encompassed an implacable opposition to the political process and a revolutionary insistence that the workers must seize power directly through strikes and sabotage, ultimately

THE PROGRESSIVE AGENDA

Eugene Victor Debs

culminating in the direct control of production by the workers. Despite their success in aiding striking textile workers in Lawrence, Massachusetts, in 1912, the Wobblies enjoyed only limited support. As syndicalists, they let their revolutionary rhetoric and ultra individualism take precedence over the necessary if duller tasks of organization. More important, their views and actions frightened many people. During World War I the federal government destroyed them with little complaint from the citizenry at large (see Chapter 5). The war would also weaken the forces of moderate socialism. Yet, before that, the SPA, which was established in 1901 with a membership of 10,000, was to win hundreds of local and state elections. By 1912 the party had increased its membership to more than 100,000 by attracting nonsocialist reformers who believed that neither major political party could or would accomplish necessary changes in American life.

Humanitarian Reforms and Social Control Much of the effort of progressive reformers centered on social injustice. Whether their motivation was basically secular or religious, they believed that they were indeed their brothers'—and sisters'—keepers. And if these people sometimes resented this as an intrusion into their personal lives, reformers seemed unbothered.

Settlement houses gave humanitarian reformers their finest hour. More often than not these reformers were women of solid middle-class backgrounds who sought useful outlets for their abilities and ambitions. For these reformers self-interest merged with altruism as they sought to alleviate the misery of immigrants and the urban poor.

Jane Addams

Stanton Coit founded the first settlement house in New York City in 1886, but it was Chicago's Hull House, established by Jane Addams in 1889, that provided the model for other such ventures. Beginning by using their own money and by soliciting contributions from the wealthy, Addams and her friend Ellen Gates Starr purchased a house in the immigrant section of Chicago. They then proceeded to set up a kindergarten, a day-care center, juvenile clubs, an employment bureau, and courses in adult education, all the while offering general counseling. Initially scoffed at by hard-nosed public officials and cynics, the two soon won enormous respect from an admiring nation. Other settlement houses followed, including Robert Woods's South End House (1892) in Boston and Lillian Wald's Henry Street Settlement (1893) on New York's Lower East Side. During the Progressive years thousands of these institutions emerged to care for and uplift the underprivileged and to imbue them with acceptable middle-class American values.

The humanitarian impulse took other forms as well. Some relief for the urban masses trapped in slums came through tenement house reform. Pushed, for example, by Lawrence Veiller's years spent painstakingly educating the middle and upper classes to the horrors of slum life, New York enacted a tenement law in 1901, which, among other provisions, mandated toilet facilities for all existing apartments and adequate ventilation, light, and fire protection for future ones. Other states and various municipalities followed suit. The sociologist Robert Hunter in his pathbreaking book *Poverty* (1904) suggested that as many as 10 million persons might be undernourished. His contention that some 70,000 New York City children went to school without enough food resulted in school lunches subsidized by the city. Meanwhile a corps of professional social workers sought

THE PROGRESSIVE AGENDA

to improve the quality of life for the young by fighting for parks, playgrounds, swimming pools, and improved facilities for physical and mental health.

Reform efforts also reached into the areas of crime and punishment. Police activity became more professionalized and better equipped to deal with crime. The use of policewomen and fingerprinting, for example, became more common at this time. Also, psychologists, sociologists, and jurists pioneered in the battle to win such innovations as probation and parole for certain offenders. Especially noteworthy among these reformers was Judge Ben Lindsey of Denver, who dedicated himself to preventing juvenile delinquents from leading future lives as hardened criminals.

Humanitarianism shaded into social control. Implicit in the progressive attempts to uproot social distress was the fear that unrelieved suffering and frustration could erupt into a violent attack on the fabric of society itself. Respect for order and the dread of anarchy thus provided additional motivation for progressives.

The problem of drinking offers an example of the mixed motives of reformers. Since its origins the United States has never lacked for advocates of temperance or abstinence. In the years after the Civil War the crusade took on renewed fervor, as antidrinking champions cited the harmful effects of liquor to health, the close connection between saloons and prostitution, the high rates of individual accidents and workdays lost due to drink, the depletion of the precious wages of the lower classes, and the disturbing incidence of wife- and child-beatings at the hands of drunken husbands and fathers. Then, too, the movement had strong ties with fundamental Protestantism, which closely linked liquor with sin. Frances Willard resigned her position as president of the Evanston College for Ladies to join the powerful Women's Christian Temperance Union (WCTU). She subsequently served as its president from 1879 to her death in 1898.

Even more effective in the crusade against Demon Rum was the Anti-Saloon League (ASL), which was established in 1893. Male opponents who sneered as women members sang "The Lips That Touch Liquor Must Never Touch Mine" came to regret it. The ASL, fortified by large contributions, including some $350,000 donated by John D. Rockefeller, showed a flair for organization, timing, and strategy. Initially it favored local option or state prohibition. But it took advantage of the World War I need to conserve grain to push through Congress in 1917 the Eighteenth Amendment banning the manufacture, sale, or transportation of intoxicating liquors. Two years later the amendment became part of the Constitution. Reformers had not been deterred because many individuals, including large numbers of native and immigrant workers, objected vehemently to what they regarded as an infringement upon their personal liberties.

Ambivalent attitudes toward immigrants, particularly those from southern and eastern Europe, also characterized progressive impulse for social control. From 1901 until 1910 nearly as many immigrants reached the United States as had arrived during the last twenty years of the previous century. Most progressives freely accepted the new arrivals. Some, like Jane Addams, even welcomed the rich ethnic diversity they brought with them, assuming, however, that they ultimately would fuse into the cultural melting pot and become good American citizens. As Theodore Roosevelt pronounced: "We have a right to ask all of these immigrants and the sons of these immigrants that they become Americans and nothing else. . . ."

Yet not all progressives believed immigrants should have the right to become Americans. Liberal reformers like John R. Commons and Edward A. Ross were generally hostile to them, as was the popular novelist Jack London, whose belief in the superiority of Nordic and Anglo-Saxon peoples reached even greater explicitness in the writings of Madison Grant and Lothrop Stoddard. A number of nativists, following in the wake of late-nineteenth-century exclusionist groups, called for stronger restrictions or even total curtailment of immigration. A movement for a literacy requirement gained momentum after the 41-volume Report on Immigration (1911) by the Dillingham Commission cited the dangers of unlimited immigration, particularly among the semieducated. Despite vetoes by both Presidents Taft and Wilson, Congress passed a literacy requirement over the latter's veto in 1917. Meanwhile nativists, some of whom were avid progressive reformers, fought to limit the political clout of immigrants already here through the adoption of state literacy tests and other restrictionist measures. Xenophobic progressives were so largely because they viewed the newcomers as sources of poverty and crime, as well as political corruption and dangerous beliefs.

Blacks and Progressivism   As nativists worked to limit the political influence of immigrants, racists in the South completed the disfranchisement and segregation of blacks begun in the 1890s. Ironically, many who deprived blacks of their political and civil rights did so in the name of reform. Before progressive changes could take place, they reasoned, the issue of white supremacy must be settled so as not to permit conservative foes of reform to distract voters by playing upon questions of race.

Blacks found no help from the federal government. Initially they took heart when President Roosevelt appointed several blacks to important positions and denounced lynchings. In a display of immense symbolic value he had also invited Booker T. Washington for dinner at the White House in 1901. The event outraged many. Fumed South Carolina's Senator Ben Tillman: ''The action of President Roosevelt in entertaining that nigger will necessitate our killing a thousand niggers in the South before they will learn their place again.'' Roosevelt never extended a second invitation.

More serious in dashing the hopes of blacks was the Brownsville, Texas, riot of August 13, 1906. After days of taunting by angry whites, a small group of black soldiers from the 25th U.S. Infantry went on a shooting spree in the town, killing one white civilian. Eyewitness reports and relevant evidence were sketchy, and no soldier would offer information during the official investigation that followed. Finally, on November 5, the day before congressional elections, Roosevelt ordered all 160 black soldiers of the companies in question discharged without honor or pension. Included in the group were 6 Medal of Honor winners as well as 13 who held certificates of merit for courageous action. Though some Republicans, such as Ohio's Senator Joseph B. Foraker, strongly protested, the presidential order stood.

Blacks fared no better under Roosevelt's successor, William Howard Taft, who reduced their political patronage. Taft's successor, the Democrat Woodrow Wilson, appointed no blacks to office, and out of deference to his Southern supporters in Congress, accepted, and perhaps even encouraged, the segregation of black government workers in the District of Columbia.

Yet even by the time of the Brownsville affair many people had lost faith in Booker T. Washington's policy of patience and accommodation. Foremost among them was W. E. B. DuBois, a young black sociologist who sarcastically referred to Washington as the most popular southerner since Jefferson Davis. DuBois's philosophy provided an alternative to that of the famed educator at Tuskegee.

W. E. B. DuBois

Born in Massachusetts of mixed black and white ancestry, DuBois, unlike Washington, never directly knew the blight of slavery. He grew up poor but was generally accepted by white townspeople, some of whom contributed money to send him to Fisk University. In 1895 DuBois became the first black to receive a doctorate from Harvard University, writing his dissertation on "The Suppression of the African Slave Trade to the U.S.A., 1638–1870." He then pursued further study at the University of Berlin. Despite or perhaps because of his unusual background, DuBois perceived the situation for blacks differently than Washington: he insisted that blacks settle for nothing short of full equality. As he stated in *The Souls of Black Folk* (1903), the black man "simply wishes to make it possible for a man to be both a Negro and an American . . . without having the doors of Opportunity closed roughly in his face." Instead of being satisfied with manual and industrial training, as Washington advised, able blacks should demand a liberal arts education and seek training for the professions. DuBois was an acknowledged elitist. Having little faith in the masses, he stressed that leadership should come from the "talented tenth" of the black population.

In 1905 DuBois called upon black leaders to meet in Niagara Falls to discuss a program for combating racial discrimination. Lacking grass-roots support and incurring much hostility from Washington, the meeting proved a fiasco. Yet four years later, on the centennial of Abraham Lincoln's birth, a new group met and pledged itself to work for an end to segregation, the achievement of equal educational opportunities, and the enforcement of the Fourteenth and Fifteenth Amendments. The group called itself the National Association for the Advancement of Colored People (NAACP). Biracial in membership, it included such prominent whites as Jane Addams, William Dean Howells, John Dewey, and Oswald Garrison Villard, grandson of the famed abolitionist William Lloyd Garrison. The NAACP named DuBois as an officer and editor of its official publication, *The Crisis*.

With the death of Booker T. Washington in 1915 an era seemed at an end. Blacks, driven by implacable hostility encountered in the South, began migrating. Between 1890 and 1909 some 200,000 largely rural blacks moved to the North, particularly to its cities. During the next decade perhaps a half million more made the same trek. The National Urban League was established in 1911 to help these newcomers adapt to their strange surroundings.

Who was right, Washington or DuBois? Was Washington cowardly in his public acceptance of the abuse of blacks (he privately and quietly fought against it), or was he a realist making the best of a hopeless situation? Was DuBois a courageous leader intent on leading his people out of the wilderness of pain and suffering, or was he a visionary too far ahead of his time? Historians, then and now, have debated these questions heatedly. But many fully agree with DuBois's assessment that ''the problem of the twentieth century is the problem of the color line.''

Women and Reform   Women contributed significantly to the progressive impulse. Active in every major reform cause of the period, they fought on behalf of others as well as themselves. Like blacks, they were the objects of long-standing and pervasive discrimination. Also like blacks, women were divided by considerations of class, education, and personal temperament, as well as by questions of overall goals and tactics. Yet, unlike blacks, women achieved some notable victories in their struggle against inequality.

Though most men and many women themselves continued to believe that the proper place for women was at home tending to domestic chores, a surprisingly large number of women were entering the work force. In 1890 some 4 million of them held jobs. That figure rose to 7.4 million by 1910. Qualitative changes accompanied this increase, as more women left domestic work to enter factories, offices, and the professions. Many regarded these positions as liberating, despite receiving discriminatory wages and treatment. As the prominent writer and reformer Charlotte Perkins Gilman explained, ''there is nothing more absolutely in the way of social progress to-day than . . . the economically dependent woman.'' Sharing Gilman's concern, others fought against the economic exploitation of women. Notable among them was the resourceful Florence Kelley, general secretary of the National Consumers' League. The Women's Trade Union League, established in 1903, also brought together working-class women with upper- and middle-class reformers in an effort to encourage workers to unionize.

The women's struggle went well beyond economic issues, extending to such vital and divisive concerns as marriage, sexuality, and childbearing. Marriage, considered by many the foundation of society, showed signs of stress. The Census of 1890 revealed only 33,000 divorces, but by 1920 that figure had risen sharply to 170,000. A more vivid statistic was the ratio between divorce and marriage. In 1900 there was one divorce for every seventeen marriages; twenty years later the figure had more than doubled. Whatever threat a rising divorce rate posed to the moral and social order, it did not

THE PROGRESSIVE AGENDA

necessarily mean that married couples were less happy—only that they were less willing to endure their misery.

Sexual questions troubled feminists. Some reflected a Victorian prudery and distaste for sex, associating it with overbearing, insensitive husbands; the less they heard about sex the better. Other women went beyond this Victorian mode of thinking and called for more honest sexual relationships that would gratify both partners. Few feminists, however, could accept the radical doctrine of free love, preached and practiced by the notorious anarchist Emma Goldman. Yet some were clearly willing to challenge traditional taboos. Alfred C. Kinsey's *Sexual Behavior in the Human Female* (1953) revealed that for women born between 1900 and 1917 instances of premarital sex doubled or trebled.

Birth control spoke to the question of both marriage and sex. Led by the pioneering efforts of Margaret Sanger, the movement to provide contraceptive information and devices gained strength despite considerable obstacles, legal and otherwise. Some reformers supported contraception primarily as a hygienic measure; others viewed it principally as a means of advancing sexual freedom and enjoyment. Some women asked: Are our bodies our own? Yet many women as well as men continued to condemn contraception on religious and moral grounds, arguing that sex was intended for procreation within marriage and not for fornication.

For many women nothing better illustrated their subservience than not being able to vote. Suffragists had been arguing this point since the Seneca Falls convention of July 1848. Elizabeth Cady Stanton and Susan B. Anthony organized the National Woman Suffrage Association in 1869, which in 1890 became the National American Woman Suffrage Association (NAWSA). Yet by 1900 only four states had allowed women's suffrage. The movement accelerated during the Progressive era as astute leaders like Carrie Chapman Catt and Dr. Anna Howard Shaw turned NAWSA into a more effective political force. Disaffected by NAWSA's tactics of moderation, the radical Alice Paul broke with the organization and formed her own group, the Congressional Union, which later became the National Woman's party. Paul was opposed to NAWSA's policy of fighting for suffrage on a state-by-state basis and demanded a constitutional amendment. She pressured individual politicians, including President Wilson, and dramatized her cause through such drastic measures as hunger strikes. Thus she complemented and influenced the activities of NAWSA, which by 1917 had more than two million members. Prodded by Wilson, Congress in 1918 passed the Nineteenth Amendment granting women the vote, and by 1920 the amendment became part of the Constitution.

Winning the suffrage did not solve every feminist problem, as some had hoped. Few issues elicited a solid "woman's vote." Moreover, many women accepted suffrage as their ultimate goal and disdained further reform efforts. Some feminists thought otherwise, believing that winning political rights was but the first step toward full equality. In 1923 the National Woman's party advocated an Equal Rights Amendment (ERA), which would make discrimination on the basis of sex illegal. To date the amendment remains in limbo. Yet even Alice Paul, a fervent supporter of the ERA, admitted that the gains women had made during the Progressive years were real, if limited. Looking back half a century later, she saw their efforts as "a sort of mosaic. Each of us puts in one little stone, and then you get a great mosaic at the end."

In a sense Alice Paul's description applies to the progressive movement as a whole, with various individuals and groups contributing different stones to form a rich pattern

BIOGRAPHICAL SKETCH

MARGARET HIGGINS SANGER · *1883–1966*

Born in Corning, New York, the sixth of 11 children, to a family of very limited financial means, Margaret Sanger later blamed the large number of children for her family's economic woes and for the death of her exhausted mother at age 49. But it was a searing incident experienced as a nurse working on New York's impoverished Lower East Side that turned her into a crusader for birth control. The episode involved a lower-class woman dying in her arms after a self-induced abortion. Unable to prevent this death, the young nurse was determined to keep others from meeting a similar fate.

Many Americans during the Progressive era condemned birth control on moral grounds and argued that it would invite "race suicide" by lowering the nation's birthrate. Further, the Comstock Act of 1873 made it illegal to send contraceptive information or devices through the mails. Sanger frequently ran afoul of both public opinion and the law, going to jail on several occasions for her activities. Nonetheless, she continued to write and speak on birth control. A prewar socialist, she received strong support from various radicals, including Emma Goldman. She also traveled to Europe, where she gained valuable insights from such knowledgeable figures as the English psychologist Havelock Ellis. In 1915 she opened the first birth control clinic in the United States in Brownsville, a section of Brooklyn that was heavily populated by poor immigrants. Authorities soon closed the clinic, but in 1917 Sanger founded the National Birth Control League, which later became the Planned Parenthood Federation of America.

Though a supporter of a variety of progressive causes, Margaret Sanger continued to make sexual reforms her priority. Women,

she argued, must possess the unequivocal right to secure full sexual knowledge, to decide whether or not to bear children, and to consummate their physical urges with whomever they chose. But believing that lower-class women either could not or would not accept her views, she increasingly turned to upper-class, educated women for support. For nearly half a century she actively championed her pioneering program, despite continued opposition. At home she challenged anti-birth control laws in the courts and encouraged the formation of birth control clinics, as well as the dissemination of contraceptive instruction. Abroad she organized the International Planned Parenthood Federation and campaigned widely for limiting the world's population. The last major achievement of this controversial reformer involved the promotion of birth control pills, which first reached the United States in 1960.

SUGGESTED READINGS

of reform impulses. Diverse as they were, what knitted these impulses together was the understanding that exposés, statistical studies, and consciousness-raising were critically important but not sufficient for achieving solutions. Only the political process, most thought, could provide these.

SUGGESTED READINGS

Numerous general and interpretive works on progressivism exist. For brief but extremely readable accounts of the era, see Samuel P. Hays, *The Response to Industrialism: 1885–1914* (1957); William L. O'Neill, *The Progressive Years* (1975); and Arthur S. Link and Richard L. McCormick, *Progressivism* (1983). George E. Mowry, *The California Progressives* (1951), and Richard Hofstadter, *The Age of Reform* (1955), interpret progressivism from the point of view of class status. John D. Buenker, *Urban Liberalism and Progressive Reform* (1973), notes the importance of workers and immigrants as components of the movement. Robert H. Wiebe, *Business and Reform* (1962), focuses on businessmen as progressives, while Gabriel Kolko, *The Triumph of Conservatism* (1963), a stimulating though strongly biased work, sees progressivism as the tool of businessmen. Other important interpretive works include Wiebe's *The Search for Order* (1967) and David P. Thelen's *The New Citizenship* (1972).

Louis Filler, *Crusaders for American Liberalism* (1939), and David M. Chalmers, *The Social and Political Ideas of the Muckrakers* (1964), deal in detail with muckraking. For related studies, see Peter Lyon, *Success Story: The Life and Times of S.S. McClure* (1963), and Lincoln Steffens, *Autobiography* (1931). Arthur and Lila Weinberg, eds., *The Muckrakers* (1961), offers a useful sampling of representative writings.

A difficult but rewarding work, Morton White, *Social Thought in America* (1949), provides a keen analysis of progressive thought, as do Richard Hofstadter, *The Progressive Historians* (1968); David W. Marcell, *Progress and Pragmatism* (1974); and David W. Noble, *The Progressive Mind: 1890–1917* (rev. ed., 1981).

For other works on some of the intellectuals discussed in this chapter, see Sudhir Kakar, *Frederick Taylor* (1970); Joseph Dorfman, *Thorstein Veblen and His America* (1961); and Gay Wilson Allen, *William James* (1967).

Henry F. May, *Protestant Churches and Industrial America* (1949); Charles H. Hopkins, *The Rise of the Social Gospel in American Protestantism, 1865–1915* (1940); and Aaron I. Abell, *American Catholicism and Social Action* (1960), detail the Social Gospel movement. Robert D. Cross, ed., *The Church and the City* (1967), contains some good selections of pertinent primary sources.

For the business "impulse" to reform, in addition to the Wiebe and Kolko books cited above, see James Weinstein, *The Corporate Ideal in the Liberal State, 1900–1918* (1968). Samuel Haber, *Efficiency and Uplift* (1964), and Samuel P. Hays, *Conservation and the Gospel of Efficiency* (1959), examine the ideal of efficiency as an influence on progressive thought.

Labor and socialism have received extensive coverage. Relevant sections of Melvyn Dubofsky, *Industrialism and the American Worker, 1865–1920* (1975), and Herbert G. Gutman, *Work, Culture, and Society in Industrializing America* (1976), as previously noted, offer important insights into the conditions of workers. For the lives of prominent labor leaders, see Samuel Gompers, *Seventy Years of Life and Labor* (1925), and Nick Salvatore, *Eugene V. Debs* (1983). David A. Shannon, *The Socialist Party of America* (1955), and James Weinstein, *The Decline of Socialism in America, 1912–1925* (1967), examine the fate of radicalism at this time, as does the fine study of the IWW by Melvyn Dubofsky, *We Shall Be All* (1969).

The literature on humanitarian reforms is vast. Robert H. Bremner, *From the Depths* (1956), analyzes the attempts to identify and understand poverty, while Allen F. Davis, *Spearheads for Reform* (1967), examines settlement houses. Davis's *American Heroine: The Life and Legend of*

Jane Addams (1973), is a valuable complement to Jane Addams, *Twenty Years at Hull House* (1910). Roy Lubove, *The Progressives and the Slums* (1962), looks at tenement conditions in New York. Jeremy P. Felt, *Hostages of Fortune* (1965), also looks at New York, this time in terms of its child labor problems. John F. McClymer, *War and Welfare* (1980), is one of the more recent of several good studies chronicling the rise of professional social workers.

For insights into prohibition as a means of social control, see Joseph R. Gusfield, *Symbolic Crusade* (1963); James H. Timberlake, *Prohibition and the Progressive Movement, 1900–1920* (1963); and Norman H. Clark, *Deliver Us From Evil* (1976). Anti-immigrant feelings are touched upon in numerous studies, but John Higham, *Strangers in the Land* (1955), remains the preeminent study of nativism. C. Vann Woodward, *The Strange Career of Jim Crow* (3d ed., 1974) is a classic analysis of the rise of segregation in the South, but see also Jack T. Kirby, *Darkness at the Dawning* (1972), and J. Morgan Kousser, *The Shaping of Southern Politics* (1974), which illustrates the uses of quantitative history at its best. The response of blacks is carefully explored in August Meier, *Negro Thought in America, 1880–1915* (1963), and James M. McPherson, *The Abolitionist Legacy* (1975). See also Elliot M. Rudwick, *W. E. B. DuBois* (1963).

Studies of women and women's reforms have proliferated over the past two decades. Sheila M. Rothman's *Woman's Proper Place* (1978) is a solid study of the changing ways in which women have been perceived and have perceived themselves since the late nineteenth century. William L. O'Neill has written two exemplary works in *Divorce in the Progressive Era* (1967) and *Everyone Was Brave* (1969). Good studies of individual reformers include Josephine C. Goldmark, *Impatient Crusader: Florence Kelley's Life Story* (1953); Richard Drinnon, *Rebel in Paradise: A Biography of Emma Goldman* (1961); and David M. Kennedy, *Birth Control in America: The Career of Margaret Sanger* (1970). Students of woman's suffrage will benefit from Aileen S. Kraditor, *The Ideas of the Woman Suffrage Movement, 1890–1920* (1965), Ellen Carol DuBois, *Feminism and Suffrage* (1978), and Lois Banner, *Elizabeth Cady Stanton* (1980).

3

The Politics of Reform

Progressives, as noted in the previous chapter, differed sharply as to what kind of reforms they wanted. Most did agree, however, that politics provided an important means for obtaining desired change. But to change society and its institutions through politics, it was also necessary to change politics itself—at the city, state, and national levels. The various attempts to reform American political life constitute an essential part of progressivism and provide a clearer understanding of what that movement hoped to achieve.

REFORMING THE CITIES

Political Machines: Critics and Defenders   Lord James Bryce, a distinguished British visitor in the late 1880s, noted that "the government of cities is the one conspicuous failure of the United States." Many Americans agreed. Looking around, they found their major cities teeming with tenements and slums, plagued with vice, squalor, and poverty, and saddled with insufficient basic public services. Few doubted that these urban ills stemmed from misgovernment by political bosses and their machines.

Boss rule rested on a combination of patronage and special favors. Well-rewarded lieutenants skillfully organized voters at district and ward levels. Money to pay these henchmen and, if necessary, to purchase votes came from favors, particularly those granted to businessmen. Since the boss controlled the machinery of government, he could, for example, make deals involving utilities or transportation franchises, sell contracts for municipal building or repairs, or simply demand outright bribes and kickbacks. Corruption need not be that blatant. George Washington Plunkitt, a colorful Tammany Hall figure who made a fortune in New York real estate, defended "honest graft," such as profiting from inside information. If you learned that the city was going to purchase

49

Fifth Avenue in New York City at the beginning of the twentieth century.

a certain building, he argued, buy the building first and then sell it to the city at a handsome profit. Said Plunkitt proudly of himself, "I seen my opportunities and I took 'em."

Yet boss rule did provide benefits. Often the boss understood the needs of the common people, especially the immigrants, far better than his middle-class critics. He was present at festive occasions, and when there was illness, death, the loss of a job, or trouble with the police, he gave advice and assistance, asking only to be remembered at election time. Even blacks, ignored by most progressives, received favors and protection from bosses like James Pendergast of Kansas City and George B. Cox of Cincinnati. Given the enormously complex problems facing cities, even honest civic officials might not have fared any better than the machine politicians.

Reformers disagreed. Machine politics debased democracy by corrupting officials, favor-seeking businessmen, and ordinary citizens alike. "The spirit of graft and of lawlessness is the American spirit," concluded the muckraker Lincoln Steffens in *The Shame of the Cities* (1904). The cities "shamed" by Steffens's exposés included St. Louis, Minneapolis, Pittsburgh, Philadelphia, Chicago, and New York, but few doubted that he might have added almost any large city to his list. Reformers concurred that only the destruction of machine rule could save urban America.

REFORMING THE CITIES

POPULATION OF THE 15 LARGEST AMERICAN CITIES: 1900

New York	3,437,202
Chicago	1,698,575
Philadelphia	1,293,697
St. Louis	575,238
Boston	560,892
Baltimore	508,957
Cleveland	381,768
Buffalo	352,387
San Francisco	342,782
Cincinnati	325,902
Pittsburgh	321,616
New Orleans	287,104
Detroit	285,704
Milwaukee	285,315
Washington, D.C.	278,718

Reform Mayors   Progressive reform began in the 1890s and accelerated during the years before World War I. Sometimes citizens' groups assumed leadership, as when aroused Chicagoans kept Charles T. Yerkes from gaining control of a 100-year, tax-free franchise for the city's street railways. More often reform mayors, who were frequently businessmen or occasionally socialists, led nonpartisan battles for good government and improved civic services. Both Seth Low and John Purroy Mitchel prescribed and served large doses of honest administration for a rapidly growing New York, which by 1900 numbered almost 3.5 million inhabitants. Honest, efficient government also benefited Milwaukee under Socialist mayor Emil Seidel, while San Francisco regained respectability when irate citizens, led by the journalist Fremont Older and the sugar magnate Ruldolph Spreckels, broke the power of the notorious Boss Abe Ruef and sent him to prison. Other cities also elected reform mayors, probably none more esteemed than two from Ohio: Samuel M. Jones of Toledo and Tom L. Johnson of Cleveland.

Dubbed ''Golden Rule'' for his efforts to bring Christian ethics to politics, Jones served as Toledo's mayor from 1897 until his death in 1905. Unsuccessful in his quest for municipal ownership of utilities, he did achieve an eight-hour day and minimum wage standards for city employees. He also established free kindergartens, public parks, and outdoor concerts for the benefit and enjoyment of all. Although a wealthy man, he subscribed to Christian socialism. Tom Johnson, another millionaire, won four consecutive two-year terms in office in Cleveland between 1901 and 1909. He fared better than Jones against the utilities interests, bringing street railways under closer supervision and lowering costs for riders. Steffens called Johnson the ''best mayor of the best-governed city in America.''

Institutional Reforms   While supporting the work of reform mayors, many progressives turned to structural changes and expertise to achieve more lasting improvements. After a devastating tidal wave in 1900, the citizens of Galveston, Texas, replaced the mayor and aldermen with a special board of five commissioners to govern the city on an emergency basis. Proving successful, this commission form of government became permanent three years later. Other cities followed Galveston's example, and by 1914 over 300 municipalities had adopted some form of commission government. For other reformers, the city manager plan of government, first adopted in 1913 by Dayton, Ohio, seemed attractive. Under this plan a popularly elected commission or city council appointed an executive to conduct the city's affairs. Within ten years more than 300 cities had opted for this arrangement.

Reformers enlisted the services of nonpartisan experts to cope with the perplexing questions of public service, taxation, and social problems. Public-spirited research groups, such as the National Municipal League and a host of local bureaus designed to do research and provide technical assistance for solving these problems, organized throughout the nation's cities. At the same time, the number of municipal workers owing their positions to civil service examination rather than party patronage increased. To achieve reform, the progressives were trying to take the politics out of politics.

But did they succeed? While a greater degree of honesty and efficiency crowned reform efforts in some American cities, others clearly remained under the domination of machines and special interests, while continuing to suffer from incompetent rule. New civil servants, moreover, sometimes formed an entrenched bureaucracy that hindered future reform efforts. Municipal ''reform'' sometimes diminished the political role of the lower and lower-middle classes, as well as ethnic and racial minorities, especially as it struck at ward representation in city councils. Then, too, hostile state legislatures continued to thwart urban reformers even after the latter had secured home rule for their cities. Still, they had made a beginning. Public awareness had grown, and even some bosses and machines, like Charles F. Murphy and his Tammany Hall, began to respond more positively to public needs.

STATE REFORM

Progressives at the state level faced many of the same kinds of problems as their counterparts in cities. Like municipal reformers, they fought to establish governments purged of corruption, guided by experts, and responsive to the needs of the people rather than the special interests.

Democratizing Politics   Believing that the cure for democracy was more democracy, progressives battled to change the electoral process. By 1900 they had forced nearly all states to adopt the Australian (or secret) ballot and many to adopt the short ballot, which simplified the voting procedure. By 1914 two-thirds of the states had also enacted direct primary and presidential preference laws, thought it soon became painfully clear that boss rule and machine politics could dominate those preelection contests, much as southern suffrage restrictionists could subvert the intent of the Australian ballot and use it to reduce voter turnout.

A trio of innovations—the initiative, referendum, and recall—theoretically brought government even closer to the people. The initiative empowered voters to force a state legislature to consider a proposal. The referendum, on the other hand, gave them the opportunity to pass judgment on laws already passed or to vote yes or no on an issue not yet decided. The recall allowed voters to remove a corrupt or unresponsive official before his term expired. By 1914 more than twenty states had adopted the initiative or referendum or both, while more than ten had secured the recall. Yet it should also be remembered that well-organized minority interest groups sometimes thwarted the democratic intent of the initiative and referendum.

Progressives achieved another victory by ending the practice of having state legislatures select United States senators. Cliques of opportunistic politicians in league with business interests frequently pushed their choices through the legislatures regardless of public opinion. In 1906 David Graham Phillips wrote a series of muckraking articles, "The Treason of the Senate," for William Randolph Hearst's *Cosmopolitan* magazine. Naming names and describing the United States Senate as the "millionaire's club," he insisted: "Treason is a strong word, but not too strong . . . to characterize the situation in which the Senate is the eager, resourceful, indefatigable agent of interests as hostile to the American people as any invading army could be, and vastly more dangerous. . . ." Senators, according to Phillips, better represented moneyed interests—oil, steel, banking, railroads, lumber, and sugar, for example—than their respective constituencies. His articles fueled a cause already well underway. By 1912 more than thirty states passed bills calling for the direct election of senators. The next year the Seventeenth Amendment became part of the Constitution.

Progressive Governors Concerned with bringing governments closer to the people, reformers also wished to provide governments which would safeguard and advance the public interest. During the Progressive era many states elected governors to do just that. In the East, New York's Governor Charles Evans Hughes, who had earlier exposed fraudulent practices among insurance companies, now instituted a strong public utilities commission. In New Jersey, Woodrow Wilson obtained laws for direct primaries, the regulation of public utilities, and workmen's compensation. The South and Southwest also produced several reform governors like Hoke Smith of Georgia and "Alfalfa" Bill Murray of Oklahoma, who fought corrupt politicians and entrenched special interests. In the West, Hiram W. Johnson of California successfully curtailed some of the immense privileges of the Southern Pacific Railroad, which for decades had dominated the state's politics.

No area of the country exhibited a greater progressive fervor than the Midwest, and no governor of any state proved as successful a progressive reformer as Robert M. La Follette of Wisconsin. Having served four terms as congressman, La Follette bucked Republican bosses to gain the statehouse in 1900. Before leaving for Washington and a Senate seat six years later, "Fighting Bob" turned Wisconsin into a laboratory for democracy and a model of state progressivism by developing the "Wisconsin Idea," which combined political reform with social legislation. Under this program La Follette obtained the initiative, referendum, and recall, as well as direct primary, civil service reform, and corrupt political practices laws. He also forced business interests, especially railroads, lumber companies, and public utilities, to pay a fairer share of taxes. Farmers received such benefits as lower railroad rates and conservation programs, while labor enjoyed laws limiting hours of work for women, granting workmen's compensation, and banning child labor. In addition, La Follette used the resources of the University of Wisconsin to bring expertise to complex issues. Political scientists, for example, helped

Robert M. La Follette

draft legislation, while economists focused on fiscal matters and agronomists aided farmers. Although La Follette broke the powerful Republican state machine only to replace it with his own, most electors seemed not to mind.

Social Reforms   So extensive was the social legislation enacted at the state level that it can only be summarized. Though as varied as tenement and prison reforms, most of this legislation tried to protect workers through a web of safety codes and laws pertaining to health and accident insurance, maximum hours and minimum wages, and survivors' benefits. Work hazards for women and children particularly concerned progressives, who found it easier to convince the courts to protect weaker groups. (It was ironic for the women's movement that equal treatment or protection required that gender distinctions be drawn.) In 1908 Louis D. Brandeis, a brilliant crusading lawyer, convinced the U.S. Supreme Court in *Muller* v. *Oregon* to uphold a state law that limited hours of work for women. Then after the tragic fire at the Triangle Shirtwaist Company in New York on March 25, 1911 cost the lives of 146 persons, mostly young immigrant women, a number of states passed stricter safety codes for factories. Children also obtained greater protection at this time. By 1914 virtually all states had minimum-age laws, while many had prohibited child labor from dangerous or late-hour work.

In spite of these successes, state reformers also encountered failures. Sometimes they quarreled or worked at cross-purposes; more frequently they ran into stubborn opposition from such groups as the National Association of Manufacturers, which vehemently opposed prolabor legislation. The courts also thwarted reformers, as in the previously cited *Lochner* v. *New York* (1905), in which the Supreme Court invalidated a law designed to protect the health of bakers. Given these difficulties, many progressives increasingly looked to the national government for reform leadership.

Progressives fought the problem of vicious child labor conditions.

THEODORE ROOSEVELT AND THE MODERN PRESIDENCY

Learning of President McKinley's choice of running mate for the 1900 election, an annoyed Mark Hanna fumed: "Don't any of you realize that there's only one life between this madman and the White House?" The worst fears of this powerful Ohio businessman and politician soon became reality. On September 14, 1901, McKinley, who had been shot by the anarchist Leon Czolgosz several days earlier, died and Theodore Roosevelt—"that damned cowboy," as Hanna called him—assumed the presidency.

Roosevelt: Career and Personality At 42, Roosevelt became the youngest chief executive in the nation's history. Yet he had already experienced a richly varied and successful life. After graduating from Harvard in 1880, he tried cattle ranching in North Dakota, wrote several books, and served three terms as a New York state assemblyman. Unsuccessful as a mayoralty candidate in New York in 1886, he became a federal civil service commissioner, New York police commissioner, assistant secretary of the navy under McKinley, and a national hero following his deeds in Cuba during the Spanish-American War. Capitalizing on his newly acquired fame, he won the New York gubernatorial race in 1898 and two years later agreed to run for vice-president of the United States, a position which had usually proved a political dead end.

It seemed a foregone conclusion in light of his background and values that the Roosevelt presidency would be an active one. To compensate for the frailties of asthma

Theodore Roosevelt

and poor eyesight, Roosevelt constantly sought the strenuous life, whether it was skating in subzero temperatures at Harvard or hunting wild game in the West. With an enormous zest for life, everything appeared "perfectly bully," including the White House, which he envisioned as a "bully pulpit" from which he could lecture fellow citizens. This penchant for moralizing, along with a sense of what was popular and practical, colored his political style and informed his values, which were those of an enlightened conservative who accepts necessary changes to prevent radical upheaval.

"Square Deal" Possessing comfortable means but not enormous wealth, the patrician Roosevelt identified with the solid middle class, which sensed itself caught between the plutocrats on the one hand and a working class seemingly drifting toward radicalism on the other. Horrified by potential class warfare and the subsequent undermining of the nation's stability, Roosevelt concluded that "the government must now interfere to protect labor, to subordinate the big corporation to the public welfare, and to shackle cunning and fraud." To achieve this he promised a "square deal," under which the government would act to defend the interests of all groups—business, labor, and consumers alike.

Events soon tested this resolve. On May 14, 1902, the United Mine Workers of America (UMW), with nearly 150,000 members, struck the anthracite coalfields of Pennsylvania when coal operators refused their demands for a 20 percent pay increase, reduction of daily work hours from ten to nine, and recognition of the UMW as the bargaining agent for the workers. UMW president John Mitchell was willing to negotiate, but the operators refused. George Baer, one of the operators, informed miners that their interests would be best served "not by the labor agitators, but by the Christian men to whom God, in His infinite wisdom, has given the control of the property interests of the country."

Roosevelt, dreading a severe fuel shortage for the oncoming winter and irked by the mine owners' intransigence, summoned both sides to the White House. The operators remained adamant. Knowing that public sentiment now was shifting to the side of the workers, the president threatened to use troops to reopen the mines. This threat, along with pressure from the financier J. P. Morgan, induced the owners to yield. Arbitration brought the workers their nine-hour day but only a 10 percent wage increase and no union recognition. The arbitrators further recommended that owners increase anthracite prices by 10 percent, and the owners happily complied.

Roosevelt Takes On Big Business   Roosevelt's experience with the coal operators convinced him that to defend capitalism it was necessary to reform it. The problem of the trusts afforded him the opportunity to translate theory into practice.

After a costly struggle for control of the Northern Pacific railroad between the forces of J. P. Morgan and James J. Hill pitted against those of E. H. Harriman, the three entrepreneurs joined to create the Northern Securities Company, a holding company of railroads valued at $400 million. In 1902 Roosevelt ordered Attorney General Philander C. Knox to prosecute this organization, which virtually monopolized transportation in the Northwest, for violation of the Sherman Antitrust Act. A surprised Morgan sent word to the president that "if we have done anything wrong, send your man to my man and they can fix it up." The suit proceeded, however. In *Northern Securities Co*. v. *U.S.* (1904), the Supreme Court, by a five-to-four vote, agreed that violation of the

J. P. Morgan wielded such enormous power that many considered him more important than the nation's presidents.

Sherman Act had occurred and ordered the dissolution of the huge enterprise. Before leaving the presidency, Roosevelt would initiate more than forty antitrust suits and would win twenty-five indictments against such giants as the Beef Trust, the American Tobacco Company, and John D. Rockefeller's immensely unpopular Standard Oil. Few trusts were actually dissolved—they frequently found ways to circumvent decisions—but Roosevelt won the nickname "trust buster" for his efforts.

Trust-busting activities notwithstanding, some 300 business mergers took place in the United States between 1895 and 1905. Roosevelt never opposed bigness per se, regarding it as a natural and inevitable outgrowth of the intense competition which raged during the late nineteenth century. To attempt to recapture the pre-Civil War circumstances of small enterprise was impossible in any case. What Roosevelt preferred was to distinguish between "good" and "bad" trusts. "Good" trusts served the public interest by providing products efficiently and at reasonable cost or by helping the nation grow stronger in international trade; "bad" trusts merely sought their own selfish aggrandizement at the public's expense. He hoped that business would police itself. If not, he would publicize its wrongdoings through the investigations of the Bureau of Corporations, established in 1903 as part of the newly created Department of Commerce and Labor. Trust busting was a last resort.

Through patronage and the allegiance of both Old Guard and progressive Republicans, Roosevelt assured himself of renomination in 1904. His only threat had been a possible challenge from Mark Hanna, but in February 1904 Hanna died. The Democrats abandoned the reformer William Jennings Bryan, who had been their unsuccessful candidate in 1896 and 1900, and nominated Alton B. Parker, a conservative New York judge. After a bland campaign the incumbent handily defeated his opponent, winning roughly 58 percent of the popular vote in the greatest presidential victory to that time. A grateful Roosevelt could now enjoy a full term in office, secure in the knowledge that he was no longer "His Accidency." Buoyed by his triumph, Roosevelt pressed for further reforms.

Railroad Regulation Railroad abuses presented a particular concern since courts had eroded much of the regulatory powers of the Interstate Commerce Commission (ICC). Yet regulation was never a simple question of reformers versus railroads. Small-scale shippers, as well as many railroads themselves, bitterly opposed the rebates that filtered back to powerful shipping interests. The Elkins Act of 1903 did impose fines on those who either offered or received rebates. Under this law Judge Kenesaw Mountain Landis, a future commissioner of baseball, fined Standard Oil more than $29 million in 1907, only to have a higher court set aside judgment. The courts, in fact, increasingly frustrated attempts by the ICC to abolish rebates.

Railroad rates provided an even more serious problem than rebates, as shippers, especially farmers and manufacturers from the progressive midwestern states, demanded relief from what they deemed exorbitant rates. Railroads, in turn, argued that they needed rate increases to offset their huge bonded indebtedness and the depreciation of equipment. Prodded by Roosevelt, Congress passed the Hepburn Act in 1906. This act expanded ICC membership and permitted it to determine maximum rates subject to court review, to inspect company records, and to include sleeping car companies, express companies, storage facilities, and oil pipelines within its jurisdiction. By prohibiting free railroad passes to all but employees, it also diminished the opportunity for bribery.

THEODORE ROOSEVELT AND THE MODERN PRESIDENCY

Roosevelt's role in the passage of the Hepburn Act illustrates both his commitment to moderate reform and to keeping the Republican party intact. When the strong House version of the bill reached the Senate, the railroad lobby, aided by staunchly conservative Republicans like Nelson W. Aldrich of Rhode Island, set out to emasculate it. These conservatives did obtain the right to have the rates set by the ICC reviewed by circuit courts and the U.S. Supreme Court, which might then decide in favor of the railroads; yet Roosevelt made sure that they obtained no more. Some progressives, especially La Follette, resented that he had compromised with conservatives at all and that he had not won for the ICC the power to evaluate the physical properties of the railroads to determine more accurately their costs of operation. Still, the Hepburn Act represented a major victory for reformers and shippers. For the first time since its inception in 1887, the ICC had genuine power to determine rates, and the burden of proof now shifted from the government and shippers to the railroads. Within a few years the number of rate complaints received by the ICC soared from fewer than a hundred to more than a thousand. Yet the Hepburn Act may have proved too successful. According to some historians, it initiated the long process of decline for the railroads.

"I'm pizened."   Moderate but real reform also characterized Roosevelt's position with regard to food and drugs. Various muckraking exposés and the findings of Dr. Harvey Wiley, chief chemist for the Department of Agriculture, had pointed to the widespread adulteration of food and patent medicines. Yet until the publication of *The Jungle* by Upton Sinclair in early 1906, the public remained generally apathetic. Sinclair intended his best-selling book, which described the misfortunes of a Lithuanian immigrant worker in the harsh meatpacking industry in Chicago, to win converts for socialism. Instead, by depicting such revolting scenes as those in which rats and various portions of human bodies found their way into meat products, he merely nauseated most readers. As the novelist ruefully observed, he had aimed an arrow at the public's heart but had hit its stomach.

One such injured stomach belonged to the nation's president. According to Mr. Dooley, the fictional Irish-American saloon keeper created by humorist Finley Peter Dunne: "Tiddy was toying with a light breakfast an' idly turnin' over th' pages iv th' new book with both hands. Suddenly he rose fr'm th' table, an cryin': 'I'm pizened,' began throwin' sausages out iv' th' window." By threatening to disclose additional grisly details uncovered by federal agents, Roosevelt broke the stubborn opposition to regulation on the part of the meatpacking interests in Congress. The Meat Inspection Act, which passed in July 1906, provided government inspection for all meat shipped in interstate or foreign commerce. Yet Roosevelt did compromise with the packers in that the government, not business, was to pay for inspections. The Pure Food and Drug Act also passed at this time. Unfortunately, it contained little provision for enforcement and, like the Meat Inspection Act, proved only moderately successful for many years to come. Nevertheless, both laws underscore a willingness on the part of both the president and Congress to use expanded federal powers to safeguard the public interest.

Conserving Resources   Roosevelt's finest and most enduring achievements as president came in the area of conservation. When he entered office, the nation had exhausted three-fourths of its original 800 million acres of forests, and private owners possessed four-fifths of what remained. No coherent conservation policy existed, nor did the public seem overly concerned. All this was to change, thanks in no small measure to this outdoorsman residing in the White House.

Sensing that something had to be done to preserve the nation's natural heritage, Congress had passed the Forest Reserve Act in 1891, empowering the president to set aside forest lands. Presidents Harrison, Cleveland, and McKinley preserved roughly 46 million acres of such land; Roosevelt nearly trebled that amount. At Senator La Follette's suggestion, he provisionally withdrew an additional 85 million acres located in the Northwest and in Alaska. In 1905, after the revelation of private looting of the public domain, he ordered control of forest lands transferred from the Interior Department to the new U.S. Forest Service in the Department of Agriculture and appointed the capable Gifford Pinchot as chief forester. Pinchot, who had once decked Roosevelt in a friendly boxing match, believed in using the nation's resources, but in a more rational manner. Some conservationists, like John Muir, who founded the Sierra Club and helped establish Yosemite National Park, called for the preservation of a pure wilderness rather than its planned use, however rational.

Roosevelt's achievements in conservation extended well beyond forest preservation. In 1902 he pushed the Newlands Act through Congress. It called for irrigation projects in arid states to be financed by the sale of public lands. From this law came a number of dams, such as the Roosevelt Dam in Arizona. In 1907 Roosevelt appointed an Inland Waterways Commission to study broad questions of river and power development. The following year he focused national attention on conservation by convening a governors' conference, from which emerged more than 40 state conservation commissions, the National Conservation Association, and the National Conservation Commission, with Pinchot as its leader. In addition, Roosevelt established 5 new national parks, 4 special game preserves, and more than 50 bird refuges. The battle for conservation and the intelligent consumption of the nation's finite resources had begun in earnest.

Panic, Recovery, and the 1908 Election   In 1907 a brief but sharp economic panic struck. Roosevelt denounced the ''malefactors of great wealth'' for having precipitated the crisis; the latter blamed the president for having undermined business confidence through his ''radical'' pronouncements. As matters worsened, J. P. Morgan wielded his enormous influence to stabilize the New York financial community. During this process he inquired if the government would invoke the Sherman Act should his gigantic U.S. Steel buy out one of its competitors, the Tennessee Coal and Iron Company. The trust would profit of course, but if the important brokerage house of Moore & Schley that held a good deal of the depressed shares of Tennessee Coal and Iron Company collapsed, as it seemed in danger of doing, the panic might spread. Roosevelt reluctantly assented to the acquisition, and by the following year the recession ended.

Reformers berated Roosevelt for having yielded to the Morgan and financial interests, much as they earlier had attacked him for not having secured tougher legislation apropos of railroads and the meatpacking industry. They applauded his call for stronger laws to protect workers, as well as for legislation to regulate the stock market and to impose income and inheritance taxes, but deplored his failure to convince Congress to enact these measures. Indeed, the overall legislative accomplishments of his years in office—the Hepburn Act and conservation statutes excepted—were hardly extraordinary.

But there was considerably more to the Roosevelt presidency than laws. For one thing, he used his office and persuasive rhetoric to create a national forum and favorable atmosphere for progressivism. For another, he successfully steered a treacherous course between the extremes of socialism and unregulated capitalism, thereby demonstrating the feasibility of moderate but meaningful reform. Roosevelt, who proved himself the strongest chief executive since Lincoln, thoroughly revitalized the presidency and took long strides toward creating a responsible interventionist state. In addition, he resolutely advanced America's coming of age as a world power (see Chapter 4). Few would dispute the lasting significance of these achievements.

Impulsively having pledged after his 1904 victory not to seek another term, a disappointed Roosevelt contented himself with handpicking William Howard Taft as his successor in 1908. The Democrats again turned to William Jennings Bryan. Taft won easily with 321 electoral and nearly 7.7 million popular votes to 162 electoral and 6.4 million popular votes for his opponent. Although the Republicans did lose House seats, they remained in control of both houses of Congress as they had since the 1894 elections. Presuming that Taft and his party would continue his policies, Roosevelt set out for a safari in Africa.

THE TRIALS OF WILLIAM HOWARD TAFT

William Howard Taft never aspired to the presidency. A dedicated jurist, he had a distinguished record as a lawyer and judge. He had also displayed a flair for administration, serving as both governor-general of the Philippines and secretary of war under

William Howard Taft

Roosevelt. Unlike the latter, he did not relish the hurly-burly of politics, much preferring to serve on the Supreme Court. (He ultimately served as Chief Justice from 1921 to 1930.) His ambitious wife, however, coaxed him into accepting Roosevelt's offer. Enough voters then responded to the intent of his campaign slogan, ''Get on the Raft with Taft, Boys''—quite a feat since this genial candidate weighed well over 300 pounds—to please Roosevelt, Mrs. Taft, and, by that time, probably even Taft himself.

Taft the Conservative   Taft sincerely hoped to expand the progressive program launched by his predecessor, and he actually achieved much during his term in office. For example, he instituted 90 antitrust cases in four years, whereas Roosevelt had begun only half that number in nearly twice the time. Taft also strongly supported the Sixteenth and Seventeenth Amendments, which procured the income tax and direct election of senators. The Mann-Elkins Act of 1910, further strengthening the ICC by allowing it to void rate increases even before receiving complaints, won his support. So, too, did the decision to divide the Department of Commerce and Labor into separate units, and bills to expand civil service, create a postal savings bank and parcel post, and solidify work and safety benefits for labor.

Yet Taft, by temperament and training, was a conservative who believed deeply in the sanctity of the law and doubted the legality of certain progressive measures. Caught between the conflicting views of conservatives and progressives within his party, he proved politically inept, lacking both the judgment and conciliatory talents of his predecessor. Few presidents ever have illustrated better than this well-meaning man how the road to political ruin is often paved with the best of intentions.

Tariff Fiasco   Roosevelt had used the threat of tariff revision to prod conservative Republicans into enacting railroad regulation. Taft now decided revision was inescapable as he noted growing consumer dissatisfaction—the cost of living had risen nearly 40 percent since 1897—and the protests of midwestern farmers bitter at the high prices paid for imported manufactured goods and lower prices received for their agricultural exports. He was gratified to see a dramatically lower schedule of duties emerge from the House in the form of the Payne bill in March 1909. Matters looked much different when Senator Aldrich and his conservative cohorts made some 800 changes, more than 600 of them upward.

Believing that a better tariff was not forthcoming and fearing that a veto would further divide the party, Taft signed the Payne-Aldrich Tariff into law in August 1909. Political wisdom now dictated silence amid the fury of progressives. Instead, Taft foolishly began to defend his actions. Speaking before a crowd in Winona, Minnesota, in the heart of progressive territory, he praised Congress's handiwork as ''the best tariff bill that the Republican party has ever passed.'' Hostilities intensified between the president and Republican progressives. When Taft supported a projected reciprocity treaty that would have opened up midwestern food and dairy products to greater Canadian competition, matters only worsened.

''Cannonism''   Taft and the progressives also quarreled over the issue of ''Cannonism.'' The last Speaker of the House to avail himself of a spitoon, ''Uncle Joe'' Cannon ruled the lower house of Congress with an iron hand. Like Aldrich in the Senate, he did

THE TRIALS OF WILLIAM HOWARD TAFT

his best to stifle liberal reform through a variety of techniques, most notably his right to appoint the powerful Rules Committee, which largely defined the issues and terms of debate for the House. Determined to overthrow this curmudgeon from Illinois, progressives sought Taft's aid in 1909. At first sympathetic, Taft hesitated and then rescued Cannon from defeat. The following year, however, reformers, led by Representative George W. Norris of Nebraska and allied with friendly Democrats, stripped Cannon of his seat on the Rules Committee. This meant that he could no longer appoint members of various standing committees and that the Rules Committee itself would now elect the Speaker of the House.

Ballinger-Pinchot Controversy   Conservation formed another bone of contention between the embattled president and his critics. Once more it provides an example of good intentions gone awry. Taft was very much a friend to the conservation movement, setting aside new lands and vital resources such as oil. Yet Richard A. Ballinger, his secretary of the interior, seemed insensitive when he withdrew from government protection a million acres of land in Wyoming and Montana and permitted valuable coalfields in Alaska to be leased to a wealthy private syndicate. Louis Glavis, an investigator for the Interior Department, protested, as did Pinchot. When Attorney General George C. Wickersham found no collusion or conflict of interest on Ballinger's part, Taft sided with his secretary of the interior and dismissed Glavis. After Pinchot leaked the story to the press and called upon Congress to investigate, Taft fired him too.

Having bagged more than three thousand animals and birds in Africa, Roosevelt decided to return home, instructing a friend that "if there is to be a great crowd, do arrange so that the whole crowd has a chance to see me and that there is as little disappointment as possible." On June 18, 1910, he confronted swarms of enthusiastic people waiting when his boat docked in New York harbor. He also found his party in total disarray.

Taft-Progressive Split   In late winter 1910 Taft declared war on Republican progressives, denying them patronage and vowing to campaign against them in the upcoming primaries. Through letters received while on safari, Roosevelt had followed the political situation with growing alarm. The dismissal of Pinchot appalled him; the widening rift within Republican ranks dismayed him. Still, he carefully refrained from taking sides when he returned and agreed to campaign for the party. At Osawatomie, Kansas, on August 31, he delivered a major speech (written for him by Pinchot) in which he called for a "New Nationalism." Asserting that the "true friend of property, the true conservative, is he who insists that property shall be the servant and not the master of the commonwealth," he cheered progressives by calling for the national government to protect laboring men, women, and children more adequately, to regulate corporations and politics more closely, and to tax the wealthy more freely. Old Guard Republicans denounced him when he further proposed applying the recall to unpopular state judicial decisions.

The 1910 congressional elections brought the Old Guard more grief. Republican wrangling gave the Democrats control of the House for the first time in 16 years, while control of the Senate rested with a coalition of progressive Republicans and Democrats. In January 1911 a group of insurgents formed the National Progressive Republican

CHAPTER 3: THE POLITICS OF REFORM

League to deny Taft renomination. Since Roosevelt politely refused to join, insurgents assumed that he would not be a candidate in 1912. Robert La Follette then announced his candidacy.

ELECTION OF 1912

"Bull Moose" Party   Yet many progressives really preferred Roosevelt, believing that only he could defeat Taft. Increasingly sympathetic to the progressive cause, Roosevelt hesitated to break with Taft until the latter precipitated the rift by instituting an antitrust suit against U.S. Steel in October 1911, partially on grounds of its having acquired the Tennessee Coal and Iron Company in 1907. An annoyed Roosevelt then quietly maneuvered behind the scenes to wrest the backing of the Progressive League from La Follette. When the Wisconsin senator, exhausted and worried abut his ailing daughter, suffered a temporary nervous collapse while speaking in Philadelphia, Roosevelt entered the race. He immediately won the support of most insurgents, who had been waiting for a convenient excuse to defect from La Follette. The latter never forgave Roosevelt for his perfidy.

Victories in 13 state primaries (including Taft's home state of Ohio) and the overwhelming backing of rank-and-file party members made Roosevelt's nomination seem likely. Yet he was still 100 delegates away from his prize when the Republicans convened in Chicago in June. As the incumbent, Taft controlled the party machinery, which promptly awarded him 235 of 254 disputed delegates. This assured his victory. Roosevelt, who had told backers that "We stand at Armageddon and we battle for the Lord," called Taft's triumph "naked theft." He stormed out of the convention but initially refused a third-party nomination from his loyal adherents.

Roosevelt changed his mind when the wealthy George W. Perkins, a former partner of J. P. Morgan, and the publisher Frank Munsey offered financial support. In August about two thousand enthusiasts from across the nation met once more in the Windy City to tender the Progressive party nomination to their hero. The convention resembled a revival meeting, as delegates paraded thrugh the hall singing "John Brown's Body," "The Battle Hymn of the Republic," and "Onward Christian Soldiers." Businessmen were there; so, too, were social reformers like Jane Addams, who offered a seconding speech for the nominee. In advertently giving the party its popular nickname by announcing that he felt "fit as a bull moose," Roosevelt received Hiram Johnson as his running mate. He also accepted a platform calling for sweeping reforms: the initiative, referendum, and recall; the recall of judicial decisions; child labor legislation; women's suffrage; workmen's compensation and social insurance; the eight-hour day; and tariff and trade commissions to regulate business. Even the socialist Eugene V. Debs thought the platform radical, and by the standards of the day it was.

Two episodes dampened the convention's exuberance. First, some in attendance opposed Roosevelt's acceptance of all-white, rather than racially mixed, southern delegations. More, including Gifford Pinchot, resented his deletion of a strong antitrust plank from the platform. They erroneously believed that this decision stemmed from the influence of Perkins and other businessmen. In fact, Roosevelt now more than ever favored regulation rather than dissolution. Nevertheless, most delegates remained firmly committed to their Bull Moose candidate.

Democrats Nominate Wilson   Only a few weeks after the brawl Republicans enacted in Chicago, Democrats staged their own donnybrook in Baltimore. Several candidates—notably House Speaker Champ Clark of Missouri, Representative Oscar W. Underwood of Alabama, and Governor Woodrow Wilson of New Jersey—vied for the presidential nomination. Democrats groaned under the weight of an ancient party rule which required nomination by two-thirds of the delegates. Though the lackluster Clark took an early lead in the balloting, he could not secure enough votes to win. On the fourteenth ballot William Jennings Bryan deserted Clark for Wilson, but with little effect. Finally, the Underwood forces switched to the New Jersey governor, giving him the victory on the forty-sixth ballot.

Few astute observers could doubt the election outcome. Roosevelt's decision to run as the Bull Moose candidate had severely split Republicans. As "Uncle Joe" Cannon remarked, it only remained to see which corpse, Taft or Roosevelt, got more flowers. With but a slim hope for victory, Roosevelt needed support from substantial numbers of progressive Democrats. But the candidacy of Woodrow Wilson eliminated that possibility.

Thomas Woodrow Wilson was born in Virginia in 1856 to a strongly religious family. His father and maternal grandfather were both Presbyterian ministers. Shunning the ministry for himself, he first trained for the law but then turned to history and received his doctorate from Johns Hopkins University in 1886. Wilson next taught at Bryn Mawr, Wesleyan, and Princeton, and achieved a distinguished scholarly reputation for works in political science, notably *Congressional Government* (1885). From 1902 until 1910 he served as president of Princeton, where he fought unsuccessfully to abolish the university's aristocratic eating clubs and to merge the graduate and undergraduate campuses.

Originally conservative in his politics, Wilson at one time or another had denounced Bryan and the farmers, opposed a closed shop for labor, and fretted over the massive influx of immigrants. These views caught the attention of George Harvey, the wealthy head of Harper and Brothers publishing firm. The powerful Harvey launched Wilson's political career and helped him secure the New Jersey Democratic gubernatorial nomination in 1910. When Wilson made campaign speeches promising liberal reforms, few believed he would or could enact them—but he did.

New Freedom or New Nationalism?   With Taft resigned to defeat, the 1912 campaign centered on Wilson and Roosevelt. Wilson, greatly influenced by the ideas of Louis Brandeis, wooed voters with a program he termed the New Freedom. In its strictest sense, this called for the restoration of a competitive economy devoid of trusts, which, according to Wilson, were too large to be efficient. The New Freedom was a "forward-looking return to the past," and the past the Democratic nominee had in mind was the Jeffersonian past of smallness and individualism. Beyond restoring competition, the program envisioned no major social changes.

The New Nationalism of Roosevelt contrasted sharply with the New Freedom. Like *The Promise of American Life* (1909), the work of the progressive writer Herbert Croly that it had earlier inspired, the New Nationalism called for Hamiltonian means to achieve Jeffersonian ends—that is, for an interventionist state to safeguard the general well-being of the individual. More specifically, Roosevelt wished to augment the powers of government to regulate trusts and also to protect citizens against the ravages of industrialism.

In practice the position of the candidates became blurred. Wilson backed away from demanding the dissolution of all trusts; Roosevelt agreed that some trusts deserved dissolution. William Allen White, the respected Kansas newspaperman, wryly observed that the two programs presented all the differences of Tweedledum and Tweedledee.

For all the campaign excitement, fewer than 59 percent of the eligible electorate bothered to vote, the lowest percentage since before the Civil War. This was partly due to the widespread conviction that Wilson was a certain winner and was partly a manifestation of the generally low voter turnout for presidential elections during this era. But the election results did generate some surprises. Debs, the Socialist candidate, polled 900,000 votes, or 6 percent of the total cast, a remarkably high figure in light of the two reform candidates on the ballot. There were other surprises. A vindictive Robert La Follette voted for Wilson, as did W. E. B. DuBois, the first major black figure since Reconstruction to back a Democratic presidential nominee. Wilson's triumph was not a surprise. In becoming the first Democratic president since Cleveland in 1892, he received 435 electoral votes to 88 and 8 for Roosevelt and Taft, respectively. Roosevelt and Taft, however, polled slightly more than 50 percent of the popular vote, while Wilson garnered slightly less than 42 percent, the smallest for any victor since Lincoln in 1860. Thanks to the Republican split, Democrats, who had gained control of the House in 1910, also won the Senate. This gave them control of both houses of Congress for the first time in 20 years and facilitated Wilson's reform plans.

WILSONIAN DEMOCRACY

Wilson was not a showman like Roosevelt, but he proved an adept political leader. He possessed intelligence, a grasp of political intricacies, and an oratorical style marked by a gift for memorable phrases. Like the Rough Rider, he also had weaknesses. He suffered from a strain of self-righteousness, a difficulty in accepting others as equals, and a distaste for compromise. An admirer of the British parliamentary system, Wilson believed that the American president, like the prime minister, must enjoy overwhelming support from his party, regardless of internal differences, and must appeal directly to the people should Congress block his policies. Armed with these views, he proposed major reforms involving the tariff, banking and currency, and trusts.

Underwood-Simmons Tariff On April 8, 1913, Wilson became the first president since John Adams to speak before Congress. In his speech he vigorously attacked the system of protective tariffs, which had not been revised substantially downward since before the Civil War. The House quickly passed the Underwood bill, which would have dramatically lowered duties, only to have the Senate prepare to restore cuts, much as had happened with the Payne-Aldrich Tariff. Wilson intervened, lashing out at lobbyists for special groups and calling upon citizens to pressure lawmakers.

The Underwood-Simmons Tariff, which finally passed in October 1913, lowered the average duty from 37 percent to 27 percent, with reductions outnumbering increases by better than a 10–1 margin. Most iron and steel products, cottons and woolens, shoes and sugar, and other important consumer items entered free or nearly so. Only luxuries suffered increased duties. To compensate for the anticipated loss in government revenue, Congress appended an income tax measure, the first since the recent ratification of the

Woodrow Wilson

Sixteenth Amendment. (Congress had adopted an income tax measure in 1894, but the Supreme Court invalidated it the following year.) This rider levied a tax of 1 percent on incomes of $4,000 or more, with a surtax ranging from 1 percent to 6 percent added to incomes of over $20,000. While hardly a radical measure, the Underwood-Simmons Tariff brought lower prices to consumers and initiated a modest provision for progressive taxation.

Banking and Currency Reform Another major Wilsonian reform involved the nation's finances. The lack of a flexible currency had contributed heavily to previous panics, including that of 1907. Finding an acceptable solution to this problem proved difficult. In 1912 the National Monetary Commission, headed by Senator Aldrich, recommended a single central bank with branches, both under the control of private bankers. For progressives this was a monstrous proposal, conjuring up images of a "Money Trust." The following year a House committee chaired by Representative Arsène Pujo reported that such a trust already existed. Morgan and Rockefeller interests, it disclosed, held 118 directorships in 34 banks and trust companies with assets of more than $4.5 billion. They also controlled 341 directorships of 112 corporations with capitalization of more than $22 billion.

After considering matters, Wilson threw his support behind the position adopted by William Jennings Bryan, whom he had appointed secretary of state. This position called for a decentralized reserve system controlled by the government. "Control," insisted the president, "must be vested in the Government itself, so that the banks may be the instruments, not the masters of business and of individual enterprise and initiative." Wilson, deploying patronage and persuasion to keep conservative party members in line, secured the Federal Reserve Act in late December 1913. This act provided for a Federal Reserve Board appointed by the president and located in Washington, with 12 regional Federal Reserve Banks owned by member banks and located throughout the country. National banks had to join; others were encouraged to do so. Federal Reserve notes promised to make currency more available outside the Northeast. The financial community, originally opposed to this measure, soon recognized its merits, particularly as Wilson appointed men acceptable to them to the Federal Reserve Board. Within ten years the Federal Reserve system encompassed 70 percent of the nation's banking resources. Though problems remained, such as the lack of deposit insurance, a more flexible currency and centralized banking operation had come to pass.

Attacking Big Business   Wilson next turned to the still thriving trusts. Determined to root out the worst abuses, Wilson secured passage of the Clayton Act of 1914. This law prohibited price discrimination and other practices that might lessen competition and also restricted interlocking directorates. Corporation officers were now legally liable for antitrust violations. Pressured by both unions and progressives, a reluctant Wilson accepted as part of the measure provisions that specifically exempted labor from prosecution under the Sherman Act and forbade injunctions against strikes and peaceful picketing, "unless necessary to protect irreparable injury to property." Samuel Gompers hailed the Clayton Act as "Labor's Magna Carta." Yet it proved disappointing. Filled with loopholes and ambiguities, the law frequently permitted business violators to escape prosecution and courts to rule against labor.

Doubting the ultimate effectiveness of the Clayton Act even as it was being passed, Wilson followed Brandeis's suggestion to seek a regulatory commission. As a result, the Federal Trade Commission Act of September 1914 outlawed (but did not define) "unfair" practices and established a Federal Trade Commission to investigate abuses and issue "cease and desist" orders. By implicitly accepting the regulation rather than the destruction of monopoly, this body represented a victory of sorts for the New Nationalism over the New Freedom.

By the end of 1914 Wilson was satisfied, while other reformers were disappointed that reforms pertaining to social justice or meant to benefit special groups had been conspicuously absent from his program. He had accepted the prolabor provisions of the Clayton Act under duress but had successfully withstood demands to support rural credits for farmers, women's suffrage, child labor legislation, or federal positions for blacks.

The New Nationalism Triumphs   Few things are more conducive to a political change of heart than a forthcoming election. Republicans seemed to be healing their wounds and had made impressive congressional and gubernatorial gains in 1914. Pressured by progressives within his own party and needing to gain Republican progressive votes to win reelection in 1916, Wilson did an about-face. Election year found him supporting the Keating-Owen Child Labor Act (declared unconstitutional in 1918 in *Hammer* v. *Dagenhart*), which prohibited the interstate shipment of goods produced by child labor; the Adamson Act, which granted the eight-hour day to railroad workers; and a Rural Credits Act for farmers. He further impressed progressives by naming Louis D. Brandeis, the first Jew so appointed, to the Supreme Court. Finally, he publicly endorsed women's suffrage. Whether more out of conviction or electoral necessity, the advocate of the New Freedom entered the 1916 campaign as the champion of the New Nationalism. Like Theodore Roosevelt earlier, he had come to accept the need for a more active, interventionist government.

BIOGRAPHICAL SKETCH

LOUIS DEMBITZ BRANDEIS · *1856–1941*

Brandeis was born in Louisville, Kentucky, to Jewish parents who had emigrated from Prague after the unsuccessful revolutions of 1848. Without benefit of undergraduate education, young Brandeis in 1875 completed Harvard Law School before his twentieth birthday and three years later established a law practice in Boston with a former classmate. Family wealth and professional success brought Brandeis an average yearly income of $50,000 by 1900, at a time when most lawyers earned less than $5,000 a year. This financial security enabled him to take many legal cases for little or no fee and to devote himself to reform efforts.

During the late nineteenth century the plight of workers and the social criticism of Henry George, Henry Demarest Lloyd, and others aroused his conscience. He became convinced that the law must respond to changing conditions and protect human welfare. In 1908 his "Brandeis Brief," presented in *Muller* v. *Oregon,* underscored the dangers of long hours to the health of female workers. The brief devoted only a few pages to legal principles but more than one hundred to statistics and expert testimony, providing a novel sociological approach to juridical argument.

Deeply committed to progressivism, Brandeis represented Louis Glavis before a joint congressional hearing on the Ballinger-Pinchot controversy. He also wrote *Other People's Money and How Bankers Use It* (1914) in response to the Pujo Committee findings. A collection of articles, the work offered both important documentation and an incisive analysis of key economic problems. Progressives deemed this book of major importance to their crusade against monopoly. An admiring President Wilson appointed Brandeis to the Supreme Court in 1916, though he had difficulty obtaining confirmation due to his Jewish religion and liberal views.

Brandeis's distinguished career on the Court spanned more than twenty years. Frequently remembered for his minority dissents, he in fact sided with the majority of his fellow justices in over 90 percent of the 528 opinions he ultimately wrote. His most famous opinions defended freedom of expression and opposed the concentration of wealth. During the Great Depression of the 1930s he looked skeptically at the economic planning that characterized the First New Deal but generally supported the reform measures that marked the Second New Deal. At the time he also worked quietly but effectively to defeat the court-packing scheme of President Franklin D. Roosevelt.

Zionism provided another major concern for Brandeis. Somewhere between 1910 and 1912 he espoused the idea of a homeland for Jews, and by 1914 he had become a prominent Zionist. He retired from the Court in 1939 to devote his last years to this cause.

CHAPTER 3: THE POLITICS OF REFORM

Woodrow Wilson had presided over more far-reaching domestic legislation than had Roosevelt, thanks both to the strength of Democrats in Congress and to his ability to manage them. A pedagogue by profession, he had used his talent for patient, careful explanation to educate and persuade party members to his points of view. In the process he, like his onetime Bull Moose opponent, contributed handsomely to the emergence of a dynamic twentieth-century presidency.

But, with the passage of the diverse legislation of 1916, progressivism reached its zenith. By the following year the nation turned increasingly and then overwhelmingly to a war that would generate progressive measures but would also sound the death knell for the movement. Looking back, one can see the balance sheet for progressivism check-ered with pluses and minuses. None of the fundamental problems that reformers had struggled against had disappeared, and for groups such as blacks conditions may have actually worsened. Some of their approaches and proposed solutions to problems now seem naïve or misguided. Still, if the progressives solved nothing, they ameliorated many conditions. Politics had become somewhat less corrupt; government had become more efficient and more responsive to the needs of citizens; social legislation had improved the quality of life for many; greedy businessmen and organizations could rarely act with total impunity; and conservation had become a significant public issue. In his perceptive *Drift and Mastery* (1914), the young journalist Walter Lippmann called on Americans to control the chaotic forces of change and dislocation that swirled about them. By the end of the Progressive era reformers had largely stopped the "drift." The elusive battle for "mastery" remained for future generations to wage.

SUGGESTED READINGS

The previously cited John D. Buenker, *Urban Liberalism and Progressive Reform* (1973), provides a general description of the politics of municipal reform, but one should also read Lincoln Steffens, *The Shame of the Cities* (1904), for a classic muckraking exposé of corruption. William L. Riordon, *Plunkitt of Tammany Hall* (1905), offers the entertainingly candid self-disclosures of a wily machine politician. Some other good studies of municipal politics include W. E. Bean, *Boss Ruef's San Francisco* (1952); Zane Miller, *Boss Cox's Cincinnati* (1968); Melvin G. Holli, *Reform in Detroit* (1969); and J. Joseph Huthmacher, *Senator Robert F. Wagner and the Rise of Urban Liberalism* (1971). Martin J. Schiesl, *The Politics of Efficiency* (1977), and Bradley R. Rice, *Progressive Cities* (1977), analyze innovations in municipal government.

Books on state progressivism are numerous. George E. Mowry, *The California Progressives* (1951), and Russell B. Nye, *Midwestern Progressive Politics* (1951), are somewhat dated but still useful. Other important related works include Sheldon Hackney, *Populism to Progressivism in Alabama* (1969); Robert S. Maxwell, *La Follette and the Rise of Progressivism in Wisconsin* (1956); Herbert F. Margulies, *The Decline of the Progressive Movement in Wisconsin, 1890–1920* (1968); David P. Thelen, *The New Citizenship: Origins of Progressivism in Wisconsin, 1885–1900* (1972); Ransom E. Wilson, *New Jersey Progressivism Before Wilson* (1946); Robert F. Wesser, *Charles Evans Hughes: Politics and Reform in New York State, 1905–1910* (1967); and Richard L. McCormick, *From Realignment to Reform: Political Change in New York State, 1893–1910* (1981).

Theodore Roosevelt has never lacked attention. Henry F. Pringle's *Theodore Roosevelt* (rev. ed., 1956) is an older but highly satisfying biography. William H. Harbaugh's *The Life and Times of Theodore Roosevelt* (rev. ed., 1975) remains a solid study, as do George E. Mowry, *The Era of Theodore Roosevelt* (1958), and the briefer John M. Blum, *The Republican Roosevelt* (rev. ed.

SUGGESTED READINGS

1977). Two especially good recent works are Edmund Morris, *The Rise of Theodore Roosevelt* (1979), and David McCullough, *Mornings on Horseback* (1981), both of which deal with their subject in his pre-presidential years. David W. Levy, *Herbert Croly of The New Republic* (1985), is a solid biography of a major progressive social thinker. For studies of two important conservatives during the Roosevelt administrations, see Nathaniel W. Stephenson, *Nelson W. Aldrich* (1930), and Frederick Lewis Allen, *The Great Pierpont Morgan* (1949). For an example of how differently historians can interpret a problem, see Albro Martin, *Enterprise Denied* (1971), and Gabriel Kolko, *Railroads and Regulation* (1965).

Henry F. Pringle has also written a fine and favorable two-volume study of Roosevelt's successor, *The Life and Times of William Howard Taft* (1938). Other good biographies include Donald E. Anderson, *William Howard Taft* (1973), and Paolo Coletta, *The Presidency of William Howard Taft* (1973). William Manner's *TR and Will* (1969) chronicles the ups and downs of a troubled friendship. Norman Wilensky's *Conservatives in the Progressive Era* (1965) provides balance to the studies of Taft's foes, who are the subjects of David P. Thelen, *Robert La Follette and the Insurgent Spirit* (1976), and Richard Lowitt, *George W. Norris* (1971). James Penick, Jr., *Progressive Politics and Conservation* (1968), examines the controversial Ballinger-Pinchot affair. See also Harold T. Pinkett, *Gifford Pinchot* (1970). The split among Republicans is treated in Amos Pinchot, *The History of the Progressive Party, 1912–1916* (1958).

Like Roosevelt, Woodrow Wilson has been the subject of many studies. The foremost Wilson scholar is Arthur S. Link, whose magisterial *Wilson* (5 vols., 1947–1965) is as yet incomplete. For a broader look at Wilson and his times, see Link's *Woodrow Wilson and the Progressive Era* (1954). John M. Blum's *Woodrow Wilson and the Politics of Morality* (1956) and John A. Garraty's *Woodrow Wilson* (1965) are briefer but insightful. William Diamond's *The Economic Thought of Woodrow Wilson* (1943) is a competent, more specialized work. John M. Blum's *Joseph Tumulty and the Wilson Era* (1951) offers additional information on Wilson from the vantage point of his personal secretary. Alpheus T. Mason, *Brandeis* (1946) and two more recent works, Melvyn I. Urofsky, *Louis D. Brandeis and the Progressive Tradition* (1980), and Philippa Strum, *Louis D. Brandeis* (1984), are model studies of the eminent jurist and friend of progressivism.

4

Foreign Policy Comes of Age

Foreign affairs began to assume greater importance for the United States as the twentieth century began. Victory in the Spanish-American War had transformed the nation into an imperial republic with far-ranging overseas possessions, increased opportunities for trade and investments, and the chance to play a greater role in international politics. Profits and prestige accompanied this new position, but so did problems and responsibilities. In the years between the conflict with Spain and World War I the United States struggled with questions of formal and informal empire, sought to increase economic and strategic interests in Latin America and the Far East, and tried to maintain an equilibrium among international forces. Some Americans objected to parts or all of this complex foreign policy. For others it was an acceptable price for coming of age as a major power.

GOVERNING THE NEW EMPIRE

The peace with Spain brought the United States possession of the Philippines, Guam, and Puerto Rico, as well as the responsibility for determining the fate of Cuba. These territories, along with the acquisitions of Hawaii (1898) and a portion of Samoa (1900), comprised a small but not insignificant empire. Yet sharp contradictions characterized the nation's colonial experiment. On the one hand Americans exploited native peoples, thwarted their wishes, and despised their cultures. But they also manifested a genuine desire to bring them the benefits of modern Western society. In addition, they could not agree whether their empire represented a permanent condition or a passing phenomenon.

The nation's experience with the Philippines demonstrated its ambiguity and discomfort as a colonial power. American troops finally subdued Emilio Aguinaldo and his

American soldiers supervising the burial of slain Filipino rebels during the brutal aftermath of the Spanish-American War.

rebel forces in 1902 after three years of savage fighting that witnessed grotesque cruelties and hardships on both sides. Casualties were heavy, but particularly among Filipinos. At the same time Americans were also extending the olive branch of peace and promising the benefits of material and moral progress to the Filipinos. As General Arthur MacArthur, military governor of the Philippines and father of future general Douglas MacArthur, explained, "inspiration and hope go with our flag." The United States did indeed pour millions of dollars into the islands to repair the ravages of war. They also increased landholding among the poor through sales on reasonable terms.

More striking was the fact that the nation began preparing the Philippines for independence even before their pacification. In 1900 President McKinley appointed William Howard Taft as governor-general and head of a committee to prepare the islands for self-government. The Organic Act of 1902 subsequently provided the limited beginnings of self-rule, though real power continued to rest with the colonial administration. The Filipinos themselves remained restive and continued to demand complete independence. Many Americans, moreover, continued to sympathize with Aguinaldo and the former rebels. Meanwhile the Philippines began to seem less important strategically to some makers of foreign policy. Theodore Roosevelt, for example, who had clamored for the annexation of the islands after the war with Spain, now decided that they represented a "heel of Achilles"—vulnerable to attack and impossible to defend. Both Republicans and Democrats increasingly spoke of Philippine independence. The Jones Act of 1916, strongly supported by President Wilson, promised freedom as soon as the islands achieved a "stable" government. Independence finally came on July 4, 1946.

The Cuban Protectorate   The United States encountered no rebellion among liberated Cubans, but it did face a host of difficult problems after the Spanish evacuated the island. The Teller Amendment, adopted just a few days before the war declaration of April 25, 1898, explicitly renounced any intention of annexing the island, and the subsequent peace treaty promised Cuba its independence. Yet the victors found the island in desperate straits after the war. Years of Spanish misrule and fighting had brought disease, hunger, and chaos, convincing many that an immediate American withdrawal from Cuba would be disastrous. This considerably muddied the waters for Cuban self-rule.

Responsibility for formulating a Cuban policy fell to Secretary of War Elihu Root, who in 1900 appointed General Leonard Wood military governor of the former Spanish colony. Wood firmly believed that the United States should annex Cuba but dutifully bowed to the decision of his civilian superiors to train Cubans for self-rule. By the time he left his position in 1902 he had accomplished much. An excellent administrator, Wood had improved health conditions, built roads, hospitals, and schools, and ferreted out the considerable corruption that had derived from American adventurers as well as Cubans themselves.

Yet complete independence for Cuba proved unacceptable to many Americans. Policymakers feared that political, social, and economic stability was unlikely in Cuba, and that European powers would be tempted to intervene. The United States wished to forestall this potential threat to the Monroe Doctrine and to growing American interests in Latin America. At the same time it wanted to avoid the charges of hypocrisy that it would face in annexing Cuba.

The Platt Amendment of 1901, largely the work of Secretary Root, offered a solution. The measure, which avoided any mention of annexation, secured America's dominant position in Cuba in several ways. It forbade Cuba to enter into foreign treaties without American acquiescence or to contract large debts that would invite the intervention of creditors. Cuba also had to provide the United States with naval bases and grant it the "right to intervene for the preservation of Cuban independence" and the "maintenance of a government adequate for the protection of life, property, and individual liberty." Cuba, knowing that agreement was the price for ending military rule, accepted the Platt Amendment in 1903. It remained in effect until 1934. The United States took advantage of its provisions during these years, sending troops on three occasions (1906–1909, 1912, and 1917–1922) and building an imposing naval base at Guantánamo Bay. Meanwhile Cuba became part of the United States' informal empire, as trade and investments tied the two nations closely together. Cuban exports (mostly sugar) to the United States grew from $31 million in 1900 to $131 million in 1914, while American exports to the island soared from $50 million in 1898 to $1.25 billion by the mid-1920s.

Other American acquisitions proved easier to manage. Hawaii, for example, received territorial status in 1901 as its inhabitants acquired citizenship. Meanwhile the Foraker Act of 1900 brought Puerto Rico under American jurisdiction. In 1917 the Jones Act granted it territorial status and citizenship to its inhabitants. The less-inhabited possessions—Guam and Samoa—simply came under military jurisdiction.

THE OPEN DOOR AND THE FAR EAST

General MacArthur, while defending American involvement in the Philippines, promised that a "magnificent and mighty destiny awaits us in the East." The general was speaking of imperial power and responsibility. Many Americans agreed with his assessment but defined "destiny" largely in dollar terms. The dream of lucrative trade with China had beguiled Americans from the earliest years of the republic. The dream survived into the nineteenth century, but the returns from the China trade remained meager.

China declined rapidly toward the end of the nineteenth century. Yet its misfortunes kindled hopes for expanded commerce. Humiliated and severely weakened by defeat in the Sino-Japanese War (1894–95), it no longer could defend itself against the encroachments of Western nations and Japan. These imperial powers successfully demanded spheres of influence, which were enclaves of economic and legal privilege along the Chinese coast. Among the major nations, only the United States failed to secure a foothold. As a result, it feared exclusion from the China market, or at least curtailment of the "most favored nation" trading rights that it had enjoyed since 1844.

John Hay, secretary of state under McKinley, took steps to prevent this. In September 1899 he initiated his Open Door policy by calling upon Great Britain, France, Germany, Italy, Russia, and Japan to respect the rights of other powers in their respective spheres of influence and not to discriminate against them in such matters as import duties and railroad rates. Italy, which had a limited stake in China, readily accepted Hay's proposals; Russia flatly rejected them. Each of the other nations agreed to accept if the others would. Secretary Hay, rather than alluding to his failure to secure unanimity, cleverly announced in March 1900 that the powers had agreed in principle to safeguard an Open Door for China.

That Hay failed to consult with China itself at this time underscores his and the West's general contempt for that nation. (Hay privately referred to the Chinese as Chinks.) The Chinese, long scornful of outsiders and humiliated by the concessions forced upon them, seethed with indignation. In the summer of 1900 the Boxers, a secret group of Chinese patriots, openly rebelled, vowing to force foreigners from the country. They killed over 200 Western missionaries and civilians in North China and Manchuria, and then besieged foreign residences in Peking. Chinese officials disclaimed responsibility for the uprising but did nothing to stop it. Meanwhile some 19,000 Western and Japanese troops, including 2,500 Americans dispatched from the Philippines, fought their way to the Chinese capital and lifted the siege that had lasted for nearly two months. Foreign nations imposed an indemnity of $333 million on China. The United States returned more than half the $25 million it had been allocated on the grounds that its share was excessive. A grateful Chinese government earmarked the returned funds for the education of Chinese students in American universities.

Secretary Hay feared that other nations would take advantage of the Boxer Rebellion to wring further economic concessions from China or even demand outright territorial acquisitions. He accordingly issued a second Open Door note during the uprising. This note called for the extension of Open Door trading privileges and respect for China's independence. Hay also persuaded the powers to accept a financial indemnity rather than additional territory.

The Open Door policy represented a partial diplomatic victory for John Hay. The international powers, at least for the time being, had acceded to American wishes for access to the China market and for the preservation of China as a ''territorial and administrative entity.'' Yet that agreement ultimately hinged on preserving the balance among the various nations interested in China and the Far East, and not upon Hay's proposals. Many, including Hay himself, doubted that the United States would use armed force to maintain the accord.

REFORMING THE ARMY AND NAVY

A prerequisite for empire was a larger and more efficient military. It was essential to administering the nation's newly acquired possessions and interests. The Spanish-American War, despite having culminated in victory, underscored certain military weaknesses. A special commission convened in 1898 to investigate the inefficiency and scandals surrounding the War Department and its secretary, Russell A. Alger. The following year the commission reported to President McKinley that substantial army reforms must take place.

The task of reforming the army belonged to Alger's successor, Elihu Root, a lawyer who was to serve as secretary of war from 1899 until 1904. During his tenure Root initiated several significant changes. In 1901 he persuaded Congress to enlarge the army to reflect its new responsibilities. The army had never had a peacetime force exceeding 28,000. Congress now authorized a force of from 60,000 to 100,000 men. Root also introduced the practice of rotating officers between field and staff work, arguing that a good soldier should be competent in both warfare and administrative matters. A modern officer, he believed, also needed up-to-date knowledge of strategy and tactics. Thus in 1901 he ordered the establishment of the Army War College in Washington, D.C., as well as new and upgraded training schools for select branches of the service. In 1903 Root persuaded Congress to recognize the National Guard as the nation's reserve force and to authorize its strength at between 250,000 and 300,000. Finally, he developed a general staff in an effort to procure efficient chain-of-command procedures.

Root had succeeded in imposing more rational features on the army and bringing to it a heightened sense of professionalism. Certain problems—interservice rivalries, for example—eluded immediate solution. Yet Root's strenuous efforts had resulted in an army more attuned to the nation's increasingly complex needs and responsibilities.

The navy also underwent far-reaching changes during the early years of the twentieth century. Substantial naval reforms had begun in the 1880s with the building of a larger and more technically modern fleet. The Naval War College at Newport, Rhode Island, had also been established in 1884. Meanwhile Captain (later Admiral) Alfred Thayer Mahan, the internationally celebrated naval historian and president of the Naval War College, insisted that the United States needed an even stronger navy. This navy would not merely protect the nation's Atlantic coast, Mahan explained, but it could also protect its seaborne commerce and fight an offensive war. When war broke out with Spain, the navy possessed a strong fighting fleet, owing in no small measure to Mahan's influence on prominent figures like Henry Cabot Lodge and Theodore Roosevelt.

As president, Roosevelt successfully prodded Congress to continue increasing naval strength. By 1905 Congress had sanctioned the construction of 10 battleships, 4 cruisers, and 17 smaller vessels. Naval appropriations rose from $85 million to $118 million

Alfred Thayer Mahan

annually, despite vigorous opposition both inside and outside Congress. Enlistments also surged from 25,000 in 1901 to 44,500 in 1909. Roosevelt, moreover, forged a stronger fighting fleet through reorganization. The European and South Atlantic Fleets merged with the North Atlantic Squadron to form a more unified and manageable Atlantic Fleet. This, in turn, complemented a growing Pacific Fleet.

Roosevelt's successors proved unable or unwilling to sustain his program of naval expansion. President Taft wanted to continue the pace but became too mired in domestic concerns and political infighting. President Wilson and many Democrats, in contrast, seemed amenable to the pre-Mahan position of a navy for coastal defense only. Nevertheless, there was no serious erosion in naval strength between 1900 and 1914.

ROOSEVELT: THE RESPONSIBILITIES OF POWER

Theodore Roosevelt exclaimed in an address to the Naval War College in 1897 that ''no triumph of peace is quite so great as the supreme triumph of war.'' Later he would say, ''speak softly and carry a big stick, and you will go far.'' Roosevelt has thus been portrayed as one of the nation's most bellicose and aggressive presidents. Yet he was also responsible for returning a portion of the Boxer indemnity to China, for seeking an international agreement to limit naval armaments, and for supporting arbitration treaties, world conferences on peace, and the establishment of a world court. He also mediated the Russo-Japanese War, for which he won the Nobel Peace Prize. His policies were, in fact, generally more moderate than his pronouncements. Force and diplomacy formed opposite sides of the same coin, and the coin, according to Roosevelt, was to be spent in pursuing goals of national self-interest and an expanded role as a world power. Nowhere did Roosevelt more vigorously pursue these goals than in Latin America. In doing so, he forged an indisputable U.S. dominance in the hemisphere. Its price was enduring mistrust and even hatred from the nation's southern neighbors.

Acquiring a Canal Americans had dreamed of an isthmian canal linking the Atlantic and Pacific since the gold rush of the mid-nineteenth century. The dream took on more urgency as a result of the war with Spain, when the battleship *Oregon* required 71 days to sail the 14,000 miles from San Francisco to Cuba via Cape Horn. An interoceanic canal now seemed essential to protect the nation's Atlantic and Pacific possessions, as well as to facilitate its real and anticipated world trade. Serious obstacles, however, stood in the way of building a canal.

Great Britain presented one obstacle. The Clayton-Bulwer Treaty of 1850 had given the United States and Great Britain joint rights in any isthmian venture. By the end of the century Great Britain seemed more agreeable to unilateral American action. The unpopular Boer War and the rise of Germany dramatized Great Britain's isolation and lack of friends. Consequently, the British were willing to forget past animosities and seek a rapprochement with the United States. This renewed goodwill resulted in two treaties negotiated by American Secretary of State John Hay and British Ambassador to the United States Sir Julian Pauncefote. The Senate rejected the Hay-Pauncefote Treaty of 1900. It gave the United States the right to build but not fortify a canal. The second treaty, ratified by the Senate a year later, allowed the United States to fortify the canal, provided all nations would have equal access to it and receive equal treatment.

A second obstacle involved the location of the canal. Some believed Nicaragua provided the best site, while others preferred the Colombian province of Panama. Advocates of a Nicaraguan route pointed out that it would allow sea-level construction, while the Panamanian route would require numerous locks. A French company led by the efforts of Ferdinand De Lesseps, builder of the Suez Canal, had failed to construct a canal through Panama in the late nineteenth century. Now the New Panama Canal Company, which succeeded the original company, was demanding $109 million for the rights to its concession. The Nicaraguan route seemed assured since the McKinley-appointed Isthmian Canal Commission, the House of Representatives, and President Roosevelt all favored it.

Advocates of a Panamanian canal acted quickly. The New Panama Canal Company lowered the asking price for its concession to $40 million, while William Nelson Cromwell, a prominent New York attorney and chief lobbyist for the company, won congressmen over to the Panamanian cause. The Panama lobby also shrewdly distributed postage stamps depicting an active volcano in Nicaragua, a state of affairs made more ominous by the sudden eruption of a major volcano on Martinique. In late June, Congress passed the Spooner Act authorizing the purchase of the Panama Canal Company's conces-

ROOSEVELT: THE RESPONSIBILITIES OF POWER 79

sion for $40 million if Colombia would grant the land within an acceptable period of time. If not, the president was to turn to the Nicaraguan route.

Secretary of State Hay and Colombian diplomat Thomas Herrán concluded the Hay-Herrán Treaty signed in January 1903. By its terms the United States was to receive a 99-year renewable lease on a canal zone for which it would pay Colombia $10 million and a yearly rental of $250,000, beginning nine years after ratification of the treaty. The U.S. Senate readily agreed to the treaty, but the Colombian Senate rejected it unanimously and demanded more compensation. The Panama Canal Company, it pointed out, was to receive a lump sum payment four times that offered their country.

Roosevelt was furious. He denounced the Colombians as ''bandits,'' ''dagos,'' and ''foolish and homicidal corruptionists,'' and considered asking Congress for the right to use force. While Roosevelt fumed, others, aware of the president's feelings, acted. A cabal led by Philippe Bunau-Varilla, the principal agent for the Panama Canal Company, induced Panama to revolt against Colombia. Technically speaking, Roosevelt and Hay did not plot the rebellion. Yet they certainly knew of its existence. American warships prevented Colombian troops from suppressing the rebellion when it broke out in Panama City on November 3, 1903. On November 6, the United States recognized the independence of Panama. Twelve days later Bunau-Varilla, now the Panamanian minister to the United States, signed a treaty with Hay that granted Americans the ''use, occupation, and control'' of the zone ''in perpetuity.'' Panama, in return, received the same financial terms offered Colombia. The treaty, with strong support from Roosevelt and Republicans but with some opposition from Democrats, received Senate ratification on February 23, 1904. Ten years later the Panama Canal opened.

The construction of the Panama Canal, achieved after years of battling tropical diseases and baffling engineering problems, rightfully filled Americans with wonder and pride. The circumstances surrounding the acquisition of the canal zone appeared less glorious. Roosevelt, after describing events to his cabinet, asked Elihu Root if he had defended himself effectively. ''You certainly have, Mr. President,'' replied the secretary of war. ''You have shown that you were accused of seduction and you have conclusively proved that you were guilty of rape.'' Roosevelt later boasted, ''I took the Canal Zone and let Congress debate. . . . '' Yet many of the president's countrymen remained troubled. William Jennings Bryan, secretary of state under Woodrow Wilson, negotiated a treaty with Colombia in 1914 that would grant the South American republic $25 million and would extend regrets for what had happened. Republicans, loyal to Roosevelt, blocked the treaty. In 1921, two years after Roosevelt's death, the Harding administration indemnified Colombia with that $25 million but without apologies. Meanwhile the entire episode had won the United States enormous fear and distrust from its Latin American neighbors.

The Monroe Doctrine Redefined Protecting the approaches to the Panama Canal became a vital concern of United States foreign policy. Naval power and bases formed an essential part of this strategy, as did the preservation of stability in the Caribbean. In 1902 Venezuela threatened that stability when its dictator Cipriano Castro, described by Roosevelt as a ''villainous monkey,'' reneged on loan payments to Germany and Great Britain. The two European nations resorted to a coastal blockade and the bombardment of a Venezuelan port to force the issue. Roosevelt convinced the parties to arbitrate. In 1904 the Hague Tribunal awarded scaled-down remunerations to the Europeans.

Constructing the Panama Canal proved a colossal undertaking.

Events in the Dominican Republic also threatened the status quo in the Caribbean. Revolutionary turmoil had rocked the Dominican Republic since 1899, and in early 1904 the government defaulted on a $32 million debt owed mainly to European creditors. Roosevelt decided that the United States could not stand idly by as European nations spoke of armed intervention to collect their debts. On December 6, 1904, a month after his reelection, he put before Congress what later became known as the Roosevelt Corollary to the Monroe Doctrine. Citing the restrictions imposed by the original Monroe Doctrine on European involvement in the New World, the president asserted that the United States must assume the powers of an international policeman. It must intervene in the affairs of those nations in the Western Hemisphere that were guilty of "chronic wrongdoing." More specifically, this meant that the United States would intervene to prevent European intervention when Latin American countries defaulted on debts or when revolutions in that region threatened the lives and properties of foreigners. Roosevelt had added a novel twist to one of the cornerstones of the nation's foreign policy. The original intent to the Monroe Doctrine had been to protect Latin American countries from European interference. But now, asked some, who would protect them from that of the United States?

Application of the new policy was not long in coming. The deteriorating Dominican situation convinced Roosevelt to intervene, though with the approval of Dominican authorities. In 1905 the United States assumed the receivership of Dominican customs collections. It successfully reorganized that nation's finances and restructured its debts. Democratic opposition in Congress had forced Roosevelt to do this by executive agreement, but a 1907 treaty granted the United States essentially the same rights. Meanwhile revolutionary disturbances in Cuba led the president to invoke the Platt Amendment and land troops in 1906. They remained until 1909.

Under Roosevelt the United States had maintained a formal and informal empire in Latin America, consolidating its hold on Puerto Rico and turning Cuba, Panama, and the Dominican Republic into protectorates. American trade and commerce flourished in these areas. Between 1900 and 1914 the value of American exports to Latin America increased from $132 million to $309 million. Yet Roosevelt was concerned primarily with safeguarding the Panama Canal and its approaches. Military strength and geographical proximity assured the nation a paramount position in Latin America. This was not the case with the Far East.

Roosevelt and the Far East   Roosevelt hoped to maintain a proverbial foot in the Far East through the principles of the Open Door, but understood that only an equilibrium among other powers would allow this in the face of the nation's distance from the Orient and lack of a major Pacific fleet. He became concerned first with Russian expansion into the Chinese province of Manchuria in 1902 and then with the growing differences between Russia and Japan over both Manchuria and Korea. These differences gravely threatened the balance of power in the Far East. In February 1904 the Japanese launched a surprise attack on the Russian fleet at Port Arthur as a prelude to declaring war. (Japan had similarly attacked China in 1894 and would do the same to the United States in 1941.) The United States adopted an official stance of neutrality toward the belligerents. Roosevelt, who hoped Japan would protect American economic interests in Manchuria, privately confided his belief that ''Japan is playing our game.'' He also warned France and Germany against intervening on the side of Russia. Japan did well in battle but soon began to feel the economic and military strains of continued warfare. Russia, in addition to its military reversals abroad, was facing revolution at home. Peace seemed a welcome prospect to both sides when Japan asked Roosevelt to mediate.

Roosevelt's mediation proved successful, and in the summer of 1905 the warring parties signed the Treaty of Portsmouth (New Hampshire). Russia agreed to Japanese primacy in Manchuria and Korea and ceded half of the island of Sakhalin to Japan but refused to pay an indemnity. Japan, for its part, agreed to end the fighting and not to expand further. The Japanese government accepted the treaty, but massive riots occurred among disappointed Japanese citizens, who were led to believe that their nation would receive a large indemnity and all of Sakhalin. Nonetheless, Roosevelt received the Nobel Peace Prize in 1906 for his efforts.

Japan had now emerged as the dominant power in the Far East. Earlier, Roosevelt's ardor for Japan had begun to cool when he realized the threat to the status quo a Japanese victory over Russia would pose. He had obtained a secret agreement from the Japanese to respect American rights in Manchuria as the price for his mediation of the war. At the same time he sought to protect America's vulnerable Pacific interests. In the secret Taft-Katsura Agreement of July 1905, arranged between the American secretary of war and the Japanese prime minister, the United States accepted Japanese dominance in Korea in exchange for recognition of American control over the Philippines. The arrangement

The "Great White Fleet."

tacitly and realistically acknowledged that the United States would not press the Open Door policy in Korea. In return it received assurances for the security of its major possession in the East.

An unexpected event soon threatened this accord. In 1906 the San Francisco School Board, bowing to the prejudices of white Americans who fretted over a "Yellow Peril," ordered the segregation of all Oriental children in the city's schools. Japan angrily protested, citing this as a violation of earlier guarantees. Roosevelt agreed but felt largely powerless since education was under state jurisdiction. Finally, he was able to reach a compromise with San Francisco officials. The city agreed in 1907 to rescind its segregation order if Japan restricted its laborers from immigrating to the United States. Japan acquiesced, and the so-called gentlemen's agreement took effect.

Roosevelt feared that Japan might mistake his willingness to compromise for weakness. He decided on a show of strength to prevent this and also to pressure Congress into increasing appropriations for a navy second only to Great Britain's. (The Japanese navy ranked fifth.) His plan involved assembling a large flotilla and sending it on a world cruise. This "Great White Fleet," consisting of 16 battleships and 12 smaller vessels,

TAFT'S DOLLAR DIPLOMACY

circumnavigated the globe on a voyage that began in December 1907 and lasted until February 1909. Japan greeted the fleet warmly. More than 10,000 Japanese school children waving American flags assembled at Tokyo to sing "Hail, Columbia," while 50,000 others marched in welcome through the city.

On the day of the fleet's departure Japan made overtures for further understandings. The Root-Takahira Agreement of 1908, reached by the American secretary of state and the Japanese ambassador to the United States, promised that the two nations would respect each other's possessions in the Far East and observe the independence of China and the Open Door. The pact, by reaffirming the status quo, appeared to restore Japanese-American harmony.

Roosevelt and Europe   Roosevelt, like most Americans of that time, accepted Thomas Jefferson's warning against entangling alliances as a principal foundation of national foreign policy. Yet Roosevelt rejected a policy of isolationism, believing that if the United States were to enjoy the privileges of a great power, it also had to assume corresponding obligations. The Moroccan crisis of 1905–1906 tested his resolve.

The Anglo-French entente of 1904 provided for French dominance in Morocco. Kaiser Wilhelm II, in an effort to protect German interests there, objected to the French role and appealed to the American president for assistance. Roosevelt did not wish to become embroiled, but fear of a general war led him to convene the Algeciras Conference in Spain in early 1906. Theoretically impartial, the United States actually sided strongly with France. The resulting agreement preserved nominal independence and an open-door policy for Morocco. In reality, it paved the way for a French protectorate while granting Germany minor concessions. Yet it did avoid the war Roosevelt had feared. The Senate accepted the agreement but warned that acceptance did not constitute any change in the nation's traditional policy of noninvolvement in European affairs. When a second Moroccan crisis broke out in 1911, President Taft carefully remained aloof.

TAFT'S DOLLAR DIPLOMACY

Taft, like his predecessor, wished to expand American interests in both Latin America and the Far East. Yet he and Roosevelt reversed priorities. The more conservative Taft emphasized American financial investments abroad as the best means of maintaining international peace and the nation's strategic interests. Roosevelt, in contrast, stressed American military and geopolitical strengths and treated the export of capital as secondary. One further difference distinguished their respective foreign policies: Roosevelt's usually succeeded, while Taft's generally failed.

Latin America represented a critical area for "dollar diplomacy." Taft and Secretary of State Philander C. Knox, a lawyer with close ties to the business community, believed that the United States should replace European nations as the principal investors there. This would result in the consolidation of American power in the area and the removal of any real threat to the Panama Canal. Taft and Knox successfully prodded American businessmen to invest in the area, but unforeseen problems often arose. In Nicaragua, for example, the United States welcomed an uprising in 1909 against the dictator Zelaya, who had threatened American business interests and had amassed an alarming debt to Europeans. Knox sent naval forces to help the insurgents after the dictator killed two Americans. Adolfo Díaz, the new Nicaraguan strongman, willingly granted concessions to Americans, including control of customs collections, in return for financial assistance. His opponents, partly in response to these concessions, rebelled. American marines arrived in 1912 to quell the disturbance and remained to safeguard stability until 1925. Nicaragua, too, had become an American protectorate.

Taft and Knox also encouraged American financiers to invest in other Latin nations, principally Haiti and Honduras, in order to stabilize their economies and political regimes. Secretary Knox pointed to the successful American receivership of Dominican customs initiated by his predecessor in 1905. Indeed, a stable government and a viable economy had lasted there until 1911, when the assassination of the president plunged the country into yet another civil war. By 1912 President Taft deemed it necessary to send in troops. The examples of both Nicaragua and the Dominican Republic point to the underlying practical weakness of dollar diplomacy: Designed to substitute dollars for bullets, the policy needed bullets to back up dollars.

Dollar diplomacy also found its way to the Far East. Taft, who had visited the Orient in 1905 and believed in the possibilities of a significant China market, was determined to uphold the Open Door policy in order to promote American commercial interests. In 1909 Secretary Knox made a proposal that would have given the United States, through its bankers, access to financing Manchurian railroads. The proposal failed because Japan and Russia had already carved out spheres of influence there. Great Britain, France, and even China had accepted this development. So had the United States, at least implicitly in the Root-Takahira Agreement. Taft and Knox, finding no support, backed down.

Yet Taft and Knox seemed undeterred. By 1911 Knox was insisting that Great Britain, France, and Germany admit his nation into a consortium to finance other railroad projects in China. The Chinese Revolution of 1911 that toppled the Manchu dynasty and led to a republic found the secretary of state willing to include Japan and Russia in his arrangements. The matter was still undecided when Woodrow Wilson succeeded Taft in 1913. The new president, viewing the six-power consortium as a violation of China's sovereignty, withdrew the United States from the project and dashed any lingering hope for further penetration of the China market through the murky channels of dollar diplomacy.

Reciprocity and Arbitration   Matching the failure of dollar diplomacy were Taft's diplomatic efforts along the lines of reciprocity and arbitration. In 1911, for example, the United States and Canada concluded a reciprocity treaty that would have strengthened ties of friendship and brought economic advantages to both. The complex agreement essentially would have facilitated the exportation of American manufactured goods northward in exchange for Canadian raw materials. Producers of goods left unprotected by this arrangement, especially Canadian industrialists and American midwestern farmers already furious with the president for the Payne-Aldrich Tariff of 1909, protested hotly on both sides of the border. Taft nevertheless secured congressional passage of the agreement, thanks to the cooperation of enough Democrats. Among prominent Democrats, Speaker of the House Champ Clark favored the measure, which he thought would hasten ''the day when the American flag will float over every square foot of the British

WILSON AND MISSIONARY DIPLOMACY

North American possessions clear to the North Pole.'' Clark's tactless enthusiasm so galled Canadians that their parliament roundly defeated the reciprocity accord.

The unfortunate Taft fared no better in his attempts to strengthen arbitration in international affairs. The Hague Peace Conference of 1899 had established the Permanent Court of Arbitration for nations to settle their differences without resorting to war. The principle of arbitration won acceptance from the world powers, including the United States, but no nation seemed willing to submit issues deemed vital to its national interests. Roosevelt's secretaries of state, Hay and Root, negotiated a number of arbitration pacts with other countries but made certain that the United States would maintain the right to decide which issues were arbitrable. Taft moved more boldly. Secretary Knox, acting on presidential instructions, negotiated treaties with both Great Britain and France that, in effect, pledged the signatories to a broader range of negotiable issues. The Senate, however, quickly amended the agreements to preserve American control over such matters as immigration and the Monroe Doctrine. An embarrassed Taft withdrew the treaties rather than present them to Great Britain and France in their revised form.

WILSON AND MISSIONARY DIPLOMACY

No American president has ever brought higher ideals to foreign policy than Woodrow Wilson. The vision of a world order guided by fair play and cooperation suited Wilson, who was both deeply religious and a member of the American Peace Society. Idealism and national self-interest were not incompatible, he believed. On the contrary, the United States could strengthen its own moral, political, and economic position by serving as an example and by spreading democracy and hope to less fortunate lands. This ''missionary diplomacy'' would also regain the respect and popularity that the United States had lost through the ''big stick'' and dollar diplomacy policies of Roosevelt and Taft. Ironically, Wilson's efforts frequently seemed a mere continuation of these policies.

Wilson the Moralist Wilson promised a major departure in foreign policy. Only a few days after his inauguration in March 1913 he pledged an end to dollar diplomacy and assured Latin American nations ''that the United States will never again seek one additional foot of territory by conquest.'' His unsuccessful attempt to compensate Colombia provided a dramatic example of his sincere efforts to make amends and restore Latin American confidence in the United States. He similarly pursued a moralistic policy with regard to China by renouncing American participation in the six-power consortium fashioned by Knox. He also forced Japan to back down on harsh demands it had tried to impose on the newly established republic. Wilson also took steps toward self-determination for those under American rule. In 1916, for instance, he induced Congress to pass the Jones Act granting the Philippines self-government and promising future independence. (Wilson announced in 1920 that the time for Philippine independence had arrived, but the next administration thought otherwise.) The year following the Jones Act, Wilson convinced Congress to grant citizenship to the inhabitants of Puerto Rico.

Wilson also sought diplomatic means to serve the cause of world peace. Secretary of State William Jennings Bryan more than shared Wilson's enthusiasm on this issue. Bryan, too, was a committed Christian and member of the American Peace Society. Unlike Wilson, he also had become a pacifist—the only one ever to head the State

Department. Within two years this three-time presidential candidate negotiated 30 separate treaties of conciliation. These agreements lacked any power of enforcement but clearly indicated the administration's resolve for peace by calling upon each signatory to observe a six-month or full-year ''cooling-off'' period before resorting to armed force.

The vexing question of canal tolls also tested the president's determination to improve the nation's tarnished international image. An act of 1912 exempted American ships engaged in coastal trade from paying tolls when passing through the Panama Canal. Great Britain protested, insisting that the Hay-Pauncefote Treaty of 1901 had guaranteed the same tolls for all nations. The United States replied that *all* excluded the United States. Furthermore, foreign nations could not legally engage in American coastal trade and therefore were not the objects of discrimination. Such arguments did not placate the British. Then Wilson became convinced that the legislation of 1912 was petty and unfair. In 1914 he persuaded Congress to repeal the act, thus strengthening the Anglo-American rapprochement and further committing himself to the cause of international harmony.

Wilson the Nationalist   For all his idealism, Wilson remained wedded to the dictates of national self-interest, particularly in Latin America. The Panama Canal was a fact of life, and Wilson felt obliged to defend it and the surrounding area against foreign intrigues or internal subversions. He did so well in this region that his policies fundamentally extended those of Roosevelt and Taft. The United States, despite Wilson's early rhetoric and lofty intentions, actually tightened its grip on the Western Hemisphere by the time he departed from office.

Both the president and Bryan, though sincerely disliking dollar diplomacy, proved adept dollar diplomats with regard to Nicaragua. They kept the marines in place and tried to induce American bankers to provide loans to the beleaguered Díaz government. Bryan also continued negotiations begun under Knox to secure the exclusive rights to any isthmian canal built through Nicaragua. The Bryan-Chamorro Treaty, signed in 1914 and ratified two years later, was remarkably favorable to American interests. For $3 million the United States obtained a 99-year renewable lease to construct a canal, the right to build a naval base on Nicaraguan soil, and permission to monitor Nicaragua's expenditure of the $3 million. Nothing could disguise the fact that this Central American republic had also become an American protectorate.

The same fate awaited Haiti. That improverished country owed huge debts to Germany and France, and suffered from the rapacity of a particularly cruel dictator. In 1915 Secretary Bryan sought to ameliorate conditions by asking the Haitians to permit American intervention, if only to preclude European interference. Before any decision could be reached Haitian revolutionaries overthrew and dismembered their dictator, who had just ruthlessly killed nearly 200 political prisoners. American marines landed the same day and remained until 1934. The United States subsequently imposed a treaty on Haiti with provisions similar to the Platt Amendment, including the right to intervene.

Anarchic conditions in the Dominican Republic, which shared the island of Hispaniola with Haiti, led Wilson to ask for more American authority in that country also. Troops landed when revolution erupted in 1916, and they remained until 1924. The Dominican Republic, like its neighbor, had lost much of its sovereignty, a victim of Wilson's missionary diplomacy.

WILSON AND MISSIONARY DIPLOMACY

Trouble with Mexico   On March 11, 1913 Wilson vowed that he would "teach the South American republics to elect good men." He specifically had in mind Mexico, which was in the throes of revolutionary upheavals. For the next several years Mexico's problems became America's problems, as the president sought a solution to difficulties that nearly embroiled the United States in war. In the process Wilson displayed his missionary diplomacy at its very best—and worst.

The rule of Porfirio Díaz, president and dictator of Mexico since 1877, came to an end in 1911. For more than three decades the Mexican ruler had maintained stability at the price of liberty. His policies pleased some: large landowners, the Catholic Church, and foreign investors. They alienated others: constitutionalists, nationalists, and many landless peasants, who formed the vast majority of the nation's population. Francesco I. Madero, a middle-class constitutionalist supported by angry peasants, deposed Díaz but then proved unable to govern effectively or to satisfy the land hunger of the poor. General Victoriano Huerta, backed by conservative Mexicans and foreign investors, overthrew Madero in February 1913 and promptly had him assassinated.

Ambassador Henry Lane Wilson, a supporter of the counterrevolution, urged the United States to follow other nations and recognize the Huerta government. After all, Americans owned roughly 40 percent of Mexico's land, and there were perhaps 50,000 Americans living there and in need of protection. President Taft seemed about to grant recognition. Then Venustiano Carranza, a high Mexican official and constitutionalist, revolted. Amid this confusion Taft left office and gladly bequeathed the Mexican tangle to his successor.

Wilson broke with traditional diplomatic practice by insisting on moral considerations as a prerequisite for granting diplomatic recognition. He flatly refused to recognize the Huerta regime, which he termed a "government of butchers." In the summer of 1913 the president recalled Ambassador Wilson and set terms for recognition: a military armistice, free elections, and Huerta's promise to vacate office. Huerta dismissed Wilson's offer, as did Carranza, whose dislike for Huerta was matched only by his hatred of Yankee interference in Mexican affairs. Wilson's antipathy for Huerta deepened when the latter arrested his opponents in the legislature and established a military dictatorship. The president then lifted an arms embargo to permit Huerta's enemies to obtain weapons in the United States. He also forced Great Britain to withdraw its support for the dictator, partly as the price for his leniency on the Panama Canal tolls. The United States now embarked on a policy of "watchful waiting."

The waiting came to an end in April 1914 when Mexican authorities in Tampico arrested a few American sailors who had gone ashore without securing permission. The authorities quickly apologized and released the crewmen, but the American naval commander demanded a twenty-one gun salute and a stronger apology. Huerta refused to comply. Wilson then asked Congress for permission to use force. Almost simultaneously he received the alarming news that a German ship filled with armaments was about to dock at Veracruz. He immediately ordered naval forces to seize the city. Marines took Veracruz on April 21, and Congress legalized the act by granting the president power to use force in Mexico. Wilson mistakenly believed that Veracruz would fall without bloodshed since the Mexican commandant had promised to withdraw his troops. Some soldiers remained, however, and fighting took the lives of 19 Americans and some 200 Mexicans.

War seemed inevitable until the ABC powers—Argentina, Brazil, and Chile—offered to mediate. Representatives from these nations, along with those from Mexico and the United States, met at Niagara Falls, New York, in May. No concrete solutions emerged, but the talks had a pacifying effect. In July, Huerta, harassed by his foes and deprived of weapons and credits because of the war situation in Europe, fled Mexico. The following month the victorious Carranza became president, and Americans breathed a little easier.

But not for long. Francisco ("Pancho") Villa, a former bandit and backer of Carranza, and Emiliano Zapata, a dedicated friend of the downtrodden, refused to accept the new government and each began to attack it. The United States briefly considered recognizing the wily Villa, but a series of government victories convinced Wilson to extend a limited de facto recognition to Carranza in October 1915. Relations between the two neighboring countries slowly improved until January 1916, when Villa, hoping to stir up trouble, robbed a Mexican train and killed 16 Americans. Two months later he boldly rode across the border to Columbus, New Mexico, where he and his forces killed 17 Americans. Wilson dispatched General John J. Pershing and 6,000 troops to pursue Villa. Carranza, though he grudgingly granted permission for the foray, strongly resented the presence of American soldiers on Mexican soil. Twice the forces of the two countries clashed in the spring of 1916, and war once again appeared imminent. But even as war approached both sides backed away from hostilities and established a commission to discuss differences. Pershing failed to capture Villa, but Mexican government forces broke the strength of the bandit's army. By January 1917 Wilson felt it was time to recall Pershing, who had marched more than 300 miles beyond the Rio Grande; by April he decided it was time to grant full recognition to Carranza.

Wilson's handling of the Mexican situation won few supporters. Some complained that he simply should have recognized Huerta from the outset. Others berated him for

Motorcycle messengers served with General Pershing in his pursuit of Pancho Villa.

his failure to use greater military force and perhaps to annex portions of Mexico. Still others condemned him for having intervened in the internal matters of an independent nation. Yet Wilson, for all his errors of judgment and self-righteous tones, had acted from principle. He had defied the propertied interests at home and a military dictator abroad in the hope of saving a revolution dedicated to liberty and a higher standard of living for the masses. He had also ultimately refused to entangle the country in a war with Mexico. This decision, however, may have stemmed more from the fact that the United States was about to get involved in a larger war, a titanic struggle "to make the world safe for democracy."

Meanwhile, in the single generation between the 1890s and World War I, the United States had moved beyond its continental boundaries and onto the center stage of world politics. Like other Western powers it acquired both formal possessions and informal spheres of preeminence. Important strategic interests, naked economic exploitation, and decent humanitarian concerns served unevenly and uneasily as wellsprings for action in the Caribbean and Latin America, the Pacific, and the Far East. Seemingly less important at the time was a growing willingness to become involved in European diplomatic problems. Many Americans protested the turn of events as a betrayal of the nation's heritage and finest principles. Others either silently acquiesced or vigorously defended the change as the fulfillment of a manifest destiny that would bring benefits to all concerned.

BIOGRAPHICAL SKETCH

ELIHU ROOT · *1845–1937*

Root was born in Clinton, New York, where his father was a professor of mathematics at Hamilton College. Seeing no service in the Civil War, he graduated from Hamilton in 1864 and received a degree from the New York University Law School three years later. In 1871 he assisted in the unsuccessful legal defense of the notorious Boss Tweed. Root won acclaim over the next three decades not as a trial lawyer but as a counsel for numerous corporations. A staunch believer in the sanctity of private property, he skillfully aided such powerful business clients as the Sugar Trust.

Root's career as a public figure began in 1899 when President McKinley appointed him secretary of war. The New York attorney had no direct political experience, but his qualifications included an astute mind, an ability to reconcile divergent people and points of view, and a solid Republican allegiance. His friendships with leading party figures like Henry Cabot Lodge and especially Theodore Roosevelt made him even more appealing. (Ironically, Root was the first choice of many party leaders for the vice-presidential nomination to the 1900 ticket. Had he accepted, he, rather than Roosevelt, would have become president after McKinley's assassination.) His stints as secretary of war (1899–1904) and secretary of state (1905–1909) led both Roosevelt and William Howard Taft to consider him the most capable statesman of the era.

This public servant from upstate New York did not fare so well in politics. He sponsored no significant legislation during his one term in the Senate (1909–1915), where he won the enmity of progressives for his pro-business views and opposition to such democratic reforms as the direct election of senators. In 1912 he presided over the tumultuous Republican convention but failed to keep Roosevelt from bolting. Their long and fruitful friendship ended when Root remained a party regular rather than support the Bull Moose cause.

Root was dedicated to the cause of international peace, although some of his critics saw him as an architect of American militarism and imperialism. In 1912 he became the second American to win the Nobel Peace Prize. He received the honor in recognition of his long record as a statesman, as well as for specific achievements that included arbitrating a difficult dispute between the United States and Great Britain over fishing rights in North America. Root served as president of the Carnegie Endowment for Peace (1910–1925), supported America's entry into the League of Nations (though with the Lodge Reservations), and helped to establish the Permanent Court of International Justice for the League of Nations in 1920. Among his last official duties was an appointment to the International Conference on Limitation of Armaments in 1921.

SUGGESTED READINGS

For an older but still useful study of the American empire, see Julius Ward Pratt, *America's Colonial Experiment* (1950). Emily S. Rosenberg, *Spreading the American Dream: American Economic and Cultural Expansion, 1890–1945* (1982), complements Pratt's work. Cuba is the focus of both David Healy, *The United States in Cuba, 1898–1902* (1963), and James H. Hitchman, *Leonard Wood and Cuban Independence, 1898–1902* (1971). Detailed studies of involvement in the Philippines include Peter Stanley, *A Nation in the Making: The Philippines and the United States, 1899–1921* (1974); Richard E. Welch, Jr., *Response to Imperialism: The United States and the Philippine-American War, 1899–1902* (1979); and Stuart Creighton Miller, *"Benevolent Assimilation": The American Conquest of the Philippines, 1899–1903* (1982).

Military affairs provide the subject for Richard D. Challener, *Admirals, Generals, and American Foreign Policy, 1898–1914* (1973), and William R. Braisted, *The United States Navy in the Pacific, 1897–1909* (1958). See also the relevant chapters in Harold and Margaret Sprout, *The Rise of American Naval Power, 1776–1918* (1939), as well as W. D. Puleston, *Mahan* (1939). For two fine studies of the principal architect of military reforms at this time, see Richard W. Leopold, *Elihu Root and the Conservative Tradition* (1954) and the statesman's official biography, Philip C. Jessup, *Elihu Root* (2 vols., 1938).

SUGGESTED READINGS

There are many instructive works dealing with Sino-American relations. Tyler Dennett, *John Hay* (1938), is a standard life of the eminent secretary of state. The China market is the focus of Paul A. Varg, *The Making of a Myth: The United States and China, 1897–1912* (1968); Thomas J. McCormick, *China Market* (1967); and Marilyn B. Young, *The Rhetoric of Empire: America's China Policy, 1895–1901* (1968). Robert McClellan, *The Heathen Chinee: A Study of American Attitudes Toward China, 1890–1905* (1971), and Paul A. Varg, *Missionaries, Chinese, and Diplomats* (1958), concentrate on some noneconomic aspects of America's complex relationship with the Middle Kingdom.

Most of the biographical studies of Roosevelt cited in previous chapters cover foreign affairs, though to varying degrees. Three fine studies specifically treating Roosevelt's foreign policy are Howard K. Beale, *Theodore Roosevelt and the Rise of America to World Power* (1956); David H. Burton, *Theodore Roosevelt: Confident Imperialist* (1968); and Frederick Marks, III, *Velvet on Iron: The Diplomacy of Theodore Roosevelt* (1979). The Panama Canal episode receives careful analysis from Dwight C. Miner, *Fight for the Panama Route* (1940), and Walter LaFeber, *The Panama Canal* (1978). David McCullough, *The Path Between the Seas: The Creation of the Panama Canal, 1870–1914* (1977), offers a fascinating account of the problems involved in constructing the canal. Dexter Perkins, *The Monroe Doctrine, 1867–1907,* covers Roosevelt's reinterpretation of that far-reaching document.

Relations with Japan are well described in Raymond A. Esthus, *Theodore Roosevelt and Japan* (1966); Charles E. Neu, *An Uncertain Friendship: Roosevelt and Japan, 1906–1909* (1967); and Akira Iriye, *Pacific Estrangement: Japanese and American Expansion, 1897–1911* (1972). More specialized studies include Eugene P. Trani, *The Treaty of Portsmouth* (1969); Robert A. Hart, *The Great White Fleet* (1965); and Roger Daniels, *The Politics of Prejudice: The Anti-Japanese Movement in California and the Struggle for Japanese Exclusion* (1962).

For Roosevelt and European affairs, see Eugene N. Anderson, *The First Moroccan Crisis, 1904–1906* (1930). Anglo-American relations receive close attention in Bradford Perkins, *The Great Rapprochement: England and the United States, 1895–1914* (1968). Calvin Davis's *The United States and the First Hague Peace Conference* (1962) and *The United States and the Second Hague Peace Conference* (1976) analyze the American role in two major international gatherings.

Walter and Marie Scholes, *The Foreign Policies of the Taft Administration* (1970), is a good overall study of Roosevelt's successor. Other accounts of Taft's diplomacy appear in his biographies and in general works dealing with foreign policy during the Progressive era. Two of the latter that detail Taft's handiwork are Dana C. Munro, *Intervention and Dollar Diplomacy in the Caribbean: 1900–1921* (1964), and A. Whitney Griswold, *The Far Eastern Policy of the United States* (1938).

Numerous studies of Wilson's foreign policy treat the Mexican question. A few of the more important ones are Robert E. Quirk, *An Affair of Honor: Woodrow Wilson and the Occupation of Veracruz* (1962); Clarence C. Clendenen, *The United States and Pancho Villa* (1961); Kenneth J. Grieb, *The United States and Huerta* (1969); and Friedrich Katz, *The Secret War in Mexico: Europe, the United States, and the Mexican Revolution* (1981).

Other aspects of Wilsonian foreign policy can be found principally in biographical studies, notably those by Arthur S. Link. Yet one should also see David Healy, *Gunboat Diplomacy in the Wilson Era: The U.S. Navy in Haiti, 1915–1916* (1976); Bruce J. Calder, *The Impact of Intervention: The Dominican Republic During the U.S. Occupation of 1916–1924* (1984); and Roy W. Curry, *Woodrow Wilson and Far Eastern Policy, 1913–1921* (1957). Paolo Coletta's *William Jennings Bryan: Progressive Politician and Moral Statesman, 1909–1915* (1969) analyzes, among other things, ''the Great Commoner'' as secretary of state.

Finally, one should see John Milton Cooper, Jr., *The Warrior and the Priest: Woodrow Wilson and Theodore Roosevelt* (1983), for interesting and instructive comparisons.

5

Making the World Safe for Democracy

On June 28, 1914, Gavrilo Princip, member of a secret terrorist organization, forever altered the course of history by assassinating Archduke Franz Ferdinand, heir to the throne of Austria-Hungary. Princip believed he was striking a blow for Serbian nationalism against the hated Austrians. He did not foresee that his act of violence in the Bosnian city of Sarajevo would assume gigantic proportions. On July 28, Austria, supported by a "blank check" from Germany, declared war on Serbia after the latter had rejected a set of harsh demands. Three days later Germany declared war on Russia, which had vowed to back the Serbs and had ordered the full mobilization of troops. Germany next declared war against France on August 3 and invaded neutral Belgium the following day. It hoped to strike a quick knockout blow against France through this unexpected invasion route. Instead, it precipitated a war declaration from Great Britain, which could not afford the presence of a powerful opponent so near home. All diplomatic efforts had failed to prevent what Europeans had long dreaded: armed hostilities between the rival Central Powers (Germany and Austria-Hungary) and the Allies (Great Britain, France, and Russia).

The conflict of 1914–1918 came to be known as the Great War. (It assumed the title World War I only after there was a World War II.) The war was "great" both in the scope of its fighting and in the magnitude of its consequences. To the aid of the Central Powers came Turkey and Bulgaria; to the Allied cause rallied 32 nations in all. The belligerents on both sides mobilized forces that totaled 58.5 million. Their casualties were equally astounding: 7.7 million dead and 20.2 million wounded. Germany, Austria-Hungary, and Turkey lost their empires; Russia underwent revolution and lost its czar. The total economic costs were incalculable, as were the costs in human suffering. Nor could one reckon the damage to the belief in human progress that had characterized European society at the beginning of the twentieth century. Given the enormity of this upheaval, no major country could escape untouched.

FROM NEUTRALITY TO INVOLVEMENT

An Unneutral Neutrality   President Wilson reacted to the war in Europe by proclaiming American neutrality and by calling upon Americans to be "impartial in thought" as well as in action. It was relatively simple in the early period of the war to remain impartial in action since few Americans wanted to fight. Impartiality of thought was another matter. Wilson himself was a fervent admirer of the culture, history, and institutions of Great Britain. Millions of other Americans, with similar Anglo-Saxon roots, shared his preferences. Many also sympathized with France, remembering the valuable assistance rendered during the American Revolution. Germany also had its supporters when war broke out. In 1914 the U.S. population counted more than 8 million German-Americans, who were either born in Germany or had one or both parents born there, and who now cheered the cause of the Fatherland. Many of the 4.5 million Irish-Americans, angered by Great Britain's persistent refusal to grant home rule to Ireland, also made no secret of their prejudices in favor of the Central Powers.

Yet Germany badly hurt its cause in the United States. It shocked Americans by invading Belgium and deriding the treaty that had guaranteed its neutrality as merely a "scrap of paper." More disturbing were accounts—most of them false or exaggerated— of the atrocities committed by German troops against Belgian civilians, especially women and children. The execution of British nurse Edith Cavell for helping Allied prisoners of war to escape only worsened the German image as the "savage Hun." Effective British propaganda depicted the struggle as one of democracy versus autocracy.

Problems pertaining to the rights of neutrals also made it difficult for Americans to remain impartial in their deeds. As a neutral nation the United States had the right to trade with any belligerent. But the Allies, thanks to Great Britain's dominance of the seas, benefited most from this trade. Between 1914 and 1916, for example, American trade with the Allies skyrocketed from $825 million to $3.2 billion. American trade with Germany, in contrast, plunged at the same time from $345 million to less than $2 million. By 1916, moreover, munitions represented approximately 40 percent of the trade with the Allies. This activity, while perfectly legal, linked the United States more closely to the Allied cause and threw its stance of strict neutrality into doubt.

The question of wartime loans also made a mockery of this neutrality. The British had used their impressive wealth to underwrite the war in its early stages, but they rapidly depleted their financial reserves as fighting stalemated on the Western Front and both sides dug in for a prolonged period of trench warfare. Great Britain turned to the United States for loans. Secretary of State William Jennings Bryan very early counseled bankers against such loans, warning that they were inconsistent with, and might ultimately threaten, the nation's neutrality. Nevertheless, J. P. Morgan and other financiers floated loans and bond sales to aid the Allies. Government opposition to the loans melted away once the pro-Allied Robert Lansing replaced Bryan, who resigned during the summer of

1915. Many Americans accepted the loans because of their immediate economic benefits. The economy was in a mild recession in 1914, and the nation still owed foreign creditors more than $3 billion, though that debt was constantly shrinking. Between 1914 and the nation's entry into war, the United States lent the Allies $2.3 billion and the Central Powers only $27 million. Most of the loans to the Allies were secured. Yet any substantial default on the loans or loss of the lucrative wartime trade with the Allies might plunge the country into a recession. Policymakers could not discount this possibility as they steered the course of neutrality.

Freedom of the Seas American demands for neutral shipping rights necessarily clashed with British determination to deny goods to their enemies. International law had never been totally precise with regard to neutral rights. Great Britain—arguing that it stood with its back to the wall—now bent, broke, and redefined those rules. For example, it expanded the definition of contraband to include food and such items as cotton, which was a major export of southern farmers. Great Britain also brought many ships suspected of carrying contraband into port, where their search resulted in extensive delays for shippers. Redefining the concept of continuous voyage, the British also intercepted neutral shipping headed for the ports of other neutrals, such as Holland, Denmark, and Sweden, for fear that goods unloaded in those countries might find their way to the Central Powers. Finally, they mined the North Sea, an act of dubious international legality.

The United States had options in responding to Great Britain's violations of its neutral rights. They included challenging Great Britain either through armed force or, more likely, by a partial or total trade embargo. Such an embargo, particularly on munitions, would severely strain the British ability to make war and might lead to an end of its maritime abuses against American shipping. Some Americans called for President Wilson to invoke this option, as did the German government. Another option called for the United States to protest British violations, to hope for their redress, but ultimately to accept them. Advocates of this position pointed to the enormous pressure Great Britain was under and to the efforts the British had made to pay for confiscated American goods. They also noted the ever-growing disparity between trade with the Allies and with the Central Powers. Strong cultural and emotional ties also militated against a firmer stand for neutral rights. Finally, and perhaps most important, there was Germany's use of a terrifying new weapon: the submarine.

Germany possessed only 21 submarines, or U-boats as they were more commonly known, at the outset of the fighting. Naval officials foresaw no major use for these weapons in a war that most believed would end quickly. However, the military stalemate on land, coupled with the British dominance of the seas (most of the German fleet was bottled up in port by superior British forces) and an increasingly effective blockade, occasioned a change in tactics. U-boats, relying on the element of surprise, seemed the best hope for breaking the British stranglehold. In addition, this new kind of warfare might turn the tables on the British and prevent goods from reaching their shores, thus bringing the war to a successful conclusion.

Germany announced on February 4, 1915 that the waters around the British Isles constituted a war zone and that it would sink without warning all Allied ships entering

FROM NEUTRALITY TO INVOLVEMENT

that zone. Germany advised neutrals to stay clear of the area for fear that their ships might accidentally be torpedoed, a distinct possibility since the British sometimes flew the flags of neutrals to confuse the enemy. President Wilson responded to the German announcement with anger. On February 10 he promised to hold Germany to "strict accountability" for "property endangered or lives lost." He had not used such strong language to protest British maritime violations, both because he quietly sympathized with Great Britain and because the German policy seemed destined to destroy lives.

Events soon put Wilson's warning to the test. The president, heeding the advice of Bryan, registered no formal protest when a German U-boat sank the British ship *Falaba* on March 28 with the loss of one American life. On May 7, however, the Germans sank without warning the luxury liner *Lusitania* in the Irish Sea with a loss of nearly 1200 persons, including 128 Americans. German officials justified the action on grounds that the liner was carrying munitions and other war material. Indeed, the *Lusitania* had been transporting more than 5,000 cases of ammunition, and German officials in the United States had placed notices in newspapers advising Americans not to travel on the ship. These justifications, whatever their legitimacy, did not mollify public opinion. Outraged citizens like Theodore Roosevelt demanded war, while others called for less extreme but vigorous countermeasures.

Wilson probably could have obtained from Congress a declaration of war over the *Lusitania* incident. Instead, he announced that "there is such a thing as a man being too proud to fight" and opted for diplomatic pressure. He pressed Germany for a promise that a similar tragedy would not occur. Germany vacillated. A second and stronger note failed to elicit the desired response, but it did occasion the resignation of the pacifist Bryan, who now feared war and also resented the growing influence of Wilson's advisor and confidant, Colonel Edward M. House. On August 19 two Americans died when Germans sank the *Arabic,* another British liner. This time German Chancellor Bethmann-Hollweg stood firm against the military and agreed to Wilson's demand that Germany cease attacking liners without warning and without providing for the safety of those aboard. Failure to agree, Wilson had warned, would lead to a break in diplomatic relations.

Germany's acceptance of Wilson's demands constituted a major concession. Submarines were effective only as long as they remained submerged. Once surfaced, they were vulnerable to gunfire or even to ramming, and there was no guarantee that liners or merchant ships would not attempt to destroy them once they abandoned their concealed position. Further, ships might relay the position of the submarines to armed ships while the passengers and crews were being rescued.

Germany deemed the risk acceptable and curbed the excesses of its deadly raiders. Then, on March 24, 1916, a U-boat torpedoed the unarmed French ship *Sussex,* which it mistook for a minelaying vessel. The blast injured several Americans, and President Wilson threatened to sever diplomatic ties unless Germany ceased submarine warfare against *all* merchant and passenger ships. Germany, fearing that America's entrance into the war would adversely tip the scales, agreed to Wilson's demands in the *Sussex* pledge of May 4. In return it demanded that the president hold the British liable for their violations. Wilson ignored this stipulation, but for the remainder of 1916 Germany fulfilled its pledge. Meanwhile Great Britain's treatment of neutral rights became more high-handed and insensitive, as evidenced by its blacklisting of more than 80 American citizens and firms suspected of trading with the enemy. Wilson confessed that the "blacklist business is the last straw" and that he was "about at the end of my patience with Great Britain and the Allies."

Mediation, Preparedness, and Politics   Wilson had unsuccessfully offered American mediation for the European conflict almost as soon as hostilities erupted. Undeterred, he sent Colonel House to London in early 1915 to renew the offer. Once again it was refused. In early 1916 the pro-Allied House recrossed the Atlantic and met with both British and French officials. The resulting House-Grey Memorandum of February 22 stated that the United States, "on hearing from France and England that the moment was opportune," would convene a conference of the belligerents. House promised that if Germany refused to attend or if the conference failed to achieve peace on terms "not unfavorable to the Allies," the United States would probably enter the war against the Central Powers. Yet British Foreign Secretary Grey wanted no conference while the German military position remained strong. Wilson had hoped that the belligerents would accept a negotiated settlement and end the carnage. But as casualties multiplied, the various war leaders found it impossible to tell their people that there would be no spoils of war to compensate for their losses.

The prolongation of the war, as well as the threats to American neutrality, forced a reluctant Wilson to turn to preparedness. The *Lusitania* tragedy sparked the formation of several private groups advocating military readiness. The Plattsburg (New York) idea of establishing training camps for civilians sprouted in the summer of 1916. Numerous citizens attended these camps and voiced their readiness to fight. On December 7, Wilson called upon Congress to upgrade the state of the military. Over the next several months Congress increased the size of the army to more than 200,000, brought the national guard under strong federal control, and accepted the Plattsburg program of establishing summer training camps. In addition, it authorized an ambitious program for the construction of military and merchant vessels. Finally, it provided for a Council of National Defense to coordinate efforts if the nation went to war.

Preparedness by no means pleased everyone. Pacifists and pro-Germans opposed this policy, as did isolationists. Other critics included progressives who stressed the costs of preparedness and the economic boon it presented to business. No large and effective antipreparedness organization existed, but incidents such as Henry Ford's quixotic chartering of a "peace ship," which he sent to Europe in late 1914 in the vain hope of securing a negotiated settlement, publicized the cause of peace. In early 1916 the Gore-McLemore resolution, which strove to avoid war by forbidding Americans to travel on the ships of belligerents, came before Congress. Wilson pressured Congress to defeat it.

Domestic concerns complicated foreign policy, and the principal domestic concern for Wilson in 1916 was the presidential election. At the Democratic convention that year a party speaker described the incumbent in words that were to become a campaign slogan: "He kept us out of war." The party also pointed to the recent social legislation championed by Wilson. The Democrats wrote a liberal platform that called on voters to elect the man who had brought them peace, prosperity, and progressivism.

Republicans still suffered from the split that had divided them in 1912. Progressives again wanted Theodore Roosevelt as their standard-bearer, but the former Bull Mooser refused and opted to return to the GOP. Some progressives joined him; others, impressed by Wilson's achievements, turned to the Democratic party. The Republicans nominated

Charles Evans Hughes, who had been a liberal governor of New York, but who now seemed an acceptable moderate because of his decisions as a justice of the U.S. Supreme Court. Republicans in their platform denounced the liberal legislation espoused by Wilson, as well as his failure to take a stronger stand against both Mexico and Germany.

The Republicans, still the dominant party, considered Wilson's victory in 1912 a fluke and foresaw triumph in 1916. And there was much reason for their optimism: Wilson had alienated isolationists and internationalists alike, as well as German-Americans and much of the business community. Hughes, however, proved a poor campaigner. Generally lackluster in his appearances, he tried to be all things to all people, especially in his foreign policy pronouncements. His foes jeeringly called him Charles "Evasive" Hughes. Theodore Roosevelt, who campaigned for him, privately mocked him as "the bearded iceberg" and "the kind of a man who would vote for Wilson."

Wilson meanwhile impressed voters with his liberal record and the promise of continued peace and prosperity, though he never promised that the nation could avoid entering the war. Labor rallied to his side, as did women, who appreciated his strong if belated support for women's suffrage. Nevertheless, Wilson went to sleep on election night reconciled to defeat as the returns from the East pointed to a victory for Hughes. The next day he awoke to find himself reelected. California, by the slimmest of margins—fewer than 4,000 of the nearly one million votes cast—had provided Wilson with his margin of victory. In all, he secured 277 electoral votes to 254 for Hughes, and 9.1 million popular votes to Hughes's 8.5 million.

War Comes   With the election behind him, Wilson resumed his quest for peace. In December he asked both sides to state their terms but received no satisfactory reply. Then on January 22, 1917 he called for "peace without victory." The conditions of that peace, which largely incorporated his Fourteen Points, included freedom of the seas, self-determination for suppressed nationalities, and an organization to preserve peace. On January 31 Germany stunned the United States by revoking the *Sussex* pledge and announcing that it would sink all merchant ships, armed or not, that ventured into the war zone. The military had outargued the civilians in Germany, promising that the submarine fleet, now grown to more than a hundred, could force Great Britain into suing for peace within six months. The military agreed that this presented a risk since the United States might declare war. But the effective entry of American forces into battle, they promised, would come too late to save the Allies.

Wilson responded to the new German provocation by breaking diplomatic relations on February 3. He still entertained hopes of avoiding war, particularly since Germany promised safe conduct to a certain number of American passenger ships and promised not to attack American merchant ships until the middle of March. Wilson also reasoned that Germany might back down entirely on its threat to American ships as it realized the foolishness of pushing the United States into war.

Events in February and March destroyed Wilson's wishful thinking. In late February the British passed along a decoded copy of the Zimmermann telegram. This note, written by the German foreign minister, asked Mexico to fight with Germany against the United States if war broke out. In return, Mexico would receive Texas, Arizona, and New Mexico after the war. (Japan would switch from the Allied side to Germany's, according to the plan.) Many Americans clamored for war after Wilson released the note on March 1.

Americans also responded to the growing threat of economic recession. Merchant shipowners, fearful of unrestricted submarine warfare, refused to carry cargo or to import goods from abroad. Shortages of food and other materials appeared. Wilson asked Congress for the power to arm merchant ships. The House gave its approval, but isolationists in the Senate, led by Robert La Follette, successfully filibustered against the measure. Wilson, after denouncing this "little group of willful men," found an old statute that permitted the chief executive to arm merchant ships without congressional approval. He implemented this law in early March. That month the Germans also made good their threat to attack American ships entering the war zone. By the end of the month they had sunk several still unarmed vessels with the subsequent loss of three dozen American lives.

Wilson no longer believed war could be avoided. Armed neutrality was not working; submarine warfare was destroying Great Britain's ability to receive necessary imports. Moreover, the overthrow of the autocratic Russian Czar Nicholas II in March now made it more plausible for the Allies to claim that they were the more democratic of the two sides in the conflict. Wilson went before a packed joint session of Congress on April 2 to ask for a declaration of war against Germany. Americans had no quarrel with the German people, he stressed, nor were they serving selfish ends. Germany had forced the United States into war through its unacceptable behavior. The American cause now was to "vindicate the principles of peace and justice." "The world," solemnly intoned the president, "must be made safe for democracy." Toward that end, he noted, "America is privileged to spend her blood and her might. . . ." The speech drew great applause, but a somber Wilson privately confessed: "My message today was a message of death for our young men. How strange it seems to applaud that."

Congress debated the president's request. Most members voiced their support, but pacifists, isolationists, and some progressives balked. Senator George W. Norris of Nebraska, for example, feared that American participation would only bring further profits to financiers, industrialists, and Wall Street speculators, while saddling future generations with enormous debts. Representative Jeanette Rankin of Montana voted her pacifist disapproval of war, an act she would repeat a generation later at the time of the Japanese attack on Pearl Harbor. Nonetheless, the Senate voted for war on April 4 by a vote of 82–6. Two days later, on Good Friday, the House followed suit by a majority of 373–50.

Some have questioned the wisdom of Woodrow Wilson's foreign policy and how, desiring peace, he ultimately led the nation into war. Wilson had successfully resisted earlier pressures to ask for war. But by 1917 Germany clearly had adopted a more provocative stance with its declaration of a resumed unrestricted submarine warfare, its subsequent sinking of American ships, and the inflammatory Zimmerman note. Also, many more Americans by this time had come to believe that Germany was decidedly the aggressor among the belligerents. Wilson spoke for some of them when he envisioned the war as a struggle for the survival of democracy. But was it? Even if Germany could have won a decisive military victory it would have had to expend tremendous energy and resources to impose its rule on the Allies. And despite the presence of some spies and saboteurs on American soil it would have experienced even greater difficulty in attempting to extend its dominion to the Western Hemisphere; nor in such an undertaking could it have counted on much support from strife-torn Mexico. The United States, then, had ample reason to declare war on Germany on moral and legal grounds. The grounds of self-interest were considerably less tenable.

Historians Debate

AMERICAN INTERVENTION IN WORLD WAR I

Few issues have provoked more controversy among historians than the decision of the United States to enter World War I. Debate over American intervention has fallen into three main categories: (1) The United States went to war because of Germany's ruthless submarine warfare and threats to democratic values. (2) The United States intervened for reasons of vital national self-interest to prevent German hegemony in Europe and control of the Atlantic. (3) War came as Woodrow Wilson jettisoned nonintervention because of his bias for the Allies and willingness to protect the investments of financiers.

The first argument was largely dominant during the 1920s, but yielded to revisionist scholarship during the next decade. Charles Beard, C. Hartley Grattan, Walter Millis, and Charles C. Tansill, among others, concluded that involvement had been a serious mistake, dooming progressive reform and needlessly embroiling the nation in the internecine quarrels of the Old World. President Wilson, as Millis noted in *The Road to War* (1935), had unwisely seized upon "the easy, the profoundly tempting alternative—of making war." Like most Americans of the 1930s, these revisionists hoped that the bitter lessons to be drawn from entanglement in the Great War would preclude involvement in any other such cataclysm.

The advent of World War II and the subsequent Cold War brought to the fore the thesis that intervention had stemmed largely from realistic considerations of self-interest. Tending to equate the threat of Kaiser Wilhelm's Germany with that of Adolf Hitler, some scholars agreed with Walter Lippmann's argument, first offered in 1917, that the nation

had entered World War I in order not to "betray the Atlantic community" and give Germany dominion in the West. The fear of communism during the postwar era provided an added impetus to the "realist" argument, as evidenced in *American Diplomacy, 1900–1950* (1952), by diplomat-historian George F. Kennan, and in several works authored by the eminent Wilson scholar Arthur S. Link. Some concurred with John Morton Blum, whose *Woodrow Wilson and the Politics of Morality* (1956) attacked the president's foreign policy for having contained too much idealism. Others agreed with the subtle and basically favorable analysis of Wilson's blending of realism with idealism as presented in Robert E. Osgood's *Ideals and Self-Interest in America's Foreign Relations* (1953) and Ernest R. May's *The World War and American Isolation, 1914–1917* (1959).

Given the upheavals that affected American society during the 1960s, it was not surprising that radical historians joined the debate. Both William Appleman Williams, in *The Tragedy of American Diplomacy* (1962), and N. Gordon Levin, Jr., in *Woodrow Wilson and World Politics* (1968), stressed Wilson's desire to establish a stable world order based on liberal capitalism. For these scholars the origins of intervention seemed intimately linked with the peacemaking that followed. Still other scholars added new dimensions to the historical debate by eschewing economics for science. Alexander L. George and Juliette L. George, for example, interpreted the president's actions in psychoanalytical terms in *Woodrow Wilson and Colonel House* (1956); Edwin A. Weinstein skillfully pointed to the possible effects of Wilson's health on policymaking in "Woodrow Wilson's Neurological Illness" [*Journal of American History* 57 (September 1970): 324–351].

In light of the sharply conflicting interpretations that have characterized the debate over intervention, it seems most unlikely that any one point of view is destined to predominate. Older interpretations reappear in newer forms; new syntheses arise, phoenix-like, from the ashes of past ideas once largely out of favor. But what has clearly emerged from the debate is agreement that the decision to go to war was much more complex than once believed.

THE NATION AT WAR

Many Americans misjudged the sufferings and sacrifices that war would bring. They agreed that Germany must be punished for its barbarous submarine attacks and that the Allies must continue to receive American aid to insure their survival. But few imagined that 4.8 million of their fellow citizens ultimately would serve in the war and that domestic hardships and strife were also in store. Victory would be theirs—but at a price.

The War at Sea German submarines were exacting a grim toll by the time the United States declared war. U-boats sank 881,000 tons of British shipping in April, more than double the amount destroyed at the beginning of the year, before unrestricted warfare was resumed. Great Britain had enough grain for only two months, and officials estimated that the country could no longer fight beyond 1917 if the situation did not change dramatically.

The American response to Britain's plight snatched victory from defeat. Rear Admiral William S. Sims convinced the British to adopt a convoy system to protect their merchant shipping. By this method, cruisers and destroyers, which were more than a match for submarines, patrolled the movements of vulnerable merchant freighters. So effective was this convoy system that British shipping losses fell to 289,000 tons by November. Meanwhile an increasing number of American warships, which eventually would total 2,000, became active, sinking their first U-boats. The navy also began experimenting with various forms of radar and planes to chart the position of enemy boats. By the spring of 1918 it had virtually closed off the North Sea to German submarines. Most important, it was safely transporting men and material through the war zone.

The War on Land Germany's gamble that the United States could not train and deploy an effective army before it was too late did not seem farfetched. Many Americans assumed their soldiers would never go overseas, and even General Tasker Bliss of the General Staff recommended two years of training for troops before departure to the western front. Nonetheless, the nation launched a campaign to expand its regular army, which, along with the national guard, totaled 378,000 when the war began. Wilson asked for 500,000 troops in his war message but turned down the request of a bitterly disappointed Theodore Roosevelt, then nearly 60 years old, to lead a group of volunteers into battle.

Congress responded to Wilson's request by passing the Selective Service Act the following month. This act required all males between ages 18 and 45 to register. On

THE NATION AT WAR

June 5 nearly 10 million Americans registered, and on June 20 blindfolded Secretary of War Newton Baker drew the first number. The draft initially called men between ages 21 and 30 but later extended the range to the ages of 18 to 45. All those drafted were unmarried. Thirteen percent of the draftees were blacks, who constituted only 10 percent of the entire population. This imbalance stemmed from the inability of blacks to procure exemptions as readily as whites, as well as the difficulty they sometimes encountered when trying to volunteer. Other noteworthy facts revealed by the draft included a shockingly high total incidence of venereal disease and an illiteracy rate of 25 percent.

General John J. Pershing received command of the American Expeditionary Force (AEF), composed of regular army units as well as draftees. Pershing, for both political and professional reasons, resisted all efforts to merge the AEF with the Allied forces. Instead, he promised that his independent troops would coordinate their activities with British and French soldiers. (The relatively small number of American troops who were integrated into Allied units, thanks largely to the latter's experience and more solid leadership, suffered comparatively fewer losses than those who were not.) Only a limited contingent of American troops, or "doughboys" as they were called, reached France in the first few months after the American declaration of war. But on July 4, 1917, Pershing reviewed an American battalion as it marched through Parisian streets to the wild cheerings of the French. "Lafayette, we are here," quipped one of his aides.

Training camps sprang up throughout the country in 1917 to transform raw recruits into soldiers and to swell the trickle of AEF troops into a river of fighting forces. Recruits, often arriving to the tune "Johnny Get Your Gun," quickly turned to booze and sex for relief from the alternating rigors and tedium of martial life. The army soon forbade the sale of liquor to uniformed men and worked feverishly to combat venereal diseases. Morale remained generally high as camaraderie bonded the recruits. Groups such as the YMCA arrived to entertain the troops, and there were also athletic programs and movies. Hit songs of the day reflected the high spirits. True, soldiers grumbled "Oh, How I Hate to Get Up in the Morning." On the other hand, George M. Cohan's immensely popular "Over There" reflected a real eagerness to get on with the work of winning the war.

The first AEF units reached France in late 1917, only a few months after the regular army had sustained its initial casualties. French life, particularly the cosmopolitanism of Paris, excited the doughboys. So, too, did the French women, as the troops sang the splendors of "Mademoiselle from Armentières" and wondered, as the popular song of 1919 would ask, "How Ya Gonna Keep 'Em Down on the Farm?" after they had seen Paris. But American soldiers were there for more serious reasons. Between March and October 1918 some 1,750,000 of them arrived, probably just in time to save the Allies from defeat. The Bolshevik Revolution of November 1917 led directly to the Treaty of Brest-Litovsk a month later. The treaty resulted in peace with Germany and Russian withdrawal from the war. By March 1918, 40 German divisions from the eastern front joined those on the western front in a huge offensive designed to end the stalemate. Americans helped blunt the offensive in such battles as Château-Thierry and Belleau Wood. In July they joined Allied troops in a huge counteroffensive. By late September more than a million doughboys helped in the Meuse-Argonne thrust that broke through enemy lines and cleared the way for an invasion of Germany itself.

Faced with this grave situation, Germany asked for and received an armistice on November 11, 1918. Four years and three months after it had begun, the most murderous

Citizens entertaining American troops. Note the photograph of Theodore Roosevelt, and not Woodrow Wilson, above the piano. Most blacks considered themselves Republicans.

American troops fighting in the Argonne sector.

THE NATION AT WAR

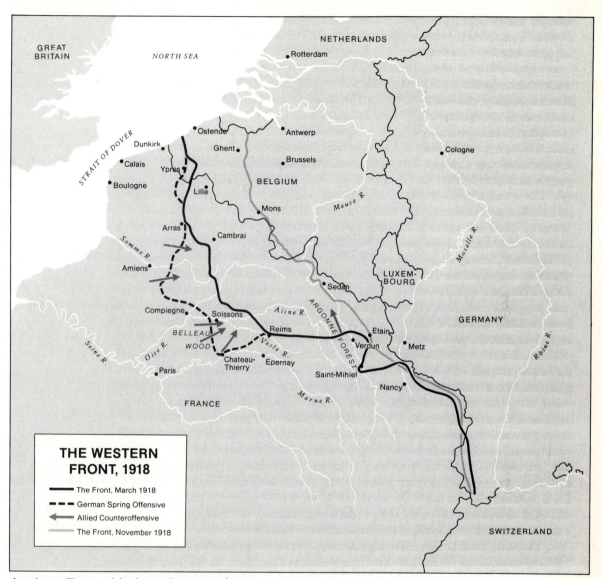

American military participation on the western front.

war in history had come to its painful close. American deaths totaled 112,000, nearly half of them from disease. (The great influenza epidemic of 1918 killed some 50,000 American troops and 20 million civilians throughout the world.) The wounded numbered 230,000. These figures, dreadful though they were, paled before the staggering battle losses for the other combatants: Britain and the Commonwealth countries lost 900,000; Russia, 1.7 million; Germany, 1.6 million; France, 1.38 million; Austria, 800,000; and Italy, 460,000.

The War at Home   The military success of both the AEF and the Allies depended on the successful mobilization of civilians and essential goods at home. To provide this mobilization, government intervened in the daily affairs of people as it had not done since the Civil War. World War I tested the willingness of Americans to accept a powerful interventionist state. Many—government officials and private citizens alike—remained uneasy with this new approach, questioning the extent to which intrusion was necessary and hoping for a return to the pre-1917 status quo. Still, most accepted the restraints and the sacrifices that allowed them to triumph over the Central Powers.

Mobilizing the Economy   Congress granted the president broad powers to organize the war effort. Wilson toiled endlessly and imaginatively to find ways to make that effort a success. During most of 1917 the government relied on the voluntary cooperation of the private sector to meet war needs. The following year it turned to stronger controls. A Council for National Defense, consisting of several cabinet officers and advisors, received a mandate from Wilson to establish agencies to determine priorities, allocate supplies, fix prices, oversee distribution, and run the nation's transportation and communication systems. By war's end some 500 agencies had come into existence.

One major agency was the War Industries Board, which in the summer of 1917 received the gargantuan charge of military production and supply. The astute Bernard Baruch became its chairman in March 1918. A remarkably successful stock market speculator, Baruch won the confidence of businessmen and eased some of the worst obstacles to production efficiency. More than 30,000 articles fell within the scope of the War Industries Board, though its powers were circumscribed. The chairman, for instance, could not fix prices without the advice of a special committee. Nonetheless, the board did bring increasing order to an initially chaotic war effort.

The government also attempted to impose order and efficiency on vital resources and on the transportation system. Harry A. Garfield, president of Williams College and son of the assassinated president, became head of the Fuel Administration. Garfield's primary job was to increase coal production and insure that war-related industries received enough coal to meet their needs. ''Fuel Will Win the War'' became the Fuel Administration's motto, as Garfield called for greater sacrifices. ''Heatless'' days and ''lightless'' nights resulted; so did the widespread adoption of ''daylight saving time'' and ''gasless Sundays.'' Some factories closed, numerous civilians ran short of fuel, and tempers flared. However, Garfield brought an end to the overall bottlenecking of coal.

Railroads were proving unable to coordinate the complex movement of troops and supplies. The government then decided to take over the running of the railroads in December 1917. Wilson delegated responsibility for untangling the railroads to his hard-working son-in-law, William G. McAdoo, who was also serving as secretary of treasury. A viable system emerged under McAdoo's Railroad Administration, though it did not please everyone. For example, McAdoo passed along to irate shippers and passengers the more than $700 million in costs and benefits granted to the companies and workers. The Railroad Administration also took over responsibility for directing other vital services such as telephones and telegrams.

The government additionally assumed the planning for ship and airplane construction. The Shipping Board, which was established in 1916, set up the Emergency Fleet Corporation the following year. Besides seizing enemy merchant vessels, the new agency undertook the building of a "bridge of ships" to cross the Atlantic. Despite bureaucratic confusions and the need to move ahead at a breakneck pace, the corporation did manage to build more ships than enemy submarines could sink, and it was becoming more effective by the end of the war. Less fruitful were the efforts of the Aircraft Production Board, which was able to construct fewer than 2,000 planes by the summer of 1918, only one-tenth the number it had promised.

The management of the nation's food resources provided another dramatic example of government intervention in domestic affairs. The Allies desperately needed food, as would the AEF. Compounding this problem were the poor grain harvests of 1916 and 1917. In May 1917 Wilson appointed Herbert Clark Hoover to head the recently created Food Administration. Hoover had overcome an unhappy childhood as a poor orphan to become a world-famous mining engineer and millionaire. At the outset of the war he successfully organized the Belgian Relief Commission, winning a well-deserved reputation for his humanitarian endeavors. He again used his skills to achieve desired ends as director of the Food Administration. Low-keyed in tone, he successfully urged Americans to make needed sacrifices. "Wheatless Mondays," "meatless Tuesdays," and "porkless Thursdays" became standard. "Victory gardens" of homegrown foodstuffs also underscored the willingness of citizens to do their part to insure an Allied victory. Avoiding rationing, Hoover stimulated production through price-fixing, quotas, and ingenious purchasing methods. As a result the United States was able to export three times as much food to Europe during the war as before. The Miracle Man, as people dubbed him, became one of the great war heroes and a likely future candidate for high public office.

The war witnessed a significant change in the government's attitude toward labor. In order to secure labor peace and harmonious industrial operations, the government responded positively to the demands of workers. It offered them collective bargaining rights and guaranteed the eight-hour day where it already existed in exchange for promises to forgo strikes. The agreement, supported by Samuel Gompers and his AFL, worked imperfectly because some employers refused to grant these concessions while some workers thought the concessions inadequate. More than 4,400 strikes occurred in 1917. Most of these were brief, however, as the National War Labor Board helped to arbitrate more than 1,500 cases. The real income of workers rose nearly 20 percent from prewar levels as a result of wartime needs and the friendly attitude of government. Union membership also increased from 2.7 million in 1916 to 4 million in 1919.

Women and Blacks: Limited Opportunities   The war created a vast demand for labor. The huge, steady immigration from Europe to America that had characterized the previous thirty years dried up, thanks to the need for manpower in Europe itself and the U-boat menace in the Atlantic. The drafting of millions of able-bodied American males worsened the labor shortage, bringing about a near-emergency situation.

Women helped to relieve this shortage. "A woman's place is in the war" replaced "A woman's place is in the home" as a slogan for the times. Some 11,000 women ("yeomanettes") joined the navy, while others ("farmerettes") took agricultural jobs. Many served as nurses or Red Cross volunteers; many more quietly knitted clothing for the soldiers overseas. More significant were the large numbers who entered the industrial work force. Eight million women worked during the war. Many white women shifted

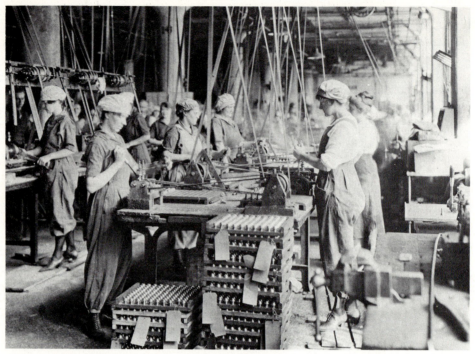
Women provided a significant addition to the civilian work force during World War I.

from domestic to factory employment, with black women assuming their vacated positions. Organized labor, especially the AFL, opposed the widespread hiring of women, fearing that this would generate lower wages for males. Their fears usually proved groundless: Employers simply paid women less. In New York, for example, only 9 percent of women workers received the equal pay they were promised.

After the war, society urged women to return to their place in the home. The "war to make the world safe for democracy" had not brought women equal economic opportunities with men. Yet women did obtain one substantial democratic triumph: suffrage.

The war also promised new opportunities for blacks. Some questioned whether in the light of their second-class citizenship at home they should serve, spill their blood, and die abroad. Various developments reinforced these doubts. A riot in Houston in 1917 cost the lives of 17 white civilians and 2 black soldiers. Whites had provoked the incident, but more than 100 blacks received courts-martial for murder or mutiny. Thirteen of these were executed and 41 were given life sentences. Nonetheless, nearly 400,000 blacks either enlisted or were drafted into the military. Most of them obtained menial positions, and only 20,000 actively fought. Yet many won honors for their valor on the battlefield. Some 170 officers and soldiers in the distinguished 369th New York Regiment, for instance, received medals. All black troops served in segregated units. Despite this, W. E. B. DuBois urged blacks to support the war in every way possible, believing that white Americans would respond by granting them full rights and respect once the fighting ended. That more than 100 blacks were lynched during the war years did not augur well for his hopes.

THE NATION AT WAR

Still, the labor shortage at home provided benefits for many blacks who did not serve in the military. Responding to the abundance of jobs, as well as to the segregation and lynchings prevalent in the South, blacks migrated northward as never before. Northern and western states, according to the census of 1920, reported a gain of 330,000 blacks during the previous decade. Blacks secured employment but faced discrimination and violence at the hands of northern whites who resented job competition and the presence of these darker-skinned strangers. In 1917, for instance, angry white mobs in East St. Louis, Illinois, attacked blacks who had been hired by a local factory. At least 40 of the latter died during the riot, including a two-year-old who was shot. Race relations worsened once the war ended. Returning black servicemen, aware of their martial contributions and filled with greater self-pride, were less likely to accept insults and mistreatment. This changed attitude angered many whites, particularly soldiers who now found that blacks had moved into both their jobs and their neighborhoods. More than two dozen cities and towns experienced racial riots in 1919. Especially hard hit was Chicago, where after days of violence 38 people were dead and more than 500 injured. In all, hundreds died as a result of the 1919 riots.

Financing the War   Disagreement arose as to how best to finance the war, whose direct costs came to roughly $33 billion. (Indirect costs—pensions, bonuses, debt interest— surpassed that amount.) Progressives wanted the wealthy to bear the brunt in the form of higher taxation. Conservatives favored greater borrowing to lower costs. Compromise resulted. Taxes accounted for approximately one-third of the war financing. Congress taxed luxury items such as gasoline, liquor, and entertainment. It also passed new corporate taxes, with rates reaching a maximum of 65 percent. More surprising was the Revenue Act of 1918, which raised the rates on personal income to an unprecedented maximum of 77 percent.

The government also turned to the small investor for financial assistance. Over 65 million individuals subscribed more than $20 billion to the five loan drives that took place between 1917 and 1919. Popular enthusiasm for these bond-selling campaigns was enormous. There was also much popular pressure on reluctant bond purchasers. Miranda, heroine of Katherine Anne Porter's *Pale Horse, Pale Rider* (1939), received intimidating exhortations to purchase a Liberty Bond. She protested that she lacked funds. ''That's no excuse, no excuse at all, and you know it, with the Huns overrunning martyred Belgium,'' warned a superpatriotic bond salesman. Others in real life were physically beaten and forced to subscribe.

Shaping Public Opinion   The government pressured Americans to subscribe to the ideals and sentiments of the war, as well as its finances. Many Americans originally failed to see the justice of the Allied cause or at least the necessity of American assistance to the Allies. Socialists like Eugene V. Debs, pacifists like Jane Addams, progressives like Robert La Follette, German-American and Irish-American hyphenates, and millions of others doubtlessly belonged in this category. To achieve greater national unity Congress established the Committee on Public Information (CPI) on April 14, 1917, and the president appointed George Creel as its head. It was ironic that Creel, a progressive journalist and defender of the radical ''Big Bill'' Haywood and his IWW, would help foment wartime hysteria and intolerance.

Creel and the CPI designed an elaborate system to unify public opinion. They issued over 75 million copies of more than 30 pamphlets in different languages to mold the nation's thinking and sent out 75,000 "four-minute men" to speak at public gatherings. It is estimated that these volunteers gave more than 750,000 speeches to audiences that eventually totaled over three million. Creel's organization also enlisted artists and professionals to create eye-catching graphics and news releases. The CPI initially stressed factual information, promising that "no hymn of hate accompanies our message." This soon changed. Facts yielded to propaganda; tolerance gave way to bigotry. In 1917 Creel and his cohorts produced such positive films as *Pershing's Crusaders* and *Our Colored Fighters*. The following year they turned out *The Kaiser, the Beast of Berlin* and *The Prussian Cur,* and instructed their "four-minute men" to recount incidents of atrocities.

The CPI proved all too successful in its attempts to instill in Americans a fanatical hatred of the Germans. Schools could no longer teach German, and it became a crime in several states to speak German over the telephone. The mayor of Jersey City refused to let Fritz Kreisler, the noted Austrian composer, perform in public. Superpatriots renamed sauerkraut "liberty cabbage" and German measles "patriotic measles," while the dachshund became the "liberty pup." There were reported incidents, both in the United States and Great Britain, of frenzied crowds stoning dachshunds to death.

Violence extended to humans as well. In April 1918 a mob of 500 stripped a German-American, draped him in an American flag, dragged him through the streets, and lynched him. A jury verdict that took 25 minutes to reach later acquitted the mob leaders of murder. In August a handful of zealots seized an IWW official in Butte, Montana, dragged him behind an automobile until they destroyed his kneecaps, and then hanged him. No attempt was made to apprehend the perpetrators. The American Protective League, at one time boasting a membership of 250,000, continually harassed German-Americans and conscientious objectors. (Nearly 500 of the latter received prison terms during the war.) Such groups as the Sedition Slammers and Boy Spies of America abetted the league in the quest to enforce their rigid definition of Americanism.

The government denounced lynchings and headed off attempts to establish military courts within the United States. Yet its overall record on civil liberties reflected a sad mixture of fear and hysteria. Instances of sedition and spying did occur, but they were uncommon. The Espionage Act of June 1917 made it illegal to spy or to interfere with the draft. It also empowered the postmaster general to deny mailing privileges to material he deemed treasonous or harmful to the war effort. The Sedition Act of 1918 made it a crime to impede bond sales or to "utter, print, write or publish any disloyal, profane, scurrilous or abusive language about the form of government of the United States, or the Constitution, or the flag, or the uniform of the Army or Navy. . . ." Both acts carried a maximum penalty of 20 years in jail and a $10,000 fine. Under the terms of these laws nearly 2,000 persons were indicted, of whom roughly 1,000 were found guilty. Most received pardons after the war, but some continued to serve sentences long afterwards.

The government zealously enforced the Espionage and Sedition acts against antiwar radicals. Postmaster General Albert S. Burleson freely censored the mails and withheld the use of cheaper mailing privileges from two socialist newspapers. The government also prosecuted two of the most prominent Socialists, Debs and Victor Berger. Debs was tried, found guilty, and sentenced to 10 years in jail for obstructing the draft. Berger, a

THE NATION AT WAR

The young man in the stocks represented a symbolic warning to inhabitants of Cincinnati who opposed the war effort. The warning was also meant for opponents in general.

Socialist from Milwaukee, received a 20-year sentence for denouncing the war as a capitalist venture. Twice elected as a congressman, he was denied his seat by the Wisconsin state legislature. A similar fate awaited several duly elected Socialists from New York City. The New York state assembly expelled them for their antiwar positions.

The IWW fared worse. Local officials and vigilante groups regularly persecuted the Wobblies for their labor strikes and antiwar sentiments. More than a thousand Wobbly strikers in Bisbee, Arizona, for instance, were herded onto a train and taken to the desert, where they remained foodless for more than a day. The federal government broke the power of the IWW in 1917 when it rounded up Haywood and other Wobbly leaders throughout the country and indicted them under the Espionage Act the following year. Half of them were convicted and sentenced to prison terms. Haywood jumped bail and fled to Russia, which was then under Bolshevik rule. His ashes, like those of John Reed, the radical American correspondent who covered the Bolshevik Revolution, remain interred in the Kremlin.

Civil libertarians challenged the government's repressive measures, but usually in vain. The Supreme Court upheld the Espionage Act in *Schenck* v. *U.S.* (1919). Justice Oliver Wendell Holmes, speaking for a unanimous court, ruled that the defendant, by obstructing the draft, had represented "a clear and present danger" to the nation during a wartime situation. Holmes joined Justice Louis Brandeis that same year in dissenting from their fellow justices in *Abrams* v. *U.S.* Holmes pointed to the necessity of enjoying a "free trade in ideas." The majority of the court, however, ruled against the defendant and validated the Sedition Act.

THE SEARCH FOR PEACE

Wilsonian Idealism   Seeking peace was no less important to President Wilson than waging war. And despite the widespread incidences of violence and suppression of civil liberties at home, he was determined to achieve a just and democratic settlement abroad. On January 8, 1918 Wilson went before Congress and proposed his Fourteen Points as the basis for future peace. Half the points dealt with postwar boundaries and territorial settlements. Others enunciated high-minded principles such as no secret treaties, freedom of the seas, and a general armaments reduction. The final point, Wilson's most cherished, called for the creation of a League of Nations to prevent wars. Wilson hoped that his speech would both encourage the Allies and convince the Germans that they could obtain fair treatment if they stopped fighting. So stirring were his ideas and words that even Debs believed that they "deserve the unqualified approval of everyone believing in the rule of the people, Socialists included."

By the end of the war Wilson was optimistic that his idealism would win the day. Germany had sought an armistice based on his Fourteen Points; the masses of people in the Allied countries were hailing Wilson and American soldiers as their saviors. But the president faced serious obstacles. Allied leaders believed Germany must pay a steep price for the grief and suffering it had precipitated. They scoffed, moreover, at Wilson's high ideals and at what they considered his naïveté. French Premier Georges Clemenceau privately jeered that Wilson had Fourteen Points, while God only had Ten Commandments. The president also needlessly alienated Republicans at home. He pleaded with voters to elect Democrats to Congress in the 1918 elections, although Republicans had given him strong support for his wartime measures. The November returns provided Republicans with a 49–47 margin in the Senate and a 240–190 margin in the House. Wilson increased his difficulties with Republicans a month later when he sailed for Paris and the upcoming peace conference. He knew that the Republican-dominated Senate would have to ratify any treaty. Nonetheless, he failed to select even one senator for the delegation and chose only one minor Republican to join the group.

Wilson and the Peace Conference   Wilson sailed for France on December 13, 1918. He took with him four other official members of the peace delegation (all "yes men," according to one critic) and hundreds of experts to render advice. No doubt existed, however, that Wilson alone would decide questions of policy. After a triumphant tour of various European cities, where he received tumultuous welcomes from crowds, the president returned to Paris for the opening of the peace conference on January 18, 1919.

THE SEARCH FOR PEACE

Turmoil and bitterness greeted American delegates. Chaotic conditions prevailed throughout eastern Europe. The Allies meanwhile refused to seat defeated Germany or Russia. The latter had withdrawn from the war and was currently in the throes of a civil conflict between Bolsheviks and non-Bolsheviks. The staunchly anti-Bolshevik Wilson had earlier sent more than 10,000 American troops to Russia, ostensibly to safeguard supplies from falling into the hands of the Germans and to guarantee the exit of a pro-Allied Czech contingent of prisoners of war trapped in Siberia. He had ordered the troops not to intervene directly in the civil war. Still, he hoped for an anti-Bolshevik victory and embargoed aid for the Bolsheviks. The last troops left Russia only in 1920. The president's antibolshevism and subsequent shunning of the Bolsheviks at the Paris peace conference very early poisoned Soviet-American relations, leaving a legacy of distrust and hostility to this day.

With Russia and Germany excluded from proceedings, the Big Four—Wilson, Clemenceau (France), David Lloyd George (Great Britain), and Vittorio Orlando (Italy)—quickly assumed control and hammered out one of the most complex and controversial peace treaties in modern history. At first, Wilson's moderation seemed triumphant over the more selfish goals of the Allied leaders. Within a month Wilson obtained an agreement from them that they would not receive Germany's existing colonies as outright possessions but as mandated territories to be governed with a view toward eventual independence. More significant, he convinced them to include within the treaty itself provisions for a League of Nations. Internationalists throughout the world had been calling for such an organization during the war years, but now Wilson, a figure of tremendous prestige and popularity, seemed able to translate the dream into reality. The League would perform several functions, most notably guaranteeing world peace. Article X of its Covenant stated that ''members of the League undertake to respect and preserve as against external aggression the territorial integrity and existing political independence of all the members.''

Wilson returned home in late February during a lull in the activities to sign congressional bills into law. Senator Henry Cabot Lodge of Massachusetts, chairman of the powerful Foreign Relations Committee and a strong foe of Wilson, warned the president that the Senate would not ratify the treaty as it stood. In March three dozen senators joined with Lodge in signing a resolution to that effect. They demanded, among other guarantees, that the nation be permitted to withdraw from the League and that its special concerns, such as immigration and the Monroe Doctrine, be protected. Wilson reluctantly promised to ask the Allies to accept the proposed changes.

The Allies acceded to the changes but in turn presented stiffer demands of their own. At one point an angry Wilson threatened to return to the United States. The vindicative, territory-seeking Allies vitiated many of the Fourteen Points. There were no promises to remove tariffs, reduce armaments, or maintain freedom of the seas. The principle of national self-determination did find acceptance in the establishment of several eastern European states carved out of the defeated Austro-Hungarian Empire, but nothing was said about a free state for Ireland, for the 200,000 German-speaking inhabitants of the Tyrol placed under Italian rule, for the Chinese who resented the Japanese occupation of former German holdings in their country, or for the many German inhabitants now included in the restored nation of Poland and the self-governing ''free city'' of Danzig. Wilson did keep Italy from obtaining the Adriatic port of Fiume and France from annexing

Delegates signed the peace treaty ending World War I in the Hall of Mirrors at Versailles.

the Rhineland; but France did recover from Germany the provinces of Alsace and Lorraine, which had been lost during the Franco-Prussian War. France also received the right to exploit the coal-rich Saar region in Germany and to have the Rhineland declared a demilitarized zone. The Allies also exacted an admission from Germany that it alone was responsible for the war, as well as exorbitant reparations that amounted to $33 billion. In June the humiliated German delegates signed the dictated Treaty of Versailles in the palatial Hall of Mirrors.

    The victors had written a harsh peace, though terms were less punitive than those Germany had imposed on Russia and might have imposed on the Allies had the war ended differently. This was despite Wilson's best efforts. Still, the president may have achieved as much as possible under the circumstances. Poland was re-created as a nation; other long-repressed peoples in eastern Europe received states of their own; former German colonies inched toward self-determination via the mandate system. Meanwhile the Allies had given Wilson what he most wanted: the League as a foundation for world peace. It only remained for the Senate to ratify the treaty, and as Wilson remarked, "The Senate must take its medicine." Doctor Wilson had grossly underestimated what poor patients senators could be.

The Fight for Ratification The Senate divided into three basic positions on the issue of the treaty. At one extreme were 40 or so Wilsonian Democrats who supported the president's version. The "irreconcilables," or "Battalion of Death" as they were also called, occupied the other end of the spectrum. These were a group of somewhat more than a dozen senators, mainly progressive Republicans such as La Follette, Hiram Johnson, and Edgar Borah, who opposed the adoption of any treaty committing the nation to internationalism. In between stood most of the Republicans, who were either "mild" or "strong" reservationists. At any given moment more than the required two-thirds of the Senate were prepared to commit the nation to participation in some kind of League. Only the bitter clash between Senator Lodge and President Wilson could—and did—prevent this.

The patrician Henry Cabot Lodge, a descendant of one of Massachusetts's most distinguished families, was a scholarly Harvard graduate. A staunch conservative, he was also a dedicated Republican determined that the Democrats not receive any credit for the treaty that might help them in the 1920 elections. The senator was, moreover, a strong nationalist who believed that the United States should play an active role in world affairs but must maintain the supremacy of its self-interests. Lodge had also come to despise Wilson. He had detested his handling of the nation's problems with Mexico. And after the president's failure to take a firmer stand against Germany following the sinking of the *Lusitania,* he fumed: "WW is a self-seeking, unprincipled, egotistical, timid, and narrow-minded politician. . . . In domestic matters he is a demagogue, in foreign affairs a coward." Wilson's war message failed to change his opinion. He wrote to Theodore Roosevelt (who equally hated the president): "He is a mean soul and the fact that he delivered a good message does not alter his character."

Henry Cabot Lodge

Wilson's dislike for Lodge stemmed basically from the struggle over the League. He could not forgive Lodge for demanding changes in the League's Covenant, which he regarded as nearly sacrosanct. Any changes, he argued, would bring dishonor to the United States and represent a setback for the cause of world peace. It has also been suggested that Wilson refused to compromise because he perceived Lodge as the figurative reincarnation of the strongly authoritarian minister-father who had dominated the president's youth.

Wilson officially presented the treaty to the Senate on July 10, asking with more than a little hyperbole: ''Dare we reject it and break the heart of the world?'' Lodge knew that most Americans wanted a League in some form. He also sensed that delays could aid him in revising or defeating Wilson's version. For two months the wily senator procrastinated. First he spent two weeks reading the 264 pages of the treaty to the members of the Foreign Relations Committee, even though each had his own copy. Next he held public hearings for six weeks.

Wilson chafed at the delay. Earlier he had informed the French ambassador that he would consent to none of the revisions. As it became clear that the Foreign Relations Committee would append amendments and reservations to the treaty, the president decided to take his case to the people. In early September he embarked on a tour of the Middle and Far West, visiting city after city and sometimes speaking several times a day. The strain proved too much for one who was weary and not in robust health to begin with. On September 25, Wilson collapsed after a speech in Pueblo, Colorado. The presidential train rushed the ailing chief executive back to Washington, where a few days later he suffered a stroke that left his body paralyzed on one side. For several weeks he remained in seclusion, guarded by his protective wife, who served as an intermediary between her husband and his friends and foes in the Senate.

By mid-September the Foreign Relations Committee had attached a host of changes to the treaty, and by November had narrowed the changes to 14 reservations. The most controversial of these reiterated that the United States under no circumstances would be bound by Article X of the League Covenant. It is impossible to say whether any of the reservations would have destroyed the integrity of the League, but Wilson certainly thought so. The ailing leader ordered his Senate followers to spurn all changes. The vote came on November 19. First the Wilsonian Democrats and the irreconcilables defeated the treaty with the Lodge reservations by a vote of 55–39. Next the reservationists and the irreconcilables defeated the treaty without the reservations by a 53–38 vote.

Many Americans who wanted the nation to join the League were appalled. Former president Taft denounced both Lodge and Wilson for having put ''their personal prestige and the saving of their ugly faces above the welfare of the country and the world.'' Lodge remained unmoved. Meanwhile neither Colonel House nor Sir Edward Grey, whom the British had dispatched to the United States, could convince Wilson to change his mind. Individual Democratic senators also fruitlessly urged compromise. On March 19, 1920 the Senate took one final vote. This time the treaty, with the reservations, lost by a margin of 49–35, seven short of ratification.

Historians continue to argue over whose fault it was that the United States failed to ratify the Treaty of Versailles and thereby join the League. Certainly the irreconcilables must share in the blame. For some, Senator Lodge has been the chief villain. Finally, there are those who point the accusing finger at President Wilson for having refused compromise even before his health broke. As the diplomatic historian Thomas A. Bailey noted, Wilson stood guilty of the "supreme infanticide": he had killed his own child. In the last analysis the primary responsibility for the fiasco belonged to the president.

The 1920 Election: The "Solemn Referendum"   Wilson refused to accept defeat. He termed the 1920 election a "solemn referendum" on the issue of the League and called upon the electorate to uphold him. Although ill, he himself desired renomination for a third term in office. The party denied him his wish, nominating instead the liberal governor of Ohio, James M. Cox. For vice-president they chose the affable assistant secretary of the navy, Franklin D. Roosevelt. Cox supported the Wilsonian League without the reservations, though the party platform seemed to accept the League with the proposed changes.

Several strong candidates vied for the Republican presidential nomination. Theodore Roosevelt would have been the candidate in all likelihood, but he had died of an embolism in the early morning hours of January 6, 1919. General Leonard Wood was a leading contender, as was Governor Frank O. Lowden of Illinois. The progressive Senator Hiram Johnson drew some support, particularly from fellow irreconcilables. Other Republicans spoke of nominating Herbert Hoover. Ultimately a clique of party politicos chose Senator Warren Gamaliel Harding of Ohio, whose one term in the Senate had been distinguished by little more than party regularity and a handsome face that falsely implied statesmanship. For vice-president the party nominated Massachusetts Governor Calvin Coolidge, who recently had come into national prominence thanks to his handling of the Boston police strike (see Chapter 6). Republicans, sharply divided between irreconcilables and reservationists of one intensity or another, straddled the issue of the League, hoping that the voters would mistake vagueness for wisdom. Harding, a strong reservationist during the treaty fight, proved as skillful a straddler as his party brethren.

The 1920 election brought Harding a stunning victory, one of the most lopsided in national history. The Ohio senator outpolled the Ohio governor in the popular vote 16,152,000 to 9,147,000, and in the electoral column by 404 votes to 127 votes. Debs became the first candidate to run for president while serving a prison term. From his cell in Atlanta Penitentiary the Socialist candidate learned that he had received 919,799 votes.

The election results had not provided any "solemn referendum" on the League. Rather, they reflected the Republican position as the normal majority party and, perhaps more, the deep resentment nourished by many against Wilson. Angry Irish-Americans and Italian-Americans, usually Democratic, switched allegiance in large numbers because of Wilson's stance on Ireland and Italy during the Paris conference. Midwestern farmers also deserted the Democrats because of the ceilings Wilson had earlier imposed on wheat prices. Black voters, disfranchised in the South but able to vote as they came northward, spurned Wilson and his segregationist policies in favor of the party of Lincoln. Finally, many voters simply may have disassociated themselves from Wilson and the Democrats, who had come to symbolize war and sacrifice. What they wanted was what Harding promised: a "return to normalcy."

Congress passed a joint resolution officially ending the war against Germany on August 25, 1921. The Great Crusade, as American participation in World War I has been called, was over. The United States and the Allies had triumphed militarily, but as the title of a famous 1924 antiwar drama by Maxwell Anderson and Laurence Stallings would ask: *What Price Glory?* The victors, as well as the vanquished, had suffered enormous casualties—physical, psychological, and moral. Looking at the widespread unrest and political uncertainties that marked the conflict's immediate aftermath, in addition to the shattering of idealism that had taken place at the Paris peace conference, few believed that the world had been made safe for democracy. This postwar disillusionment affected numerous Americans and made possible the intense isolationist sentiment that was to pervade the 1930s.

The Great Crusade also occasioned both the culmination of progressivism and its demise. On the one hand, such major progressive concerns as women's suffrage and prohibition became law during and partly because of the war. Involvement also led to the further growth of government power and intervention in the traditionally private sectors of the economy, a development that reformers had long been urging. But the conflict also resulted in the strong if temporary curtailment of civil liberties. In the longer run, it seriously depleted enthusiasm and energies for continued ameliorative ventures. As the 1920s began, many Americans were saying good-by to progressive reform at home and idealistic crusades abroad. They were about to embark upon what F. Scott Fitzgerald would call "the greatest, gaudiest spree in history."

BIOGRAPHICAL SKETCH

JOHN JOSEPH PERSHING · *1860–1948*

Pershing was born in Laclede, Missouri, where as a child he witnessed Confederate raids during the Civil War. He also saw the Panic of 1873 destroy his father's precarious position as a businessman, thus ending his mother's hopes for his formal education. Pershing, the eldest of six children, spent the next decade teaching in rural schools and performing odd jobs.

Pershing's fortunes improved in 1882 when he received an appointment to West Point. He was stationed in the West following his graduation in 1886. There he engaged in skirmishes with various Indian tribes but also received a law degree from the University of Nebraska in 1893. In 1897 he returned to West Point as an instructor. At this time he received the nickname "Black Jack" both because he had commanded a cavalry of black troops in Montana and because of his tough disciplinarian methods. (Pershing always believed in the fighting abilities of black soldiers.)

The Spanish-American War brought Pershing the Silver Star and promotion to the rank of major because of his valor at San Juan Hill and later in the capture of Santiago. The army soon sent him to the Philippines, where between 1899 and 1903 he helped to subdue the ferocious Moro warriors and performed ably as an administrator. President Theodore

Roosevelt next dispatched him to observe the fighting during the Russo-Japanese War. So impressive were Pershing's reports that the president passed over 800 other candidates to promote him to the rank of brigadier general in 1906. Between March 1916 and February 1917 Pershing attracted much national attention for his pursuit of Pancho Villa deep into Mexico.

The culmination of Pershing's distinguished military career came as commander of the American Expeditionary Force during World War I. He persistently irritated Allied generals by his unwillingness to merge his troops with theirs. Several called for his dismissal, but his popularity with President Wilson and Secretary of War Baker saved him. Pershing, in turn, deplored the trench warfare of the Allied strategists and itched for American soldiers to take the offensive. He got his wish with the spectacular offensive in the Meuse-Argonne sector from September 26 to November 11, 1918. American casualties were high, but the fighting, most of which was done by the British, forced Germany to seek an armistice. For his exploits the AEF commander received the title of "General of the Armies," the highest rank accorded any military figure since George Washington.

Age forced Pershing to retire from active service in 1924 after having served as chief of staff from 1921. He later won the Pulitzer Prize in history for his two-volume *My Experiences in the World War* (1931) and was involved in causes to memorialize the American contributions to the war. Historians generally have judged him an admirable leader and tactician, as well as a wise advocate of up-to-date education and training for the military.

SUGGESTED READINGS

The literature on America's road from neutrality to World War I is voluminous. Excellent studies include: Ross Gregory, *The Origins of American Intervention in the First World War* (1971); John Milton Cooper, Jr., *The Vanity of Power: American Isolation and the First World War* (1969); Ernest R. May, *The World War and American Isolation, 1914–1917* (1959); and Daniel M. Smith, *The Great Departure: The United States and World War I, 1914–1920.* One should also consult works on Wilson. In addition to those cited in previous chapters, see Arthur S. Link, *Wilson the Diplomatist* (1957) and *Woodrow Wilson: Revolution, War, and Peace* (1979), as well as Edward H. Buehring, ed., *Wilson's Foreign Policy in Perspective* (1957), and Patrick Devlin, *Too Proud to Fight: Woodrow Wilson's Neutrality* (1975). Two strongly anti-Wilson studies are Walter Millis, *The Road to War* (1935), and Charles C. Tansill, *America Goes to War* (1938).

The American military involvement in the war is examined in Harvey A. De Weerd, *President Wilson Fights His War* (1968), and Edward M. Coffman, *The War to End All Wars* (1969). The black military experience receives sympathetic treatment in A. E. Barbeau and Florette Henri, *The Unknown Soldiers: Black American Troops in World War I* (1974). The prewar preparedness movement is the theme of J. Garry Clifford, *The Citizen Soldiers: The Plattsburg Training Camp Movement, 1913–1920* (1972), while pacifism during the war is covered in Charles De Benedetti, *Origins of the Modern American Peace Movement, 1915–1929* (1978). For good biographies of the nation's military leaders, see Elting E. Morison, *Admiral Sims and the Modern American Navy* (1942), Frank E. Vandiver, *Black Jack: The Life and Times of John J. Pershing,* 2 vols. (1977), and Donald Smythe, *Pershing* (1986).

The best treatment of the home front during the war can be found in David M. Kennedy, *Over Here: The First World War and American Society* (1980). But see also Robert H. Ferrell, *Woodrow Wilson and World War I: 1917–1921* (1985). Much older but still useful works are Preston Slosson, *The Great Crusade and After, 1914–1928* (1930), and Frederic L. Paxson, *Amer-*

ican Democracy and the World War, 3 vols. (1936–1948). A more specific work is Robert D. Cuff, *The War Industries Board: Business-Government Relations During World War I* (1973). Jordan Schwarz, *The Speculator: Bernard M. Baruch in Washington, 1917–1965* (1981), details the colorful life of the WIB's director. David Burner's *Herbert Hoover* (1978) contains a helpful account of the wartime activities of the head of the Food Administration. Other relevant works depicting the effort to mobilize the economy for war include Charles Gilbert, *American Financing of World War I* (1970), and Daniel Beaver, *Newton D. Baker and the American War Effort, 1917–1919* (1966). Seward D. Livermore, *Politics Is Adjourned: Woodrow Wilson and the War Congress* (1966), adroitly details wartime politics at the national level. Labor and the war provide the topic for Frank L. Grubbs, Jr., *The Struggle for Labor Loyalty* (1968). The role of women during the war receives careful attention from Maurine W. Greenwald, *Women, War, and Work* (1980). Two works that examine the hostility encountered by blacks as they migrated northward are Eliot M. Rudwick, *Race Riot at East St. Louis, July 2, 1917* (1964), and William M. Tuttle, *Race Riot: Chicago in the Red Summer of 1919* (1970).

George Creel, *How We Advertised America* (1920), recounts the battle to shape public opinion. A later, more scholarly work is Stephen Vaughn, *Holding Fast the Inner Lines: Democracy, Nationalism, and the Committee on Public Information* (1980). Those interested in the wartime assault on civil liberties can turn to H. C. Peterson and Gilbert C. Fite, *Opponents of War, 1917–1918* (1957); Zechariah Chafee, *Free Speech in the United States* (1941); and Paul L. Murphy, *World War I and the Origins of Civil Liberties in the United States* (1979). For the effect of the war on German-Americans, see Frederick Luebke, *Bonds of Loyalty* (1974).

Numerous works on postwar diplomacy and peacemaking exist. Two very readable and incisive works are Thomas A. Bailey, *Woodrow Wilson and the Lost Peace* (1944), and *Woodrow Wilson and the Great Betrayal* (1945). N. Gordon Levin, Jr., *Woodrow Wilson and World Politics* (1968), is both thoughtful and provocative. Other useful works include: Inga Floto, *Colonel House in Paris* (1980); Herbert Hoover, *The Ordeal of Woodrow Wilson* (1958); Warren F. Kuehl, *Seeking World Order: The United States and International Organization to 1920* (1969); and Lawrence E. Gelfand, *The Inquiry: American Preparations for Peace* (1963). For Wilson's views on Bolshevism and the American intervention in Russia, see: Arno Mayer, *Wilson vs. Lenin* (1959) and *Politics and Diplomacy of Peacemaking* (1967); George F. Kennan, *The Decision to Intervene* (1958); John L. Gaddis, *Russia, the Soviet Union, and the United States* (1978); John Thompson, *Russia, Bolshevism, and the Versailles Peace* (1966); and Betty M. Unterberger, *America's Siberian Expedition* (1956). The fullest accounts of the battle for ratification of the Treaty of Versailles can be found in Denna F. Fleming, *The United States and the League of Nations* (1932), and Ralph Stone, *The Irreconcilables: The Fight Against the League of Nations* (1970). The previously cited John A. Garraty, *Henry Cabot Lodge* (1953), and W. C. Widenor, *Henry Cabot Lodge and the Search for an American Foreign Policy* (1980), are generally sympathetic to the role played by the Massachusetts senator in the ratification drama.

6

Life in the New Era

Probably no decade has captured the popular imagination as much as the 1920s. ''Jazz Age,'' ''Roaring Twenties,'' and ''Lost Generation'' are colorful labels that convey the sense of drama and excitement associated with the years between the Treaty of Versailles and the stock market crash of 1929. It was the time of illegal liquor and bootlegging gangsters, flapper girls and their naughty ways, hot jazz and haunting rhythms, fads and manias, experimental writing and disillusioned writers. As the writer Floyd Dell noted: ''Life . . . consisted so largely of spilt milk that there is no use crying over it—we might just as well celebrate the magnificent inevitability of the spilling.''

But the 1920s represented more than Dell's bittersweet lament or F. Scott Fitzgerald's assertion that it was the ''greatest, gaudiest spree in history.'' Great uncertainty also marked these years. Americans turned from the politics of progressivism and involvement in World War I to face the challenges and opportunities of the New Era, as many termed the decade. Transitions that already were evident before the war, as well as those generated by the war, were causing them to reassess established values and attitudes. Some welcomed these changes; others fought them. All formed part of a generation caught between the continuity and discontinuity of history.

THE NEW PROSPERITY

Strong prosperity characterized the New Era, although the aftermath of World War I occasioned some severe dislocations and hardships. The end of the fighting brought a termination of wartime contracts for business, as well as the cessation of most government involvement in the major sectors of the economy. Unemployment, exacerbated by the return of servicemen, soared in 1919, but consumer spending and new European demands

119

for American goods soon refueled economic activity. Steep inflation ensued, only to be followed by a sharp recession that lasted from late 1920 until 1922. From that point until 1929, however, the nation experienced a generally uninterrupted period of growth and prosperity.

The rise in the GNP from $54.2 billion in 1919 to $103.4 billion in 1929 underscored the leap in economic growth. Per capita income and real wages increased significantly, while the average number of work hours declined. Industrial production nearly doubled. Not everyone, however, shared equally in this growth and its subsequent benefits. The income of workers did rise 11 percent between 1923 and 1929, but at the same time corporate profits and dividends climbed 62 and 65 percent, respectively. Other groups—notably farmers—also failed to enjoy the fruits of prosperity. Still, many believed that good times would only get better. Some predicated their faith on the astounding growth enjoyed by several industries.

The Automobile Revolution   The phenomenal growth of the automobile industry provided the keystone for the prosperity of the 1920s. Automobile production reached 4.8 million units in 1929, compared with only 4,000 in 1900. Meanwhile the number of registered cars during the decade nearly trebled from 8.2 million to 23.1 million. By 1929 one American in five owned a car, as compared with one in every 7,000 Russians. Henry Ford had perfected the principles of assembly-line production and interchangeable parts—as early as 1914 it took only 93 minutes to produce a car—and, as previously noted, he had made his Model T affordable to the working class as well as to the more affluent. Americans were so in awe of the entrepreneur's genius that half a million of them made down payments on his more stylish new Model A car without having seen it. Yet Ford's preeminence in the field was no longer unquestioned: General Motors and Chrysler were producing highly competitive models.

Booming automobile sales accounted for numerous jobs. During the 1920s more than 300,000 Americans found direct employment in this industry. Other jobs were closely tied to the industry. Automobiles utilized tires, glass, and gasoline; they also required servicing. Moreover, an estimated 15 percent of the nation's steel production went into automobile production during the decade. In all, probably several million workers owed their positions to the internal combustion machine.

The automobile also transformed American society. Greater mobility was one such change. Many people, especially from the middle class, departed from increasingly crowded cities to the suburbs, hoping that a switch in residence would provide a new life style combining the best urban and rural features. The automobile continued to shape leisure-time activities. It widened the dimensions of travel for many, but critics complained that cars were destroying the close-knit family and were lending themselves to sexual activities. They also pointed to the alarming growth in highway accidents and fatalities. Like many innovations, the automobile offered mixed blessings.

Henry Ford mirrored the ambiguity of his product. Born on a Michigan farm in 1863, he detested farming but loved tinkering with machinery. Later he would declare that ''machinery is the new Messiah.'' By the 1920s he came to symbolize the awesome world of technology. Yet for all his futuristic and mechanistic orientation, Ford retained many of the values associated with rural and small-town America. His fears and prejudices were deep-seated. He hated Jews, Catholics, and Wall Street bankers. There was

Fashionable flapper girl standing beside her roadster.

also the irony of his Greenfield Village, a costly reproduction of a nineteenth-century community that celebrated individual craftsmanship. Janus-faced, Ford spoke for countless Americans who clung to a vanishing past as, literally and figuratively, they drove full-speed into the future.

Newer Growth Industries The growth of other new industries likewise promoted affluence in the 1920s. For example, the decade witnessed a threefold increase in the production of electrical power. In 1900 electricity ran the machinery in only 5 percent of the nation's factories. By 1929 the figure had risen to 70 percent. Much of this electrical power was flowing to homes, as Americans devoured the latest in such modern appliances as refrigerators, vacuum cleaners, and washing machines. And the electricity was being generated by larger and larger companies. During this period more than 3,000 electrical power companies disappeared. By decade's end the 10 largest utility companies controlled more than 70 percent of the nation's electrical power.

The chemical industry also spurted during the 1920s. During the war Americans had been unable to import chemicals from Germany, then the world's leader in the industry. American firms thus developed their own products, greatly aided by the government, which turned over confiscated German patents. By the 1920s American firms were pioneering in such new products as plastics and razors.

Less profitable but much more exciting was the airplane. The dream of air travel had filled the minds of adventurers and entrepreneurs alike ever since the celebrated flight of the Wright Brothers at Kitty Hawk, North Carolina, in 1903. The military had found a use for airplanes during the war. Afterwards limited passenger and airmail service took effect, while barnstormers did their amazing solo stunts.

But no daredevil or service did more to boost the fortunes of the airline industry than Charles A. Lindbergh, the son of a former Minnesota congressman. On May 21, 1927 Lindbergh landed his small monoplane, *The Spirit of St. Louis,* outside Paris after a transatlantic flight of 33 hours from New York. Frenzied crowds mobbed the ''Lone Eagle'' when he swooped out of the sky at Paris's Le Bourget field, as well as when he returned to the United States. Several others had earlier crossed the Atlantic in an airplane or dirigible, but it was ''Lucky Lindy'' who became one of the decade's chief heroes. A partial explanation rests with the values he stood for, which like those of Henry Ford looked both forward and backward. On the one hand, his solo flight represented a self-sufficient individualism conquering the newest frontier. On the other hand, Lindbergh's achievement dramatized yet another overwhelming technological triumph and pointed to man's increased dependence on machines. Whatever the explanation for its popularity, his solo flight kindled the growth of the aviation industry. By 1930 more than 100 commercial airlines were flying mail and passengers to more than 300 American cities.

Consumerism Consumerism came of age during the 1920s. Before then problems of production dominated the economy. Now much of the emphasis shifted to convincing Americans to buy products, including those for which they may have had no clear need. The advertising industry greatly accelerated this change. Well-known prewar firms like J. Walter Thompson, along with newer ones like Batten, Barton, Durstine & Osborn (BBD&O) vigorously promoted their clients' wares. By the end of the 1920s advertising had become a major industry, having expended nearly $1.8 billion during the decade.

If Americans needed to be convinced to buy—and many did not—other publicists helped whet their appetites. Bruce Barton, for example, a partner in BBD&O, wrote *The Man Nobody Knows* (1925). This best seller depicted Jesus as ''the founder of modern business'' and an incomparable salesman who forged his disciples into a group ''that conquered the world.'' Some thought the comparisons sacrilegious. Others accepted it as part of what another best seller called ''Our Business Civilization.''

CULTURAL CONFLICTS IN THE NEW ERA

Few Americans objected to the material prosperity of the New Era. Many, however, vehemently opposed other changes that threatened traditional values and norms. These changes frequently underscored urban and rural animosities at a time when urban life was becoming dominant. (The census of 1920 revealed that for the first time urban inhabitants, who numbered 51.2 percent of the nation's population, were in the majority.) However useful, overemphasis upon the city/country conflict can be misleading. Recent urbanites brought their rural values with them; some rural dwellers held views usually associated with city dwellers. What remains clear is that the cultural conflicts of the 1920s provoked intense bitterness and a new wave of intolerance.

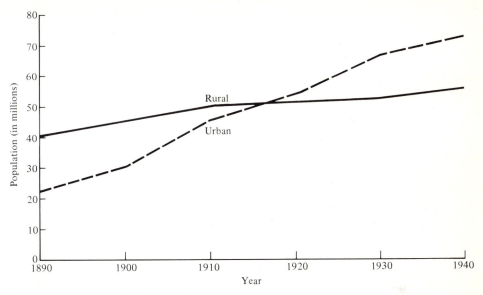

Rural and urban population: 1890–1940.

Radicalism and the Red Scare One bitter conflict focused on labor. Workers, no longer constrained by wartime controls, pressed their demands during the immediate postwar boom. Most of their more than 3,600 strikes in 1919 were local and short-lived. Others, however, gained national attention and filled many Americans with fears of radical upheaval. On May Day, for example, a general strike paralyzed Seattle, forcing Mayor Ole Hanson to request federal troops to restore order and services. A crisis also struck Boston, whose policemen were notoriously underpaid and subject to poor working conditions. (A starting policeman, for example, received an average wage of only $21 per week and had to purchase his uniform and equipment, which cost more than $200.) Thwarted in their demands to unionize, more than three-quarters of the police force walked off their jobs in early September. During the next two days 8 persons died and more than 50 were injured, while looting and destruction cost more than $300,000. Governor Calvin Coolidge sent in the national guard and proclaimed tersely that "there is no right to strike against the public safety by anybody, anywhere, anytime." Not one striking policeman ever regained his job. That same month some 350,000 steelworkers struck in several midwestern cities after failing to obtain an 8-hour day (most worked 12 hours) and the right to bargain collectively. Elbert H. Gary, president of U.S. Steel, led the industry's fight to break the strike, which collapsed by January 1920, but not before 18 strikers were slain in Gary, Indiana.

Antilabor businessmen and others equated strikes and sporadic violence with wild-eyed radicalism. Workers' demands, they claimed, were aimed at undermining the economic and social structure. Many blamed the AFL for supporting an abortive postwar attempt to nationalize the railroads. Ironically, the AFL was itself antiradical.

But radicalism was not an idle threat. Radicals were determined to spread the Bolshevik revolution. Unsuccessful uprisings took place in Germany and eastern Europe immediately after the war, and a leading Russian Bolshevik boasted that the money for the German uprising "was as nothing compared to the funds transmitted to New York for the purpose of spreading bolshevism in the United States." American radicals organized both a Communist and Communist Labor party in 1919. More ominous, some radicals turned to direct violence. More than three dozen bombs addressed to such public figures as John D. Rockefeller and Justice Oliver Wendell Holmes, Jr. were discovered in post offices. A bomb was also found in Mayor Ole Hanson's mail, while another blew the hands off a Georgia senator's servant. Even Attorney General A. Mitchell Palmer was not safe: a bomb exploded on his front porch in June. Then in September a blast on Wall Street killed 38 persons and injured hundreds.

Reaction to the Red Scare was swift. Numerous states passed antiradical measures and jailed suspects. There were race riots, attacks on individual radicals, suppressions of radical literature, and expulsions of socialist legislators from several state houses. Attorney General Palmer, prodded by fearful citizens and officials, as well as by his own frightening experience, also moved to suppress radicalism. In August he appointed young J. Edgar Hoover as head of the Intelligence Division of the Department of Justice.

Hoover soon reported that the country was full of dangerous revolutionaries. Between November 1919 and early 1920 federal agents arrested 6,000 real or alleged radicals in cities throughout the country. The government eventually deported 556 persons. Among these were 249 aliens (including Emma Goldman), who were sent to the Soviet Union aboard the so-called Soviet Ark (the *Buford*). The itch to become president struck Palmer, who now had a vested interest in maintaining public fear. His reputation and presidential aspirations sank, however, once the huge radical uprising he had predicted for May Day failed to materialize.

May also witnessed one of the most celebrated episodes of the Red Scare. Two Italian immigrants, Nicola Sacco and Bartolomeo Vanzetti, were arrested and charged

Nicola Sacco and Bartolomeo Vanzetti

CULTURAL CONFLICTS IN THE NEW ERA

with the murders of a paymaster and guard in South Braintree, Massachusetts. Both were convicted and sentenced to death after a trial marked by gross prejudice. (Presiding Judge Webster Thayer, for example, referred to the defendants as ''anarchistic bastards'' and ''damned dagos.'') The verdict pleased some, such as evangelist Billy Sunday, who stormed: ''Give 'em the juice. Burn them if they're guilty. That's the way to handle it. I'm tired of hearing these foreigners, these radicals, coming over here and telling us what we should do.'' Many strongly believed that the verdict represented a condemnation of the political views and ethnicity of the defendants rather than a finding of their guilt. For six years supporters unsuccessfully fought to win a new trial for the pair. Their cause won worldwide sympathy, as civil libertarians denounced trial procedures and the state's unwillingness to reopen the case. Finally, on August 23, 1927, Sacco and Vanzetti, the shoemaker and fish peddler, died in the electric chair. More recent evidence has linked Sacco to the murders. Nothing, however, has diminished the general belief that the trial was unfair and that they were found guilty for their background and views.

The Sacco and Vanzetti episode notwithstanding, the Red Scare ebbed rapidly after Attorney General Palmer's May Day prediction of 1920 proved groundless. Nonetheless, it had the effect of virtually destroying the radical movement in the United States and of seriously weakening organized labor for the remainder of the decade. It also showed the difficulty many had in distinguishing between those who wanted peaceful change and those who desired revolution. The same difficulty would resurface during the Cold War.

Nativism   World War I all but ended the influx of immigrants to the United States, but the flood resumed immediately afterward. In 1919, 110,000 immigrants arrived; in 1921 the figure shot up to 805,000, of whom two-thirds were from southern and eastern Europe. The earlier nativist hostility to these new arrivals continued. Books like Madison Grant's *The Passing of the Great Race* (1916) and Lothrop Stoddard's *The Rising Tide of Color Against White World Supremacy* (1920) fanned the flames of prejudice, convincing many Americans of older stock that they were about to be overwhelmed by inferior immigrants from southern or eastern European stock, along with blacks, Orientals, and other undesirables.

Jews and Italians particularly suffered the stigma of stereotyping. Radicalism existed among immigrant Jews, but the Red Scare exaggerated its extent and stimulated anti-Semitism. During this period the fraudulent *Protocols of the Elders of Zion*, which depicted a conspiracy to establish Jewish dominance throughout the world, circulated. Henry Ford published the *Protocols* in his *Dearborn Independent* newspaper, and many gullible readers accepted it as fact. Meanwhile both Italians and Jews became synonymous with organized crime for simple-minded and bigoted people, for whom Al Capone represented all Italians and Arnold Rothstein all Jews.

With strong public backing Congress took steps to limit the influx of these undesired immigrants. A law of 1921 limited immigration from each country to three percent of its nationals living in the United States in 1910. The National Origins Act of 1924 went further. Reducing the percentage from three to two, it based the new quota on the 1890 census, which reflected far fewer immigrants from southern and eastern Europe. The act also excluded Orientals. In 1929 Congress legislated an even more draconian measure that set the yearly immigration quota at 150,000, with the proportion of entering nationals based on the 1920 census. Italy, for example, could send 6,000 immigrants under this

ORAL HISTORY
Growing Up in the Twentieth Century

JOSEPH GALANTE · *born 1910*

I was born in Sicily. My father had been in the army in Italy—he was a career man—and he saw what was coming in 1914. He thought, "If war breaks out, I'm going to get hooked here, and we'll never get over to the United States." We were two children, my brother and myself, my mother and father. We already had family in Chestnut Hill and that's why we came here. My father first got a job around 1916 on the Houston estate. [Henry Howard Houston was an immensely wealthy entrepreneur and director of the Pennsylvania Railroad.] He was in charge of their chickens and worked there until he died in 1938.

We were the first Italian family on Springfield Avenue, and we had to buy that property through "straw" people. You talk about prejudice! Today these minority people, so called—they have no idea what went on in those days. The neighbors were real cool at first and we minded our own business. But we maintained our property to such a level that it made you proud to be around there. We had beautiful flowers and lawns and gardens, and people began to say, "Hey, they keep their place well." We helped out neighbors any way we could and we got to have a lovely relationship for years and years.

We had an enormous kitchen at home; we could sit twelve around the table in there. The kitchen was a kind of family room in those days. The parlor, as we called it, was never used. The dining room was only used on special occasions. Even our holiday meals were in the kitchen. My father sat at the head of the table and he and my mother did most of the talking at meal time. We also had two men that lived with us. I had to get up and make their coffee in the morning so they could leave the house by 6:30 and be at their jobs at 7:00. We children all had plenty of chores.

I had many jobs as a youngster. I started helping the milkman at four o'clock in the morning—until seven. I also did part-time work with the baker—delivering bread. Around the Christmas holiday I used to help the mailman. Then, in the wintertime, snow was a great thing and it made me very proud to go out and shovel some of these walks and make myself $8.00 or $10.00 when my father was getting only $4.00 a day. I used to take it home and give it to my mother. I kept maybe a quarter for myself.

CULTURAL CONFLICTS IN THE NEW ERA

My father was quite strict about dating. He was especially strict with the girls. He was strict with us boys, too, but we had a little more freedom than the girls. My father had Italian friends who had children and this was the way we were supposed to meet young girls or young fellows. And then, of course, they tried the matchmakers, but it didn't work. I married a woman who was mostly German and my parents were real angry. But after our first child was born, that mellowed everything.

Then I went to work for the Houstons in March of 1930. Mr. Kraut, the superintendent, liked me and he took me under his wing and made me his assistant. The Houston family also took quite a liking to me. My father had been there now for about 20 years. When he died I had to assume all his responsibilities. I had to run the incubators, run the chickens, plus my own landscaping work, plus a lot of other activities I had to do around there as Mr. Kraut's right-hand man. That

place back there—the Houston's place—was like a little town. We had our own rubbish collection; we had cows; we had greenhouses; we had formal gardens in the summertime; and we had truck gardens. Then there was the farm over in Roxborough which belonged to Mr. Houston.

I got along well with the Houston children and grandchildren. In fact, they used to always ask if I would go up their place in Maine in the summertime. "When are you going to come up and spend your vacation with us," they'd ask? But I knew you didn't intermingle like that. No, no, you kept apart. So I kept a very good relationship with them. I stayed with the Houstons about 11 years— till '41.

That's when I started a business on my own—a grocery store. I was very, very insistent that we carry nothing but the best, and wait on the customers and give them service. That's been our formula and it has stood us in good stead.

law, although hundreds of thousands wished to enter. These various laws brought an end to an historical epoch. The United States would no longer serve as a haven for all who wished to enter.

The Ku Klux Klan and Black Nationalism While restrictionists attempted to protect America from further contamination by hordes of unwanted newcomers, others battled immigrants who were already here and whose values or life styles frequently stood in contrast to those of old-stock Americans. Many of the latter joined the Ku Klux Klan, the most feared and most intolerant nativist group of the 1920s.

The modern Klan was organized in 1915 by William J. Simmons, a one-time Methodist minister, on Stone Mountain, outside Atlanta, Georgia. All "native born, white, gentile Americans" were eligible for membership, but few took advantage. The Klan had only 5,000 members by 1920. Postwar hysteria gave an impetus to the organization, as did entrepreneurial changes that brought higher dues and modern techniques of salesmanship to stimulate growth. Membership increased to slightly more than 100,000 by the time Hiram W. Evans, a Texas dentist, replaced Simmons as Grand Wizard in 1922.

The Klan drew up a hate list of those who supposedly threatened traditional Americanism. Like its Reconstruction predecessor, it was strongly antiblack. The Klan resented the attitudes of returning black servicemen who refused to accept second-class citizenship,

Klan members march along Pennsylvania Avenue in Washington, D.C., in 1928.

as well as the strident black nationalism of Marcus Garvey. But the Klan also shared the fears and prejudices of contemporary Americans against Catholics, Jews, foreigners, "wets" (those who opposed prohibition), and large-city dwellers. Its white gowns and hoods were more than ritualistic emblems: they stood for a purity of life now threatened by alien elements. To preserve that purity the Klan resorted to threats, cross-burnings, beatings, kidnappings, mutilations, and murders.

The Klan attained the height of its power in the mid-1920s when membership reached 4.5 million. The organization's greatest strength lay not in the South but in the Midwest, Southwest, and Far West, where it was partly a response to poor local government. It enjoyed its greatest success in Indiana, whose politics it dominated until Klan leader David Stephenson created a major scandal. He kidnapped and raped a young woman, who later died after attempting suicide. Stephenson was found guilty of second-degree murder. Subsequent state investigations found Klan politicians guilty of wide-

CULTURAL CONFLICTS IN THE NEW ERA

spread graft and malfeasance. The resulting stigma of immorality and corruption, along with concentrated attacks by anti-Klan groups, led to the decline of the Klan as the decade ended. Nonetheless, it still was able to thwart the Democratic candidacy of Alfred E. Smith in 1928 (see Chapter 7).

Some blacks agreed with the Klan that racial segregation was desirable. Foremost among them was Jamaican-born Marcus Garvey, who came to the United States in 1917. The charismatic Garvey, believing that whites would never accept blacks as equals and, pointing to postwar violence as evidence, called on blacks to develop racial pride and a sense of separateness. He organized a Universal Negro Improvement Association (UNIA) for this purpose, with the ultimate aim of establishing an independent black nation in Africa. Hundreds of thousands joined the UNIA (Garvey put membership at several million). Huge rallies took place in Harlem, where Garvey, wearing fancy paramilitary outfits, captured the enthusiasm of the masses of poor blacks. Middle-class black integrationists like W. E. B. DuBois scorned Garvey as a demagogue, denounced his separatist message, and continued to encourage blacks to fight for their rights in the United States.

It was the government, however, that brought about Garvey's downfall. In 1922 it brought suit against him for mail fraud, claiming that he had sold worthless shares in his Black Star Line that transported blacks to Africa. UNIA declined as Garvey had to devote his energies and resources to fighting the case. He was finally convicted in 1927 and deported to Jamaica. Despite his failure, Garvey had done much to make many blacks aware of their past heritage and present plight. He had demonstrated that the black urban masses could be galvanized and organized, and given a message that had some relevance to their condition. Along with the Klan, he had also seriously questioned the desirability and viability of a biracial society.

Fundamentalism The clash between modern science and religion provided still another focus for the cultural conflicts of the 1920s. More specifically, the struggle centered around Darwinism versus Biblical beliefs. Charles Darwin's *Origin of Species* (1859) had upset traditional believers in various ways. In it Darwin rejected the Genesis account of creation, positing a gradual evolution of species after a period of several million years. Nonetheless, many modern Christians had reconciled the differences by accepting the Bible as divinely inspired but not literally true. Many others, however, rejected any compromise with Darwinism. These fundamentalists clung to a simple, comforting view that the truths of the Bible were all one needed to know.

Fundamentalists were numerous during the 1920s. As the celebrated journalist H. L. Mencken noted, you could ''heave an egg out of a Pullman and you will hit a Fundamentalist almost everywhere in the United States.'' Fundamentalism prevailed mainly in small towns and rural areas, thus underscoring the clash between urban and rural America. But cities also provided bastions for antimodernists, as evidenced by the Moody Bible Institute of Chicago and a host of fundamentalist urban ministries. Further, one must remember that many urban inhabitants had but recently arrived from the hinterlands and had brought their traditional beliefs with them. Nonetheless, it was the small town of Dayton, Tennessee, that played host to the great controversy between science and religion.

In the early 1920s William Jennings Bryan and other fundamentalists had fueled this controversy by crusading for laws that would prohibit the teaching of Darwinism in public schools. Several states, particularly in the South, subsequently enacted such legislation. In 1925 John Thomas Scopes, a high school teacher in Dayton, agreed to test the validity of his state's antievolution statute. Arrested and put on trial, Scopes was defended by lawyers of the recently formed American Civil Liberties Union and also by Clarence Darrow, the nation's foremost trial lawyer. Bryan, whom Mencken sneeringly called ''the Fundamentalist Pope,'' joined the prosecution.

The Monkey Trial, as it was dubbed, received national attention, thanks to both its famous participants and the nature of the case. Bryan himself unwisely agreed to take the stand. Though he cleverly jested about being more interested in the Rock of Ages than in the age of rocks, Darrow's clever questioning and Mencken's prejudiced reports to his readers made Bryan seem foolish to the more sophisticated public. Ultimately, and not surprisingly, Scopes was convicted and fined $100, although a higher court later dismissed the case. Bryan failed to survive the ordeal of the heat and emotional pressure of the mid-summer trial and died five days after the verdict. Bryan's death deprived the antievolution forces of their greatest leader. But the controversy did not end. Several other states passed antievolution laws before the decade ended.

Fundamentalism continued to hold the allegiance of millions of Americans, thanks in part to the work of extraordinary revivalists. Billy Sunday, whom Americans in a poll of 1914 ranked as the eighth greatest of their living countrymen, remained the premier revivalist until the 1920s. Afterwards the Canadian-born Aimee Semple McPherson eclipsed him in popularity. The flamboyant McPherson, dressed in flowing robes, preached her Four Square Gospel of God, home, school, and government from her huge temple outside Los Angeles. She combined Hollywood showmanship, New York advertising, and old-fashioned religion to become the nation's most famous revivalist by the end of the decade. Being described as the ''world's most pulchritudinous evangelist'' did not hurt her cause, nor apparently did her three marriages, two divorces, reputed kidnapping, and financial misadventures.

Prohibition Another cultural conflict of the 1920s revolved around prohibition, which probably divided Americans more sharply during that decade than any other issue. Prohibition especially exacerbated the urban-rural tensions. ''Wets'' and ''drys'' inhabited all parts of the country, but their respective strongholds were urban and rural America. Rural drys strongly associated their wet opponents with the urban values of the foreign-born, especially those who were Catholics. (Some drys tried to ban the sale of wine for religious rites.) On the other hand, many wets—wine-drinking Italians, beer-drinking Irish and Germans—bitterly resented this intrusion upon their personal liberties.

Prohibition also occasioned a growth in crime. Drinking itself was legal, and many Americans enjoyed homemade brew (although it not infrequently resulted in blindness) or the liquor they had carefully stockpiled before the passage of the Eighteenth Amendment. But many wished to drink outside their home, and selling liquor was illegal. Whatever the law, anyone who wanted a drink did not have to go dry, as ''speakeasies'' proliferated and ''bootleg'' liquor became a major industry. Canada, Mexico, and the Caribbean provided convenient sources for booze-running, which was developed into a high art by proficient gangsters.

CULTURAL CONFLICTS IN THE NEW ERA

The most legendary and powerful of these prohibition gangsters was Al ("Scarface") Capone. He rose from the ranks of small-time hoodlum to become kingpin of Chicago, having corrupted politicians and liquidated rival mobsters. In the notorious St. Valentine's Day Massacre of 1929, Capone's henchmen brutally killed seven members of another gang. Capone, who later went to prison for income tax evasion, was only the most famous of a long line of notorious criminals operating in the nation's cities during these years. Enormous profits from illegal liquor also made it possible for organized crime to expand its activities in the areas of prostitution, loan sharking, gambling, protection, and drugs.

The attempt to enforce prohibition proved a failure. Federal agents never numbered more than a few thousand. Many local agents, moreover, were corrupt or unwilling to enforce the law. The criminals, in contrast, were numerous, dedicated, and efficiently organized. People wavered over whether to continue the "noble experiment," as prohibition was called. In 1931 the Wickersham Commission, established by President Hoover, compounded the confusion when it concluded that crime and corruption were rampant and enforcement a failure, but that prohibition should continue. By this time, however, most Americans were more concerned with the ravages of the Great Depression than with a continued battle for a dubious cause. General disillusionment with prohibition

Al Capone became the most notorious criminal in the United States during the Prohibition Era.

and the argument that governments needed revenue from liquor taxes led enough citizens to reverse their position on the question. The Twenty-First Amendment, repealing prohibition, was adopted in December 1933. Yet for all its weaknesses and unpopularity, prohibition, it should be noted, was effective in reducing alcoholism, deaths from alcohol-related diseases, and traffic fatalities. This resulted largely from having made liquor too expensive for the working classes.

The New Morality Few matters more interested and distressed Americans during the 1920s than did changing life styles and attitudes. Traditionalists predicted ruin as they pointed a finger at the loosening of family ties, the rebellion of youth, preoccupation with sexual matters, drinking, wild new dances, and the novel rights demanded by some women. Others welcomed the liberating mores of the Jazz Age. Actually, the initial breakdown of Victorian manners and morals had preceded World War I. The war experience accelerated the process of change and the 1920s provided the crucible for more distinct transformations. Nonetheless, the new morality was less revolutionary than many feared—or would have liked. How far it extended beyond middle-class whites also remains in doubt.

The celebration of youth formed a basic part of the new morality. Indeed, the 1920s feted youth as had no previous period. More naughty than angry, the young were seeking to establish their own codes of behavior and morality. Their colorful dress, illegal drinking, and dancing to the exuberant Charleston and other upbeat music spoke more to changing tastes than to contempt for the traditions and behavior of their elders. So too did the rage for fraternities and zany antics that characterized college life in a period that saw the number of college students increase from 600,000 in 1918 to twice that figure in 1930. When it came to politics, college students were no more radical than their elders. But people worried about the sexual mores of the young, which were in fact changing. More avant-garde youth rejected the sexual taboos—in speech and, to a degree, in action—that their parents had accepted. Yet their sexual rebellion was expressed primarily through ''necking'' and ''petting,'' not through an upsurge of premarital sex. And unlike the prior generation they drew more of a connection between greater sexual candor and finding a suitable mate for marriage.

In addition to a cult of youth, the 1920s witnessed the emergence of a ''new woman,'' though how new remained debatable. Women did benefit from general economic prosperity. Technology and increased family income made it possible for them to escape some of the worst drudgery of household chores. Many continued the prewar trend of entering the work force. By 1930, 10.8 million women held jobs, a fivefold increase since 1914 and an increase of two million since 1920. Most held lower-rank work positions, but there was an increase of women in the professions; however, lower wages and job discrimination remained widespread.

Politics also brought mixed results for the new woman. A few women, like Belle Moskowitz, an important advisor to New York Governor Alfred E. Smith, and Governor Nellie Ross of Wyoming, did attain political prominence, but women's suffrage had not radically altered the male-dominated power structure. Feminists fought unsuccessfully for an equal rights amendment and for more unified political action by women.

But the new woman did cause traditionalists much consternation by challenging long-accepted patterns of appearance and behavior. Bobbed hair, cosmetics, and short

POPULAR AMUSEMENTS AND THE ARTS

133

skirts or flapper dresses that muted the body's natural curves became the rage. (The flapper dress, in part, was less an act of rebellion than a reflection of the passion for Egyptian styles occasioned by the opening of King Tut's tomb in the early 1920s.) The new woman smoked publicly and went to speakeasies, where she drank illegally and practiced the latest dances that, according to one disapproving minister, brought "the bodies of men and women in unusual relations to each other."

But it was the fear of sexual emancipation that caused most concern. Some extreme feminists, who deemed sex humiliating, shared this fear. Others—both men and women—lamented the real or supposed threat to premarital innocence and marital monogamy. Meanwhile the number of divorces doubled between 1914 and 1929. Birth control measures, while still under heavy attack, had attained a level of acceptability not granted during the previous decade. Family size declined accordingly during the 1920s as the birthrate fell from less than 24 per thousand in 1920 to less than 19 per thousand in 1930. Traditionalists concluded gloomily that the new woman and the new morality were undermining the well-being of society. Others were pleased at the greater freedom and frankness.

The obsession of numerous Americans with psychology, particularly the Freudian variety, provided support for the new morality. Freud had visited the United States briefly in 1909 but without much impact. However, the socialite Mabel Dodge helped to popularize his ideas through stimulating gatherings in her New York Fifth Avenue salon. By 1916 an estimated 500 psychoanalysts were practicing their craft, mainly in New York. Nonetheless, Freud's ideas and influence failed to reach a larger audience until the 1920s. By then, however, Freudianism had become a mania. The public, misunderstanding the complexities of the irrational and the unconscious, grossly simplified what they believed the famed Viennese doctor had said. For many, Freud meant that they should avoid sexual repressions at all costs. The reduction of Freud's ideas to triviality and downright nonsense reached the point where one person accounted for the popularity of the song. "Yes, We Have No Bananas," as being the result of a nation's inferiority complex. A Sears Roebuck catalog meanwhile advertised publications entitled *Sex Problems Solved* and *Ten Thousand Dreams Interpreted*. Freudianism exercised a generally more positive influence on serious literature, but even there oversimplification frequently reduced criticism to a purely sexual focus.

Freud did not lack for challengers. The views of other psychologists, such as Carl Jung and Alfred Adler, also proved attractive to a number of Americans. Probably most influential among these non-Freudians was John B. Watson. His *Behaviorism*, originally published in 1914, helped to persuade many that environment was the critical factor in shaping both individual lives and society. His ideas had a much greater impact than Freud's on child-rearing practices during the 1920s.

POPULAR AMUSEMENTS AND THE ARTS

People remember the 1920s as much for their vital popular amusements and artistic achievements as for their conflicts. Silly manias and crazes marked these years, but so did an appreciation for entertainments that remain an integral part of American life today. Developments in serious culture, especially literature, have left a similarly lasting impression.

The Silver Screen and Radio   Movies in the 1920s continued to enjoy great popularity. Comedies and adventures remained favorites, but films with sexual episodes represented a distinct break with previous works. Innocent-looking Mary Pickford had been "America's Sweetheart" to many prewar moviegoers, but numerous fans of the twenties looked more to the sensual, come-hither stares of "The Vamp" (Theda Bara) and the "It" girl (Clara Bow). No more powerful sexual symbol existed than Rudolph Valentino, the screen's "Great Lover." A seventeen-year-old high school girl reported that Valentino's film, *The Son of the Sheik*, made her wonder, as it doubtlessly did millions of other women, "what it would be like to be in his arms, if he gave wet kisses or dry ones, if he smacked his lips or merely held them tightly. . . . "

Many Americans feared that Hollywood's pandering to the taste for sexuality would erode the nation's morals. Glamorous sex stars provided unhealthy role models for the young to emulate, they warned, while films with such suggestive titles as *A Shocking Night* and *Up in Mabel's Room* were considered dangerously suggestive. Personal scandals of a sexual nature involving movie celebrities such as comedian Roscoe ("Fatty") Arbuckle only worsened Hollywood's image. To counter this adverse publicity movie moguls opted for self-censorship. They induced Postmaster General Will H. Hays to leave his cabinet position in the Harding administration to become their designated censor. Good intentions to the contrary, Hollywood really did not tone down the sex content of its productions. It did, however, make them more palatable by insuring that each film had an acceptable moral ending.

Technical innovations also separated the films of the 1920s from their predecessors. The most sweeping of these involved the change from silence to sound. The early movies relied on imaginative camera work, snatches of written dialogue, and some form of musical accompaniment (usually a piano) to complement the acting. In 1927, however, *The Jazz Singer*, featuring popular Al Jolson, was introduced as the first full-length sound movie. Many both within and without the movie industry resisted this revolutionary development. Some traditional moviegoers preferred the silents; theater owners bemoaned the expensive new equipment; actors and actresses wondered whether they could learn their lines and deliver them well. Some of the latter failed to do so, and saw their careers ruined. Nonetheless, the "talkies" had become a fixed feature of cinema by the end of the twenties, just as movies themselves were a permanent part of American life. By 1921 an estimated 95 million persons were flocking weekly to movie houses.

Listening to the radio offered another popular amusement during the twenties. Pittsburgh-based Westinghouse station KDKA provided the nation's first public radio broadcast when it reported the presidential election of 1920. The initial commercial broadcasts came two years later, and the industry grew quickly. The National Broadcasting Company was founded in 1926, and the Columbia Broadcasting Company in 1930. Meanwhile, listeners became addicted to their favorites, such as Rudy Vallee crooning the decade's hit songs and Graham McNamee announcing its major sporting events. Annual radio sales climbed from $60 million in 1922 to a staggering $842 million in 1929.

The Sports Craze and Other Manias   Americans also amused themselves during the 1920s with an array of manias, some of which seemed to defy reason. One year found them fascinated by self-help advice from Emil Coué, who intoned: "Day by day in every way I am getting better and better." Couéism soon became a fad, only to be replaced

POPULAR AMUSEMENTS AND THE ARTS

135

by a national passion for Mah-Jongg and then for crossword puzzles. The rage for marathon dancing became as compelling—and more tiring. No fad, however, rivaled for bizarreness the passion for sitting atop flagpoles. The record was set in 1927 when one Baltimore ''sitter'' managed to stay up for 23 days and 7 hours.

But no mania could challenge the overall national obsession with spectator sports. As society became more urban and collective, nostalgia for the free-spirited, untamed individual became more pronounced. Americans, in short, were looking for heroes to worship. They found them in Charles Lindbergh, Henry Ford, and in various Hollywood stars. They also discovered them in a host of athletes, both men and women, who made the decade one of spectacular sporting achievements: Bobby Jones and Walter Hagen (golf); ''Big'' Bill Tilden and Alice Marble (tennis); and Gertrude Ederle and Johnny Weissmuller (swimming).

Boxing also provided heroes, perhaps reminding Americans of days when a man prevailed by physical prowess. No boxer received more adulation than Jack Dempsey, the tough ''Manassa Mauler'' from Colorado. His appeal stemmed from his reputation as the ''giant killer'' who had won the heavyweight crown from huge Jess Willard (who, in turn, had dethroned the also huge Jack Johnson), and from the modest, unassuming ways he maintained despite the glamorous, publicity-filled life he led. During the twenties his two grueling championship bouts with Gene Tunney proved enormously popular. The soft-spoken Tunney, who later would lecture on Shakespeare to Yale students, won both fights. The referee's famous ''long count'' may have cost Dempsey the second fight when he knocked Tunney to the canvas but failed to go immediately to a neutral corner. Promoters, in any event, were not disappointed. Perhaps as many as 150,000 people had paid $2.6 million to see that match in Chicago in 1927 (120,000 fans had paid slightly less than $2 million to see their fight in Philadelphia the previous year).

Another popular spectator sport was football. By the 1920s most major colleges fielded teams, a few of which won nationwide followings. One such gridiron eleven was Notre Dame's, led to fame by its fabled coach Knute Rockne and by its ''Four Horsemen'' in the backfield. Team effort tended to downplay individual achievement, but Americans still found such heroes to cheer as running back Red Grange, the celebrated ''Galloping Ghost'' from the University of Illinois. Albie Booth of Yale, the most noted black football player of the decade, was another such hero. The erection of large stadiums, as well as the establishment of the first professional league in 1920, gave further indication that football would become an enduring amusement.

Football, for all its popularity, could not rival baseball as the national pastime, despite a scandal that jeopardized the latter's reputation as the decade began. In September 1920 three Chicago White Sox players confessed to a grand jury that they and five teammates had accepted money from gamblers and had thrown the World Series of 1919 to their opponents, the Cincinnati Reds. One apocryphal story had a youngster capturing the stunned public's disbelief when he cried out to ''Shoeless'' Joe Jackson, the White Sox's star outfielder: ''Say it ain't so, Joe.'' But it was so, as Jackson admitted. A jury acquitted the players in 1921, but the retired judge Kenesaw Mountain Landis, newly appointed first commissioner of baseball, barred them permanently from further participation in the game.

A number of heroes were ruined by the 1919 ''Black Sox'' scandal, but Babe Ruth was not. The ''Bambino,'' as Ruth came to be known, switched from being a successful southpaw pitcher to being the most celebrated slugger of his day or, arguably, in baseball

Babe Ruth with Secretary of War George H. Dern in 1934.

history. This "Sultan of Swat" powered 59 home runs in 1921, only to shatter that record with his 60 home runs of 1927 and help make his New York Yankees one of the most feared teams of that era. His simplicity and geniality, as well as the countless stories of his gargantuan appetite for food, drink, and carousing, further helped elevate this remarkable player to legendary status. So, too, did his annual salary, which by 1930 had reached the then awesome sum of $80,000.

Such good fortune did not extend to black or dark-skinned Latin players. As early as the 1880s white players refused to play with or against their black counterparts. Deprived of the benefits of playing in the major leagues, blacks established the Negro National League in 1920. This made possible the emergence of such stars as Satchell Paige, Josh Gibson, and "Cool Papa" Bell, all of whom were ultimately inducted into baseball's Hall of Fame. But despite the abilities of these and other black players, racial segregation ruled major league baseball until 1947 when Jackie Robinson broke the color line by joining the Brooklyn Dodgers.

Music The music of the 1920s continued some of the trends of the prewar years but also took off in new directions. The popularity of fast-paced dances remained undiluted, particularly the Charleston, which became the favorite new dance of the period. Similarly, Tin Pan Alley tunes and musical theater enjoyed continued success. Such composers as Irving Berlin, Richard Rodgers, Lorenz Hart, Cole Porter, and Jerome Kern introduced works in the twenties that remain staples of the contemporary popular musical repertoire.

It was jazz, however, that offered the nation's most distinct, indigenous contribution to music. Like its predecessor, ragtime, this idiom sprang from the rhythms of

POPULAR AMUSEMENTS AND THE ARTS

black musicians living in the South. One of them, W. C. Handy, composed "St. Louis Blues," which soon won national acclaim. Yet it was only after jazz moved northward and was altered by white musicians and composers that it became acceptable to large numbers of white listeners. Aptly named Paul Whiteman, the "King of Jazz," took the lead in this direction, much to the displeasure of jazz purists. In 1924 he introduced audiences to *Rhapsody in Blue*, the compelling jazz composition of Brooklyn-born George Gershwin. The latter was to become America's finest composer of serious jazz and, for some, America's finest original composer. His *Porgy and Bess* and *An American in Paris* continue to enjoy widespread appeal.

Classical music also flourished. Composers like Aaron Copland, Henry Cowell, Howard Hanson, Walter Piston, Roy Harris, and Roger Sessions debuted impressive compositions during these years. Meanwhile an increasing number of American cities formed symphony orchestras, and conductors like Walter Damrosch and Serge Koussevitzky educated listeners to both traditional and new works by European and American composers. The growing availability of recordings also made it possible for music lovers to hear their favorites in the comfort of their homes.

Art and Architecture   The visual arts, for the most part, followed prewar directions rather than pointing in new directions. In painting, for example, American artists tended to follow in the footsteps of European modernists or to echo the indigenous Ash Can School. There were, however, some genuinely creative native talents. Both Charles Demuth and Joseph Stella produced fine works in the cubist tradition. Charles Sheeler, another abstract painter, proved adept at capturing the nuances of contemporary technology. His depictions of Henry Ford's River Rouge factory outside Detroit combined clean geometric lines with a sense of powerful industrial forces. Other noteworthy painters of the period included the versatile John Marin, who specialized in water colors, and Georgia O'Keeffe, who brought a unique sensibility to her renderings of the harsh beauty of the Southwest.

Several members of the prewar Ash Can School continued their realist traditions. Among these was George Bellows, whose dramatic *Dempsey and Firpo* portrayed the South American challenger knocking the North American champion out of the ring. (Dempsey later won the fight by a knockout.) Newer realists who emerged during the decade included Edward Hopper, who captured the depressing loneliness and shabbiness of urban life, and Charles Burchfield, who suffused everyday scenes in an aura of poignant nostalgia. Regionalist painters also received attention by the late 1920s, although their heyday would not arrive until the thirties.

In architecture the battle between tradition and modernism that had characterized the prewar era seemed to favor the conservatives in the 1920s. The modernist Louis Sullivan died unhonored and in poverty in 1924. His disciple Frank Lloyd Wright found little respect among fellow countrymen, who preferred the time-honored styles of Gothic, classical, and colonial to the international style of functional building that enjoyed current favor in Europe. Traditional in their tastes for style, American architects and clients were ambivalent toward technological novelties. They readily adopted air-conditioning, acoustics, insulation, and newer types of glass and textiles; they generally failed to take advantage of mass production, standardization of parts, and the latest trends in machine-inspired design. One preference remained constant: skyscrapers. By 1929 the United

States could boast 377 skyscrapers of more than 20 stories. New York alone accounted for half of these structures, 15 of which rose more than 500 feet skyward. Two years later the 102-story Empire State Building was dedicated, and it remained the world's tallest building for several decades.

Literature: Rebellion and Liberation   The serious literature of the 1920s continued the prewar rebellion against the canons of traditional literary tastes. The shock of the war added a strong note of disillusionment to the rebellion, prompting American-born Gertrude Stein, who resided in Paris, to describe young American writers as "a lost generation." A few, like the talented and flamboyant Harry Crosby who ended as a suicide, were truly adrift. Most were never really "lost," but only in search of self-expression. Rebelling in order to create, they fashioned a literature during the 1920s that no decade has surpassed in its novelty and richness.

That so many young American writers became expatriates seemed to give credence to the idea of a lost generation. Major talents like Henry James, Edith Wharton, Ezra Pound, and T. S. Eliot had opted to live in Europe before the war began. Now many more writers joined their ranks, gravitating especially to Paris or southern France. These writers often complained about the crassness of American life and insisted that the Old World was more stimulating to creative minds. A more practical consideration underlay their exile: Europe provided much cheaper living quarters for struggling artists. Nostalgia and a lack of funds, however, soon caused most of them to return home. Many then settled in New York's Greenwich Village, whose inexpensive food and accommodations, bohemian life style, and air of artistic and intellectual liberation appealed to them.

Still, one should not underestimate the sense of disillusionment felt by some of the decade's outstanding writers. Ernest Hemingway, perhaps the most celebrated American writer of the twenties, best captured the sense of loss following World War I. In *A Farewell to Arms* (1929) Hemingway, using terse, simple sentences that were to make his style widely imitated, portrayed both the grimness of the war and its enervation of the human spirit. As his hero Lieutenant Henry noted: "I was always embarrassed by the words sacred, glorious, and sacrifice and expression in vain. . . . Abstract words such as glory, honor, courage, or hollow were obscene." Hemingway's *The Sun Also Rises* (1926) had likewise etched a portrait of despair. All the major characters seemed hopelessly lost. Jake Barnes is impotent because of a war wound; Lady Brett Ashley loves Barnes but moves promiscuously from man to man in a futile effort to find fulfillment.

F. Scott Fitzgerald, one of Hemingway's expatriate friends and rival for literary fame, also captured the air of postwar disillusionment. In his several novels and numerous short stories (for which he was handsomely paid), Minnesota-born Fitzgerald analyzed the corrupting effects of riches, commercialism, and social climbing in the "sad young men" and their equally sad women. His novel *The Great Gatsby* (1925) adroitly depicts the tragic fate of a once innocent American destroyed by forces seemingly beyond control. Hero Jay Gatsby, whose roots remain mysterious, devotes himself to regaining his prewar girlfriend Daisy, now unhappily married to a rich, vulgar, and domineering man. He fails; in the end both he and his dream are destroyed.

While Hemingway and Fitzgerald focused on personal alienation, others launched a wider denunciation of contemporary society. Many of these writers, most of them

F. Scott Fitzgerald with wife Zelda and daughter Scottie.

realists or naturalists, continued the "revolt from the village" that had begun in prewar years. Small towns and farming areas, they contended, were cesspools of narrow-minded prejudice and cultural dry rot. Sherwood Anderson's *Winesburg, Ohio* (1919) demonstrated the warping effects of small-town life on the inhabitants of a mythical backwater. Sinclair Lewis, a Minnesotan, extended this perception. In *Main Street* (1920) his culturally alive heroine is stifled by the complacency and narrow-mindedness of a provincial midwestern town that seemed to symbolize all small American communities. *Babbitt*

(1922), his next and most famous novel, delineated the life of a boring mediocrity, a small-town businessman loyal to his Boosters' Club, his profits, and his tasteless furnishings. For many, George Babbitt was the prototypical small-town businessman. Lewis also penned a savage indictment of the medical profession in *Arrowsmith* (1925) and of a hypocritical clergyman in *Elmer Gantry* (1927). In *Dodsworth* (1929), however, he portrayed a retired businessman sympathetically. Lewis received wide acclaim for his penetrating portraits of national life and in 1930 became the first American to win a Nobel Prize in literature.

No writer more fiercely attacked small-town and rural America than Henry Louis Mencken, who once declared that the farmer did not belong to the human race and that the South was ruled by ''Baptist and Methodist barbarism.'' Mencken, as a newspaperman and editor of the widely read *American Mercury* magazine, consistently titillated his many followers with his denunciations of fundamentalism, prohibition, nativism, the Klan, and literary censorship—all, so he argued, a bedrock of faith for nonurban Americans. His prejudices extended elsewhere, too. His scorn of politicians, for example, seemed limitless. President Wilson was ''the Archangel Woodrow''; President Hoover looked like ''a fat Coolidge.'' A persistent critic of mass society, he railed at the shortcomings of democracy and the ''booboisie.'' Often outrageous but never dull, this iconoclast from Baltimore engaged the interests of serious readers as well as those seeking lighthearted entertainment.

Not all writers condemned the traditions and values of rural and small-town America. Indeed, a number of southerners vigorously defended their region. These included the self-styled ''Agrarians,'' among them Allen Tate, Robert Penn Warren, and John Crowe Ransom. The Agrarians, several of whom taught at Vanderbilt University, denounced the corrosive effects of technology and modernism on the South. In *I'll Take My Stand* (1930) they asked fellow southerners to take pride in the past and reject the onslaught of industrialism. Thomas Wolfe, however, felt less charitably toward his native South, leaving Asheville, North Carolina, for study at Harvard and then residence in New York. His autobiographical *Look Homeward, Angel* (1929) describes the meanness and petty cruelties of small-town southern life, though not without bittersweet touches.

The 1920s also witnessed the emergence of William Faulkner, who was to become one of the South's and the nation's greatest writers. In 1950 he would receive worldwide applause as the recipient of the Nobel Prize for literature. Faulkner served as a pilot with the Canadian Royal Air Force during World War I, after which he returned to his native Mississippi rather than lead an expatriate's life in Europe. His *Soldier's Pay* (1926) was a searing indictment of war. But it was *The Sound and the Fury* (1929) that won him enormous critical praise. In this work he depicted the degeneration of the Compson family by utilizing the stream-of-consciousness technique employed so brilliantly earlier in the decade by European writers like James Joyce and Virginia Woolf. His subject matter—the conflicting values of the old and modern South—as well as the difficulty of his style, would become his trademark in a long series of novels to follow.

During the 1920s black Americans also produced a vital literature, one which expressed renewed pride in race and cultural achievement. Harlem at this time became the most important black urban center in the country, attracting aspiring black artists from all over the nation. Soon a community of writers, musicians, and painters coalesced, and from this emerged the ''Harlem Renaissance.'' The ''New Negro'' was urbane and middle-class, and proud to draw upon sources of Afro-American culture. There were

BIOGRAPHICAL SKETCH

RUDOLPH VALENTINO · *1895–1926*

Like other heroes of the 1920s, Valentino made it possible for millions of Americans to identify with what they admired but did not possess. In Valentino's case identification mingled freely with fantasy and brought color to the otherwise drab and unexciting lives of moviegoers. Hollywood had become a shrine for make-believe in more ways than one. Where else could an Italian immigrant like Valentino, surrounded by Jewish producers and directors, enjoy the devotion of so many Americans who simultaneously scorned other arrivals from southern and eastern Europe?

Valentino was born in Italy as Rodolpho Gugliemi di Valentina d'Antonguolla. This future movie idol migrated in 1913 to the United States, where his first jobs included sweeping saloons for fifty cents a day and gardening on a Long Island estate. He then turned to entertainment and became a vaudeville dancer. By 1918, however, he was appearing as a bit player in movies, which typecast him in sinister roles: blackmailer, thief, and gigolo. Valentino performed credibly as a villain, but he wished to assume more heroic roles. The director D. W. Griffith, for one, doubted if Americans would accept a Latin as a hero, and Valentino, with his dark, pomaded hair and sideburns, was unmistakably ethnic in appearance.

Young Valentino's fortunes changed in 1921. That year found him playing a major role in *The Four Horsemen of the Apocalypse*. More important, it also saw him starring in *The Sheik*, a movie that launched his career and catapulted him to fame. His sultry good looks, smoldering glances, and macho treatment of women fulfilled some female romantic fantasies and caused numerous men to change their hairstyles and grow sideburns. Valentino's graceful dancing also helped popularize the tango.

Later films did not disappoint his fans. *Blood and Sand* (1922) captivated audiences, as did *The Eagle* (1925). Meanwhile he became a subject of countless speculations and gossip, much of it focusing on his marital life. In 1926 Hollywood's most famous leading man starred in *The Son of the Sheik*, in which he played the roles of both father and son. Valentino traveled to New York that year to attend the opening of the film but died unexpectedly from a ruptured ulcer on August 23. Lines of mourners stretched for more than ten blocks in New York to catch one final glimpse of their departed hero. Mobs rioted in the streets, injuring scores of persons. They also gutted the funeral chapel in search of flowers and other mementos. A second funeral held in Hollywood found the crowds more restrained.

poets, novelists, essayists, sociologists. The list of important contributors to the Harlem Renaissance was substantial, including Countee Cullen, Zora Neale Hurston, Claude McKay, James Weldon Johnson, Langston Hughes, Alain Locke, and W. E. B. DuBois, to name several. Jazz musicians like Louis Armstrong and Edward "Duke" Ellington added a special quality to the Harlem Renaissance (though few black writers were interested in jazz at the time); so did a few painters like Aaron Douglass. The New Negro of the 1920s had taken important steps in search of both a heritage and a larger role in the nation's artistic expression.

Poetry achieved major advances in the 1920s, too. The decade witnessed the flowering of such original poets as Wallace Stevens, E. E. Cummings, and Robert Frost, as well as popular, more traditional ones like Edna St. Vincent Millay and Carl Sandburg. Ezra Pound and T. S. Eliot continued their careers as expatriates. Many regarded St. Louis-born Eliot's *The Waste Land* (1922) as the single most important poem of the twenties. In 400 or so dense, difficult lines he presented a world of cultural despair and nihilism. Most thought he was depicting a prostrate West after World War I. It now seems more likely that his gloom came chiefly from a miserably unhappy marriage.

The American theater also flourished. By far the most important and innovative playwright was Eugene O'Neill. Princeton-educated and the son of an actor, O'Neill remained remarkably open to a variety of sources, including naturalism, symbolism, Greek tragedy, and Freudianism. Several of his plays stressed the importance of the irrational or developed themes of incest and Oedipal conflict. During the 1920s he received the Pulitzer Prize for *Beyond the Horizon* (1920), *Anna Christie* (1921), and *Strange Interlude* (1928). His talents assured O'Neill of personal popularity long after the twenties faded. They also richly contributed to the overall diversity and creativity that characterized artistic developments during the New Era.

SUGGESTED READINGS

For general reading about the 1920s, Frederick Lewis Allen's *Only Yesterday* (1931) presents a lively but largely descriptive portrait. William E. Leuchtenburg's *The Perils of Prosperity, 1914–32* (1958) is equally readable and more scholarly. Both Paul A. Carter, *Another Part of the Twenties* (1977), and Roderick Nash, *The Nervous Generation: American Thought, 1917–1930* (1970), challenge the Allen-Leuchtenburg position that the decade was one of ballyhoo and sharp breaks with the past. *The Aspirin Age* (1949), edited by Isabel Leighton, contains useful essays that can supplement these works.

For the general economic developments of the era, see George Soule, *Prosperity Decade* (1947). James W. Prothro, *The Dollar Decade: Business Ideas in the 1920s* (1954), skillfully analyzes the ideology of the business community, while Alfred D. Chandler, *Strategy and Structure* (1962), concentrates on corporate developments. Labor receives careful treatment in Irving L. Bernstein, *A History of the American Worker, 1920–1933* (1960). See also Leslie Woodcock Tentler, *Wage-Earning Women: Industrial Work and Family Life in the United States, 1900–1930* (1979). Both John Rae, *The Road and the Car in American Life* (1971), and James J. Flink, *The Car Culture* (1975), examine the impact of the automobile on American society. Allan Nevins and Frank E. Hill, *Ford* (3 vols., 1954–1962), presents a very sympathetic account of the industrialist and folk hero of the twenties. See Kenneth S. Davis's *The Hero, Charles A. Lindbergh* (1959) for the life of another symbol of the era. Otis Pease, *The Responsibilities of American Advertising* (1958), offers insights into the growth of one of the decade's major industries.

SUGGESTED READINGS

The literature on social and cultural conflicts is rich and diverse. For postwar radicalism, see Robert K. Murray, *The Red Scare* (1955); Stanley Coben, *A. Mitchell Palmer* (1963); Robert L. Friedham, *The Seattle General Strike* (1965); David Brody, *Labor in Crisis: The Steel Strike of 1919* (1965); and Francis Russell, *A City in Terror: 1919—The Boston Police Strike* (1975). Several studies, including G. L. Joughin and E. M. Morgan, *The Legacy of Sacco and Vanzetti* (1948), are highly sympathetic to the decade's two most famous Italian-born anarchists. Francis Russell, in contrast, argues that Sacco was guilty and Vanzetti innocent in his *Tragedy in Dedham* (1962) and *Sacco and Vanzetti: The Case Resolved* (1986). The best account of nativism can be found in the previously cited John Higham, *Strangers in the Land* (1955). Both Kenneth Jackson, *The Ku Klux Klan* (1965), and David Chalmers, *Hooded Americanism* (1965), analyze the growth of the Klan. E. David Cronon, *Black Moses: The Story of Marcus Garvey* (1955), and Theodore Vincent, *Black Power and the Garvey Movement* (1971), examine black nationalism and its principal leader. Fundamentalism finds its fullest account in Norman F. Furniss, *The Fundamentalist Controversy, 1918–1931* (1954), but also see Ray Ginger, *Six Days or Forever?* (1958) for an incisive look at the Scopes Trial. Studies of prohibition seem endless. In addition to previously cited works, see Charles Merz, *Dry Decade* (1931), and Andrew Sinclair, *Prohibition: The Era of Excess* (1962). Literature on the new morality is also extensive. For more works on feminism and the role of women in society, see J. Stanley Lemons, *The Woman Citizen: Social Feminism in the 1920s* (1973). Paula S. Fass's *The Damned and the Beautiful: American Youth in the 1920s* (1977) is an important study of a topic that generally has been neglected. Robert S. and Helen M. Lynd's *Middletown: A Study in Contemporary American Culture* (1929), a portrait of Muncie, Indiana, provides a sociological study of the values and norms of Main Street America during these years.

The decade's amusements and artistic achievements have also spawned a burgeoning literature. Robert Sklar, *Movie-Made America* (1975), treats the development of the cinema during the 1920s. Radio has received less attention than movies, though Erik Barnouw's *A Tower of Babel: A History of Broadcasting in the United States to 1933* (1966) is thorough. For developments in sports, see John R. Tunis, *The American Way in Sport* (1958). Two fine biographies of great sports heroes of the 1920s are Robert Creamer, *Babe* (1974), and Randy Roberts, *Jack Dempsey* (1979). A lively account of the general culture of the era is Gilbert Seldes, *The Seven Lively Arts* (rev. ed., 1957).

Literature has received the lion's share of attention from cultural and intellectual historians of the twenties. Frederick J. Hoffman's *The Twenties: American Writing in the Postwar Decade* (rev. ed., 1962) provides comprehensive coverage. See also his excellent *Freudianism and the Literary Mind* (1945). Alfred Kazin's *On Native Grounds* (1942) also offers a survey of the literature of the period. Malcolm Cowley's *Exile's Return* (1934) is the classic account of expatriate life during the postwar years. Studies of major writers and literary figures include Carlos Baker, *Ernest Hemingway: A Life Story* (1969); Arthur Mizener, *The Far Side of Paradise: A Biography of F. Scott Fitzgerald* (1962); Mark Schorer, *Sinclair Lewis* (1961); William Manchester, *Disturber of the Peace: The Life of H. L. Mencken* (1951); Andrew Turnbull, *Thomas Wolfe* (1968); and Joseph Blotner, *Faulkner: A Biography* (2 vols., 1974). John Stewart's *The Burden of Time* (1965) examines the southern Agrarians. Nathan Irvin Huggins, *Harlem Renaissance* (1971), carefully analyzes black cultural developments during the decade. A fine supplementary work is Gilbert Osofsky, *Harlem: The Making of a Ghetto* (1965). Arthur and Barbara Gelb's *O'Neill* (1962) is a lengthy life study of America's most famous playwright.

7

From Normalcy to Depression

Tension and conflict marked the politics of the New Era. Conservatives controlled the Republican party during this period, and the party, in turn, dominated national politics under the probusiness presidencies of Harding, Coolidge, and Hoover. But progressives, although greatly weakened by the wartime experience and by internal dissension, provided a significant minority opposition. Throughout the 1920s their forces, consisting largely of farmers, workers, ethnics, and dissenting intellectuals, fought for and obtained reforms. Nonetheless, conservatives remained firmly in the saddle, thanks to the decade's economic prosperity. Then the terrible economic crash of 1929 burst the bubble of prosperity, and the politics of normalcy gave way to the politics of depression.

THE HARDING YEARS

The Politics of Normalcy   Warren G. Harding lacked the credentials to be an outstanding statesman. He possessed limited intellectual abilities. His speeches, scoffed a critic, left ''the impression of an army of pompous phrases moving over the landscape in search of an idea. . . . '' He also possessed a character flawed by, among other weaknesses, a too trusting nature and an inability to say no to friends. Harding accepted his shortcomings, admitting that while he could not be a great president he hoped to be ''one of the best loved.'' His impressive victory in the 1920 election gave promise of fulfilling this hope.

Part of Harding's appeal to the electorate was his pledge of a ''return to normalcy.'' This did not mean a return to the past, according to the candidate, but ''a regular steady order of things . . . normal procedure, the natural way, without excess.'' However awkwardly stated, these sentiments reflected Harding's belief in moderation and a limited

Warren G. Harding

role for the presidency. The chief executive, he explained, generally should defer to Congress and should act principally to conciliate opposing points of view both within and without the government. He should also rely on the advice of his advisors. Some of the Ohio president's cabinet appointments proved assets to his administration: Charles Evans Hughes (State), Herbert Hoover (Commerce), and Henry C. Wallace (Agriculture). Others were disastrous: Harry Daugherty (Attorney General), Albert Fall (Interior), and Edwin Denby (Navy). One—Andrew Mellon (Treasury)—became a superb executor of dubious policies.

    In keeping with his passive views of the presidency, Harding espoused a program that he hoped would help the nation weather the storm of postwar readjustment. Toward that end he made probusiness appointments both to the federal courts and to key regulatory agencies like the Interstate Commerce Commission, as well as the Federal Reserve Board. The Budget and Accounting Act of 1921 reflected Harding's desire to bring more efficient, businesslike practices to government. This measure established a budget bureau and made it mandatory for the president to submit an annual budget to Congress. Harding named Charles Dawes, an Illinois banker, as the first budget director. The new budget chief soon made significant cuts in government costs. More controversial was Harding's support for the Fordney-McCumber Tariff of 1922 that increased the duties on both agricultural and industrial imports. The act erected a powerful wall of protectionism around the United States at the very time when European nations desperately needed larger American purchases of their goods. They argued that they could not pay back war debts if the latter did not purchase their commodities (see Chapter 9).

As another part of the normalcy program, Harding announced his intention to extricate government from its wartime involvement in the traditionally private sectors of the economy. The nation, he declared, needed "less government in business and more business in government." Under Harding the government in fact maintained its close relations with private enterprise, though the emphasis shifted from regulation to cooperation. Secretary of Commerce Hoover epitomized this change. Hoover, influenced by his experiences as an engineer and wartime administrator, saw the future of capitalism as one of cooperation rather than competition, with the goal being more wealth for more people. Efficiency and planning, though not price fixing, were necessary means to this end, and the government should encourage trade associations. Businesses, for their own good as well as that of the public, should share information and coordinate marketing and production strategies.

Business found another champion in Harding's enormously wealthy secretary of the treasury, Andrew Mellon, who had amassed a fortune through steel, banking, and aluminum ventures. Mellon envisioned a rejuvenated private enterprise in which the benefits obtained by big business and wealthy individuals would trickle down to other sectors and classes of society. The Budget and Accounting Act reflected his desire to cut waste, reduce expenditures, and enhance efficiency in government operations as a prelude to reducing the nation's wartime debts. The Fordney-McCumber Tariff was less to his liking because it afforded greater protection to agriculture than industry.

The most controversial aspect of Mellon's program involved plans to reduce high wartime taxes on both business and wealthy individuals. These plans originally met with only partial success. Congress did abolish excess-profits taxes and reduced the maximum surtax rate on individual income taxes from 73 percent to 50 percent. But it disappointed Mellon by not lowering the direct rate of taxation on personal income, corporations, or private inheritances. Nonetheless, the Revenue Act of 1921 provided tax relief that amounted to more than $800 per capita in its first year of operation. Rightly or wrongly, many credited the Harding administration in general and Mellon in particular for the economic recovery that took root in 1922 and solidified the following year.

Harding's generous and compassionate nature further impressed many, as when he granted a pardon on Christmas Eve 1921 to Eugene V. Debs and other radicals who were serving prison terms for their earlier antiwar activities. Also welcomed were his largely successful efforts to persuade the steel industry to abolish its 12-hour workday.

The Harding Scandals Administration scandals soon made Americans forget Harding's positive achievements and endearing personal traits. The scandals involved appointees who were either unqualified for office or whose primary qualification was a friendship that dated back to the president's Ohio days. News of the first scandal broke in early 1923, when it was discovered that Colonel Charles R. Forbes, director of the Veterans'

CALVIN COOLIDGE AND THE POLITICS OF RESTRAINT

Bureau, had defrauded the government of more than $200 million. Forbes fled the country but returned to stand trial. He was convicted and served a short term in Leavenworth Prison. Charles F. Cramer, an assistant to Forbes, committed suicide rather than face a possible trial. Meanwhile Colonel Thomas W. Miller, the Alien Property Custodian, also was tried and convicted for having accepted a bribe. He, too, served a brief prison sentence.

Scandal also enveloped the "Ohio Gang," as several of Harding's liquor-drinking, poker-playing cronies were called. Jesse Smith, a close friend of Attorney General Daugherty, used his connections to solicit bribes from those who sought special favors from the government. He later killed himself. Daugherty himself stood trial in 1927 on charges of having pocketed bribes. Refusing to testify, he was acquitted by a hung jury.

No scandal proved more odious than the one involving government oil reserves held aside to meet future naval needs. In 1921 Secretary of the Interior Albert B. Fall persuaded a pliable Secretary of the Navy Edwin Denby to transfer some oil reserves held at Teapot Dome (Wyoming) and Elk Hills (California) to Fall's department. Fall then leased Teapot Dome and Elk Hills to Harry F. Sinclair and Edward L. Doheny respectively. (Both men were major contributors to the Republican party.) A Senate committee headed by Democrat Thomas J. Walsh of Montana began an investigation in the autumn of 1923. The committee learned that Fall had received a "loan" of $100,000 in cash from Doheny and more than $300,000 in cash and securities from Sinclair. Meanwhile the two oil men had hatched a plot that would have netted each millions of dollars. A jury later acquitted Doheny and Sinclair of bribery and conspiracy charges, although Sinclair was to spend several months in jail for having attempted to bribe the jury. Fall stood trial in 1929 and received a one-year sentence, as well as a fine of $100,000 for his attempts to cheat the government. The Supreme Court meanwhile returned the oil reserve leases to the government in 1927.

By mid-1923 Harding felt betrayed by those "damn friends" whom he had trusted. He suspected Fall, and one reporter claimed to have seen Harding choking Forbes in the White House after learning of the latter's embezzlements. But the public remained ignorant of this skulduggery as the worried Harding left for a speaking tour in the Midwest and West. On the return trip he collapsed. His physician, a crony whom he had appointed surgeon general, misdiagnosed his illness as ptomaine poisoning instead of a heart attack. The president suffered a second heart attack before dying in San Francisco on August 2.

The nation mourned its fallen chief executive but became disillusioned as the scandals began coming to light. Some concluded that Harding had committed suicide. Others believed that his wife and physician had administered poison to spare him the shame of the forthcoming disclosures. Later a few decided that Mrs. Harding had acted alone because of her husband's extramarital activities. No convincing proof exists for any of these allegations.

CALVIN COOLIDGE AND THE POLITICS OF RESTRAINT

Calvin Coolidge presented a sharp contrast to his predecessor. Unlike the handsome, affable, pleasure-loving Harding, Coolidge was a dour Vermonter who, according to one wit, looked as if he had been weaned on a pickle. Privately, he displayed a dry wit. To the public, however, his silence was legendary. "Silent Cal," a man of few words, was

Calvin Coolidge

fond of the adage "If you don't say anything, you won't be called on to repeat it." There were other contrasts. Harding was an extrovert who enjoyed socializing; Coolidge, who suffered from various ailments, was chronically tired and frequently required 10 or 11 hours of sleep daily. More important, Harding, although not personally corrupt, had assumed an aura of scandal; Coolidge presented an image of scrupulous honesty. Finally, Harding was probusiness but strove for balance among various sectors of the economy. Coolidge, on the other hand, was more ideologically conservative and unabashedly probusiness. His laconic statement "The business of America is business" captured the spirit and substance of his administration.

The Election of 1924 Had Harding lived, the scandals of his administration might have badly divided the Republican party and seriously affected its chances for victory in the 1924 election. Coolidge, however, offered a respectable, if not exciting, candidate around whom most party members could rally. For his vice-presidential running mate the party selected Charles G. Dawes, Harding's budget director. Making no mention of the deceased president's woes, Republicans advised voters to "Keep Cool and Keep Coolidge" and to enjoy four years of "Coolidge Prosperity."

CALVIN COOLIDGE AND THE POLITICS OF RESTRAINT

Unlike Republicans, Democrats suffered from serious rifts reflecting the tensions that characterized the decade's social and cultural developments. First, they bickered at the convention over whether or not to denounce the Ku Klux Klan by name, with condemnation failing by a single vote. Next delegates battled bitterly over the choice of a standard-bearer. Rural delegates and those from the Midwest and Far West backed William Gibbs McAdoo, who was both a Protestant and a "dry." Urban delegates lined up behind New York's Governor Alfred E. Smith, a Catholic, a "wet," and a champion of recent immigrants. After days of deadlock and 103 ballots, the weary participants turned to John W. Davis, a prominent lawyer with strong ties to the Morgan financial interests. The party denounced the scandals of the Harding administration but, by having chosen the conservative Davis, seemed to offer no real alternative to Coolidge.

Liberals were appalled at the prospect of having to choose between Coolidge and Davis. So also were other groups, especially railroad workers, farmers, and socialists. As early as 1922 these disaffected elements had contemplated the formation of a third party. In 1924 they coalesced to form a new Progressive party, and nominated the aging Robert M. La Follette and Burton K. Wheeler, a Democratic senator from Montana, as their presidential and vice-presidential candidates. Their platform called for more aid to farmers, government ownership of railroads, the right of collective bargaining for labor, an end to injunctions in labor disputes, and a constitutional amendment that would permit Congress to override Supreme Court decisions. The platform also strongly denounced monopoly.

La Follette and the Progressives, attacked by both Republicans and Democrats as radicals, waged a strenuous but futile campaign. A lack of funds hurt their cause, but no more so than internal weaknesses. (Labor, for instance, helped much less than expected.) The outcome of the election was never seriously in doubt. Coolidge, riding the wave of economic good times, polled 54 percent of the popular vote and 382 electoral votes, as compared with Davis's less than 29 percent of the popular vote and 136 electoral votes. La Follette, running a distant third, garnered nearly 5 million popular votes but carried only his home state of Wisconsin. The electorate had said yes to conservatism.

Coolidge and Prosperity   Coolidge presided over an increasingly prosperous nation during his full term in office. Industry continued to boom as the gross national product climbed from $93.3 billion in 1925 to $103.4 billion in 1929. A get-rich-quick fever also spread. Some Americans speculated wildly in Florida real estate during these years, and many went bankrupt as a result. The stock market attracted even more gamblers. Perhaps a million Americans were playing the market by the time Coolidge left office. The value of stocks soared 300 percent during his presidency, and market participants, trusting that the future was even brighter, increasingly began buying stocks on credit.

Many believed that the primary responsibility for present and future prosperity rested with the business community. Businessmen, they sensed, had increased national wealth through improved methods of productivity and other efficiencies, while turning from fierce competition to cooperation among themselves and with their employees. Even the octogenarian John D. Rockefeller, once among the most vilified individuals in the land, had now become a figure of veneration for some of his countrymen.

The Coolidge administration agreed that business wisdom was responsible for prosperity. Accordingly, it adopted a strongly probusiness stance in its policies and vowed to adopt business goals and techniques in running the government. Budgets were slashed, although a vote-conscious Congress did override Coolidge's veto of a bonus for veterans. Austerity measures also helped to reduce by half the deficits incurred during World War I. Thanks to these economies and the return of prosperity, the government found itself with a budget surplus. Secretary Mellon, who was chiefly responsible for fiscal conditions, subsequently obtained congressional passage of the Revenue Acts of 1926 and 1928, which substantially reduced levies on personal income and estates. These tax cuts particularly benefited the rich, who understandably lauded Mellon as the "greatest secretary of the treasury since Alexander Hamilton."

Not everyone approved of the New Era's policies or shared wholly in its prosperity. Advocates of public power, for example, resolutely opposed the plans of all three New Era presidents. President Harding had intended to lease to private entrepreneurs the government-constructed nitrate plants located on the Tennessee River at Muscle Shoals, Alabama. In 1924 Congress nearly passed a bill that would have turned over these sites to Henry Ford, who promised to produce cheap fertilizers and develop the hydroelectric resources of the region. Senator George W. Norris successfully fought the bill, arguing that the government, not private industry, should be responsible for this huge undertaking. Four years later the progressive Nebraskan managed to get Congress to pass a bill to have the government operate the Muscle Shoals facilities, but Coolidge vetoed the measure. Congress passed a similar bill in 1931, only to have President Hoover respond with another veto. Norris, however, would find a more sympathetic chief executive in Hoover's successor.

The New Era also disappointed labor. A series of unfavorable Supreme Court decisions invalidated a minimum-wage law for women and children, outlawed secondary boycotts, and upheld the widespread use of injunctions to halt strikes. Membership in organized labor fell markedly during this period. The pivotal American Federation of Labor (AFL) witnessed a decline in its ranks from roughly four million to three million between 1920 and 1929. Internal and external forces contributed to this situation. Samuel Gompers, president of the AFL, who stubbornly clung to his belief in craft unionism and "voluntarism," continued to oppose welfare legislation. He died in 1924, but his successor, William Green, continued his conservative policies and failed to achieve significant gains in union membership.

Company unions further weakened organized labor. More than 1.5 million workers belonged to these associations by 1928. Sometimes workers joined as a result of their employers' coercive methods. Often, however, companies won their employees' loyalty by positive means, including attractive profit-sharing and pension plans, as well as the introduction of such amenities as cafeterias and recreational facilities. Despite earnings of less than $1,500 annually in 1929, the typical industrial worker enjoyed increased real wages of more than 10 percent since 1923 and a shorter work week. Both militated against his support for independent unions and encouraged his acceptance of company unions and the open-shop policy of his employer.

Labor suffered real problems, but no economic group fared worse during the 1920s than the farmers, whose share of the nation's income plummeted from 16 percent in 1919 to less than 9 percent a decade later. Farmers had enjoyed high prices and sustained demand for their goods during the war. Afterward, renewed worldwide competition, coupled with greater yields resulting from increased technological efficiency, found farm-

CALVIN COOLIDGE AND THE POLITICS OF RESTRAINT

151

ers suffering from overproduction, low prices, and indebtedness on land and machinery. A farm bloc emerged during the 1920s and secured such remedial legislation as the protectionist Fordney-McCumber Tariff and laws to ease credit for farmers and regulate packers and speculators.

But the problems of agricultural surpluses and low prices remained. Ultimately the farm bloc endorsed a plan to have the government purchase various staples at a given price and then sell the surplus abroad at the lower world price. An "equalization fee" imposed on farmers would compensate for the difference in the two prices. Twice—in 1927 and 1928—Congress passed the McNary-Haugen bill that contained these provisions, but President Coolidge vetoed the measures. The second time Congress almost overrode the veto, an indication of the seriousness of the farmers' problems, the strength of the farm bloc, and the willingness of legislators to extend the scope of federal intervention in the nation's economy.

The Election of 1928 President Coolidge shocked the country in August 1927 when he announced, "I do not choose to run for president in 1928." Historians now suspect that he would have accepted a draft, but Republicans at that time took his terse statement at face value. At the 1928 convention, delegates nominated his secretary of commerce, Herbert Hoover, and wrote a conservative platform that promised sustained prosperity. The platform also pledged continued support for prohibition.

The Democrats in 1928 managed to avoid most of the bitter factionalism that had divided them four years earlier, thanks to McAdoo's refusal to run. The party now had little choice but to turn to its other available candidate with a national reputation: Al Smith. It nominated the exuberant New York governor on the first ballot and balanced the ticket by naming a southerner, Senator Joseph T. Robinson of Arkansas, as his running mate. The Democratic platform was conservative on most economic issues. It also defended prohibition, despite the opposition of Smith, who warned that he might urge repeal of the Eighteenth Amendment.

Since both party platforms were quite similar, the campaign focused on the backgrounds and personalities of the candidates. Here sharp disparities emerged. Hoover started his life in rural Iowa, the son of native-born Quaker parents. In 1928 he was a committed "dry." Smith, in contrast, was a product of New York's Lower East Side, a Catholic, and the offspring of recent immigrants. He was one of the nation's leading "wets." Further, Hoover seemed aloof from the hurly-burly of politics; Smith enjoyed close ties with Tammany Hall. Strong differences in appearance and style also existed. The secretary of commerce always appeared dignified and self-contained, somewhat like the impeccably starched collars he wore. His opponent was more ebullient—the "Happy Warrior," as he was called—and sported a jaunty brown derby hat and cigar, as well as a pronounced New York accent.

For many Americans who were citizens from birth, Smith's background, social views, and style embodied all that menaced American life and values. Most Republicans discreetly refrained from attacking Smith on these grounds, but many of his fellow Democrats did not. Southern Protestants, in particular, disliked his urbanism and immigrant background. Often angry opponents assailed "Alcohol Smith" for his stand on drinking and reviled his Catholicism, warning that he would be subservient to the pope.

Noted for his easygoing ways, Alfred E. (Al) Smith was aptly called "The Happy Warrior."

Smith brought this "whispering campaign" into the open in September and reminded the electorate that he strongly supported the separation of church and state. Nonetheless, the bigoted attacks continued as Smith fought to win the northeastern states and hold the traditionally Democratic Solid South.

Election day brought defeat for Smith and the Democrats. Hoover won 444 electoral votes to his opponent's 87, and his 21 million popular votes topped Smith's by more than 6 million. Hoover also made the first significant Republican inroads into the South since Reconstruction by winning five former Confederate states (Texas, North Carolina, Florida, Tennessee, and Virginia). Smith held onto the remaining six ex-Confederate states but won only Massachusetts and Rhode Island in addition.

The election results were deceptively one-sided, however. Smith had polled a greater proportional popular vote than the Democratic candidates in 1920 and 1924. More significantly, he won a plurality of the votes in the nation's 12 largest cities, where Coolidge had easily triumphed in 1924. This dramatic turnabout resulted largely from the enthusiastic support given Smith by recent immigrants. A number of Republican midwestern farmers, angry at Hoover's failure to back a system of price supports for agricultural goods, also voted for the Democratic candidate.

Smith's various identifications, especially his Catholicism and his stand against prohibition, had hurt him. They were not the factors that cost him the election, however. Given the economic good times, Hoover's personal credentials, and the Republican status as the majority party, no Democratic presidential aspirant could have won in 1928.

HOOVER AND THE POLITICS OF DEPRESSION

In accepting his presidential nomination, Hoover declared: "We in America today are nearer to the final triumph over poverty than ever before in the history of any land. . . ." The candidate's optimism, shared by many, proved illusory: Herbert Hoover was to preside over the worst depression in this nation's history.

The Roots of Economic Disaster Serious flaws threatened the structure of the economy at the time Hoover took office. Certain vital industries, such as automobiles and housing, showed signs of weakness; other areas of the economy, notably the coal and textile industries, remained in the doldrums. The general imbalance between supply and demand worsened with the failure of businesses to cut prices and thus provide a greater incentive for consumers to buy. A major part of the problem, moreover, was the unequal distribution of wealth that kept many from being or becoming active consumers. Business, for example, allocated proportionately more of its profits for capital investment and dividends than for wages. Hard-pressed farmers also made poor consumers as the glut in agricultural production forced them to accept decreasing prices for their goods. Persistently high unemployment further contributed to the failure of demand to keep pace with supply. At no time during the 1920s did unemployment fall below one million persons, and in 1928 the figure rose to two million. Put more starkly, perhaps 7 out of every 10 Americans lived at subsistence level—or worse. The wealthiest 5 percent of the population, in contrast, received more than 25 percent of the nation's total personal income. Their purchases of luxury items, while useful to the economy, failed to compensate for lack of consumer demand elsewhere.

Herbert Hoover enjoying a rather rare happy moment as president.

In retrospect, government policies may also have contributed to the coming economic disaster. Secretary Mellon's tax policies favored the well-to-do over those of modest means, thereby failing to encourage the latter to buy more American goods. Protectionism weakened the ability of American business in the area of international trade. Finding high American tariffs erected against their exports, Europeans retaliated. Huge American loans had propped up international trade, but by decade's end a number of debtors had defaulted on their obligations and had imperiled the delicate structure of goods and credits. Many foreign loans were of dubious wisdom or legality, as investors bet on continuing prosperity. At home, investors similarly gambled. The pyramiding of holding companies made certain enterprises appear sounder than they actually were. Ultimately some, like those of Chicago public utilities magnate Samuel Insull, collapsed and spread widening circles of panic and financial doom.

The Great Crash   Structural weaknesses pointed to the underlying unsoundness of the American economy. Yet it was the stock market crash of 1929 that undermined prosperity and heralded the coming depression. Believing in the strength of the nation's economy and in the miracle of quick profits, Americans invested heavily in the stock market throughout the 1920s. Between 1923 and 1930 trading on the New York Stock Exchange quadrupled. Stock prices nearly trebled between 1925 and 1929, with two-thirds of that increase coming between December 1928 and September 1929. Brimming with confidence, the American investor, like the American consumer, increasingly began to purchase stocks on credit. Buying "on margin" meant that the investor put down a certain amount of money toward the purchase of a stock (sometimes as little as 10 percent of the cost) and received a "loan" from his broker to cover the remainder of the transaction. If the stock rose in price, the investor paid off his broker and kept the remainder as profit. If the stock fell, the investor still had to pay back the broker's loan and might incur substantial losses or even ruin. The Federal Reserve Board did nothing to curb the frenzied speculation in securities, despite the promptings of President Hoover, who got Secretary Mellon to advise the public to switch from stocks to bonds. Hoover also asked the president of the New York Stock Exchange, Richard Whitney, to "curb the manipulation of stocks." Nonetheless, only a few shrewd investors (like Joseph P. Kennedy) began divesting themselves of their stock holdings.

In the fall of 1929 the stock market collapsed. It showed signs of weakening on October 21, recovered slightly, weakened again, and then crashed on October 29. That day, known as Black Tuesday, more than 16 million shares were traded, and the industrial average of stocks plummeted 43 points. Within a few days the value of stocks on the New York Stock Exchange had declined from $87 billion to $55 billion. By the end of the year the market had lost $40 billion. Investors were ruined; so were brokers who had unwisely permitted overgenerous margin terms to their clients. Most stocks would lose 90 percent of their worth within three years.

Many believed that the recession that followed the stock market crash would be brief and manageable. By the summer of 1931, however, severe recession was turning into profound depression. Enormous economic and fiscal problems occurred in Europe, particularly in Great Britain, Germany, and Austria, as American exports of capital and goods dropped sharply. Great Britain abandoned the gold standard, an act that precipitated

STOCK MARKET DEBACLE

	1929 High	1932 Low
American Telephone and Telegraph	310¼	70¼
Anaconda Copper	140	3
Auburn Auto	514	28¾
Chrysler	135	5
Du Pont	231	22
General Motors	91¾	7⅝
International Telephone and Telegraph	149¼	2⅝
Johns-Manville	242¾	10
Montgomery Ward	156⅞	3½
New York Central	256½	8¾
Pennsylvania Railroad	110	6½
United States Steel	261¾	21¼
White Sewing Machine	48	¼
Woolworth	103⅞	22
Zenith Radio	52¾	½

a further decline in international commerce. In the first three years of the Great Depression the value of American foreign trade fell from $9 billion to $3 billion. These developments insured that the United States would confront a catastrophic depression.

The Statistics of Misery   Statistics attest to the depth of the Great Depression. Between 1929 and 1933 the GNP fell from almost $104 billion to $74 billion. Wholesale commodity prices decreased by nearly one-third, while the price of farm goods diminished by more than one-half. The per capita income of the nation's 122 million Americans was $857 in 1929; in 1933 the country's 131 million inhabitants showed a per capita income of only $590. More than 100,000 businesses and 5,000 banks failed during these years. Perhaps most shocking, unemployment soared from 3 percent to 25 percent (35 percent for blacks). *Fortune* magazine in September 1933 estimated that 34 million people (28 percent of the population) had no income whatever. The figure did not take into account the nation's 11 million farm families, many of whom were also in dire straits.

Other evidence substantiated the calamitous nature of the depression. A typical worker in manufacturing earned $25.03 weekly in 1929 but only $16.73 in 1933. Female workers, as usual, tended to fare worse than their male counterparts. In Brooklyn, for example, some women earned only $2.39 for a 50-hour workweek; across the river in Manhattan 50,000 female garment workers labored under grim sweatshop conditions. Teachers in rural Kansas were earning only $280 a year. Worse still, cities frequently defaulted on teachers' salaries. By 1933 Chicago, which had dismissed a thousand teachers, owed its educators more than $20 million in back salaries, some of which would not be paid for a decade.

Unemployment presented an even greater problem than substandard or deferred wages. City after city, large and small, coped as best it could with its unemployed, but efforts fell far short of success. As unemployment grew, relief allowances diminished. New York could take care of only half of its qualified needy families by 1932, and these families received only $2.39 a week. Philadelphia's families, which received $5.50 per week, did somewhat better. Mississippi families, in contrast, obtained only $1.50 but were more fortunate than those in Detroit who received a pathetic 60 cents. One survey, moreover, reckoned that only one in every four qualified families was getting any financial aid.

Relief assistance was not only frequently too little, it was also degrading. Most Americans cherished the values of independence and self-help, and going on the dole brought humiliation and sometimes despair. A New York dentist and his wife killed themselves after leaving a note that explained: "We want to get out of the way before we are forced to accept relief money." Others sought less drastic solutions to their woes. The poor, the middle class, and those rich who had fallen on hard times were willing to accept any menial jobs, such as selling apples on street corners.

Often the unemployed became homeless. Landlords sometimes deferred rents, but evictions were frequent, as were foreclosures on homes whose owners could not meet mortgage payments. The homeless took to sleeping on park benches with newspapers for blankets, or in the dingiest of shanties in dumps or delapidated sections of cities and towns. These shantytowns consisted of cardboard boxes and assorted bits of metal and wood. By day the vagrants wandered the streets or queued in long lines to receive soup and bread provided by charitable organizations.

The depression uprooted many others as well. Searching for work, perhaps more than a million people roamed the land, sometimes on foot, often as hobos furtively hopping railroad freight cars. By the mid-1930s entire families were becoming nomads, particularly those from the Great Plains and parts of Arkansas, Oklahoma, and Texas. Since 1930 incredibly arid conditions had turned large portions of these areas into a

Migratory family as captured by the famous Depression photographer, Dorothea Lange.

HOOVER AND THE POLITICS OF DEPRESSION

gigantic Dust Bowl, where agriculture could not thrive because of the lost topsoil. So heavy were dust storms that the sun sometimes became invisible. In 1938, the worst year for these disasters, erosion claimed an estimated 850 million tons of soil. Many "Arkies" and "Okies" abandoned ruined farmlands and headed for California. There, most eked out a meager living toiling long hours as despised migrant workers. Lamented one of the characters in John Steinbeck's *The Grapes of Wrath* (1939): "Okie use' ta mean you was from Oklahoma. Now it means you're scum."

The migrants were not the only farmers to suffer from the depression. Agricultural prices reached historic lows during this period, as the market for farm products kept weakening. By 1932 wheat was worth only 38 cents a bushel and cotton 6 cents a bale. Farmers burned their grain for heat or dumped their milk in ditches because the price of hauling these goods to market was greater than their selling price. Some slaughtered their livestock since they could not afford to feed them. (Relatedly, some cities killed zoo animals because they, too, could not feed them.) So reduced was farm income during these years that roughly one-third of all farms were foreclosed.

"Nobody is actually starving," protested President Hoover, but the statistics of misery told a different story. Reports circulated from various parts of the country that people were eating wildflowers and weeds, as well as scarcely edible animals. People fought over the contents of garbage pails. One newspaper suggested establishing a center for leftovers where the needy could forage freely. Sometimes the evidence was grimmer. In 1932 the New York City Welfare Council reported that 29 persons had starved to death and that more than 100 had died from malnutrition. *Fortune* magazine publicly termed Hoover a liar.

The Hoover Program It is ironic that Herbert Hoover, the "Great Humanitarian" as people called him for his World War I service, had become indissolubly linked to one of the profoundest tragedies in national history. A man who genuinely cared about the suffering of his fellow humans, he was perceived as cold and unsympathetic, a president whose chief—some said only—concern was for big business. There was a further irony. Hoover championed the doctrine of "rugged individualism," but by greatly expanding the role of the government in domestic affairs, he helped prepare the way for the New Deal.

Voluntarism formed the heart of Hoover's philosophy. According to Hoover, the "new" individualism of the 1920s centered on the individual as part of a cooperative society that the state encouraged but did not coerce. As secretary of commerce he had urged businesses to form voluntary, mutually beneficial associations. When the depression erupted he used his persuasive powers to induce employers to refrain from cutting wages or employment. Similarly, he tried to prevail upon workers not to press wage demands. (Conditions worsened, however, and few businessmen or labor leaders were willing or able to hold the line.)

His voluntarism notwithstanding, Hoover disagreed with orthodox economists who said that the depression was a natural development that must run its course. He strongly believed in a balanced budget. Yet, in view of the economic catastrophe that enveloped the land, he ultimately asked Congress for $2.25 billion in funds for public works construction, much to the distress of stricter conservatives. Hoover also acted to assist farmers, arguing that "the farm is more than a business; it is a state of living." Calling

Congress into special session in April 1929, several months before the stock market debacle, he urged it to pass the Agricultural Marketing Act. By this measure a Federal Farm Board, consisting of the secretary of agriculture and eight other members, could aid in the marketing of farm goods through various cooperatives and corporations. Congress earmarked a revolving fund of $500 million for the board to buy surpluses and thereby increase the price of farm goods. The program failed, however, in part because farmers were loath to curb production. The board ceased purchasing goods in 1931 and terminated its activities altogether in 1933 after having lost $350 million.

The Hawley-Smoot Tariff of 1930 was also designed to aid farmers by protecting them against foreign competition. In its final form, however, the act proved exorbitantly protectionist, featuring rates well above those of the steep Fordney-McCumber Tariff of 1922. Other countries responded with their own protectionist policies, thus further hurting American agricultural and industrial exports. Hoover himself disliked the tariff measure but signed it.

On two issues the president remained adamantly conservative. First, he refused to accept any scheme to raise the price of goods by inflating the currency. The nation, he insisted, must remain on the gold standard. Secondly, he denounced the suggestion of direct federal aid to the unemployed. He believed that charity, literally and figuratively, should begin at home with private groups and, if necessary, local and state governments providing for the needy. To furnish people with federal relief, he argued, would transform individuals into wards of the state. These individuals would be selling their birthright of freedom for dangerous short-term benefits. Besides, he promised, ''prosperity is just around the corner.''

Political Paralysis By the first half of 1931 the recession showed a few signs of abating, and Hoover's policies seemed justified. Soon the financial panic and depression that had struck Europe intensified American economic woes. Hoover began to blame domestic weaknesses on international conditions. To remedy matters, he announced a moratorium on all war debts and reparations. The moratorium failed to improve the situation, and by the end of 1931 Hoover felt obliged to redirect his focus and to expand government activity on the home front. In 1932 he got Congress to pass the Federal Home Loan Bank Act and to increase funding for federal land banks. These measures averted the collapse of numerous mortgage-holding financial institutions and the loss of many private properties through an infusion of government funds. The Glass-Steagall Act of February 1932 added $1 billion of gold to the money supply and made it possible for domestic banks to meet the tide of foreign withdrawals that by 1931 had exceeded $1.5 billion. In all, the various emergency banking and fiscal laws helped forestall possible financial panic and collapse.

The most prominent measure supported by Hoover at this time involved the creation of the Reconstruction Finance Corporation (RFC). Established by Congress in 1932, the RFC began with $500 million of capital and could borrow $1.5 billion. Its purpose was to lend money to banks, insurance companies, railroads, and large corporations to prevent their collapse. The RFC loans did save a number of the nation's large financial and business concerns but provided no help for smaller companies. Moreover, only those institutions with sufficient collateral could receive loans, prompting critics to label the agency the ''bread line for big business.'' The RFC also granted funds for public works but no direct aid for the unemployed.

The RFC's loans to big business rather than to isolated individuals made economic sense. But like so much of Hoover's philosophy and overall program, it proved unpopular. As the economy worsened, many began to blame Hoover for having caused the depression. Others simply, but just as unfairly, concluded that he was callous toward suffering. The "Great Engineer," they scoffed, had "ditched, drained, and damned the country." They described the growing number of shantytowns as "Hoovervilles" and the newspapers with which people covered themselves as "Hoover blankets." Their cruel jokes about the chief executive betrayed their own pain and bitterness. One such story had Hoover asking Mellon for a nickel so that he might telephone a friend; the secretary of the treasury gave Hoover a dime so that he might call *all* his friends.

In 1932 an incident involving World War I veterans and the government further diminished Hoover's popularity. Eight years before, Congress had approved a deferred bonus for veterans to be paid in 1945. In 1931 it passed legislation that allowed these former soldiers to borrow as much as 50 percent against their bonuses, an increase from the earlier 22 percent borrowing privilege. The president noted that this would cost the government more than $1 billion and vetoed the measure. Veterans then asked for an immediate payment of their bonuses. Twenty thousand of them marched as a "Bonus Army" on Washington in June, but most dispersed the following month after Congress narrowly defeated a bill that would have granted their request.

Those who did not leave—a few thousand men, women, and children—bivouacked on the Anacostia Flats outside the city. Their huge camp did provide some threat to public health, and there were likely some undesirables among them. But a nervous Hoover also concluded that communists and criminals riddled the Bonus Army. Overreacting, he asked the local police to clear the marchers from several federal buildings. Violence subsequently erupted, and two of the squatters were killed. Hoover then ordered the United States Army to aid the police in dispersing all the protesters.

Policemen clash with members of the Bonus Army.

CHAPTER 7: FROM NORMALCY TO DEPRESSION

General Douglas MacArthur, the army chief of staff, commanded a force of 1,000 troops, who came equipped with bayonets, tear gas, swords, machine guns, and six tanks. Also present were MacArthur's aide, Dwight David Eisenhower, and the commander of the Third Cavalry, George S. Patton. The regular army easily broke up the Bonus Army, burning the latter's camp, injuring 100 of them, and accidentally asphyxiating a baby with tear gas. The Bonus Army no longer presented any threat to the government; but Hoover no longer presented any credibility for many citizens.

The Election of 1932   Voters in the 1930 congressional elections had given Democrats control of the House and, in alliance with progressive Republicans, control of the Senate. By the summer of 1932 it was evident that Hoover and his party faced even more serious political trouble. Nonetheless, the Republicans had no alternative but to renominate Hoover, pleading that he had done his best in the face of an unprecedented crisis and that prosperity would soon return. They also called for the repeal of national prohibition and the restoration of liquor control to the states.

Several candidates contended for the Democratic presidential nomination. Al Smith carried over some support from his previous presidential bid; Speaker of the House John Nance Garner of Texas also enjoyed popularity, especially among delegates who resented Smith for his religion and views on prohibition. The leading candidate, however, was Governor Franklin D. Roosevelt of New York.

A distant cousin of Theodore Roosevelt, Franklin Roosevelt was born to a prominent family of considerable wealth and had attended a prestigious private school (Groton), Harvard College, and Columbia Law School. He rose quickly in politics, serving as assistant secretary of the navy under Woodrow Wilson and then as James Cox's vice-presidential running mate in 1920. Polio struck the genial, self-assured Roosevelt in 1921 and threatened to end his career. He fought back courageously and returned to politics. In 1928, a predominantly Republican year, he won a close gubernatorial election in New York with the crucial support of his friend Al Smith. Two years later he won reelection by a landslide, as voters responded to his attempts to combat the depression.

Roosevelt gained his party's 1932 presidential nomination on the fourth ballot, despite the bitter opposition of Smith, who felt that he deserved the nomination and that Roosevelt had betrayed him. Garner had released his delegates to the New York governor and consequently received the vice-presidential nomination as a reward. The party platform castigated Hoover and the Republicans not only for failing to achieve a balanced budget but even more for failing to cure the depression. The platform pledged that Democrats would balance the budget, maintain a sound currency, and still end the depression. It also called for repeal of prohibition. Much more dramatic than the platform was the precedent-shattering appearance of Roosevelt at the Chicago convention to accept the nomination in person. In his acceptance speech the candidate promised to remember the "forgotten man on the bottom of the economic pyramid." He also committed himself to a "new deal for the American people."

Hoover and Roosevelt campaigned arduously. The incumbent patiently explained and defended his policies but rarely drew more than polite applause. His opponent fared better. It was not that Roosevelt offered the electorate radical departures from Hoover's program. Roosevelt was as economically conservative as Hoover and attacked his rival

BIOGRAPHICAL SKETCH

ANDREW WILLIAM MELLON · *(1855–1937)*

Mellon was born in Pittsburgh, Pennsylvania, one of eight children in a family of Presbyterians whose values included work, thrift, and education. Mellon's father was a successful lawyer, judge, and banker, who also expected success from his children and built his own schoolhouse to educate them. Andrew's decision to quit college (Western University of Pittsburgh) in 1872, only a few months before graduation, disappointed his father. But the senior Mellon recognized his son's aptitude for business and took him into the family bank in 1874, giving him full control in 1882.

Andrew Mellon's extraordinary success in business fully vindicated his father's judgment. He and his close friend, the steel magnate Henry Clay Frick, formed the Union Bank of Pittsburgh, which, along with the Mellon National Bank and another local bank, soon made Mellon one of the most prominent American financiers. He used his financial acumen to invest in a host of small but promising ventures. He helped establish the Union Steel Company, which later became part of United States Steel, the Gulf Oil Corporation, and the Aluminum Company of America. He eventually obtained control of the latter, which reorganized as Alcoa and enjoyed a monopoly in the aluminum industry for a number of years. Mellon also held financial interests in companies that constructed both the Panama Canal locks and New York's George Washington Bridge. By 1920 he was an officer of 60 corporations capitalized at $2 billion. He was also one of the richest men in the United States.

"Conservative Republican" described Mellon politically. Yet, as a reserved man who suffered from a slight speech impedi-

ment, he had no interest in assuming any active political role. "It's always a mistake," he noted, "for a good businessman to enter politics." Nonetheless, he yielded to party pressure and agreed to serve as Harding's secretary of the treasury. At the time he did not anticipate a particularly long stint in the cabinet. In the end he served longer than anyone since Albert Gallatin, who held the same position under Jefferson and Madison.

A belief that taxation should be used only for revenue and not for social engineering lay at the heart of Mellon's fiscal beliefs and practices. Heavy taxes, he warned, would force the wealthy into excessively cautious investments and thereby fail to generate employment and increased income for the less fortunate. Progressives denounced this viewpoint as benefiting only the well-to-do. Others attacked his high tariff policies, as well as his proposals on reparations and war debts. Critics further complained when Mellon used an Internal Revenue official to help him in personal tax preparation. Even more distressing were charges that he had granted financial aid to Colombia in exchange for concessions for his Gulf Oil Corporation. The House Judiciary Committee considered impeachment proceedings. This, along with his failure to foresee the Great Depression and his consequent unpopularity, led President Hoover to replace him as secretary of the treasury in 1932 and appoint him ambassador to Great Britain.

Like J. P. Morgan, Andrew Mellon was not only a titan of finance but a connoisseur of art as well. He developed a serious taste for art in 1880 on a youthful trip to Europe. Afterward he became an inveterate collector, amassing during his lifetime a collection valued at an estimated $35 million. Prominent among his treasures were Renaissance paintings and works secured from the Hermitage after the Bolshevik Revolution. In the year of his death he donated $19 million worth of art, as well as a massive building, to form the core of the National Gallery of Art in Washington, D.C. His fortune and that of his two children were estimated at the time at approximately $500 million.

as a big spender. He also dubiously promised to balance the budget while aiding the unemployed. But Roosevelt did indicate a willingness to experiment with new programs. And there was his self-assurance and charm—a soothing voice and captivating smile that inspired hope and promised a better future. Fittingly, the Democratic campaign song was ''Happy Days Are Here Again.''

Roosevelt won a staggering victory. He bested Hoover by more than 7 million popular votes and by an electoral margin of 472 to 59. The large cities continued their new trend of voting Democratic, and significant numbers of black voters began supporting Democrats as well. Democrats also gained control of both houses of Congress by wide margins. Yet the vote was probably more anti-Hoover than pro-Roosevelt. Additionally, it reflected the nonrevolutionary mood of the American people. Norman Thomas, the Socialist candidate, won only 2 percent of the popular vote. The Communist party candidate, William Z. Foster, did worse, winning only 100,000 votes, or 0.25 percent of the total cast.

As a lame duck president, Hoover failed to get a single bill passed by Congress. Nor did he obtain the cooperation of the newly elected chief executive. Roosevelt, not wishing to tie his hands, carefully refused to pledge support for any Hoover policies. To have done so might have precluded the ''new deal'' that he had promised a country moving perilously toward economic destruction.

SUGGESTED READINGS

Readings on the politics of the New Era are abundant. In addition to general works cited in Chapter 6, see for a highly readable, liberal interpretation, Arthur M. Schlesinger, Jr., *The Crisis of the Old Order, 1919–1933* (1957). John D. Hicks's *Republican Ascendancy, 1921–1933* (1960) is comprehensive and balanced but less colorful.

Warren G. Harding does not lack biographies. Two popular ones are Andrew Sinclair, *The Available Man* (1965), and Francis Russell, *The Shadow of Blooming Grove* (1968). Robert K.

SUGGESTED READINGS

163

Murray's *The Harding Era* (1969) and *The Politics of Normalcy: Governmental Theory and Practice in the Harding-Coolidge Era* (1973) are decidedly pro-Harding. For a look at the corruption that tainted Harding and his administration, see Samuel H. Adams, *Incredible Era* (1939); Karl Schriftgiesser, *This Was Normalcy* (1948); and Burl Noggle, *Teapot Dome* (1962).

Two good studies of Calvin Coolidge are William Allen White, *A Puritan in Babylon* (1938), and the more recent Donald R. McCoy, *Calvin Coolidge; The Quiet President* (1967). Farm problems and politics in the 1920s receive careful analysis in Theodore Saloutos and John D. Hicks, *Twentieth Century Populism: Agricultural Discontent in the Middle West, 1900–1939* (1951). For detailed treatment of the 1924 election, see Kenneth C. MacKay, *The Progressive Movement of 1924* (1947). The bitter election of 1928 is the subject of Allan J. Lichtman, *Prejudice and the Old Politics: The Presidential Election of 1928* (1979), and Edmund A. Moore, *A Catholic Runs for President* (1956). Oscar Handlin's *Al Smith and His America* (1958) is brief but quite cogent. David Burner's *The Politics of Provincialism: The Democratic Party in Transition* (1968) is an incisive study of the problems, aspirations, and restructuring of the Democratic party in the New Era.

Historians continue to debate the causes of the Great Depression. John Kenneth Galbraith, *The Great Crash* (1954), offers a penetrating analysis of the debacle. Milton Friedman and Anna Schwartz, in *The Great Contraction, 1929–1933* (1965), put forth a controversial argument from the point of view of monetarism. Peter Temin, *Did Monetary Forces Cause the Great Depression?* (1976), disputes this position. See also Lester V. Chandler, *America's Greatest Depression* (1970), and Broadus Mitchell, *Depression Decade* (1947), which, though dated, provides a useful overview. Among the numerous accounts of the personal suffering occasioned by the depression, several of the best include: Studs Terkel, *Hard Times: An Oral History of the Great Depression* (1970); Caroline Bird, *The Invisible Scar* (1967); Dixon Wector, *The Age of the Great Depression* (1948); and David A. Shannon, ed., *The Great Depression* (1960).

Herbert Hoover and his administration remain popular subjects for historians. Richard Norton Smith's *An Uncommon Man: The Triumph of Herbert Hoover* (1984) is an objective study, with good insights into its subject's personality and character. George H. Nash, *The Life of Herbert Hoover: The Engineer, 1874–1914* (1983), provides ample details of Hoover's early years. Harris G. Warren, *Herbert Hoover and the Great Depression* (1959), and Albert U. Romasco, *The Poverty of Abundance* (1965), are critical but fair in their assessments. David Burner, *Herbert Hoover: A Public Life* (1978), is more sympathetic to the embattled president, as is Joan Hoff Wilson, *Herbert Hoover: Forgotten Progressive* (1975). Hoover's *Memoirs: The Great Depression, 1929–1941* (1952) is important but highly apologetic and defensive in tone. Jordan A. Schwarz, *The Interregnum of Despair: Hoover, Congress, and the Depression* (1970), carefully analyzes the complex relationship between the executive and legislative branches of government during these critical years. For more specific topics, see Roger Daniels, *The Bonus March* (1971), and James Olson, *Herbert Hoover and the Reconstruction Finance Corporation* (1977).

A number of works listed above cover the 1932 election, as do many of the works cited in the following chapter. Roosevelt's prepresidential years are examined in detail in the earlier volumes of Frank Freidel, *Franklin D. Roosevelt* (4 vols., 1952–1973), and in Geoffrey C. Ward, *Before the Trumpet: Young Franklin Roosevelt, 1882–1905* (1985). See also Bernard Bellush, *Franklin D. Roosevelt as Governor of New York* (1955), and Kenneth S. Davis, *FDR: The New York Years, 1928–1933* (1985). Useful studies of the postelection lame duck period are Eliot Rosen, *Hoover, Roosevelt, and the Brains Trust: From Depression to the New Deal* (1977), and Frank Freidel, *Launching the New Deal* (1973).

8

New Deal America

A deepening economic crisis enveloped the nation as Franklin D. Roosevelt took the presidential oath of office on March 4, 1933. Unemployment was climbing, agricultural goods lay rotting and unmarketed, banks and businesses were failing in unprecedented numbers. Yet the president-elect assured Americans in his inaugural address that "the only thing we have to fear is fear itself." He promised to call Congress into special session to attack the problems of the depression and to grant him "broad Executive power to wage a war against the emergency, as great as the power that would be given me if we were in fact invaded by a foreign foe." Roosevelt's "new deal" had begun.

Historians have questioned the "newness" of the New Deal. Its most salient characteristic — a willingness to deploy the forces of the government for extensive intervention in the economy — was hardly novel. The Populists had called for such intervention, as had progressives. World War I witnessed an explosion of government activity that the New Era, conservative rhetoric notwithstanding, continued and the Great Depression accelerated. Rexford Guy Tugwell, one of Roosevelt's advisors, later acknowledged that most New Deal programs derived from those of Herbert Hoover, although the latter steadfastly denounced the New Deal and denied any relationship.

The New Deal, then, did not represent a distinct break with the past. But it was not simply a continuation of established practices. Under it the pace and scope of government peacetime activity ranged far beyond any of its predecessors. In the last year of the Hoover administration the government spent $4.6 billion, an outlay that brought stinging rebukes from Democrats. Three years later the Roosevelt administration expended $8.5 billion. Further, the New Deal not only spent more, it initiated entirely new programs and took on responsibilities that no administration had previously assumed.

The New Deal did not represent a program of clearly defined principles or policies, due in part to the clashing views of those who counseled the president. During the 1932 campaign and early years of his presidency Roosevelt surrounded himself with his "Brains Trust," an informal group of advisors that included Columbia professors Tugwell, Adolf A. Berle, Jr., and Raymond Moley, as well as Harvard Law School professor Felix Frankfurter. He also received important advice from key cabinet officials: Henry Morgenthau, Jr. (Treasury), Henry A. Wallace (Agriculture), Harold L. Ickes (Interior), and the first woman to enjoy cabinet rank, Frances Perkins (Labor). Budget director Lewis Douglas, the social worker Harry L. Hopkins, and the jurist Samuel I. Rosenman, who was the president's major speech writer, were other prominent advisors. All contributed to the tone and direction of the New Deal, but Roosevelt was beholden to none. He listened and then selected his own course of action, often to the dismay of those who believed that he had accepted their arguments. Like most of his advisors, Roosevelt rejected theory for practice. Unwed to any one plan for ending the depression, he experimented with options that he hoped would produce relief, recovery, and reform.

LAUNCHING THE NEW DEAL

What many historians have termed the First New Deal lasted from Roosevelt's inauguration to the spring of 1935. During these two years Roosevelt built on previous programs and initiated new ones. This First New Deal reflected the needs and dictates of special interest groups, presidential advisors, and party politics. It also bore out the president's willingness to experiment and cast aside ideas that had failed or had worked ineffectively.

Franklin D. Roosevelt, with Rexford Guy Tugwell at left.

The Banking Crisis   Roosevelt's first action as president was to order all banks closed from March 6–10 and to forbid the export of gold. During this "bank holiday" he convened a special session of Congress that on March 9 passed the Emergency Banking Relief Act to stabilize the nation's financial institutions. The measure outlawed the exportation of gold and authorized both the Federal Reserve system and the Reconstruction Finance Corporation to strengthen banks in various ways. Most significant was the provision empowering the Treasury Department to reopen only those banks it deemed solvent.

On Sunday evening March 12 Roosevelt explained this situation to the American people in the first of his highly successful "fireside chats," radio addresses that reached tens of millions of listeners and numbered more than 100 in his first administration alone. The president's soothing and optimistic tones were to become his hallmark, cementing his popularity and winning converts to his cause. (President Hoover had delivered nearly as many radio broadcasts as Roosevelt but without favorable results.) His chat of March 12 convinced many that it was safe to leave their money in banks. The crisis had receded. By summer the Treasury Department permitted most of the nation's banks to reopen, people stopped their panicky withdrawals, and few new bank failures occurred.

Roosevelt's handling of the bank crisis represented a moderate approach. Some critics were disappointed that he had not opted for a more radical restructuring of the banking system, perhaps even nationalization. But the president was essentially conservative in economic matters, wishing to reform as well as safeguard traditional institutions. On March 10 this conservative approach again manifested itself as he asked Congress to pass the Economy Act. Influenced by budget director Douglas, Roosevelt called for cuts in veterans' benefits and government employees' salaries that would amount to $500 million. The bill passed both houses in less than a week. Congress also responded to the president's request for revenue-producing taxes by enacting the Beer-Wine Revenue Act on March 22. This measure, which passed after Congress had proposed the repeal of prohibition, legalized the sale of wine and beer, and levied taxes on them.

The Emergency Banking Relief Act stemmed the panic among bank investors, and the Economy Act and Beer-Wine Act indicated an effort on the part of Democrats to redeem their party platform pledge to balance the budget. All three were palliative measures only. In the "Hundred Days" between Roosevelt's inauguration and mid-June, however, a pliant Congress enacted a host of administration-backed measures that would have widespread repercussions on agriculture, industry, labor, banking and taxation, public power, and unemployment. Along with later New Deal legislation, they would profoundly affect future generations.

Aiding the Farmers   Roosevelt believed that the disproportion between agricultural and industrial prices constituted an enormous flaw in the nation's economy. Secretary of Agriculture Wallace, after obtaining the views of various farm leaders, offered a proposal that Congress enacted on May 12 as the Agricultural Adjustment Act (AAA). By its provisions farmers would receive payments to curtail production of wheat, cotton, corn, hogs, and other staples. These payments aimed at "parity" between agricultural and industrial products, based on the prosperous period 1909–1914, when farm items were more or less equal in worth to manufactured goods. A tax on processors, such as millers or meatpackers, was to finance these subsidies. The processors could then pass along their burden to consumers in the form of higher prices. The AAA hoped to assist farmers through direct subsidy payments and indirectly through the higher prices that diminished production supposedly would fetch. Conservatives complained that the measure was socialistic, but people supported it as a necessary attempt to help the embattled farmer.

Unfortunately for the farmer, the AAA became law too late to affect the spring planting season. Farmers plowed under nearly one-fourth of their cotton production and slaughtered more than six million pigs. Many were outraged. Although the government distributed some of the destroyed livestock to the needy, a gnawing question remained: What kind of system permitted the destruction of food, especially during hard times?

The administration defended its actions by citing the need to save farmers and ultimately the nation's ability to feed itself. Farm prices did in fact begin to rise as supplies dwindled, thanks to both government policies and the drought that would culminate in the Dust Bowl. Farmers consequently increased production, but in 1934 the government imposed production quotas and fines for violators. Farmers took more than 30 million acres out of production in 1934 and 1935, receiving more than $1.1 billion in government subsidies. Meanwhile the value of their goods rose further. A bushel of wheat climbed in price from $0.38 in 1932 to $1.02 in 1936, while the price of hogs surged from $3.34 to $9.37 per hundredweight. The net income of farmers during this period rose from $1.8 billion to $5 billion.

The New Deal assisted farmers in other ways as well. The Farm Credit Act of June 16, 1933 facilitated credits for production and marketing. This allowed numerous farmers to refinance existing mortgages or to save their farms from foreclosure. The Frazier-Lemke Farm Bankruptcy Act, passed by Congress the following year, extended credit provisions and enabled the repurchase of foreclosed farms on reasonable terms.

All these measures brought relief and recovery to many farmers during the years of the First New Deal. Still, those who benefited were mainly larger farmers. The New Deal as yet had done little to relieve the plight of small farmers, tenants, or sharecroppers. In fact, by reducing the cultivation of acreage, the AAA unintentionally had made their lot more precarious.

Aiding Industry   Mixed results also characterized New Deal attempts to assist industry. Like agriculture, American industry suffered from low prices that in turn created lower wages and unemployment. This led to the vicious circle of decreased consumer purchasing power and still lower industrial prices. Roosevelt and his advisors spurned the growing congressional demand for a 30-hour work week, believing that it would forestall recovery. They turned instead to a more comprehensive plan.

The National Industrial Recovery Act (NIRA), enacted on June 16, 1933, represented an ambitious effort to revivify industrial activity. The measure, which created the National Recovery Administration (NRA), drew on Hoover's ideas for trade associations, although it exchanged his voluntarism for compulsory compliance. Tinges of corporatism that marked the Italian fascism of Benito Mussolini also colored the NIRA, which called for capital and labor to cooperate under the watchful but beneficial aegis of government.

Specifically, the NIRA empowered the NRA to permit trade associations to draw up codes for the nation's basic industries. These codes were to establish production and marketing goals, thereby indirectly encouraging price-fixing. The NIRA seemed in clear violation of the Sherman Antitrust Act, but the government accepted these transgressions in order to aid recovery. Partially to offset anticipated criticism, the NIRA also provided for codes of fair practices and their enforcement through government licensing. These codes called for minimum-wage and maximum-hour standards throughout respective industries, and the elimination of sweatshop conditions. Section 7(a) of the act offered a major concession to labor by acknowledging its right to form unions and to bargain collectively. The NIRA also sought economic recovery and relief by instituting a Public Works Administration (PWA). Headed by Secretary of the Interior Ickes, the PWA was designed to stimulate both employment and consumer spending by using its initial funding of $3.3 million for various public construction projects.

The NIRA was a bold experiment. Roosevelt declared that "history would probably record it as the most important and far-reaching legislation ever enacted by the American Congress." To head the NRA the president selected General Hugh S. Johnson, a no-nonsense administrator who had helped organize selective service during World War I and afterward became a successful businessman. Enthusiastic and energetic, Johnson set about drafting codes and getting businesses to agree to improved working conditions, wages-and-hours provisions, and stipulations that avoided cutthroat competition. Some basic industries, such as automobiles and coal, initially demurred. Within a year, however, more than 500 codes covering businesses that employed more than 20 million workers had been enacted. Firms pledging themselves to abide by these codes could proudly display the NRA's symbolic Blue Eagle and its motto, "We Do Our Part."

Despite initial enthusiasm engendered by the NRA, its policies soon came under fire. Small businessmen complained that larger competitors used industry codes for their own purposes, specifically to arrange for favorable production, marketing, and price-fixing agreements. Maximum hours and minimum wages further hurt the small businessmen's ability to compete. Consumers meanwhile were complaining that prices were too high, the result of deliberate cutbacks in production. And women and minorities, workers who enjoyed no safeguards in code provisions, continued to suffer from discrimination. By late 1933 the powerful newspaper magnate William Randolph Hearst was referring to the NRA as the "National Run Around," while others dismissed it as "No Recovery Allowed." Feuding between businessmen and the abrasive Johnson also diminished the effectiveness of the NRA. A National Recovery Review Board chaired by Clarence Darrow reported in mid-1934 that large businesses were in fact dominating their smaller rivals and establishing monopolies. The besieged Johnson resigned in September.

In May 1935 the Supreme Court invalidated the NIRA in *Schechter* v. *United States*. The Court found the law unconstitutional on two grounds. First, the Brooklyn-based Schechter brothers had sold their poultry wholly within New York State, and hence the commerce clause of the Constitution that gives Congress the right to regulate interstate commerce did not apply. Second, the Court ruled that Congress had unlawfully delegated power to draft the NRA codes to the executive branch. This "sick chicken" decision, though denounced by Roosevelt, only hastened the demise of the already mortally ailing NRA. The agency had helped raise industrial prices, but the increase was limited and was accompanied by adverse side effects. At best it had granted temporary relief and recovery rather than an enduring solution. Still, it scored real and substantial achievements—the virtual elimination of child labor and sweatshops, a model for future maximum-hour and minimum-wage laws, and the assertion of labor's legitimate rights.

LAUNCHING THE NEW DEAL **169**

Financial Reforms Extensive government intervention also characterized the New Deal's approach to the nation's financial institutions and fiscal conditions. The Emergency Banking Relief Act had stopped the run on banks and had halted financial panic, but it had done nothing to stimulate recovery or achieve much needed reforms. During the course of the First New Deal various advisors persuaded Roosevelt to use his powers to effect these changes. In the end the reforms brought mixed results.

Currency manipulation, like production control, emerged as one of the means for stimulating a badly deflated economy. But opinions varied with respect to the proper means for achieving this. Many called for a substantial infusion of paper money or silver to inflate the currency. The president, fearing too much inflation, proceeded more cautiously. On April 18, 1933 he officially took the United States off the gold standard, hoping that the dollar would decline abroad and stimulate higher prices at home. When only a limited decline occurred, he embarked upon a domestic gold-purchasing program. This, too, failed. Finally, the Gold Reserve Act of January 1934 authorized the president to buy gold at $35 an ounce and fixed the dollar's gold content at 59.06 percent of its 1932 value. This move produced no significant increase for domestic prices, although it did effectively commit the government to greater involvement in monetary matters.

The New Deal fared better with respect to financial reforms and safeguards. The Glass-Steagall Act of June 16, 1933 separated commercial and investment banking, and mandated restrictions on banking speculation. The act promised further guarantees to depositors by establishing the Federal Deposit Insurance Corporation (FDIC), which insured individual deposits in participating banks up to $2,500. The Banking Act of 1935, chronologically a part of the Second New Deal, represented another major reform. It greatly strengthened the Federal Reserve Board. Renamed the Board of Governors, this agency further centralized the nation's banking system through extended powers over regional member banks and control of reserve requirements and interest rates. Given these protections, any future collapse of financial institutions seemed unlikely.

The New Deal also extended protection to those Americans who still had a taste for playing the stock market. The Federal Securities Act of May 27, 1933, commonly called ''The Truth in Securities Act,'' forced sellers of securities to disclose all pertinent information. The following year the Securities Exchange Act provided added protection by creating the Securities Exchange Commission (SEC) to oversee stock market operations. Included in the SEC's broad powers was authority to license all stock exchanges, to register all securities, and to regulate all trading. Seeking someone skilled in the ways of the market, Roosevelt named Joseph P. Kennedy as the SEC's first chairman.

The New Deal and Public Power Franklin Roosevelt, like his cousin Theodore, was a staunch advocate of conservation. Several major dams, including the Boulder and Grand Coulee, were completed with his backing. More controversial was his support for the Tennessee Valley Authority (TVA), the multipurpose project enacted by Congress during the Hundred Days.

The origins of the TVA dated back to the struggle for public control of hydroelectric power waged during the 1920s and early 1930s by Senator George W. Norris and other progressives. Advocates of public power had pointed to the exorbitant rates charged by private utility companies. The collapse of Samuel Insull's huge pyramid of utility holding companies in 1932 further helped move the pendulum from New Era conservatism to New Deal reform.

The Tennessee River cut through seven southern states and affected the lives of millions of people, a large number or whom were impoverished. On May 18, 1933 Congress established the TVA to harness the river's power for the public benefit. Among its multifarious operations the agency improved and built dams (one of them named for Senator Norris), provided cheap fertilizers, reforested barren areas, furthered soil conservation, advanced public health, and gave employment to local inhabitants. Its most radical function involved the production and distribution of electricity. Its relatively cheap rates—the cheapest in the country—served as a ''yardstick'' by which to measure the rates charged by private companies. The latter denounced the TVA as socialistic. The government, in turn, assailed the greed of the companies. In any case, the TVA represented the most radical domestic measure of the Hundred Days and perhaps of the entire Roosevelt presidency.

The New Deal and Relief No problem of the Great Depression outweighed unemployment. Conscious of the pain and fear felt by millions of the unemployed and their families, Roosevelt went before Congress soon after his inauguration with a relief program. He proposed direct federal involvement as well as federal cooperation with the states to attack this urgent problem.

The Civilian Conservation Corps (CCC), established on March 31, 1933, was the most innovative of the New Deal relief measures. Originally authorized to employ 250,000 young men between ages 18 and 25, by 1941 the CCC had given jobs to more than 2 million youths, some of whom otherwise might have turned to a life of hopelessness and crime. The agency took them to camps, outfitted them with uniforms, and put them to work on useful projects: road construction, reforestation, park rehabilitation, tree planting, and soil replenishment. The CCC proved immensely popular for its imaginative utilization of the unemployed.

A Civilian Conservation Corps camp in Colorado.

The Federal Emergency Relief Act (FERA) of May 12, 1933, committed the government to aiding the states in the war against unemployment. Unlike Hoover's policy of granting loans, the FERA provided direct and matching grants to the beleaguered states. Harry Hopkins, who had headed the New York relief agency, was placed in charge of the program, which received an appropriation of $500 million. Neither Hopkins nor Roosevelt felt entirely comfortable with direct relief, fearing, like Hoover before them, that those on the dole might become permanent wards of the state. This fear, coupled with continued high unemployment rates, led to the creation of an emergency Civil Works Administration (CWA) in November. With Hopkins as its administrator, the CWA put 4 million of the unemployed to work on public works projects between late fall 1933 and early spring 1934. Some of these projects seemed eminently worthwhile—building and decorating post offices and schools, for example; others, such as raking leaves, drew the wrath of the budget-conscious. Roosevelt, himself concerned with the budget, terminated the agency after it had spent nearly $1 billion.

The Public Works Administration (PWA), created as part of the NIRA, was another example of "pump-priming." Congress appropriated $3.3 billion for the PWA to spend on diverse construction work as a means of combating unemployment and lagging consumer demand. Ultimately the PWA spent $4.25 billion, but most of it in the later 1930s. Its administrator, Secretary of the Interior Ickes—people called him "Honest Harold"—initially expended little of the allocated funds for fear that the public might regard his projects as boondoggles.

New Deal programs also assisted property owners. Besides the legislation pertaining to farm mortgages and foreclosed farms, Congress enacted two major measures affecting home owners. Established in June 1933, the Home Owners' Loan Corporation (HOLC) helped refinance home mortgages, granting loans on more than a million mortgages before going out of existence in 1936. The National Housing Act of 1934 established the Federal Housing Administration (FHA) to insure home mortgages. This measure brought relief to home owners and also stimulated the badly depressed construction industry.

Opposition to the New Deal   Roosevelt and his policies received strong support during his first two years in office. The elections of 1934 confirmed this popularity as Democrats maintained control of Congress, winning nine additional seats in both the Senate and House. The president had adroitly used his persuasive powers with press and public, and he had dispensed patronage with skill. He had also played the "honest broker" to various interest groups—farmers, businessmen, labor, public power advocates, the unemployed—and had won widespread approval from within their ranks. Nonetheless, opposition to the president and his policies was increasing by the end of 1934. The country had weathered the worst of the depression, but persistently high unemployment and the failure to achieve full recovery intensified criticism from both the left and the right.

A belief that Roosevelt and the New Deal had not done enough to combat the depression underlay the disapproval on the left. Blunt, radical Governor Floyd Olson of Minnesota liked Roosevelt, but confessed: "I hope the present system of government goes right down to hell." He preferred a socialistic commonwealth. Socialism was also the goal of novelist Upton Sinclair, who ran a strong but unsuccessful race for governor of California in 1934 on his EPIC (End Poverty in California) platform. The Socialist party, led by Norman Thomas, continued to maintain its historic position of seeking a

ORAL HISTORY
Growing Up in the Twentieth Century

RUTH H. RINEHART · *born 1918*

Dad had always worked for the Logan Gas Company as a foreman on their pipe-laying crews. Dad had a nice income every year, and we had a nice two-story, white frame house with a large backyard. We bought nice things: We bought a piano; my brother Miles and I took music lessons. We bought an automobile, built a garage and driveway, and had pretty much everything we needed—a comfortable life. I would think, in fact, that we were a little better off than most of the other neighbors.

Then about 1930 the Logan Gas Company decided to sell out to the Ohio Fuel Gas Company. Dad lost his job along with everybody else. He kept going to the office and they'd say, "We'll get you something, we'll get you something." But they never did. So we lived on our savings for about two years. That was the beginning of the depression for us.

Mom was always a country girl, and they talked about buying a place in the country. Well, Dad found this place on the Columbus Pike—25 acres and he mortgaged our house in town and bought those 25 acres up there. He built a filling station on the property because he knew he wasn't a farmer. And so he stayed up there all the time, and Mom would drive up there, and my brother and I would go up there with her, and Dad would come home once in a while. He also had a farmer plant corn up there—on the shares. It sold for a few cents a bushel. Everything started to go to pot, and he had to sell the place for less than he paid for it, and there was still a mortgage on the house. So there

we were in the middle of the depression—no work, no money, and all that. We thought we'd lose our house and we were scared to death. No wonder Mom lost weight.

Mom would never let us tell anybody when we started not having money. It was nobody's business outside the house. And what was said inside the house was supposed to stay there. We didn't tell any of the neighborhood kids about what was going on at home, and so everybody thought we were very nice comfortable people, and they didn't know we were suffering from the depression.

I remember the worry, the gloom that fell over our house. Then in 1933 Franklin Delano Roosevelt came in for his first term and the economy was in such bad shape. He started all these programs to get the economy going again. He started the Home Owners Loan Corporation. It gave government-subsidized loans. The government took over the loan from the bank where you owed the mortgage and your payments were just a little each month. And if it wasn't for that particular program during Roosevelt's administration, we would have lost our house. (I forget how many years—twenty more years, I think, for Mom and Dad to pay off that little bitty loan.) Then Dad worked a while for the WPA, and then Uncle Grover, who worked for the state highway department, got him a job as a cook for the highway crews.

When I think of my early life, I like to think of the younger years, because I didn't like the high school years, the depression, those years of turmoil where everything went sour in our family. Before the depression Dad was a happy, carefree person. He made a garden. He fixed up everything really nice. He worked hard and he was happy, and he sang all the time. We had phonograph records—all operatic arias. He loved music. And he joked a lot, and then all at once he didn't joke any more. Mom used to be happy, and she was helpful and sweet and loving, and then all at once that was gone. And so I suppose in everybody's family this was the way things happened.

The thing was, Dad started out big—not really big but comfortable, and he went down hill from then on. You give up after so long a time. Yes, the depression and everything that went along with it. It just sort of broke everybody's spirit, and we didn't recover right. I can't put the blame on anybody, and I won't blame my parents for what happened in our family, because I think they did their best.

---

peaceful overthrow of capitalism through education and political action. Yet the party lost strength during the depression, its membership declining to fewer than 20,000 by 1936.

Communism provided an attractive ideology for some who wished to jettison the entire capitalist system. Membership in the Communist party increased between 1928 and 1938 from 8,000 to 75,000. During the thirties the movement made fairly strong inroads into labor and won converts among leading intellectuals and some Hollywood figures. At first communists perceived Roosevelt as capitalism's best friend, a "social fascist" who propped up a decadent system in order to thwart radical change. Later in the decade many of them, taking their cue from Moscow or for independent reasons, toned down their criticism of the president and sought a "common front" of liberals, socialists, and communists to fight the growing menace of fascism in Europe.

Rightist opposition to the president and the New Deal stemmed largely from the business community and others who feared too much centralized power. The libertarian writer Albert Jay Nock expressed the concerns of many in the title of his book, *Our Enemy, The State* (1934), a work that warned of the dangers posed by big government. Similarly, H. L. Mencken spoke for opponents of welfarism when he derided the Roosevelt administration as "a milch cow with 125,000,000 teats." Organized right-wing opposition came largely from the American Liberty League, an association founded in

Communists demonstrate in front of the St. Louis City Hall.

August 1934 by a coalition of wealthy businessmen and conservative Democrats, including former presidential candidates Al Smith and John W. Davis. The league was avowedly nonpartisan in its denunciation of the Roosevelt program. Viewing the New Deal as a threat to free enterprise, it declared itself a supporter of freedom and the Constitution. Sneered one critic of the league: "They were deeply moved about the Constitution of the United States. They had just discovered it."

Yet a minority of the business community supported Roosevelt and his policies. Leaders of newer enterprises like Thomas A. Watson, founder of International Business Machines, backed the president, as did the department store magnate Edward Filene and his wealthy fellow Bostonian, Joseph P. Kennedy. Various southern and western businessmen, resentful of eastern industrial and financial power, also accepted the New Deal. Prominent among these were A. P. Giannini, the head of Bank of America, and Jesse Jones, the imaginative Texas banker whom Roosevelt appointed to run the Reconstruction Finance Corporation.

Indeed, Roosevelt's greatest challenge did not come from political parties or groups like the American Liberty League; rather, it came from three highly diverse individuals. What linked the three, besides a conviction that the New Deal had failed to solve the problems of the depression, was an ability to win a mass following.

One of these challengers was Dr. Francis E. Townsend, a mild-mannered physician from Long Beach, California, who was in his later sixties. He proposed a plan in 1934 that would have the federal government grant a $200 monthly pension to individuals over

60 years of age on the condition that they retire and spend their entire stipend. A 2 percent tax on business activities would finance this Old Age Revolving Pension proposal. Further, the retirement of the elderly would create jobs for the young. It was not the recovery aspect of Townsend's plan that captured popular attention, but the idea of a guaranteed pension for the elderly. Roosevelt and others doubted the feasibility of his ideas, but not so the more than three million Americans the doctor claimed as supporters.

Father Charles E. Coughlin presented even more serious problems for Roosevelt. From his small parish in Royal Oak, Michigan, a suburb of depression-torn Detroit, the "Radio Priest" broadcast controversial weekly sermons. At first an ardent champion of the president, by 1934 he began attacking Roosevelt for being too timid and for not pursuing a bold inflation of the currency through silver. Coughlin also lashed out at communists in broadcasts that reached an estimated 30–45 million listeners on a typical Sunday. To further his aims he organized the National Union for Social Justice to serve as a pressure group.

More formidable than either Father Coughlin or Dr. Townsend was the "Kingfish," Huey P. Long of Louisiana. Like Coughlin, Long had a populistic dislike for entrenched interests and used his oratorical powers to establish a mass following. He rose from a modest rural background to defeat the economic forces (mainly oil and public utilities) that controlled Louisiana politics. Elected governor in 1928, he improved education, roads, and health services, and achieved fairer taxation in one of the nation's poorest states. He also brought Louisiana dictatorial rule. First as governor and then after 1930 as a U.S. senator, he controlled the state as his personal fief, silencing critics through intimidation.

Like Coughlin and Townsend, Long believed that New Deal policies were inadequate. Breaking with Roosevelt, he organized a Share Our Wealth Society. This program promised each needy family an initial $5,000 and a guaranteed annual income of $2,500. Confiscatory taxes on income and inheritance would benefit the underprivileged at the expense of the rich and would make "Every Man a King." Filled with presidential ambitions and hinting at a third-party candidacy, the Kingfish posed a clear threat to Franklin Roosevelt's political future.

The Second New Deal Frustration and necessity spawned the Second New Deal. Between the 1934 congressional elections and the spring of 1935 both recovery and New Deal activity remained sluggish. The Supreme Court also invalidated the NIRA, as opposition from the business community and other groups and individuals intensified. Stung by their attacks, Roosevelt confessed: "I am fighting Communism, Huey Longism, Coughlinism, Townsendism. I want to save our system, the capitalist system. . . . To do so he launched what historians have called the Second New Deal.

The Second New Deal, which lasted from mid-1935 to 1938, did not represent a complete break with the First New Deal. Some reforms derived from those of the earlier New Deal or were already under consideration. Still, the Second New Deal found Roosevelt no longer playing the "honest broker," but acting as the leader of a coalition that increasingly looked to the needs of organized labor, small farmers, the unemployed, and the elderly. In addition, the president turned from seeking the cooperation of big business to seeking its reform.

The Public Utility Holding Company Act of August 28, 1935, for example, resulted from Roosevelt's attack on the electric power industry. Oligopoly characterized this industry, with the 13 largest companies controlling 75 percent of the nation's electricity through pyramiding holding companies. The administration proposed a "death sentence" clause that would have forced the dissolution of any holding company that after five years could not prove its usefulness or efficiency. The power companies fought back, spending over $1.5 million in lobbying efforts. At length the bill passed in weakened form and gave Roosevelt only a limited victory.

The Revenue Act (Wealth Tax Act) of 1935, enacted two days after the Public Utility Holding Company Act, also drew denunciations from economic conservatives, particularly wealthy ones. Roosevelt believed that a fairer distribution of the tax burden was in order and persuaded Congress to increase rates for large corporations. More controversial were the increased surtax on incomes over $50,000 and the increased gift and estate taxes. More controversial still were the graduated increases on millionaires' incomes, with rates soaring to 75 percent for incomes exceeding $5 million. Few doubted that Roosevelt was prepared to incur the wrath of the moneyed class, if only to offset the popularity of Huey Long's Share Our Wealth plan.

The National Labor Relations Act, better known as the Wagner Act (named for Senator Robert F. Wagner of New York), originally drew little support from either Roosevelt or Secretary of Labor Perkins, and it elicited even less from conservatives. The act established a National Labor Relations Board (NLRB) with far-reaching powers to protect workers against their employers. The NLRB, for example, could safeguard employees from having to join company unions. It also could supervise disputed elections and certify union representatives. To prevent employers from using a divide-and-conquer policy, this Second New Deal measure also mandated that the union receiving the majority of votes in an election would represent all the workers. Company unions soon began to give way to independent unions. Overall, the Wagner Act represents the most important prolabor law ever passed in the nation's history.

The Second New Deal also benefited farmers, including many who had derived no advantage from the AAA. The Resettlement Administration (RA), established by executive order on May 1, 1935, and headed by Undersecretary of Agriculture Rexford Guy Tugwell, helped impoverished rural families in a variety of ways. It granted loans to sharecroppers, tenants, and farm laborers for the purchase of land or equipment, and it also provided for outright resettlement. That same month Roosevelt also established the Rural Electrification Administration (REA) to bring affordable electricity to certain isolated rural areas.

In January 1936 the Supreme Court dealt the Roosevelt administration a serious blow by invalidating the AAA in *United States* v. *Butler*. In its decision the Court ruled that the tax on processors of agricultural goods was unconstitutional. Undaunted, Roosevelt and his supporters met the objection by pushing through Congress the Soil Conservation and Domestic Allotment Act of 1936 that committed the government to direct payments to farmers who curtailed production through various soil-conservation practices. The second Agricultural Adjustment Act of 1938 continued payments for soil conservation and added new measures, such as select parity payments, to increase farmers' income. Similarly, the Bankhead-Jones Farm Tenant Act of 1937 established the Farm Security Administration (FSA), which incorporated the RA and continued the battle to aid small farmers and to help migrant workers achieve a decent life.

LAUNCHING THE NEW DEAL

The Second New Deal also brought renewed government assistance to the unemployed. The Works Progress Administration (WPA), established by Congress on April 8, 1935, as part of the Emergency Relief Appropriation Act, represented an innovative program of work relief. Under Harry L. Hopkins the agency began hiring the unemployed for a variety of tasks. In existence until 1943, the WPA at one time or another employed 8.5 million persons and spent more than $10 billion. Its workers built 650,000 miles of road and constructed or improved more than 100,000 bridges and 100,000 public buildings.

The WPA also committed itself to the culturally creative. First, it provided jobs for artists, actors, musicians, and writers. Among those benefiting were such literary figures as Conrad Aiken, Richard Wright, Ralph Ellison, and John Cheever. The Federal Theatre Project, Federal Music Project, and WPA Dance Theatre brought culture and entertainment to millions. The WPA, in addition, was responsible for preserving invaluable local histories and folklore, as well as for advancing black studies. Wartime needs, denunciations of the leftist leanings of some participating artists, and charges that the agency spent far too much ultimately led Congress to end the WPA, but not before an important precedent had been set for government patronage of the arts.

No Second New Deal measure proved more important and far-reaching than the Social Security Act of August 14, 1935. The most significant of its complex provisions focused on old-age and survivors' insurance, for which employers and employees paid equally. Beginning in 1942 those insured could retire at age 65 with monthly benefits ranging from $10 to $85. The Social Security Act also committed the government to helping the states care for indigent persons 65 years old or more, as well as for dependent children and the physically handicapped. Finally, the act promoted a more uniform code of unemployment compensation through a tax on employers and direct grants to the states.

The Social Security Act was conservative in certain respects. Employers and employees, rather than the government, paid for old-age insurance. Also, the act initially excluded from coverage many workers, such as servants, farm laborers, migrants, and white-collar professionals. Many other countries already had enacted similar welfare programs—Germany a half-century earlier. Nonetheless, conservatives bitterly denounced this New Deal measure that had laid the cornerstone for a genuine welfare state.

A Landslide Victory   Few doubted the outcome of Roosevelt's bid for reelection. Agricultural and industrial prices were up, unemployment was down, and the flurry of legislation during the Second New Deal convinced many that the president needed a second term to complete the nation's economic recovery and to complete his program of reform. A confident Roosevelt accepted his party's renomination with the stirring promise that the American people had ''a rendezvous with destiny.''

Meeting in Cleveland, Republicans were considerably less confident. They repudiated Hoover and the implacable anti-New Deal wing of the party, and named Kansas governor Alfred M. Landon as their presidential candidate, with Colonel Frank Knox, a Chicago newspaper publisher, as his vice-presidential running mate. Both Landon and Knox had been Bull Moose supporters of Theodore Roosevelt and had maintained progressive views. Landon, while denouncing the cost and centralizing tendencies of the New Deal, pledged himself to carrying out Roosevelt's policies, only more cheaply and more efficiently.

Landon campaigned vigorously. He picked up the support of dissident Democrats like Al Smith, William Randolph Hearst, and former Brains Truster Raymond Moley. The Liberty League also worked to defeat ''that man,'' as critics frequently called Roosevelt. But the president's vocal opponents had limited powers to deliver votes. The same weakness applied to the Socialist candidate, Norman Thomas, and Earl Browder, presidential nominee of the Communist party.

Huey Long had been assassinated in 1935, leaving one major source of serious opposition to the president in disarray. Father Coughlin attempted to pick up the pieces by launching the Union party, which nominated Republican Representative William Lemke of North Dakota for president. Coughlin had hoped to mesh his forces with those of Dr. Townsend and Gerald L. K. Smith, the self-appointed successor to Long. But the Townsendites were disintegrating, thanks in part to a trusted advisor of the doctor who absconded with the organization's funds, and to Father Coughlin's distrust of Smith. Nonetheless, the Radio Priest remained optimistic in public, promising that he would quit broadcasting should Lemke receive fewer than 9 million votes.

The election results forced Coughlin to retire (but only briefly). Roosevelt won an extraordinary victory, capturing nearly 61 percent of the popular vote and carrying every state except rockbound-Republican Maine and Vermont. Landon won 36 percent of the vote. Lemke's 882,000 popular votes—one-tenth of the total predicted by Coughlin—represented slightly less than 2 percent of the votes cast but three times as many as the miniscule number of votes garnered by the Socialist and Communist candidates.

A powerful new coalition had emerged. It consisted of traditional liberals and ethnics, but now added increased numbers of urbanites, farmers, organized workers, unemployed, and for the first time a strong majority of black voters. It brought victory to Roosevelt and overwhelming dominance to Democrats in Congress. The president interpreted both as a clear mandate for continued reform.

THE SECOND ADMINISTRATION

Packing the Court The Supreme Court posed a major challenge to further reform as well as to existing programs. Alternating between broad and narrow interpretations of the Constitution, the Court had invalidated several key laws, including the AAA, NIRA, and a New York minimum-wage measure. Drawn up in haste, some of the laws, like the NIRA, were patently unconstitutional and were invalidated by 9–0 decisions. Others, decided by 6–3 or 5–4 margins, seemed to reflect the biases of the justices, four of whom were strongly anti-New Deal, three sympathetic to the New Deal, and two—Chief Justice Charles Evans Hughes and Justice Owen J. Roberts—not firmly committed. Still to be judged were several crucial cases.

Roosevelt had earlier expressed his dismay at the Court's decisions, but his call in February 1937 for changes in the judiciary caught all but a few close advisors by surprise. Citing the heavy backlog of cases facing the federal courts and the magnitude of work imposed upon judges, he offered various proposals, the most drastic of which involved the Supreme Court itself. This proposal would permit all justices to retire with full pay at age 70. For each eligible justice who chose not to retire within six months of having reached that age, the president could appoint a new justice until the Court reached a maximum membership of 15. Reasonable on the surface, the president's plan lacked candor. It was, as critics correctly charged, a ''court-packing'' bill.

THE SECOND ADMINISTRATION

179

Usually a master politician, Roosevelt had blundered badly. He had expected fierce opposition from conservatives, but he had failed to anticipate similar opposition from liberals. The Supreme Court, for all its unpopular decisions, had become sacrosanct to many. Liberals and conservatives alike respected the independence of the judicial branch of government and resented attempts to politicize it. Lawyers and judges throughout the country denounced the plan, as did many members of Congress. For some the measure seemed like the handiwork of a would-be dictator. Criticism came from the Court, too. Chief Justice Hughes eloquently defended its integrity, and 70-year-old Justice Louis D. Brandeis, a strong New Deal supporter, chided the president for implicitly questioning the abilities of older Americans.

Despite this niagara of protest, the president continued to defend his plan, whose outcome was far from certain. Many New Dealers loyally backed his efforts, including Senate majority leader Joseph T. Robinson of Arkansas, to whom Roosevelt promised the first vacant justiceship but who died in July. Many, moreover, strongly resented the actions of the ''Nine Old Men'' on the Court for having overturned popular legislation.

What doomed Roosevelt's plan, ironically, was a turnabout by the Court itself, leading one wit to suggest that ''a switch in time saves Nine.'' In the spring of 1937 the Court narrowly upheld the Wagner Act, the Social Security Act, and a state of Washington minimum-wage law for women. The fruits of the Second New Deal seemed secure. The court-packing proposal appeared even less necessary when conservative Justice Willis Van Devanter announced his retirement. The bill died in committee. In August, Congress passed a politically innocuous measure affecting the lower federal courts but not the Supreme Court.

Roosevelt claimed victory. His bill had not passed, but the Court, under pressure, had declared important New Deal measures constitutional and Van Devanter's resignation had led to the appointment of a committed liberal, Senator Hugo L. Black of Alabama. Further vacancies during the next four years allowed the appointment of six additional justices who were pro-New Deal in their sympathies. Roosevelt boasted that he had lost the battle but had won the war. James McGregor Burns, a Roosevelt scholar, was probably more accurate in claiming that the president had lost the battle, won the campaign, and lost the war. True, the Supreme Court did not invalidate any further important New Deal legislation. Alienated Democrats, however, would join Republicans in bringing the New Deal to a halt.

The Growth of Labor If the New Deal scored only an ambiguous victory in its fight with the Court, it did much better in its efforts to promote organized labor. Roosevelt originally tried to remain neutral between business and labor. But the growing hostility of businessmen, the advice of persuasive figures like Senator Wagner, and the political support given him by labor tilted the scales. The New Deal, especially after 1935, provided a favorable atmosphere for labor to press its demands.

Yet labor also had to put its own house in order. The conservative AFL remained dedicated to craft unionism and skilled workers. Unskilled workers, however, became more aggressive once unemployment began to recede and the Wagner Act took effect. Sympathetic leaders like John L. Lewis, the tough head of the United Mine Workers (UMW), clamored for the parent AFL to organize unskilled workers, particularly in mass industries like automobiles, steel, textiles, and rubber, where independent unionism did not exist. Rebuffed by the AFL at its Atlantic City convention in 1935, Lewis stormed out, but not before knocking down William L. Hutcheson of the carpenters' union. Soon afterward Lewis formed the Committee for Industrial Organization (CIO) to exert pressure on the AFL from within. The following year the AFL suspended the new group, which renamed itself the Congress of Industrial Organizations. All efforts at reconciliation failed, and in 1938 the rift became official. By then the CIO enjoyed a membership of 3.7 million, some 300,000 more than the rival AFL.

The surge in CIO membership resulted primarily from the unionization of unskilled workers in the automobile and steel industries. By 1936 the United Auto Workers (UAW) had emerged as the dominant union in the industry but had failed to obtain employer recognition. It turned to a new tactic: the sit-down strike. (In this kind of strike, widely used in Europe but infrequently in the United States, workers remain idle on the job, thus preventing strikebreakers from taking over.) After a 44-day sit-down strike, General Motors conceded defeat and agreed to recognize the UAW. Aiding the resolute strikers was the sympathy of both President Roosevelt and the liberal Michigan governor and future Supreme Court justice, Frank Murphy, who refused to send troops to disperse the strikers. Buoyed by its spectacular victory, the UAW won recognition from Chrysler later the same year and from Ford in 1940.

Attempts to unionize the steel industry proved somewhat less successful and considerably more violent. Labor took heart in 1937 when it gained union recognition from U.S. Steel after only a few months of strikes. The industry giant had caved in rather than continue a costly struggle. "Little Steel," the smaller companies in the industry, remained more firmly opposed to unionization and more willing to use force. On Memorial Day 1937 police clubbed and shot steelworkers and their families who were demonstrating outside the Republic Steel plant in Chicago. The "Memorial Day Massacre" left 10 persons dead and nearly 100 injured. Many Americans were shocked at the carnage, but Little Steel remained adamant. Only in 1941 did steelworkers win union recognition from these rivals of U.S. Steel.

John L. Lewis

Labor gains continued despite the setback at the hands of Little Steel. Workers emerged the winners in most of the more than 4,700 strikes involving nearly 2 million workers that occurred in 1937. Encouraged to join unions by New Dealers, many continued to flock to both the CIO and AFL. By 1941 membership in organized labor stood at nearly 10.5 million, a figure far surpassing the 3.6-million membership in 1930. Unions were less successful in obtaining major gains in wages and hours. But the New Deal-sponsored Fair Labor Standards Act (Wages and Hours Act) of 1938 called for a minimum wage of 40 cents an hour and a 40-hour maximum workweek. More important, it marked the first time that the federal government had legislated these matters.

Roosevelt, the New Deal, and Minorities   The government made a much less decisive commitment to alleviating the problems of blacks and other minorities. Roosevelt was sympathetic toward blacks, but he was unwilling to embark on any substantial crusade to improve their overall situation for fear of alienating his white southern supporters in Congress. He denounced lynching but refused to push for an antilynching bill, one of the chief concerns of civil rights advocates during the 1930s. He also refused to campaign against the poll tax. Certain New Deal programs even discriminated against blacks. Some of the NRA codes, for example, allowed blacks to receive lower wages than whites; the CCC established segregated camps for its black youths.

Yet Roosevelt and the New Deal did help black people. Unemployed or otherwise needy blacks were the recipients of relief benefits, which New Dealers like Harry Hopkins and Harold Ickes administered without prejudice. The president meanwhile created a ''Black Cabinet,'' a group of able women and men like Mary McLeod Bethune and Robert C. Weaver. By their presence these subcabinet officials symbolized that blacks had not been totally excluded from the corridors of power. They also served as spokespersons for black needs. And no New Dealer more forcefully popularized the plight of blacks than the president's wife. In addition to campaigning tirelessly for civil rights, Eleanor Roosevelt resigned from the Daughters of the American Revolution when the latter refused to permit Marian Anderson, the noted black singer, to perform in a Washington, D.C. building the organization owned. Fittingly, she and Secretary Ickes then arranged for Anderson to give her concert at the Lincoln Memorial on Easter Sunday 1939.

Black voters showed their gratitude for these benefits and recognitions. Abandoning their traditional allegiance to the Republican party, they solidly realigned themselves with the Democratic party and, like so many other Americans, looked upon Roosevelt with a respect that bordered on worship. Their old problem remained: ''last hired, first fired.'' But the president and the New Deal had given them hope.

The New Deal also gave hope to the most downtrodden of the nation's minorities: the Native Americans. With the onset of the depression, Hoover applied his policy of ''rugged individualism'' to a race whose individualism another race had all but destroyed. Only in 1931 did Congress allocate relief funds for their Native American wards. Roosevelt's appointment of John Collier as Indian commissioner effected a remarkable change in policy. Immensely sympathetic to their problems, the crusading Collier brought an end to the disastrous policy of individual land ownership provided for by the Dawes Severalty Act of 1887. Too many Native Americans had sold their lands for a pittance, and by the depression era they held, overall, precious little land, much of it arid. The Indian Reorganization Act (Wheeler-Howard Act) of 1934 restored their right of collec-

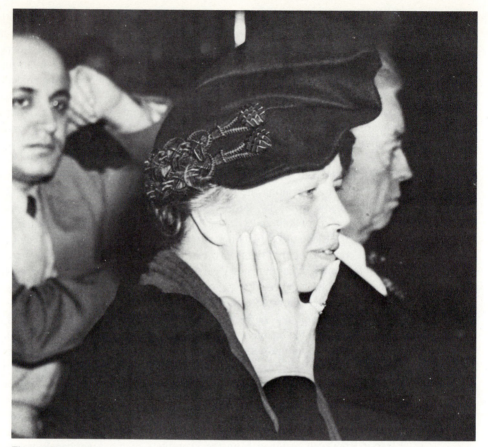
Eleanor Roosevelt

tive land ownership. The act also encouraged greater self-government and provided funding for education and cultural programs.

Mexican-Americans, in contrast, received little assistance from the New Deal. During the 1920s their numbers increased. As immigrants, legal and illegal, they crossed into the United States and settled mainly in California and the Southwest. Welcomed then as a source of cheap agricultural labor, they were despised by competing local workers once the depression began. Perhaps as many as 500,000 of these migrants were forcefully returned to Mexico during the 1930s. Many businessmen, irritated by the growing militancy of these workers, supported the move. Those migrants who remained occasionally benefited, like their Native American counterparts, from New Deal agencies like the Farm Security Administration, which tried to establish decent camps for them. But basically they represented Roosevelt's "forgotten man," whom the government had failed to remember.

The End of the New Deal "I see one-third of a nation ill-housed, ill-clad, ill-nourished," Roosevelt had declared in his second inaugural address. By the following year he and others could see visible improvements as the New Deal programs increasingly

THE SECOND ADMINISTRATION

took effect. The GNP had risen markedly from its lowest levels in 1932, unemployment had slackened, and industrial and farm prices had climbed. Roosevelt believed that the worst of the depression was over. He also was sensitive to the $4 billion budget deficit amassed in 1936 and to the critics of his spending policies. Reverting to his earlier economic conservatism, he trimmed programs, especially the WPA and PWA, and persuaded the Federal Reserve to adopt a deflationary policy by raising interest rates in order to tighten credit. At the same time, business cut back on capital investments, in part because of the new Social Security taxes. The president had overestimated the strength of the economic recovery and underestimated the extent to which the recovery depended on government spending.

Roosevelt's policies induced a severe recession that lasted from the fall of 1937 to the spring of 1938. Unemployment rose by more than 2 million and industrial production declined by one-third. The president received conflicting advice. Secretary of the Treasury Morgenthau and other conservatives pressed for financial orthodoxy. Others, like Federal Reserve Chairman Marriner Eccles, urged him to adopt the ideas of noted British economist John Maynard Keynes, which called for government deficit spending to compensate for diminished outlays in the private sector. Roosevelt reluctantly committed himself to the latter course in the spring of 1938. Congress, at his request, appropriated more than $3 billion for public works and WPA programs. The recession eased, but full recovery did not follow.

Yet it was mounting conservative opposition, not the recession, that most imperiled the New Deal. Many conservative Democrats in Congress had long disapproved of Roosevelt's policies but were afraid to voice or vote their disapprobation. The court-packing plan, the widespread public outcries against the administration's prolabor bias, and the failure to avert the economic downturn in 1937 emboldened them. Joining forces with Republicans, they stymied attempts to pass legislation in 1937. The following year they thwarted the president's plan to reorganize the executive branch of government. The Senate narrowly passed the measure, but the House, led by critics who accused Roosevelt of seeking dictatorial powers, defeated it by a vote of 204–196.

The defeat of this innocuous bill represented a humiliation for Roosevelt. Stunned, he declared war on conservative Democrats in the upcoming congressional elections. On June 24, 1938, the president announced that he would tour the country on behalf of various pro-New Deal candidates but in opposition to those who had obstructed his policies. The campaign ended in failure. He helped to unseat one anti-New Dealer but failed to unseat several others. Meanwhile the election found Republicans gaining 75 House and 7 Senate seats, mainly the result of the recent recession, higher unemployment, and a resurgence in traditional Republican strength, but also in reaction to Roosevelt's clumsy meddling. Critics charged that the president, like Soviet dictator Joseph Stalin, had been conducting a ''purge'' of his enemies. A rejuvenated Republican party and hostile Democrats honed their political knives. Generally unable to destroy existing New Deal programs, they settled for a stalemate. The New Deal had ended.

The New Deal Assessed Whatever else it may have been, the New Deal was not a revolution. Concerned with problem solving through practical and experimental programs, it left the quest for permanent solutions to the extremists. For the most part, it presented a blend of liberal and conservative elements. Like a true conservative, Franklin Roosevelt understood that it was necessary to change in order to preserve.

CHAPTER 8: NEW DEAL AMERICA

But to deny that the New Deal was revolutionary is not to deny that it effected major changes in American institutions, perceptions, and values. The New Deal resulted in a tremendous growth of executive authority. No peacetime president had ever exercised nearly so much power as Roosevelt did. Similarly, the government bureaucracy grew apace, as critics were quick to point out. The proliferation of New Deal "alphabet soup" agencies led to a huge increase in the number of federal employees and a corresponding growth in red tape and inefficiency.

The New Deal also greatly affected the nation's two major parties. The Republicans had enjoyed political dominance between the mid-1890s and the Great Depression. Since the New Deal the Democrats, thanks to Roosevelt's leadership and the coalition he fashioned, have constituted the majority party. Republicans have elected several presidents since then, but Democrats have fared better in terms of congressional strength. For only four years—1947–1949 and 1953–1955—has the GOP controlled both houses of Congress.

Building on the Populist and progressive traditions, the New Deal firmly established the principle that the government should promote the well-being of its citizens. Much New Deal legislation was temporary in nature, makeshift solutions to the most pressing problems of human suffering. But many of the innovations—FDIC, Wagner Act, TVA, FHA, SEC, Social Security, and others—outlasted the depression to become fixtures in American life. The New Deal also served notice that big business could not count on government neutrality when it posed a threat to the common welfare.

The most important achievement of the New Deal in the short run was to inspire hope in a nation ravaged by a shattering economic disaster. The New Deal did not achieve full industrial and agricultural recovery, nor did it effectively end unemployment, which stood at 8.1 million, or nearly 15 percent of the total work force, as late as 1940. Ironically, only another disaster—World War II—would restore genuine prosperity and bring about full employment. But the realization that the government did care for its citizens and was trying to solve perplexing problems restored confidence, preserved faith in traditional institutions and beliefs, and kept radicalism at bay. As Eleanor Roosevelt noted in 1939: "I never believed the Federal government could solve the whole problem. It bought us time to think."

LIFE AND CULTURE OF THE THIRTIES

The life and culture of New Deal America offered dramatic changes from that of the New Era. Continuities existed, but the realities of the depression colored the 1930s, dampening the exuberance and carefree tenor of life in the Jazz Age. Sobered by suffering, the generation of the thirties questioned values taken for granted by its predecessors. Yet for all its doubts and malaise, this generation made rich contributions to the nation's cultural heritage and ongoing quest for identity.

Historians Debate

THE NEW DEAL

The historical debate over the New Deal has paralleled the diverse ideological points of view that emerged during the 1930s. Then and since, liberals have extolled Franklin D. Roosevelt for his accomplishments in the face of unprecedented economic disaster. Yet sharp dissent from both the left and the right has also characterized scholarly judgments.

From the liberal perspective, no historian has championed Roosevelt and the New Deal more resolutely or articulately than has Arthur M. Schlesinger, Jr., in his three completed volumes of *The Age of Roosevelt* (1957–1960). For Schlesinger, Roosevelt steered an heroic, slightly left-of-center course that enabled the United States to avoid revolutionary upheaval or tyranny. He argued that the president, "a liberal pragmatist *par excellence*," had pursued a policy in which "a managed and modified capitalist order achieved by piecemeal experiment could combine personal freedom and economic growth." Roosevelt, claimed Schlesinger, had tamed the "economic royalists" and brought tangible benefits to the needy.

Other liberal historians tempered their favorable assessments. In *Franklin D. Roosevelt and the New Deal* (1963), William E. Leuchtenburg concurred with Schlesinger that Roosevelt was an astute leader who had restored public confidence, introduced or supported measures necessary for recovery, relief, and reform, and firmly established the principle of government intervention in the economy. But Pulitzer Prize winner Leuchtenburg also noted the shortcomings of the president's policies. Only World War II restored prosperity to the nation, and while Roosevelt's programs aided many—numerous farmers, laborers, the broad middle class—they did little for such submerged groups as blacks and poorer farmers. In sum, the New Deal was a "halfway revolution."

Radical historians have accentuated the reservations of liberals like Leuchtenburg. For them the glass was not half full but half empty—or even more so. During the 1960s the New Left scholar Paul Conkin agreed with Old Left critics from the thirties who castigated Roosevelt for having failed to achieve further social reforms and for having proppped up a tottering capitalist system that, thanks to the president, ultimately survived with its basic structure intact. In *The New Deal* (1967), Conkin did note that "plausible alternatives to the New Deal are not easily suggested." Still, he concluded that it had "solved a few problems, ameliorated a few more, obscured many, and created new ones."

Conservatives, too, have focused on the failings of the New Deal. Virtually all their criticisms speak to a few key points: the expansion of presidential powers at the expense of Congress; the emergence of a bloated, costly, and inefficient federal bureaucracy; and the intrusion of government into formerly private spheres of activity. Substantial scholarly critiques from this vantage point have been relatively few. Among the more incisive have been the moderately pitched *After Seven Years* (1939) by Raymond Moley, an important early advisor to Roosevelt, and *The Roosevelt Myth* (1956), a stinging diatribe by John T. Flynn that depicts the president as a dictator.

Fifty years after its inception the New Deal continues to engage the attention of historians. Numerous biographies and monographs have considerably augmented our knowledge of New Deal America and are spawning further research. Nonetheless, historical debate as to the larger meaning of the New Deal still essentially clings to the paths hewn during the dark years of the depression.

Literature The serious literature of the 1930s reflected the concerns of the depression. Some writers turned to communism and socialism; others remained less radical. Economic and social distress and the need for the redress of grievances provided the common focus. Erskine Caldwell portrayed the grim life of southern poor whites in *Tobacco Road* (1932) and *God's Little Acre* (1933), while Richard Wright, the most prominent black author of the decade, showed the tragic effects of poverty and racism on blacks. Driven by these forces, Wright's Bigger Thomas, Chicago-dwelling protagonist of *Native Son* (1940), turns to murder. The naturalist James T. Farrell also depicted the harsh brutalities of his native Chicago in the *Studs Lonigan* trilogy (1932–1935). John Dos Passos, who had been a noted writer in the twenties, offered another trilogy that castigated American life. His *U.S.A.* (1930–1936) vilified capitalism and its failures through a rich newsreel-style technique of narration. The plays of Clifford Odets, particularly *Waiting for Lefty* (1935), showed deep sympathy for the underdog, as did Jack Conroy's proletarian novel *The Disinherited* (1933). John Steinbeck's *The Grapes of Wrath* (1939), probably the decade's most renowned work of social fiction, captured the travail of the Okies, much as his other writings similarly focused on outcasts and losers.

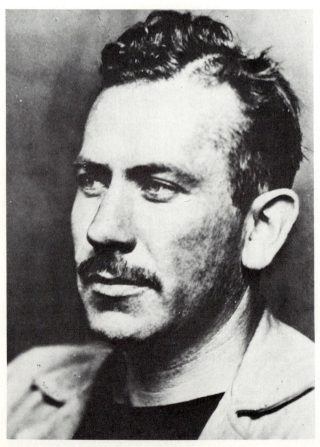

John Steinbeck

LIFE AND CULTURE OF THE THIRTIES

Not all writers were, or remained, disenchanted. Wright was to disavow communism; Dos Passos would turn from youthful radicalism to a later conservatism that pilloried Marxism and the Soviet system. Literary critic Granville Hicks would also disclaim his communism, while fellow critic Van Wyck Brooks, who once scoffed at the nation's literary past, exalted its artistic accomplishments in *The Flowering of New England* (1936). Other writers, still unhappy with American life and institutions, generally muted their criticisms after their disillusionment with the Moscow purge trials and the Soviet-German nonaggression pact of 1939.

Popular literature seemed more concerned with escapism and self-help than with social criticism and reform. Pearl Buck's *The Good Earth* (1931) gained immense popularity as it transplanted depression readers to faraway China. The best-seller status accorded Ely Culbertson's books on bridge similarly reflected the desire for diversion. Readers also popularized books of self-help and advancement. Dale Carnegie's *How to Win Friends and Influence People* (1937), for example, became a major best seller. Americans also sought to improve their fortunes through such new fads as bingo, marathon dancing, and the Irish Sweepstakes. And however badly capitalism may have treated them, many enjoyed Parker Brothers' new game, Monopoly.

In turning to both history and historical novels, readers showed a renewed appreciation for their past. Charles and Mary Beard's *The Rise of American Civilization* (1930) was a best seller, as were James Truslow Adams's *The Epic of America* (1932) and *The March of Democracy* (1933), and Douglas Southall Freeman's *R. E. Lee* (1934). Readers also savored such historical recreations of the past as Walter D. Edmunds's *Drums Along the Mohawk* (1936) and Kenneth Roberts's *Northwest Passage* (1938). Neither, however, gained the popularity of an Atlanta-born woman's first and only novel, Margaret Mitchell's *Gone with the Wind* (1936).

Music The depression gave direction to American music as well. Country music captured the pain and sorrows of poor folk, particularly those from the rural South and those uprooted from the Dust Bowl. Oklahoma-born folksinger Woodrow Wilson (Woody) Guthrie caught the plight of the latter in ''Dust Bowl Refugee'' and ''I Ain't Got No Home in This World Anymore,'' much as folksinger Huddie Ledbetter was expressing the woes of his fellow blacks.

But there was a market for upbeat popular music, too, as Americans sensed that the depression was finite. ''Brother Can You Spare a Dime'' was popular in 1932 when the depression had reached its nadir. Six years later ''Somewhere Over the Rainbow,'' from the hit movie *The Wizard of Oz,* assured people that a happier future lay ahead. Hopeful or not, many of the decade's popular hits reflected a collective concern with money: ''I Found a Million Dollar Baby—In a Five and Ten Cents Store,'' ''I've Got Five Dollars,'' ''We're in the Money,'' ''Love and a Dime,'' ''Pennies from Heaven,'' and ''There's a Gold Mine in the Sky.''

Radio, Movies, and Visual Arts The radio, movies, and the visual arts also provided depression-weary Americans with escape and entertainment, as well as with serious documentation of their conditions. By tens of millions they tuned to President Roosevelt's fireside chats and to the sermons of Father Coughlin. But they also turned to lighter fare, listening to soap operas like "Romance of Helen Trent" and "The Goldbergs." Some preferred adventures like "The Lone Ranger," in which a mysterious masked man, aided by a faithful Indian companion, brought justice to the West and doled out punishment to villains—a parable, so some thought, for Roosevelt righting the wrongs of the depression and scourging those who had been responsible for it. "Amos 'n' Andy," which began in 1929, remained a favorite for audiences in search of comedy. Radio once proved perhaps too diverting. On October 30, 1938, the actor Orson Welles and his Mercury Theater dramatized H. G. Wells's *The War of the Worlds,* a science fiction fantasy that described a Martian invasion of earth. So realistic was the broadcast that thousands of panicked listeners called their radio stations and local authorities for help.

Between 60 and 80 million Americans were going to movies weekly even during the worst period of the depression, and once the economy began improving, so did movie attendance. For the most part, audiences preferred films that either permitted them a respite from their own problems or allowed them to see these problems in a less serious vein. Frothy musicals like Busby Berkeley's *Gold Diggers of 1933, 42nd Street, Footlight Parade,* and *Gold Diggers of 1937* offered engaging singing and dancing, laughter, and happy endings. The same was true for the movie musicals featuring sophisticated Fred Astaire and his partner, Ginger Rogers. Outstanding comedians like W. C. Fields, Laurel and Hardy, Charlie Chaplin, Will Rogers, and the Marx Brothers brought laughter to countless Americans, as did the offbeat films of Frank Capra. Small wonder that Hollywood censor Will Hays boasted in 1934 that "no medium has contributed more greatly than film to the maintenance of the national morale during a period featured by revolution, riot and political turmoil in other countries." Only occasionally, as in *The Grapes of Wrath,* did Hollywood emphasize the more somber aspects of the decade.

Other visual arts did not flinch from depicting the sufferings of the depression. The Farm Security Administration sent photographers, including Walker Evans, Dorothea Lange, and Margaret Bourke-White, to document the bleakness and poverty of the rural South. The writer James Agee created a compelling narrative for Evans's photographs of impoverished farmers in what was to become a classic portrait of the decade, *Let Us Now Praise Famous Men* (1941). Detailed visual documentaries of depression America also filled the pages of *Life* magazine and "The March of Time" newsreels that appeared regularly in movie houses. Some painters portrayed the devastations of the depression. But the most prominent of the new regionalists—Grant Wood of Iowa, John Steuart Curry of Kansas, and Thomas Hart Benton of Missouri—also caught the individual courage of rural and frontier Americans, as well as the rich tradition of the past.

Cutting across the various cultural expressions of the depression years was the search for a usable past that would knit Americans closer together in the present. In the private works of individual artists and in the variety of WPA-sponsored group projects, in both serious and escapist art and entertainment, the nation looked for unifying themes, while not forgetting the grimness of current conditions. Many of the artists of the 1920s had turned their backs on a heritage they professed to despise; those of the 1930s avidly sought to recover and build a better future upon an inheritance they increasingly respected. Meanwhile, events abroad furthered American cultural nationalism. The rumblings of strife that were to culminate in World War II aroused many to the need for preserving not only the legacy of their past but their current and future freedom as well.

BIOGRAPHICAL SKETCH

CHARLES EDWARD COUGHLIN · *1891–1979*

Coughlin was born in Hamilton, Ontario, the son of an American seaman and a Canadian mother. He studied religion at St. Michael's College, Toronto, where he received instruction emphasizing the Catholic Church's commitment to social justice. Ordained, Coughlin taught at a Canadian college for a few years before receiving a pastorate in 1926 in the small Detroit suburb of Royal Oaks. That year he began his career as the spellbinding "Radio Priest" by denouncing the Ku Klux Klan for having burned a cross in the churchyard.

The Great Depression turned the direction of Coughlin's broadcasts from religion to politics. So popular were they that by 1930 CBS started airing them nationally. After his "Hoover Prosperity Means Another War" talk, he received 1.2 million letters. Contemptuous of Hoover's efforts to end the depression, he coined the phrase "Roosevelt or Ruin," confident that the New York governor would restore economic well-being if elected president.

Coughlin increasingly became disillusioned with Roosevelt and the New Deal, though he had once declared that "the New Deal is Christ's Deal." His panaceas for the nation's woes—broad inflation of the currency and nationalization of banks—never became part of Roosevelt's program. By 1934 the priest was denouncing the president along with "every money-changer in Wall Street." On Armistice Day of that year he established the National Union for Social Justice. The program, for all its generous concerns, assumed fascist overtones and attacked the selfishness of labor unions, the greed of capitalists, and especially the atheism of com-

munism. Concerned largely with middle-class Americans, Coughlin paradoxically hoped to increase the powers of government to restore the individual's control over his destiny. His organization supported politicians on a nonpartisan basis, but he turned to more direct political action with the formation of the Union party and the ill-fated candidacy of William Lemke.

After the 1936 election Coughlin was even more opposed to Roosevelt, whom he described as "anti-God." He assailed the president's court-packing plan and his toleration for the sit-in strikes in the automobile industry. Coughlin also became overtly anti-Semitic. His *Social Justice* magazine praised Hitler and reprinted the notorious *Protocols of the Elders of Zion*. He sympathized with Christian Front rowdies who bullied and brutalized Jews both before and after the outbreak of World War II. An isolationist, Coughlin denounced America's participation in the war as the result of a conspiracy forged by Roosevelt, the British, and the Jews. In 1942 the government invoked the Espionage Act to bar his magazine from the mails. That same year Church authorities forbade the controversial clergyman from speaking publicly on political matters.

Father Coughlin retired as pastor of the Shrine of the Little Flower in 1966 after 40 years of service. Banned from radio broadcasting, in his later years he wrote pamphlets reviling communism as well as the pronounced changes in the Roman Catholic Church occasioned by Vatican II.

SUGGESTED READINGS

William E. Leuchtenburg, *Franklin D. Roosevelt and the New Deal* (1963), offers the finest single-volume critical analysis of the New Deal. Another invaluable study is the yet uncompleted Arthur M. Schlesinger, Jr., *The Age of Roosevelt* (3 vols., 1957–1960). James MacGregor Burns, *Roosevelt: The Lion and the Fox* (1956), presents astute insights from the vantage point of a political scientist. Denis W. Brogan, *The Era of Franklin D. Roosevelt* (1951), looks at the New Deal from a foreign (British) perspective. Negative perceptions of Roosevelt and his policies can be found in Paul Conkin, The *New Deal* (1967), and Edgar E. Robinson, *The Roosevelt Leadership, 1932–1945* (1955). See also the previously cited Frank Freidel, *Franklin D. Roosevelt* (4 vols., 1952–1973).

Biographies, autobiographies, and reminiscences shed light on Roosevelt and the New Deal. See, for example, the moving Joseph P. Lash, *Eleanor and Franklin* (1971), as well as the First Lady's, *This I Remember* (1949). Also consult: Frances Perkins, *The Roosevelt I Knew* (1946); Rexford Guy Tugwell, *The Brains Trust* (1968) and *In Search of Roosevelt* (1972); Raymond Moley, *After Seven Years* (1939); J. Joseph Huthmacher, *Senator Robert F. Wagner and the Rise of Urban Liberalism* (1968); Searle F. Charles, *Minister of Relief: Harry Hopkins and the Depression* (1963); John M. Blum, *From the Morgenthau Diaries* (3 vols., 1959–1967); Harold L. Ickes, *The Secret Diary of Harold L. Ickes* (1953–1954); and Otis L. Graham, Jr., *An Encore for Reform: The Old Progressives and the New Deal* (1967).

Numerous specialized studies of the New Deal exist. For farm problems, see Richard S. Kirkendall, *Social Scientists and Farm Politics in the Age of Roosevelt* (1966); Christiana M. Campbell, *The Farm Bureaus: A Study of the Making of National Farm Policy, 1933–1940* (1962); David E. Conrad, *The Forgotten Farmers: The Story of Sharecroppers in the New Deal* (1965); and Walter J. Stein, *California and the Dust Bowl Migration* (1973). For the NRA, see John Kennedy Ohl, *Hugh S. Johnson and the New Deal* (1985), and Bernard Bellush, *The Failure of the NRA* (1975). Ellis Hawley, *The New Deal and the Problem of Monopoly* (1966), is most helpful for understanding the New Deal vis-à-vis business. Ralph F. De Bedt's's *The New Deal's SEC* (1964) and Michael Parrish's *Securities Regulation and the New Deal* (1970) are useful on the New Deal and the financial community. Thomas K. McCraw's *TVA and the Power Fight* (1970) is another enlightening work. Monty Noam Penkower, *The Federal Writers' Project: A Study in Government Patronage of the Arts* (1977), and Roy Lubove, *The Struggle for Social Security* (1968), examine key welfare measures. Irving Bernstein, *Turbulent Years: A History of the American Worker, 1933–1941* (1970), offers the most detailed account of labor during this period. But see also Melvin Dubofsky and Warren Van Tine, *John L. Lewis* (1977); Walter Galenson, *The CIO Challenge to the AFL* (1960); Jerold S. Auerbach, *Labor and Liberty: The La Follette Committee and the New Deal* (1966); and Sidney Fine, *Sit-Down: The General Motors Strike of 1936–1937* (1969).

Many studies exist on the opposition to Roosevelt and the New Deal. For opposition from the left, see Harvey Klehr, *The Heyday of American Communism: The Depression Decade* (1985); David A. Shannon, *The Socialist Party of America* (1955); Daniel Bell, *Marxian Socialism in the*

United States (1967); and Donald R. McCoy, *Angry Voices: Left-of-Center Politics in the New Deal Era* (1958). For right-wing opposition, consult George Wolfskill and John A. Hudson, *All but the People* (1969), and Wolfskill's study of the Liberty League, *The Revolt of the Conservatives* (1962). Other major dissent from the New Deal provides the theme for Alan Brinkley, *Voices of Protest: Huey Long, Father Coughlin and the Great Depression* (1982); Abraham Holtzman, *The Townsend Movement* (1963); and David H. Bennett, *Demagogues in the Depression: American Radicals and the Union Party, 1932–1936* (1969). Good biographies of dissenters include T. Harry Williams, *Huey Long* (1969), and Charles J. Tull, *Father Coughlin and the New Deal* (1965).

Studies of the New Deal and minorities are growing in number. For the New Deal and blacks, see Harvard Sitkoff, *A New Deal for Blacks* (1978), and James B. Kirby, *Black Americans in the Roosevelt Era: Liberalism and Race* (1980). Kenneth Philip's *John Collier's Crusade for Indian Reform, 1920–1954* (1977) is a substantial work, as is Abraham Hoffman's *Unwanted Mexican-Americans in the Great Depression: Repatriation Pressures, 1929–1939* (1974).

Studies of events during Roosevelt's second term are less abundant. But see Leonard Baker, *Back to Back: The Duel between FDR and the Supreme Court* (1967), for one such important study. Administrative reform is the subject of both Richard Polenberg's *Reorganizing Roosevelt's Government* (1966) and Barry Karl's *Executive Reorganization and Reform in the New Deal* (1963). James T. Patterson, *Congressional Conservativism and the New Deal* (1967) critically analyzes the growth of the anti-New Deal coalition.

The life and culture of New Deal America have generated strong interest. Richard H. Pells, *Radical Visions and American Dreams: Culture and Social Thought in the Depression Years* (1973), provides astute insights into the decade's artistic and intellectual life. Daniel Aaron's *Writers on the Left: Episodes in American Literary Communism* (1961) and Leo Gurko's *The Angry Decade* (1947) are good older studies of the literature of the thirties. Robert Sklar, *Movie-Made America* (1975), and Andrew Bergman, *We're in the Money: Depression America and Its Films* (1971), satisfactorily cover cinematic developments.

9

Foreign Affairs Between the World Wars

The widely held belief that the United States pursued a foreign policy of isolationism after World War I is simplistic and distorted. The nation did heed the hallowed advice to avoid entangling alliances. But it simultaneously involved itself in a host of thorny international issues that included disarmament and the search for peace, as well as the settlement of war debts and reparations. It also continued its prewar activism in the Western Hemisphere and its pursuit of global opportunities for markets and investments.

Isolationism became more pronounced during the 1930s as domestic concerns stemming from the Great Depression took precedent. The threat to world peace posed by aggressors in Europe and the Far East also stiffened American resolve to stay out of foreign disputes. The coming of World War II, however, led many to question the feasibility of remaining aloof. All doubts came to an end on Sunday morning December 7, 1941, when Japan launched a surprise attack on the American military base at Pearl Harbor.

POSTWAR DIPLOMACY

Naval Disarmament   The decision not to join the League of Nations underscored the nation's determination to shun enmeshing foreign commitments. But it still had to face the prospect of a costly, peace-threatening naval armaments race with Japan and Great Britain as the New Era began. The Japanese were already disappointed at having failed to win certain concessions at the Paris Peace Conference. They also grew alarmed when the United States began to shift the bulk of its navy to the Pacific Ocean and appeared ready to fortify both the Philippines and Guam. Great Britain, burdened with staggering wartime debts, dreaded the anticipated expenses required to maintain naval supremacy over the United States and Japan, its two major challengers. Meanwhile the United States, desirous of lower taxes and a balanced budget, chafed at the prospective costs of maintaining its position as the world's second greatest naval power. In the spring of 1921 Congress called upon President Harding to invite Great Britain and Japan to discuss reductions in seapower. Charles Evans Hughes, Harding's secretary of state, responded by asking not only Great Britain and Japan, but also France, Italy, China, Portugal, Belgium, and the Netherlands to consider arms limitations and general problems in the Far East.

Secretary Hughes convened the Washington Naval Conference on November 12, 1921. Lasting nearly three months, it produced several significant results. In his opening address Hughes shocked delegates by announcing that the United States would scrap 30 capital ships (large warships of more than 10,000 tons or with guns whose bore exceeded eight inches), and that Great Britain and Japan should destroy 23 and 25 such ships, respectively. Hughes's dramatic proposal called for the scrapping of two million tons of warships, prompting the observation that he "sank in thirty-five minutes more ships than all the admirals of the world have sunk in a cycle of centuries." After complex negotiations the Five-Power Treaty resulted. This arrangement provided for a 10-year "holiday" on building capital ships and established a tonnage ratio of 5:5:3:1.75:1.75 for Great Britain, the United States, Japan, France, and Italy. The agreement gave the United States parity with Great Britain while relegating Japan to a seemingly inferior position. The latter agreed to terms because geography dictated reality: the Japanese navy would be dominant in the Pacific. Great Britain and the United States also agreed not to fortify their Pacific possessions, but did not require Japan to do likewise.

Other agreements followed. The Four-Power Treaty compelled the United States, Great Britain, Japan, and France to respect each other's Far Eastern possessions. To the relief of Americans, the treaty also abrogated the Anglo-Japanese Alliance of 1902, which conceivably could have compelled Great Britain to support Japan in a war against the United States. A Nine-Power Treaty pledged all the nations attending the conference to respect the Open Door in China as well as the latter's territorial integrity. Japan further agreed to return to China the Shantung Province, an area that Japan had seized from Germany during World War I, and to withdraw its troops from Russian territories in Siberia and on Sakhalin Island.

The Washington Conference, by limiting the naval armaments race and seeking stability in the Far East, represented perhaps the most noteworthy achievement of the Harding administration. But it left some problems unsettled and created several new ones. The delegates set tonnage limits for capital ships but failed to do so for destroyers, cruisers, or submarines. Furthermore, the Nine-Power Treaty lacked provisions for enforcement. Also, by limiting its naval strength and by agreeing not to fortify its Pacific holdings, the United States wagered that it could avoid conflict with Japan. Diplomatic tensions with the Flower Kingdom did ease during the 1920s, while Americans were able to escape the added taxation necessary to support a naval buildup. The United States might not have been able to challenge Japan's Far Eastern position short of using force in any case, and the use of force seemed unthinkable to most war-weary Americans.

Further attempts at naval disarmament followed the Washington Conference. In 1927 President Coolidge called for a reduction in submarine, cruiser, and destroyer tonnage among the Five-Power Treaty signatories. The resulting Geneva Conference

Washington Naval Conference. Secretary of State Charles Evans Hughes is fifth from the left, facing front, at the large table. Henry Cabot Lodge and Elihu Root are to his immediate right.

ended in failure when France and Italy refused to attend and those who did could reach no agreement. The London Naval Conference of 1930 fared better. A complicated formula prorated the construction of noncapital warships by the United States, Great Britain, and Japan, and extended the moratorium on capital ship construction until the end of 1936. These three powers also agreed to scrap a total of nine battleships.

Outlawing War Peace advocates pursued other forms of international cooperation besides arms reductions. Despite both President Harding's vow that the United States would not enter the League of Nations "by the side door, or the back door, or the cellar door," and the isolationist sentiment that kept the nation from joining the World Court, by 1930 more than 200 Americans had served as official delegates to more than 40 conferences held by the League. Five permanent officials, in addition, remained at the League's headquarters in Geneva. Private organizations were also active. The Carnegie Endowment for International Peace, generously funded by the steel magnate whose name it bore, dedicated itself to the "speedy abolition of international war between so-called civilized nations." The Woodrow Wilson Foundation pursued a similar goal.

Such champions of peace scored an ambiguous triumph with the passage of the Kellogg-Briand Pact in 1928. The previous year James T. Shotwell, a Columbia University professor who was an official of the Carnegie Endowment for International Peace as well, convinced French Foreign Minister Aristide Briand to seek a treaty with the United States that would outlaw war. Fearful of a future German war of revenge, the French foreign minister hoped to transform Shotwell's suggestion into a mutual security treaty between his nation and the United States. Coolidge's secretary of state, Frank B. Kellogg, was unenthusiastic but could not turn a deaf ear to the groundswell of popular approval for a pact to prohibit war. Cleverly, he expanded Briand's proposal into a call for an international pledge for peace. Briand, in turn, could not reject Kellogg's overture, which also won widespread acclaim. Delegates from 62 nations met in Paris and in August 1928 renounced war "as an instrument of national policy."

The Kellogg-Briand Pact exempted wars of self-defense from its provisions and provided no means of enforcement against violations. In reality the accord represented little more than pious hopes, committing its signatories only to good faith. For this reason Senate isolationists had no difficulty in joining with internationalists to approve the treaty in January 1929 by a lopsided vote of 85–1. Peace advocates understood the shortcomings of the agreement but viewed the pact as a critical first step. So, apparently, did the Nobel Peace Prize committee, which tendered the award for 1929 to Secretary Kellogg.

War Debts, Reparations, and Investments The problems of war debts and reparations proved as difficult as those of disarmament and the quest for peace. World War I, as noted previously, had transformed the United States from a debtor to a creditor nation. European citizens owed their American counterparts $3 billion by the war's end, while European states, principally Great Britain and France, owed the United States government $10 billion. The Allies, arguing that the war had been a common cause and pointing out that they had sustained far greater casualties in the fighting, asked for a generous forgiveness of the debts. The United States refused. As an unmoved President Coolidge explained: "They hired the money, didn't they?"

Linked to the question of war debts were the reparations that the victorious Allies imposed upon vanquished Germany. The Allies called for a huge indemnity of $33 billion, which they then could use to pay their obligations to the United States (or "Uncle Shylock," as embittered debtors sneered). But economic dislocations, as well as internal resentment, led Germany to default on its payments. France and Belgium retaliated by occupying the heavily industrialized Ruhr Valley in 1923. Ruinous inflation resulted for much of the German middle class, while the default on reparations, coupled with the protectionist tariff policy of the United States, made any reduction of the war debts even more difficult. The Allies pleaded that they needed greater penetration of the American market if debt reduction were to be successful, but the United States was much more concerned with safeguarding and extending its domestic interests. Claimed one congressman, "to give up our home market, which is the best in the world, for the encouragement of foreign trade would be not only a poor but a perilous policy."

The Dawes Plan of 1924 attempted to achieve stability in the face of this impending financial chaos. Soon to be named Coolidge's vice-presidential running mate, Charles G. Dawes devised an arrangement by which Germany agreed to pay approximately $250 million yearly in reparations. At the same time it would receive a loan of $200 million from the United States to stabilize its currency. In 1929 the Young Plan, named for the American industrialist Owen D. Young, revised the Dawes Plan, which scaled back total German reparations to a more manageable $9 billion payable over a 59-year period at a $5\frac{1}{2}$ percent rate of interest.

Yet the success of the Dawes and Young plans was limited. Both had linked reparations and war debts more tightly than ever. American loans permitted Germany to pay indemnities to the Allies, who, in turn, could repay debts to the United States. When the Great Depression struck, this triangular arrangement began to unravel. American investments in Europe failed and the sources of investments dried up. Germany and the Allies, no longer able to meet their respective obligations, defaulted on reparations and war debts. President Hoover's announcement of a moratorium on the debts in 1931 only legitimized what already was taking place. Only Finland ultimately paid off its indebtedness. Between 1918 and 1931 the United States received a mere $2.6 billion in repaid war debts, a rather small sum in light of the larger reservoir of ill will it had generated.

War debts and reparations told only part of the story of American concerns with international economics during the New Era. Having emerged from the war as the sole victor in financial terms, the United States proceeded to reap further rewards during the 1920s. By the decade's end it was the leading exporter of goods, as well as the center of world finance. Exporting 15 percent of its total exports, Americans also produced 46 percent of the world's industrial products. Hardly an area of the globe escaped the effects of American commercial dominance.

Even the Soviet Union provided a field for American investments, although its government had not received official recognition from the United States. After the war the Bolsheviks reneged on more than $600 million in debts that they and the previous czarist government owed the United States and its citizens. Secretary of Commerce Herbert Hoover nevertheless organized a massive relief program for victims of the Russian civil war. The Bolsheviks, communist ideology notwithstanding, subsequently opened their borders to American capitalists. Major corporations like Du Pont and General Electric sold to the Soviets, as did Henry Ford, who contracted to help build automobiles and trucks and eventually lost more than $500,000. Americans in 1928 were responsible for nearly 25 percent of all foreign investments in the Soviet Union.

For all its obvious importance the tremendous expansion of American overseas trade during the 1920s must be kept in perspective. This trade represented somewhat less than 10 percent of the GNP for the decade, as businessmen concentrated on domestic markets. In part they gauged that greater profits were available at home. But some also feared the uncertainties of a postwar world economy. The economics of internationalism, for them, presented no open-ended opportunity.

Latin American Relations   American investments ballooned in Latin America between the Versailles Conference and the Great Depression. Investments there nearly trebled from a prewar 1914 figure of $1.2 billion to $3.5 billion in 1929. During that time Americans controlled more than a thousand businesses in the area, ranging from Chilean copper and nitrates to Cuban sugar and utilities, to the agricultural products and extensive lands held by the United Fruit Company in Central America. Investors and government officials argued that much of the wealth generated by American firms helped the economies of Latin American countries, which benefited from improved roads, health facilities, schools, and employment. This was true—but misleading. American businesses extracted more profits and resources than they invested. More of the benefits engendered, moreover, never reached the bulk of the destitute masses but further enriched wealthy landowners and businessmen, as well as military dictators and corrupt officials.

The American military presence in Latin America, initiated in the years following the Spanish-American War, also continued. As investments in the area increased, so did the need to protect them against revolution or expropriation. American troops safeguarded private commercial interests in Honduras and in Haiti. Elsewhere the United States counted on Latin American dictators and the military to preserve order. In the Dominican Republic, for example, the United States removed its troops in 1924 but left a native military government in control. From the tangle of Dominican politics emerged Rafael Leonidas Trujillo, who became his nation's president in 1930 and ruled with the aid of American backing until his assassination 31 years later. Nicaragua offered a parallel scenario. President Coolidge removed American troops from that country in 1925 after an occupation that dated back to 1912. Civil war the following year led him to redeploy military personnel, who remained until 1933. American-supported General Anastasio Somoza then crushed the anti-American rebellion led by Augusto Sandino. Somoza's ferocious and corrupt rule lasted until 1979, when anti-American revolutionaries toppled him and his powerful family.

The United States, despite occasional military intervention, increasingly looked to settle its Latin American disputes amicably. Trouble with Mexico severely tested this resolve. The Mexican Constitution of 1917 declared that Mexico owned all rights to its natural resources. This jeopardized hundreds of millions of dollars of American investments, particularly in oil. The declaration remained ineffective until 1926, when Mexican president Plutarco Elías Calles moved to expropriate American interests. He further angered many Americans by persecuting the Roman Catholic Church in his country.

Secretary of State Kellogg, soon to be noted for his peace efforts, charged that communists were at work and hinted at military intervention. In early 1927, however, the Senate unanimously voted for arbitration. President Coolidge then named Dwight W. Morrow, his former college classmate, as ambassador to Mexico. Despite close ties with the Morgan financial interests, the affable, urbane Morrow had denounced dollar diplomacy and was now determined to settle the Mexican situation peacefully. Using tact and goodwill, Morrow obtained compromise agreements that were favorable to American business interests and that promised an end to attacks on the Catholic Church. Morrow's handiwork remained intact until 1938, when another Mexican president confiscated all foreign oil holdings.

Other attempts to improve Latin American relations followed the Morrow mission. Late in 1928 Under Secretary of State J. Reuben Clark prepared a memorandum that repudiated the Roosevelt Corollary to the Monroe Doctrine. The Clark Memorandum, published in 1930, reaffirmed the meaning of the original document by stressing its intent to prevent intervention by non-Western Hemispheric powers rather than to provide an excuse for such intervention by the United States.

Herbert Hoover translated the conciliatory language of the Clark Memorandum into action. Genuinely interested in Latin America—unlike most of his presidential predecessors—he toured the area in the months between his election and inauguration. As president, he supported treaties of arbitration and conciliation between the United States and its southern neighbors, and agreed in principle to nonintervention in their domestic and foreign affairs. In 1931 he refrained from military action when several countries defaulted on their debts. The following year he sponsored a new treaty with Haiti, leading to the removal of American troops two years later. In words and in deed, Hoover had adopted a ''Good Neighbor Policy'' (a phrase he coined) that he hoped would roll back the swelling tide of anti-Yankeeism.

Trouble in the Far East   Successful in Latin America, Hoover's diplomatic efforts proved futile in the Far East, where Japan and China clashed over Manchuria. Nominally under Chinese control, Manchuria had actually been under Japanese domination since the Russo-Japanese War of 1904–1905. By the late 1920s it furnished Japan with badly needed raw materials and an outlet for more than 50 percent of its foreign investments. Strategically, it offered a buffer against the Soviet Union, whose ideology and power Japan deemed a threat. At this time Nationalist Chinese leader Chiang Kai-shek was endeavoring to unite a country torn by civil war, corruption, and chaos. In the process he encouraged a boycott of Japanese goods and challenged Japanese hegemony in Manchuria. On September 18, 1931, the Japanese army in Manchuria captured some Chinese troops after an alleged act of sabotage. Fearful of its military, which had recently assassinated a prime minister, the Japanese government then permitted a full-scale invasion of Manchuria that culminated in victory by early 1932.

Japan's actions constituted a clear violation of the Nine-Power Treaty, the Kellogg-Briand Pact, and the Covenant of the League of Nations. Neither the League nor any individual nation was willing to use force to repel the Japanese incursion. Hoover's secretary of state, Henry L. Stimson, knew that American military intervention was out of the question but suggested economic sanctions since Japan needed American oil and exported 40 percent of its goods to the United States. Hoover, fearing war, squelched the proposal and opted for moral persuasion instead. Through the Hoover-Stimson Doctrine (usually referred to as only the Stimson Doctrine) of January 7, 1932, the United States refused to recognize any impairment of either American rights under the Open Door policy or China's territorial integrity. Undaunted, Japan responded to a Chinese boycott of their goods by a savage bombing of Shanghai. Later that year Japan reorganized Manchuria into the puppet state of Manchukuo. The League of Nations adopted the Stimson Doctrine but also recognized the legitimacy of Japan's interests in Manchuria and made no attempt to repel its encroachments. In early 1933 Japan announced that it was withdrawing from the League. Mired in the throes of the depression, few Americans really cared.

THE GREAT DEPRESSION AND FOREIGN POLICY

The Great Depression transformed the international order during the 1930s, shaking and sometimes undermining political institutions and social foundations. Hard times, for example, had been instrumental in allowing Japan's militarists to increase their power at the expense of their nation's fragile democratic government. Germany's postwar Weimar Republic, the only truly democratic government that nation had enjoyed since its unification in 1871, also fell victim to debilitating economic conditions that permitted Adolf Hitler and his National Socialist party, or Nazis, to come to power in 1933. Austrian-born Hitler, who had served in the German army during World War I, pledged to restore prosperity as well as to resuscitate Germany as a world power. Contemptuous of democratic methods, he also promised to wage war against communists and Jews, who, he claimed, had polluted the purity of the Aryan race. In 1936 he joined with Benito Mussolini, Fascist leader of Italy since 1922, to form the Rome-Berlin Axis. Like Hitler, Mussolini despised both communists and democrats but was considerably less anti-Semitic.

Adolf Hitler and Benito Mussolini

Other European countries also experienced growing threats from left- and right-wing extremists during these years, due likewise to the demoralizing and destabilizing effects of the depression. The depression did not destroy democratic government in the United States, but it did effect a retreat from the more international mood of the prosperous 1920s. Economic nationalism became the new order of the day.

Even Franklin D. Roosevelt, originally a Wilsonian internationalist, espoused economic nationalism soon after becoming president. More than 60 nations, including the United States, sent delegates to the London Economic Conference, which met in the summer of 1933. The primary purpose of the meeting was to seek a stable currency as a means of reviving world trade. Roosevelt, who had initially welcomed the conference, destroyed it by announcing that the United States would not adhere to the gold standard. The president realized that American products could compete more favorably in international trade if gold were devalued abroad. The next year he underscored his conversion to economic nationalism by signing the Johnson Debt Default Act that prohibited loans to any nation that was behind on its war debts.

The search for economic recovery also colored foreign relations with the Soviet Union. During the 1920s the United States was the sole major Western nation that refused to recognize the new Bolshevik regime, although informal ties and trade existed between the two countries. Most of that trade evaporated during the depression. Roosevelt was eager to increase American exports and to improve relations with a nation that might serve as a deterrent to Japanese aggression in the Far East. In late 1933 he and Maxim Litvinov, the Soviet foreign minister, concluded an agreement that granted the Soviet Union diplomatic recognition. The Soviets, in turn, promised to cease their propaganda activities in the United States and to negotiate their debts.

The results of this diplomatic accord proved disappointing. American bankers were reluctant to grant new loans to a government built on an ideology that promised an end to capitalism. This virtually insured that the Soviets would not accept large amounts of American goods or prove amenable to paying back their debts. The brutal Soviet purge trials of the mid-1930s further convinced many Americans that diplomatic recognition had been of dubious value, if not a mistake altogether.

Secretary of State Cordell Hull vigorously pursued American interests in other foreign markets, but not through economic nationalism. A committed internationalist, this Tennessean firmly believed that reciprocal trade agreements would aid the United States economically and at the same time further the cause of world peace. At his urging, Congress in 1934 passed the Regional Trade Agreements Act. This measure permitted the president to lower duties by as much as 50 percent on the goods of those nations that did the same for American products. A most-favored-nation clause also meant that the signatories would not levy lower tariffs on the goods of any other countries. By the end of the decade the United States had negotiated reciprocity pacts with 21 nations, among them, Canada, the Soviet Union, and a number of Latin American states. American exports to its southern neighbors alone increased in value from $244 million in 1933 to $642 million in 1938, in part due to reciprocity and in part due to loans obtained by Latin American countries through the Export-Import Bank, which was established in 1934 to advance overseas trade.

Yet the United States achieved more than trade benefits from Latin America during the 1930s. More goodwill and less animosity flowed northward as Roosevelt continued the Good Neighbor Policy initiated by his predecessor. The United States officially repudiated the Roosevelt Corollary to the Monroe Doctrine at the Montevideo Inter-American Conference of 1933. There, Secretary Hull agreed to the stipulation that ''no state has the right to intervene in the internal or external affairs of another.'' Roosevelt showed his commitment to this pledge the following year by withdrawing troops from Haiti and by refusing to send them to Cuba, which was in the throes of revolution. He displayed even greater restraint by refusing to intervene militarily in Mexico, which from 1934 onward was seizing American-owned oil and real estate. Meanwhile various hemispheric conferences resulted in further agreements calling for restraint and consultation. The success of the Good Neighbor Policy became evident during World War II. Soon after the United States entered the conflict, Latin American nations either declared war on, or broke diplomatic relations with, the Axis powers. The two exceptions were Argentina and Chile, which severed ties only toward the war's end.

Isolationism and Neutrality Legislation Isolationism in nonhemispheric matters characterized American foreign policy during much of the 1930s. By then a growing number of Americans—nearly two out of every three, according to a Gallup poll of 1937—had concluded that participation in World War I had been a mistake, as evidenced by the

THE GREAT DEPRESSION AND FOREIGN POLICY

punitive peace treaty and defeat of Wilsonian idealism, as well as by the reluctance or inability of the Allies to make good on their war debts. Businessmen indirectly helped to strengthen this isolationism. Republican Senator Gerald P. Nye of North Dakota chaired a committee that from 1934 to 1936 conducted investigations of the arms trade over the previous 20 years. Their findings disclosed that these "merchants of death," together with foreign arms dealers, had formed a "blood brotherhood" and had amassed gargantuan profits. Nye charged that American arms dealers, along with bankers who had tendered massive loans to the Allies, had been responsible for the nation's entry into the war. He and his committee had no incontrovertible proof for this allegation, but many Americans believed the accusation. Other sources also helped convince citizens that they had been duped into entering the war. Journalist Walter Millis's best-selling *Road to War: America, 1914–1917* (1935), for instance, forcefully suggested that economic factors, propaganda, and the pro-Allied biases of leading figures had been responsible for involvement.

Isolationism appealed to Americans for other reasons as well. Domestic reformers, mindful of World War I experiences, feared that foreign embroilment might weaken New Deal reform efforts and undermine civil liberties. Extremist groups and their sympathizers, for one reason or another, also embraced isolationism for much of the decade. So did pacifists, whose dedication to peace transcended other considerations. Pulitzer Prize dramatist Robert E. Sherwood skillfully portrayed the dilemmas of peace-minded citizens living in a troubled world in *Idiot's Delight* (1936) and *Abe Lincoln in Illinois* (1938).

The American commitment to isolation grew as international order diminished. During the 1930s both Hitler and Mussolini remorselessly undermined the postwar settlement. In 1935 the Nazi dictator announced that Germany would no longer abide by the disarmament limits imposed by the Versailles Treaty. That same year the Italian dictator sent troops into Ethiopia, which lost its independence after barbarous warfare on both sides. The League of Nations condemned Italian actions, and Italy promptly resigned from the League. Great Britain and France, fearful of a German-Italian alliance, refused to act. The following year Germany again violated the Versailles Treaty, this time by sending troops into the demilitarized Rhineland. Once more Great Britain and France did nothing.

The year 1936 also witnessed the outbreak of the Spanish Civil War, a bloody, protracted conflict between Loyalists who supported the republican government and rebels who opposed it. Before the war ended in 1939 with a victory for the rebels, Europe's totalitarian states intervened. The Soviet Union gave assistance to the Loyalists. Germany and Italy sent arms and men to the republic's opponents, whose leaders included Fascist-leaning General Francisco Franco and whose supporters numbered large segments of the military and the Catholic Church, as well as wealthy landowners and businessmen. Meanwhile Hitler and Mussolini concluded their Rome-Berlin Axis of 1936, turning Anglo-French fears to reality. The following year Germany and Japan signed the Anti-Comintern Pact that was openly directed against international communism and covertly aimed at the Soviet Union.

In the face of these threats to world peace most Americans sought noninvolvement. Because war eventually did come, later generations would blame them for short-sightedness. Yet at the time they believed that Europe's problems were not their own and that the United States could successfully avoid entanglement. Recollecting the experiences of World War I, they strongly supported the efforts of Congress to legislate neutrality.

The Ethiopian crisis led to the Neutrality Act of 1935. President Roosevelt wanted discretionary powers to invoke an arms embargo against one or more of the belligerents in any conflict, but Congress enacted a measure that made such an embargo mandatory on all belligerents once the president had officially announced that a state of war existed. The act also forbade American ships from conveying munitions to the belligerents and gave the president the power to prohibit American citizens from traveling on belligerent ships. The law, which was to expire after six months, failed to prohibit the export of goods such as steel and oil that were critical for waging war. This failure unwittingly favored the more industrialized Italians over their Ethiopian foes. Hoping for voluntary cooperation, Secretary of State Hull unsuccessfully encouraged American businessmen to refrain from trading these goods with Italy.

The Neutrality Act of 1936 strengthened the position of the isolationists by extending the provisions of the earlier neutrality measure and by expressly forbidding loans to belligerents. Congress was determined that neither munitions makers not financiers should embroil the nation in a foreign conflict to protect their profits. Meanwhile President Roosevelt seemed a convert to the isolationist cause. Declaring ''I hate war,'' he told Americans that ''we shun political commitments that might entangle us in foreign wars. . . .''

The Spanish Civil War tested Roosevelt's words. The applicability of existing neutrality legislation was in doubt since the fighting represented a civil war rather than a traditional one. A number of Loyalist sympathizers, including the isolationist Senator Nye, called for aid to the Spanish government. Yet Roosevelt, aware of Catholic dislike for the anticlerical Spanish republicans, convinced Congress to enlarge the scope of the neutrality laws to cover the Spanish fighting. Then on May 1, 1937, Congress enacted the third Neutrality Act. This law extended the embargo on arms and loans to belligerents and made mandatory the prohibition against traveling on the ships of belligerents. Finally, it added a ''cash-and-carry'' provision on nonmilitary goods that was to last for two years. Congress, again mindful of the origins of the nation's involvement in World War I, was resolved to keep American ships from entering war zones.

More Trouble with Japan   Relations between the United States and Japan had improved after the Manchurian crisis of the early 1930s, but in July 1937 fighting erupted between Japan and China after a skirmish near the Marco Polo Bridge in Peking. Within a month, superior Japanese forces captured Peking and were attacking Shanghai. This time Roosevelt refused to invoke neutrality legislation, thus permitting a small amount of supplies to continue to reach China. Outraged like many other Americans, the president publicly condemned Japanese aggression and in October called for a ''quarantine'' against those responsible for an ''epidemic of world lawlessness.'' By ''quarantine'' he probably had in mind an economic boycott. His strong words, however, aroused isolationist fears that he might take military action. Faced with unfavorable reactions—some called for his impeachment—Roosevelt muted his opposition to Japan. In November he did send representatives to an international conference to discuss the situation, but the meeting achieved nothing.

The *Panay* just before sinking.

War scares mounted in December when Japanese pilots deliberately attacked the *Panay,* an American gunboat that was escorting three Standard Oil Company tankers on the Yangtze River. The *Panay* sank, with a loss of 2 crewmen and 30 wounded. The Japanese government quickly apologized and offered an indemnity as well as assurances that similar incidents would not recur. On Christmas Day Secretary Hull accepted Japan's response: He understood the nation's mood.

Isolationism reached new heights in January 1938 when Republican Representative Louis Ludlow of Indiana introduced a constitutional amendment stating that Congress could declare war only if the United States or its possessions were attacked. Otherwise, a declaration of war would be valid only if upheld by a national referendum. Ludlow had first introduced his resolution in 1935. A survey two years later found 73 percent of those polled in favor of such an amendment. By 1938 Roosevelt was unable to keep the resolution from reaching the House floor, where it was narrowly defeated by a margin of 209–188.

Europe Goes to War As the Ludlow Resolution reached the House floor, the situation in Europe grew more ominous. German troops occupied Austria in March and Hitler announced a union or *Anschluss*. In September he demanded the Sudetenland, the western portion of Czechoslovakia in which many ethnic Germans lived. The Czechs were determined to defend their country. In late September British Prime Minister Neville Chamberlain and French Premier Edouard Daladier traveled to Munich to confer with Hitler and Mussolini. Unprepared to fight and encouraged to seek a settlement by Roosevelt among others, Great Britain and France yielded to Hitler's demands for Czechoslovakia. The Führer promised that this was his "last territorial claim . . . in Europe," while Chamberlain explained that the accord had brought "peace in our time." Without the assistance of the British and French the Czechs were forced to cede the Sudetenland. Six months later, in March 1939, German forces occupied the remainder of their truncated country.

Unfairly or not, "Munich" has become a synonym for shameful appeasement. For Hitler had no intention of stopping with Czechoslovakia. In the spring of 1939 he demanded the return of the former German possessions of the free city of Danzig and the Polish Corridor that the Versailles Treaty had granted the recreated nation of Poland after World War I. Great Britain and France, harboring no further illusions about Hitler, promised to aid Poland if attacked and pushed ahead to strengthen their own armed forces. They also sought to thwart German expansion by reaching an understanding with Germany's sworn enemy in the East, the Soviet Union. But in a shocking diplomatic turnabout, the Soviet Union and Germany signed a nonaggression pact in August 1939. Germany no longer had to worry about a two-front war. Using a trumped-up border incident as an excuse, it invaded Poland two weeks later, on September 1, 1939. Great Britain and France then declared war on Germany, and the greatest war in human history began.

Neutrality in Jeopardy Two years and three months elapsed between the invasion of Poland and the United States' entry into World War II. Americans were overwhelmingly hostile to Nazi aggression in Europe and the continuing Japanese invasion of China. A public opinion poll in October 1939 revealed that 84 percent of the respondents wanted the Allies to win, 2 percent favored Germany, and 14 percent had no opinion. The following month Congress enacted a new Neutrality Act to replace the act of 1937, now expired. This measure lifted the embargo on munitions, permitting their sale on a "cash-and-carry" basis. This aided the Allies alone, since they controlled the Atlantic Ocean. Yet it would require an attack on Pearl Harbor to propel the United States into war. To the very end, Americans hoped to avoid open conflict, abandoning their peaceful stance only after events gave them no other choice.

The long and tortuous road to war provoked numerous criticisms at the time and continues to intrigue historians today. Internationalists have faulted President Roosevelt for not acting earlier and more vigorously against Germany and Japan. Isolationists, on the other hand, have denounced Roosevelt as a warmonger from start to finish. Most recent historians have taken a more balanced view. Roosevelt, they admit, sympathized with Great Britain and France from the beginning; yet he sincerely wished to avoid war. When it became clear that the western European democracies could not withstand the Nazi onslaught, he launched a gradually escalating campaign to assist them. A strong public desire for peace and lack of military preparedness kept him from moving more rapidly. So, too, did a powerful isolationist bloc in Congress, which at least until the fall of France in the late spring of 1940 offered some plausible and persuasive arguments against involvement. Then, with Hitler having secured dominion over the European continent in the west and with threats to American interests in the Western Hemisphere becoming more ominous, their cause became less tenable. But whatever the controversies

THE GREAT DEPRESSION AND FOREIGN POLICY

surrounding American entry into World War II, the nation's steady movement toward belligerency is quite clear in retrospect.

From September of 1939 until the spring of 1940 the United States pursued a policy of watchful waiting. The Nazi blitzkrieg in Poland both horrified and awed the American public, while Stalin's simultaneous invasion of eastern Poland elicited widespread outrage. A Russian attack on Finland that winter and subsequent reannexation of Latvia, Lithuania, and Estonia made Stalin look little better than Hitler in American eyes. Yet Roosevelt and the State Department were careful not to denounce the Soviet Union, believing that Hitler and Stalin would soon come to blows. In that case the Russians might become valuable allies in the fight against fascism.

Meanwhile Secretary of State Hull turned his attention to Latin America, hoping to create greater solidarity in case of war. At a meeting of foreign ministers in Panama, the United States joined the other American republics to declare a security zone around the entire Western Hemisphere south of Canada. This would later permit the U.S. Navy to patrol large areas of the western Atlantic.

On other fronts American diplomacy entered a relative lull that stemmed from the surprising dearth of military action after the fall of Poland. The West expected Germany to repeat the tactics of 1914 and launch an immediate attack on France. But nothing happened. This "phony war" lasted until April 1940 when the Nazis invaded Denmark and Norway. On May 10 they swept into Belgium and broke through French lines near Sedan on the 14th. They then began a push toward the English Channel, trapping over 300,000 British troops on the beaches at Dunkirk. Under Winston Churchill, who had replaced the discredited Neville Chamberlain, Great Britain rescued most of its soldiers but lost much matériel in one of the most dramatic exploits of the war. Thousands of small vessels, including fishing boats and pleasure craft, braved heavy German fire to ferry British troops home.

The "miracle" at Dunkirk did nothing to save France. Paris fell on June 14, the French government sued for peace, and the Germans occupied approximately three-fifths of the country. To the south and west a considerable portion of France remained nominally free under the puppet regime of Marshal Henri Philippe Pétain, a hero of World War I. In one of the more painful decisions of his presidency, Roosevelt decided to recognize this controversial government with its capital at Vichy. A diplomatic presence in France permitted the United States to gather valuable information on German activities. Later, relations with Vichy France would save many American lives during the invasion of North Africa.

Britain now braced itself for a German invasion. But lacking sufficient landing craft as well as air supremacy over the Channel, Hitler began an assault on the Royal Air Force and its bases in the south of England. When this failed, the Germans began to bomb London and other urban centers, aiming to cripple British industry and terrorize the civilian population. Churchill vowed that the British people would never surrender.

Renewed German attacks in the spring of 1940 reawakened Americans to the Nazi threat and provoked considerable sympathy for Britain and France. Passionate debates over how the nation should respond also erupted. Isolationists were more determined than ever to keep the United States out of the conflict, while internationalists demanded increased aid for embattled Britain. The arguments eventually focused around two rival organizations. The first of these was founded by William Allen White, famous editor of the *Emporia Gazette*. His Committee to Defend America by Aiding the Allies was an immediate success. Between mid-May and early July of 1940 the Committee enlisted over 300 local chapters. Well-known supporters ranged from financier J. P. Morgan, Jr., to David Dubinsky, president of the International Ladies Garment Workers. The committee and its members insisted that the country's best defense lay in massive financial and material aid to Britain and its allies.

In early September a rival group appeared. Called the America First Committee, its chief organizer was Robert E. Wood, board chairman of Sears Roebuck. Drawing its greatest support from isolationist Republicans and midwesterners, its most effective spokesman was the legendary Charles A. Lindbergh. This powerful group believed that intervention in the European conflict would be highly detrimental to American interests.

President Roosevelt, ever mindful of public opinion, tried to walk a tightrope between these conflicting camps. By the late summer of 1940 he thought it was safe to ask Congress to give Britain 50 overage destroyers in exchange for 99-year leases on eight bases ranging from Newfoundland to Bermuda to the West Indies. Isolationists raged that the "destroyer deal" was a flagrant violation of neutrality and a dangerous step toward war. Yet the public supported the exchange, with opinion polls indicating 70 percent approval.

Congress also was taking more decisive steps in the direction of combating aggression and possible internal subversion. After the fall of France it agreed to Roosevelt's request for increased military appropriations. In June it passed the Smith Act, which required aliens to be fingerprinted and made it a crime to teach the violent overthrow of the government. Three months later it enacted the first peacetime draft in the nation's history in order to train two million troops for the army.

The summer of 1940 also brought a tougher line with Japan. The impressive German victories that spring electrified the Japanese, and they were determined to take advantage of the British, French, and Dutch possessions in Asia and the Pacific. In June they forced Vichy France to stop supplying the Chinese by railroad from Indochina. They also pressured the British into closing the Burma Road, the only other land route into China. Several of Roosevelt's advisors urged him to retaliate by stopping shipments of crucial oil and scrap iron to Japan. The abrogation of a 1911 trade treaty with Japan, effective the preceding January, would have made this decision entirely legal. But Secretary Hull and others feared that such drastic action would force the Japanese to attack the oil-rich Dutch East Indies, and they urged Roosevelt to refrain for the time being. By September, however, the president had imposed an embargo on all steel and scrap iron.

The trade sanctions did nothing to stop the Japanese. In August they demanded and secured air bases in southern Indochina. And on September 27 they signed an alliance with Germany and Italy. This Tripartite Pact aimed to neutralize the United States by threatening the country with a two-front war. If the United States attacked any of the three powers, it would have to fight in Europe, Asia, and the Pacific.

The Election of 1940   In strong competition with the war news that summer and autumn was the upcoming presidential election. The big question was whether Franklin Roosevelt would seek a third term. There was no Constitutional impediment, but George Wash-

THE GREAT DEPRESSION AND FOREIGN POLICY

ington had established an increasingly hallowed precedent when he refused to run for a third time.

Roosevelt had already shattered precedents. War in Europe, growing trouble in the Far East, and personal ambition now led him to conclude that the country needed him in the White House for another four years. He also feared a Republican victory unless his name headed the ticket. Such a victory might undermine the New Deal. Nevertheless, he had to proceed cautiously. Republicans as well as conservative Democrats had already labeled him a dictator; a bold leap into the political fray would only confirm their suspicions. The president had to make it look as if his party and the nation had drafted him for a third try.

Roosevelt engineered a draft by encouraging several other Democrats to seek the nomination. None of them enjoyed a commanding lead by convention time. Roosevelt still denied that he wanted the nomination, insisting that he was looking forward to a long retirement on his Hyde Park estate. When a statement to this effect was read at the convention, delegates broke into a ''spontaneous'' demonstration for the president. They nominated him on the first ballot by an overwhelming vote. At Roosevelt's bidding, and over the protests of party conservatives, Secretary of Agriculture Henry A. Wallace received the vice-presidential nod.

Leading contenders for the Republican nomination that year were Senator Robert A. Taft of Ohio, Senator Arthur Vandenberg of Michigan, and New York State District Attorney Thomas E. Dewey. But a dark horse named Wendell Willkie stole the nomination after a wild demonstration from supporters who had packed the galleries.

Born and reared in a small town in southern Indiana, Willkie had risen from humble origins to the presidency of the Commonwealth and Southern Corporation, a giant utility holding company. Throughout the New Deal years he had attacked the Tennessee Valley Authority in particular and government regulation of business in general. Yet he accepted much of the New Deal, including Social Security, the National Labor Relations Act, and other benefits to American workers. Unlike the other Republican contenders for the presidential nomination, he was an internationalist in foreign policy, urging preparedness for the United States and aid for Great Britain. All in all, Willkie represented the liberal-to-moderate wing of the Republican party. Like Landon in 1936, he attacked the excesses and inefficiencies of the New Deal, and claimed that his party could administer the programs better. Conservative Republicans dubbed him a ''me-tooer.''

Since Willkie agreed with Roosevelt on so many issues it was hard for him to denounce the president. In the end he leveled three charges against him: Roosevelt was trying to become a dictator; the administration had failed to end unemployment; the country was not rearming quickly enough. The incumbent refused to answer any of these charges. At the same time events blunted Willkie's criticisms. Unemployment began to decline as defense industries and steel plants raced to meet military orders. The unpreparedness issue also rang hollow when Roosevelt signed the Selective Service Act. Charges of dictatorship appealed to the president's enemies, but they did nothing to deter his supporters. As the possibility of war increased, many Americans instinctively rallied around the president.

Toward the end of the campaign, a desperate Willkie began to claim that Roosevelt was a warmonger—one area where the president was vulnerable. Although Americans wanted a strong defense, they still opposed war overwhelmingly. Roosevelt was reluctant

Cartoon depicting Wendell Willkie capturing the 1940 Republican presidential nomination to the disappointment of rivals Thomas E. Dewey, Robert A. Taft, and Arthur H. Vandenberg.

to respond, but political advisors insisted. In Boston, on October 31, he tried to assure mothers and fathers of his peaceful intentions: "I have said it before, but I shall say it again and again and again: Your boys are not going to be sent into any foreign wars." Events soon would damage Roosevelt's reputation for honesty.

But on election day Roosevelt won an impressive victory, rolling up a popular vote of 27,243,466 to Willkie's 22,304,755. The electoral vote count was 449–82. Willkie carried Maine, Vermont, Indiana, and six sparsely populated western states. Nonetheless, Roosevelt's margin was smaller than in 1936, with many middle-class voters returning to the Republican fold as the depression finally began to fade. Roosevelt did best among lower-income groups who had benefited most from the New Deal.

From Isolation to Involvement The president saw the election as a mandate for his foreign policy and growing desire to help Great Britain. Prime Minister Churchill had already warned that Britain would soon run out of dollars for purchasing supplies, and with the election over, Roosevelt was determined to help. The neutrality laws, which forbade loans to belligerents, posed a formidable barrier, but in a press conference on

December 16 the president revealed an ingenious plan. If a neighbor's house were on fire, he explained, others would gladly lend their garden hose to help put it out. They would not quibble over terms but would simply ask the neighbor to return the hose after the fire.

In this way the lend-lease program was born. Roosevelt asked Congress for authority to "lease, lend or otherwise dispose of" any items not vital to the nation's defense. The defeated Willkie and other internationalist Republicans warmly supported the bill, which initially authorized an appropriation of $7 billion and which passed both houses by a wide margin. The president signed the Lend-Lease Act on March 11, 1941.

The isolationists charged that lend-lease was merely another step in the president's plot to drag the United States into war. And on one level, the isolationists were right. The program was clearly an unneutral act by the United States, and it would lead to even more belligerent positions within several months. Complained isolationist Senator Burton K. Wheeler of Montana, the measure was "the New Deal's triple A foreign policy; it will plow under every fourth American boy."

As the isolationists suspected, Britain would not remain satisfied for long. Lend-lease supplies began streaming out of American ports in the spring of 1941, but German submarines sank an appalling number of British ships and their lend-lease supplies. Churchill, not having enough destroyers to protect them, appealed for American assistance. The Committee to Defend America and several of Roosevelt's cabinet officials urged American naval convoys. Fearing the wrath of the isolationists, the president hedged. Instead, on April 17 he pushed the hemispheric safety zone into the middle of the Atlantic Ocean. American vessels were to locate German submarines and radio their positions to British destroyers. Meanwhile the United States, at the request of the Danish government in exile, extended a protectorate over Greenland in order to preclude German occupation. As the "battle of the Atlantic" continued into the spring, Roosevelt proclaimed an "unlimited national emergency." The emergency grew more real when a German submarine sank the *Robin Moor,* an American merchant ship, on May 21.

The summer of 1941 opened with a stunning German attack on Russia. Armored units knifed through the open plains of western Russia, frequently encountering little or no resistance. Many Americans viewed the invasion as poetic justice for a country that had so recently perpetrated aggressions of its own. Some hoped that the Nazis and the Communists would simply obliterate each other. The junior senator from Missouri, Harry S Truman, reflected these sentiments. "If we see that Germany is winning," he advised, "we should help Russia. . . . If Russia is winning we ought to help Germany and that way let them kill as many as possible, although I don't want to see Hitler victorious under any circumstances." Nor was Roosevelt fond of the Soviets and their political system. Yet he believed that Germany was the greater threat to the United States, and he soon authorized lend-lease aid to the Soviet Union.

Also, 1941 saw the first strategy sessions between American and British staff officers. They met in Washington from late January through the end of March and worked out plans for possible military operations. They also proposed to concentrate on beating Germany first in case the United States went to war in both Europe and Asia.

In August the president himself met with Prime Minister Churchill off the coast of Newfoundland. They discussed the need for American convoys in the North Atlantic and agreed to coordinate their responses to an expected Japanese attack in Southeast Asia.

Historians Debate

PEARL HARBOR

Bitter controversy has surrounded the tragic events of December 7, 1941. Even as the nation united to wage the ensuing war, some questioned whether American actions had made hostilities inevitable. Related doubts also arose as to whether the Roosevelt administration knew beforehand of the Japanese attack and, if so, whether it took all possible measures to warn military authorities on the scene.

In the years since World War II revisionist historians have affixed much blame to Roosevelt and his subordinates for the disaster at Pearl Harbor. Charles C. Tansill, for one, in his *Back Door to War* (1952) accused Roosevelt of gross duplicity. Unable to persuade Congress to declare war against Germany, the president pursued an intransigent policy against Japan. By freezing their assets and by denying them oil and scrap iron, he ultimately insured that the Japanese would have to render the United States impotent in the Pacific in order to achieve their goal of expansion. The subsequent conflict with Japan, reasoned Tansill, allowed Roosevelt to enter the fray against Japan's chief Axis ally in Europe.

Some revisionists have also charged the Roosevelt administration with having failed, perhaps willfully so, to defend Pearl Harbor properly. Having broken its secret code, the United States knew that Japan would attack somewhere on December 7. John Toland claims in the most recent major revisionist study, *Infamy: Pearl Harbor and Its Aftermath* (1982), that signals intercepted several days before the assault provided knowledge that the Japanese fleet was bound for Pearl

Harbor. Why, then, were American forces not better prepared? The fact that Chief of Staff George A. Marshall used less reliable commercial rather than government communications to alert military commanders at Pearl Harbor and that he was away from his office for a few crucial hours on the day of the attack further stoked revisionist charges of the government's dereliction of duty—if not worse.

Other historians have rejected, totally or in part, the claims of revisionists. Roosevelt's determined opposition to Japanese expansion, they argue, was both principled and preferable to dubious efforts at compromise or appeasement. Further, it was important for moral and psychological reasons that Japan rather than the United States should initiate hostilities. In *Pearl Harbor: Warning and Decision* (1962), Roberta Wohlstetter strengthened the antirevisionist position by noting that intelligence experts simply misconstrued the voluminous Japanese messages that they received and decoded. Gordon W. Prange's *At Dawn We Slept* (1981), the most detailed study of the events at Pearl Harbor to date, also concluded that the government had been guilty of serious errors but not purposeful malfeasance.

The historical debate over Pearl Harbor has not ended. Thus far historians generally have rejected the most extreme revisionist contentions as lacking incontrovertible proof. But many do concur that grave miscalculations and lapses in judgment took place. Yet as Hans L. Trefousse has noted in *Pearl Harbor: The Continuing Controversy* (1982): "The greatest error of all . . . was committed in Tokyo. It was the decision to challenge the might of the United States."

Most importantly, they worked out a statement of principles, popularly known as the Atlantic Charter, which condemned aggression, endorsed national self-determination, and reiterated the belief in self-government and freedom of speech. The leaders made no formal commitments with regard to questions of trade and a postwar settlement, but their talks represented a new plateau in Anglo-American understanding.

Within three months of the Newfoundland conference the United States and Germany were virtually at war. In early September the U.S. Navy invited British cargo ships to join American convoys. Despite these provocations, Hitler ordered his submarine commanders not to fire at the Americans, whom he did not wish to fight unless he absolutely had to. In October, however, two American ships were attacked. The *Kearney* lost 11 men, sustained heavy damage, and barely limped back to Iceland. The *Reuben James* went down with a loss of 115 American lives after being torpedoed. The president ordered all merchant ships armed, and it looked as though German submarine warfare would once again produce war.

The Road to Pearl Harbor   Relations with Japan had also deteriorated over the past year and a half. At the end of 1940 the United States increased its aid to China and extended its embargo against Japan to include iron ore, pig iron, and finished steel products. In January 1941 copper and brass joined the prohibited list. But the administration continued to permit petroleum sales, fearing that any further curtailment would compel the Japanese to invade the Dutch East Indies. Still, Japanese industry was beginning to experience raw material shortages by the spring of 1941.

Japan responded to these mounting embargoes by sending Kichisaburo Nomura as its new ambassador to the United States. Nomura had long admired the American people, and he eagerly entered into informal discussions with Secretary Hull. The Japanese wanted the United States to rescind its trade embargoes, give Japan a free hand in China, and use its influence to make Chiang Kai-shek accept Japanese demands. Hull rejected all three proposals, and the talks eventually broke down. At the same time the Japanese cabinet decided to move against Indochina and the Dutch East Indies, laying the foundation for a ''Greater East Asia Co-Prosperity Sphere.'' Both the name and the idea were wholly propagandistic: Japan would enjoy greater prosperity at the expense of its Asian neighbors.

In late July, Washington learned that Japan had demanded air bases in southern Indochina. Roosevelt froze all Japanese monetary assets in the United States, and on September 5 the State Department stopped all oil shipments to Japan. Knowing that they must strike before their oil supplies ran out, the Japanese government decided to attack on a wide front. General Hideke Tojo, a militant expansionist, became prime minister.

Although there was virtually no movement on the diplomatic front during the late summer and early autumn of 1941, the Japanese continued their charade in Washington. In mid-November they sent Saburo Kurusu to the United States as a special envoy to assist Nomura with negotiations. By this time the United States had deciphered the Japanese diplomatic code and knew that they planned attacks in Southeast Asia and the South Pacific. The State Department also knew exactly what the Japanese diplomats were going to propose. On November 20 they submitted their final terms: Japan again asked for a free hand in China and a full restoration of trade with the United States, including stated amounts of oil. In return they would withdraw their troops from Indochina and make no further advances to the south or east. Roosevelt was interested in some kind of stopgap, if only to buy time for military preparations, but Chiang Kai-shek utterly refused to compromise. On November 26 the United States responded to the latest Japanese proposals by reiterating demands for withdrawal from China and Indochina. In return the United States would give Japan greater trade and financial assistance.

There was no chance that Japan would accept this offer. The State Department also knew from a decoded message that Tokyo had imposed a November 29 deadline. If there were not some favorable agreement with the United States, the dispatch read, "things are automatically going to happen." In fact, a Japanese armada left the Kurile Islands on November 25 and headed for Hawaii. Most American officials guessed that the attack would come against the Philippines or British Malaya. But on December 7, at about 8:00 A.M. Honolulu time, Japanese planes swooped down on the U.S. Pacific fleet, peacefully anchored at Pearl Harbor. Four battleships went down and three suffered serious damage. At nearby Hickham Field the Japanese bombed and strafed American aircraft that were lined up in tidy rows. Only a few managed to take off. About 2,200 Americans lost their lives and over 1,000 were wounded. Fortunately, there were no American aircraft carriers at Pearl Harbor that morning. En route to the Philippines to deliver airplanes, all were spared for future action.

The U.S.S. *Shaw* exploding at Pearl Harbor.

The next day President Roosevelt went before Congress to ask for a declaration of war. Calling December 7, 1941, a day "which will live in infamy," the president denounced the Japanese surprise attack. After a sobering account of American losses, he ended on a note of righteous optimism: "With confidence in our armed forces—with the unbounding determination of our people—we will gain the inevitable triumph—so help us God."

Certainly the American people needed all the optimism their president could muster. On December 11, Germany and Italy declared war on the United States. Meanwhile the Japanese struck unopposed throughout Asia and the South Pacific. Within six months they would conquer Hong Kong, Malaya, Singapore, Burma, the Dutch East Indies, Guam, Wake Island, the Gilberts, and the Philippines. And for the time being the United States was helpless to stop them.

BIOGRAPHICAL SKETCH

CHARLES AUGUSTUS LINDBERGH · *1902–1974*

Lindbergh was born in Detroit, Michigan, but grew up in rural Little Falls, Minnesota. His Swedish-born father served five terms as a Republican in the U.S. House of Representatives, where he became noted for his progressive politics and his opposition to American participation in World War I. After graduating from high school young Lindbergh studied engineering at the University of Wisconsin but left college during his second year. Long interested in the new field of aviation, he became a barnstorming pilot and afterward a second lieutenant in the U.S. Army upon graduation from military flying school in 1925.

Two years later Lindbergh set out to capture a $25,000 prize offered for the first nonstop transatlantic flight from the United States to France. Several aviators had already perished or failed in attempts to cross the Atlantic. Undaunted, he convinced several St. Louis businessmen to finance the construction of a plane, which he aptly named *The Spirit of St. Louis*. Flying this single-engine aircraft from San Diego to St. Louis and on to New York, he broke existing records for the longest and speediest solo flights.

On May 21, 1927, with food and water but no parachute, Lindbergh took off from Roosevelt Field, Long Island, on what would be an historic flight. Thousands of frenzied admirers were on hand to greet the "Lone Eagle" when he landed outside Paris some 33 hours later. After his return home Americans outdid the French in celebrating his feat with a ticker tape parade along Broadway. Lindbergh seemed the perfect hero to his countrymen. He had mastered the newest in technology but still maintained the traditional values of courage and self-reliance. Noted one writer: "He is the dream that is in our hearts."

In 1929 Lindbergh married Dwight Morrow's daughter, Anne, by whom he was to have six children. His first child and namesake was kidnapped and found murdered in 1932. Bruno Richard Hauptmann, an obscure carpenter, was tried, found guilty, and executed for this shocking crime. But more recent evidence indicates that Hauptmann, who maintained his innocence, may not have been guilty.

Pestered mercilessly throughout their ordeal by newspaper reporters, the Lindberghs left the United States for self-imposed exile in England in 1935. Charles visited Germany on several occasions during the next few years at the request of an American official. Once, without his preknowledge, he received a medal from the high-ranking Nazi, Reichsmarshal Hermann Göring. This drew angry criticism from Americans, as did his warnings that the German air force was superior to that of other nations.

Convinced that war in Europe was imminent, Lindbergh returned to the United States in April 1939. When war did erupt, he allied himself with the America First Committee to keep the United States from becoming involved. The famed aviator proved a popular speaker until an address in Des Moines, Iowa, on September 11, 1941, during which he attacked Roosevelt, the British, and the Jews for plotting to embroil the nation in war. Some denounced him as a Nazi and an anti-Semite, and he received a stinging public rebuke from President Roosevelt.

The president refused Lindbergh's request to serve in the military once the United States entered World War II. Disappointed, he nevertheless worked with Henry Ford to produce B-24 bombers and also tested planes. Unknown to Roosevelt, he flew 50 missions in the Pacific war theater in a civilian capacity and shot down a Japanese fighter plane.

After the war Lindbergh enjoyed the quiet life he had long sought. His wife became a well-known writer during these years, and he won the Pulitzer Prize for Literature for his autobiographical *The Spirit of St. Louis* (1953). In 1954 President Dwight D. Eisenhower named him a brigadier general in the U.S. Air Force. During the last decade of his life this controversial hero became an ardent conservationist.

SUGGESTED READINGS

For general works on the diplomacy of the New Era, see L. Ethan Ellis, *Republican Foreign Policy, 1921–1933* (1968), and William Appleman Williams, *The Tragedy of American Diplomacy* (rev. ed., 1962). Thomas H. Buckley, *The United States and the Washington Conference, 1921–1922* (1970), and Roger Dingman, *Power in the Pacific: The Origins of Naval Arms Limitations, 1914–1922* (1976), carefully analyze the diplomacy of naval arms reductions. Also see Akira Iriye's important *After Imperialism: The Search for a New Order in the Far East, 1921–1931* (1965). L. Ethan Ellis, *Frank B. Kellogg and American Foreign Relations, 1925–1929* (1961), and Robert H. Ferrell, *Peace in Their Time: The Origins of the Kellogg-Briand Pact* (1952), focus on the attempt to outlaw war. Consult also Harold Josephson, *James T. Shotwell and the Rise of Internationalism in America* (1976). A number of solid studies pertaining to the economic aspects of foreign policy exist. Three such works are: Joan Hoff Wilson, *American Business and Foreign*

SUGGESTED READINGS

Policy, 1920–1933 (1971); Herbert Feis, *The Diplomacy of the Dollar, 1919–1929* (1950); and Derek H. Aldcroft, *From Versailles to Wall Street, 1919–1929* (1977).

Foreign relations with Latin America between the world wars have received much attention. Joseph Tulchin's *The Aftermath of War: World War I and U.S. Policy toward Latin America* (1971) is a good introduction. Bryce Wood, *The Making of the Good Neighbor Policy* (1961), and Irwin F. Gellman, *Good Neighbor Diplomacy: United States Policies in Latin America, 1933–1945* (1979), examine attempts by the United States to improve relations with its southern neighbors. Other informative studies include: Dana Munro, *United States and the Caribbean Republics, 1921–1933* (1974); Thomas L. Karnes, *Tropical Enterprise: The Standard Fruit and Steamship Company in Latin America* (1978); and Lorenzo Meyer, *Mexico and the United States in the Oil Controversy, 1917–1942* (1977).

Numerous studies of Japanese-American relations cover the Manchurian crisis, but for detailed coverage, see Armin Rappaport, *Henry L. Stimson and Japan, 1931–1933* (1963). Similarly, there is no lack of works treating Soviet-American relations during these years. A few particularly helpful works are: Peter Filene, *Americans and the Soviet Experiment, 1917–1933* (1967); Thomas R. Maddux, *Years of Estrangement: American Relations with the Soviet Union, 1933–1941* (1980); and Donald G. Bishop, *The Roosevelt-Litvinov Agreements* (1965).

The most comprehensive examination of foreign policy during the Roosevelt years is Robert Dallek's *Franklin D. Roosevelt and American Foreign Policy, 1932–1945* (1979). John Wiltz's *From Isolation to War, 1931–1941* (1968) is a brief but readable overview. See also appropriate sections of previously cited works about Roosevelt.

The isolationism of the 1930s has proved a popular subject. Selig Adler, *The Isolationist Impulse* (1957), and the more recent Thomas N. Guinsburg, *The Pursuit of Isolationism in the United States Senate from Versailles to Pearl Harbor* (1981), are richly detailed. Other reliable works include Manfred Jonas's *Isolationism in America, 1935–1941* (1966) and Robert A. Divine's related studies, *The Illusion of Neutrality* (1962) and *The Reluctant Belligerent* (2d ed., 1979). Warren Cohen, *The American Revisionists* (1967), examines key isolationists. Wayne S. Cole's *America First* (1953), *Roosevelt and the Isolationists, 1932–1945* (1983) and *Charles A. Lindbergh and the Battle Against American Intervention in World War II* (1974) are sympathetic in their appraisals of isolationists, as is his *Senator Gerald P. Nye and American Foreign Relations* (1962).

There is considerable literature tracing the transition from isolation to involvement. Two standard works are William L. Langer and S. Everett Gleason, *The Challenge to Isolation, 1937–1940* (1952), and *The Undeclared War, 1940–1941* (1953). James V. Compton, *The Swastika and the Eagle: Hitler, the United States, and the Origins of World War II* (1967), is also valuable. Allen Guttmann, *The Wound in the Heart: America and the Spanish Civil War* (1962), examines American attitudes toward that brutal conflict. Warren F. Kimball's *The Most Unsordid Act: Lend Lease, 1939–1941* (1969) is another important work. Joseph P. Lash, *Roosevelt and Churchill, 1939–1941* (1976), looks at growing Anglo-American cooperation in the face of the fascist challenge, while Thomas A. Bailey's and Paul B. Ryan's *Hitler vs. Roosevelt: The Undeclared Naval War* (1979) sheds additional light on the period between the invasion of Poland and Pearl Harbor.

Books on Pearl Harbor are profuse and frequently provocative. Herbert Feis's *The Road to Pearl Harbor* (1950) is an older but balanced study, as is the more recent, highly detailed Gordon W. Prange, *At Dawn We Slept: The Untold Story of Pearl Harbor* (1981). Both Paul W. Schroeder, *The Axis Alliance and Japanese-American Relations, 1941* (1958), and Bruce M. Russett, *No Clear and Present Danger: A Skeptical View of the U.S. Entry into World War II* (1972), are critical of Roosevelt. Even more so is Charles A. Beard's *President Roosevelt and the Coming of the War, 1941* (1948), which charges Roosevelt with virtually treasonous behavior. Basil Rauch, *Roosevelt: From Munich to Pearl Harbor* (1950), is highly defensive of the president's actions. Roberta Wohlstetter, *Pearl Harbor: Warning and Decision* (1962), provides a fine analysis of intelligence information and misinformation.

10

America in a World at War

The bombing at Pearl Harbor ended the months of quarreling and indecision, uniting the American people as nothing else could have. For the next four years the United States would wage relentless warfare against far-flung enemies in several theaters of battle. The country and its allies would emerge victorious in the end. But Axis capitulation brought much more than military triumph. The war would transform the United States, as well as the world at large, while at home the war extinguished the Great Depression overnight and sowed the seeds for unparalleled affluence in peacetime. The war also created serious disruptions, leading to a painful reassessment of traditional attitudes toward women, blacks, and other minorities. The postwar baby boom, with its manifold impact on American life, likewise had its roots in the war. Finally, the scope of the U.S. government, and especially the power of the presidency, expanded dramatically during the war years and left an unsettling legacy for future generations.

Changes wrought by the war beyond American borders affected the nation, too. Germany, Italy, and Japan would cease to be world powers; Great Britain and France were considerably weakened and would have to shed nearly all their overseas possessions within two decades following peace. Only the United States and the Soviet Union could claim true great power status in 1945, and during ensuing decades both would try to fill the vacuum left by defeated nations and crumbling empires. The so-called cold war would thus be another important consequence of World War II.

DEFEATING THE THIRD REICH

Winston Churchill was understandably jubilant over the American declaration of war. The prime minister promptly left for Washington, where he and President Roosevelt

DEFEATING THE THIRD REICH 217

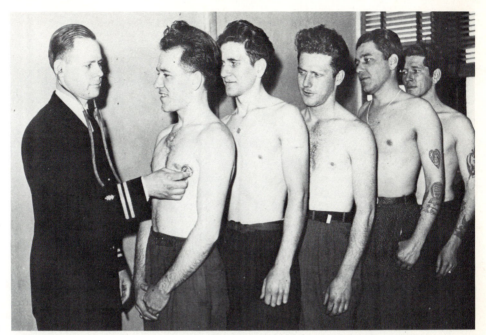

Five of the more than 16 million young Americans who passed their military physicals.

reiterated their earlier decision to concentrate on defeating Germany first. Some critics have charged that racial prejudice lay behind this decision, contending that the United States and Great Britain preferred to rescue white Europeans before liberating the yellow and brown peoples of the Pacific and Far East. But the decision made good strategic sense. Britain was fighting for its life at the time and could spare few resources for the war in the east. The only possible theater of cooperation was therefore Europe and adjoining areas. The United States and Great Britain would smash Hitler first and then turn to Japan.

Superficially, the plan for defeating Hitler was quite simple. Allied forces would converge on Germany from all sides, trapping the Germans in a great viselike movement and ultimately pushing them back into the Reich itself. There was, of course, much room for disagreement within the overall scheme. The Soviets, who would soon lift the siege of Stalingrad and begin their long campaign to drive the Nazis out of the Soviet Union, agitated for an early Anglo-American invasion of France. In this way, the Allies could force Hitler to transfer more troops to the west and thereby alleviate some of the pressure on the Red armies. But Roosevelt and Churchill estimated that they would not have sufficient forces for an invasion of France before 1943.

Many Americans strategists wanted to postpone any large military undertaking until there were enough forces massed in Britain for a cross-Channel invasion of the French coast. Churchill maintained, however, that the Anglo-American team must open a front in the west whenever it was feasible, and for him North Africa was the most logical choice. Besides relieving the Russians somewhat, a North African campaign would open up the Mediterranean to Allied shipping and allow the transport of lend-lease materials

The war in Europe.

to the Soviet Union through the Persian Gulf. Victory in North Africa would also afford bases for an early invasion of Italy. In addition, North African landings would assist the British Eighth Army, already fighting in Libya. Roosevelt approved the invasion and plans were begun in July 1942.

Crusade in North Africa Allied landings took place on November 8, with simultaneous assaults at three points: one in Morocco near Casablanca; the other two at Oran and Algiers, both in Algeria. Ironically, these invasions were not in enemy territory, but in lands governed by Vichy France. General Dwight David Eisenhower, the commander of Allied armies in North Africa, took advantage of "friendly" relations with the Vichyites to seek cooperation with French authorities in Algiers. After several days of delicate negotiations, the French agreed to assist the Allies and allow use of northwest Africa as a base for operations against the Germans. In exchange, the United States and Great Britain recognized continued French rule there, with Fleet Admiral Jean Darlan in charge. This deal with Vichy officials outraged some American liberals, but it probably saved many lives and shortened the war in Africa.

From Algeria, American and British forces drove toward Tunisia and its port at Tunis, a crucial link in German supply lines to North Africa. At the same time British troops in Libya began moving west, and by mid-May of 1943 Allied armies had surrounded the Germans in Tunisia. Over a quarter million Germans surrendered, despite Hitler's orders to fight to the last man.

The Struggle for Italy Sicily and the Italian boot itself were but a small jump from Tunisia. American planners had grave doubts about invading Sicily and Italy, fearing that such a campaign would become an unending drain on Anglo-American men and

American invaders hitting the Normandy beaches on D-Day, June 6, 1944.

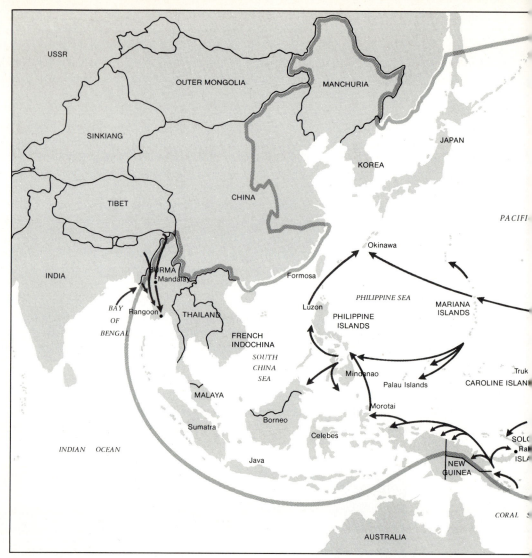

The war in the Pacific.

materiel. But Churchill insisted. The Italians might be forced into an early surrender; Germany could then be threatened from the south. Churchill also viewed Italy and adjacent Yugoslavia as the "soft underbelly" of Europe—a point where Axis forces were weak and vulnerable. At the same time, Churchill had postwar strategies in mind, asserting that attacks through Italy and Yugoslavia would keep the Soviets from penetrating too deeply into western and central Europe. Finally, an Italian operation would give Anglo-American forces another opportunity to engage the enemy while preparing for the cross-Channel invasion.

Everything went smoothly at first. Allied troops landed in Sicily on June 10, 1943, and encountered only weak resistance. In less than two weeks Allied armies pushed across Sicily, took Palermo on July 22, and captured Messina a month later. The Allied conquest of Sicily meanwhile fed a growing opposition to Mussolini, who was driven

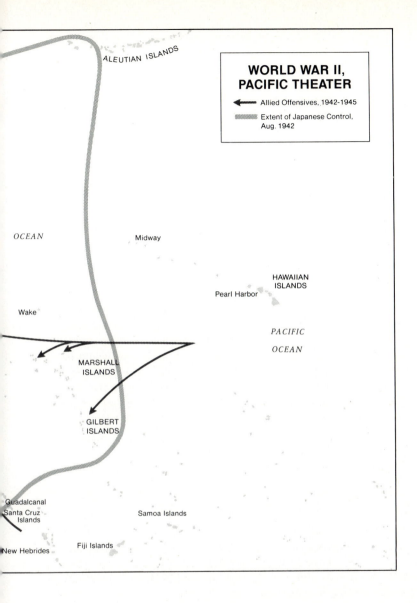

from power. On September 8, Italy surrendered to the Allies. The Germans then rescued the Duce from prison, setting him up as the head of a puppet government in northern Italy. German troops poured into Italy and took charge of the war there.

The battle for the Italian peninsula itself, again under the direction of General Eisenhower, proved more difficult than anyone had predicted. Attacks on Anzio and Monte Cassino were particularly costly for the Anglo-American armies, and they did not take Rome until June 1944. At the time of the German surrender in 1945, all of Italy north of the Po River still lay in enemy hands.

From Normandy to Victory in Europe   The very moment that Allied troops were marching into Rome, a vast armada was poised on the southern shores of England for the long-awaited assault on Nazi-occupied France. Led by General Eisenhower, now

Supreme Allied Commander in Europe, the attack began in the early hours of June 6, 1944 (D-Day). Some 1,200 warships and 4,000 landing craft, representing the largest amphibious operation in history, dispatched thousands of British and American troops at five points along France's Normandy coast. After costly fighting on the beaches, Allied forces began driving inland and captured the principal Norman port at Cherbourg on June 26. Exactly two months later they liberated Paris.

Defeats in northern France stunned the Germans, who retreated toward their own frontiers during the summer and autumn of 1944. By year's end, Anglo-American forces were at the very gates of Hitler's Reich. But on December 16 the Germans mounted a powerful counteroffensive in Belgium's Ardennes Forest, resulting in the now famous Battle of the Bulge. By December 23 American reinforcements had stemmed the enemy advance. The costs were high—77,000 casualties for the Allies and over 100,000 for the Germans—but the way was now open to Germany itself. The drive to cross the Rhine River began in February 1945, and in late March the first units crossed the river at Remagen.

While Allied troops were closing in on Germany, British and American bombing of the Third Reich reached its climax, the worst single attack of the war coming at Dresden in February 1945. Combined raids by British and American bombers virtually destroyed the city and killed tens of thousands of civilians. Such carnage would have outraged the world in the early 1930s, but the bombing of civilian populations had become so commonplace that few thought twice about it. This steady pounding from the air and the inexorable advance of Soviet, American, and British arms sealed Germany's fate by April 1945. As Soviet troops fought their way through the streets of Berlin, Hitler committed suicide in his bunker deep beneath the Reich Chancellery. On May 8 the Germans officially surrendered to the Allies in the French city of Rheims.

TURNABOUT IN THE EAST

Americans rejoiced over the Nazi collapse, but the war with Japan remained to be won. During the first six months after Pearl Harbor, the Japanese had appeared invincible. Lack of men and equipment, in addition to the "Germany first" commitment, meant that the United States could only hope to fight a holding action against Japan for the time being. And because the British were already overextended in Europe, most of the fighting in Asia and the Pacific fell to American forces.

Japan Halted   As 1942 began, there seemed no end to Japanese victories. In May, American troops in the Philippines were forced to surrender. The Japanese then created an immense defense perimeter. Resembling a bloated semiellipse, it ran from the Kurile Islands in the north to Wake Island in the east, to the Dutch East Indies in the south. Well fortified behind their island bastion, the Japanese hoped to repulse all attacks and gradually break American resolve.

American forces were clearly in no position as 1942 began to push back the contours of a swollen Japanese empire, but strategists were determined to halt the enemy advance and, in particular, to keep Australia from falling into Japanese hands. At the battles of the Coral Sea (May 3–8, 1942) and Midway (June 4, 1942), the U.S. Navy accomplished both of these objectives. In the Coral Sea, just north and east of Australia,

American prisoners of war beginning the hellish Philippine "death march."

U.S. naval aircraft destroyed a large Japanese carrier, but enemy planes were also successful, sinking the U.S. carrier *Lexington* and severely damaging the *Yorktown*. Although the United States suffered greater material losses than their opponents, Japanese plans to invade Australia were thwarted. At Midway Island in the Central Pacific, where American planes destroyed four large Japanese carriers, U.S. naval forces more than made up for their losses in the Coral Sea. The United States lost the *Yorktown,* but the Japanese Navy never wholly recovered, and from that moment forward they lost their initiative at sea.

Island Hopping in the Pacific Once in control of the seas around Australia and nearby New Guinea, the United States launched a campaign to occupy a string of Pacific islands, each one a little closer to Japan itself. This strategy required a superior massing of troops for assaults against each targeted island. Air bases could be established once the enemy was overcome and used to support the next island campaign. Once within striking distance of Japan, planes could begin strategic bombing of Japanese cities and industries. The plan, however, did not require attacks on all Japanese-held islands; after the most important ones had fallen, isolated enemy troops could be left behind on the other islands.

The first successful attack came at Guadalcanal in the Solomons. From there Marines advanced to New Britain, Saipan, Iwo Jima, and Okinawa—among other islands. In late 1944 and early 1945 the United States recaptured the Philippines. With aircraft

ORAL HISTORY
Growing Up in the Twentieth Century

RALPH SHUPING · *born 1920*

I went into the service in December 1940. I was trained in radar. We were the original radar unit in the Army Signal Corps. In May 1941 we left for the Philippines as experimental units—to see if radar would work in the tropics.

As it got close to December 1941, we could tell that something was going on. We heard about the Pearl Harbor bombing on the seventh and then the Japanese hit us the next day. On the morning they came in to bomb us, I was in the radar unit. I picked them up about 250 miles out. There was a big swarm of bombers coming. I called Clark Field and talked to the general and he said he was sorry: he couldn't send any interception planes; Congress hadn't declared war yet, and he didn't feel he had the authority to declare war on Japan himself. So the Japs came in and blasted our Air Force on the second day of the war.

The Japs bombed us every day. All we had to hold them off were 1917 and 1918 ammunition and hand grenades. And then we ran out of food. If it wasn't for the twenty-sixth Cavalry, we wouldn't have had anything to eat. We ate the horses. That's where we got the name BBBs—Battling Bastards of Bataan!

All up and down Bataan the Japanese tried different landings and we were able to repulse them. They didn't get into us completely until the ninth of April. There were 250,000 Japanese against 27,000 Americans. We were pushed clear back against Manila Bay and had no place to go. So we had no choice but surrender.

The Japs congregated us on this airfield. You didn't know what was going to happen—

where you were going to go, what they were going to do, how they were going to be toward us. They beat us around pretty good on the airstrip. They searched us and took everything away from us—all our wristwatches, rings, eyeglasses, and cameras. We got no food or water. On the tenth they started the "death march." The march out of Bataan lasted nine days and nine nights. It was about 200 miles, and we walked day and night. The only water that we had was when it rained: we scooped water out of the ditch and drank it.

At our first prison camp—Camp O'Donnell—there would be as many as 100 to 125 men a day who were dying of malnutrition and disease. The Japanese didn't allow the American doctors who were with us to have any medicine. The camp was originally a Philippine army camp. They had just bamboo shacks, and there was just one water faucet for the whole company. You'd stand in line for hours and hours just to fill one canteen. It was a day or two after we reached camp that we got any food at all, and that was just a bowl of rice.

Later they sent us to Japan as slave labor. We lost so many men in the shipment from the Philippines to Japan. We were on unmarked freighters, and the American ships and submarines attacked them. Conditions in the ships were terrible. We were locked into a small hold; there were 300 men down there. You couldn't lie down—no food, no water, not a thing. Men suffocated and died. The only thing we could do is pass the bodies up, and the Japs would throw them into the ocean. After eight days at sea we landed in the southern part of Honshu, and from there they put us on a train for Tokyo. And then they put us on display downtown on the Ginza. Kids came down and threw rocks at us. We were there for two days, and then they moved us out to the work camps. I went to a town called Ashio, where we worked in the copper mines and copper factories until the war ended.

We had no idea how the war was going—or what was happening back home. In the four years that I was a prisoner of war, I got two postcards from home. I was considered missing in action for 11 months before word got through the Red Cross that I was still alive. In my own mind, I never had any idea I was not going home. I just lived from day to day.

On the fifteenth of August 1945—we didn't know about V-J Day yet—they locked us in the camp and all of the guards disappeared—all except the camp commander, who had lived in California and spoke good English. Then on the twenty-ninth American planes flew over and dropped in magazines, newspapers, and other literature. They dropped food and cigarettes and everything. Everybody went outside and jumped around. I weighed 90 pounds and was sick with maleria, dysentery, and beriberi.

I still have nightmares about it all: I'm refighting the war and refighting the prison camps. Sometimes it really gets bad.

now in striking distance of Japan, American bombers began a relentless devastation of enemy cities. On March 9, 1945, over 300 B-29 bombers raided Tokyo. Incendiary bombs leveled about one-fourth of the buildings and killed as many as 80,000 civilians. By the late summer of 1945 many other Japanese cities lay in ruins.

Victory over Japan   American forces now braced themselves for a projected invasion of Japan, with some strategists estimating that it would take several years to subdue the Japanese and cost over a million American casualties. But the dropping of two atomic bombs, one on Hiroshima on August 6, 1945, and the other at Nagasaki three days later, convinced the Japanese to give up before the invasion had to be launched. Estimates vary, but the bomb may have taken upwards of 70,000 lives in each city.

Development of this terrible weapon had begun back in 1939 when Albert Einstein, a Jewish refugee from Nazi Germany, wrote to President Roosevelt that the Germans might be capable of building atomic weapons of unprecedented power. Roosevelt promptly appointed a committee to oversee atomic research, and in March 1942 the president, with strong encouragement from the army, threw his support behind a $2 billion program to create an atomic bomb. The resulting Manhattan Project was top secret, funds being taken piecemeal from other appropriations. Indeed, many who worked on various portions of the Manhattan Project knew nothing about the bomb itself.

Atomic "mushroom" cloud over Nagasaki, Japan, August 9, 1945.

The decision to drop atomic bombs on Japan remains controversial. Some have charged that continued conventional bombing would have brought the Japanese to their knees within a very short period. Of course, such bombing might have inflicted even more devastation than the two atomic blasts. Others contend that the United States should have warned the Japanese by demonstrating the bomb's destructive power at some uninhabited site, but such a demonstration would have demanded an unusual degree of cooperation between fighting nations. Japanese leaders, along with knowledgeable Japanese scientists, would have to be induced to witness the trial run, and there was always a possibility that the bomb would fail to explode, making American threats seem ludi-

BIG THREE DIPLOMACY 227

crous. In the end, President Harry S Truman, who had come into the White House following Roosevelt's death on April 12, 1945, contended that dropping the bomb would shorten the war and save lives. A few scholars assert that he also used the bomb in order to demonstrate its power to the Soviets and thus obtain their acquiescence on postwar boundaries and other disputed issues.

Whether necessary or not, the two atomic bombs fell on Japan and no doubt hastened the Japanese capitulation. They accepted American terms on August 14 (V-J Day) and surrendered formally on September 2 aboard the battleship *Missouri* in Tokyo Bay. Nearly four years after the United States had entered the conflict, World War II came to an end. Over 16 million Americans served in the armed forces during that period, and more than 400,000 lost their lives.

BIG THREE DIPLOMACY

Success on the battlefield was not the only key to victory. Delicate wartime diplomacy, as well as effective mobilization of the home front, were essential for triumph in the field, and of particular importance on the diplomatic front were the summit meetings among Allied leaders.

The first such gathering had taken place between Roosevelt and Churchill off Newfoundland before American entry into the war (see Chapter 9). They met a second time in Washington just after Pearl Harbor, and a third bilateral meeting took place at Casablanca in French Morocco during January 1943. The two Allied chiefs invited Joseph Stalin to join them, but he declined, citing the crucial military situation in the Soviet Union. At Casablanca, Roosevelt and Churchill agreed to launch an Italian campaign and, at the president's instigation, called for unconditional surrender of the Axis powers. Some have contended that this demand for surrender without conditions prolonged the war. The possibility of a negotiated peace, such critics assert, might have induced the enemy to ask for peace earlier. Whatever the case, unconditional surrender required the total defeat of Germany and Japan, which in turn created large power vacuums in Europe and Asia. After the war the Soviets would exploit the situation with telling results.

In November 1943 Roosevelt and Churchill met with Chiang Kai-shek in Cairo to discuss postwar settlements for Asia and the Pacific. The Japanese, they concluded, would lose all Pacific islands acquired since 1914 and would evacuate China, including Manchuria. The three leaders also pledged eventual independence for Korea, governed since 1905 by Japan.

Immediately after the Cairo meeting, Roosevelt and Churchill flew to Teheran for a Big Three conference with Stalin. There the president had a long-awaited opportunity to meet the Soviet dictator, hoping that the famous Roosevelt charm would work as effectively with "Uncle Joe" (his private nickname for Stalin) as it did with politicians back home. The initial formalities over, the two Western leaders pleased Stalin by making a final commitment to invade France the following spring, and Stalin agreed to coordinate the invasion with a Soviet offensive in eastern Europe. These mutual pledges helped for the time being to dispel some of the suspicions that had grown up between the eastern and western Allies.

Churchill, Roosevelt, and Stalin at Yalta, February 1945.

The Big Three met a second time at Yalta, a Russian resort on the Crimean Sea in February 1945. Knowing that their armies would soon converge on Germany, the Allied leaders agreed to divide the country into zones of occupation. The city of Berlin, deep within the Russian zone, would become a microcosm of Germany at large, with American, British, French, and Russian occupations of the former capital.

The Big Three also discussed the fate of Poland at Yalta. The Soviets had already occupied the country and had since installed a Communist regime known as the Lublin government. Churchill and Roosevelt urged Stalin to invite non-Communist Polish leaders (most of whom had spent the war in exile in London) to join the government. Stalin accepted in principle and also promised to hold free elections in Poland at some future date, but he added that any such arrangements must be consistent with Soviet security needs. The agreement on Poland was thus vague and open to different interpretations. Stalin doubtless left Yalta believing that he had a free hand there.

The Yalta formula for Japan and the Far East was much clearer. The Soviet Union would declare war on Japan within three months of a German surrender. In compensation, the Soviets would regain territories lost in the Russo-Japanese War 40 years earlier. In addition, the Soviets would receive Japan's Kurile Islands, several of which had once belonged to Russia. Finally, Stalin agreed to cooperate with the Nationalist Chinese (rather than the Chinese Communists under Mao Tse-tung) in defeating the Japanese, as well as in the postwar period.

The Big Three held a final meeting in the Berlin suburb of Potsdam in July 1945.

FIGHTING THE WAR AT HOME

President Truman now represented the United States, and part way through the conference Clement Atlee replaced Churchill, who had lost his post as prime minister as a result of the first British elections since the war began. At the meeting Stalin reaffirmed his promise to enter the war against Japan. The Big Three also worked out a plan to de-Nazify and disarm Germany, as well as to punish German leaders and war criminals. German resources, it was agreed, would be used to compensate for damages that the Nazis had inflicted on other countries during the war. Finally, the three leaders completed the discussions they had begun at Teheran on Poland's postwar boundaries. The Soviet Union obtained a large slice of eastern Poland, with the Poles receiving a chunk of German territory as compensation. It would be clear within months that these and other wartime agreements among the Allies did little to insure cordial relations among the victorious powers.

FIGHTING THE WAR AT HOME

At home the American people played an essential role in winning the war. It was they who forged the weapons, grew the food, raised the money, shipped crucial supplies, and kept democracy alive. These new responsibilities placed a large strain on American society. But in comparison to the population of other belligerent nations, the American people suffered very little during the war. Despite some serious shortages, they were well housed, well fed, and well paid. The United States was not invaded or bombed; Americans at home were not tortured, enslaved, or expelled from their homeland.

Economic Mobilization   The most important domestic task was mobilizing the nation's industries and economy. In this respect the country was fortunate to enter the war with unused industrial capacity and unemployed workers, for both plants and workers could be employed to produce war goods with little immediate strain on either. But demands for war materiel would soon outrun productive capacity if vigorous measures were not taken. Accordingly, President Roosevelt created the War Production Board (WPB) in January 1942, placing Donald Nelson of Sears, Roebuck at its head. The WPB tried to coordinate military procurement, allocate scarce resources, and determine industrial priorities. Unfortunately, the Army and Navy maintained a large degree of autonomy over purchases, resulting in lack of coordination and wasteful duplication. And Nelson himself proved inadequate for the job. Eventually the WPB was superseded by several other authorities, the most important of which was the Office of War Mobilization, headed by former senator and Supreme Court justice James M. Byrnes.

Agencies outside the WPB also tried to regulate various aspects of production. The War Food Administration sought to increase supplies and alleviate shortages, while the War Manpower Commission oversaw mobilization of civilian personnel for both commercial and military purposes. The Office of Scientific Research, under Dr. Vannevar Bush, recruited scientists and engineers, assigned research tasks, and mandated new wartime technologies. The Office of War Information attempted to coordinate the dissemination of war news and information. The press was censored and the FBI was on the lookout for disloyal citizens, but the widespread assaults on civil liberties that had occurred during World War I were generally not repeated, except in the unfortunate case of Japanese-Americans.

These and other agencies were the targets of much criticism and dissatisfaction, but they were necessary to insure a high volume of military production and civilian cooperation. And the flow of war goods was truly astounding. By 1945 American industry had turned out 300,000 airplanes, 12,000 ships, 64,000 landing craft, 86,000 tanks, and millions of rifles, machine guns, and side arms, as well as mountains of ammunition and bombs. Defense contractors gave most of their orders to big business, for it was the larger concerns that had the capital, the plant capacity, and the pool of skilled labor. In order to reduce risk and encourage production, the government offered private industry generous "cost plus" contracts. Uncle Sam would cover the complete cost of production and guarantee a reasonable profit. The antitrust laws were also suspended for the most part in order to avoid confusion and encourage the business community. A special Senate committee headed by Senator Harry S Truman investigated corruption and malfeasance in defense industries, and it was generally quite effective.

Labor also cooperated well, pledging not to strike for the duration of the war. And with few exceptions—notably two strikes by John L. Lewis's United Mine Workers—labor kept its word. Meanwhile the ranks of organized labor grew impressively, as millions of industrial workers found jobs after the long years of depression. Union membership grew from just under 9 million in 1940 to about 14.8 million in 1945.

Under the stimulation of wartime production, the nation's GNP reached unprecedented levels. Between 1939 and 1944, the peak year of military production, GNP soared from $88.6 billion to just under $200 billion. Approximately 45 percent of it represented government spending.

Paying for the War   The total financial cost of World War II was therefore quite large. In addition to weapons and other military equipment, the federal government had to pay the salaries of millions of service personnel, not to mention the costs of fuel, medical care, and other services for the military. The final price tag stood at about $288 billion as 1945 came to a close. In the decades ahead the American people would have to pay out billions more for pensions, veterans' benefits, and interest on the debt.

The United States covered the initial costs of World War II through both taxation and borrowing. Approximately 40 percent derived from tax revenues; the other 60 percent came from the sale of bonds. Roosevelt had wanted a higher proportion to come out of increased income taxes, but Congress balked. Even so, millions of Americans found themselves owing federal income taxes for the first time in their lives. The 1942 Revenue Act made all annual incomes over $600 liable for taxation, and many were shocked at the end of the year to find that they were in debt to the Internal Revenue Service. In order to ease the burden and to insure a steady flow of revenue into the Treasury, Congress ordered employers to withhold taxes from each paycheck. The withholding tax continued after the war to become a permanent feature of the tax system.

Wartime Shopping   Increased federal demands for money and materiel inevitably created shortages in civilian markets. The government ordered automakers to stop manufacturing cars in early 1942 and convert to war production. Auto manufacture did not resume until 1946, forcing motorists to make existing vehicles last for the duration of the conflict. Under the circumstances, the used-car market boomed as never before.

FIGHTING THE WAR AT HOME

Rubber was also in short supply, as many sources of raw rubber fell into Japanese hands. The government launched a crash program to develop and manufacture synthetic rubber (made from petroleum), but it did not ease the shortage of rubber tires for civilian use. Highway speed limits were reduced to 35 miles per hour to save wear on tires, as well as to conserve gasoline. Authorities also began to ration gasoline itself. Amounts available to drivers depended on need, but most received only three gallons per week. Commuters formed car pools or switched to public transportation, and families doubled up for pleasure trips.

Other scarce items were rationed, too. Local rationing boards distributed booklets of stamps each month to residents in their area, and consumers had to surrender the appropriate stamps, along with the purchase price, when buying rationed commodities. Meat, coffee, sugar, and shoes were among these items. Other products simply disappeared from the market. Nylon stockings fell victim to the need for thousands of parachutes; still other commodities were altered or abbreviated. Skirts and dresses grew shorter in order to save cloth, while in men's apparel the popular double-breasted, wide-lapeled jacket gave way to more streamlined models. Trouser cuffs were also forbidden in the name of economy. Some citizens purchased scarce goods from illegal sources (the black market), but widespread patriotism and general support for the war kept such behavior to a minimum.

Certain industries felt the pinch of shortages as much as consumers. Many small manufacturers, without the plant capacity or the capital to convert to war production, frequently suffered financial reverses or had to close altogether. Protests from small business led to Senate hearings and congressional action on the problem. The Murray-Patman Act of 1942 established a Smaller Plant Corporation under the War Production Board. It received a fund of $150 million to finance the conversion of small industries for war work, but the measure did not begin to address the problem–nor could it change the fact that big businesses were simply better prepared to meet the challenge of military production.

Battling Inflation   Accompanying the shortages was an ever-present danger of inflation, for as goods and services became scarce, prices began to rise. At the same time, consumers had more money than ever before. Full employment, good wages, and lots of overtime pay gave workers a flood of dollars with which to demand scarce goods and services. Unless something were done quickly, prices might rise to astronomical levels, placing real hardships on consumers and making the war itself more costly to the American people.

The federal government took several steps to control inflation. President Roosevelt created an Office of Price Administration (OPA) in April 1941, several months before Pearl Harbor. The following January Congress gave OPA power to fix wages, prices, and rents. War bond drives also helped to reduce the threat of inflation. The Treasury did need the revenue from these sales, but money put into bonds was taken out of circulation and could not be used to bid up prices of scarce goods. The large aggregate savings represented by these bonds would later help to fuel a postwar economic boom.

Selling the War   Bond sales played still other roles on the domestic front. The government used bond drives to give civilians a sense of personal sacrifice and participation in the war effort. Hollywood stars and radio personalities appeared at huge bond rallies, made jibes at Hitler and Tojo, and urged the nation on to victory. Nonetheless, the government tried not to oversell the conflict. Roosevelt himself believed that efforts to transform World War I into a great crusade for peace and democracy had backfired, leading to disillusionment in the 1920s and 1930s. In World War II the emphasis was thus placed on winning the war and returning to familiar patterns of life. For most Americans, then, the war was a grim but necessary fight to preserve the status quo.

Commercial advertising repeated this same theme again and again. In the early years of the war, companies devoted whole advertisements to bond sales or patriotic messages, if only to keep their names before the public. But as the war seemed to be winding down in 1944, firms began to fill their copy with promises of material bounty in peacetime. A full-color ad for Cannon bath towels appearing in *Life* magazine showed a slender, well-proportioned young woman as she stepped out of a shower into a sparkling clean bathroom, filled with all the latest fixtures. Wrapped in a large fluffy towel and dreaming of the day when her husband (or boyfriend) returns from the service, she vows that they'll have the best of everything in their home—including Cannon towels, of course. Kelvinator held out visions of a shiny new refrigerator for former soldiers and their families, while Ford Motor Company assured them that there would soon be a Ford in their life.

If advertising was any gauge, Americans definitely did not see World War II in revolutionary terms. They would beat the Germans and the Japanese and go back to the homes they remembered. Despite these longings for ''normalcy,'' the war was working powerful changes in American society, changes that few intended or anticipated.

Family Strains   Family life, for instance, endured considerable disruption during the war years. An already mobile people now began moving around the country at record pace. Wives and sweethearts followed their men from one military base to another, while others uprooted themselves and their families for higher-paying jobs in other states. Young children had no choice but to go along with wandering parents and were jostled from school to school and neighborhood to neighborhood with bewildering speed. Day-care centers and nursery schools cropped up in many areas for the first time in order to look after the smallest children of working parents. But thousands of school-age children were simply given house keys so they could let themselves in after school and await the return of one parent or both. Some communities responded with special school programs. The Board of Education in New York City ordered all its schools to stay open until late afternoon.

Children with absent fathers had to find male role models in other members of the family, and would later have difficulty accepting ''Daddy'' back into the family fold. Such absences also placed a great strain on marriages. Indeed, at a time when premarital sex was much less tolerated than today, some couples married after only a few encounters in order to legitimize their passions before the young man was shipped off for combat. When the war was over, many found that they had very little in common and were divorced within a brief period. The divorce rate rose from 2.2 persons per thousand in 1941 to 3.5 per thousand in 1945, and then soared to 4.3 per thousand in 1946. And although there are no reliable statistics on the subject, incidents of adultery and premarital sex undoubtedly increased during the war.

FIGHTING THE WAR AT HOME 233

Women working at Douglas Aircraft in Long Beach, California.

Women in Wartime Beyond the family per se, the war affected women and minority groups significantly, though the full ramifications might not be felt for a generation or more. Women streamed into the labor force as the demand for war goods accelerated and as many young men left for the armed services. The number of women in the work force leaped by over 7 million between 1941 and 1945. Most of them took jobs believing that they were purely temporary. Yet for many unmarried women, as well as for female heads of households, these jobs often meant a welcome and much needed increase in their standard of living, and they eagerly took advantage of the new opportunities.

The federal government did take steps to insure equal pay for women in defense plants, but it could not stop employers from relegating women to the less skilled and therefore lower-paying positions. On the positive side, Americans became accustomed to women's performing all sorts of tasks which traditionally had been considered beyond their capacity. Women drove buses and ambulances, worked in the fields planting and harvesting crops, welded airplanes together, and joined the Army (as WACs) and the Navy (as WAVEs). (Women did not go into combat, but worked in support positions behind the lines.) These women often found a new sense of independence and pride in earning and spending their own money. Women would be fired wholesale in 1946 as the troops returned, but many would remember their wartime jobs and return to the labor market during the prosperous years of peace. Whatever their fate, women were vital to war industries and the not so mythical ''Rosie the Riveter'' became a popular heroine.

Black America Goes to War   The war also provided new opportunities for black Americans, the majority of whom continued to live in the rural South when the war began. After Pearl Harbor thousands of blacks moved to defense jobs in northern cities like Philadelphia, Chicago, and Detroit. There they hoped to find better positions and a higher standard of living. Yet they had to confront many obstacles from the beginning. Segregation might not exist by law in the North, but it was the custom in most communities. Black defense workers and their dependents were crowded into substandard, segregated housing, were paid less than white workers, and frequently were denied membership in all-white unions.

Black leaders tried to address the problem of unequal pay. A. Philip Randolph, head of the wholly black Brotherhood of Sleeping Car Porters, threatened to organize thousands of blacks for a march on the Washington Monument in the spring of 1941 to protest discrimination in defense plants. In June of that year President Roosevelt, who had wanted to play down the race issue so as not to arouse the ire of southern Democrats, finally acted. He issued Executive Order 8802, which forbade racial or sexual discrimination in defense industries and authorized a Fair Employment Practices Committee (FEPC) to hear complaints and take appropriate action. Both the order and the committee resulted in greater equality for blacks in defense work, but the FEPC was too often defied by white labor unions and clever employers, though reorganization in 1943 did make the FEPC a bit more effective than earlier in the war.

The FEPC was also powerless to address living conditions for black defense workers; nor could it erase the bigotry and hatred that many white laborers felt toward their new black neighbors. Race riots erupted in several northern cities, the worst in Detroit in June 1943. Following several incidents at a municipal park, involving both blacks and whites, rumors spread through the city that whites had killed three blacks. Angry blacks began to smash windows, loot stores, and assault white trolley car riders. Whites retaliated by rampaging through black neighborhoods, beating and shooting indiscriminately. The governor of Michigan asked for federal troops, who finally restored order. Thirty people died in the two days of rioting.

Blacks in the armed services fared little better than workers back home. Over a million of them served during World War II, and because of the great demand for combat troops, blacks had more of an opportunity to prove themselves on the battlefield than in the past. (In previous wars there had been a tendency to use blacks as servants or to employ them in menial support functions.) Still, blacks fought in segregated units, despite the fact that the United States was waging a war against the racist Nazis. The military establishment claimed that any attempts at desegregation in the ranks would anger southerners and create tremendous morale problems.

Racial segregation thus prevailed in the armed services throughout the war and was enforced even in northern states where it was technically against the law. In addition, black soldiers and sailors often received substandard housing on bases, were given fewer opportunities to leave their quarters, and had to bear the insults of white officers and enlisted men. Some were abused physically by bigoted white superiors. Yet blacks fought bravely and well during the war. Thousands gave their lives for the United States and thousands more were injured or maimed. Many returned from the service with a heightened sense of racial injustice and vowed to work against it in peacetime. Numerous whites, perhaps shamed by the insidious parallels between American and Nazi racism, were prepared to join with them.

FIGHTING THE WAR AT HOME   **235**

Rage Against Hispanics   Mexican-Americans on the West Coast also became the victims of white prejudice during the war. In June 1943, just before the riots in Detroit, white servicemen in Los Angeles began attacking Mexican-American youths, many of them wearing outlandish outfits called zoot suits. These suits consisted of long, double-breasted jackets and billowy trousers that were tightly pegged at the ankle. Zooters often sported gaudy watch chains and wore their hair long, plastering it down with hair cream and combing it back into ducktails. Some of them belonged to youthful gangs, many of them entirely harmless. Bored sailors and other servicemen from nearby bases began roaming through Mexican neighborhoods, accosting and beating any teenagers they happened to meet. The local press, sharing the racial prejudices of most southern Californians, blamed the violence on the Mexican-American community alone. The Los Angeles police, meanwhile, looked on and did nothing to stop the beatings.

"Concentration Camp, U.S.A."   The worst treatment of the war was reserved for Japanese-Americans. Even more alarming, these assaults on human dignity and civil rights were carried out by the U.S. government. Many inhabitants of the western states had long despised the Japanese who had settled there, and the bombing of Pearl Harbor only intensified their hatred. Unfounded rumors of Japanese-American collaborators and

The Mochida family awaiting their internment.

saboteurs then led to demands for their relocation and confinement. On February 19, 1942, President Roosevelt authorized the Army to remove ''any and all persons'' who might pose a threat to national security. Approximately 120,000 Japanese, two-thirds of them born in the United States and therefore citizens, were moved into ten barbed-wire-enclosed camps in the middle of the desert. Because of their rapid relocation, most had no choice but to leave the bulk of their possessions behind. Those who sold property and other belongings did so at great loss.

During the course of the war most of the Japanese-Americans were released when it became obvious that they posed no security threat. Several thousand young men were cleared for military duty and fought bravely on the Italian front. Despite the patent injustice of their removal, the U.S. Supreme Court upheld the evacuations. In 1968 the Court and the nation partly redeemed themselves by ordering some restitution for the property the internees had lost.

Germans and Italians   The Japanese relocation was even more remarkable when one considers that the much more numerous Japanese population of Hawaii, so recently attacked by Japan and much more vulnerable to invasion, was neither removed nor persecuted. And contrary to their experience in World War I, German-Americans were not molested at all. This was due, in part, to the much larger numbers of German-Americans and to their greater assimilation by the 1940s. Unlike Japanese-Americans, they were also white Europeans.

Italian-Americans, on the other hand, did not fare quite so well as the Germans. As late as 1940 over 80 percent of the Italian-language newspapers in the United States were pro-Axis. Furthermore, most Italians had arrived in America fairly recently, continued to speak their native tongue, and lived largely in ethnic neighborhoods. All these factors made them suspect to some extent and singled some out for verbal abuse. An executive order of December 8, 1941, designating all noncitizens from Axis nations as enemy aliens, also fell heavily on Italian communities, since a considerable percentage had not become naturalized. (This was because many hoped to return to Italy after prospering for some years in the United States.) Still, there was no reign of terror against Italian-Americans, and the enemy-alien classification was lifted as a political gesture on Columbus Day 1942.

War and Class   All in all, the United States remained dominated by its citizens of Anglo-Saxon background. While the majority of Americans no longer traced their ancestry to the British Isles, white Anglo-Saxon Protestants (WASPs) continued to control society, business, and the higher echelons of education and politics. However, rising taxes and the ''desertion'' of servants for the military or for more lucrative defense jobs greatly disrupted the life styles of prosperous WASP Americans. More significantly, the war gave unparalleled opportunities to members of white ethnic groups. The desperate need for talent in both the military and private sectors allowed non-WASPs to occupy positions for which they would not have been considered before the war. A young man with an Italian or Polish surname might serve as an army officer or even an aviator and after the war become a bank president, a lawyer, or a college professor. A young woman from the same background would have to wait another generation, and more, for similar opportunities.

FIGHTING THE WAR AT HOME **237**

The Home Folks at Play   Americans of all classes entertained themselves during the war much as they had before. Radio audiences grew even larger since citizens were forced to spend more time at home because of gasoline rationing. Listeners continued to enjoy comedian Jack Benny and singer Kate Smith. The popular but racist ''Amos 'n' Andy'' show survived the war, too, as did ''Fibber McGee and Molly,'' a combination situation comedy and soap opera. Stay-at-homes also played cards and board games such as Monopoly to pass the evening hours.

Like radio, the movies more than held their own. The Hollywood studios donated prints of all their pictures for free distribution to the armed forces, and many stars toured the bases and camps to entertain the troops. Comedian Bob Hope trekked to the far corners of the earth to cheer the men and women in uniform, as did Betty Grable, famous for her long and shapely legs.

Film audiences at home and abroad understandably preferred escapist themes in their movies. Crime thrillers, musical spectaculars, westerns, romances, and comedies were still favorites. Most of these titles do not deserve mention. But among the more memorable was *Yankee Doodle Dandy,* a 1942 production depicting the life of songwriter George M. Cohan and starring James Cagney. A 1944 success was *National Velvet,* a touching and sometimes teary-eyed story about a girl and her horse. It featured Micky Rooney and Elizabeth Taylor, already beautiful in her early teens. The public also responded favorably that year to *Going My Way,* a film about two parish priests in New York City, with Bing Crosby in the leading role.

Despite popular preferences, Hollywood also tried to delineate the war itself. Most of the war pictures were merely contemporary versions of ''blood and guts'' melodramas, with the Germans and the Japanese taking the place of more traditional ''bad guys.'' One of the better war movies was *Mrs. Miniver* (1942), which introduced Americans to the trials of total war in Britain. Starring Greer Garson and Walter Pidgeon, the film did display a degree of contrived sentimentality. Warner Brothers' *Action in the North Atlantic* (1943) was a highly realistic release about the merchant marine—so realistic that it was later used as a training film. Perhaps the best movies about the war were done by the armed services themselves, often under the supervision of former Hollywood directors. Among these was John Ford's *Battle of Midway,* made for the Army, and Darryl Zanuck's *At the Front,* commissioned by the Signal Corps.

Spectator sports remained very popular during this period. Baseball and football declined, however, when a large number of the young players joined the service or were drafted. But military needs had no effect on the number or the quality of racehorses, as attendance at the tracks boomed. With few luxuries to spend their money on, the newly affluent seemed to enjoy spending their extra income on trackside betting. The federal government finally closed the tracks for several months because of all the gasoline that was squandered going to the races.

The Printed Word   In spite of large attendances at the racetracks and movies houses, Americans read a great deal during these pretelevision days. Nonfiction was more popular than ever before, a reflection of the nation's concern with the war and the general state of the world. Heading the nonfiction list on Pearl Harbor day was William L. Shirer's *Berlin Diary,* the account of a radio broadcaster's experiences in the Nazi capital from 1934 to 1941. Its successor was yet another diary, that of Joseph Davies, American ambassador to the Soviet Union. His *Mission to Moscow* (1942) praised the Soviets for their courage and resourcefulness during the German invasion, while playing down the brutalities and privations of Soviet life before the war. In 1943 Davies's book came out as a highly controversial movie. Even more successful was Wendell Willkie's *One World* (1943), an account of the former candidate's recent travels around the world and a plea for international cooperation after the war. Several other best-selling titles in the non-fiction category were vivid accounts of crucial battles. Among the most applauded were Richard Tregaskis's *Guadalcanal Diary* and Ernie Pyle's *Here's Your War,* both published in 1943. Bill Mauldin's *Up Front,* which appeared in 1945, gave readers a glimpse of the combat soldier's irreverence for officers, contempt for troops in the rear echelons, and frequent bitterness toward civilians back home.

In the fiction column there were several religious novels that had wide appeal to a public in the throes of war. Leading the list was Lloyd C. Douglas's *The Robe* (1942). John Steinbeck's *The Moon is Down* (1942) dealt with the Nazi invasion of Norway and angered some readers by failing to paint all Germans as irredeemably wicked. In *A Bell for Adano* (1944) John Hersey explored cultural differences and ethnic animosities during the American conquest of Sicily. Richard Wright's *Black Boy* (1945), a thinly fictionalized account of the author's own deprived boyhood in the South, pointed to a growing awareness of the plight of black Americans.

POLITICS AS USUAL

Domestic politics also felt the effects of war, but there were no real departures from the patterns of the early 1940s. Indeed, the relative political quietude of the war years was a testament to American democracy in a world torn asunder by terror and death.

A Fourth Term for the Commander in Chief   Franklin Roosevelt's decision to run for a fourth term in 1944 presented fewer obstacles than his bid for reelection in 1940. He had already broken the no-third-term precedent, and with the country at war, he could seek another four years in the White House by merely offering to stand by his post, like any good soldier. There were no serious competitors for the Democratic nomination and the president won it handily. Instead, the most exciting contest during the summer of 1944 was the race for second spot on the Democratic ticket.

The chief contender for second place was Vice-President Henry Wallace, who very much wanted to continue in office, believing that it would put him in a good position for the 1948 presidential nomination. But Wallace was much too liberal for increasingly powerful conservatives in the party. Also in the running were Supreme Court Justice William O. Douglas and Speaker of the House Sam Rayburn. As he had done with his presidential rivals in 1940, Roosevelt encouraged all of the vice-presidential contenders in 1944, including Wallace, whom he secretly opposed. Meanwhile the wily president settled on Senator Truman as the best candidate. Truman had won great respect for his investigations of war industries without, at the same time, embarrassing Roosevelt or the Democratic party. And hailing from a border state like Missouri, he could attract votes from both the South and the Midwest. Roosevelt's machinations succeeded once again, and Truman received the vice-presidential nod.

The Republicans nominated Thomas E. Dewey on a ticket with Ohio's Governor John W. Bricker. Willkie had sought the nomination, too, but alienated the party with his frequent attacks on conservative Republican members of Congress. Dewey meanwhile had grown in stature and experience. In 1942 he had been elected governor of New York and could claim to be a young but seasoned politician. He was capable, energetic, and determined, but certain personality quirks hindered him seriously. At times he could appear stiff and humorless, while his proper attire and dark waxy mustache caused many to remark that he looked like the groom atop a wedding cake.

Like Willkie, Dewey accepted the principal results of the New Deal and was an internationalist in foreign affairs. In many ways, Dewey would mount another me-too campaign, agreeing with Roosevelt on most of the issues but promising that he and the Republicans could administer the system better. He soon discovered, like Willkie before him, that such an approach left few issues on which to attack the president. Dewey thus concentrated on Roosevelt's health and the longevity of Democratic rule.

Dewey's speculations about the president's health were all too true, though the public was largely ignorant about the matter. In June 1944, while on an inspection trip to San Diego, Roosevelt experienced severe chest pains. A couple of weeks later he complained of a seizure, with pain radiating into both shoulders—doubtless an attack of angina pectoris. Photographs also showed the president looking haggard and tired. Yet he managed to rally for a few carefully staged campaign appearances. To demonstrate his stamina, he rode standing up in an open car for four hours through New York streets, seemingly oblivious to a cold and driving rain. And in response to Dewey's charges that his Democratic administration was old and tired, he pointed to American landings in Normandy and the impending liberation of the Philippines.

Failing to make headway on the health and longevity issues, a desperate Dewey tried to tar the New Deal with the brush of communism. Some conservative Republicans had charged for years that the New Deal was socialistic or even communistic. Dewey added to these more general charges by reminding the electorate that Roosevelt had pardoned Earl Browder, leader of the American Communist party, and further criticized the president for courting the left-leaning CIO. Such charges of communism through vague or even imagined association would become common within a few short years, but they failed in 1944. Roosevelt's supporters simply refused to believe that he was tainted with communism, socialism, or subversion of any color. As commander in chief of victorious American armies, he appeared the very embodiment of patriotism.

Besides reassuring the public about his health and democratic principles, Roosevelt promised the country a continuation of the good life after the war. He would provide the nation with 60 million jobs, enough for anyone who wanted work. Government would assist in the building of new homes, highways, airports, and hospitals. The Missouri, Arkansas, and Columbia River basins would be developed along the lines of the Tennessee Valley Authority. His administration would also try to stimulate foreign trade and help small businesses. Finally, the president would ask Congress to make the Fair Employment Practices Committee permanent. There would be something for nearly everyone in a Democratic victory.

When the votes came in, Roosevelt proved as victorious as his troops, but the majority was a bit smaller than in 1940, representing less than 53 percent of the popular vote. He carried 36 states with 432 electoral votes to Dewey's 12 states and 99 electoral votes. Roosevelt again won big among lower-income groups and in urban areas. A large vote of confidence from the soldiers, whose voting had been facilitated by the mass mailing of special absentee ballots, helped, too.

No Change on Capitol Hill   The Democrats also maintained their congressional majorities in 1944. But as in the last three elections, including the off-year balloting of 1942, Democratic majorities were of little solace to New Dealers and liberals, for conservative Democrats continued to vote with Republicans to defeat most social legislation, and they would continue to do so for decades. It was this coalition that refused to increase income taxes in 1944 and sounded the death knell for several surviving New Deal agencies. Congress refused to extend the Civilian Conservative Corps in 1942 and the National Youth Administration a year later, despite plans to overhaul both agencies for wartime projects. And in 1944 and 1945 the conservative coalition would fail to authorize extensive planning for the postwar period; nor would it implement any of the programs that President Roosevelt outlined in his 1944 campaign. Of course, Roosevelt had seen the writing on the wall sometime before. Knowing that domestic reform was probably dead for the time being, he himself had declared that ''Dr. New Deal'' had to stand aside for ''Dr. Win-the-War.''

PLANNING FOR PEACE

The G.I. Bill   In one area, however, Congress was willing to open its pocketbook wide. It and a grateful nation would gladly assist the returning soldiers to readjust to civilian life. Powerful veterans' organizations had lobbied since the beginning of the war for generous benefits, and no sensible legislator wanted to alienate millions of returning troops and their families. In June 1944 Congress passed and President Roosevelt signed the so-called G.I. Bill of Rights. (G.I., short for ''general issue,'' was a slang term for soldiers and sailors during World War II.) Instead of promising bonuses at some future date, the act provided veterans with a number of more immediate benefits, several of which would have long-term consequences.

The most innovative and far-reaching feature of the G.I. Bill pertained to education. The government would pay for at least one year of education (or training of any kind) for every veteran. He or she was entitled to an additional year of schooling for every year served, up to a total of four years. This provision would entice many returnees onto college campuses and out of the job market while business and industry retooled for a peacetime economy. It also permitted thousands of young people, who might never have had a chance to attend college, to obtain a higher education.

Along with schooling, former G.I.s could collect unemployment compensation for one year after their release from the military. Thus they would enjoy some income while looking for a job and the economy would benefit from their expenditures, however meager. Yet another portion of the G.I. Bill established federal guarantees for home mortgages and business loans. This easy credit helped veterans to buy farms, establish commercial enterprises, and purchase millions of new homes, all of which contributed greatly to the postwar housing boom and general prosperity. Finally, the G.I. Bill mandated employment counseling for former service personnel, as well as new veterans hospitals and a wide array of health benefits.

Many liberals wanted to extend such features to the population at large. It was the only way, they claimed, to prevent a return to mass unemployment and depression. But Congress and the country were in no mood for extensive economic planning or social welfare schemes.

Bretton Woods   When it came to the international situation, there was a bit more willingness to anticipate and plan for the future. The twentieth century, not yet half over, had already witnessed two devastating world wars and no one wanted to see a third. Few advocated a return to the isolationism of the 1920s and 1930s, a stance that had played into the hands of aggressor nations. Hence there was much support within government, and without, for international cooperation to promote peace and prosperity.

Many experts believed that high tarriffs and economic warfare had helped to cause both world wars. President Roosevelt went even further, asserting that ''commerce is the lifeblood of a free society.'' The country had to insure ''that the arteries which carry the bloodstream are not clogged again.'' Pursuing such sentiments, representatives from 44 countries met at Bretton Woods, New Hampshire, in July 1944. The British delegation, headed by the brilliant economist John Maynard Keynes, proposed a huge international clearinghouse to extend credit and facilitate exchange. The Americans, however, insisted on more conservative arrangements that were beneficial to the United States.

Two institutions came out of the Bretton Woods Conference. The Intenational Monetary Fund, financed and controlled by member governments, would attempt to stimulate trade through currency loans. The International Bank for Reconstruction and Development (popularly known as the World Bank) would try to salvage war-torn economies and assist their future development. From the start the United States controlled both. Voting in the Intenational Monetary Fund was weighted according to each nation's contribution, the United States receiving a large plurality of the votes because of its substantial funding. The wealth and prestige of American banks also assured them leadership of the World Bank. The two organizations were a step in the right direction, but they would soon prove inadequate to the needs of postwar trade and reconstruction.

Forging the United Nations   Most Americans at the time also believed that failure to join the League of Nations had been a costly mistake, and support grew during the war for a new peacekeeping organization. In October 1944 representatives from the United States, Great Britain, China, and the Soviet Union gathered at Dumbarton Oaks, a mansion in the Georgetown section of Washington, D.C., and held initial discussions for such an organization. The Big Four agreed to create a Security Council, responsible for settling crises and maintaining peace, along with a General Assembly that could discuss other questions of international concern. The Big Four, plus France, would enjoy permanent seats on the Security Council, while all members would be represented in the General Assembly.

The Soviets created considerable commotion by demanding a veto over all proposals brought before the Security Council. The United States held out for a veto on purely substantive and not procedural questions. The Soviet Union also requested 16 votes in the General Assembly, one for each of the Soviet Republics. These were necessary, the Soviets asserted, to counteract the votes of the British Commonwealth countries, as well as the U.S.–Latin American bloc. Both topics were postponed for future discussion. Power politics and regional jealousies would plague the United Nations throughout its existence. Nevertheless, the first meeting of the new organization was held in San Francisco on April 25, 1945, with some 50 nations signing the United Nations Charter.

BIOGRAPHICAL SKETCH

GEORGE S. PATTON · *1885–1945*

Even before his untimely death at the end of 1945, General George S. Patton had become a legendary figure. Born in Pasadena, California, Patton hailed from a long line of military men, including high officers in both the American Revolution and the Civil War Confederacy. Patton entered Virginia Military Institute like his father and grandfather before him, but transferred to West Point after his freshman year. Known at West Point for his physical strength and athletic prowess, Patton represented the United States at the Stockholm Olympic Games in 1912, placing fifth in the military pentathelon.

Patton's first experience under fire came in 1916 when he accompanied General John J. Pershing on a punitive expedition into Mexico against Pancho Villa, attracting considerable notice after shooting three of Villa's bodyguards in a gunfight. In 1917 Patton followed Pershing to France and concentrated on tank warfare. There he formed the 304th U.S. Tank Brigade and distinguished himself in battle. During the 1920s and 1930s he took various assignments in the cavalry (later the tank corps), continuing his interest in mechanized welfare.

World War II allowed Patton to demonstrate his great talents as a battlefield commander. In November 1942 he directed a large amphibious landing at Casablanca. Several months later, in Tunisia, he rallied the Second Tank Corps after a stinging defeat at the Kasserine Pass and led them to several brilliant victories against the Germans. The second half of 1943 found him in Sicily, where his mechanized units swept across the western part of the island to take Palermo and then wheeled east for a lightning attack on Messina. Yet it was in Sicily that Patton nearly

General George S. Patton

lost his command. While touring military hospitals he slapped a soldier suffering from battle fatigue and verbally upbraided two others. He later explained that he was trying to shock them back into good health.

In preparation for D-Day Patton took charge of the Third Army. Once in Normandy, he encircled the German Seventh Army and began driving east through France, stopping only when his armored columns outran their supply lines. The war ended with Patton deep into Austria and western Czechoslovakia.

During the first weeks of peace Patton grew suspicious of Soviet activities in eastern Europe and called for the United States to join the Germans in a crusade to push the Russians back into their own territory. He also advised the Army to employ more former Nazis in the occupation of Germany. Only they, he contended, could provide the necessary bulwark against Communist subversion. Because of his outspoken and controversial opinions, Patton was relieved of his command. Soon thereafter he broke his neck in an automobile accident and died 12 days later.

Temperamentally, Patton was a curious blend of tough warrior and sentimental romantic. He could be deeply religious at times, but was frequently profane in his speech and personal behavior. His colorful yet contradictory personality has led to a growing body of Patton literature. The movie *Patton* (1970), starring George C. Scott, was a box office hit that appealed to the postwar generation as well as to those old enough to remember the war. The Patton mystique will doubtless live on for some time.

Crimes Against Humanity   As the United Nations got under way, American troops were liberating the most tragic victims of Nazi tyranny. For over six million Jews the liberation came too late. Shot, starved to death, and gassed, they had been brutally killed as part of Hitler's plan to exterminate Europe's Jews. Although these persecutions had begun well before the war, the United States refused to increase immigration quotas to admit the helpless targets of Hitler's wrath, citing the continuing economic depression as the most frequent excuse; nor would the government relent and admit large numbers of Jewish refugees into the country after the war. Even so, these atrocities, generally known in the postwar Jewish community as the Holocaust, reinforced the Allied decision to de-Nazify Germany. The occupying powers would discredit Nazi ideology and punish party as well as military leaders.

The most notorious Nazis stood trial at Nuremberg before a special tribunal of Allied judges, with Supreme Court Justice Robert H. Jackson representing the United States. Accused of crimes against humanity and the rules of civilized warfare, 12 Nazi chieftains received death sentences and another 7 went to jail for long terms. In the years ahead, hundreds of lesser Nazis would be tried and convicted.

These judicial proceedings prompted a degree of criticism in the United States. Some described the Nuremberg trials as mere window dressing by a victorious coalition that had determined their prisoners' guilt long before the court assembled, while others objected that international law did not provide for such a tribunal. But most Americans believed that the Nazis got what they deserved.

No one, of course, could guess just what the postwar era would bring. But few predicted the train of crises that would puncture the peace almost as soon as it began and threaten the very existence of humankind.

SUGGESTED READINGS

Sources on World War II are voluminous. The most comprehensive military history is Russell A. Buchanan, *The United States and World War II* (2 vols., 1964). Other overviews are Basil Collier, *The Second World War: A Military History* (1967), and Kent R. Greenfield, *American Strategy in World War II* (1963). On the war at sea there is Samuel Eliot Morison's *The Two Ocean War* (2 vols., 1963). The importance of naval air power is treated in Clark G. Reynolds, *The Fast Carriers: The Forging of an Air Navy* (1968). On air power in general there is David Macisaac, *Strategic Bombing in World War II* (1976). For analyses of the atomic bomb and its immediate consequences, see Herbert Feis, *The Atomic Bomb and the End of World War II* (1966), and Martin J. Sherwin, *A World Destroyed* (1975).

A number of studies focus on the top American commanders during World War II. Among these are Stephen E. Ambrose, *The Supreme Commander: The War Years of General Dwight D. Eisenhower* (1970); Dwight D. Eisenhower, *Crusade in Europe* (1948); Russell F. Weigley, *Eisenhower's Lieutenants* (1983); James D. Clayton, *The Years of MacArthur*, Vol. 2, 1941–1945 (1975); William Manchester, *American Caesar: Douglas MacArthur, 1880–1964* (1978); and E.B. Potter, *Nimitz* (1976).

Overviews of World War II diplomacy may be found in Robert Dallek, *Franklin D. Roosevelt and American Foreign Policy, 1932–1945* (1979); Robert Divine, *Second Chance: The Triumph of Internationalism in America during World War II* (1967); and Gaddis Smith, *American Diplomacy during World War II* (1963). Anglo-American relations in particular are delineated in Theodore A. Wilson, *The First Summit; Roosevelt and Churchill at Placenta Bay, 1941* (1969), and Christopher Thorne, *Allies of a Kind: The United States, Britain, and the War Against Japan* (1978). On relations among the United States, Great Britain, and the Soviet Union, there are Robert Beisner, *The Uneasy Alliance: America, Britain, and Russia, 1941–1943* (1972); Herbert Feis, *Churchill, Roosevelt, and Stalin* (1967); and William L. Neumann, *After Victory: Churchill, Roosevelt, Stalin and the Making of the Peace* (1969). For the two crucial summits during the last year of the war, one should consult Diane Clemens, *Yalta* (1970), and Herbert Feis, *Between War and Peace: The Potsdam Conference* (1969). A revisionistic and highly critical view of wartime diplomacy is Gabriel Kolko, *The Politics of War* (1968).

An assessment of the impact of war on domestic politics may be had in Robert A. Divine's *Foreign Policy and U.S. Presidential Elections, 1940–1948* (1974). On Roosevelt as a political leader during this period, see James M. Burns, *Roosevelt: The Soldier of Freedom* (1970). For Willkie there is Steve Neal's *Dark Horse: A Biography of Wendell Willkie* (1984). A good starting point for examining Congressional politics is David L. Porter, *Congress and the Waning of the New Deal* (1980).

On propaganda and image making, see Akira Iriye, *Power and Culture: The Japanese-American War, 1941–1945* (1981); Michael Leigh, *Mobilizing Consent* (1976); Ralph B. Levering, *American Opinion and the Russian Alliance, 1939–1945* (1967); and Allan M. Winkler, *The Politics of Propaganda: The Office of War Information, 1942–1945* (1978).

General studies of wartime society are John M. Blum, *V Was for Victory* (1976), and Richard Polenberg, *War and Society: The United States, 1941–1945* (1972). Oral accounts from men and women who lived through the war may be had in Studs Terkel, *The Good War* (1984). On women and the war at home, see Chester W. Gregory, *Women in Defense Work during World War II* (1974). The black experience during the war years is examined in Richard Dalfiume, *Desegregation of the Armed Forces, 1939–1953* (1969); Mary P. Motey, *The Invisible Soldier* (1975); and Neil A. Wynn, *The Afro-American and the Second World War* (1976). Accounts of the internment of Japanese Americans may be found in Roger Daniels, *Concentration Camps USA: Japanese Americans and World War II* (1971); Edward Spencer, *Impounded People: Japanese Americans in the Relocation Centers* (1969); and Michi Weglyn, *Years of Infamy: The Untold Story of America's Concentration Camps* (1976). Wartime movies and their effects are considered in Joel Greenberg, *Hollywood in the Forties* (1968), and Lawrence H. Suid, *Guts and Glory: Great American War Movies* (1978).

On postwar planning there are Alfred E. Eckles, *A Search for Solvency: Bretton Woods and the International Monetary Fund, 1941–1971* (1973); Keith W. Orson, *The G.I. Bill, the Veterans, and the Colleges* (1974); and David Ross, *Preparing for Ulysses: Politics and Veterans During World War II* (1969). Those interested in the Nuremberg trials should read Bradley F. Smith, *Reaching Judgment at Nuremberg* (1977). On the Jewish Holocaust, see Arthur D. Morse, *Six Million Died* (1967), and David S. Wyman, *The Abandonment of the Jews: America and the Holocaust* (1984).

11

War to Cold War

Americans greeted the end of World War II with wild jubilation, as President Truman's announcement of V-J Day sent them into the streets of every city and village in the land. They sang, shouted, danced, and hugged total strangers in a spontaneous outpouring of joy and relief. The legions of darkness had been destroyed; lasting peace seemed at hand.

Within months world events began to cast a long shadow over the peace. By 1947 many Americans would conclude that the Soviet Union had replaced Germany and Japan as the world's number one menace, while another three years would see open warfare between the United States and Communist North Korea. And looming in the background would be the very real possibility of war with the Soviet Union. It looked as if the United States had vanquished one set of tyrants, only to be confronted with the equally dangerous threat of totalitarian communism. Victory in World War II had not assured decades of tranquility. The postwar years would crackle with international tension, witness numerous local conflicts, and generate the growing specter of nuclear annihilation.

Although an open clash between the United States and the Soviet Union did not occur during these years, their conflicting policies and views erupted in what was soon called the cold war. This simmering contention between the two superpowers and their allies would dominate American foreign policy for decades and would touch many facets of domestic life. Wars in Korea and Vietnam, the escalating nuclear arms race, political and ideological intolerance at home, and the dangers of runaway inflation all stemmed in one way or another from the cold war.

245

Historians Debate

THE ORIGINS OF THE COLD WAR

Just who and what caused the cold war has been a subject of contention among historians for several decades. Although there are many shades of opinion, most accounts of the cold war fall into two broad schools—traditionalists and revisionists. Traditionalists place the greater share of blame on the Soviet Union, while revisionists have pointed to American attitudes and decisions. Both sides, however, agree that the trouble began in Eastern Europe following the collapse of Hitler's Reich.

Typical of the traditionalists is Herbert Feis, whose *From Trust to Terror* (1970) contrasts American attempts to create a free and prosperous world with Stalin's ruthless suppression of political and economic liberty in lands bordering the Soviet Union. Arthur M. Schlesinger, Jr., in his "Origins of the Cold War" (*Foreign Affairs,* Oct. 1967), echoes Feis's thesis. For Schlesinger the cold war was a clear case of right against wrong. It was, he wrote, "the brave and essential response of free men to communist aggression."

Revisionists, on the other hand, make much of Soviet concerns for their future security and of American failure to appreciate their need for "buffer states" as a guarantee against attacks from the West. Gar Alperovitz's *Atomic Diplomacy* (1965) goes further, to charge that the American monopoly on atomic weapons at the end of the World War II, combined with veiled threats to use them against the Soviet Union, caused Stalin to become even more rigid and suspicious of the United States.

Yet the major thrust of revisionist historiography is economic. Writing in the anticapitalist atmosphere of the 1960s, Joyce and Gabriel Kolko, William A. Williams, and others believed that the cold war originated in American attempts to extend the "open door" into Eastern Europe and thereby dominate the area economically. This thesis is presented in the Kolkos's *Limits of Power* (1971) and Williams's *Tragedy of American Diplomacy* (1962).

Some historians have refused to fall in with either camp. Among these is Geir Lunderstad, whose *American Non-Policy Toward Eastern Europe* (1978) finds inconsistency and lack of direction in American diplomacy as a principal cause of misunderstanding and friction between the United States and the Soviet Union. John Lukacs's *History of the Cold War* (1961) likewise faults the irregular nature of American policy in Eastern Europe. Lukacs's work, which was the first real history of the cold war in English, also explores the conflict within a cultural and historical context that reaches all the way back to the eighteenth century. Rejected by both traditionalists and revisionists, his account still deserves serious attention.

THE ROOTS OF ENMITY

At the center of the conflict was increasing enmity between the United States and the Soviet Union. Historians have traced its most immediate causes to World War II and its aftermath, but hard feelings between the two countries had long antedated the war. Both nations had pursued expansionistic policies for centuries. As the Americans moved west from the Atlantic coast, the Russians pushed east into Siberia and across the Bering Strait into Alaska and eventually as far south as California. The United States protested through the Monroe Doctrine and Russia eventually retreated from North America, the Russians selling Alaska in 1867 for what turned out to be a bargain price. Two generations later American support for Japan during the Russo-Japanese War placed a further strain on relations. Russian pogroms against Jews and the persecution of other subject peoples outraged most Americans.

The outbreak of World War I in 1914 did little to improve American opinions of czarist Russia. The Russian alliance with Great Britain and France was an embarrassment to Americans who wanted to see the war as a crusade against autocracy. The Bolshevik Revolution in 1917 alarmed most Americans, and the following year President Wilson contributed 10,000 American troops to an anti-Bolshevist expeditionary force that landed in Siberia to aid czarist partisans, an armed invasion that the Soviets would not soon forget. Then, despite the Bolshevik triumph in Russia, Wilson refused to recognize the revolutionary government.

Finally, in 1933, the Roosevelt administration extended diplomatic recognition to the Soviet Union. But in the years immediately thereafter, the United States and the western European democracies ignored Soviet calls for concerted action against Germany and Japan. Nevertheless, Stalin shocked Americans when he signed a nonagression pact with Hitler in the summer of 1939, and the Soviets' subsequent invasion of Poland and Finland made them seem little better than the Nazis.

Legacy of War The bombing of Pearl Harbor forced Americans to revise some of their attitudes toward the Soviet Union. The Germans and the Japanese posed a much greater threat to American security than the Soviets, and the United States could now join the Soviet Union in its struggle against fascism. From the very beginning, however, the collaboration betrayed numerous signs of misunderstanding and stress. Stalin suspected that Anglo-American reluctance to open a second front in France was part of a conspiracy to let the Nazis weaken the Soviet Union as much as possible. The Soviets, on the other hand, horrified the Western Allies when they halted their advance outside Warsaw while the Germans slaughtered Polish resistance fighters. It appeared that the Soviets did not want to face the political claims of Polish war heroes.

Unfortunately, President Roosevelt tried to avoid serious thinking about postwar relations with the Soviets. This was understandable at first: Recovering from the Japanese attack at Pearl Harbor and rallying the nation were his primary responsibilities, but as the months passed, Roosevelt continued to shrink from a confrontation with the Soviet question. He always disliked direct encounters, preferring to charm rather than to fight. Nevertheless, even Roosevelt became alarmed over Soviet activities in Eastern Europe during the late winter and early spring of 1945.

Churchill, on the contrary, had been wary of the Soviets from the beginning. As political leader of the British Empire—and himself a staunch imperialist—Churchill suspected that the Soviets would try to advance their own imperial interests in Eastern Europe and elsewhere. Churchill also tended to divide the world into spheres of infuence, and he knew that the war would alter the prevailing distribution. This is why he had urged Roosevelt to join in an attack through the "soft underbelly" of Europe and thereby beat the Soviets at their own game. When Roosevelt consistently refused to play openly at this kind of international power politics, the prime minister took the initiative and flew to Moscow in October 1944 for a meeting with Stalin. There he agreed to Soviet predominance in Bulgaria and Rumania in exchange for British control of Greece. Roosevelt, according to some sources, was not pleased. He not only opposed Soviet expansion into Eastern Europe, but had consistently taken a dim view of British imperialism, believing that the time had come for Britain, France, and the other colonial powers to relinquish their possessions. He therefore saw this arrangement between Churchill and Stalin as a cynical bargain between two imperialist powers.

Even when Roosevelt was present at meetings between Churchill and Stalin, their agreements did little to insure better feelings between the United States and the Soviet Union. They have also provided much ammunition for postwar critics. The most vociferous detractors, for example, have labeled the Yalta agreements a complete sellout to the Soviets. Roosevelt, they contend, was a dupe to the Communists, perhaps even a knowing collaborator in a worldwide Communist conspiracy. Such charges are wholly untrue, for Roosevelt was clearly neither a Communist nor a Socialist. He had done everything he could in the 1930s to save American capitalism, while his Christian faith and belief in democratic institutions ran counter to most everything that Marx, Lenin, or Stalin espoused. Nonetheless, Roosevelt was tired and ill at Yalta, and he may not have held his ground as strongly as he might have under better circumstances. Within two months of the summit he would be dead.

Much more significant than Roosevelt's health at Yalta, however, were the strategic realities in early 1945. The Soviets had pushed the Germans out of Eastern Europe and were well on their way to Berlin. Behind them were 125 divisions of seasoned troops, and it would take far more than strong talk to dislodge them. Besides such matters of military strength, the United States had wholly different postwar strategies in mind than the Soviets. American economic and diplomatic planners had called for freer trade and democratic governments in Eastern Europe, while the Soviets were intent on maintaining tight control over the region as a guarantee against future German attacks. Meanwhile the Pacific war dragged on, with the United States bracing for a costly invasion of the Japanese homeland. Anxious for a Soviet declaration of war against the Japanese, Roosevelt believed that he had to accommodate them somewhat in eastern Europe—at least for the time being.

GETTING TOUGH WITH THE SOVIETS

Harry S Truman was more than stunned when he learned of Roosevelt's death. "I'm not big enough for the job," he said to an old friend. Reporters heard him complain that he "felt like the moon and stars and all the planets had fallen on me." Truman also lacked Roosevelt's polish and air of cultivated gentility. Born on a farm near Lamar, Missouri,

A somber Harry S Truman, with wife and daughter beside him, taking the oath of office following President Roosevelt's death on April 12, 1945.

the new president had served as an artillery officer in World War I. After the war he had opened a men's clothing store in Kansas City, only to have the business collapse in the steep recession of 1923. He then went into local politics with the blessings of the notorious Pendergast machine. Elected to the United States Senate in 1934, he went on to become a faithful supporter of the New Deal, voting for nearly every administrative measure under Roosevelt.

Even so, Roosevelt would be a hard act to follow. Above all, Truman vowed to act like a president, and to him that meant a decisive pose. There would be none of the procrastination that marked Roosevelt's conduct at times; Truman would get tough with the Soviets. When Soviet Foreign Minister Vyacheslav Molotov paid a visit to the White House on April 23, Truman delivered a blistering lecture on Soviet failures to observe the Yalta agreements in Poland. An astonished Molotov protested that no one had ever talked to him like that. The president answered bluntly: "Carry out your agreements and you won't get talked to like that." By June, however, Truman was ready to compromise. He accepted Stalin's plan to add several non-Communist Poles to the Lublin government and promised to recognize it officially.

The United Nations Is Born At the same time, Truman had to finish plans for the opening meeting of the United Nations in San Francisco on April 25. The San Francisco meeting proved stormy from the start, as Soviet-American differences interfered immediately with the infant organization. Earlier the Soviets had demanded 16 votes in the General Assembly, but finally agreed to accept 3 votes instead. They also continued to demand a veto over all questions brought before the Security Council. The result was another compromise with the United States. The five permanent members of the Council could veto substantive but not procedural motions; that is, they could veto specific resolutions or other questions of policy, but not whether or how a matter should be discussed by the group.

Another troublesome question at San Francisco concerned the status of allegedly backward peoples. The Soviets urged swift independence for colonial populations and used the occasion to denounce Western imperialism, conveniently ignoring their own expansionist drives. The United States answered that many underdeveloped areas were not yet prepared to stand alone. Besides, both Truman and the State Department wanted to retain a number of Pacific islands captured from the Japanese. The two sides finally compromised on a trusteeship arrangement, not unlike the old League of Nations mandate system. The United States and other ''advanced'' nations could govern backward peoples, with vague promises of future independence. In the meantime, they would have to file periodic reports with the United Nations Trusteeship Council.

In the end, some 50 countries signed the United Nations Charter. Already the organization had become an arena in the emerging cold war, and in the years to come it would be manipulated shamelessly by both sides.

Meeting at Potsdam   In addition to his worries over the San Francisco meeting, Truman had to spend considerable time during the spring and early summer of 1945 preparing for the final gathering of Allied leaders at Potsdam. Once there, the Big Three soon fell to quarreling over Poland. Roosevelt and Churchill had already approved Soviet annexation of Poland up to the Curzon Line, a demarcation proposed by Great Britain after World War I. They had also agreed that Poland should receive compensation in the west at the expense of Germany. There the Polish frontier would extend to the confluence of the Oder and Eastern Neisse rivers. But the Soviets had pushed beyond that point, occupying lands as far as the Western Neisse and turning it over to Polish administration. Truman and Churchill protested, but could do nothing in the face of Soviet military superiority in the region.

The three leaders also differed over the Dardanelles, a narrow strait that connects the Black Sea to the Mediterranean. The Soviets wanted to replace Turkish control with some kind of international agreement. Truman did not openly object and used the question to introduce an American proposal—the unrestricted navigation of all inland waters. His most immediate goal was free navigation of the Danube, which ran for much of its length through Soviet-controlled territory. Stalin agreed to ponder the idea and then rejected it.

One of the most heated debates between Truman and Stalin focused on comparisons between Italy and Soviet-dominated Eastern Europe. Truman wanted to recognize the Italian government even though there had been no free elections. Stalin demanded equal recognition for Rumania, Bulgaria, and Hungary, where there also had been no free elections. Truman insisted that the situations were very different. The Soviets had unlimited access to Italy, while the western Allies were barred from countries under Soviet control. The United States would not recognize these satellite regimes until they were reorganized on more democratic lines and until free elections were held. Churchill further complained that an ''iron curtain'' (or ''iron fence,'' according to American accounts) had descended around Rumania. ''All fairy tales,'' Stalin retorted.

Yet the Potsdam conferees did reach a consensus on German reparations. At first the Soviets insisted on $20 billion worth of capital equipment and other goods. The

United States rejected a specific figure and proposed a percentage arrangement. The Soviets could take whatever they liked from their own zone. They could also have 10 percent of the industrial equipment in the western zones, in addition to another 15 percent that they would have to pay for in food and coal from their zone in eastern Germany.

It was at Potsdam, too, that Truman received news that the United States had successfully tested its first atomic bomb. In some respects the timing could not have been worse. The bomb probably gave Truman a false sense of superiority over the Soviets. The bomb also added to Soviet insecurity, reinforcing their fears of ''capitalistic encirclement.'' Stalin decided to build his own bomb; in the meantime he would keep large conventional forces in Europe.

Some of Truman's detractors would later say that he had been too lenient with the Soviets at Potsdam. Right then and there, they contend, the United States should have threatened to use force against the Communists. Such armchair critics forget that the country was still very much at war against Japan. In spite of the atomic bomb, military authorities wanted the Soviets to enter the war in the East. Besides, American public opinion would not have supported a hard line against the Soviets. The Soviet Union was an ally, and many Americans continued to admire the Red Army's stand against the Nazi invaders. More importantly, the United States would soon disband most of its military forces. And even before the Japanese surrender, American troops in Europe began protesting their impending transfer to the Pacific theater. Once Japan capitulated, the cries to go home grew louder. Troops at a number of outposts protested angrily and demanded to be mustered out right away; House members and senators received thousands of letters from mothers, wives, and sweethearts wanting to know why their men had not returned. The Soviet dictatorship, of course, did not have to worry about irate parents and spouses. By mid-1946 the giant American military and naval force of 12 million men and women had shrunk to about 1.5 million, certainly no match for Stalin's legions.

By the end of World War II, then, the political boundaries of Europe were already quite rigid. With few exceptions, Soviet power corresponded to the high-water mark of the Red Army. President Truman and his successors, both Democrat and Republican, would try to alter this accomplished fact through arms buildups and diplomatic pressure, but to no avail. Their efforts helped to feed Soviet insecurity and reinforced their resolve to stand firm.

THE LINES HARDEN

Nevertheless, as 1945 came to an end, American public and politicians alike believed that there was some room for maneuver with the Soviets. However, 1946 marked a crucial turning point in the evolving cold war. There were mutual charges of imperialism and ideological conspiracy, accompanied by declining expectations of an early or easy solution to Soviet-American differences.

Stalin fired the first salvo on February 9, when he declared in an impassioned speech that war was inevitable so long as capitalism lasted. The Soviet people must therefore face further sacrifices. Instead of turning out long-anticipated consumer goods, Soviet workers must again concentrate on iron, steel, and coal, and the weapons necessary to block capitalist aggression.

Winston Churchill answered for the West on March 5 in his now celebrated address at Westminster College in Fulton, Missouri. "From Stettin in the Baltic to Trieste on the Adriatic," the British statesman warned, "an iron curtain has descended across the Continent." Bulgaria, Rumania, Poland, Albania, Yugoslavia, Hungary, eastern Germany, and parts of Austria had all fallen into the Soviet grip, and to redress the balance, Churchill proposed an alliance of English-speaking peoples. Stalin promptly branded the former prime minister a warmonger.

To Contain Communism Not quite two weeks before, Truman had received another alarming indication of Soviet intentions in Europe and beyond. It came from young George Kennan, a scholar attached to the American embassy in Moscow. In a long telegram, which Truman had solicited earlier in the year, Kennan endeavored to explain recent Soviet behavior. The Kremlin, he observed, took a "neurotic" view of the international scene. Victory over the Germans had not changed the Soviets' "traditional and instinctive . . . sense of insecurity." They would not only cling to their acquisitions in Eastern Europe, but might try to obtain bases in Turkey and Iran, while also seeking to weaken Western influence among underdeveloped peoples. Finally, they would attempt to undermine American democracy itself. However, Kennan added, the Soviets respected force, and they tended to back down "when strong resistance is encountered at any point." The United States could therefore hope to contain Soviet expansion. Here was the seed of the "containment policy." It was not proclaimed in any great address or announced in a major position paper and would become policy only gradually, but containment was destined to become the mainstay of American foreign policy for decades to come.

Truman read the "long telegram," as Kennan's observations came to be known, but it was Secretary of the Navy James V. Forrestal who rang the alarm. He sent copies to hundreds, perhaps thousands, of high officials as required reading. Kennan's disquieting message would receive even wider coverage when the author published essentially the same analysis in the July 1947 issue of *Foreign Affairs* magazine.

In the years since, Kennan himself has analyzed his role in promoting the doctrine of containment. He has denied recommending the use of armed force in response to Soviet adventures and depreciates any role that he might have played in escalating cold war tensions. Whatever he intended, both the article and telegram had a great impact on American thinking about the Soviet Union.

The Nuclear Threat It was also in 1946 that the United States and the Soviet Union came to a deadlock on atomic energy and weapons. Many of the very people who had helped to create the atomic bomb were appalled at the prospect of nuclear war and hoped that the United States and other nations might learn to use atomic energy more constructively. Truman and the State Department were willing to explore international control of atomic energy and the eventual limitation of nuclear weapons. Under the coordination of Dean Acheson, then assistant secretary of state, and David Lilienthal, director of the Tennessee Valley Authority, a plan for international controls emerged. The final report was largely the work of J. Robert Oppenheimer, who had headed the Los Alamos Laboratory, where the first atomic bomb had been assembled.

The report recommended an Atomic Development Authority under the United Nations. In specified stages, the authority would take control of all fissionable materials, direct atomic research, and issue licenses to nations that wanted to use the atom peacefully. Individual governments were forbidden to build atomic bombs. Since the Soviets were likely to reject international sanctions or inspections, enforcement was left to individual countries. Until the plan was fully implemented, the United States would continue its monopoly on the atomic bomb.

Truman chose Wall Street banker and sometime presidential advisor Bernard Baruch to present the American scheme to the United Nations. Acheson and Lilienthal were disturbed at the choice, fearing that Baruch would render the proposal unacceptable to the Soviets. But Baruch had the support of influencial conservatives in the Senate, in addition to the strong backing of his friend, Secretary of State James F. Byrnes.

Baruch did just as Acheson and Lilienthal feared. He insisted on international sanctions against violators and opposed any veto over the punishment of guilty parties. The Soviets objected at once. Yet, even without the Baruch amendments, the Soviets may well have refused international controls on atomic energy. By the summer of 1946 they had lost nearly all trust in the United States and had already decided to build their own bomb. They also feared that an international atomic agency would fall under the control of Western governments who would then deny them licenses or fissionable materials. Finally, they opposed an interim American monopoly on nuclear weapons. International control of the atom became another victim of the cold war.

AN ANTI-COMMUNIST BLOC

Until 1947 American opposition to Soviet actions was largely strategic and geopolitical. Certainly, there were protests against the imposition of Communist governments in Eastern Europe, and there were numerous American denunciations of communism per se. But it was not until the second year of peace that most Americans began to see all Soviet actions as part of a worldwide Communist conspiracy. At the same time, the United States government became a prisoner of its own anti-Communist rhetoric. For once officials had thoroughly alarmed the public over the Communist menace, any overture to the Soviets or any response to their peace initiatives invited public and partisan attack. Thus Truman and his entire administration were frequently accused of being ''soft on communism,'' as were subsequent administrations of both parties. In the Kremlin, too, failure to take a harsher line against the capitalists became a political liability, as factions within the Communist hierarchy vied for power.

The Truman Doctrine   The campaign against international communism stemmed most immediately from President Truman's decision to aid Greece in February 1947. Great Britain had informed the State Department that it could no longer assist the conservative Greek government in its civil war against a Marxist National Liberation Front. There was no evidence that the rebels were receiving direct help from the Soviets, but it was certain that Communist Yugoslavia was sending them arms and supplies. Under the circumstances, Truman agreed to assume Britain's role in Greece and try to save the country from Communist subversion.

The first obstacle was Congress. The Republican Congress elected the previous November was determined to curb federal expenditures. The president therefore decided to use their fear of communism as a lever to obtain money for Greece. As Senator Arthur H. Vandenberg advised, Truman should go to Capitol Hill and "scare the hell out of them." And while he was at it, he should ask Congress to help the Turks, too. The Soviets had been pressing Turkey for joint control over the Dardanelles, and although the Turks had resisted, Truman anticipated future Soviet threats in the area. Besides, the president wanted to entice Turkey squarely into the Western camp.

On March 12, 1947, Truman appeared before a joint session of Congress and, as planned, warned of a massive Communist conspiracy. He did not attack the Soviet Union by name, but his protests against violations of the Yalta accords clearly pointed to the Soviets. His denunciations of "totalitarian regimes" were also unmistakable. Such governments, he added, "undermine the foundations of international peace and hence the security of the United States." Americans must therefore stand up and "support free peoples who are resisting attempted subjugation by armed minorities or by outside pressures."

This so-called Truman Doctrine was aimed against Soviet expansion and subversion. But interpreted broadly, it condemned all violent revolution, whatever its cause or source. Any uprising might disrupt world order and hurt American interests; in the following decades the United States would frequently oppose revolutionary movements in the name of international stability.

Not everyone in the foreign policy establishment was happy about Truman's statement. George Kennan, who had helped to sound the alarm a year earlier, disliked the strident ideological tone of the president's address. He believed that the open-ended pledge to uphold freedom was overly ambitious and potentially dangerous. Kennan thus echoed some of the concerns that Secretary of Commerce Henry Wallace had aired the previous September at a political rally in New York's Madison Square Garden. The secretary insisted that the United States had to accept the status quo in Eastern Europe or risk World War III. Pressure against the Soviets to retreat would only stiffen their resolve. "The tougher we get," Wallace declared, "the tougher the Russians will get. . . ."

Truman, of course, did not want war with the Soviet Union any more than Henry Wallace did. He was not asking Congress to commit American troops to either Greece or Turkey. "Our aid," he assured the legislators, "should be primarily . . . economic and financial." By a large majority, Congress approved a $400 million aid package.

Marshall Aid   The administration's next major foreign policy initiative—the Marshall Plan—followed logically from the Truman Doctrine, for, according to some analysts, Western Europe was as vulnerable to Communist threats as Turkey or Greece. Nearly two years after the war's end the Western European economy was in shambles. Several large American loans, along with substantial relief monies through the United Nations, had done little for industrial recovery. Europe was sinking into discontent, despair, and seemingly hopeless poverty. If conditions did not change rapidly, local Communist parties might increase their already large followings, especially in Italy and France. The Soviets would undoubtedly exploit this indigenous communism and try to seduce Western Europeans away from the American side. Finally, an impoverished Europe could not

AN ANTI-COMMUNIST BLOC

afford the arms to protect itself from a Soviet invasion. Economic and military recovery thus went hand in hand.

Secretary of State George C. Marshall (who replaced Byrnes in January 1947) dramatized Europe's plight in a commencement address at Harvard University. Massive aid from the United States would be necessary to put Europe back on its feet. There was considerable opposition to the plan in Congress. Republican Senator Robert Taft of Ohio and other conservatives opposed this massive ''welfare scheme'' for Europe, much as they had tried to block domestic welfare programs during the New Deal. On the left, Henry Wallace and his supporters charged that the plan would only inflame the Soviets further. But a Soviet-led coup against non-Communist Czech parties in February 1948, followed by the suicide or murder of the widely respected Czech foreign minister Jan Masaryk, horrified most Americans and lent urgency to what became known as the Marshall Plan, which cleared Capitol Hill in March.

European governments responded enthusiastically to the Marshall Plan. In late June of 1947, delegates from interested nations assembled in Paris to discuss their economic needs and make proposals to the United States. This included the Soviets, who had been invited despite mounting tensions. Ostracizing them would make the recovery plan seem like just another ploy in the East-West confrontation—which, to a large extent, it was. Secretly, the State Department hoped that the Soviets would refuse to take part in the program, and in the end, they did. They balked at opening their financial records to American scrutiny and claimed that the plan violated national sovereignty. They also feared that the United States would use the promise of economic assistance to lure the satellite nations away from the Soviet orbit. After several sessions the Soviets left the Paris meeting and forced their Eastern European clients to follow suit. In January 1949 they countered with their own aid package for Eastern Europe, the Council for Mutual Economic Assistance (COMENCON). The lines between East and West had been drawn even tighter.

While the Marshall Plan was taking shape the Truman administration proposed a similar but far less ambitious program to discourage Communist appeals in Latin America. In his inaugural address of January 1949 the president proposed to send scientific and technical aid to the nation's southern neighbors. Through such programs the Latin republics could ''produce more food, more clothing, and more . . . housing''—all ''through their own efforts.'' Known as Point Four aid because of its position on a list of administration proposals, the plan did not clear Congress until May 1950, and its initial appropriation of $26.9 million was far short of what Truman wanted. Nevertheless, Point Four became the first stage in an unfolding national policy to assist the economic development of poorer countries.

Both the Truman Doctrine and the Marshall Plan alarmed the Soviets, who feared that the West was planning to rearm Germany as part of an anti-Soviet coalition. Germany had invaded Russia twice since the beginning of the century. Visions of a reunified and rearmed Germany did little to comfort the Soviets, while American assurances of peaceful intent had no impression on the security-conscious Soviets. The Kremlin's response to these new arrangements in Germany provoked the most dangerous crisis thus far. On June 24, 1948, the Soviets blocked all rail and highway routes to the Western zones of Berlin. Western access to the city had not been guaranteed by treaty, but the United States was determined to remain in Berlin.

An American cargo plane being loaded with vital supplies for a besieged Berlin.

President Truman had several options. He could send in the tanks and attempt to blast open the routes to Berlin, or he could try negotiations. The first might lead to full-scale war with the Soviet Union, while the second might produce only a diplomatic standoff. He decided to launch a massive airlift of all necessary supplies into the city, hoping that the Soviets would not shoot down the American planes. For the next 11 months cargo planes flew 13,000 tons of food, fuel, and other supplies into Berlin each day, including coal for the winter months. The Soviets did not resist, and in June 1949 they lifted the blockade. Later that summer the Federal Republic of Germany was born, as West Germans held elections and began governing themselves once again.

The NATO Response Soviet actions in Berlin led President Truman to propose a military buildup in Western Germany. Britain, France, and the Benelux countries (Belgium, the Netherlands, and Luxemburg) had already taken the initiative by signing a mutual defense pact in March 1948, and the following summer American representatives began discussions to include the United States and other interested parties. On April 4, 1949, the United States, Canada, Italy, Norway, Denmark, Iceland, and Portugal joined the original five in signing the North Atlantic Treaty. (Italy, of course, was not an Atlantic nation, nor were several others that joined the alliance later.) The U.S. Senate approved the treaty by an impressive 82–13 vote.

Several years would pass before the North Atlantic Treaty Organization (NATO) became an effective military force. Yet approval of the NATO treaty was an unprecedented step for the American people. One hundred fifty years after Washington and Jefferson warned fellow citizens to avoid permanent and entangling alliances, the nation committed itself to the defense of Western Europe. Isolationism seemed utterly dead. The rise of fascism and the horrors of World War II had convinced most Americans that they could not simply mind their own business and remain untouched by powerful events beyond their borders. And whatever yearnings they might have for a simpler past, the consequences of a violent decade could not be undone. The United States had gone to war, had played a large role in defeating Germany and Japan, and thereby had helped to shape the postwar world. If the nation did not take some responsibility for world conditions, it was quite certain that the Soviets would not shrink from the task.

Recognizing Israel   It was fear that the Soviet Union would try to manipulate unsettled conditions in the Middle East, for instance, that helped convince the United States to recognize the state of Israel in May 1948. The emergence of this new nation had roots that went all the way back to the Jews' expulsion from their homeland in the first century after Christ. The dream of returning someday had never died entirely, and in the late nineteenth century several Jewish leaders inaugurated the Zionist movement. Their goal was to create a Jewish nation, and in the aftermath of World War I, small bands of emigrants began moving to Palestine, by then a British mandate under the League of Nations. The Nazi Holocaust and the large number of Jewish refugees at the end of World War II gave even more impetus to the Zionist dream. Despite objections by the British and the local Arab population, thousands of Jews found their way into Palestine, and by the spring of 1948 their leaders were determined to carve out a new state of Israel. When the Soviets made it clear that they were ready to recognize such a government, Truman decided to beat them to it and head off any special relationship between the Soviet Union and the Israelis. Thus on May 14, 1948, the president recognized the Jewish nation.

There were, of course, other reasons for the American recognition of Israel. The Democrats were anxious to please Jewish voters in the United States, and there was genuine sympathy for the victims of the Holocaust. Foreign policy strategists also welcomed the presence of a democratic and highly westernized people in the Middle East. Whatever the reasons for recognition, the American relationship with Israel would grow closer with the years and bring advantages as well as difficulties.

A NOT SO COLD WAR IN ASIA

As Israel was being born in the Middle East, events in Asia created the specter of another Communist triumph. For the next 25 years American leaders would insist that these advances in the Far East were engineered from Moscow as part of a monolithic Communist conspiracy. The United States would go to war in both Korea and Vietnam in largely futile attempts to stem the tide, while plunging the nation into the most divisive debate over foreign policy in the twentieth century.

China Goes Communist   Most shocking of all was the news that China had fallen to Communist rebels in the summer of 1949—despite numerous indications of an impending Communist victory. Much of the consternation had deep historical roots. For decades the United States had seen China as a kind of pet project. Some, with China's vast population in mind, hoped to carve out great commercial empires. John Hay's Open Door notes and later American espousals of the Open Door policy had tried to ensure free access to Chinese markets. Christian missionaries waxed eloquent over their plans to convert the ''heathen Chinese,'' while others felt genuine sympathy for a land that had taken so much abuse from its more powerful neighbors. Many of these looked forward to a day when China would be free, independent, and despite centuries of autocratic rule, somehow democratic. Indeed, the United States had fought a war with Japan to liberate China and restore the Open Door. The Communist takeover had destroyed American hopes for the Chinese and made the recent victory over Japan seem hollow. China had been delivered from its tormentors only to fall into the hands of the Communists, who most Americans assumed took their orders directly from Moscow.

Critics of the Truman administration charged that the president and his advisors had failed to support Chiang Kai-shek vigorously enough—that they had, in effect, "lost" China to the Communists. But Truman had aided the Nationalists so long as there was any hope for victory. After World War II the United States had transported Chiang and his armies into Manchuria so that they could take control of the area once the Japanese and Russians left. Truman even dispatched 100,000 American troops to China and provided logistical support. Despite such efforts, Mao and the Communists won the race for Manchuria. When the Russians left in the spring of 1946, Mao inherited a huge cache of Japanese arms and other equipment.

Earlier that year Truman had sent General of the Army George C. Marshall to China on a diplomatic and fact-finding mission. Marshall tried to reconcile Mao and Chiang to some sort of coalition government, but a tentative agreement collapsed when Chiang decided that he could retake Manchuria by force.

According to Marshall and many other American observers, Chiang was his own worst enemy. His rule was corrupt, incompetent, and tyrannical and he could not attract the support of the Chinese masses, who increasingly sided with Mao and the Communists. By the end of 1946 Marshall concluded that Chiang could not win the Chinese civil war without massive American assistance, including ground troops and air strikes. Indeed, Marshall warned Truman that the United States would virtually have "to take over the Chinese government" and remain there indefinitely in the face of continued Communist attacks. Given later American difficulties against a much smaller group of insurgents in Vietnam, Marshall's hesitations appear quite valid. American participation in the Chinese civil war would have become an endless quagmire and Truman knew it. The administration continued to send Chiang small amounts of aid but believed his cause was lost.

Following his victory, Mao made overtures to the United States and even invited the U.S. ambassador to China for informal talks. Truman nearly gave his permission and then changed his mind, supposing that Mao was already firmly in the Soviet camp. Still, the State Department discussed the possibility of recognition as soon as conditions warranted. Deteriorating relations between East and West would force postponement for a quarter of a century, for the fall of China was only the most recent event in a series of crises and disappointments for the American people.

NSC-68 In a little over a year, there had been the Berlin Blockade, with its threat of war with the Soviet Union, and the Communist victory in China. If this were not enough, the Soviets exploded their first atomic bomb in late August 1949, depriving the United States of its atomic monopoly; henceforth Americans would have to live in fear of a nuclear holocaust. Truman countered by authorizing an even more destructive hydrogen bomb and also ordered the National Security Council to reevaluate the nation's policies toward the Soviet Union and its Communist allies. The final report, known as NSC-68, would provide a framework for the nation's foreign policy for the next two and a half decades.

NSC-68 was largely the work of Secretary of State Dean Acheson, who replaced Marshall in January 1949. The document asserted, without any hard evidence, that the Soviets were bent on dominating the entire Eurasian land mass. Negotiating with the Soviets would accomplish nothing. They were fanatical Communists who could never be trusted, and who would not be satisfied until they had conquered most of the globe. The United States must therefore rebuild its military, stockpiling nuclear weapons and increasing conventional forces to fend off local Communist attacks. Additional alliances with non-Communist countries would supplement American rearmament. Finally, the nation should launch an all-out public opinion drive to alert citizens to the dangers of international communism. At the same time, the United States should try to undermine the allegiance of the Soviet people to their Communist masters. Communism had to be contained at all costs, and perhaps overthrown in the Soviet Union itself.

The new campaign called for extraordinary efforts and massive appropriations, and there was little chance that Congress would fund the undertaking. Then, in June 1950, South Korea was invaded by Communist forces from the north. Here was further proof of Communist aggression in Asia. The invasion now guaranteed abundant support for the steps outlined in NSC-68.

War in Korea: Initial Phase   The resulting Korean conflict was another remnant of World War II, yet it also had roots in a more distant past. For years Korea had been a bone of contention between Russia and Japan. Korea lay due west of Japan and was Japan's nearest port of entry to the Asian mainland. To the north of Korea was Chinese Manchuria, an underdeveloped but potentially rich land. In the northeastern corner of the country, Korea and the Soviet Union shared a short stretch of border. Understandably, Korea became a source of friction between the Russians and Japanese. Japan forced a protectorate on Korea following the Russo-Japanese War of 1904–1905, and in 1910 Japan annexed the peninsula outright.

The Soviets' declaration of war against Japan in the late summer of 1945 entitled them to occupy the northern portion of Korea, as American troops took up positions in the south. The occupying powers hastily agreed on the 38th parallel as the dividing line between their two zones. The Soviets, who wanted a buffer in North Korea against any possible Japanese resurgence, erected a Communist government above the 38th parallel. The United States responded in the south by installing a government under Syngman Rhee, an uncompromising Korean nationalist who had spent decades away from his homeland as an exile in the United States. The government that he established was by no means democratic, at least by American standards. It was corrupt, dictatorial, and favored wealthy conservatives.

By the end of 1948 the situation in Korea appeared fairly stable. In December the Soviets withdrew their last troops from the north, and in June 1949 the United States followed suit. The State Department was so confident about Korea that Secretary Acheson declared in early 1950 that the Korean peninsula was outside America's first line of defense in Asia—though not beyond the concern and protection of the United Nations. General MacArthur, now commander of Americn forces in Japan, had made a similar statement the year before. The North Koreans probably took these pronouncements to mean that the United States would not defend the South militarily, and on June 25, 1950, they invaded.

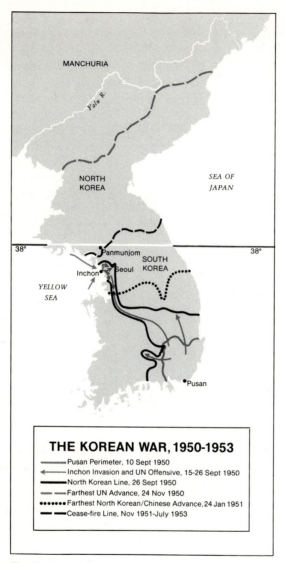

The Korean conflict.

President Truman concluded immediately that the Soviets were behind the invasion, though the nature and extent of Soviet involvement has remained unclear. He decided to act quickly, reasoning that a Communist takeover would put them within easy bombing range of Japan and would represent one more victory for the Soviets. On June 27 the President directed General MacArthur to assist the South Koreans with naval and air power. The same day the United Nations, in response to an American resolution, called upon member nations to join in resisting the invaders. (The Soviets, who surely would have vetoed such a measure, had walked out of the Security Council to protest a United

American troops advancing over the rough Korean terrain.

Nations refusal to seat Communist China.) Truman now had international approval for his countermeasures in Korea. Several other countries did, in fact, respond to the call and fought beside American units, but 90 percent of the troops and most of the funds came from the United States.

Unfortunately, Truman did not ask Congress for a declaration of war. Several congressional leaders said it was unnecessary and the president feared that a legislative debate might delay his response to the North Korean onslaught. There is little doubt, however, that Congress would have assented. Without their declaration Truman lacked the official support of Capitol Hill and opened himself to much criticism and abuse from Republicans. Truman himself invited such attacks when he called the war a "police action." A later generation would charge that he had usurped the power of Congress and helped lay the ground for an "Imperial Presidency."

For several months the military situation in Korea was grim. At the end of June Truman sent the first American troops from Japan, but they and their South Korean allies suffered heavy casualties and were forced to retreat day after day. They finally fell back to a corner of southeast Korea and established a defense perimeter around the port city of Pusan. On September 15 MacArthur stunned the enemy with a brilliant amphibious landing at Inchon, behind North Korean lines. The trapped Communists surrendered or fled across the 38th parallel.

Soon-to-be-dismissed General Douglas MacArthur receiving a medal from President Truman on Wake Island.

China Enters the War At this juncture Truman had to decide whether MacArthur should pursue the retreating North Koreans above the 38th parallel. If he did not, some analysts warned, the Communists might regroup and attack South Korea again. Complete victory over the Communists and a reunification of Korea under Rhee would also give the Truman administration a much-needed boost following its ''defeat'' in China. Yet the United Nations resolution had only called for the restoration of previous boundaries. Besides, an invasion of the North might invite a direct Soviet or Chinese counterattack. However, Secretary of State Acheson assured the president that the Chinese were too exhausted from their long ordeal to intervene, while Stalin had already declared that the Soviet Union would not enter Korea's ''civil war.'' Truman issued orders to cross the 38th parallel, with the United Nations concurring in late October.

The Chinese did not behave as predicted. The closer the Americans came to their boundaries in Manchuria, the more anxious they became. They warned the United States through India that an American march to the Yalu River (the boundary between North Korea and Manchuria) would provoke Chinese retaliation. The State Department dismissed these warnings and the campaign into North Korea continued. Then late in October and early November several hundred thousand Chinese troops streamed across the Yalu, driving the Americans and South Koreans back below the 38th parallel. In hard and costly fighting, UN forces managed to push the enemy back to the notorious parallel, where the lines finally stabilized.

BIOGRAPHICAL SKETCH

J. ROBERT OPPENHEIMER · *1904–1967*

More than anyone else in the scientific community, J. Robert Oppenheimer could claim credit for creating the world's first atomic bomb, and he emerged from his laboratory at the end of World War II as a minor celebrity. Yet within a decade he became the pawn of cold war suspicion and intolerance.

Born in 1904 to a wealthy New York family, Oppenheimer was a bright and precocious child. At Harvard he pursued a broad and demanding curriculum that included numerous courses outside the sciences, but nevertheless completed his college program in three years, graduating *summa cum laude*. He spent the next four years in Europe, where he studied physics with several outstanding researchers and developed a lifelong interest in atomic theory. He also found time to earn a Ph.D from the University of Göttingen in Germany.

In 1929 Oppenheimer began a distinguished teaching career when he accepted positions at the University of California at Berkeley and the California Institute of Technology. He was a brilliant lecturer, attracting many students through his provocative questions, intellectual integrity, and personal charm. It was during this period that Oppenheimer grew interested in politics and world affairs; like many intellectuals in the 1930s he was drawn to several left-wing causes.

Oppenheimer's research in atomic physics led him into the Manhattan Project. In order to obtain quicker and more efficient results, Oppenheimer advised the Army to concentrate all research for the atomic bomb at one location near Los Alamos, New Mexico. He was made director of the facility and immediately assembled an outstanding team of scientists.

The first successful test of the atomic bomb filled the sensitive Oppenheimer with a mixture of exhilaration and dread. Even so, he advised the Army to use the new weapon against the Japanese, believing that it would shorten the war and save lives. After the war, however, he worked to halt nuclear proliferation and hoped that the atom would be harnessed for peaceful uses. He was therefore delighted to cooperate with the State Department on its plan for international control of atomic energy, and in the late 1940s he opposed building a hydrogen bomb.

Oppenheimer's resistance to the hydrogen bomb, in addition to his prewar associations with radical groups, made him suspect in the early 1950s. In December 1953 the Atomic Energy Commission (AEC), under tremendous political pressure to prove its loyalty, revoked his security clearance, citing "defects of character." There was no evidence then or subsequently that Oppenheimer had ever compromised the security of the United States or engaged in disloyal activities.

Oppenheimer spent the rest of his professional life as director of Princeton's Institute for Advanced Studies, a position he had held since 1947. There he continued as a highly effective administrator and teacher. In 1963 the AEC made partial amends by selecting him for the Enrico Fermi Award and President John F. Kennedy bestowed the honor at a special White House ceremony. Oppenheimer died four years later of throat cancer, displaying the same intellectual curiosity about the deadly disease as he had about so many other troublesome issues during his life.

General MacArthur then insisted that Chinese entry called for new and drastic tactics. He wanted to bomb Chinese bases and supply depots in Manchuria, blockade the China coast, and do whatever else was necessary to achieve victory, but Truman refused permission. The Western European nations strenuously opposed any escalation of the conflict, and Truman himself feared a full-scale war with China, or even the Soviet Union. When MacArthur publicly criticized the decision, Truman fired him, provoking a storm of criticism at home.

Truman had no choice but to revert to his original goal in Korea—a restoration of boundaries at the 38th parallel. Truce talks began on June 23, 1951, at the urging of the Soviets, but negotiations dragged on for over two years as fighting continued along the parallel and the two sides argued over repatriation of prisoners and other details. On July 27, 1953, the deadly stalemate came to an end. By then over a million Americans had fought in Korea and had suffered 140,000 casualties, 34,000 losing their lives.

Korean Consequences   The Korean conflict would have a large impact on American cold war policy. Truman had presented the war as a necessary response to a worldwide Communist conspiracy directed from the Kremlin. Communism, the administration argued, was monolithic, a seamless cloth which neither nationalism nor local interests could pierce. Truman's successors would echo the same message—the United States must contain communism and try to undermine it where it already existed. Even non-Communist revolutionaries were suspect, for they might provide the Communists with an opening; to fight communism anywhere was thus to fight it everywhere.

It is understandable that Americans would find communism offensive during this era and after. Both in theory and practice it violated nearly every tenet of the American political and economic system. Stalin's bloody purges and the brutal tactics that the Soviets used to gain and hold power beyond their borders did much to alienate American opinion. At the same time, it is unfortunate that the United States could not appreciate Soviet concerns for their security in Europe and elsewhere. It was also unfortunate that both sides overestimated the strength and misunderstood the intentions of the other. The results were mutual charges of worldwide conspiracy, paralleled by constant attempts to force the other to back down or retreat. Ensuing decades would witness further ideological and military warfare, with periodic escalations in the nuclear arms race. Before long the cold war would threaten the entire human race.

SUGGESTED READINGS

There are several overviews of the cold war. Louis J. Halle's *Cold War as History* (1967) was an early attempt to put the conflict into a larger historical perspective. Lawrence S. Wittner's *Cold War America: From Hiroshima to Watergate* (1974) takes the account into the Nixon years. Especially insightful is John Lukacs, *A History of the Cold War* (1961).

Other works focus on the origins of the cold war. Among these are Roy Douglas, *From War to Cold War, 1942–48* (1981); John L. Gaddis, *The United States and the Origins of the Cold War, 1941–1947* (1972); Thomas T. Hammond, ed., *Witnesses to the Origins of the Cold War* (1982); Robert J. Maddox, *The Unknown War: Wilson's Siberian Intervention* (1977); Lisle A. Rose, *Dubious Victory: The United States and the End of World War II* (1973); and Daniel Yergin, *Shattered Peace: The Origins of the Cold War and the National Security State* (1977).

Still other authors have concentrated on contention between the United States and the Soviet Union. These are John L. Gaddis, *Russia, the Soviet Union, and the United States* (1978); Walter LeFeber, *America, Russia, and the Cold War, 1945–1980* (1980); Adam B. Ulam, *The Rivals: America and Russia since World War II* (1971); and Bernard A. Weisberger, *Cold War, Cold Peace: The United States and Russia since 1945* (1984). Vojtech Masny's *Russia's Road to the Cold War* (1979) is a useful volume by a Soviet historian.

On the early diplomacy of the period, see Terry H. Anderson, *The United States, Great Britain, and the Cold War, 1944–1947* (1981); Lloyd C. Gardner, *Architects of Illusion: Men and Ideas in American Foreign Policy, 1941–1949* (1970); and Gabriel Kolko, *The Limits of Power: The Cold War and United States Foreign Policy, 1945–1954* (1972). The last is particularly critical of American actions in the postwar world. Studies of the Marshall Plan in particular are Thomas A. Bailey, *The Marshall Plan Summer* (1978), and John Gimbel, *The Origins of the Marshall Plan* (1976). On the formation of NATO, see Timothy P. Ireland, *Creating the Entangling Alliance: The Origins of the North Atlantic Treaty Alliance* (1981); Lawrence S. Kaplan, *The United States and NATO: The Formative Years* (1984); and Robert E. Osgood, *NATO: The Entangling Alliance* (1962).

Several major figures of the era wrote memoirs. Of particular significance are Dean Acheson, *Present at the Creation* (1969); Charles Bohlen, *Witness to History* (1973); George F. Kennan, *Memoirs, 1925–1950* (1967); and Harry S Truman, *Memoirs: A Year of Decisions* (1955). The latter should be read in conjunction with Robert J. Donovan, *Conflict and Crisis: The Presidency of Harry S Truman, 1945–1948* (1977). Also illuminating in this regard is Richard V. Walton, *Henry Wallace, Harry Truman, and the Cold War* (1976).

Books that concentrate on Asia are Akira Iriye, *The Cold War in Asia* (1974), and Herbert Feis, *The China Triangle* (1966). The Korean conflict per se is treated in Bruce Cummings, *The Origins of the Korean War* (1981); Francis H. Heller, *The Korean War: A 25 Year Perspective* (1977); Glenn Paige, *The Korean Decision* (1968); and David Rees, *Korea: The Limited War* (1964).

12

From the Fair Deal to the Middle Way

Politics in the postwar period offered both continuities and departures. One constant was the overwhelming dominance of Democratic voters, who outnumbered Republicans more than two to one by the early 1960s. Not surprisingly, the Democrats controlled both houses of Congress for all but four years between 1945 and 1960. Yet this voter consistency did not translate into a new flurry of liberal legislation, for the combination of Republicans and conservative Democrats that first emerged in the late 1930s maintained its hold on Capitol Hill and blocked most liberal measures. Widespread prosperity and a renewed commitment to capitalism also dampened the liberal agenda.

At first glance the relationship between voter registrations and presidential elections during this period also appears perplexing. A large Democratic affiliation would logically produce huge majorities for Democratic nominees; yet Harry Truman barely won reelection in 1948. Republican Dwight Eisenhower's landslide elections in 1952 and 1956 likewise defied the registration statistics. It was as if citizens voted for Democratic Congresses in order to keep New Deal programs, while sending the more moderate Eisenhower to the White House in order to signal their opposition to further social reform. And in some ways this explanation makes sense. The postwar period was a time of political consolidation. Most Americans were happy with the social reforms of the 1930s, but were not sure if they wanted to go any further.

Cold war anxieties also exerted a powerful effect on American politics. Any criticism of American political life might be denounced as unwitting assistance to the Communist propaganda machine. Cold war rhetoric had also engendered an inflexible foreign policy, making it difficult for Democrats and Republicans alike to compromise with the Soviets or to seek a workable disarmament scheme.

TRUMAN TAKES CHARGE

Besides contending with such realities, President Truman had to manage a series of crises that arose out of the country's swift transition to peacetime. In nearly all of them Truman acted as a practical politician rather than as an ideologue of the right or left. This surprised many in light of Truman's consistent support for Roosevelt and the New Deal, but it is now clear that his support had owed as much to party loyalty as to personal conviction. Nevertheless, he thought that government could and should assist less fortunate members of society. He also believed that government must protect all citizens from the irresponsible power of both big business and organized labor. Above all, Truman detested professional liberals who seemed blind to the realities of everyday politics.

The Battle over Prices and Labor   No one knew better than President Truman just what these realities were or how swiftly they could overtake a new chief executive. Truman's own initiation came shortly after V-J Day in a battle over wages and prices.

The various measures to control inflation during the war had been quite effective, but peace brought sharp demands for an end to all controls. The most obvious target was the Office of Price Administration (OPA). Truman wanted the OPA to continue setting prices until reconversion was well under way; otherwise pent-up demand, combined with various shortages, might unleash a dangerous bout of inflation. Congress voted to extend the life of the OPA but greatly reduced its authority. Truman vetoed the bill because it was both ineffective and misleading. As he put it, the measure gave the people only "a choice between inflation with a statute and inflation without one." Controls ended in June 1946 and prices soared immediately, touching off loud complaints from consumers. Congress responded with another weak control bill, and the President reluctantly signed it. As Truman predicted, it had little effect.

But rising prices were not the only threat to family budgets. Peace had brought fewer overtime hours for industrial workers, resulting in as much as a 30 percent cut in take-home pay. These same workers also resented having had to hold the line on wages while stockholders earned handsome dividends during the war. They now wanted to stay ahead of inflation, recoup their overtime pay, and make up for wage sacrifices during the war. The result was a wave of strikes in 1946. By year's end, over 116 million days of work had been lost to labor walkouts. Auto workers struck early in the year, followed by coal miners in April and railroad workers in May. Although the auto strike posed a serious setback to reconversion, the rail and mine workers' strikes were far graver. The nation still depended on coal for most of its energy needs, and the railroads continued to haul most of the freight. Prolonged stoppages in either industry would cripple the entire economy.

Truman had always been sympathetic toward workers and had enjoyed considerable union support while in the Senate, but he could not allow labor demands to endanger the public welfare. On May 21 he seized the coal mines and ordered the miners back to work as government employees. All went well until United Mine Workers president John L. Lewis called the workers out again, this time on a technicality in the contract. Truman obtained a federal court injunction, U.S. attorneys arguing that recent labor legislation barred injunctions only on behalf of private employers. The courts cited Lewis and the union for contempt and imposed heavy fines. Lewis gave up and sent the men back into the pits.

The president took equally drastic action against the railroad workers. He went before Congress on May 25 and asked for authority to draft the strikers into the Army and then order them to run the trains, but as he spoke the two sides came to an agreement and the stoppage ended. Truman's plan outraged organized labor, as well as many legislators, who found his solution downright dictatorial.

Despite misgivings over Truman's methods, many senators and representatives concluded that the time had come to curb the unions through remedial legislation. The president vetoed the resultant Case bill in June 1946, believing that it was vindictive and ineffectual. A year later Congress passed a somewhat similar measure in the form of the Taft-Hartley Act. This law forbade union membership as a prerequisite for employment (the closed shop), made union leaders liable to law suits for violating contracts, outlawed union contributions to federal election campaigns, and permitted the president to seek an 80-day cooling-off period when an impending strike threatened the national welfare. Truman vetoed the bill, but Congress overrode him with votes to spare. On June 23, 1947, the Taft-Hartley Act became law, but it did little to weaken the unions and was a disappointment to many of its sponsors.

Legislating Full Employment   While members of Congress worried about the power of organized labor, a number of economists feared that the postwar era would witness another devastating depression. Drastic cuts in defense spending, combined with the return of 12 million men and women from the armed services, seemed destined to touch off an unprecedented wave of unemployment. Liberal economists urged legislation that would require the federal government to take specific actions whenever the economy appeared in danger. Among such measures would be tax cuts, deficit spending, extension of unemployment benefits, public works projects, and the like.

The final legislation fell short of what they wanted, but the Employment Act of February 1946 established an important precedent. In the past the question of whether or not to respond to economic emergencies was up to individual presidents and legislators; there was no legal requirement for them to act. The new law specifically declared that it was the ''responsibility of the Federal Government . . . to promote maximum employment, production, and purchasing power.'' The act also created a Council of Economic Advisors to help presidents to achieve these goals. Of course, it was up to each administration to implement the act and use the council effectively. Still, the legislation lent dramatic support to the idea that the federal government must play an active role in maintaining economic well-being, and in this sense it was clearly an extension of New Deal thinking.

Troubles in the Inner Circle   Meanwhile Truman was having plenty of trouble within his own official family. In February 1946 Secretary of the Interior Harold Ickes, who had remained at Truman's request following Roosevelt's death, submitted his resignation after opposing the president's appointment of Edwin Pauley as assistant secretary of the navy. Pauley had invested heavily in California oil wells, and Ickes feared a repeat of the Teapot Dome scandals. Unfortunately for Truman, Ickes shared his suspicions fully with the Senate and press. Ickes resigned his cabinet post in protest and Pauley failed to win confirmation.

In September the president forced Henry Wallace to resign from the Commerce Department. In a highly controversial speech that Truman approved after a cursory reading, Wallace criticized the administration's harsh line against the Soviets. Wallace continued his strictures even after he had assured Truman that he would keep silent on foreign affairs, leaving the president no choice but to fire him.

Ickes and Wallace were not the only ones to defy the president openly. Truman had decided to streamline the defense bureaucracy by creating a separate division for the Air Force and then to combine all three services (Army, Navy, and Air Force) under a single secretary of defense. Secretary of the Navy James Forrestal publicly opposed the plan, fearing that the Navy would lose its own air wing and much of its prestige. Several top-ranking naval officers also testified against the scheme. In the end Truman secured the National Security Act of 1947 which authorized a single Department of Defense. Nevertheless, the Army, Navy, and Air Force maintained bureaucratic autonomy as separate subdepartments. It would take several years of intramural bickering and a 1949 amendment to the National Security Act before the Department of Defense became a viable cabinet department with sufficient authority to oversee its three subdivisions.

Elections of 1946   By late 1946 the Truman administration seemed in disarray. Labor resented the president's tactics against striking rail and mine workers, and on the international scene, it looked as if Stalin were robbing the nation of its hard-earned victory in World War II. Republicans saw a golden opportunity to translate this discontent into votes during the off-year congressional elections. Voters had "had enough," Republicans insisted—enough strikes, enough shortages, enough high prices, enough incompetence, and enough communism. On November 5 citizens vented their frustrations against the Democrats, giving the Republicans control of Congress for the first time since 1928. They rolled up 246 House seats to the Democrats' 188, and in the Senate the balance was 51 to 45. The Republicans were jubilant, with conservatives vowing to repeal much of the New Deal. Among the House freshmen that year was California's Richard M. Nixon. Young John F. Kennedy of Massachusetts managed to buck the Republican tide and entered the House for the first time as well.

Promoting Civil Rights and National Loyalty   The 80th Congress, which convened in January 1947, was a constant thorn for Truman. One of their confrontations was over civil rights. That year the President ordered desegregation in the armed forces and appointed a civil rights commission to investigate discrimination throughout the United States. In October the committee delivered its report, aptly entitled "To Secure These Rights." It called for an ambitious legislative and judicial campaign against racism in America, and on February 2, 1948, Truman followed up the report with a ten-point message to Congress. He asked for a strong anti-lynching law, for a fair employment practices committee, for an end to racial segregation in interstate transportation, and for federal protection of black voting rights. As Truman feared, his proposals went nowhere in the conservative 80th Congress.

In seeming contrast to Truman's civil rights message was his loyalty program for the federal bureaucracy. Charges of communism in government were already filling the halls of Congress and Truman decided to initiate his own guidelines for federal employees, if only to head off the Republicans on Capitol Hill. In March of 1947 he established a Federal Employee Loyalty Program, with loyalty boards within each agency to hear charges against employees. By the end of Truman's term these boards had reviewed some 9,000 complaints of disloyalty but failed to uncover a single case of espionage. Nevertheless, about 1,200 civil servants were dismissed over the next decade as security risks, while another 6,000 resigned under pressure. Unfortunately, too many of these complaints were motivated by personal animosities within the bureaucracy. And the review proceedings were often grueling affairs that ruined the reputations of those who were innocently accused. Such hunts for possible Communists in government would become even more abusive in the years just ahead.

Truman's Surprise Victory   Amidst the furor over communism in government and the administration's civil rights bill, Truman decided to run for reelection. The outlook was not good. To some, Truman's personality was his greatest handicap. There were still many who regarded him as a crude upstart from the Midwest, and the president's blunt public comments often made him look rude and irresponsible. A classic incident involved his daughter Margaret's Washington début as an opera singer. When a local critic panned the performance, Truman wrote him a scathing letter, threatening the reviewer with a black eye and other bodily injuries. The letter duly appeared in the newspaper and confirmed opinions of the president's bad manners and ill-considered rhetoric. Others, remembering that the president was also a father, cheered his defense of his daughter. Nevertheless, there was widespread opinion that Truman simply had not been an effective or a particularly dignified president. ''I'm just mild about Harry'' was typical of the one liners that circulated at the time; ''To err is Truman'' was another of the popular quips.

Such controversies over Truman's behavior sowed much doubt in the minds of professional politicians, some of whom wanted to replace him with a more attractive candidate. A few had even courted General Eisenhower, whose political affiliation was then unclear. If this were not enough, the civil rights question split the Democratic party wide open when liberals like Hubert Humphrey of Minnesota insisted on a strong civil rights statement in the platform. Senator Strom Thurmond of South Carolina and 34 other southern delegates left the convention and formed their own Dixiecrat party, which promptly nominated Thurmond for president. The remaining Democrats nevertheless nominated Truman, with Senator Alben Barkley of Kentucky in the second spot.

A united and serenely confident Republican convention turned once again to Thomas E. Dewey, with California Governor Earl Warren for vice-president. Since 1944 Dewey had won another term as governor of New York and had skillfully presided over the state's transition from war to peace. He had also persuaded the legislature to pass a controversial law that banned racial discrimination in the workplace, the first law of its kind in the nation and a model for other states. And in his capacity as titular head of the Republican party, he had embraced the United Nations and the need for a more active foreign policy in peacetime. His own record, combined with the growing disarray in Democratic ranks, convinced Dewey and most other Republicans that he and the party

A dapper Thomas E. Dewey.

would have an easy time defeating Truman. Dewey therefore decided to run a quiet campaign and avoid the issues as much as possible.

But Truman came out fighting. At the Democratic convention he told a cheering audience that he would convene a special session of Congress that summer and propose a host of measures that he knew the opposition would oppose, thus giving him a highly visible issue to use against them.

The Republicans fumed at the idea, but the president called the special session on July 26. He asked for federal aid to education, national health insurance, civil rights legislation, an increase in the minimum wage, extended Social Security coverage with increased benefits, and federal development of cheap electrical power. As Truman expected and secretly hoped, the Congress did little during its two-week session, giving the Democratic candidate a convenient and effective target.

Truman then took to the rails in the nation's last great whistle-stop campaign. Everywhere he denounced the "no-good, do-nothing 80th Congress," warning voters that the Republicans were bent on sabotaging the New Deal. He told farmers they would lose their price supports under a Republican regime, and he led many elderly Americans to believe that the Republicans would destroy Social Security as soon as they had the chance. Candidates always exaggerate, but Truman pulled out all the stops. As the campaign progressed, the crowds grew larger. Audiences begged the president to give the Republicans ''hell,'' and he gleefully obliged. The result was a surprising victory for Truman. He won 24,106,000 votes to Dewey's 21,970,000; the electoral count was 303–189. The Democrats also regained control of both houses of Congress and would maintain their majorities in the 1950 off-year elections.

Truman took personal credit for the victory and deserved much of it, for his strenuous campaign had made all the difference. Yet in many respects, it was the old Roosevelt coalition that had sent him back to the White House. Americans might not have been in a particularly liberal mood in 1948, but most did not want to lose the benefits that had come their way under the New Deal. It did not seem to matter that Dewey represented the moderate wing of the Republican party and had accepted most of the Roosevelt reforms. An electorate frightened by recent Soviet actions in Czechoslovakia and Berlin may have also been attracted by Truman's tough stand against communism.

TRUMAN'S SECOND TERM

By the time Truman won the election of 1948, the most immediate postwar crises were behind him; nevertheless, his second term would be marked by continuing conflict and controversy. The president continued to struggle with a recalcitrant Congress and had to face a growing hysteria over domestic communism and internal subversion.

The Fair Deal   Despite these handicaps, Truman was determined to press ahead with his domestic program. In his State of the Union Message for 1949 he declared, ''Every segment of our population and every individual has the right to expect from our government a fair deal.'' The press picked up the term ''fair deal'' and used it as a convenient tag for the administration's domestic proposals. It was a fitting label in any case, for Truman saw his legislative package as a logical extension of New Deal programs. The president reiterated his calls for civil rights legislation, national health insurance, federal aid to education, expansion of Social Security, a higher minimum wage, and federal development of electrical power. He also asked for low-cost housing, federal control of unemployment compensation, and repeal of the Taft-Hartley Act. He fared little better with Democratic majorities than he had with the ''do-nothing'' 80th Congress, as conservative Democrats joined with Republicans to block the Fair Deal. Not until the mid-1960s would liberals overcome the opposition and enact many of Truman's proposals.

Corruption and Labor Strife   Besides castigating the Fair Deal, Truman's critics also charged that the administration was riddled with corruption. In 1949 newspapers revealed that minor government officials made a practice of securing government contracts for favored companies in return for a percentage of the sale. It was discovered at about the same time that Truman's old friend and military aid Harry Vaughn had arranged for a wealthy business associate to give Mrs. Truman a freezer. All of this was minor compared to allegations about the Internal Revenue Department, as two top tax collectors were indicated for bribery and fraud.

Such revelations retreated to the background after the Korean War broke out and

ANTICOMMUNISM AND COLD WAR SPIES

Truman spent his last two and a half years embroiled in the politics of war. His last real domestic crisis came in the spring of 1952 when steelworkers walked off the job. Citing the need for steel in wartime, the president seized the mills, but a federal district court declared the act unconstitutional and the Supreme Court sustained its ruling in *Youngstown Sheet and Tube Company* v. *Sawyer* (1952).

ANTICOMMUNISM AND COLD WAR SPIES

It was also during Truman's second term that the nation began to feel the full fury of anticommunism. As tensions mounted between the United States and the Soviet Union, Americans grew increasingly convinced of a worldwide Communist conspiracy. This exaggerated fear of communism is understandable in retrospect. Many Americans naively believed that World War II would rid the globe of evil dictators and open the way to American-style democracy almost everywhere. It now seemed that Stalin had merely replaced Hitler. When the Truman administration failed to halt the spread of communism, critics charged that the government itself was riddled with Communists and Communist sympathizers.

Cries of Communist conspiracy also became a convenient excuse for the nation's own shortcomings. There was nothing wrong with America, many were able to conclude; rather, it was the Communists who fomented unrest among the labor unions, the blacks, and other discontented elements of society. Politicians also leaped on the Communist issue, as Republicans in particular found it a convenient club with which to hammer away at the administration. Former isolationists, who had had to accept at least a veneer of internationalism after the war, likewise jumped onto the anti-Communist bandwagon. Many of them charged that the United Nations was a tool of the Communists, demanded increased defense expenditures, and found ready audiences for their glowing tributes to the American way of life. Then there were powerful religious groups who found a perfect, modern-day devil in the Communist system, while wealthy and even moderately well-off Americans feared a Communist-inspired onslaught against free enterprise. Finally, poor and uneducated citizens, many of them living in small towns and rural backwaters, vaguely associated the Communist menace with foreign radicals, homosexuals, and Ivy League intellectuals on the East Coast. All in all, the anti-Communist campaign fed on a multitude of fears and resentments.

This is not to deny that there were real Communist spies at work in the United States. Two spectacular espionage cases, both of which reached a climax early in 1950, focused attention on the problem and appeared to substantiate suspicions of a widespread Communist conspiracy. The first involved Alger Hiss, a high official in the State Department. In many ways Hiss was a perfect target. Born into a socially prominent but no longer wealthy Baltimore family, he went on to become an honors student at Johns Hopkins University and Harvard University Law School. He served as a law clerk for Supreme Court Justice Oliver Wendell Holmes, Jr., and later went to work for several New Deal agencies. He held senior posts in the State Department during World War II and organized the opening meeting of the United Nations in San Francisco. Handsome, slender, well dressed, and unfailingly polite, Hiss became the stereotypical eastern snob to his detractors. He was charged with passing classified State Department documents to a member of the Communist underground named Whittaker Chambers.

Chambers himself was from a respectable Long Island family, but he was otherwise quite different from Hiss. He had dropped out of Columbia University before graduating and became a radical, sometimes romantic social reformer. Unlike Hiss, the short and pudgy Chambers was often careless about his attire. He joined the Communist party and became an underground agent. News of Stalin's bloody purges led him to defect, and in 1938 he went to work as an editor for *Time* magazine. Then, in exchange for immunity from prosecution, Chambers began to name government officials who had passed classified information to Soviet agents. Included on the list was Alger Hiss.

When questioned by a federal grand jury in New York, Hiss denied that he had ever known Chambers, but the House Committee on Un-American Activities (HUAC) decided to pursue the testimony further. Among the committee members was Congressman Richard Nixon, who took a personal dislike to Hiss and launched a crusade to unmask him. It was Nixon who arranged a confrontation between Hiss and Chambers in a private hotel room, and it was Nixon who drove out to Chambers's Maryland farm to retrieve incriminating microfilms from a hollowed-out pumpkin in the Chambers garden.

In the end Congressman Nixon and the other members of HUAC forced Hiss to admit that he had indeed known Chambers, though allegedly under a different name. Hiss was then tried for having lied to the grand jury about his friendship with Chambers. After one hung jury, Hiss was found guilty of perjury and sentenced to prison. Because the statute of limitations had run out, the government was unable to try him for espionage. Throughout the HUAC hearings and the two perjury trials, the Hiss case made constant headlines, causing many citizens to conclude that the entire U.S. government was riddled with Communists. The publicity was also a great spur to Richard Nixon's political career. Indeed, it was his "victory" over Hiss that catapulted him into the vice-presidency and launched him on his ultimately successful bid for the White House.

Accused spies Ethel and Julius Rosenberg (right).

ANTICOMMUNISM AND COLD WAR SPIES

Equally sensational was the case of Julius and Ethel Rosenberg. It began when a physicist named Klaus Fuchs, who had worked on the atomic bomb at Los Alamos, confessed to the British that he had given valuable information about the Manhattan Project to the Soviets. He then implicated several others, including the Rosenbergs. They were charged with entering into a conspiracy to transmit atomic secrets to the Soviet Union. Their confessed motive had been to share the atomic bomb with the Soviets so that no one nation could use its nuclear monopoly against another, thereby sparing the world from atomic warfare. They were fund guilty of espionage in March 1951 and were executed two years later.

Most Americans thought that the Rosenbergs got what they deserved, but others objected to the death sentence, protesting that it was far too severe. Some charged that the Rosenbergs, both the children of Jewish immigrants, were victims of anti-Semitism and many felt genuine concern for their two small children, who were orphaned by their parents' execution.

The McCarthy "Witch Hunts"   All too many politicians were willing to exacerbate the anti-Communist hysteria and use it for partisan gain. The most notorious of these was Joseph R. McCarthy, a Repubican senator from Wisconsin. Born into a poor farm family with nine children, he had worked his way through college and law school. He was elected a county judge in 1939 and enlisted in the Marine Corps shortly after Pearl Harbor. Though he served mainly as a desk clerk in the South Pacific, McCarthy went on to invent a glorious combat record for himself, claiming to have been a tail gunner with over 50 combat missions. He also said that he had been wounded several times, and walked with a fake limp for a while after the war. Calling himself "Tail Gunner Joe," McCarthy won a U.S. Senate seat in the Republican landslide of 1946.

From the beginning of his Senate career, McCarthy was skillful at manipulating the press and calling attention to himself. Even so, he was worried about reelection, and by early 1950 he was casting around for an issue on which to launch his campaign. It was then that he hit on the idea of exposing domestic communism. He launched his anti-Communist crusade on February 9, 1950, during a speech in Wheeling, West Virginia. There he produced a document that he said contained the names of 205 Communists employed by the State Department. He later reduced the number to 81 and then to 57, but he persistently refused to show the list to anyone else and failed to uncover even one Communist in the department.

Despite his failure, McCarthy used his membership on the Government Operations Committee to launch a probe into subversion in government. Once again he proved to be a master at manipulating the press, throwing out enough tantalizing information each day to keep reporters and their editors interested in what he was doing. He found nothing of any substance, but ruined many innocent witnesses through character assassination and guilt by association. If witnesses refused to testify against themselves, a right guaranteed by the Fifth Amendment to the U.S. Constitution, McCarthy and his supporters took this refusal as automatic proof of guilt. McCarthy himself often bullied and intimidated his hapless victims in a mockery of proper procedure.

Even esteemed public servants like General Marshall came in for rebuke. In June 1951 McCarthy charged that Marshall, while secretary of defense, was part of a "conspiracy so immense and an infamy so black as to dwarf any previous such venture in the history of man." President Truman particularly resented this slander and on several

Senator Joseph R. McCarthy raising a "point of order."

occasions denied the senator's accusations against Marshall. But Truman's remarks fell on deaf ears, for too many Americans wanted to believe McCarthy's charges and were unconcerned about his unjust and abusive tactics. McCarthyism has thus become a byword for the sort of unprincipled crusades led by the Wisconsin senator and his imitators.

Further Investigations   McCarthy's investigations were only the best-known probes into domestic communism during the late 1940s and early 1950s. Besides HUAC there was the Senate Internal Security Subcommittee probes. These and other legislative investigations delved into nearly every corner of national life in an effort to uncover subversive activities, but the most spectacular was HUAC's investigations of the movie industry, which commenced in 1947.

Arguing that many recent movies, including the laudatory *Mission to Moscow,* were filled with Communist propaganda, the committee sought to expose the perpetrators. Their targets were the Hollywood scriptwriters, many of whom had belonged to the Communist party or other left-wing organizations at some time during their lives. None of them had engaged in disloyal acts or had advocated the violent overthrow of the United States government. Rather, like so many who were examined by congressional committees, they were being persecuted for their political opinions—opinions which should have been protected by the First Amendment. Ten of them refused to answer the committee's questions and loudly denounced the hearings. They were cited for contempt and indicted by a grand jury. At this point a number of film stars rallied to their defense, including John Huston, Gene Kelly, and Humphrey Bogart. But their efforts proved fruitless, as all ten went to jail following their unsuccessful appeals to the Supreme Court. In 1951 HUAC launched a second investigation of the movies. With the example of the Hollywood Ten in mind, most witnesses cooperated fully. The studios were thrown into a panic and began to "blacklist" any writers or performers who were suspected of having belonged to left-wing organizations.

Congressional committees also made extensive inquiries about Communist infiltration of labor unions and the scientific community. Meanwhile the individual states established their own investigations of possible subversion. Their principal targets were university professors and public school teachers. Again, the familiar tactics were used: innuendo, character assassination, guilt by association, and persecution for holding unpopular political beliefs. Once again, many innocent people lost their jobs or suffered public humiliation and private anguish.

The feverish search for Communists and other subversives would continue far into the 1950s. Tragically, the campaign to rid the government of spies was often turned against people who had never engaged in any sort of espionage or subversive activity. Thousands of innocent men and women suffered, while others in high office shamefully abused their public prerogatives.

VICTORIOUS REPUBLICANS

Truman's second term in office thus came to an end amidst cries of communism and corruption in high places. Even so, Truman considered running again in 1952. The Twenty-Second Amendment, ratified the year before, limited a president to two terms, but it did not apply retroactively to Truman. A disastrous showing in the early primaries convinced him that he had only a slight chance of winning. Besides, he looked forward to retirement.

The man from Missouri had presided over eight of the most difficult years in the nation's history, and despite his mistakes and the often vituperative criticism from his opponents, he had generally handled the office quite well. Large numbers failed to appreciate him at the time; but his strong stands, personal honesty, and inveterate courage would later appeal to a nation beleaguered by Watergate and humiliated by defeat in Vietnam.

The Republicans, after 20 years in the political wilderness, now believed that they had a good chance to recapture the presidency. Indeed, many Americans asserted that the party's survival and, with it, the continuance of a healthy two-party system depended on a Republican victory.

Ohio's Senator Robert A. Taft was clearly the Republican front-runner as 1952 began. To many conservatives, this son of President William Howard Taft *was* the Republican party: for them he was Mr. Republican. Taft had sought the party's nomination in 1940, 1944, and 1948, and he was determined to succeed in 1952. But moderates in the party feared he would prove too conservative for the populace at large and wanting to take no chances, they persuaded General Eisenhower to run for the nomination.

Eisenhower and Stevenson Like Truman, Eisenhower hailed from a small midwestern town, in this case Abilene, Kansas. His leading role in the victory over Germany in World War II had made him an instant hero, and even before the war was over, both political parties had talked of running him for president. Since 1945 he had served as Army Chief of Staff, president of Columbia University, and commander of NATO. His decision to seek the nomination stemmed from personal distaste for Truman's style and a belief that he could provide the dignified leadership that the nation needed and craved. Taft did not accept the challenge lightly, and the two battled all the way to the convention floor. Eisenhower won the nomination only after a credentials committee awarded him a number of disputed southern delegates. Senator Richard M. Nixon received the vice-presidential nomination. The Republicans promised to clean up the "mess in Washington," a clear reference to corruption under Truman and the Democrats' supposed lack of vigor against the Communists. The GOP would not be content with mere containment of communism, but would try to push the Soviets out of eastern Europe and vowed to assist Chiang Kai-shek in a reconquest of mainland China.

With Truman out of the race, two Democratic front-runners emerged. They were Senator Estes Kefauver of Tennessee and Governor Adlai Stevenson of Illinois. Kefauver had attracted much publicity for his investigations into organized crime in 1950 and 1951, but his probes had uncovered embarrassing ties between Democratic bosses and the criminal underworld, making him unacceptable to many party regulars. That left Stevenson, who captured the Democratic nomination with little difficulty. Senator John J. Sparkman of Alabama received the vice-presidential nomination.

Stevenson descended from a long line of notable Democrats. His grandfather had been a member of the House of Representatives and vice-president during President Cleveland's second term. A moderate on domestic issues, Stevenson accepted the New Deal reforms and promised to maintain many social programs. He was also a fierce anti-Communist. Finally, he attracted the support of Democratic liberals, who were charmed by his witty speeches and impressed by his Princeton degree. Besides, they had no alternative.

Stumping for Votes As the campaign unfolded, Eisenhower, too, embraced much of the New Deal program, promising to preserve the "solid floor that keeps us all from falling into a pit of disaster." Nevertheless, he had no intention of extending the New Deal. He would seek a "middle way," eschewing the reactionary pose of those who wanted to return to the politics of Herbert Hoover or William McKinley. He also would go to Korea after the election. He did not promise to bring peace, but a war-weary public wanted to believe that he could. If anyone could put an end to the Korean mess, many voters reasoned, it was General Ike.

Eisenhower himself refrained from attacking the Democrats on the Communist issue, but Nixon had no reservations. He called Stevenson a "Ph.D. [graduate] from Dean Acheson's College of Cowardly Containment." Nixon also promised that the Republicans would restore clean language to the White House, apparently meaning that Eisenhower would not swear as much as Truman had.

Before the campaign ended, Nixon himself was the target of serious charges. It was said that he had used political contributions for personal expenses while in the House and Senate. Eisenhower seriously considered dropping him from the ticket, but Nixon saved himself by going on nationwide radio and television to explain his finances. He

Candidate Adlai E. Stevenson and dog during 1952 campaign.

interlarded the facts with highly emotional references to his mother, wife, and young daughters. He admitted that a supporter had given the Nixon girls a little dog named Checkers and challenged anyone to take it away from them. He concluded with a plea for messages of support to the Republican National Committee—not to Eisenhower himself who had planned to determine Nixon's fate following the broadcast. The committee was deluged with letters and telegrams in favor of the would-be vice-president and Eisenhower was forced to keep him on the ticket, but he never quite forgave Nixon for appealing over his head to rank-and-file Republicans.

    The election was a complete rout for the Democrats. Eisenhower won 39 of the 48 states, with a total of 33,936,000 popular votes and 442 electoral votes. Stevenson carried only the Deep South, plus Kentucky and West Virginia. He received 27,315,000 popular votes, with a mere 89 votes in the electoral college. The Republicans also won control of both House and Senate, leading many party leaders to hope that there had been a realignment of voter strength, with the Republicans once again in the majority. Congressional elections in 1954 and 1956 would prove them quite wrong.

A smiling President Eisenhower with son John and two grandchildren.

EISENHOWER'S MIDDLE WAY

Eisenhower's warm, grandfatherly smile, unaffected demeanor, and reputation as a military leader convinced most Americans that the country would be in good hands. His moderate course also pleased the great majority. After decades of depression and war, voters were tired of noble crusades and heroic sacrifice. Most agreed that America was just fine the way it was, and they wanted a president who would let them enjoy it. Eisenhower was quite willing to oblige.

Slashing the Budget One of the keys to his middle way, Eisenhower believed, was a balanced budget. This would require cuts in defense spending, an end to the Korean War, and no new social welfare programs. The first hurdle was Korea.

Eisenhower did go to Korea after the election. He observed the battlefields, talked with top-ranking generals, visited the troops, and found the situation intolerable. The war had to end. Upon assuming the presidency, Eisenhower hinted to the Chinese that he would use atomic weapons to break the stalemate, and in April 1953 the peace talks resumed. On July 26 the two sides finally signed an armistice. There was no official agreement on Korea's future, and the country remained divided near the 38th parallel; nor were there any guarantees against subsequent attacks from the North. But few Americans cared; all that mattered was peace.

With the war over, Eisenhower went to work slashing the defense budget. Pentagon officials opposed him at almost every turn and frequently went over his head and appealed to Congress. But Eisenhower fought excessive defense expenditures throughout his eight years in office and, in particular, tried to reduce manpower costs in the military. In order to make up for lower troop strengths, the country would rely more on atomic weapons. As his Secretary of State John Foster Dulles put it, the United States would employ "massive retaliation" against any attempts to advance communism or threaten free governments. This "new look" in defense, as it was called, would betray serious weaknesses in the long run, but for the time being it promised considerable savings. Eisenhower was able to balance the budget in 1956 and showed a billion dollar surplus in 1960. His fight for balanced budgets helped to keep inflation low, and in comparison with escalating costs in the 1980s, his success was quite impressive.

Farm Aid and Public Power   Eisenhower also hoped to make cuts in the farm program, with an eye to restoring a free market in agriculture. He believed that his secretary of agriculture, Ezra Taft Benson, was well suited for this task. Benson was a successful large-scale farmer, an elder in the Mormon Church, and a political conservative. Yet neither he nor Eisenhower succeeded in dismantling the farm program established under the New Deal. Congressional Democrats defeated their plan for more flexible price supports that would vary in accordance with market conditions. Toward the end of his second term Eisenhower proposed a "soil bank" program that paid farmers for taking land out of production and using it to plant trees or construct farm ponds. The scheme turned out to be quite costly, benefited large cultivators more than small- or medium-sized farmers, and generally removed only the most unproductive land from cultivation.

Eisenhower met with more success in blocking the expansion of public power. Republicans had raged against the Tennessee Valley Authority (TVA) for over 20 years and pointed to it as a prime example of unwarranted socialism. Eisenhower could not dismantle the TVA, but he did limit its expansion and opposed the creation of similar regional authorities. His attempts to check the TVA, however, involved the administration in a minor scandal. It began when Eisenhower refused to allow the TVA to build another generating plant to meet the growing needs of Memphis, Tennessee. Instead he authorized a contract with Edgar Dixon and Eugene Yates, who then formed a company to provide Memphis with additional electric power. In 1955 a Democratic investigating committee discovered that one of the Dixon-Yates consultants had also advised the Bureau of the Budget on the Memphis project, resulting in conflict of interest allegations. Eisenhower himself had nothing to do with the impropriety and ordered the contract cancelled as soon as he learned of the conflict. Of course, the Democrats tried to take every advantage of the "Dixon-Yates affair."

From More Social Security to Better Highways   In some areas, however, Eisenhower did urge increased expenditures, and in this sense he departed somewhat from the middle way. One area was Social Security. In August 1953 he asked Congress to add 10.5 million more Americans to the rolls and to increase overall benefits. Conservatives balked, but Congress approved the expansion in the spring of 1954. Eisenhower had earlier received legislative approval for a Department of Health, Education, and Welfare, the first new cabinet position in over 40 years. The president appointed Oveta Culp Hobby, former head of the Women's Army Corps, as its first secretary. Both acts demonstrated how widely accepted the social welfare state had become by the early 1950s.

Still, both pieces of legislation merely extended or altered a system already in place, and in this sense they were not a vast departure from the middle way.

More far-reaching, and undoubtedly the most important domestic program initiated under Eisenhower, was the interstate highway system. The president had been impressed with the German autobahns during World War II and believed that the United States needed a similar system of four-lane, divided highways. Few could argue with the need for better roads. Most of the nation's highways were narrow, two-lane pavements that commonly took drivers through the most congested areas of large cities, with the unhappy consequences of massive traffic jams, numerous accidents, and mounting highway death tolls. The president began urging Congress to pass an interstate highway bill in 1955. Besides providing the country with better roads, he claimed that the new highways were necessary for defense. They would permit more rapid movement of troops and supplies in time of war and would ease the evacuation of cities in case of nuclear attack. Finally, he asserted that this massive public works project could be accelerated or held back so as to even out the economy's peaks and troughs.

The highway bill ran into disputes over money, but Congress finally passed it in June 1956, securing funds through a federal gasoline tax. Neither the president nor Congress foresaw the total impact of the 41,000 mile ribbon of superhighways. It encouraged the purchase and use of even more automobiles and thereby helped to undermine already declining passenger rail lines. And by extending the interstate highways into urban centers, the system accelerated the move into suburbia and the concomitant decay of older neighborhoods.

Technically, the interstate highway system was state socialism on a massive scale, but Americans had grown so used to public road building that few considered it as such. Whether one called the program socialistic or not, the new highways would transform the nation in ways that the moderate Eisenhower and his advisors never imagined.

"With All Deliberate Speed"   The impending civil rights revolution would also alter American society immensely, but here Eisenhower was less than enthusiastic. It is true that he completed integration of the armed services and ordered the desegregation of public facilities in Washington, D.C. It is also true that the president was genuinely outraged at the continuing disfranchisement of southern blacks and at the numerous assaults against black citizens. Yet he was reluctant to take vigorous action.

In the first place, Eisenhower did not think it was necessary for blacks and whites to mix socially, and he sympathized with a number of southern friends who recoiled at the thought of integrated schools and other public facilities. Time and time again, the president declared that the law could not change people's minds about race, that legal coercion would only inflame whites and make the situation worse. Finally, he wanted to strengthen the Republican party in the South and feared that outspoken support for civil rights would alienate southern voters.

Particularly vexing for Eisenhower was the Supreme Court's decision in *Brown* v. *Board of Education of Topeka* (1954). Thurgood Marshall and other lawyers from the NAACP had argued before the court that racial segregation was not only unconstitutional, but that separating children in the schools gave black youngsters an indelible sense of inferiority. As a consequence, their ambition and self-esteem were seriously undermined. In order to buttress their testimony, NAACP lawyers cited extensive sociological evi-

Black youths protesting segregated swimming pool.

dence, and in a unanimous decision the Court agreed with the NAACP position. The resultant *Brown* decision explicitly overturned *Plessy* v. *Ferguson,* an 1896 case holding that segregation was constitutional so long as facilities were "separate but equal." In 1955 the Court followed up the initial *Brown* v. *Board of Education* decision by ordering desegregation of the public schools with "all deliberate speed." (Ironically, the decision was coordinated and written by Chief Justice Earl Warren, whom Eisenhower had appointed in 1953. The Warren Court would hand down a number of other decisions that were much too liberal for Eisenhower and the president regretted in private that he had ever appointed Warren.)

Despite the crucial importance of *Brown* v. *Board of Education,* Eisenhower refused to comment publicly on the decision for the entire six and a half years that he remained in office. He contended that any statement on his part would violate the separation of powers between the executive and judicial branches; nor did he press the Justice Department to give school desegregation top priority.

Segregationists in the South no doubt interpreted the president's silence as sympathy for their point of view and were thus encouraged in their resistance to integration. In this respect, Eisenhower's refusal to speak out on desegregation forced him to take the strongest possible action in Little Rock, Arkansas. There, in September 1957, a large and angry mob of whites tried to stop eight black students from integrating Central High

School. When Governor Orval Faubus defied Eisenhower and failed to restore order, the president sent U.S. Army units into the riot-torn city to protect the students and keep the peace.

Earlier that year, Eisenhower had decided to support the first civil rights bill since Reconstruction. It was a mild bill, as the president constantly reassured southerners, that allowed individual blacks to sue in the federal courts if they were denied the right to vote. The Senate weakened the bill even further by permitting state election officials to demand a jury trial if charged with violating black voting rights. Since jurors were likely to be all white (jurors being chosen from lists of registered voters), there was little likelihood of conviction. Nevertheless, Eisenhower signed the bill.

Eisenhower and McCarthy   When it came to Senator Joseph R. McCarthy and his tactics, Eisenhower also failed to take a strong stand. He approved of congressional investigations into Communist activity, but deplored the senator's behavior and particularly resented his attacks on General Marshall, the man most responsible for making Eisenhower Supreme Allied Commander in Europe. Yet, when he found himself sharing a campaign platform with McCarthy, the Republican presidential candidate deleted a segment of his speech that praised General Marshall. Eisenhower later explained that he did not want to damage party harmony in Wisconsin.

As president, Eisenhower decided to maintain complete public silence on McCarthy, again citing separation of powers, this time between the White House and Capitol Hill. He also asserted that presidential criticism would only pander to McCarthy's insatiable appetite for publicity and give the senator still more recognition. Even after McCarthy began to assault members of Eisenhower's own administration, the president continued to hold his tongue. By then many of Eisenhower's advisors believed that silence had been a mistake and urged him to speak out. Many observers since have agreed, contending that a strong reprimand from the widely respected Eisenhower might have curbed McCarthy.

McCarthy's downfall finally came without any help from the president. His demise was triggered by the so-called Army-McCarthy hearings in the late spring of 1954. Amid wild and groundless charges that the U.S. Army was full of Communists, McCarthy attempted to bully high-ranking officers and Defense Department personnel. The televised hearings were seen by as many as 20 million viewers each day. These proceedings soon degenerated into a kind of brutal circus, and in the process McCarthy exposed himself for the reckless demagogue that he was. In December the Senate voted overwhelmingly to condemn McCarthy's behavior. Thereafter McCarthy was a broken and powerless man. He began drinking heavily and died in April 1957.

Eisenhower Again   Yet another failure of leadership involved the entire Republican party. Eisenhower wanted Republicans to pursue a moderate course on issues and thus appeal to the majority of voters who occupied the middle of the political spectrum. Conservative Republicans in Congress frequently thwarted him, wrecking his legislative proposals while continuing to attack the memory of Roosevelt and the New Deal. As a result the Republicans made no headway against Democratic registrations and lost control of Congress during the off-year elections of 1954 and 1958. They even failed to regain their majorities in the presidential election of 1956, when Eisenhower won by a huge majority.

EISENHOWER AND THE WORLD

If nothing else, the results in 1956 showed that Eisenhower's success at the polls was largely personal. Despite a serious heart attack in September 1955 and surgery for an intestinal ailment in June 1956, he managed to mount an effective campaign and squelch rumors that he was too old and sick to serve a second term. He also decided to share the ticket once again with Vice-President Richard Nixon.

The Democrats turned again to Stevenson, with Estes Kefauver as his running mate. The Democratic nominee tried to attack Eisenhower on defense, calling for an end to the draft and a moratorium on nuclear testing. Then, seeming to contradict himself, he criticized the administration for not placing enough emphasis on missile development. Eisenhower insisted that such proposals were dangerous as well as unsound economically, and the voters agreed with the former general. In November, the president received 35,590,000 votes to Stevenon's 26,022,000. Stevenson took only seven southern states with 74 electoral votes, as compared to Eisenhower's 457. The president's sweep was even greater than in 1952 and represented the largest majority since Roosevelt's landslide in 1936.

EISENHOWER AND THE WORLD

Eisenhower's foreign policies were much more consistent than his record in domestic areas, and it is his conduct of foreign affairs that will probably assure him the greatest approval from future generations. He ended the war in Korea and kept the nation at peace for the remainder of his two terms in office.

Crisis in Vietnam   Eisenhower's first international crisis came over Vietnam. Since 1946, when the French forced their way back into Indochina, the United States had spent millions trying to help them defeat a native uprising under Ho Chi Minh in exchange for French support of American policies in Europe. Both a Marxist and a fierce nationalist, Ho had led a popular resistance against the Japanese during World War II and enlarged his following after the war. Truman and Eisenhower pressed the French to make liberal reforms in Vietnam and to promise its people eventual independence, but the French were determined to hold on to their empire in Southeast Asia and consistently rejected American advice. The fighting continued between the French and Ho's Vietminh, as the rebels were then called, until the French lost a decisive battle at Dien Bien Phu in May 1954. At a peace conference in Geneva, Switzerland, diplomats decided to divide Vietnam temporarily along the 17th parallel. All sides agreed to hold free elections in two years to decide the political fate of the entire country.

The United States sent an observer to the Geneva conference but refused to sign the final peace accords. Still, American leaders pledged that their government would respect the agreements on Vietnam and would do nothing to interfere with their implementation. Within a year the United States reneged, as American intelligence reported that even the freest elections would result in overwhelming victory for Ho Chi Minh in both North and South Vietnam, and Eisenhower backed the South Vietnamese government in its refusal to hold elections there. Despite Ho's great popularity, Eisenhower vowed to prevent a Communist victory.

By this time Eisenhower was convinced that communism in one area would inevitably spread to neighboring regions, and during a press conference in April 1954 he compared this process to the chain reaction of a row of falling dominoes. ''You knock over the first one,'' he warned, ''and what will happen to the last one is certainly that it will go over very quickly [to communism].'' The phrase caught on, and soon the ''domino theory'' was applied widely to justify the doctrine of containment.

Trouble with Communist China Meanwhile Eisenhower spearheaded a new alliance system in Southeast Asia. Like NATO in Europe, it would attempt to halt the spread of communism on the opposite side of the globe. By early September 1954, eight nations had committed themselves to a Southeast Asian Treaty Organization (SEATO). Besides the United States, there were Great Britain, France, Australia, New Zealand, Thailand, the Philippines, and Pakistan. They pledged to defend the region, specifically extending their protection to Laos, Cambodia, and South Vietnam, none of which belonged to the SEATO alliance itself. By signing the treaty, the United States was laying the groundwork for possible armed intervention in Southeast Asia. For the remainder of his presidency, however, Eisenhower refused to commit more than a couple of hundred advisors to an increasingly besieged Vietnam.

While the United States was concluding the SEATO agreements, another crisis erupted in Asia. This time it involved Quemoy and Matsu, two tiny islands just off the coast of mainland (Communist) China. Since fleeing from the mainland in 1949, Chiang Kai-shek had held the islands with large garrisons, hoping to use them as stepping-stones to a reconquest of China. On September 3, 1954, the Chinese Communists began bombarding Quemoy and Matsu from coastal batteries. Chiang insisted that the artillery barrage was the opening wedge in an attack on Nationalist-held Formosa (Taiwan), and he asked for American help. Senator William Knowland of California and other conservatives called for an American blockade of the Chinese coast, but Eisenhower refused, insisting that such a drastic move might provoke war with Mao Tse-tung. Counseling patience, the president responded less dramatically by signing a mutual defense pact with Chiang and the Chinese Nationalists. The United States would defend Formosa and nearby islands from Communist attack, but the treaty was curiously silent about Quemoy and Matsu. Eisenhower did not believe they were essential to Formosa's defense and would not risk war to save them from the Communists. Mao would threaten the islands several more times during the Eisenhower administration, but the president remained calm. The Communists did not invade Quemoy and Matsu, and the United States stayed at peace with China.

Coups in Iran and Guatemala In areas where Eisenhower believed that he could overthrow objectionable regimes without direct American involvement, he was more than willing to act. In the spring of 1953 he approved a plot by the Central Intelligence Agency (CIA) to topple the Iranian prime minister, Mohammed Mossadegh. Mossadegh had nationalized oil fields and refineries belonging to the Anglo-Iranian Oil Company, and Great Britain asked for American help in retrieving them. Eisenhower was particularly receptive to British pleas because he believed that Mossadegh was leaning toward communism. The prime minister had recognized the Iranian Communist party and accepted financial aid from the Soviet Union. By cooperating with conservative forces around the young Shah of Iran, the CIA successfully ousted Mossadegh and restored the

Shah to full power. As a reuslt, American oil companies received a 40 percent share in Iran's oil production, with another 40 percent going to the British and the remaining 20 percent to Dutch and French companies.

In the summer of 1954 Eisenhower authorized another CIA operation against supposed Communists, this time in Guatemala. Their target was Jacobo Arbenz, Guatemala's democratically elected president. He had legalized his country's Communist party, had accepted arms from the Soviets, and then had embarked on moderate land reform that included the nationalization of property belonging to the American-owned United Fruit Company. By placing his support behind Colonel Carlos Castillo Armas and a handful of counterrevolutionaries, the CIA helped to drive Arbenz from power.

Suez and a Changing Middle East Nationalization of foreign real estate did not always lead to American intervention. In July 1956 Egypt's Gamal Abdel Nasser seized the Suez Canal, owned for decades by an Anglo-French company, and the United States did nothing to stop him. In this case there was no possibility of covert operations, and Eisenhower feared that any moves to assist the British or French would turn much of the underdeveloped ''third world'' against the United States. He urged Britain and France not to take retaliatory measures against Egypt. Even when Britain and France joined Israel in an attack on Egypt at the end of October, the president refused to support them, verbally or otherwise. Instead he pressured all three invaders to pull out of Egypt and advocated a United Nations peace-keeping force to replace them. By November the crisis was over. The British and French had strained the North Atlantic Alliance and were feeling the financial costs of the invasion. None of the parties wanted to endure the political and economic burdens of an indefinite occupation and agreed to withdraw in favor of a UN force.

Throughout the Suez crisis, Eisenhower feared Soviet intervention in the Middle East and after the smoke had cleared, he decided to ask Congress for discretionary authority to protect that region against Communist encroachments. He appeared before Congress on January 5, 1957, to dramatize his request. He wanted economic and military assistance for ''any nation or group of nations which desires such aid,'' along with blanket permission to use American armed forces ''to secure and protect the territorial integrity and personal independence of such nations . . . against overt armed aggression from any nation controlled by International Communism.'' He hoped that congressional approval would warn the Communists that the United States would not tolerate aggression in the Middle East. On March 9 the Senate passed the president's resolution and sent it to the House for the necessary funding. Such broad latitude to commit troops in time of peace was unparalleled, and in the future many Congressmen would regret the precedent.

Circumstances did not require the president to invoke the Eisenhower Doctrine per se, but internal conflict in Lebanon persuaded him to land troops there in July 1958. He believed, without any hard evidence, that Moslem riots against a Christian government under President Camille Chamoun were Communist-inspired. The situation in Lebanon cooled considerably, and by October the last American troops were withdrawn. In the last analysis, Eisenhower may have sent them in as a mere show of force, demonstrating that the United States could deploy troops on short notice throughout the eastern Mediterranean.

CONFRONTING THE SOVIETS

Eisenhower also faced a number of tense moments with the Soviet Union, many of them over the status of postwar Germany. Even before he became president, Eisenhower had wanted to rearm Germany and make it part of the Western defense system. While at NATO headquarters in the early 1950s, he had pushed for a Western European army, known more properly as the European Defense Community (EDC). But the French legislature, still fearing a German resurgence, refused to ratify the scheme. After his inauguration, Eisenhower proposed to bring Germany directly into the NATO alliance. He allayed French fears by promising to limit German participation to 12 divisions, and on April 1, 1955, the U.S. Senate ratified the agreement. The security-conscious Soviets predictably denounced the arrangement as part of an ongoing capitalist encirclement.

To the Summit   At the very time Eisenhower was pushing German rearmament, he became increasingly alarmed over the nuclear arms race between the United States and the Soviet Union. In a speech before the UN General Assembly in December 1953, he had proposed an ''atoms for peace'' program. Instead of building increasingly destructive weapons, he declared that the nuclear powers should donate fissionable materials to an international pool under UN control. Other nations could then draw from it for peaceful purposes. The Soviets did not respond.

Nevertheless, the Soviets indicated that they wanted to explore peaceful solutions to their differences with the United States. Stalin died in March 1953, and his immediate successor, Georgi Malenkov, soon announced that he wanted to negotiate seriously with the United States. Eisenhower made no objections, but insisted on some tangible indication that the Soviets were sincere. They subsequently made several gestures, including their acceptance of an Austrian State Treaty in May 1955. Austria had been occupied since World War II by American, British, French, and Soviet forces. These were pulled out as Austria became an independent but neutral country. This accomplishment convinced Eisenhower that the Soviets were ready for constructive talks, and he agreed to a European summit meeting.

The summit opened in Geneva on July 18, 1955, attended by American, British, French, and Soviet leaders. Eisenhower and Soviet premier Nikolai Bulganin began at once to discuss the German question. Eisenhower proposed to unify Germany through free elections, but the Soviets refused, saying that the Germans had not yet had time to appreciate the benefits of socialism. Still disturbed over German entry into NATO, the Soviets proposed a disarmed and neutral Germany, but Eisenhower rejected the suggestion outright.

On July 21, Eisenhower presented a carefully prepared idea for arms reduction and inspection. Both the United States and the Soviet Union would provide the other with a ''complete blueprint'' of military facilities and permit aerial photography by the other side. This way neither could cheat on any disarmament agreement. Bulganin thought the proposal had real merit and promised to study it carefully, but on the way out of the session Nikita Khrushchev, now First Secretary of the Communist Party, told Eisenhower that he opposed the plan. The president realized at once who was really running the Soviet Union, and he tried in vain to get Khrushchev to reconsider. The summit ended

CONFRONTING THE SOVIETS   289

without any substantive agreements, but Eisenhower refused to despair. In the days that followed, he spoke again and again of the ''spirit of Geneva.'' If the two sides did not accomplish anything solid, they at least had replaced confrontation with discussion and had reduced international tensions.

Uprisings in Poland and Hungary   The spirit of Geneva did not last for long. Uprisings in Poland and Hungary in October 1956 led to armed Soviet intervention and a renewal of the fierce propaganda war between the superpowers. Encouraged by what they thought was a more lenient line in the Soviet Union following Stalin's death, the Poles rioted and brought down their country's pro-Soviet government. Wladyslaw Gomulka, earlier dismissed from power by the Soviets, now took charge of Poland. He was committed to socialism, but announced that there was more than one way to achieve it, adding that the Poles would ''defend themselves with all means.'' Inspired by the Polish example, neighboring Hungarians revolted on October 23 and made Imre Nagy their premier—yet another official whom the Soviets had deposed sometime earlier. When riots continued in Hungary, the Soviets sent in troops and tanks.

The Republican party and Secretary of State Dulles had often talked about ''rolling back'' communism and employing ''massive retaliation'' in the face of Soviet aggression, but Eisenhower did nothing more than issue verbal protests against the Soviet actions in Hungary. He realized there were no contiguous land bases from which the United States could send troops or supplies into Hungary and feared that any American interference might mean war with the Soviets. Despite his party's rhetoric about liberating Eastern Europe from the Communists, Eisenhower tacitly recognized that area as a legitimate Soviet sphere.

Sputnik   In 1957 Americans were alerted to another sort of challenge from the Soviet Union—this one scientific and technological. In October the Soviets launched the world's first satellite into orbit around the earth, naming it Sputnik, the Russian word for ''traveling companion.'' This was a rude shock for Americans, who were sure of their technological superiority. If the Soviets could fire a satellite into orbit, they could also use missiles to send nuclear warheads against the United States. Press and politicians alike demanded an accelerated missile program.

American education also came in for part of the blame, as critics contended that American students did not receive nearly as much exposure to the sciences as Soviet youngsters. Congress responded with the National Defense Education Act in September 1958, which allocated about $1 billion for grants to improve instruction in science, math, and foreign languages, and also provided low-interest loans for college students.

The United States matched the Soviet space feat when it put Explorer I into orbit in January 1958, and the immediate panic began to subside. Yet the indirect consequences of Sputnik would be felt for some time. Rivalries between Army and Navy satellite programs soon prompted Eisenhower to support a separate space agency, the National Aeronautics and Space Administration (NASA), created in July 1958. Meanwhile, critics claimed that there was a dangerous ''missile gap'' between the United States and the Soviet Union. Eisenhower's immediate successor would launch a crash program to land an American on the moon.

Historians Debate

DWIGHT D. EISENHOWER

Both the presidency and individual presidents have long been a source of debate among scholars and critics. As the nation's experiences and needs have shifted, so have evaluations of various presidents. But few recent occupants of the White House have undergone such rapid changes in reputation as Dwight D. Eisenhower.

Although immensely popular with the general public when he left office in early 1961, a poll among professional historians rated him mediocre at best. And as the 1960s unfolded, Eisenhowers's image remained poor among academicians. In contrast to the young and charismatic John F. Kennedy, Eisenhower now seemed dull and unimaginative, while supporters of the reforms under Kennedy and his successor, Lyndon B. Johnson, faulted the former president for not taking vigorous action against domestic problems. In his *Ordeal of Power* (1963), for instance, speechwriter Emmet J. Hughes criticized his former boss for frequent timidity and self-doubt. Richard Neustadt came to similar conclusions in his *Presidential Power* (1960). Other detractors, like Townsend Hoopes, concentrated their fire on Eisenhower's foreign policy. His *Devil and John Foster Dulles* (1973) criticized Eisenhower for dependence on an often self-righteous and inflexible secretary of state.

The expansion of presidential authority under Lyndon Johnson and Richard Nixon, however, caused some scholars to look at Eisenhower differently. In his *Imperial Presidency* (1973) Arthur M. Schlesinger, Jr., saw Eisenhower as an abuser of presidential power. In particular, Schlesinger cited the former general for unwarranted assertions of ''executive privilege'' in the face of congressional requests for information. William L. O'Neill went even further in his *Coming Apart* (1971), branding Eisenhower as a sort of modern Machiavelli.

The opening up of primary sources on the Eisenhower presidency in 1975 permitted researchers to view him more accurately than before. Taking advantage of these materials, Elmo Richardson's *Presidency of Dwight D. Eisenhower* (1979) has become one of the more balanced accounts of those eight years.

By the time Richardson's book appeared, scholars were beginning to reevaluate the Eisenhower presidency more positively. Those who were alarmed at spiraling federal deficits began to praise Eisenhower's fiscal restraint, while others appreciated that there had been no new foreign wars or governmental crises such as Watergate. Meanwhile, a new poll among historians placed Eisenhower just below the most highly rated chief executives. Representative of these more laudatory appraisals is Stephen Ambrose's *Eisenhower the President* (1984). Ambrose gives the president especially high marks for his efforts to keep peace. A yet to be published volume on the Eisenhower presidency by his grandson David Eisenhower promises to be even more congratulatory.

A Festering Berlin The furor over Sputnik also reflected renewed tensions between the United States and the Soviet Union. In March 1958 Khrushchev alarmed the free world by threatening to give the East Germans control over access routes to West Berlin and thereby force the United States and the other Western powers to recognize the East German government. He added that the West must accept these plans by May 27.

For all his bluster over Berlin, Khrushchev also wanted peace with the West. The arms race was a heavy burden on the Soviet economy and Khrushchev recognized the folly of nuclear war as much as Eisenhower. Yet he wanted the West to admit Soviet hegemony in East Germany and was determined to advance Soviet interests in the third world. He also feared that the United States would interpret conciliation as a sign of Soviet weakness. Finally, Khrushchev liked to boast about Soviet power and tended to plunge into dangerous situations without weighing all the consequences beforehand. Most Americans took such behavior as one more proof of Soviet perfidy.

A Visit from Khrushchev Fortunately, Khrushchev let the deadline on Berlin pass, no doubt realizing that he had made a serious blunder. That summer Eisenhower invited him to visit the United States, and he accepted. He arrived on September 15 and spent ten days touring the country. The president wanted to show Khrushchev the many blessings of capitalism and took him on a helicopter ride around suburban Washington,

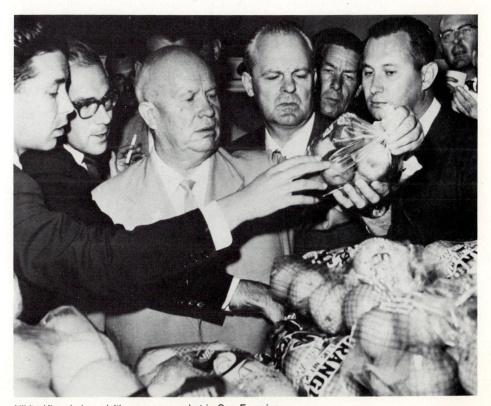

Nikita Khrushchev visiting a supermarket in San Francisco.

pointing out the thousands of shiny new cars clogging area highways and the neat rows of single-family houses. But Khrushchev was not impressed. Such possessions were wasteful, he told the president. The Soviet emphasis on public transportation and multiple housing units, he added, were more practical and economical. The visit ended with talks at Camp David, a presidential retreat in Maryland's Catoctin Mountains. Khrushchev agreed to postpone the Berlin question and to meet with Eisenhower in the spring for a second summit conference, insisting that Eisenhower and his family visit the Soviet Union immediately thereafter.

Spy Planes and a Spoiled Summit Late in 1958, Eisenhower embarked on an ambitious goodwill tour, stopping in 11 countries in Europe, Africa, and Asia, where he was universally hailed as a great peacemaker. Eisenhower meanwhile began to plan for the summit. Above all, he wanted to obtain a nuclear test ban treaty with the Soviets. He was alarmed at reports of radioactive fallout from numerous weapons tests in both countries and wanted to halt them before the atmosphere was completely poisoned. He also saw the ban as a way of limiting the nuclear arms race. The ban could halt the development of even more destructive bombs and might be followed by arms limitations talks. In particular, Eisenhower wanted to introduce an amended version of his open-skies proposal.

Disaster struck only days before the summit opened, when the Soviets shot down an American reconnaissance plane known as the U-2. The president had authorized high-altitude flights over the Soviet Union three years earlier, but the Soviets had not been able to intercept them. On May 1 they succeeded, capturing pilot Gary Francis Powers as he parachuted to safety. At first Eisenhower denied that the flights had ever taken place, but he was forced to tell the truth when the Soviets produced the pilot. Nevertheless, the summit opened in Paris on May 14. Khrushchev immediately took the floor and delivered a blistering attack on the United States for the U-2 flights. The summit broke up without any discussion of the issues, and Khrushchev withdrew Eisenhower's invitation to visit the Soviet Union.

Contention with Castro Eisenhower's last year in office also brought increasing trouble with Cuba. In early 1959 Fidel Castro overthrew the corrupt and dictatorial Fulgencio Battista. Battista was pro-American and had made Cuba into a vacation and gambling resort for wealthy Americans, while the majority of Cubans continued to live in grinding poverty. After seizing power, Castro nationalized American properties and signed a trade agreement with the Soviet Union. Although there was no proof that Castro was himself a Communist, Eisenhower concluded that the Cuban dictator had become a Soviet puppet. In early 1960 the president allowed the CIA to plan covert activities against Castro. Several assassination plots failed, and the agency decided to try to overthrow Castro with the same sort of tactics that had succeeded in Guatemala and Iran. Agents recruited anti-Castro refugees in Florida for a counterrevolutionary coup, but Eisenhower refused to allow an attack until the group could agree on a leader and a political program.

Eisenhower's Farewell Several other events marred Eisenhower's last years in office. Secretary of State Dulles died in May 1959. Eisenhower made Christian Herter his new head at State, but he missed Dulles's industry and command of the facts.

BIOGRAPHICAL SKETCH

JOHN FOSTER DULLES · *1888–1959*

More than anyone else during the 1950s, John Foster Dulles personified American foreign policy. His bold statements made headlines throughout the world; they inspired many, angered others, and left few indifferent. His name and image were seldom absent from news reports or editorial comment.

Dulles's interest in foreign affairs, as well as his moralistic stance in international relations, stemmed from powerful family influences. His father's side numbered a long line of Presbyterian preachers and missionaries, and among his mother's relatives were several important diplomats. These included Dulles's grandfather John W. Foster, who served as secretary of state under Benjamin Harrison, and his uncle Robert Lansing, who headed the State Department during most of the Wilson administration. The young Dulles was pulled in both directions and gave up plans for the ministry only after his grandfather Foster had taken him along to the Second Hague Conference in 1907.

Following graduation from Princeton, Dulles studied law at George Washington University and entered the prestigious New York firm of Sullivan and Cromwell in 1911. There he became an expert on international law. During and after World War I Dulles performed several diplomatic assignments for the Wilson administration, and in 1919 he went to Versailles as council for the American reparations committee, an assignment that lasted well into the postwar period.

Like many Wall Street lawyers in the 1930s, Dulles turned against the New Deal. He also criticized Roosevelt's foreign policy

John Foster Dulles

in the late 1930s and joined Republican isolationists in their campaign to stay out of World War II. Once the United States entered the war, he supported the effort wholeheartedly. After the war he undertook several diplomatic missions for President Truman, including negotiations for the Japanese peace treaty in 1951. The next year he drafted the Republican platform on foreign policy; condemning the policy of containment, Dulles and the Republicans committed themselves to the liberation of captive nations.

Throughout the Eisenhower years, Dulles resisted any recognition of Soviet spheres in eastern Europe and accordingly opposed a summit meeting in 1955. He was equally against compromise with the Chinese Communists, advising Eisenhower to fight for complete victory in Korea and urging a hard line on Quemoy and Matsu.

Dulles's threats of "massive retaliation" and his insistence on "rolling back" communism alarmed many in the United States and Western Europe who wanted a more flexible policy toward the Eastern bloc. Although Eisenhower usually rejected Dulles's extreme positions, he valued his secretary's knowledge and dedication. John Foster Dulles will doubtless remain a controversial figure for some time to come.

Just a year before the president had been forced to fire Sherman Adams, his principal White House assistant. In June 1958 a congressional subcommittee found that Adams had accepted gifts and other favors from New England industrialist Bernard Goldfine in return for help with the Securities and Exchange Commission. The Democrats, as well as many Republicans who had been jealous of Adams's close relationship with the president, demanded his resignation and Eisenhower reluctantly asked for it.

Three days before leaving office, Eisenhower delivered a "farewell address" over radio and television. Among other issues, he spoke of a dangerous collaboration between the military and the nation's defense industry. The danger was multifaceted, Eisenhower warned—"economic, political, and even spiritual." Government must therefore be on guard "against the acquisition of unwarranted influence" by this "military-industrial complex." The warning took many by surprise, but it should not have; for eight years Eisenhower had fought against excessive defense expenditures and had often found it impossible to restrain his own Defense Department. He knew from too many bitter experiences all about the pressure to develop and manufacture unnecessary weapons.

Despite the Adams scandal, the U-2 incident, and the aborted Paris summit, Eisenhower left office as one of the most popular presidents of all time. He had presided over nearly eight years of relative peace, had maintained a tight rein on federal spending, and left most Americans with a sense of national well-being. Professional historians did not, by and large, share this public assessment, and in the decade that followed his approval rating within the profession sank even lower. By the mid-1980s, however, Eisenhower's reputation would soar among historians. In the aftermath of Vietnam, Watergate, and Nixon's "imperial presidency," Eisenhower's policies of restraint would seem attractive indeed.

SUGGESTED READINGS

Truman's increasing popularity over the past decade has resulted in a growing list of sources. Helpful are Truman's own *Memoirs: Year of Decisions* (1955) and *Years of Trial and Hope* (1956). Robert J. Donovan has written an exhaustive two-volume account of the Truman presidency: *Conflict and Crisis* (1977) and *Tumultuous Years* (1982). The most recent and complete analysis of the Truman presidency is Donald R. McCoy, The *Presidency of Harry S Truman* (1984). Truman's daughter, Margaret Truman Daniel, has written a highly personal but revealing biography entitled *Harry S Truman* (1982). Another excellent biography is Roy Jenkins's *Truman* (1986). Focusing on Truman's domestic policies are Barton J. Bernstein, *Politics and Policies of the Truman Administration* (1970), and Harold F. Gosnell, *Truman's Crises: A Political Biography of Harry S Truman* (1980). A brief but insightful account of the Truman administration is Robert H. Ferrell, *Harry S Truman and the Modern Presidency* (1983).

Other works concentrate on particular themes of the Truman presidency. Among these are

SUGGESTED READINGS

Alonzo L. Hamby, *Beyond the New Deal: Harry S Truman and American Liberalism* (1973); Susan M. Hartman, *Truman and the 80th Congress* (1971); Richard F. Haynes, *The Awesome Power: Harry S Truman as Commander in Chief* (1973); and Maeva Marcus, *Truman and the Steel Seizure Case: The Limits of Presidential Power* (1977). On reconversion problems, see Jack S. Ballard, *The Shock of Peace: Military and Economic Demobilization after World War II* (1983).

Renewed appreciation for Eisenhower has likewise resulted in a growing body of literature. Eisenhower's memoirs concentrate on his decisions as president and the reasons behind them. These are *Mandate for Change* (1963) and *Waging Peace* (1965). The most recent and complete biography of Eisenhower's presidential years is Steven E. Ambrose, *Eisenhower the President* (1984). A succinct but thorough account of the Eisenhower administration is Elom Richardson's *The Presidency of Dwight D. Eisenhower* (1979). Fred Greenstein's *The Hidden Hand Presidency* (1982) treats Eisenhower's qualities as a political leader, as does Gary W. Reichard's *Reaffirmation of Republicanism: Eisenhower and the 83rd Congress* (1975). Emmet J. Hughes, a speechwriter during the first years of Eisenhower's presidency, writes a more critical portrait of his boss's leadership abilities in *The Ordeal of Power* (1963). Helpful, too, is Herbert S. Parmet's *Eisenhower: The Necessary President* (1972). An introduction to Eisenhower's foreign policy is Robert A. Divine's *Eisenhower and the Cold War* (1981). Background on the *Brown* decision may be found in Richard Kluger's *Simple Justice: The History of Brown v. Board of Education* (1976).

An overview of political parties during this period is given in Paul L. Murphy, ed., *Political Parties in American History, 1890–Present* (1974). James T. Patterson's *Mr. Republican: A Biography of Robert Taft* (1972) sheds much light on Republican politics in the late forties and early fifties. On the Democrats there is Herbert S. Parmet's *The Democrats: The Years After FDR* (1976). Robert A. Divine treats the influence of foreign affairs on domestic politics in a two-volume work: *Foreign Policy and U.S. Presidential Elections, 1940–1948* and *1952–1960* (1974). Similarly enlightening is Ronald J. Caridi, *The Korean War and American Politics: The Republican Party as a Case Study* (1968).

There are a number of excellent works on communism and domestic politics: David Caute, *The Great Fear: The Anti-Communist Purge under Truman and Eisenhower* (1978); Stanley I. Kutler, *The American Inquisition: Justice and Injustice in the Cold War* (1982); Alan D. Harper, *The Politics of Loyalty: The White House and the Communist Issue, 1946–1952* (1969); and Athan Theoharis, *Seeds of Repression* (1971). Studies of Senator Joseph R. McCarthy in particular are Fred J. Cook, *The Nightmare Decade: The Life and Times of Senator Joe McCarthy* (1971); David M. Oshinsky, *A Conspiracy So Immense: The World of Joe McCarthy* (1983); and Richard H. Rovere, *Senator Joe McCarthy* (1959). On McCarthy and related issues, see Edwin R. Bailey, *Joe McCarthy and the Press* (1981); Donald F. Crosby, *God, Church, and the Flag: Senator Joe McCarthy and the Catholic Church, 1950–1957* (1978); Richard M. Fried, *Men Against McCarthy* (1976); and Richard Freeland, *The Truman Doctrine and the Origins of McCarthyism* (1971).

Sources on foreign affairs under Eisenhower are extensive. Michael A. Guhin's *John Foster Dulles: A Statesman and His Times* (1972) is the most complete volume on Eisenhower's outspoken secretary of state. Concentrating on Dulles's moralistic view of world affairs is Townsend Hoopes's *The Devil and John Foster Dulles* (1973). On early decisions regarding Vietnam there is Weldon A. Brown's *Prelude to Disaster: The American Role in Vietnam, 1940–1963* (1975). For a clearer understanding of the Suez crisis, see Herman Finer, *Dulles over Suez* (1964) and Hugh Thomas, *Suez* (1967). U.S.-Cuban relations are discussed in Hugh Thomas, *Cuba* (1971) and in Philip W. Bonsal, *Cuba, Castro, and the United States* (1971). Jack Schinck's *Berlin Crisis, 1958–1962* (1971) gives a good overview of Soviet-American contention in Germany. The two Eisenhower summits are placed in a larger historical context in Keith Eubank's *The Summit Conference, 1919–1960* (1966). On arms and arms control, there are Robert A. Divine, *Blowing in the Wind: The Nuclear Test Ban Debate, 1954–1960* (1979), and Urs Schwarz, *American Strategy* (1966). The activities of the CIA under Eisenhower are explored in Harry Rosizke, *The CIA's Secret Operations: Espionage, Counter Espionage, and Covert Action* (1977).

13

A Contented Society

Despite the cold war and numerous world crises, most Americans were quite contented with national life during the 15 years following World War II. A vibrant economy and widespread prosperity came as a pleasant surprise after a decade and a half of depression and wartime scarcities. Acres and acres of new houses, tens of millions of bright new automobiles, and a bumber crop of babies all testified to the country's growing bounty. Those who shared this horn of plenty were unlikely to criticize the capitalistic system or the public policies that sustained it. Doubters also risked great unpopularity, as government and critics alike trumpeted the American way of life in an ongoing campaign against Communist ideology.

Even so, the period was not without its detractors. Some detected an unhealthy social conformity, with a corresponding lack of individual creativity, while others regretted a renewed celebration of the business ethic, with its Babbitt-like return to self-congratulation and boosterism. By the end of the 1950s many Americans began to realize that millions of fellow citizens had been passed over in the great tide of abundance. Decent wages, safer working conditions, and legal equality remained the preserve of white males from European backgrounds. Blacks, women, Hispanics, orientals, and other minorities continued to face great obstacles along the road to personal fulfillment.

Because of the era's self-satisfaction and general blindness to social deprivation, critics have tended to dismiss the immediate postwar era as bland and uninspiring, and in contrast to the tumultuous years just before and after, the period can seem quite dull. Yet the late 1940s and the 1950s were an extremely fertile time for the arts. Popular music also underwent a major upheaval, laying the basis for a musical renaissance in the 1960s. All in all, the postwar period represented a time of social transition, a breathing spell between two generations of tension and upheaval.

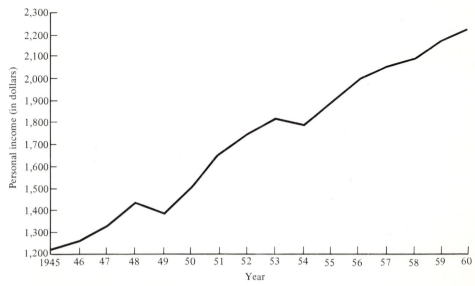

Average personal income, 1945–1960.

THE CONTOURS OF PROSPERITY

The rate of economic growth during the postwar years was truly impressive. Despite several recessions, the gross national product increased by 64 percent between 1946 and 1960, rising (in constant 1958 dollars) from $312.6 billion to $487.7 billion. During the same period, steel production climbed from 66.6 million tons to 99.3 million. Even more telling, the manufacture of automobiles soared from 2 million units in 1946 to a peak of 8 million in 1955. Meanwhile the number of car registrations more than doubled from 25 million during the last year of the war to 62 million in 1960. And while legions of drivers took to the roads, the nation's housing stock jumped by 25 million new dwellings. Average employee earnings also kept pace. Measured in constant 1914 dollars, they more than doubled from $2,359 in 1946 to $4,743 as the 1950s came to a close.

The causes of the economic boom were not hard to find. Pent-up consumer demand for many goods reached all the way back to the early 1930s. The depression had forced millions to forgo new automobiles, better housing, and a wide array of domestic appliances. World War II brought high wages, but few items were available for purchase, inducing citizens to save at record rates. Emerging from the war with billions of dollars in bank accounts and war bonds, consumers had plenty of money with which to demand goods and services. Low interest rates and the generous provisions of the G.I. Bill stimulated the economy even further. Hundreds of thousands of ex-soldiers went to college or training schools instead of entering the job market or going onto unemployment rolls. These and other veterans also took advantage of government-guaranteed mortgages in order to finance new businesses and homes.

Baby Boom Another boost to the economy was the so-called baby boom. Like the widespread prosperity of the period, a sustained increase in the birthrate took the country

ORAL HISTORY
Growing Up in the Twentieth Century

PHILIP HAZELTON · *born 1941*

Growing up in a small midwestern town in the forties and fifties was fun. We'd build huts up in the woods. We'd carry our lunch up there and spend the whole day. Cowboys and Indians was the popular thing in those days—good guys and bad guys out West. We played war. You had a lot of army and navy gear from the surplus stores or that somebody's father had around. Boys would wear this stuff all over the place; there was still very much the ethos of World War II. Many of the movies we saw were reenactments of World War II—heroic kinds of things. Even though we were too young to remember the war, we were early enough in the postwar era that the popular culture brought it across to us.

My parents didn't tell us anything about sex. There were just veiled warnings. They probably trusted that somehow, by the normal progression of things, we'd find out on our own, and we did. Somehow I knew that a man had to get with a woman to have a baby, but how that happened and how the baby came out, I didn't know. The fellows—we'd talk about it and you'd gradually, from hearing these things, put together in your mind how everything worked. The best contraception was hearing about somebody who got pregnant and the shock waves that rolled through the school and the community when the word came out. I would imagine that the 1950s and the 1930s, in terms of sexual attitudes, were very much alike.

In politics, I was told that if you were a Republican you were good and normal and clean-cut and wholesome. If you were a Democrat, you were some kind of union

rabble-rouser and ignorant. I was surprised to learn that there were some Democrats like Averell Harriman who were from wealthy families. It was Harry Truman, I was led to believe, who was the typical Democrat—kind of short, brassy, loud, and not very well-spoken or dressed. He just wasn't our kind of person. I found out much later that Harry Truman was very well-read and intelligent.

The president of the United States was the biggest, most Republican Republican of all—Dwight D. Eisenhower. We saw him as clean-cut, wholesome, and really nonpolitical—a kindly person who was above politics.

THE CONTOURS OF PROSPERITY

He was a father. He came to power when I was 11 and left office when I was 19. Throughout this whole period, there was this smiling, bald, and yet absolutely strong man you sometimes called General Eisenhower or even Ike. He was definitely *not* a Truman. I couldn't imagine anyone not voting for Ike. I was completely mystified when Nixon lost to Kennedy in 1960. He was Eisenhower's heir apparent. He also seemed to be clean-cut and wholesome—a father and a family man and all that.

We're talking here about the early 1950s: McCarthyism, the cold war, a lot of anticommunism. I know I grew up with the feeling that anyone who was different was thought to be a Communist of some sort. People who wore beards—they might be Communists. People who promoted civil rights a little too much might be Communists. And, of course, Russia was at the center of all this. I think it was built up in my mind at school. Teachers would say, "You wait until the Russian tanks come right down Broad Street . . . and you're taken off to slavery in Russia somewhere." They also told us that America was the only place where democracy existed, that America was the only place where there

was freedom of religion. When I graduated from high school in 1959 the principal hired as the commencement speaker some Hungarian freedom fighter. He told us: "You won't even live to be 25. The battle is coming between the Russians and the Americans, and you've got to be ready." I went out into the world with a very great sense of doom.

Maybe what they were trying to do was build up our courage, but what they taught us was fear. We didn't learn that America was strong and needed to stand up. The message was: "We've got to be afraid of those dirty Russians with their big tanks and jackboots; they really can come marching into our little town and take us." We still talked in terms of World War II; that's how wars were fought—with brutal, strutting invaders and their tanks. Nobody really talked about planes and atomic bombs.

There was a real sense of security in the fifties that you were growing up in a cozy little town in the valley. But there was always, always this feeling that the day would come when you would be called up and you would go marching down the street to meet the Russians, God knows where.

by surprise. The birthrate in the United States had been declining since the mid-nineteenth century and it had reached an all-time low during the depression. Wartime prosperity produced a modest increase in births and demographers predicted an even larger rise after the war as couples who had put off having children for the duration made up for lost time. What surprised the experts was the continuation of high birthrates into the early 1960s. The number of live births per thousand of population reached a high of 26.6 in 1947, up from a low of 18.4 in 1933, the worst year of the Great Depression. By the early 1950s, the birth rate had leveled off to 24 or 25 per thousand, but stayed there until the end of the decade, when it began to decline noticeably and return to more normal patterns. It was not that more parents were having five or six children; rather, the typical couple was electing to have two or three children instead of one or two—and that made all the difference.

American families were more than compensating for low fertility rates during the war and depression years, and experts were hard pressed at first to explain the facts. The ongoing prosperity of the period was clearly an important cause, as parents believed that

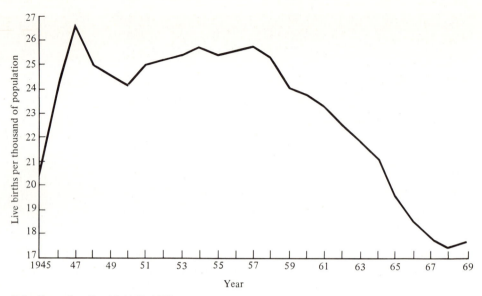

Baby "boom" or "bust," 1945–1969.

they could afford another child or two. The higher birthrates in turn stimulated the economy, for the new arrivals required mountains of food and clothing, not to mention expanded living quarters and a second car for transporting them to the swimming pool, dancing lessons, Little League, and after-school activities.

Beyond such obvious economic explanations, one must turn to more subtle reasons for increased birthrates. Some investigators have pointed to what they call a "cult of domesticity" during these years, which emphasized the emotional rewards of children and family. It arose, they conjecture, from wartime longings for the comforts of "hearth and home." Homesick, bored, and often frightened, soldiers and sailors dreamed of a quiet little house, a loving wife, and a couple of healthy, cheerful kids. Whether an accurate view or not, former G.I.s joined a virtual stampede into marriage. The average age at marriage declined year after year, while the divorce rate tumbled from 4.3 per thousand in 1946 to 2.1 in 1958.

The baby boom would have a profound effect upon American society for decades to come. The children themselves faced years of overcrowding. At first there were not enough houses and then there were too few schools or qualified teachers, followed by a shortage of college classrooms and dormitory spaces. And those born toward the end of the baby boom would encounter the frustrations of a glutted job market. As the oldest of them reached middle age, there were worries that the Social Security system might not be able to support the superabundance of retirees only 20 or 30 years ahead. Students of the baby boom have also linked it to increased crime rates in the 1960s and 1970s, pointing out quite correctly that most violent crimes are committed by people under 30. Finally, observers have associated the baby-boom generation with several other phenomena of the 1960s, ranging from the fast-food craze to rock music, campus rebellions, and the sexual revolution.

Suburban Fever   In the search for adequate housing, many parents of the baby-boom generation turned to suburbia. Suburbs were nothing new on the American scene, having emerged in the late nineteenth century as commuter trains and trolleys permitted middle-class workers to travel from outlying homes to the city proper on a daily basis. The advent of automobiles accelerated the movement at the same time that it freed suburbanites from the rigid routes of trains and trolleys. Depression and war slowed the suburban exodus considerably, but the postwar period witnessed a veritable explosion of suburban populations.

Various factors accelerated the suburban trend. In the first place, there was frequently little vacant land within older urban boundaries, forcing developers to seek locations outside city limits. Regulations on veterans' mortgages, as well as those financed through the Federal Housing Administration (FHA), also favored suburban locations. Lending authorities believed that new housing in outlying districts was a much better risk than older units in ethnic or racially mixed neighborhoods and often refused to grant mortgages for these declining areas—a practice known as "redlining." Yet another important factor was the interstate highway system which made it easier to commute by automobile than ever before. Within months of their completion, interstate routes in and around urban areas became congested commuter highways. On a personal level, postwar families were lured to the suburbs by promises of better schools, lower crime rates, more homogeneous neighborhoods, larger yards, and increased privacy.

Acres of nearly identical suburban houses.

The most spectacular of the suburban developments were those of William Levitt. The first went up on Long Island, the second outside Philadelphia in Bucks County, and the third in Willingboro, New Jersey. Levitt kept costs to a minimum by restricting buyers to two or three basic models and by employing assembly-line techniques to build his houses. Workers assembled components in on-site factories and trucked them to individual building lots, permitting Levitt to raise thousands of houses at record speed and the lowest possible prices.

Those studying the three Levittowns and communities like them remarked at the high level of social and economic homogeneity. In Levittown, Long Island, for example, two-thirds of the residents earned between $5,000 and $10,000 per year, the great majority of them falling into one level or another of the middle class. In Levittown, New Jersey, 56 percent of the workers were white collar, 18 percent qualified as professionals, and the remaining 26 percent fell into various blue-collar categories, but their incomes did not differ substantially from one another. Virtually all were Caucasian.

Among whites, who composed over 95 percent of the suburban population, there was considerable ethnic variety, but most were at least second or third generation who had assimilated the values and habits of the social mainstream. Social philosopher Will Herberg argued in *Catholic-Protestant-Jew* (1955) that suburban residents tended to submerge their ethnic origins in religious affiliations, identifying themselves instead as Catholics, Protestants, or Jews. Social status existed in suburbia, observers maintained, but it seemed to depend upon community leadership and volunteer work rather than on the more traditional factors of family name, occupation, or residence. Critics of suburbia accused residents of racism and social irresponsibility, and maintained that the new developments were veritable prisons for housewives, who remained behind while their husbands went off to work. Suburbs also lacked urban amenities such as the corner drugstore or delicatessen. But when asked, most suburbanites expressed great satisfaction with their homes and communities.

The lack of retail stores within walking distances in the suburbs was, of course, one of the factors in the automobile boom, as various commercial enterprises tried to serve the needs of a nation on wheels. Shopping centers, which had originated in the 1920s, now appeared throughout suburbia. At the same time, there was a veritable epidemic of drive-in facilities: drive-in movies, drive-in banks, drive-in restaurants, and even drive-in churches. Downtown shopping districts soon began to feel the competition. With limited parking and with retail establishments spread over a wide area, they simply could not compete with the new merchandise centers. More than ever before, the automobile was a way of life.

Urban Decay   The suburban movement hurt the cities in other ways. Between 1950 and 1960, 4 of the 15 largest cities in the country actually lost population. While cities as a whole grew by only 13 percent during this period, the suburbs increased their populations by an impressive 46 percent. It is also significant that those cities which grew the most were in the South and the West, while suburban communities in these areas also expanded more rapidly than those in the Midwest and Northeast. Comparisons between the 1940 and 1960 census returns show this trend quite clearly. New York State, for example, grew by a modest 25 percent. At the same time, the population of Texas

THE CONTOURS OF PROSPERITY   **303**

One of thousands of postwar drive-in theaters.

grew by nearly 50 percent and that of California by an astounding 127 percent. Within another decade, California would supersede New York as the country's most populous state.

As people moved out of the eastern cities into the suburbs or out of the region altogether, these older municipalities contained larger and larger percentages of poor and elderly people. Tax bases shrunk accordingly and city authorities found it difficult to pay for essential services. Many cities tried to compensate by levying wage taxes on suburbanites who worked within municipal boundaries, but even this tactic proved inadequate. By the end of the 1950s most of the nation's largest cities were in difficult financial straits.

Rural Retreat The number of people living in rural areas also declined steadily after World War II. In 1945, about 24.5 million Americans lived on farms, but by 1960 the figure had fallen to 15.6 million. For the most part it was the smaller and least productive farms that disappeared, their owners forced into nonagricultural jobs. Those who remained on the land made increased use of mechanized equipment, chemical fertilizers, and hybrid seeds to produce record yields. Remaining agriculturalists also became more like their urban compatriots, as electricity and the mass media penetrated nearly every rural home. Farmers watched the same television shows as city people, and with a car at their disposal, they shopped in many of the same retail outlets.

The Social Fabric With the growth of real incomes in the late forties and fifties, many Americans tasted middle-class life for the first time. When polled, the great bulk of respondents placed themselves in the broad middle class, whether they belonged there or not. Sociologists also reported that Americans were not particularly class-conscious and found it easy to associate with those above and below them on the social ladder, remarking further that Americans continued to have great faith in social mobility. Yet studies showed that most people experienced little if any social mobility in their own lifetimes. In a study of Oakland, California, Seymour Lipsit and Reinhard Bendix discovered that 80 percent of manual workers remained in manual occupations all their lives. The 20 percent who moved into nonmanual occupations commonly did so at the lowest levels of white-collar employment where the pay was only marginally better (and sometimes worse) than before. Those who failed to advance even this far nevertheless hoped that their children might be more fortunate. It is impossible to ascertain how many offspring did in fact achieve higher socioeconomic levels than their parents, but existing studies suggest that the majority did not. Parents' income, occupation, and social standing continued to exert a powerful effect on their children. Education proved to be the surest route to social mobility in the next generation and the higher percentages of youth graduating from college in the late forties and fifties doubtless produced a real increase in the size of the middle class.

A Segregated Society The relative lack of class consciousness quite clearly did not extend to relationships between blacks and whites. Blacks continued to earn 50 to 60 percent less than whites during the postwar era. Few could qualify financially for mortgages in the new suburban developments, and those who could were effectively excluded by prejudicial builders and real estate agents. Zoning ordinances, which required single-family dwellings and substantial lot sizes, were particularly effective in excluding lower-cost housing for blacks and other minorities.

Such segregation was only one piece of a larger policy of separation. In the South, segregation continued to exist by law and extended from the cradle to the grave. Blacks and whites lived in different neighborhoods, attended different schools, and lay buried in separate cemeteries. Blacks were excluded from hotels, restaurants, and theaters which served a white clientele. Rest rooms and drinking fountains were also segregated. Department stores would not permit black customers to try on clothes, and they could not return ill-fitting garments. Even the Red Cross kept black and white blood separate.

Despite the odds, a handful of courageous blacks began to challenge segregation. *Brown* v. *Board of Education* engendered high hopes in many, but these were soon dashed by Eisenhower's lukewarm enforcement of the decision and by white resistance. Blacks thus turned to other methods for attacking the color line. In Montgomery, Alabama, first capital of the Confederacy and a stronghold of segregation, black residents boycotted the city's bus system in the autumn of 1955. It began when a woman named Rosa Parks refused to sit in the section of a bus designated for blacks. Led by the Reverend Martin Luther King, Jr., and other members of the clergy, blacks formed car pools or walked long distances to and from work. Meanwhile lawyers from the NAACP charged that segregated buses were unconstitutional, and the U.S. Supreme Court agreed

THE CONTOURS OF PROSPERITY 305

in a November 1956 decision. After 381 days, the Montgomery bus boycott ended and the buses were integrated.

Although the participants probably did not realize it, the Montgomery bus boycott opened a new chapter in the civil rights movement. Blacks not only challenged segregation, but adopted nonviolent tactics that legitimized their crusade in the eyes of many Americans, white as well as black. Segregationists might attack the peaceful resisters with savage brutality, but it was they and not the protesters who were discredited in the public mind. As in India under Mahatma Gandhi, civil disobedience and peaceful protests would prove much more effective than rioting or violent confrontation.

In 1959 students from two black colleges in Greensboro, North Carolina, used civil disobedience to desegregate the lunch counter in a local Woolworth store. Relays of students sat at the counter silently and waited to be served. When police came in and carried them off, they went peacefully, their places at the counter being taken by another group of students. The store's management eventually relented and the lunch counter was integrated. In the years ahead, black and white youths would use similar tactics to integrate bus lines and the public facilities along their routes.

Feminist Doldrums   Most women did not have to breach a stone wall of segregation, but they still faced a formidable body of prejudice and numerous forms of discrimination. It is true that more women than ever before worked outside the home, representing 34.5 percent of the work force by 1960. Many, however, were interested solely in supplementing the family's income. Yet even those who sought full-time careers were paid less than men in similar positions and were unlikely to secure advancement to the most lucrative and prestigious positions. Women also earned relatively fewer college degrees in the 1950s than they had 30 years earlier and made little or no progress in securing elective office. All in all, women seemed to have lost ground since winning the right to vote in 1920.

There were various reasons for this dismal state of affairs. For one thing, prejudice against women continued to be quite strong. The earlier suffragists were frequently characterized in the media as quaint oddities or ridiculed as unfeminine. Securing the vote had also left the feminist movement without a rallying point. In addition, few women sought political office or voted as a bloc on feminist issues. The League of Women Voters, for instance, became a strictly nonpartisan organization, dedicated to informing voters regardless of their party or sex. Finally, most women seemed caught up in the cult of domesticity, as press and pulpit alike praised homemakers for their femininity and maternal sacrifices to the human race. To disagree and say that American housewives were not the luckiest women on earth appeared almost unpatriotic in a nation that felt compelled to extoll its virtues in the battle against communism.

Still, the feminist movement managed to survive the 1950s with something of a skeleton crew on board. The small National Women's party concentrated on an Equal Rights Amendment, pressing Congress session after session to pass the measure and send it out to the states for ratification. The National Federation of Business and Professional Clubs joined the lobbying efforts, but there was virtually no chance of success in the political climate of the McCarthy era.

SOCIAL CRITICS

General contentment and political conservatism did not mean that postwar society was entirely without critics. Among the most provocative studies of American society during this time was David Riesman's *The Lonely Crowd* (1950). Riesman, a Harvard sociologist, believed that a new kind of national character had arisen in recent decades—what he called the ''other-directed'' type. This other-directed person, who looked to others for ideas and standards of behavior, contrasted sharply with the self-made man of the nineteenth century. Living at a time of social and economic upheaval, the nineteenth-century entrepreneur had been much more ''inner-directed'' than men and women of the mid-twentieth century. In contrast to citizens of the 1950s, who took their cues from the world around them, he had carried his values within himself and thus was able to maintain an inner equilibrium despite a world awash with change.

The mid-twentieth century, observed Riesman, had brought new social realities and with it the other-directed type. Industrialization was now complete and material abundance assured. Consumption and not production was the chief pursuit of the American people, and their purchases were increasingly determined by the media and other external guides. At the same time, modern transportation and communication made the world much smaller, demanding increased cooperation among peoples at home and abroad. The competitive, inner-directed man was thus an anachronism. In the future, more and more Americans would take their values from others, and especially from the mass media. The inner-directed personality thus gave way to the other-directed type.

Another sociologist, William H. Whyte, Jr., shared many of Reisman's observations, but he was much more critical of what he saw. In *The Organization Man* (1956) Whyte described the emerging consequences of increased organization in American life. Whyte admitted that much of this organization was necessary and even beneficial. Larger economic units required more structure, greater cohesiveness, and better management, and consequently the self-made entrepreneur had been replaced by professional managers. By the mid-twentieth century, however, organization had become an end in itself; groups superseded the individual and consensus was ultimately more important than the right decision. This insistence on group consensus and cooperation, Whyte lamented, was even foisted on scientific researchers, resulting in a decline of initiative and imagination. And in the bedroom suburbs where the organization man commonly resided, being able to ''get along with others'' was a prime virtue. In nearly every aspect of life the ''Social Ethic,'' with its emphasis upon harmony and cooperation, had replaced the older ''Protestant Ethic,'' with its belief in individual competition, and hard work.

On the whole, Whyte regretted the overemphasis on group cooperation and mutual accommodation. They impeded criticism, stifled creativity, and thwarted change. Alexis de Tocqueville's worst fears seemed confirmed, as pressures to conform threatened to engulf the nation in a gentle but persistent tide of mediocrity and conformism.

Still other criticisms were primarily religious in nature. One of the most important came from Reinhold Niebuhr of New York's Union Theological Seminary. Niebuhr owed a large debt to Calvinism, with its insistence upon divine omnipotence and original sin; Americans might be prosperous and contented, but they had not overcome evil and human imperfection. In the midst of unparalleled plenty, Niebuhr pointed out, there were millions who could not escape the bonds of grinding poverty. Crime, racism, and political

POPULAR CULTURE

corruption continued unabated and human performance constantly fell short of the ideal. The cold war, with its mutual threats and recriminations, kept the world teetering on the brink of nuclear disaster. But these imperfections were no mystery for Niebuhr. In *The Irony of American History* (1952) and other works, he reminded readers that humans were prone to sin and error, that all were destined to some degree of failure or imperfection.

POPULAR CULTURE

Niebuhr enjoyed a respectable following among sophisticated readers, but most Americans preferred a more optimistic kind of religion. Preachers like Norman Vincent Peale provided them with abundant encouragement, assuring them that prayer and "positive thinking" would lead to both spiritual and worldly success. For those who wanted a more emotional approach to religion, there was the Reverend Billy Graham, who emerged as the chief evangelist of the postwar period. Like the "old-time" revivalists, he asked his audiences to come forward and make a public commitment to God. In later years he would take his crusades to millions through television.

Even President Eisenhower spoke out for religion, assuring citizens that God was on the American side. "Recognition of the Supreme Being," he pronounced, was "the most basic expression of Americanism." "Without God," he added, "there could be no American way of life." And as if to emphasize his tribute to the Almighty, he endorsed a congressional resolution that added the words "under God" to the Pledge of Allegiance.

Americans echoed their president's sentiments with a great upsurge in church affiliation and attendance. By the mid-1950s, 63 percent of the population belonged to institutionalized churches, up from 40 percent in 1940. Whether this represented a genuine increase in belief is open to question. In suburbia the new churches were as much neighborhood meeting places as they were houses of worship, while cold war anxieties sent others flocking to Sunday services.

Television   When it came to the newest electronic miracle, namely television, there could be no doubt about the nation's mass conversion. Many of the discoveries that had made television possible dated from the late nineteenth and early twentieth centuries. Experimental television appeared in the 1930s, but the depression and the war had greatly retarded commercial development. Peace and prosperity gave it an immediate boost, and by the early 1960s over 90 percent of the nation's households owned at least one television set.

In some ways television was an extension of radio. The old radio networks launched and then dominated television broadcasting, continuing to use commercial advertisements to finance the venture. And many of the early television programs were merely video versions of popular radio shows, Jack Benny, Superman, and several soap operas among them. Yet television was different from radio. A person listening to radio had to use considerable imagination, but in television, little was left to the viewer's interpretation. The new medium also imposed certain limitations on programming, especially during the early days when nearly all shows were broadcast live. Dialogue had to take place against appropriate visual backdrops, which were in turn circumscribed by the range and capabilities of the television camera.

Television has been criticized from the very beginning. Many analysts believe that it was far better during the formative period, before the networks turned to film and video recording to achieve a smoother, cinemalike effect. The earlier live broadcasts, they contend, captured some of the theater's creative spontaneity, but they were soon replaced by mindless situation comedies like "I Love Lucy," rigged quiz shows, ranging from "Twenty-One" to "The $64,000 Question," and a blur of afternoon soap operas. Yet serious drama continued to be aired throughout the 1950s. Both "Playhouse 90" and "Armstrong Circle Theater" presented excellent plays. Milton Berle offered classic comedy, while "The Ed Sullivan Show" brought the best new talent into family living rooms.

But television, even more than radio, kept Americans from reading. One magazine after another disappeared, and daily newspapers folded or merged with their competitors. Teachers complained that students were growing less adept at reading and conversation, as they found classroom activities boring in comparison to the continuous motion and excitement of television. Others contended that television violence made such behavior seem commonplace and acceptable while stimulating the morbid imaginations of juvenile delinquents and other criminals.

Still others complained that television became the only reality for millions of citizens, obscuring distinctions between truth and fiction and determining which events were newsworthy and which were not. The newscasters themselves became stars, their words and expressions vested with an aura of infallibility. Nor is it surprising that television commercials sometimes masqueraded as news events, with pseudonewscasters

Set for a "live" television drama.

POPULAR CULTURE   **309**

describing their sponsors' products against a backdrop of maps and charts much like those in the news room.

Politics also proved quite vulnerable to television. The major parties changed their convention schedules in order to conduct their most dramatic activities during prime time. Instant analyses of presidential speeches by news commentators helped to mold public opinion before viewers had had a chance to reflect on what they had just seen and heard. Contention for political office became a television event, with telegenic candidates having a distinct advantage over others. Increasingly, the presidency itself threatened to become a public relations job, as the president's image on television, not the issues or his performance in office, was what seemed to count most.

Movies Another victim of television was the movie industry, as Americans found it much easier to stay home and watch television in the evenings than to drive or walk to the movies. Men and women who had gone to the cinema two or three times a week now went only occasionally or not at all. Movie ticket sales declined from $66 million in 1948 to just under $40 million a decade later. The industry tried to win back its audience in several ways. Some producers turned to technical innovations like wider screens (CinemaScope) or three-dimensional (3-D) films. The former became a staple in movie making, but theatergoers objected to the special eyeglasses required for 3-D pictures. Cinerama created a three-dimensional effect by using a large curved screen and three projectors, equipment that most movie houses found too expensive. Smell-O-Vision, or movies accompanied by appropriate aromas squirted through the theater's ventilation system, also failed to catch on.

With revenues declining, most movie producers were afraid to experiment with new themes and therefore decided to stick with proven formulas. Attacks on the industry from the House Committee on Un-American Activities, which accused the studios of harboring Communist actors and writers, likewise convinced filmmakers to avoid controversial subjects. The western thriller returned after a brief decline during the war years, the best of these being *High Noon* (1952) and *Shane* (1953). The musical film also regained predominance through such hits as *Singin' in the Rain* (1952), a classic starring dancer Gene Kelly. A handful of titles did in fact touch upon milder social issues. In *Rebel Without a Cause* (1955) James Dean played a teenager in the throes of adolescent rebellion. Dean's death in a violent car crash a year later dramatized even more vividly the youthful zest for automobiles and daredevil driving, and Dean became something of a folk hero to millions of teenagers who identified with his portrayal of rebellion—both on and off the screen.

Sports Like the movies, sports felt the impact of television in the postwar period. Television accelerated the transformation of American athletics into big business and also favored some sports at the expense of others, sometimes inducing changes in the rules themselves. Nowhere was this more evident than in football.

Until the late 1930s college football dominated the public's attention. Professional teams were often poorer than the best college organizations, and they suffered from their origins among ethnic players from steel and mining towns in the Midwest. But football proved to be the perfect sport for television, and the professional teams profited immensely from it, as did the better college teams. Football's constant movement and building suspense (as each team fought to make first downs and advance toward the goal line) were perfect for an action-oriented medium. The action also tended to take place on a small area of the field, making it easy for the cameras to follow. With more and more viewers tuning into the play-by-play, teams earned increasing revenues from television. More skillful players like John Unitas and Otto Graham became national celebrities with salaries and promotional fees to match.

Baseball and basketball were not quite so fortunate. In comparison to football, baseball seemed a slow-paced, old-fashioned game, and the great expanses over which a play might take place also posed difficulties for early television cameras. Baseball's long season and many games made it additionally difficult for the networks to anticipate critical contests. The frequency of basketball games proved to be a similar handicap. Basketball was a fast-paced sport, but it lacked the "fourth-down crisis" of football. Nevertheless, the telecasting of baseball and basketball competitions increased their public followings and began to generate large sums of money for players and owners alike.

Perhaps the worst effects of large-scale spectator sports were felt in the colleges and universities. Campus sports had been growing in importance since the late nineteenth century. But in the postwar period, college sports (and football in particular) became big business. Coaches sought to use winning teams as a stepping-stone in their own careers, while players looked toward a profitable contract with one of the professional teams after graduation. It is no wonder that college sports officials as well as students violated amateur athletic rules with alarming frequency. Perhaps the worst scandals of all occurred during the basketball season of 1950–1951 when the New York district attorney accused 37 college basketball players of collaborating with New York City gamblers to fix scores.

On a more positive note, black professional athletes were hired by the major league teams for the first time just after World War II. The Brooklyn Dodgers broke the "color line" in 1947 when they signed Jackie Robinson, whose obvious talent and self-restraint in the face of jeers and racial slurs opened the game, along with other major league sports, to black players.

Popular Music   The growth of spectator sports did nothing to dampen the public's appetite for popular music. The immediate postwar period saw little change in musical tastes, with big bands and "swing" tunes continuing to dominate. Broadway musicals also remained popular. Indeed, the late forties and fifties were a golden age for the live musical. Leading the list was *South Pacific* (1949) by Richard Rodgers and Oscar Hammerstein II. Other hits by Rodgers and Hammerstein were *Carousel* (1945) and *The Sound of Music* (1959)—both made into highly successful movies.

Although these musicals were a far cry from the classics, their creators used many of the rules and techniques laid down by the great masters of the nineteenth century. Even the popular jazz tunes of the prewar years had been "sanitized" somewhat to fit within a loose framework of serious music. Adults were thus shocked and dismayed when rock and roll swept the nation in the mid-1950s.

Even the term *rock and roll,* a slang reference to body movements during sexual intercourse, was offensive to middle-class parents. Nor were many pleased that the new rhythms originated with black musicians and performers—though it actually was the greater acceptance of black musicians and African rhythmic traditions that helped the new music to make headway. Thus, despite parental disapproval (and in part because of it) teenagers loved the raucous beat and irreverent lyrics. Like James Dean's *Rebel Without a Cause,* the new music struck a strong chord in adolescents and became a convenient but harmless vehicle of teenage rebellion.

At the center of the rock craze was Elvis Presley. Although white, Presley was faithful to black singing styles and excited his young audiences with wild pelvic gyrations. Teenage girls screamed throughout his performances and tried to tear his clothes off as he left the stage. Presley made a fortune from records, his most popular singles being "Heartbreak Hotel" and "Hound Dog," both released in 1956. Disc jockeys, led by Alan Freed of WINS in New York, were soon blasting rock and roll all over the country. The rock movement would continue into the 1960s and take on the dimensions of a full-blown social protest.

LITERATURE AND THE ARTS

Few literary critics would give high marks to the fiction of the postwar period, as the novelists of this era suffered by comparison to the great writers of the recent past. No one emerged to take the place of a Fitzgerald, a Dos Passos, or a Hemingway. Hemingway actually lived into the 1950s and published his last novel, *The Old Man and the Sea,* in 1952, but Hemingway belonged to the past. Some even suspected that his last novel had been written several years before. John Steinbeck's *East of Eden* was published the same year, while William Faulkner's *Requiem for a Nun* appeared in 1959. Both were well received but somehow fell short of their authors' previous works.

Novels about World War II continued to come forth during these years. Among the best was James Jones's *From Here to Eternity* (1951), a highly enjoyable and sometimes moving saga about men and women caught up in the bombing of Pearl Harbor and the early days of the war. Norman Mailer's *The Naked and the Dead* (1948) also focused on the drama and power of war. Other novels continued the long tradition of criticizing the nation's commercial culture. At the top of the list was Sloan Wilson's *Man in the Gray Flannel Suit* (1955), which sadly depicted a businessman and his values. Also very popular was J. D. Salinger's *Catcher in the Rye* (1951), featuring an adolescent protagonist named Holden Caulfield who lashes out against adult hypocrisy and anticipates something of the youthful rebellion to come—though on a wholly individualistic level. Meanwhile the historical novel continued to attract a large following. Most notable was MacKinlay Kantor's *Andersonville,* a horrifying tale about life in a Confederate prisoner-of-war camp, no doubt inspired by parallels with the concentration camps of Nazi Germany.

The Beats The most critical literary figures of the day were so-called beat writers. Poets like Allen Ginsberg and Lawrence Ferlinghetti attacked the materialism and artificiality of middle-class life. But the most important of the beat writers was Jack Kerouac, who found scores of antiheroes among hoboes, prostitutes, drug addicts, alcoholics, and members of despised minority groups. Whether by choice or necessity, all had escaped the trap of middle-class conformity. For Kerouac, they were also closer to nature and perhaps even to God. This was Kerouac's particular message in *On the Road* (1957), a thinly fictionalized account of his rambles with a friend across the United States. Kerouac and the other beats were offended by the seeming hollowness and injustice of American life, but they had no remedies to propose and generally despaired at the prospects for social reform. Smoking marijuana and drifting about the country were the only things that made sense for these men and women who were alienated by the Babbitt-like atmosphere of the 1950s.

Painting Unlike the beat writers, American painters generally moved away from social criticism in the postwar epoch. The social-realist school of Ben Shahn, Thomas Hart Benton, and others appeared to have run its course when the depression ended, though some continued to work in this genre for another decade or so. The war, however, brought new influences to American art, as dozens of European painters sought a haven from fascism in the United States. With them came living examples of every major artistic movement of the recent past, ranging from cubism and surrealism to complete abstractionism. These talented émigrés taught, painted, and exhibited, and touched off a movement among their American disciples called abstract expressionism.

Practitioners of the new style tried to convey their innermost feelings without reference to physical objects or representational forms. They would, quite literally, use paint and canvas to express themselves as abstractly as possible. Among the earliest and most famous of the abstract expressionists was Jackson Pollock, who filled giant canvases, often measuring 20 feet across and 8 feet high, with exuberant swirls of color interspersed with bright splotches and spaghetti-like strands of pigment and sand. Pollock never planned his paintings, but began by applying paint to the surface and then let the work grow out of itself and his own evolving feelings. He preferred to nail his canvases to the floor and work on them from all angles—sitting, standing, crouching, and crawling about as he painted. In such works as *Sounds in the Grass* (1946) there is a shimmering dynamism, as swirling abstract shapes flicker and pulsate over the bedabbed surface. Others like Robert Motherwell employed bold but simple patterns to convey feeling or mood.

Despite the strong hold of abstract expressionism among artists, many accomplished painters chose to work in a different genre. One was Arshile Gorky, who turned to surrealism in the early 1940s. Gorky's paintings relate to real objects, but on canvas they assume distorted and often dreamlike forms. Objects are juxtaposed in unfamiliar and even ludicrous fashion, much as they might be in a dream. For example, Gorky's *Agony* (1948) depicts furniture and other objects around a glowing fireplace, yet their tormented forms convey the artist's fears of death, commingled with a life-giving sense of hearth and home.

Willem de Kooning likewise departed from abstract expressionism with his references to physical objects, but refused to be bound by traditional rules of representation. In his *Woman and Bicycle* (1952–1953), objects can be identified on canvas, yet the finished work is a gross distortion of reality. Like Pollock, de Kooning let the painting emerge out of his own feelings about the images taking shape before him. *Woman and Bicycle* is thus more interesting with respect to color and texture than for a consideration of form itself.

Still other painters remained within the broad tradition of American realism—among them, Andrew Wyeth. Both in his subjects and his use of light, Wyeth resembles the impressionists of the late nineteenth and early twentieth centuries. But unlike the impressionists, he is very careful about visual detail. Almost always his canvases combine

Willem de Kooning at work.

landscape and human figures, his people appearing in everyday surroundings as they go about accustomed routines. *Distant Thunder* (1961) and *Adam* (1963) are fine examples of his approach. In both of them, as in many of Andrew Wyeth's paintings, there is a hint of melancholy that comes from a realization that these scenes are but fleeting moments, destined to disappear in the remorseless passage of time.

Architecture The architects of the era also broke with convention. For decades architecture had lagged behind the spirit of the age, with most designers ignoring or rejecting the implications of a modern, industrial society. With few exceptions, skyscrapers continued to display acres of historical ornament that bore little or no relationship to structure and function. Then the depression and World War II brought a virtual halt to commercial construction. The 15 years or so after the Wall Street crash operated as a sort of creative moratorium that separated the architects of the early twentieth century from the practitioners of the postwar years. And like contemporary painters, the more adventuresome architects of the day took considerable inspiration from European émigrés.

Ludwig Mies van der Rohe with his Seagram Building.

By far the most influential of these new arrivals was Ludwig Mies van der Rohe, an associate of the famous Bauhaus School in Germany. Mies believed that the rapid pace of social, cultural, and economic change made it impossible to anticipate building needs beyond more than a decade or two. Structures had to be as simple and adaptable as possible, and they should make honest use of modern building materials. To Mies this meant a structure of glass and stainless steel or aluminum—the so-called international style that Mies and his German colleagues had been trying to promote for over a generation. For them it was an infinitely flexible design that was suitable for every building need anywhere in the world. Yet many Americans found the international style particularly relevant to the country's spirit, with its reputed practicality and simplicity. Corporate executives also liked the air of efficiency and modernity that the international style gave to their new office towers. The most impressive of these was Mies's Seagram Building (1954–1958) in New York City. The firm of Skidmore, Owings, and Merrill designed a number of other superb buildings along the same lines, most of them in the Chicago area. These include the Chicago Civic Center (1959–1965) and the Sears Tower (1970–1974).

But in less skilled hands the glass and steel skyscraper grew hackneyed and bland. While earlier examples of the international style often reflected the rich and varied tones of older masonry building in the area, the rows of glass towers along urban thoroughfares now mirrored one another in an endless and sterile monotony. By the 1960s some architects began to break with certain aspects of the international style, paying more attention to local eccentricities, historical references, and the desire for visual variety. Philip Johnson and John Burgee, for example, topped their AT&T Building in New York

(1978–1984) with a gigantic scrolled pediment that looks much like the decoration atop a colonial doorway, while their PPG Place in Pittsburgh (1985) is a Gothic cathedral of chrome and glass.

With all the emphasis during the period on the international style and its critics, it is easy to forget that Frank Lloyd Wright continued to design structures into the 1950s. Wright's last great work, completed shortly before his death in 1959, was the Solomon R. Guggenheim Museum in New York City. Here Wright continued his experiments with helical design, the entire museum being wrapped around an expanding spiral walkway. Visitors take an elevator to the top of the museum and view the exhibits as they walk down a gently sloping spiral ramp. Wright achieved a startling functional unity that has attracted much praise.

Despite the criticisms of American life and the controversial departures in art and architecture, most citizens were quite content with postwar society. They reveled in their reprieve from nearly two decades of disruption and hardship, and were largely oblivious to continuing injustice and deprivation. It would require another decade and a new generation to point out the nation's worst shortcomings and mount yet another program of reform.

BIOGRAPHICAL SKETCH

NORMAN VINCENT PEALE · *born 1898*

The postwar period provided fertile ground for the clergy, but none so captured the attention of middle-class Protestants as Dr. Norman Vincent Peale. Born in Bowersville, Ohio, he graduated from Ohio Wesleyan University in 1922 and was ordained a Methodist minister the same year. He proved an effective and popular preacher from the first. By 1932 he had left the Methodist fold and became pastor of the fashionable Marble Collegiate Church in New York City, a congregation affiliated with the Reformed Church in America.

After arriving in New York, Peale teamed up with Dr. Smiley Blanton to found the Religio-Psychiatric Clinic in 1937. In treating emotionally troubled parishioners, they combined selected insights from Sigmund Freud with more traditional Christian teachings. Their methods were well received and attracted much popular attention.

Following World War II Peale sought a wider audience for his message and began turning out a series of inspirational books, starting with *The Art of Modern Living* in 1948. The most successful, however, was *The Power of Positive Thinking*, which hit the best-seller list soon after its publication in 1952 and remained there for three years. To date it has sold over 5 million copies.

Critics found Peale's advice neither novel nor revolutionary, calling it a contemporary amalgam of the Protestant ethic and frontier optimism. And in fact Peale believed that the majority of emotional problems were self-induced or imagined. One could exorcise them by having faith in a better future, by taking a more optimistic view of present circumstance, and by trusting in God's help.

Peale's success as a writer catapulted him into the limelight and led to a nationwide television program, in addition to a weekly syndicated newspaper column. He also edited his own magazine, *Guideposts,* with a reputed circulation of 3.5 million by the mid-1980s.

Critics have added that Peale merely reiterated middle-class faith in self-help and rugged individualism, thereby reaffirming the widespread opposition to large-scale social reform. As such, Peale's teachings were little consolation to the victims of endemic poverty or racial discrimination. Peale himself was a conservative Republican whose writings largely ignored the "social gospel." In this sense, his message was quite congenial to the white, middle-class churches of the Eisenhower era.

Peale has flourished despite his detractors, with his publishing and broadcasting enterprises continuing to attract large audiences. Now in his eighties, Peale remains active as well as optimistic.

SUGGESTED READINGS

There are a number of general sources on postwar society and culture. Among these are Robert H. Bremner and Gary W. Reichard, eds., *Reshaping America: Society and Institutions, 1945–1960* (1982); Paul A. Carter, *Another Part of the Fifties* (1983); James Gilbert, *Another Chance: Postwar America, 1945–1968* (1981); Eric F. Goldman, *The Crucial Decade and After: America, 1945–1960* (1960); and William E. Leuchtenburg, *A Troubled Feast: American Society Since 1945* (1969).

On postwar prosperity, see John Kenneth Galbraith, *The Affluent Society* (1958) and *American Capitalism: The Concept of Countervailing Power* (1956). Vance Packard's *The Hidden Persuaders* (1957) is a well-written account of advertising in the 1950s. For insight into the automobile and the postwar era, see James J. Flink, *The Car Culture* (1975), and John B. Rae, *The American Automobile* (1965).

The best work on the baby boom is Landon Y. Jones, *Great Expectations: America and the Baby Boom Generation* (1980). Studies of the urban-suburban scene are numerous. These include William M. Dobbringer, *Class in Suburbia* (1963); Scott Donaldson, *The Suburban Myth* (1969); Herbert Gans, *The Levittowners* (1967); Mark I. Gelfand, *A Nation of Cities: The Federal Government and Urban America, 1933–1965* (1975); John Keats, *The Crack in the Picture Window* (1957); Raymond A. Mohl and James R. Richardson, eds., *The Urban Experience* (1973); Barry Schwartz, ed., *The Changing Face of the Suburbs* (1967); and Jon C. Teaford, *City and Suburb: The Political Fragmentation of Metropolitan America* (1979). For a glimpse of rural America after the war, there is John L. Shover, *First Majority Last Minority: The Transformation of Rural Life in America* (1976).

Concerning social class and social mobility are Stanley Aronowitz, *False Promises: The*

SUGGESTED READINGS

Shaping of American Working Class Consciousness (1973); Will Herberg, *Catholic-Protestant-Jew* (1955); Seymour Lipset and Reinhard Bendix, *Social Mobility in Industrial Society* (1959); C. Wright Mills, *White Collar: The American Middle Class* (1951); Vance Packard, *The Status Seekers* (1959); Richard Polenberg, *One Nation Indivisible: Class, Race, and Ethnicity in the United States Since 1938* (1980); and W. Lloyd Warner, *Class in America* (1949). The beginnings of the civil rights movement are discussed in Numan V. Bartley, *The Rise of Massive Resistance* (1969).

The most revealing criticisms of society and culture are Reinhold Niebuhr, *The Irony of American History* (1952); David Riesman, *The Lonely Crowd: A Study of the Changing American Character* (1950); and William H. Whyte, Jr., *The Organization Man* (1956).

Myron Matlaw's *American Popular Entertainment* (1979) gives a good overview of the subject. On the impact of television there are Erik Barnouw, *The Image Empire: A History of Broadcasting in the United States,* vol. 3 (1970); Daniel J. Boorstin, *The Image* (1962); Edward W. Chester, *Radio and Television and American Politics* (1974); John E. O'Connor, ed., *American History/American Television: Interpreting the Video Past* (1983); and Robert Sobel, *The Manipulators: America in the Media Age* (1976). Helpful in understanding the impact of television on the cinema is Robert Sklar, *Movie-Made America* (1975).

Overviews of sports in this period can be found in Allen Guttmann, *From Ritual to Record: The Nature of Modern Sports* (1976), and James A. Michener, *Sports in America* (1976). William O. Johnson, Jr., analyses the impact of television on sports in *Super Spectator and the Electronic Lilliputians* (1971), while Joseph Durso studies the economic aspects of sport in *The All American Dollar: The Big Business of Sports* (1971). On college athletics, see Durso's *The Sports Factory: An Investigation into College Sports* (1975).

For rock and roll music, see Carl Belz, *The Story of Rock* (1969), and Arnold Shaw, *The Rock Revolution* (1969). Beat writers are covered in Bruce Cook, *The Beat Generation* (1971); Robert A. Hipkiss, *Jack Kerouac: Prophet of the New Romanticism* (1976); and Dennis McNally, *Desolate Angel: Jack Kerouac, the Beat Generation, and America* (1979).

The following should be helpful in exploring painting and architecture: Anthony Everitt, *Abstract Expressionism* (1975); Bernard H. Friedman, *Jackson Pollock: Energy Made Visible* (1972); Carl W. Condit, *The American Building Art: The Twentieth Century* (1961); Arthur Pretler, *Ludwig Mies van der Rohe* (1960); and Robert A. M. Stern, *Pride of Place: Building the American Dream* (1986).

14

New Frontiers—At Home and Abroad

1960 was a year of expectation. The oldest man ever to occupy the presidency was stepping down after eight prosperous and peaceful years, and whoever succeeded him would be the first chief executive born in the twentieth century. Those who had become impatient with the politics of moderation hoped for a president who could invigorate government and inspire the nation; others were simply excited in the knowledge that a new generation would take up the reins of power.

As it turned out, the 1960s provided a lot more excitement than anyone had imagined. On the domestic front, the federal government launched a campaign of economic and social reform. Labeled the New Frontier under President Kennedy and the Great Society under President Johnson, this far-reaching reform rivaled Roosevelt's New Deal in its scope and implications. On the foreign front, the cold war grew hotter as the United States faced new challenges in the third world and then became entangled in a disastrous and unwinnable war in Southeast Asia. Both the war and the reforms agitated the nation profoundly, touching off wave after wave of violence and dissent.

NIXON VERSUS KENNEDY

As 1960 approached, many Republicans were sorry that they had sponsored the Twenty-second Amendment, which limited presidents to two terms in office. Eisenhower would have been a sure winner the third time around, though it is doubtful that the aging and sometimes ailing president would have accepted a third nomination. The Republicans would thus have to gamble on a new candidate. Two aspirants emerged early in the race—New York's Governor Nelson Rockefeller and Vice-President Richard M. Nixon. Rockefeller attracted scant support from party leaders and withdrew before the primaries.

The Republicans nominated Nixon on the first ballot, with former Massachusetts senator Henry Cabot Lodge as his running mate.

The Democrats drew five aspirants into the field. Adlai Stevenson's backers hoped for a third run at the presidency, but their man refused to announce his candidacy and waited in the wings for a draft that never came. The other contenders were all members of the Senate: Stuart Symington of Missouri, Hubert Humphrey of Minnesota, Lyndon Johnson of Texas, and John Kennedy of Massachusetts.

Very quickly the Democratic contest settled down to a race between Humphrey and Kennedy. The rich, well-spoken, and handsome Kennedy was by far the most appealing, yet he suffered from several handicaps. He was a Roman Catholic in a country populated largely by Protestants, and political wisdom held that a Catholic could not be elected. His record in the Senate was mediocre at best, and many considered him, at 43, too young and inexperienced.

Of all Kennedy's difficulties, however, religion was the most serious, and he had to prove to the Democratic party that his Catholicism was not an insurmountable hurdle. The crucial test came in the West Virginia primary. The state's population was 95 percent Protestant, a large number of them belonging to evangelical or fundamentalist denominations. They and many fellow Protestants throughout the country believed that a Catholic president would take orders from the pope on important national issues. Kennedy confronted this widely held myth during a carefully staged television interview, assuring West Virginians that he "would not take orders from any Pope, Cardinal, Bishop, or Priest." To do so, he added, "would be breaking [my] oath of office . . . and commit a sin against God." His convincing performance, in addition to a skillfully directed and well-financed campaign, gave Kennedy a smashing victory over Humphrey, who soon dropped out of the race. At their July convention the Democrats formally nominated Kennedy, with Lyndon Johnson as their vice-presidential candidate.

In background, as well as in style, Kennedy and Nixon could not have been more different. Born in Yorba Linda, California, the 46-year-old Nixon came from a family of modest means. He had had to work hard to finance his education at nearby Whittier College and later at Duke University Law School. Following graduation from Duke, Nixon practiced law for several years back in Whittier and then worked briefly for the Office of Price Administration. Despite his Quaker faith, he joined the Navy during World War II and served in the South Pacific as a supply officer. In 1946 he won the first of two terms in Congress, launching a successful bid for the Senate in 1950. His unrelenting pursuit of Alger Hiss brought him into the national limelight and ultimately catapulted him into the vice-presidency. Critics charged that he had taken unfair advantage of the Communist issue over the years and called particular attention to the 1946 and 1948 House campaigns, when Nixon tried to associate his left-leaning opponents with domestic communism. Such behavior, along with his reputation as a tough campaigner, won him the nickname "Tricky Dick."

Kennedy, in contrast, descended from immense wealth. Born outside Boston, he knew nothing of the financial insecurity that had plagued the young Nixon and his family. Kennedy's father, Joseph P. Kennedy, had amassed one of the world's largest fortunes through shrewd business deals and stock market speculations. Nevertheless, the Kennedys were snubbed by Boston's Protestant upper class, who considered the family to be Irish-Catholic upstarts. The parents deeply resented their social ostracism, and determined to have his revenge, Joseph P. Kennedy vowed to make one of his sons president of the United States.

John Kennedy and his three brothers were carefully groomed for important roles in American life. All graduated from Harvard University and traveled widely in Europe, especially during their father's stint as ambassador to Great Britain just before World War II. Like Nixon, Kennedy enlisted in the Navy. He saw active service in the South Pacific as the skipper of a PT boat and became a minor hero when he rescued several crew members after their boat was rammed by a Japanese destroyer. In 1946 he made good use of his wealth, personal charm, and family's political connections to win a seat in the U.S. House of Representatives. He won reelection in 1948 and 1950, advancing to the Senate two years later when he defeated incumbent Henry Cabot Lodge, the very personification of New England's Protestant establishment.

Despite their divergent backgrounds and different political affiliations, Kennedy and Nixon did not disagree widely on the issues in 1960. Both endorsed stronger civil rights legislation and both took a hard line against communism. The campaign accordingly turned more on style than substance. Nixon, who was only four years older than Kennedy, endeavored to come across as the more experienced and mature of the two candidates, while Kennedy struck a pose of freshness and vigor. Again and again Kennedy charged that the nation had lost momentum under Eisenhower and asked his audiences to help him and the Democrats "get the country moving again." Kennedy blamed the Republicans for the current economic recession and alleged that Eisenhower had permitted the Soviets to forge ahead in the deployment of nuclear missiles. These charges of a dangerous "missile gap" later turned out to be groundless.

Despite his superb campaign organization and his own fierce determination to win, Kennedy lagged in the polls as the autumn campaign began. What turned the tide was a series of televised debates between the two presidential candidates, the first to be broadcast over the medium. Throughout the four exchanges, Kennedy more than held his own against Nixon, thus dispelling the vice-president's contention that his challenger lacked judgment and maturity. Kennedy also came across as much more likable. During the first debate in particular, Nixon frequently looked angry and even sinister. He had failed to wear any substantial makeup, causing his heavy beard and prominent jowls to enshroud his face with a look of distinct hostility. Viewers generally agreed that Kennedy had "won" the debates.

Kennedy also won the November election, but by a razor-thin margin of 113,000 popular votes, making his the narrowest victory since 1888. The final tally was 34,221,000 to 34,108,000. In the electoral column the count was 303–219, with Kennedy carrying every industrial state except California and Ohio. The religious issue, it turned out, hurt as well as helped him, for Kennedy did much better among Catholics than Nixon but poorer than Nixon among Protestants. In the end, religious prejudice was not strong enough to deny him the presidency, and he became the first Roman Catholic in the country's history to occupy the White House.

GLAMOUR IN THE WHITE HOUSE

The new occupants of 1600 Pennsylvania Avenue charmed and captivated large segments of the public. First Lady Jacqueline Kennedy brought an air of beauty and grace that had been lacking in the mansion for a number of years, while her sense of history and

President John F. Kennedy and First Lady Jacqueline Kennedy

taste in the decorative arts soon inspired an ambitious campaign to restore and refurbish the White House's interior. Generous private gifts, in addition to loans from other government institutions and museums, allowed her to recapture something of the house's original flavor. Visitors came in record numbers to see the results and the First Lady hosted a televised tour of the redecorated rooms. The Kennedy's young children, Caroline and John, Jr., likewise captured the public's interest and affection. They seemed to have free rein of the house, popping into the president's office unannounced or scampering across the White House grounds in full view of press corps and visiting dignitaries.

Kennedy's cabinet and staff provoked much public interest, too, as the president brought more intellectuals and college professors to Washington than at any time since the New Deal. Among his closest advisors were Harvard historian Arthur M. Schlesinger, Jr., and economist John Kenneth Galbraith, also of Harvard. And there seemed to be Rhodes scholars in every corner of government, including Secretary of State Dean Rusk and Walt W. Rostow, the president's deputy special assistant for national security. But like many other presidents before him, Kennedy also invaded the business community for talent, taking Robert McNamara from Ford Motor Company as his secretary of defense. Treasury Secretary Douglas Dillon was a holdover from the Eisenhower administration, but Kennedy valued his ability as well as his rapport with the business community. The most controversial selection was Kennedy's choice of his brother Robert as attorney general. Critics levied charges of nepotism, and complained that the president was trying to launch a political dynasty. But most Americans found the majority of Kennedy's men to be as glamorous as his family. Kennedy himself liked to compare his administration to King Arthur's Camelot, a vision made popular at the time by a musical of the same name.

For the most part Kennedy handled criticism with good humor and enjoyed excellent relations with the press. Indeed, reporters and public alike looked forward to the president's frequently televised press conferences. The conferences were an instant hit, with Kennedy the undisputed star. He answered difficult questions with considerable wit, and even his refusals to respond were leavened with humor and goodwill. Without doubt Kennedy used the press more skillfully than any president since Franklin Roosevelt.

FACING A HOSTILE WORLD

Kennedy liked to see himself as a judicious mixture of toughness and idealism, qualities that he also admired in others and especially in his own lieutenants. Tempered by the hardships of war, he and his associates would have no illusions about the world they inherited. At the same time, Kennedy believed that the United States should use its wealth and power to promote the nation's highest ideals around the world. The road to success would be difficult, but with unyielding effort they could prevail. In his acceptance speech before the Democratic convention he had told his audience that they stood ''on the edge of a New Frontier . . . a frontier of unknown opportunities and perils—a frontier of unfulfilled hopes and threats.'' In his inaugural address he reiterated this tone of striving and sacrifice. Contending that freedom faced ''its hour of maximum danger,'' he exhorted his countrymen to ''pay any price, bear any burden, meet any hardship, support any friend, oppose any foe to assure the survival and success of liberty.'' The address dealt almost wholly with foreign affairs, and in retrospect it reads like an impassioned document of cold war rhetoric. Kennedy's inaugural remarks, as well as his campaign speeches, also make it clear that the New Frontier would concern itself as much with foreign challenges as with those nearer home.

It is easy to understand why Kennedy perceived a growing danger to world liberty. Just a year before Khrushchev had threatened a deadly confrontation over Berlin. The demise of European colonialism during the past decade and a half had meanwhile left much of the third world in disarray, as the Soviets and the Chinese both bragged that they would take every opportunity to assist Marxist insurgents in the emerging nations. It is now clear that these boasts were meant more for each other than for the United States, but Kennedy and his advisors read them as a direct challenge to American interests. In any case, Kennedy firmly believed in a monolithic Communist conspiracy and was determined to thwart Communist advances wherever he could. Realizing that empty nuclear threats would not contain indigenous rebels, he urged the development of special military forces, like the Green Berets, which could go into an area at a moment's notice and engage insurgent groups.

Alliance for Progress   But Kennedy was also willing to use economic leverage to defeat Communist influences in the third world and especially in Latin America. He feared that widespread poverty and social inequality south of the border would make inhabitants ripe for Communist appeals. His solution was an Alliance for Progress between the United

FACING A HOSTILE WORLD

States and its southern neighbors. In exchange for financial aid, Latin American governments would be asked to initiate land reform and to institute more democratic political processes. As Kennedy envisioned it on March 13, 1961, the Alliance would seek "to demonstrate to the entire world that man's unsatisfied aspiration for economic progress and social justice can best be achieved by free men working within a framework of democratic institutions." Congress agreed and authorized an expenditure of $400 billion over the next decade. The Inter-American Economic and Social Conference ratified the Alliance for Progress at an August meeting in Punta del Este, Uruguay.

Massive American aid to Western Europe after World War II had stimulated economic recovery while dampening the appeals of local Communists, but Latin America was not Western Europe. There most of the wealth and political power belonged to a privileged elite who had no intention of surrendering their traditional prerogatives. American business firms, which worked largely through these elites, also resisted attempts at reform. In the last analysis, the Alliance for Progress did little to bring about orderly change in Latin countries.

The Peace Corps A less ambitious but more effective approach to third-world problems was the Peace Corps, created by executive order in March 1961 and headed by the president's brother-in-law, Sargent Shriver. The Corps enlisted young Americans, often just out of college, and sent them into underdeveloped areas to share their knowledge of modern resources and technologies. The volunteers were enthusiastic about their assignments and were usually well received by local residents. Although Peace Corps participants were told to steer clear of politics in host countries, Kennedy saw the program as another piece of his campaign to combat communism in the third world. He hoped that the industry and dedication of these young Americans might awaken their hosts' "aspirations for a free society."

Disaster at the Bay of Pigs Cuba was another underdeveloped area that greatly concerned Kennedy, but here administration policies ended in disaster. Since seizing power in 1959, Castro had confiscated large amounts of property belonging to American companies. Thousands of anti-Castroites had meanwhile fled to the United States. Although State Department analysts did not believe that Castro posed any direct threat to American security, Eisenhower had authorized the CIA to plan an invasion of Cuba by anti-Castro forces. CIA Director Allen Dulles convinced Kennedy that the scheme was sound and the new president gave his permission for a Cuban assault.

On April 17, 1961, an army of 1,400 Cuban exiles landed at the Bay of Pigs. They hoped their bold attack would inspire a general uprising, but Castro's forces met the attackers on the beaches and overwhelmed them. Because he did not want the United States directly implicated in the attempted overthrow, Kennedy refused to order American air support for the beleaguered invaders, and they were either killed or captured. The unsuccessful attack now gave Castro an excellent propaganda weapon at home as well as abroad, while the whole fiasco cast doubt on Kennedy's ability to make effective and realistic decisions.

Danger in Berlin Kennedy feared that the Soviets would interpret his misjudgments in Cuba as signs of weakness and incompetency, and he vowed to take a tough line with Khrushchev during their June summit in Geneva. But to the president's surprise, Khrushchev used the meeting to announce that he would sign a peace treaty with the East Germans. The treaty would place access to West Berlin under East German control and thereby threaten Western access to the city.

With the Cuban humiliation fresh in his mind, Kennedy went on nationwide television on June 25 to call for a massive show of American strength. He asked Congress to vote three and a quarter billion dollars to increase military personnel. In addition, he called 160,000 reservists to active duty and sent them to reinforce American troops in Western Europe. He also ordered a military contingent of 1,500 men to drive from West Germany into Berlin as a sign that the United States meant to retain its access to the city. In the end Khrushchev dropped his threat, but on August 13, 1961, the East Germans threw up a massive concrete and barbed wire wall between East and West Berlin. They were determined to stop the flood of refugees who had been fleeing daily from East Germany into West Berlin. Americans reacted to the wall with horror and disgust, but there was nothing their government could do about it, short of full-scale war with the Soviets.

Showdown over Cuba   The showdown over Berlin was frightening enough, yet it would pale in comparison to the Cuban missile crisis of October 1962. Following the abortive Bay of Pigs invasion, Castro had turned to the Soviets for aid and protection. American aerial surveillance subsequently demonstrated that the Russians were installing nuclear missiles in Cuba. For eight days Kennedy and his advisors held nearly round-the-clock strategy sessions to decide the proper response. The military wanted to bomb the missile sites, but Kennedy and others feared that Russian technicians would be killed, thus inviting retaliation from the Soviet Union. The president's brother Robert also warned that a precipitous air strike might be viewed as a ''sneak attack'' not unlike Japan's unannounced raid on Pearl Harbor two decades earlier. Finally, and without consulting leaders in either the House or the Senate, Kennedy decided to throw a naval blockade around Cuba, promising to lift it only after the Soviets had dismantled and removed their missiles.

The ''quarantine,'' as Kennedy politely called the blockade, began on October 24. The armed forces went on full alert and preparations were made to invade Cuba. For three days the nation braced itself for the very real possibility of nuclear war with the Soviets. Then, on October 26, Kennedy received a letter from Khrushchev. The Soviet premier agreed to remove the missiles if the United States would promise not to invade Cuba. The next day Khrushchev also demanded that the United States remove its Jupiter missiles from Turkey. Kennedy decided to answer the first message and ignore the second, while Robert Kennedy privately assured Soviet Ambassador Anatoly Dobrynin that his country had decided to withdraw the Jupiter missiles some months before and that they would indeed be taken out of Turkey after a suitable interval. But there was to be no announcement of a quid pro quo.

Khrushchev then backed down and Kennedy won enormous respect for his handling of the missile crisis. The country, however, would pay a high price for Kennedy's victory. The Soviets had yielded to American pressure because they knew that the United States was far ahead of them in nuclear weapons. But the Soviets vowed never again to find themselves in such a predicament and soon launched the greatest arms buildup in their history.

The Space Race Khrushchev's blusterings over Berlin and the Cuban missile crisis a year later greatly aggravated American animosity toward the Soviet Union. Soviet feats in space added to the sense of fear and alarm. Sputnik was bad enough, but on April 12, 1961, Soviet cosmonaut Yuri Gagarin became the first man to orbit the earth and respect for Soviet technology soared around the globe. Kennedy himself feared that millions of men and women in third world countries would see this most recent Soviet accomplishment as proof of Communist superiority. Americans could take some comfort when John Glenn repeated Gagarin's success by orbiting the earth in February 1962, but second place was not good enough for Kennedy, and he asked Congress to fund a crash program to land an American on the moon by the end of the decade. He assigned Vice-President Johnson, who also headed the National Aeronautics and Space Council, to oversee the project.

The nation met this ambitious goal on July 20, 1969, when Captain Neil A. Armstrong, carried aloft in the *Apollo 11* spacecraft, became the first man to walk on the moon. For the first time a human being had stepped into a wholly alien world—without atmosphere or life. In contrast, television cameras from *Apollo 11* showed the earth as

American astronaut on lunar surface.

a brilliant turquoise sphere. For some viewers it was a compelling reminder of the earth's special place in the solar system and of the need to protect their unique and irreplaceable environment from further human destruction.

Bombs and Trade   Fortunately there was at least one bright spot in Soviet-American relations—the test ban treaty of July 1963. For years scientists had issued warnings about radioactive fallout from testing nuclear weapons in the atmosphere. There were growing demands in the United States for some kind of agreement to ban nuclear tests, but Soviet objections to on-site inspections continued to preclude any kind of accord. Now more powerful sensing devices permitted both sides to monitor nuclear explosions from outside the other's boundaries. On July 25, 1963, the United States, Great Britain, and the Soviet Union agreed to ban all nuclear weapons tests "in the atmosphere, in outer space, and under water." The agreement did not rule out underground testing, but it did result in lower levels of fallout. In the long run, however, it did nothing to halt the Soviet-American arms race.

Yet another positive initiative in American foreign policy was the Trade Expansion Act of October 1962. Fearing that the European Common Market might erect a tariff wall against the United States, President Kennedy asked Congress for the authority to negotiate trade agreements, with the goal of reducing tariff rates up to 50 percent on both sides. Hitherto reciprocal trade legislation had only permitted negotiation of individual items; now Congress authorized the president to make agreements on whole categories of goods. The act was spectacularly successful. By 1967 trade concessions to the United States were valued at $40 billion, while tariffs against American products fell by about 30 percent overall.

Misjudging Southeast Asia   The ongoing conflicts in Southeast Asia did not prove so tractable as European trade policies. Yet Kennedy was determined to halt the spread of communism. Like Eisenhower, he accepted the domino theory: if the Communists were not stopped in Southeast Asia, the contagion would soon spread to adjoining regions and from there to much of the globe. The doctrine of containment was alive and well.

One of Kennedy's first tasks as president was to cope with Communist insurgents in Laos. There Eisenhower had supported the pro-Western royal government at the same time Moscow backed the Communist Pathet Lao. Kennedy decided that the United States was not doing enough in Laos. Without consulting Congress, the president sent 400 military advisors to Laos in January 1961. By March, however, the United States helped convince the various Laotian factions to conclude a cease-fire and join a coalition government; shortly thereafter the United States and the Soviet Union agreed to a neutralized Laos.

In Vietnam, Kennedy was not so successful. In the first place, his view of the Vietnam situation was based on a colossal misconception, as he and most other Americans believed that the Communist North Vietnamese, as well as the Communist Viet Cong in South Vietnam, were simply agents of Moscow and Peking. And while it was true that both the Chinese and the Soviets aided the Vietnamese Communists, the Communist movement in Vietnam was wholly indigenous in its goals and inspiration. Besides, the Vietnamese had hated the Chinese for centuries. Despite ideological affinities, the Vietnamese Communists had no more love for the Chinese than for the non-Communists in Vietnam.

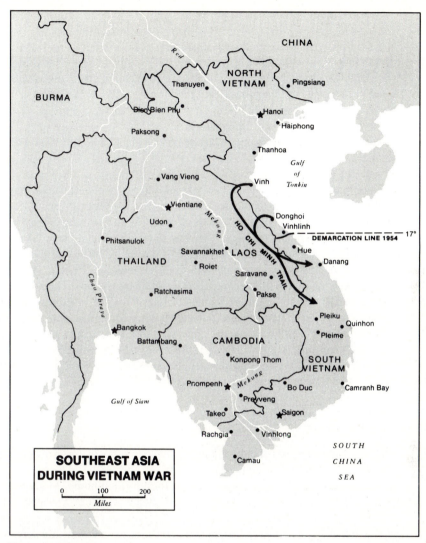

The war in Vietnam.

There was thus little likelihood that a Communist Vietnam would become some kind of Chinese puppet or client state; nor were the intensely proud and nationalistic Vietnamese about to welcome Soviet domination. A Communist Vietnam was therefore quite likely to go its own way, much like Tito's Yugoslavia. Meanwhile, China and the Soviet Union were moving farther and farther apart ideologically. Any careful weighing of the facts would have undermined American beliefs in a monolithic Communist conspiracy in Southeast Asia or elsewhere, but Kennedy and most Americans seemed blinded by 15 years of cold war rhetoric. The Vietnamese conflict was essentially a civil war and not merely another chapter in Soviet or Chinese expansion. Unfortunately, few Americans could see it that way.

CHAPTER 14: NEW FRONTIERS—AT HOME AND ABROAD

Soon after taking office Kennedy had to make some hard decisions about Vietnam. Under Secretary of State Chester Bowles and seasoned diplomat W. Averell Harriman advised a program to neutralize Vietnam, but the president, who had promised to take a hard line against communism, rejected their suggestions. The Bay of Pigs fiasco, Khrushchev's threats over Berlin, and the Soviet encouragement of Communist insurgents in the third world convinced Kennedy that he must take a firm stand in Vietnam. Some leaders, including General Maxwell D. Taylor, who had just returned from a fact-finding mission to Vietnam, urged the president to commit American combat units. The Communist Viet Cong were making serious inroads against the South Vietnamese government under Ngo Dinh Diem, and Taylor believed that American troops were needed to stem the advance. Kennedy finally decided on a middle course, sending more aid and military advisors into South Vietnam. When he took office there were about 800 such advisors in Vietnam; over the next two years the advisory force would grow to 17,000. Toward the end he also authorized American helicopter pilots to fire on enemy positions.

Viet Cong attacks in South Vietnam were not the only worries for the Kennedy administration, for the South Vietnamese government itself was both oppressive and corrupt. Numerous non-Communist factions also opposed Diem, with the Buddhists mounting the most vociferous campaigns against him. In June 1963 an elderly Buddhist monk doused himself in gasoline and set himeslf on fire in protest against the Saigon regime. That August Diem retaliated with massive raids on Buddhist temples and arrested over 1,400 of the faithful. Kennedy concluded that Diem could no longer govern effectively and threw his support behind a plot to overthrow the South Vietnamese leader. On November 1, 1963, the government fell and Diem himself was murdered. Subsequent events would demonstrate that American support for the coup was a disastrous mistake.

THE NEW FRONTIER AT HOME

Although Kennedy used the term New Frontier to refer to forward-looking policies on both the domestic and foreign fronts, historians and public alike have most associated the New Frontier with the president's plans for reform at home. Many have linked these reforms with a liberal resurgence in the 1960s, but it would be a mistake to see Kennedy as a thoroughgoing liberal. In reality, he and his closest advisors were contemptuous of the emotional liberalism that had sometimes characterized New Dealers and their ideological descendants. As historian Arthur M. Schlesinger, Jr., has explained it, Kennedy and his men proposed various domestic reforms ''more . . . because they were rational and necessary than because they were just and right.'' But it is also true that Kennedy's concern over domestic issues, and particularly those involving poverty and civil rights, intensified during his three years in office.

Challenging Congress   Even before taking office Kennedy knew that liberal legislation would face difficult sledding in a Congress that had been dominated by a coalition of Republicans and conservative Democrats since 1938. The elections of 1960 and 1962 did nothing to alter this constellation, with the Democrats adding only 12 seats to their House majority in 1960 and then losing 5 of them in 1962. In the Senate their already small margin did not change appreciably in the two elections.

THE NEW FRONTIER AT HOME **329**

Just as important as the overall strength of the conservative coalition was the fact that nearly all the powerful committee chairmen came from conservative southern states. The biggest roadblock was the House Rules Committee, which had to clear all bills before they went to the House floor for a vote. Its powerful chairman was Virginia's Congressman Howard Smith, a man renowned for his conservative views. Kennedy decided to attack the Rules Committee early in his presidency by supporting a measure to expand its membership from 12 to 15, knowing that the two additional Democrats on the committee would be northern liberals. House Speaker Sam Rayburn threw his considerable prestige behind the plan and the change went through but the reformed Rules Committee was of little real help to Kennedy. Rayburn used up much of his political capital winning approval for the change, while the obvious ploy to circumvent the conservatives made them more determined than ever to sabotage any liberal program. Critics also charged that Kennedy himself lacked the tenacity to steer his legislative agenda through a recalcitrant but sometimes malleable Congress.

Tackling the Economy   Kennedy faced troublesome economic issues throughout his three years in office. When he entered the White House, the nation was suffering through its fourth recession since World War II. Increasing prices, coupled with unemployment at around 7 percent, was clearly unacceptable. A rapidly expanding economy would no doubt reduce joblessness considerably, but certain categories of unemployment appeared permanent. This was particularly true in areas where the changing nature of the economy had eroded or even eliminated certain kinds of work. (Economists referred to this phenomenon as structural unemployment.) Coal mining was a case in point. Following World War II the widespread shift to oil and natural gas had damaged the coal industry forever. In order to stimulate general economic growth, Kennedy asked Congress to cut taxes, but the legislators refused. When it came to structural unemployment, the president called for economic redevelopment in those regions most affected, with Congress approving the Area Redevelopment Act in 1961. The bill was poorly funded, however, and it could not hope to remedy the colossal problem of structural unemployment. Nevertheless, higher federal spending and a periodic upturn in the business cycle resulted in substantial economic improvement by the autumn of 1963.

In combating inflation Kennedy employed an ''incomes policy,'' a program that urged both business and labor to temper their demands for higher wages and prices. All seemed to go well until U.S. Steel announced a price increase of $6 per ton on April 10, 1962. The administration had just engineered an agreement with steelworkers not to ask for new wage increases in exchange for an industry pledge not to raise prices. The president was understandably enraged when he heard about the price increase. He denounced the steel producers through the media, urged antitrust investigations in the House and Senate, and pressured other steel companies not to follow U.S. Steel with their own price boosts. The tactics worked and the price hike was rescinded.

Education and the Elderly   On the subjects of aid to education and medical assistance to the elderly, Kennedy hit a stone wall. Serious talk about federal aid to education had begun during the Truman administration and Kennedy renewed the campaign. Proponents pointed to the grossly inadequate funding for schools in poor districts, adding that even middle-class communities were having a difficult time building enough classrooms for

CHAPTER 14: NEW FRONTIERS—AT HOME AND ABROAD

the baby-boom generation. Despite the need for some sort of national financing, conservative states' rightists objected to federal intrusion into education; in their opinion it was dangerous to local liberties and clearly unconstitutional. There was also the religious issue. Many Constitutional experts held that federal aid to Catholic and other religious schools would violate the separation between church and state, while Catholics generally opposed federal aid unless their schools could benefit. Not surprisingly, Kennedy's bill failed to pass.

The administration's plan for medical insurance for the elderly was even more controversial. This idea, too, had been first proposed under Truman. Since then the number of senior citizens had grown even larger, as more Americans lived longer than ever before, but the same powerful forces continued to oppose federally sponsored insurance for the aged. The medical profession denounced the program as "socialized medicine," and conservatives saw it as another illegitimate extension of federal authority. The medical insurance bill also went down to defeat.

Continuing the Battle for Civil Rights Although the needs of the elderly deserved attention, it was black citizens who suffered most grievously from continuing injustices in American life. The Democratic platform in 1960 had called for vigorous action on civil rights, including more effective legislation, but at first Kennedy did not appreciate the need to move quickly. Like many other fairly enlightened whites, he deplored the continuation of racial injustice, but had no sense of a real social emergency. He believed that there would be a gradual improvement in the lives of black citizens; as both a politician and president he did not want to take actions that might anger the southerners in his party. Yet circumstances soon forced him to change his attitudes and to act decisively on behalf of civil rights.

The campaign for desegregation which had begun in earnest during the late 1950s continued and intensified as Kennedy assumed office. In 1961 black and white "freedom riders" began to challenge segregation in interstate bus lines. When blacks refused to move to the back of the bus, enraged mobs dragged them and their white companions out of their seats and beat them mercilessly. Often local police stood by and did nothing, some of the worst incidents occurring in Anniston and Montgomery, Alabama. The president ordered Attorney General Robert Kennedy to do whatever was necessary to deal with the situation. The attorney general acted swiftly, sending federal marshals into Montgomery and enjoining the Ku Klux Klan and the National States Rights party from interfering with the freedom riders. He also tried to stop the freedom rides for the time being. For a brief period the crisis subsided.

There was much more to come, however. In September 1962 an angry crowd of white supremacists tried to stop James Meredith from enrolling in the University of Mississippi. Several federal marshals were attacked and seriously injured. President Kennedy ordered in the Army to restore order, but two people were killed before they arrived. The next year Governor George Wallace of Alabama refused to allow black students to enter the state university at Tuscaloosa. After openly defying the federal marshals who had come to enforce a desegregation order, Wallace stepped aside and let the students pass.

While young men and women were challenging segregation in the colleges, others began a drive to register black voters. Since the end of Reconstruction the southern states had kept blacks from voting through poll taxes and unfairly administered literacy tests.

LYNDON JOHNSON TAKES THE HELM

When these tactics failed to work, local citizens used beatings, lynchings, and other forms of intimidation. Northern civil rights activitists then began a campaign to register southern blacks. Some were intercepted as they drove south and were assaulted or even murdered, while other segregationists bombed the churches where organizers held their meetings. Over the next couple of years the violence became widespread and often indiscriminate. On June 19, 1963, NAACP field secretary Medgar Evers was shot outside his home in Mississippi, and four black children perished when their church was bombed three months later.

By then, Kennedy had decided to push for a new civil rights act. Early in 1963 he called for a bill that would send federal referees into the South to oversee registration procedures. Conservatives successfully blocked the bill, and Kennedy died before it could be passed a year later.

Death in Dallas   Despite his growing unpopularity in the South, Kennedy decided to run for reelection in 1964. On November 22, 1963, while on an early campaign trip to ''mend fences'' in Texas, Kennedy was shot as he rode through the streets of Dallas in an open convertible accompanied by Texas Governor John Connally, who was wounded. The assassin was Lee Harvey Oswald. To compound the horror, Oswald was gunned down the next day by a man named Jack Ruby in the basement of the Houston jail, as millions of Americans witnessed this second spectacular murder over television in their own living rooms. Shocked and grief-stricken, the nation mourned its dead president and wondered what had become of their country.

A special commission headed by Chief Justice Earl Warren investigated the Kennedy assassination as thoroughly as it could and concluded that there had been no international conspiracy or foreign involvement in the murder; yet rumors would persist for decades that Communist governments were somehow involved. One recurring hypothesis held that Fidel Castro had ordered the assassination in revenge for CIA attempts on his own life. Whatever the conjectures, few Americans could imagine in the fall of 1963 that the Kennedy assassination was only the beginning of the most violent decade in recent American history.

John Kennedy died with much of his work uncompleted. It is impossible to know how he might have handled Congress in the months ahead, or if he would have managed the Vietnam situation any better than his successors. His violent and untimely death insured instant martyrdom and gave him a more favorable image than his actual accomplishments warranted. Yet he would stay forever young in the minds of those who loved and admired him. His would remain an unfinished presidency.

LYNDON JOHNSON TAKES THE HELM

For those who idolized John Kennedy, the thought of Lyndon Johnson in the White House was almost unbearable. The tall Texan had none of the Kennedy polish and youthful good looks. His southern drawl and sometimes crude mannerisms were a shocking contrast to Kennedy's public demeanor. Nevertheless, Johnson took firm control of the government, winning overwhelming popular approval within his first few months as president.

CHAPTER 14: NEW FRONTIERS—AT HOME AND ABROAD

President Lyndon B. Johnson

    The 55-year-old Johnson had been born to humble circumstances in Gillespie County, Texas. He had worked his way through San Marcos College, taught high school in Houston for a brief period, and won a seat in a special election to the U.S. House of Representatives in 1937 as a loyal Roosevelt supporter. He served six terms in the House, graduating to the Senate in 1948. From 1951 to 1953 he was the Senate minority whip and then Senate majority leader when the Democrats regained control of the upper house midway through Eisenhower's first administration.
    As Johnson saw it, his first task as president was to carry out and complete Kennedy's domestic programs. He urged Congress to pass Kennedy's bills as a monument to the slain president and used his own consummate skills as a politician to break the legislative logjam. The tax-cut bill passed in February 1964 and eventually pumped $12 billion into the economy. The Civil Rights Act of 1964 also cleared Capitol Hill and Johnson signed it on July 2. It was a comprehensive act that went well beyond Kennedy's earlier proposal, requiring equal enforcement of voting requirements and the desegregation of public facilities. It also authorized the Justice Department to file court suits in order to integrate schools and other public accommodations. Federal funds could be withheld from any state or municipality that defied the statute.

Launching the Great Society   Although proud of his legislative success, Johnson was far from satisfied with the pace of domestic reform. He had long seen public office as

LYNDON JOHNSON TAKES THE HELM

an opportunity to serve others and to win popular approval. He would now launch a massive campaign for social and economic reform and assure himself the lasting gratitude of the American people, but he first had to choose a fitting name for his great crusade. Theodore Roosevelt had had his Square Deal and Woodrow Wilson his New Freedom; more recently there had been the New Deal, the Fair Deal, and the New Frontier. One Johnson speechwriter suggested the "Great Society" for the current reform program and Johnson adopted it. He and other members of the administration used the phrase a number of times during the first months of 1964, but it did not catch on until Johnson delivered his Great Society speech at the University of Michigan commencement on May 22. There he spoke of a society "where the city of man serves not only the needs of the body and the demands of commerce but the desire for beauty and the hunger for community." Above all, Americans did not have to accept the world as they found it: "We have the power to shape the civilization that we want," he assured his listeners. Johnson's Great Society would thus go much further than Kennedy's New Frontier. Government would use its power to deliver prosperity and social justice to all, while providing a cleaner, safer, and more beautiful environment in which to live.

The War on Poverty   An essential part of the Great Society was Johnson's determination to eradicate poverty throughout the United States. For the past half-dozen years there had been growing pockets of persistent poverty that were little affected by overall economic growth. In his book *The Other America* (1962), author Michael Harrington argued quite convincingly that between one-quarter and one-fifth of the American people lived in a "culture of poverty." Yet these poor were largely invisible to middle-class citizens. They lived in the hills of Appalachia or in urban ghettos—areas that the more affluent either avoided on purpose or passed over in blissful ignorance. Many of the poor were old and forgotten, shut off by age and infirmity from the mainstream of national life. Kennedy had read Harrington's book and had grown increasingly alarmed over this mountain of poverty within a sea of plenty, but he died before executing any plans to combat it.

There is no evidence that Johnson read Harrington or that his genuine sympathy for the poor grew out of reading other reports on the subject. He had known hard times as a child and had witnessed the ravages of the Great Depression in rural Texas. His compassion for the poor was more than vicarious, and he was determined to go down as the president who had finally tackled the problem on all fronts. In his first State of the Union Message on January 8, 1964, he declared "unconditional war on poverty in America." The task would not be easy, he added, "but we shall not rest until the war is won."

Johnson won his first skirmish when Congress passed the Economic Opportunity Act in August 1964. It created 10 separate programs to be administered by an Office of Economic Opportunity (OEO). Johnson took Sargent Shriver from the Peace Corps and made him director of the OEO. Included within the act was Head Start, a preschool program geared to teach disadvantaged children the sorts of social, physical, and mental skills that they needed to enter first grade on the same level as children from more affluent homes. An Upward Bound program would concentrate on preparing poor and culturally deprived teenagers for entry into college. The Job Corps, on the other hand,

VISTA volunteer in Ridgecrest, Florida.

offered relocation and job training for young men and women. There was also VISTA, short for Volunteers in Service to America, a domestic Peace Corps that sent educated young men and women into impoverished areas. The most controversial provision of the Economic Opportunity Act called for Community Action programs that would attempt to create jobs in depressed areas and organize residents to demand better services. In such programs the poor themselves were to enjoy the "maximum feasible participation." When the Black Panthers and other radical organizations gained control of several Community Action offices, there were loud protests from Johnson's critics.

The Johnson Landslide With the war on poverty well launched, Johnson was ready to plunge into his campaign for reelection, his nomination virtually assured. In the few short months since Kennedy's assassination he had taken firm control of the executive branch, had lifted the country's morale, and had scored several stunning victories in Congress. The Democrats renominated him in an orgy of self-congratulation and named Hubert Humphrey as his running mate.

Johnson's Republican opponent that year was Arizona's Senator Barry Goldwater, with Congressman William E. Miller of New York as the vice-presidential candidate. Goldwater's nomination represented a long-awaited victory for the conservative wing of the Republican party. Since Herbert Hoover's disastrous defeat in 1932, the liberal-to-moderate wing of the party had selected the conventions and had dominated the delegates.

But in 1964 there could be no question that the conservatives had triumphed, and Goldwater pulled out all the stops, denouncing the Great Society as well as the whole liberal agenda since Roosevelt. In his *Conscience of a Conservative* (1960), he called for an end to graduated income taxes, proposed to sell the Tennessee Valley Authority, and even questioned the wisdom of Social Security. Goldwater also advocated an uncompromising stance against the Communists in Vietnam and elsewhere. In his acceptance speech before the Republican convention he boldly declared, "Extremism in the defense of liberty is no vice . . . ; moderation in the pursuit of justice is no virtue."

Johnson and Humphrey took full advantage of Goldwater's uncompromising conservatism and frequently unvarnished public remarks and successfully branded him an extremist. They charged that Goldwater would commit the country to a full-scale conflict in Southeast Asia and start a nuclear war with the Soviet Union. Many of their attacks on Goldwater were misleading as well as unfair, and within a year, Johnson himself would be waging an open-ended crusade in Vietnam.

Senator Barry Goldwater campaigning for president in Prescott, Arizona.

On election day, millions of liberal and moderate Republicans deserted the Goldwater ticket, helping Johnson to surpass even Eisenhower's landslide in 1956, thus making it the greatest electoral victory since 1936. He attracted 61.1 percent of the popular vote, the final tally standing at 43,127,000 to 27,177,000, with the electoral count at 486 to 52. Goldwater carried only Arizona and five states in the lower South. His southern strength was not lost on Republicans, who would wage vigorous campaigns in the future to convert southerners to Republicanism. The Democrats also added greatly to their majorities in Congress. In the House their lead was now an impressive 295 to 140 and in the Senate 68 to 32. Many of the new legislators were northern liberals who would support the Great Society, giving reformers a working majority for the first time in a quarter century.

The Great Society Triumphant   With a huge personal victory and large Democratic majorities in both houses of Congress, Johnson was in a prime position to complete his Great Society. The antipoverty war continued on several fronts. In 1965 came the Appalachian Regional Development Act, a measure aimed to stimulate economic growth in depressed mountainous areas stretching from western Pennsylvania into northern Alabama by pumping $1.1 billion into the region for highways, health centers, and resource development. The Public Works and Economic Development Act passed that year, too, and provided similar funds for other depressed areas.

Also, 1965 saw the enactment of two far-reaching educational acts. Both were intended to help the poor, but they would likewise benefit more prosperous segments of the population. One was the Elementary and Secondary School Act. Sponsors were able to circumvent the church-state issue through the legal fiction that funds would go to individual students rather than to educational institutions themselves. States' rights arguments were simply overcome by the large majorities in both houses who favored the bill. In its final form the act appropriated over $1 billion for textbooks, library materials, and special education programs for the handicapped. A second educational bill passed that session tackled the needs of college-age students. The Higher Education Act of 1965 provided scholarships and loans to needy students, as well as grants to college libraries and other institutional programs.

Another landmark act in 1965 established medical insurance for the elderly. Called Medicare, the long-awaited legislation provided a compulsory insurance plan for hospital stays, confinement in nursing homes, diagnostic tests, and some aspects of home health care. It was to be administered by the Social Security System and financed through increases in payroll taxes. There was also a supplementary plan that covered physicians' charges and other medical services. The supplementary plan was voluntary, with participants paying small monthly premiums. Yet a third provision of the act created Medicaid, which granted moneys to the states to help pay the medical expenses of poor residents. Congress also voted to expand preexisting benefits. Social Security payments to the elderly increased regularly, as did Aid to Families with Dependent Children (AFDC). Public assistance payments to other groups rose, too.

Nor did Congress ignore the plight of black Americans. The Voting Rights Act of 1965 authorized federal examiners to oversee registrations in states where fewer than 50 percent of adult residents had registered or voted in the 1964 elections. Over the next few years black registrations increased dramatically in the southern states.

The historic march on Washington, August 28, 1963.

Besides focusing on disadvantaged groups in the population, Great Society legislation was designed to attack the special problems of urban areas. Congress created a new cabinet-level Department of Housing and Urban Development in 1965, in part to dramatize federal concern for the cities. The Urban Development Act of that year provided federal funds for metropolitan planning, and a new housing law funded thousands of residential units, in addition to allocating sums for house repairs and rent supplements. Further, the bill provided for neighborhood health and recreation centers. The so-called Model Cities Act of 1966 authorized $1 billion for rehabilitation of blighted urban areas. Congress also created a cabinet-level Department of Transportation, while mass transit laws in 1964 and 1966 appropriated funds to improve and extend public transportation systems.

Still other laws tried to protect consumers or add new safety regulations. The Consumer Protection Act of 1968 required lenders to give full and accurate information about interest charges and other loan provisions; a commission on Consumer Finance was to oversee enforcement. The Highway Safety Act and the Traffic Safety Act, both passed in 1966, set standards for automobile manufacturers and provided funds to the states for new or improved safety programs.

Finally, Congress responded to calls for legislation to preserve the natural landscape and clean up the environment. The National Wildlife Preservation Act (1964), the Land

Conservation Act (1964), the Solid Waste Disposal Act (1965), and the Clean Water Restoration Act (1966) were all responses to these demands.

The scope of this Great Society legislation was and remains truly remarkable. Even now it is difficult to assess its impact. The civil rights acts passed under Lyndon Johnson were long overdue, and although they did not instantly solve the nation's racial problems, they went a long way towrd guaranteeing basic rights to black citizens. Federal aid to education undoubtedly helped to upgrade instruction, while federal grants and loans to college students permitted thousands of young men and women to pursue higher educations. Medicare and Medicaid did much to insure proper medical care for those least able to afford it, and despite historic opposition from the medical profession, it proved highly profitable to physicians and hospitals. The war on poverty raised a number of families above the poverty line (then defined by the federal government as an income of at least $3,000 per year), but it certainly did not end poverty in the United States. The problem was too complex and the funding far too small to eradicate poverty in a few short years. Nevertheless, the educational and job-training programs gave thousands of young Americans an opportunity to escape the hopeless cycle of poverty, ignorance, and despair.

Conservatives complained, as they had for decades, that government aid undermined the initiative and independence of recipients, but it is difficult to see how a permanently unemployed and impoverished citizen could save himself. Critics also complained about the Great Society's expense, and indeed the cost of programs initiated under Johnson would increase vastly in the years ahead, placing a growing and dangerous burden on the federal budget.

The Judicial Revolution   Many of the decisions handed down by the U.S. Supreme Court during the past decade or so reinforced the liberal legislation of the Kennedy and Johnson years. Led since 1954 by Chief Justice Earl Warren, the Court had worked a veritable revolution in American jurisprudence. Liberals were euphoric over its advanced decisions, while some conservatives vented their wrath against the Court itself. More vocal opponents demanded Warren's dismissal, a sentiment that was echoed on thousands of bumper stickers that read ''Impeach Earl Warren.'' Even many moderates believed that the Supreme Court had overstepped its judicial boundaries, entering areas that were purely political in nature and therefore the province of Congress and the state legislatures. But defenders held that the Court had always been political, as it clearly reflected the needs and opinions of the day, however much it might forge ahead or lag behind during a given period.

By the time Kennedy took office, the Court had already handed down several landmark decisions on civil rights. Many of them served to reinforce *Brown* v. *Board of Education* (1954), which had declared legal segregation of public schools to be unconstitutional. Then in *Green* v. *County Board of Education* (1968) the Court cleared the way for busing as a means of attacking de facto segregation in the schools. Other cases focused on different aspects of segregation, including housing, transportation, restaurants, and various forms of public accommodation. In *Heart of Atlanta Motel* v. *United States* (1964), the justices upheld Title II of the Civil Rights Act of 1964 which had banned racial discrimination in hotels or motels that served interstate travelers.

Chief Justice Earl Warren stands before the U.S. Supreme Court Building.

In another group of decisions the Warren Court sought to make the nation's political system more democratic and to extend most of the protections of the Bill of Rights to state judicial proceedings. Perhaps the most far-reaching of these decisions involved legislative reapportionment by the states. Many of them had not reapportioned their legislative seats for decades, despite the fact that census data revealed a large shift in population from rural to urban areas. And even in states that had reapportioned, there were often constitutional requirements for at least one representative or senator from each county, regardless of its population. This meant that some voters, usually from rural areas, had a larger voice in government than others. U.S. congressional districts, also determined by the states, likewise failed to reflect demographic shifts. Accordingly, in *Baker* v. *Carr* (1962) the Supreme Court used the "equal protection" clause of the Fourteenth Amendment to declare such practices unconstitutional, and in a series of follow-up cases the Court ordered the states to provide equal representation in their legislatures, as well as in congressional districts.

The Fourteenth Amendment also provided means for extending the "due process" provisions of the federal Bill of Rights to the states, for the amendment had forbidden the states to "deprive any person of life, liberty, or property, without the due process of law." The Supreme Court had refused to declare that these protections automatically applied to the states, and the court limited its intervention to local actions that seemed to threaten "ordered liberty." The Warren Court did not discard this rule, but found that more and more cases fitted the definition and thereby found an excuse to intervene.

Several cases involved the Fourth Amendment's protection against "unreasonable gathered without a proper search warrant, and in fact, this "exclusionary rule" had proved the only effective deterrent against constant abuse of the search-and-seizure prohibition. In *Mapp* v. *Ohio* (1961) the Supreme Court extended the exclusionary rule to state authorities, claiming that it was the only way to protect citizens' Fourth Amendment rights as applied to the states through the due process clause of the Fourteenth Amendment. Then in *Gideon* v. *Wainwright* (1963), the Court ruled that the states must extend the Sixth Amendment right to counsel in all criminal cases. The decision in *Miranda* v. *Arizona* (1966) went even further, requiring state authorities to provide counsel from the very moment of arrest. Furthermore, the arresting officer had to advise defendants of their right to counsel, as well as of their Fifth Amendment right to remain silent and not be a witness against themselves. Failure to inform suspects of these "Miranda rights" would activate the exclusionary rule, thereby forbidding authorities to use any of the evidence that they had obtained through questioning.

The *Miranda* decision was partly in reaction to brutal methods used in police interrogations, but it also rested on the centuries-old common-law proposition that the burden of proof rests with the accuser and that it is not the duty of defendants to confess. Nevertheless, many law-and-order advocates denounced the *Miranda* decision, insisting that it would now prove very difficult to obtain voluntary confessions.

In yet another set of decisions the Warren Court greatly expanded First Amendment liberties, especially the freedom to criticize and dissent. In *Yates* v. *United States* (1957) the justices held that mere advocacy of a doctrine like communism could not be prosecuted under the sedition laws; rather, one would actually have to advocate the violent overthrow of the U.S. government. *Pennsylvania* v. *Nelson* (1956) had already extended the same prohibition to the states.

This more lenient attitude toward freedom of utterance also extended to pornography, both in print and on film. In *Roth* v. *United States* (1957) the Court held that nudity or portrayal of sexual behavior could not be banned by local authorities unless "the dominant theme of the material as a whole appeals to prurient interests." The justices elaborated their definition of pornography in *Jacobellis* v. *Ohio* (1964) by declaring that the materials in question must be "utterly without social importance." As prosecutors soon learned, it became extremely difficult, if not impossible, for the state to prove its case, and pornographic films and publications began to circulate more widely than ever. Conservatives again castigated the Court for its utter abandonment of restraint, legal or traditional.

On other aspects of the First Amendment, namely in cases involving the separation of church and state, the Warren Court came down hard against school prayers, Bible reading, and other types of religious exercises in publicly supported institutions. Generally speaking, the justices held that any kind of religious observance in a public school tended toward an "establishment of religion" by the state. In *Engle* v. *Vitale* (1962) they declared even "nonsectarian" school prayers to be unconstitutional, and a year later in *Abington* v. *Schempp* (1963) they ruled against Bible reading in the public schools. Such decisions enraged many who believed that children should have the right to pray or otherwise worship God in school. But as defenders of the Court pointed out, such exercises were never wholly nonsectarian, adding that parents might do well to have their children pray before they left home in the morning or, better yet, they might send them to a church-related institution. But the question of religion in the schools would not die easily, resurfacing again and again in the years to come.

Reinforcing many of these liberal decisions, though by no means dependent upon them, were three amendments to the U.S. Constitution that widened the right to vote. The Twenty-third Amendment (1961) extended the vote in presidential elections to residents of Washington, D.C., for the first time. The Twenty-fourth Amendment (1964) outlawed poll taxes, which had been used historically to keep blacks from voting in the southern states. The Twenty-sixth Amendment (1971) then lowered the voting age for all Americans to age 18—a response to the youthful orientation of the 1960s, as well as a recognition that 18-year-olds were being called upon to fight and die in wars to which they had not consented through the ballot box.

The Twenty-fifth Amendment (1967) was also ratified. Proposed in the wake of the Kennedy assassination and the two serious illnesses of President Eisenhower, it endeavored to provide for such events in the future. In cases where the vice-president succeeded to the presidency, for example, or where he was otherwise unable to continue in office, the president was authorized to nominate a replacement, who then had to be confirmed by a majority vote in both houses of Congress. Provisions were also made for the vice-president to assume the duties of chief executive when the president was temporarily incapacitated.

THE VIETNAM QUAGMIRE

These new amendments, combined with so many landmark Supreme Court decisions, reinforced the sense of triumph that liberals felt during the Johnson years. Unfortunately, this euphoria did not extend into foreign affairs, and especially into the country's relations with Southeast Asia. At first Johnson continued Kennedy's policies in Vietnam by increasing military aid and supplying more advisors. But Diem's ouster made the situation more difficult than ever. The junta that seized power in November 1963 proved weak and incompetent and was overthrown by General Nguyen Khanh on January 29, 1964, who turned out to be only marginally better than the group that preceded him. Under the circumstances it was not surprising that the Viet Cong made steady gains throughout the following year. Indeed, it began to look as if the Communists might overwhelm the Saigon government at any time. Johnson responded by trying to build up South Vietnam's army (ARVN) and by encouraging covert operations in the North. He also considered bombing Viet Cong supply routes, along with selected targets in North Vietnam.

Since 1964 was an election year Johnson hesitated to unleash American bombers, but an incident in the Gulf of Tonkin, just off the North Vietnamese coast, gave him the opportunity to ask Congress to approve such strikes in principle. On August 1, North Vietnamese torpedo boats attacked the U.S. destroyer *Maddox,* which had been engaged for some time in electronic surveillance off the enemy coast. Three days later the *Maddox* and another destroyer, the *C. Turner Joy,* reported a second assault by North Vietnamese craft, for which hard evidence was and has remained in question. Johnson decided to retaliate swiftly and ordered American planes to bomb the torpedo-boat bases in addition to oil storage tanks nearby. He then asked Congress to authorize ''all necessary measures to repel any armed attacks against the forces of the United States and to prevent any further aggression.'' Both houses approved the resolution by wide margins after only perfunctory debate, and opinion polls showed overwhelming public approval of the president's quick action. In the years ahead Johnson and his successor Richard Nixon would interpret this Gulf of Tonkin Resolution as a blank check to wage war in Vietnam, but for the moment it did not lead to a wider American involvement. There were still the upcoming elections, and Johnson frankly doubted that the South Vietnamese were ready for a more ambitious campaign.

Americanizing the War   Johnson's reluctance in 1964 did not mean that he regarded the conflict in Vietnam as irrelevant to American interests. Like Kennedy and Eisenhower before him, he feared that a Communist victory there would play into the hands of Moscow and Peking while encouraging Communist insurgents elsewhere. He also believed that the United States must halt aggression wherever it appeared. Failure to stop aggression in the 1930s, he reasoned, had led directly to World War II, and Johnson was not about to repeat the mistakes of the isolationists. It did not seem to matter that the Viet Cong were not the Germans or the Japanese. For Johnson and for many others of his generation the lessons of the 1938 Munich agreement seemed quite simple: Failure to stop aggression, whatever its causes, would end in disaster.

Still, Johnson did not take the first fateful steps toward full American involvement in the war until February 1965. Then, using Viet Cong attacks on an American Army base at Pleiku as a pretext to act, the president ordered bombing strikes against North Vietnam. In March he ordered two Marine battalions to Vietnam to protect American bases from future attacks, and a month later he deployed 40,000 more troops, authorizing them to operate within a 50-mile radius of their bases. In July, Johnson sent an additional 50,000 troops and made plans to add yet another 50,000 by the end of the year. Meanwhile a coup in South Vietnam brought General Nguyen Van Thieu to power.

It was in 1965 also that Johnson agreed with General William Westmoreland, his top commander in Vietnam, that the United States had to abandon its defensive strategy and attack the enemy boldly. At the same time the South Vietnamese would mount a special effort to win over the rural population by sending government agents into the villages to cope with local problems. In addition, the government would provide military security while building roads, schools, and other public works—Johnson's version of the Great Society in Southeast Asia. Over the next two years American troop strength mounted and American B-52s rained tons of bombs on North Vietnam and Viet Cong positions. By the end of 1967 there were over 500,000 American troops in Vietnam, while American planes had dropped more bombs on the enemy than in all the theaters of World War II combined. And to some extent the strategy worked. The offensive had saved the South Vietnamese government from collapse and a clear-cut Viet Cong victory now seemed improbable. Even so, the Communists were far from defeated. No matter how much the United States escalated the war, the enemy would continue to bounce back. The North Vietnamese dispersed much of their industry and population into the

THE VIETNAM QUAGMIRE

343

countryside, and with 200,000 men coming of military age each year, they could match the additional American contingents.

As 1968 began, the war was no closer to being won than in 1965. Both sides faced a bloody stalemate, but neither was willing to make concessions that might bring peace. Each had lost too many lives and had invested too much of its national reputation to back down now. Johnson believed that he had to fight on indefinitely if only to avoid the humiliation of defeat.

The soaring human and financial costs of the war provoked loud protests, yet those who opposed the war did so for a variety of reasons. Many liberals insisted that the conflict in Vietnam was essentially a civil war that had little to do with monolithic communism, if in fact there was such a thing. They also charged that the war was diverting the nation's resources from a host of difficult problems at home. Critics further to the left contended that this war against a poor, third-world population was merely another example of decadent capitalism. Others objected to the nation's supporting a notoriously corrupt and autocractic government in South Vietnam, while another school argued that the United States could not expect to solve every world problem and should not try to maintain law and order around the globe. For many, the human carnage and widespread devastation were downright immoral. Then there were those who turned against the war because the United States could not or would not win. Many individuals, of course, held several of these views or combinations thereof.

Citizens and even public officials found various ways to register their opposition to the war. There were ''teach-ins'' on many college campuses where professors and students discussed the war and ways to stop it. Some students organized protest marches; others ransacked ROTC facilities or occupied administrative offices. Young men burned their draft cards, fled to Canada to avoid conscription, or defied induction and went to jail. More militant protesters lay across railroad tracks to stop troop trains or broke into local draft boards to destroy records. On October 21, 1967, 50,000 demonstrators marched on the Pentagon. And outside the White House dissidents chanted, ''Hey, hey, LBJ, how many kids did you kill today?'' In Congress there were also increasing doubts about the course of the war, and in February 1966 Chairman J. William Fulbright and his Senate Foreign Relations Committee held televised hearings on Vietnam.

The criticism on Capitol Hill was difficult enough for Johnson to take, but a massive Communist offensive in late January and early February 1968 convinced many of his loyal supporters that the war could not be won. Called the Tet offensive (after the Vietnamese lunar new year), the Viet Cong initiative was spectacularly successful at first. Armed bands infiltrated Saigon itself and besieged the American embassy. Elsewhere the Viet Cong attacked 36 of 44 provincial capitals. American and South Vietnamese forces ultimately beat back the attackers at a heavy cost to both. The Tet offensive was not a decisive victory for either side, though some analysts believed that it was really a serious defeat for North Vietnam. Still, it cast serious doubt on administration claims that the war was being won.

Weary and disgusted, Americans increasingly referred to the Vietnam conflict as Johnson's war, with one poll showing that only 27 percent of the public approved of his Vietnam policies. Despite his great victory in 1964 and his amazing legislative successes immediately thereafter, Johnson had become one of the most unpopular presidents in

CHAPTER 14: NEW FRONTIERS—AT HOME AND ABROAD

American history. Vietnam was bound to be a major issue in the upcoming election. Indeed, antiwar Senator Eugene McCarthy made no secret of his plans to deny Johnson the Democratic nomination in 1968, and in March he took the New Hampshire primary with 42 percent of the vote. Then on March 16 Robert Kennedy, who had since won a U.S. Senate seat from New York, declared his intention to enter the primaries as an antiwar candidate. On March 31 Johnson himself went on television to announce that he would seek new negotiations with the North Vietnamese and astonished listeners by stating that he would not seek reelection, ostensibly to devote full time to securing peace. Many speculated that he dropped out of the race because of mounting opposition to the war, but evidence has since revealed that worries over his health were just as crucial to Johnson's decision to retire.

NIXON'S NARROW VICTORY

Johnson had withdrawn from the contest, but he was determined to thwart both Kennedy and McCarthy. He urged Vice-President Humphrey to carry the administration standard and began rounding up support among the faithful. Meanwhile the Kennedy campaign gathered tremendous momentum, as voters fell under the growing Kennedy mystique. For millions, Robert F. Kennedy was a living link to his martyred brother, a young prince who would rekindle the Kennedy magic. In passionate and often strident appearances the younger Kennedy denounced the war in Vietnam and pleaded for social justice. Rallies in black neighborhoods combined the air of a royal procession with the hysteria of an old-fashioned revival meeting. Spectators ran after the candidate's car, chanting, shrieking, and tearing his clothes. McCarthy was clearly no match for the messianic Kennedy. Then on June 6, just after acknowledging his triumph in the California primary, Kennedy was shot and killed by a Palestinian Arab who opposed the candidate's outspoken support for Israel. Millions grieved for their slain hero, as the Kennedy legend grew to new proportions.

The horror of Robert Kennedy's murder was compounded by the assassination of civil rights leader Martin Luther King, Jr., just two months earlier on April 4, 1968. King had gone to Memphis, Tennessee, to support striking garbage workers there and was shot as he stood on a balcony of his motel. News of his death sent thousands of blacks into city streets, where many rampaged through commercial districts, smashing windows, and looting merchandise. President Johnson had to call out the Army to restore order in Washington, D.C., and armed soldiers guarded the Capitol steps for the first time since the Civil War.

In August the violence spilled over into the political arena and seriously marred the Democratic convention in Chicago. There antiwar demonstrators assembled in city parks and insisted on spending the night despite a municipal ordinance that forbade them to do so. Night after night the police chased the squatters out of the parks. On the evening of August 28 the demonstrators decided to march on the convention site. As the unruly crowd neared the convention hall and nearby hotels, local police charged into their midst and began beating the demonstrators with savage fury in full view of television crews, as the networks interrupted convention coverage to show the violence outside. Many Democrats at the convention were outraged at the police action, while others, including Chicago Mayor Richard J. Daley, sat by in defiant anger. Humphrey easily won the

NIXON'S NARROW VICTORY

nomination on a ticket with Senator Edmund Muskie of Maine, but the ugly scenes outside the convention hall provided an unfortunate backdrop for launching a presidential campaign.

On the Republican side, Richard Nixon was making a remarkable comeback. He had run for governor of California in 1962 and had been defeated in a bitterly contested election. He then announced his retirement from politics and joined a prestigious New York law firm. But over the next six years he toured the country, speaking in support of Republican candidates; now he was calling in the political favors, and his nomination was a forgone conclusion. Maryland Governor Spiro T. Agnew won the vice-presidential nomination.

Challenging both the major candidates was yet another governor, George Wallace of Alabama, who ran as the American Independent candidate. Wallace denounced federal interference with states' rights and the ''pointy-headed'' intellectuals in Washington who were bent on ruining the country. White supremacists rallied around Wallace, and for a time it looked as if northern blue-collar workers, resentful over all the federal attention paid to blacks and other minorities, might also support Wallace in large numbers.

While Wallace continued his battle against the liberal establishment, Hubert Humphrey struggled to get his campaign off the ground. This son of a small-town, South Dakota druggist had entered politics in 1945 when he became mayor of Minneapolis. He had attracted national attention in 1948 when he led a floor fight to include a strong civil rights plank in the Democratic platform, and as a U.S. senator he had gone on to champion civil rights and a variety of liberal causes.

Ironically, Humphrey became the target of left-wing protesters during the campaign. Ignoring Humphrey's liberal stands in the past, antiwar demonstrators hounded the candidate as he spoke, interrupting him time and time again with well-rehearsed and often obscene refrains. And although the vice-president had come to doubt the war in Vietnam, he refused to break with the administration—though he began to put some distance between himself and Johnson on the war issue as the campaign drew to a close. Whenever he could, Humphrey praised the Great Society and promised more reforms along the same lines.

Nixon, on the other hand, tried to avoid the issues. He decried the mounting violence in American life, called for law and order, and promised to bring the nation together again. He also claimed to have a secret plan to end the war in Vietnam. By October Nixon's low-keyed campaign began to hurt him and Humphrey made impressive gains in the polls. President Johnson's announcement of a bombing halt on October 31 also boosted Humphrey's chances. The result was an extremely close election. Nixon won 31,770,000 votes to Humphrey's 30,270,000, while Wallace ended up with 9,906,000. In the electoral college the totals were 301 for Nixon, 191 for Humphrey, and 46 for Wallace. Though victorious, Nixon would be a minority president with only 43.4 percent of the popular vote. The Democrats also retained their hold on both houses of Congress.

Nixon's election did little to lift the nation's spirits, however. The Vietnam war showed no real signs of ending, while blacks and other minorities grew increasingly restive at the slow pace of change. Events would show that foreign war and domestic strife were far from over, that the country's ''new frontiers'' had moved in perplexing and often dangerous directions.

BIOGRAPHICAL SKETCH

MARTIN LUTHER KING, JR. · *1929–1968*

By the mid-1960s the name Martin Luther King, Jr., was synonymous with the civil rights movement. Born in Atlanta, Georgia, King was the son and grandson of Baptist clergymen. He graduated from Morehouse College at age 19, went from there to Crozier Theological Seminary, and in 1955 earned a Ph.D. from Boston University. While in Boston he met and married Coretta Scott.

It was during his years at Crozier that King developed a life-long fascination with the teachings and tactics of India's Mahatma Gandhi. Like Gandhi, he believed that civil disobedience and nonviolent protest would eventually breach the wall of political and social oppression. A pastorate at the Dexter Avenue Baptist Church in Montgomery, Alabama, gave King his first opportunity to test this approach to racial injustice. There in 1955 he organized a successful campaign to desegregate the city's bus lines. Two years later he sought to broaden his movement by founding the Southern Christian Leadership Conference (SCLC). Meanwhile he moved back to Atlanta, where he served as assistant pastor to his father at the Ebinezer Baptist Church.

In conjunction with the SCLC, King organized numerous demonstrations and protests. Despite their peaceful tactics, his followers were frequently beaten and arrested, and King himself was repeatedly jailed. His campaign in 1963 to desegregate public facilities in Birmingham, Alabama, provoked savage retaliation, with police using dogs and fire hoses to disperse the peaceful marchers, many of them children. Two years later he led a historic march from Selma to Montgomery, Alabama, to protest continuing disfranchise-

Martin Luther King, Jr.

ment of southern blacks. King and his disciples were again assaulted and beaten, but their bloody trek focused nationwide attention on the need for legislation and thereby helped passage of the Voting Rights Act of 1965. In recognition for his attempts to bring about nonviolent change, King received the Nobel Peace Prize in 1964.

The most memorable event of King's career was the massive march on Washington, D.C., culminating on August 28, 1963. Standing before a throng of 250,000, with the Lincoln Memorial rising behind him, the Baptist preacher reached new heights of evangelical oratory: "Let freedom ring from every hill and mole hill in Mississippi," he implored, "from every mountainside, let freedom ring."

> Three years later King began wielding his powerful voice against the war in Vietnam, denouncing it as an inhumane and dangerous distraction from domestic reform. He also turned to the problem of poverty and planned a huge rally in Washington during the summer of 1968, but his assassination crushed the crusade in its infancy.
>
> Many whites distrusted or despised Martin Luther King, while more militant blacks chided him for his peaceful methods. But King's stature has grown to mythical proportions since his death, and he is destined to remain an authentic American hero. To honor his memory, Congress has declared his birthday, January 15, a national holiday.

SUGGESTED READINGS

There are a number of excellent analyses of presidential elections during the 1960s: Chester Lewis et al., *An American Melodrama* (1968); Jeremy Larner, *Nobody Knows: Reflections on the McCarthy Campaign of 1968* (1970); Joe McGinnis, *The Selling of the President 1968* (1969); Stephen Shadegg, *What Happened to Goldwater* (1965); Paul Tillet et al., *The National Election of 1964* (1966); and Theodore H. White's *Making of the President 1960* (1961), *Making of the President 1964* (1965), and *Making of the President 1968* (1969). Carl Solberg's *Hubert Humphrey: A Biography* (1984) also sheds much light on presidential politics. Barry Goldwater's *Conscience of a Conservative* (1964) is likewise revealing.

On the Kennedy family there is the controversial book by Peter Collier and David Horowitz, *The Kennedys: An American Drama* (1984). The most complete and well-balanced studies of John F. Kennedy are Herbert S. Parmet's *Jack: The Struggles of John F. Kennedy* (1981) and *JFK: The Presidency of John F. Kennedy* (1963). Several of Kennedy's associates have written perceptive but partisan accounts: Kenneth P. O'Donnell et al., *Johnny, We Hardly Knew Ye* (1972); Pierre Salinger, *With Kennedy* (1966); Arthur M. Schlesinger, Jr., *A Thousand Days* (1965); and Theodore Sorenson, *Kennedy* (1965). Assessments of Kennedy's leadership are found in Lewis J. Paper, *The Promise and the Performance: The Leadership of John F. Kennedy* (1969), and Bruce Miroff, *Pragmatic Illusions: The Presidential Politics of John F. Kennedy* (1976).

On Kennedy's foreign policy, see Louise Fitzsimons, *The Kennedy Doctrine* (1972); Roger Hilsman, *To Move a Nation: The Politics of Foreign Policy in the Administration of John F. Kennedy* (1967); H. B. Moulton, *From Superiority to Parity: The United States and the Strategic Arms Race, 1961–1971* (1973); and R. J. Walton, *Cold War and Counter Revolution* (1972). The latter is particularly critical of Kennedy. On the Cuban missile crisis there is Robert Kennedy's excellent *Thirteen Days* (1971), edited by R. E. Neustadt. And for a larger perspective on Cuban-American relations, see Thomas D. Boswell and James R. Curtis, *The Cuban-American Experience: Culture, Images, and Perspectives* (1984).

Among the monographs on Kennedy's domestic policy are Carl M. Brauer, *John F. Kennedy and the Second Reconstruction* (1977), and Jim Heath, *John F. Kennedy and the Business Community* (1970). On the New Frontier, see Aida Donald, *John F. Kennedy and the New Frontier* (1966). Arthur M. Schlesinger, Jr.'s *Robert Kennedy and his Times* (1978) is also helpful. For the Kennedy assassination see William Manchester, *The Death of a President* (1967) and the *Warren Commission Report* (1964).

On the Johnson years there are Lyndon Johnson's own memoirs, *The Vantage Point* (1971). The most thorough study of the Johnson administration is Vaughn D. Bornet, *The Presidency of Lyndon Johnson* (1983). Biographical treatments of Lyndon Johnson are Robert Caro, *The Path to Power: The Years of Lyndon Johnson* (1982); Doris Kearns, *Lyndon Johnson and the American Dream* (1976); and Alfred Steinberg, *Sam Johnson's Boy: A Close up of the President from Texas*

CHAPTER 14: NEW FRONTIERS—AT HOME AND ABROAD

(1968). Accounts by Johnson assistants are Eric F. Goldman, *The Tragedy of Lyndon Johnson* (1969), and Jack Valenti, *A Very Human President* (1975).

There are quite a few books about Johnson's Great Society. For an understanding of the poverty problem, see Michael Harrington, *The Other America* (1963), and James T. Patterson, *America's Struggle Against Poverty, 1900–1980* (1981). Critiques of the Great Society include: H. J. Aaron, *Politics and the Professions: The Great Society in Perspective* (1978); S. A. Levitan and Robert Taggart, *The Promise of Greatness* (1976); and Daniel P. Moynahan, *Maximum Feasible Misunderstanding* (1969). On Johnson and civil rights, see James C. Harvey, *Black Civil Rights during the Johnson Administration* (1973), and John F. Martin, *Civil Rights and the Crisis of Liberalism: The Democratic Party, 1945–1976* (1979). On education policy there is Hugh D. Graham, *The Uncertain Triumph: Federal Education Policy in the Kennedy and Johnson Years* (1984).

Foreign policy under Johnson is treated in Theodore Draper, *Abuse of Power* (1976); P. L. Geyelin, *Lyndon B. Johnson and the World* (1966); and J. William Fulbright's highly critical *Arrogance of Power* (1976). Warren I. Cohen's *Dean Rusk* (1980) is also illuminating. Concerning the Vietnam War in particular, there are Weldon A. Brown, *Prelude to Disaster: The American Role in Vietnam, 1940–1963* (1975); Lew Y. Guenter, *America in Vietnam* (1979); and George C. Herring, *America's Longest War: The United States in Vietnam, 1950–1975* (1980). A highly condemnatory account of American foreign policy during this period is Gabriel Kolko's, *The Roots of American Foreign Policy: An Analysis of Power and Purpose* (1969). Also reflecting this disappointment with the Kennedy-Johnson era is Jim F. Heath, *Decade of Disillusionment: The Kennedy-Johnson Years* (1975).

15

Revolt and Reaction

The domestic reforms under Kennedy and Johnson had raised much hope at first. Poverty, racism, and chronic unemployment—all were supposed to disappear in the flood of liberal legislation and Supreme Court decisions. Yet the latter half of the 1960s and early 1970s witnessed new eruptions of anger and discontent. Disappointed that government action did not bring immediate and far-reaching results, some disgruntled groups resorted to violent confrontation. At the same time, many middle-class youths became outspoken critics of American life. Students demonstrated loudly for black civil rights and seized campus buildings to demand changes in university rules or to protest the war in Vietnam. The youth revolt took other forms as well, ranging from unconventional clothing and socially conscious rock music to the widespread use of addictive drugs and uninhibited sexuality.

Most older and more conservative Americans reacted in horror to the loud protests and bizarre dress. Some denounced the unorthodox behavior as an unmistakable Communist plot, while others called for a return to old-fashioned morality or hid their fears beneath an unthinking superpatriotism. In politics there was a definite move away from reform, as voters elected Richard Nixon to the presidency in 1968. The new president criticized youthful protesters and openly courted their more silent critics. He also launched a campaign for law and order, but his own exaggerated fears of domestic unrest and political opposition led Nixon into a thicket of espionage, followed by a plot to conceal his misconduct. In the end Nixon was forced to resign from office or face almost certain impeachment and removal.

POWER IN MANY COLORS AND FORMS

The New Left The militant groups that emerged in the late 1960s did not share a consistent ideology, but many were influenced, if only slightly and indirectly, by an international movement known as the New Left. Although grounded in Marxism, the movement rejected orthodox communism. Its followers expressed many reservations about Marx's economic analyses, which had clearly been proven wrong by historical events, and returned to Marx's early philosophical writings, with their emphasis upon class struggle and historical dialectic. The New Left also abandoned Marx's faith in the industrial proletariat, believing that industrial workers were just as materialistic as their bourgeois employers. Third World peasants, American blacks, and other abused minorities became a new and unspoiled proletariat for them.

Above all, the new proletariat had to combat the bourgeois state. And since governments often used violence against the underprivileged, the new proletariat had to respond in kind. According to New Left spokespersons like the French Jean-Paul Sartre or the American Herbert Marcuse, such revolutionary violence was highly ethical—the only means of overthrowing the immoral forces of a reactionary society. Violence could also purify the victims of oppression, freeing them from impotence and shame.

From Civil Rights to Black Power These ideas were utterly opposed to the philosophy preached by Martin Luther King, Jr., but King's very success had led to disappointment and dissent. For many blacks progress was not rapid enough, and they began to measure results against what remained to be done rather than against what had been accomplished. Nonviolent protest also proved difficult to maintain in the face of constant beatings and insults. Unfulfilled hopes and continued frustration all helped to fuel the new black power movement.

Black power carried a variety of messages to widely differing groups: For some blacks it meant taking up arms in self-defense; to others it meant an assertion of black pride, black traditions, and black accomplishments. "Black is beautiful," they insisted with increasing frequency and volume. Still others ridiculed the goal of racial integration, believing that blacks should reject white society altogether and join to create a separate black nation.

In many respects black power had been anticipated by the Black Muslims, founded in Detroit during the 1930s by Elijah Poole. Discarding his white surname, Poole thereafter called himself Elijah Muhammad. He and his disciples denounced Christianity as the religion of their white oppressors and replaced it with their own version of the Islamic faith. The Black Muslims declared their separation from white society and urged blacks to create their own elite: It was they who first denounced the word "negro" as a white man's term and began referring to themselves as blacks.

By 1967 many other individuals and groups had embraced the goal of racial separation. Among them were the Black Panthers, who unlike the Muslims rejected the notion of a distinct black culture and nation. Yet they viewed blacks as a unique and separate people who must free themselves from oppression while refusing to be bought off or coopted by white liberals. Indeed, Panther leaders such as Bobby Seale and Huey P. Newton drew much of their ideology from a Marxist critique of capitalist society and demanded an armed rebellion against the white oppressor. Their rhetoric was much more violent than their actions, but the FBI labeled them a subversive organization and police

POWER IN MANY COLORS AND FORMS   **351**

staged raids on Panther headquarters in various cities. There were mass arrests, with 28 Panthers being shot to death in 1969 alone.

Other black power advocates worked the college campuses. Stokely Carmichael, the young chairman of the Student Non-Violent Coordinating Committee (SNCC), once a group dedicated to peaceful protest, delivered a series of defiant speeches at black universities. On April 8, 1967, students at Fisk University responded by staging a riot. At Carmichael's urging, students also revolted on several other campuses that spring. Hundreds were arrested and scores were beaten by police or expelled from school. Carmichael's successor at SNCC, H. Rap Brown, reveled in these violent confrontations with the ''establishment,'' proclaiming that violence was ''as American as cherry pie.''

Black college students were not the only ones to vent their rage. Riots erupted in several black ghettos, the worst of them in the Los Angeles suburb of Watts, where conditions were in fact terrible. Over 30 percent of adult males were unemployed and the largely white police were notorious for their brutality. Beginning on August 11, 1965, both residents and police went on a rampage. Rioters looted stores at random and set block after block of houses and shops on fire, shooting firefighters as they tried to douse the flames. When the smoke cleared, 34 lay dead and hundreds were homeless. Most of the destroyed businesses never reopened and many other shopkeepers moved out for good. The Watts explosion may have given residents a temporary sense of release and exaltation, but the destruction hurt black inhabitants far more than anyone else. In the next few years there would be similar uprisings in other cities.

The Chicano Experience   The black rights and black power movements had a galvanizing effect on other deprived minorities in the United States. Among these were the Mexican-Americans, or Chicanos (the diminutive form of ''Mexicanos''). Some Chicano leaders, like César Chavez, tried to improve the standard of living among migrant farm workers by organizing strikes against California growers. Far more militant was Reies López Tijerina, a religious mystic who found much inspiration in the black power movement. In February 1963 he founded the Alianza de Las Mercedes, an organization of Mexican-Americans in northern New Mexico whose members attempted to reclaim lands that had been seized by Anglo-American settlers a century before. At first the Alianza challenged the land titles in the courts, and when that failed they laid siege to the county courthouse at Rio Arriba on June 5, 1967. This daring assault attracted much publicity, but did nothing to further the Alianza's land claims. Nor did it address the wider sufferings of Mexican-Americans.

Red and White   Meanwhile American Indians—or Native Americans, as some preferred—began to protest against continuing poverty and deprivation. And if statistics are a reliable guide, Native Americans were clearly the poorest of the poor. In 1970 their per capita income was $1,500 a year, a full 75 percent less than the national average. Forty percent of adult Indians were unemployed, a figure that was 10 times the rate for white Americans. The American Indian Movement (AIM), founded by Dennis Means and Clyde Bellancourt, vowed to redress the situation. In November 1972 they occupied the headquarters of the Bureau of Indian Affairs (BIA) in Washington, D.C. The following February they seized the village of Wounded Knee, South Dakota, where a helpless band of Sioux had been massacred by the Army in 1890.

A member of the militant AIM at the occupation of Wounded Knee, South Dakota, March 1973.

The AIM, like many less militant groups, demanded a complete reversal of traditional government policy toward Indians. Up to this point the government had attempted to transform American Indians into middle-class WASPs. The vast majority of Indians had clearly rejected this model over the years, but members of Congress, BIA officials, and most white Americans had refused to listen. Means, Bellancourt, and their followers now hoped that they could force white America to heed their cries. They wanted strict observance of treaty rights, a halt to current efforts to destroy their tribal life, and absolute control over their own internal affairs. Their efforts met with partial success when President Nixon introduced legislation in July 1970 that granted Indian tribes a wide degree of self-determination and self-government.

New Life for the Women's Movement Protests by Indians, Chicanos, and blacks made sense to many liberal-minded Americans, even if most thought that the militants had gone too far. The women's liberation movement, however, took liberals by surprise. Since winning the right to vote in 1920, the great majority of women had seemed satisfied with, if not complacent about, their position in American life. Indeed, the post-World War II period had witnessed a veritable celebration of traditional female roles. It was true that more and more women had entered the job force, but few showed much interest in real careers during the immediate postwar period. In fact, there were relatively fewer women professionals at the end of the 1950s than there had been 30 years before. The ratio of women receiving college and graduate degrees had also declined, with 2 of every 5 bachelor's degrees and 2 of every 5 master's degrees going to women in 1930. By 1960, women earned only 1 of 3 bachelor's and master's degrees. The decline in Ph.D.'s granted to women during this period was similarly alarming, dropping from 1 in 7 to 1 in 10. And, of course, women continued to receive much lower salaries than men, even when they performed comparable tasks. In 1960 female workers, who now represented one-third of the work force, earned only about half as much as their male counterparts. If nothing else, such discrimination in pay would later provide a popular base for feminist demands.

It is not surprising that affluent, college-educated women were the first to renew the protest against their unequal station. Having been taught to think and to raise serious questions about modern society, many found themselves leading dull and unfulfilling lives as suburban housewives. At least this was the picture that Betty Friedan painted in her widely read *Feminine Mystique* (1963). Friedan believed that educated women in particular needed more creative outlets. And for most, she concluded, domestic chores or volunteer work were simply not enough. Yet continued prejudice against women, coupled with discriminatory practices in the workplace, made it difficult for them to pursue rewarding careers outside the home.

Friedan struck a kindred note for many young women, and some joined her in founding the National Organization for Women (NOW). An essentially liberal organization, many of whose members had been involved in the black civil rights movement, NOW concentrated on obtaining legislation and court decisions that would guarantee full legal equality for American women. Above all, they campaigned for an Equal Rights Amendment (ERA) to the federal Constitution that would forbid discrimination on account of sex. In this sense, their methods and goals were quite similar to those of the moderate NAACP. By the late 1960s, however, more militant women began to advocate a program that closely resembled the black power movement. Like their black counterparts, these women emphasized their unique qualities and, in some instances, insisted on the innate superiority of women over men. Militants urged "consciousness raising" sessions to alert women to their desperate plight.

One of the more radical factions adopted the name Women's International Feminist Conspiracy from Hell (WITCH). Among other things, WITCH denounced the sexual exploitation of women in entertainment and advertising. In 1968 they picketed the Miss America pageant in Atlantic City, charging that it was a sexist exploitation of the female body. Some of these same women burned their bras as a further protest against social constraint and male manipulation.

More ideologically oriented women, many of them influenced by the New Left, propounded a Marxian analysis of the situation. Among them was Shulamith Firestone. In her *Dialectic of Sex* (1970), she compared men to Marx's bourgeoisie, contending that they controlled the means of production and, through it, women's lives. Women must demand a larger share of capital and thereby burst the chains of economic oppression; only then would they be truly free. In the meantime women must not collaborate with the enemy and, accordingly, some of the more radical liberationists recommended a complete separation of the sexes. A few went further to advocate lesbianism as an alternative to dangerous and often unsatisfying relationships with men.

Another provocative assessment of women's position came in Kate Millett's *Sexual Politics* (1969). Defining politics broadly as those means through which one group dominates or governs another, Millett insisted that male power over women was essentially political in nature. From the family to the stock exchanges, she concluded, men held the real power. In the modern world this power was often subtle and unofficial, but nonetheless very real, and these patterns of male dominance were reinforced throughout the whole socialization process. Millett's analysis, though exaggerated in some respects, had a tremendous influence on other advocates of women's rights, as well as upon those who researched and wrote women's history.

Gay Rights   Yet another expression of sexual liberation was the gay rights movement. Small numbers of homosexuals had organized well before the 1960s, but the contemporary movement dates from a police raid on the Stonewall Inn in New York's Greenwich Village on June 27, 1969. In the past gays had put up little or no resistance to such raids, but this time they fought back, and for the first time many felt a sense of pride about being gay. Following the raid, members of the gay community demonstrated in the Village and shortly thereafter founded the Gay Liberation Front. Gay pride marches soon erupted in other cities, among them San Francisco, which was home to the largest concentration of gays in the nation. Within a few years gays were organizing in many states to combat discrimination against homosexuals. Contending that gays represented at least 10 percent of the population, they saw themselves as yet another oppressed minority in American life. In San Francisco as well as in several other cities, they obtained antidiscrimination ordinances. Others held that such legislation was not enough in a society suffused with antihomosexual sentiment; only a radical transformation of beliefs, they contended, would make the nation safe for gay men and women.

THE SEXUAL REVOLUTION

The gay rights and women's rights movements were actually part of a larger sexual revolution. Of course, attitudes toward sex had been changing since early in the century, and in the 1920s an earlier sexual revolution had manifested itself in many ways. World War II had served as a further catalyst, as men and women far from home found it easier to flout traditional mores. Even in the conservative 1950s, the revolt against Victorian morality continued, albeit slowly and quietly. But in the 1960s and 1970s, the sexual revolution reached a new plateau.

The roots of this change in sexual morality are deeply tangled and often elusive; yet several causes have emerged. First and foremost was the triumph of industrialization, with an increasing shift in emphasis from production to consumption. By the 1960s it was no longer necessary for the American people to defer their desires for consumer goods in order to accumulate large pools of savings and industrial capital. The problem of production was solved; the abundant life was now available to millions. Indeed, the

THE SEXUAL REVOLUTION 355

task for businesses and their advertisers was to convince the public to buy a flood of goods as they poured from the nation's assembly lines. It was now as virtuous to spend and consume as it once had been to scrimp and do without, and from every side Americans were encouraged to gratify their every desire. A popular beer commercial repeatedly reminded television viewers that they only went "around once in life" and that they had "better grab all the gusto" they could get. In such an atmosphere it seemed contradictory to insist that sexual gratification remained sinful while all other forms of sensual indulgence were healthy and beneficial.

The triumph of industrialization also meant fewer demands for labor, which ultimately translated into a lessening need for large families. At the same time, more and more Americans lived in cities. There child rearing proved much more expensive than in rural areas, where children assisted with farm work from a very young age. Meanwhile, advances in science and medicine made contraception easier and more dependable. This was particularly true of the birth control pill, introduced to the American market in 1960. When taken properly by women, it provided nearly absolute protection against pregnancy and did not require awkward or unromantic applications during sexual encounters. Abortions likewise became easier and safer, and several states made them legal by the early 1970s. With the fear of unwanted pregnancies greatly reduced, both women and men felt freer to engage in "recreational sex," within marriage or without.

Women's liberation was another important factor in the sexual revolution. For years many believed that women did not enjoy sex or experience any real sexual desires. At best, sex was a means of childbearing or an expression of marital love. Now women were seen as sexual creatures, whose desires were as real as men's. Others went on to claim that women, like men, could disassociate sex from the marriage bed or from any kind of romantic attachment. Whether men and women experience exactly the same sexual needs remains in dispute, but an increasing number of women did demand the right to sexual gratification, while more young women than ever before engaged in some form of premarital sex. In 1950, only 20 percent of women surveyed reported that they had had sexual intercourse before age 19, while 20 years later almost 50 percent reported sexual activity by that age. Surveys also showed that the pubic had grown more tolerant of premarital sex. In 1969, 68 percent of those polled believed that sex before marriage was morally wrong; in 1973, only 47 percent found the practice immoral.

Yet another product of the sexual revolution was the rise in divorce rates. From a post-World War II low of 2.1 divorces per thousand people, it reached 3.5 per thousand in 1970 and then soared to 5.3 per thousand by the early 1980s. Certainly the assertion of both partners' rights to sexual gratification caused some spouses to seek sex outside the marriage bond or to dissolve the union because of sexual incompatability. The desire of both partners for rewarding careers, and frequently children as well, placed intolerable strains on many couples. Unrealistic expectations of personal fulfillment, often vaguely defined, likewise led to marital breakdowns, as spouses blamed each other for their unhappiness or looked to a freer life style as an answer to personal problems. Greater job opportunities for women also afforded some of them more economic independence and with it the option of leaving their husbands. Finally, greater acceptability of divorce and more lenient laws, many of them providing for no-fault dissolutions, made divorce quicker, cheaper, and generally more attractive.

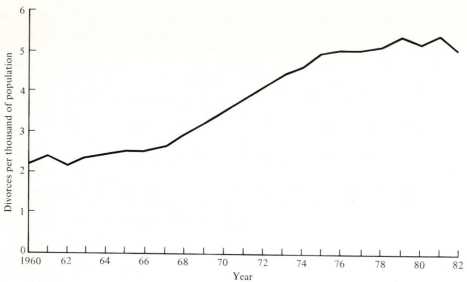

U.S. divorce rate, 1960–1982.

For some, easier access to divorce meant freedom from a hopeless union; for others, divorce left a trail of anger and emotional devastation. And for women unprepared to enter the job market, divorce frequently ended in grinding poverty. But the most unfortunate victims were the millions of children whose lives were rent by parental separation. No one could predict the full impact that the epidemic of divorce would have upon them, the family, or the social fabric.

YOUTH REBELLION AND COUNTERCULTURE

Young Americans figured prominently in the sexual revolution, as well as in various protest movements. But both phenomena were part of a larger movement that, for want of a better term, has been labeled the counterculture. Although complex and multifaceted, the counterculture movement was basically a criticism of contemporary American society. Only a minority of young people joined the counterculture per se, and those who did were generally from middle-class backgrounds, attended college, or were recent college graduates. Many nonadherents, however, adopted various ideas from the counterculture or were affected by it indirectly.

The counterculture produced a number of manifestos, but two books in particular appealed widely to the young rebels. The earlier of the two was *Growing Up Absurd* (1960) by Paul Goodman. Written before the counterculture actually emerged, Goodman's work prefigured the rebellion to come and became a sort of bible to disaffected youth in the late 1950s and early 1960s. Goodman lashed out at adult hypocrisy and the lack of inspiring national ideals. It was not surprising to him that some sensitive young people rejected middle-class life styles in favor of the beatnik world.

The second work came 10 years later, after the counterculture had reached a fever pitch. In his *Greening of America* (1970), author Charles Reich pointed with great enthusiasm to a youthful revolution that he believed was transforming the country for good. Beginning with a pseudo-Marxian interpretation of the American past, Reich proposed that the United States had passed through two stages of historical consciousness and was about to enter a third. Consciousness I, as he called it, had arisen during the late eighteenth and early nineteenth centuries. It emphasized individual competition in the marketplace and was part and parcel of the industrial revolution, with its celebration of risk-taking entrepreneurs. Consciousness II was born in the early twentieth century as an accompaniment to big business and later to big government and big labor. In this second stage individuals were told to sacrifice everything to the ''organization,'' be it economic, political, or bureaucratic. An emerging Consciousness III, now quite evident among the young, increasingly defied the stifling regimentation of Consciousness II and in some ways hearkened back to Consciousness I, with its emphasis upon the individual. But this newest form of consciousness eschewed the earlier belief in economic individualism. Instead it trumpeted the individual's right to complete self-fulfillment, while insisting on dignity and equality for all ideas and opinions.

Despite such systematic treatments of the counterculture, the movement itself often seemed contradictory in both expression and goals; yet its adherents shared a core of attitudes and beliefs. One was antimaterialism. Youthful critics contended that the nation had lost its way in a maze of commercialism and material success and, in consequence, had betrayed its higher ideals. Property rights were now more important than liberty, equality, or spiritual well-being. Closely associated with this criticism was the belief that modern society placed too much trust in reason and empirical investigation; emotion, intuition, and personal sincerity, they maintained, were far superior to cold logic. Furthermore, modern science and technology had led to nuclear weapons and the widespread destruction of the natural environment. Counterculturists also condemned the traditional American belief in personal competition, asserting that cooperation and community were far more important than contention in the marketplace.

Peace and social justice likewise ranked high within the movement. Blacks, Hispanics, women, and other oppressed minorities must be accorded basic human rights. Most immediately, the United States must withdraw from Vietnam and devote itself to peaceful programs at home and abroad. It was equally important to live in harmony with nature. People must stop exploiting the environment and live in harmony with nature's ways. A corollary to this new respect for nature was a burgeoning campaign against food additives and insecticides. Finally, self-fulfillment and emotional gratification were exalted, as traditional inhibitions and ''adult hypocrisy'' were derided or dismissed.

Few of these ideas were completely new. The ''beats'' had anticipated many of them a decade or two earlier, as had bohemians and expatriates in the 1920s. The counterculture's emphases on nature, emotion, and individual expression were also reminiscent of nineteenth-century romanticism. Just why these ideas should emerge with such intensity in the 1960s remains somewhat unclear.

To some extent, the counterculture was a sincere protest against the very real injustices of American life. Indeed, for sheltered middle-class youth who had been brought up to suppose that they lived in a land of justice and opportunity, the persistence of poverty, racism, and war seemed a complete betrayal of the national mission. And the sheer number of young people in the 1960s and 1970s meant that even a small minority of disillusioned youth could attract a great deal of attention.

ORAL HISTORY
Growing Up in the Twentieth Century

FRAN BOYCE · *born 1949*

Time magazine's article on the hippies in late '66 or early '67 influenced me a lot. I just decided I was going to be a hippie. Because that was the only thing that made any sense to me. I had no idea in what direction my life was going to go. I had quit the seminary and was in a period of tremendous rebellion against my parents and their restrictive ways. Then one day my boss said, "If you don't get a haircut, then don't bother to come back." And I didn't go back. I think a lot of kids were going through a rebellion against their parents, but only a small percentage were brave enough to cut loose and go.

I realized that there were some people out there who really wanted to build some kind of new life style, and I really wanted to find out what was going on. I was really attracted to it. The music was especially powerful. When the Beatles did the *Sergeant Pepper* album—that really pushed me over the edge. I was sitting on this kid's front porch listening to it, and I knew I was going to leave that day. They came to the song "She's Leaving Home." I heard that and thought: "Yeah, people are doing it. You go and do it!" So I went and did it.

I go to San Francisco and end up in Irving Rosenthal's house that's being used as the printing house for the Free City Digger Project. The Diggers were in the forefront of trying to build the new society. They were sort of the activist wave of the hippies. All sorts of beatnik poets came through the house. I met almost every important one except Burroughs. The Grateful Dead rock band kicked in money to keep the project going. We were trying to transform society, but I don't think that anybody had a particular political creed.

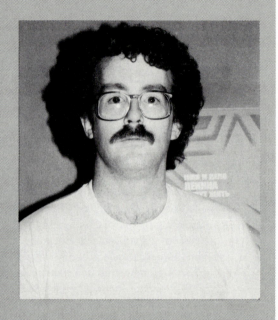

I hitchhiked back across the country to New York and then took a bus down to Philly. Then somebody laid Eldridge Cleaver on me. And that was when things really changed. Cleaver explained a lot of things to me I'd missed. Most of all there was Cleaver's incredible rage. I had been using drugs to push down all the anger against my father. I was angry with the country; I was angry with everybody. I was angry with the country because we were at war, and it was a war that seemed totally unjustified to me—a war that I didn't want to fight.

At this time there were substantial political developments. Abbie Hoffman was on the scene. The yippies were starting to make their presence known. I just loved Hoffman's outrageousness. I started looking for political groups. In September 1969 we started talking to various people, and we finally had about ten who were willing to put together a political commune of some kind. The politics weren't too well defined, but tended toward yippie, White Panther kinds of things. A little later someone decided to get a member of the radical organization Weather Underground to come and speak at Temple University. She flew in from California. What we liked about her was her policy of activism. To me, activism was the way out. This could really happen.

We were then invited to this Weather war council in Flint, Michigan, around New Year's 1970. There were a couple of hundred people there who slept on a gym floor and listened to Mark Rudd and others make speeches and debate. It was their dramatic effect that convinced me to become a Weatherman. They were action-oriented instead of just talking. They were feared; they had a persona.

We came back from Flint all fired up, and it wasn't two weeks later that we happened to notice that the "60 Minutes" show was going to do a segment by Mike Wallace on the Black Panthers. He put down their breakfast program, talked about their racism, and how they had guns.

We talked about different actions. Channel 10 was the local CBS affiliate. A lot of people had seen the show and would understand, at least, why we were doing an action against the station. Twelve of us—nine men and three women—charged into the station and threw a bunch of pamphlets around denouncing the "60 Minutes" program. We ran through the building screaming: "Power to the people!" "Free Bobby Seale!" "Free the Chicago 7!" We smashed glass display cases; we ripped phones off the wall; we destroyed everything we could see. It's clear to me now that we wanted to get caught and we wanted the publicity. That's how you get to be famous. The police showed up, arrested us, and I eventually spent a month in jail.

I know that I was incredibly naive at that time. I don't think that any of us had any idea what a real revolution would do in this country, what it would look like. I'm still left-wing politically. I'd probably like to try some form of democratic socialism. But I really don't have the foggiest idea of what would work.

Unfortunately, the counterculture had its darker sides, among them the drug cult. Advocates like Professor Timothy Leary of Harvard University proclaimed that hallucinogenic drugs such as LSD put users more in touch with their own emotions and the feelings of others. But LSD turned out to be far from benign, sometimes causing permanent brain damage in its users. Marijuana was far less harmful and was widely used by the young, but some believed that it led to more dangerous drugs. Nevertheless, many young people preferred it to alcohol, the usual adult intoxicant, and claimed that it was far less injurious than liquor. They also resented that fact that alcohol was legal, while marijuana was not—clear proof to some of an adult double standard.

The call for emotional sincerity was much less harmful. At best it encouraged individuals to be more sensitive to their own and others' feelings. At worst it led to attacks on all rational authority, striking at the very heart of academia, where rational inquiry had been the basis of research and instruction in modern universities. Some students challenged the faculty's right to judge their intellectual performance, and if rampant grade inflation were any indication of faculty attitudes, it appears that more than one professor agreed with these disgruntled students.

But much more far-reaching than inflated grades was the campus sexual revolution. The insistence on sexual freedom did little to hurt the body unless it ended in a difficult

360   CHAPTER 15: REVOLT AND REACTION

pregnancy or an illegal and deadly abortion. Yet many young people suffered moral qualms as well as emotional difficulties with the new morality. Perhaps more disquieting were the implications for the American family, as the desire for greater and greater sexual thrills undermined more stable relationships.

The Campuses Explode   The counterculture also disrupted college campuses throughout the nation. The campus became, in fact, the ideal breeding ground for antiestablishment protests. Swelled by wave after wave of baby-boom children, the colleges and universities contained the largest concentration of young men and women anywhere in the country. Enrollments more than doubled between 1960 and 1970, increasing from 3.6 to 7.9 million during that decade alone.

Like other manifestations of the counterculture, campus unrest was sometimes justifiable and even constructive, and many of the early demonstrations clearly fall into this category. Some students petitioned for the right to bring controversial speakers to campus, while others campaigned for civil rights legislation. Still others demonstrated against restrictive social regulations, including early curfews and rules against entertaining members of the opposite sex in dormitory rooms. Then there were those undergraduates who objected to large lecture classes or to the fact that many of their courses were being taught by graduate students. Later they complained that traditional academic requirements were irrelevant to modern society. To some extent these discontents with campus life were inherent in the large university, as described so well by University of California President Clark Kerr. According to Kerr, the modern ''multiversity'' became a bureaucratic monster that grew further and further away from the realm of classrooms, students, and their needs.

These and other protests were sometimes organized by local chapters of Students for a Democratic Society (SDS). The leftist ideology of the SDS led some conservative critics to denounce all campus demonstrations as Communist-inspired, but the SDS was clearly not a Communist-front organization, and most campus disorders were wholly spontaneous. Still, it was convenient to blame student protests on subversive agents, outside agitators, or other scapegoats. In that way the older generation did not have to blame themselves for their children's embarrassing behavior; nor did they have to face the very real shortcomings of higher education—or of the nation at large.

Of course, the most vocal and destructive demonstrations erupted over the Vietnam War. Students stood to lose their lives in a conflict that many sincerely questioned. Tactics ranged from peaceful marches to attacks on ROTC installations and the occupation of administrative offices, with the worst incidents occurring just after President Nixon ordered American troops into Cambodia in May 1970.

Hippies   Off campus some advocates of the counterculture decided to ''drop out'' of society for a while and adopt the latest version of the bohemian life style. In the 1960s and 1970s they were generally called ''hippies'' (from the older *hipster,* which meant someone who was ''with it''). In their manners and dress, hippies rejected everything that one might associate with the adult establishment. Men grew their hair long, tying it back in a queue or letting it fly about curly, gnarled, and unruly. Many also sported necklaces, earrings, and other jewelry, while both male and female hippies wore faded, torn, and frequently soiled blue jeans, with sweatshirts in equally tattered condition.

Students and Ohio National Guardsmen at Kent State University, May 4, 1970.

Others, identifying with oppressed minorities, donned Indian beads or African garments. They urged love and kindness on one another and everyone around them. And some, rejecting materialism as well as economic competition, lived together in communes, sharing their meager fare. Sexual communism was also important to many hippies, some of whom advocated group sex, or "love-ins." Most also shared in the drug mania and suffered all too many "bad trips." Some died from drug overdoses or slipped into serious addiction.

Rock Music Music was also central to the hippie movement, as well as to the counterculture in general. Since the mid-1950s rock and roll had been an instrument of protest for many young people, but rock music in the 1960s became a much more explicit vehicle of rebellion. At first, the lyrics contained little that was new or startling, and the majority of songs continued to focus on the trials of young love. It was rather the unorthodox dress and personal habits of rock stars that captivated audiences in the beginning. This was certainly true of the Beatles, a British rock group whose long but neatly cut hair and modish clothes swept the nation after they appeared on American television in February 1964. Later the Beatles became more raffish in appearance, wearing beads and letting their hair grow out long and wild.

The Beatles performing during their American television debut on the "Ed Sullivan Show," February 9, 1964.

But by far the most important protest singer was Bob Dylan, whose powerful lyrics attracted thousands of young protesters and social critics. Many of his songs mocked traditional assumptions of American superiority, called for peace in Vietnam, or directed attention to continuing racism in American life. Other performers graphically celebrated the sexual liberation of the 1960s. Mick Jagger of the Rolling Stones openly bragged about his sexual exploits, flaunting his body on stage, and sometimes appeared for concerts in feminine attire. He as well as other rock artists admitted taking drugs and celebrated their drug use in numerous songs.

Rock concerts themselves became an integral part of the counterculture, and often took on the proportions of a religious event, with popular rock stars as their high priests. Strung out on drugs and transfixed by the pulsating beat and flashing strobe lights, youthful audiences lost themselves in a sort of bacchanalian frenzy. The most spectacular of these concerts took place out of doors on a farm at Woodstock, New York, on August 15, 1969. About 300,000 spectators showed up. It poured rain, the grounds were sodden and jammed, and there were inadequate supplies of food and water, to say nothing of toilets. Thousands smoked marijuana, "turned on" to the music, and made love to total strangers. The crowd was quite orderly, however, and the concert promoters used helicopters to evacuate the drug casualties. For several months thereafter counterculture publicists congratulated themselves on the "spirit of Woodstock," a spontaneous expression of love and cooperation. But another outdoor concert several months later at Altamont, California, organized by the Rolling Stones, was a disaster. The Stones hired a California motorcycle gang called Hell's Angels to keep order; instead they attacked anyone who offended them and killed at least one person. There were also numerous drug overdoses and serious accidents.

YOUTH REBELLION AND COUNTERCULTURE

363

More conservative adults condemned the rock craze, insisting that its perverse message would lead to political revolution and undermine the nation's morals. Scholars continue to dispute the impact of rock music on youthful behavior, but for most young people, such music continued to be a harmless outlet, while others doubtless had their ideas confirmed by the more radical lyrics of the day.

The Arts The music of protest had no direct parallels in the art word. Instead of a return to social criticism, as one might expect, some avant-garde painters concentrated on the banal or familiar sights of the American landscape. Labeled ''pop art,'' this style concentrated on such things as comic-book heroes or commercial advertisements. The most famous of these was Andy Warhol's 3-foot-high painting of a Campbell's soup can. On one level these works were a reaction against abstract expressionism, which by the end of the 1960s had reached its artistic limitations. Yet much pop art was itself highly abstract in the sense that objects were depicted in bold colors, completely divorced from any social context. Some pop art was a humorous commentary on contemporary commercialism, while other works simply tried to please the eye through an exaggerated view of the familiar. If the pop art movement had anything in common with the counterculture, it was the importance that artists gave to everyday sights.

Some sculptors also took up the pop art mania. Andy Warhol turned out giant-sized Brillo boxes, while others like Claes Oldenburg created highly realistic but wholly synthetic food arrangements. His platters of cooked sausages or simmering Thanksgiving turkeys could look very appetizing to gallery visitors.

Movies Like the art world, movies in the 1960s betrayed no direct link to the counterculture. Yet movies did reflect the period's more lenient attitudes toward sex. There was more and more nudity in cinema and, by the end of the decade, highly explicit sexual scenes. One of the most sensational was a Swedish film entitled *I Am Curious Yellow* (1969). Religious leaders and moralists denounced this and other such films, but the federal courts took an increasingly tolerant position on pornography.

A few pictures dealt with social problems. *The Graduate* (1967), starring Dustin Hoffman, grappled quite successfully with the agonies of youthful self-definition. Others focused on the growing fear of nuclear war, often through bizarre or unintended circumstances. The best of these were *Fail Safe* (1964) and *Dr. Strangelove* (1964). The immensely popular *Bonnie and Clyde* (1967), starring Warren Beatty and Faye Dunaway, dealt skillfully with the ongoing theme of violence in national life. On one level the film is simply about two gangsters from the 1930s, but the brilliant juxtaposition of humor and grisly violence made the frequent killings all the more repulsive.

The Backlash Violent and sexy movies repelled many Americans, as did the whole counterculture movement. By the late 1960s there was an unmistakable ''backlash'' against protestors, hippies, and civil rights advocates. This reaction took several forms and ultimately had a profound impact on national politics.

Many white ethnic groups, for example, resented and feared the black civil rights movement. Some believed that black neighbors would undermine property values, or claimed that integrated schools would result in lower educational standards and thereby damage their children's chances for occupational and social mobility. They further resented special programs for blacks, along with increased welfare payments to the poor in general. Their immigrant ancestors had faced discrimination and poverty, they contended, but had overcome these handicaps through sacrifice and hard work. Apparently forgetting that their forebears had been white Europeans, they wondered why all blacks and other current minorities could not do the same thing.

White ethnic groups expressed their anger in various ways. Ironically, some of them imitated blacks, Hispanics, and women by emphasizing their uniqueness or superiority as an ethnic community. In New York City, Italians organized a giant unity rally in June 1971. Poles, Russians, Germans, Irish, and other groups reinvigorated older ethnic observations or created new ones.

To some extent the resentment of white ethnics was shared by others, and particularly those of working-class backgrounds. Their anger and general bewilderment over recent changes in national life were echoed in the immensely popular television comedy ''All in the Family,'' with its chief protagonist Archie Bunker. Played by Carroll O'Connor, himself a liberal Democrat, Archie lashed out against everything from women's liberation to integration and the decline of old-fashioned patriotism. Liberal viewers deplored Archie's unalloyed bigotry, while many blue-collar workers applauded him for expressing their own pent-up frustrations.

For a time, in fact, it looked as if white Americans were becoming as divided as blacks and whites had been. Liberals who had once seen union workers as fellow crusaders now scoffed at their petty bourgeois aspirations or wrote them off as hopeless bigots. For their own part, working-class whites came to resent the draft deferments given to middle-class college students, and many were furious about the antiwar protests. In New York City, for instance, 200 enraged construction workers attacked antiwar demonstrators on May 8, 1970, chasing them through the streets with hammers, pliers, and other tools. The local police, who generally shared the workers' anger, stood by and did nothing.

THE NIXON WHITE HOUSE

The newly elected Richard Nixon was well aware of these divisions, and in his inaugural address he promised to bring the country together again. But it was clear that he sympathized with the so-called silent majority, a term used by Vice-President Spiro Agnew to describe a great mass of citizens who worked hard, paid their taxes, and did their patriotic duty without protest. On other occasions, administration spokespersons referred to this group as ''middle Americans,'' but whatever the group was called, it was evident that Nixon wanted to curry their favor through his ''law and order'' campaign.

Instead of trying to investigate and treat the causes of crime and dissent, as some liberals advocated, Nixon chose to ''crack down'' on the nation's troublemakers. He used the Law Enforcement Assistance Administration to funnel over a billion dollars to local police forces for better equipment. His attorney general and former law partner John Mitchell authorized electronic surveillance of dissident groups and urged less stringent standards for other types of searches and seizures. Mitchell also enlisted the CIA in his crusade against dissidents, in clear violation of the CIA's legislative mandate, which forbade domestic operations.

President Richard M. Nixon delivering his inaugural address, January 1969.

A New Federalism During the campaign Nixon had also charged that too much interference from the federal government was much to blame for current domestic problems, and he promised greater autonomy for state and local governments. These pledges to restore some measure of local independence seem ironic in light of Nixon's simultaneous efforts to centralize executive authority and extend presidential prerogatives; yet Nixon did take several initiatives that promised a more equitable relationship between Washington and the state capitals. Nixon and his staff used the term New Federalism, coined by speechwriter William Safire, to describe the administration's new departure. Safire wrote several position papers on the New Federalism in 1969 and circulated them within the administration. But it was not until March 1970 that Secretary of Labor George Shultz gave the ideas a public airing during a speech at the University of Chicago. According to Shultz, the New Federalism "calls upon us to act as one nation in setting the standards of fairness, and then to act as congeries of communities in carrying out those standards." There clearly would be no return to an old-fashioned states' rights doctrine; rather, the states would receive more latitude in carrying out national policies or in funding various projects.

The New Federalism manifested itself in several ways. One was Nixon's revenue-sharing plan, a scheme to return federal tax dollars to the states, which could then spend them as they saw fit, without interference from Washington. In October 1972 Congress appropriated $5.3 billion in revenue-sharing funds. Subsequent Congresses renewed and even enlarged these grants, but never in such large amounts as Nixon wanted. Revenue sharing was attacked from both the right and left. Some conservatives did not think it went far enough in restoring states' rights, while liberals feared that it would neutralize prohibitions against the use of federal funds in segregated institutions and programs. In the longer term, revenue sharing would prove an increasing burden on the federal budget.

When it came to civil rights enforcement, Nixon also tried to restore flexibility to the states. He came out against court-ordered busing as a means of integrating public schools and proposed that the federal government should take a less adamant position on race relations. One of his chief domestic advisors, Daniel Patrick Moynihan of Harvard University, summed up the administration attitude when he proposed a policy of ''benign neglect'' in racial matters. The statement outraged liberals and black leaders, but it pleased many moderate or conservative whites, in the South and elsewhere. Nixon also opposed renewal of the Voting Rights Act of 1965, forcing Congress to override his veto. Although Nixon denied that he was trying to please southern voters, his position on civil rights was obviously part of a continuing Republican strategy to gain support in the South.

Nixon's Supreme Court appointments were likewise in the spirit of the New Federalism. The president had found the Warren Court far too liberal and objected to its frequent intrusions into local matters such as education. He was determined to make more conservative appointments to the bench, and when Chief Justice Warren retired in 1969, Nixon named Warren E. Burger, a moderate Republican from Minnesota, to replace him. When a second vacancy occurred that year, he chose Clement Haynsworth, a South Carolinian whose conservatism would have wide appeal in the South. The Senate refused to confirm him, however, citing an earlier conflict of interest. The president then proposed G. Harrold Carswell, another conservative southerner, but many found his qualifications insufficient, and the Senate again withheld confirmation. Nixon was furious and accused the Senate of ''regional discrimination.'' But he then compromised by selecting Harry Blackmun, a moderate from Minnesota, and this time the Senate concurred.

Despite Nixon's New Federalism and his clear gestures to the right, his domestic politics were not wholly conservative, for the president often proved more flexible than his rhetoric would suggest. In 1969 he proposed a Family Assistance Plan that would provide every poor family with $1,600 per year. Liberals found the support payments too meager and conservatives thought them far too generous. The bill died in the Senate, and Nixon did not try to revive it in subsequent sessions.

On the Economic Front Nixon's approach to inflation showed flexibility, too. Between 1967 and 1971 consumer prices rose 21.3 percent, then an alarming figure. The problem of inflation would play havoc with the nation's economy for more than a decade and absorb countless hours of attention from four presidential administrations. This inflation stemmed from several interrelated factors. During the war in Vietnam, President Johnson had refused to increase taxes or curb domestic consumption. As a result, the government borrowed heavily to finance the war, thus raising interest rates. Unbridled production of consumer goods in time of war also led to increases in raw material prices, as well as in the cost of finished goods. A growing balance of payments deficit, along with an increasing corporate debt, further exacerbated the inflationary pressures. Strikes then erupted as workers felt the pinch of rising prices. Their demands for higher wages led employers to raise prices even further, and these increases touched off yet another round of wage and price demands.

Long a foe of economic controls, Nixon gave in to public pressure and froze wages and prices for 90 days beginning on August 15, 1971. This initial freeze was followed by three more months of less stringent controls and then by a six-month period during which the government tried to monitor price and wage increases. Nixon also devalued the dollar by 8.57 percent in order to make American goods more affordable abroad and thus reduce the balance of payments deficit. Later he decided to let the dollar compete against other world currencies and seek its own level in the marketplace, a policy that reversed the 30-year practice of converting foreign currencies into dollars at a fixed rate. In the short run these actions were quite effective and inflation slowed to an annual rate of about 3 percent.

Meanwhile Nixon had to confront another threat to price stability, the rising price of petroleum and all its by-products. Like inflation in general, the increasing price of oil had several causes. Postwar prosperity and the shift from coal- to oil-burning furnaces and power plants had led to an ever-increasing consumption of oil. Domestic supplies also dwindled, in part because federal controls on American crude oil prices discouraged new exploration. Americans accordingly imported more oil from abroad. By 1973, one-third of the nation's oil came from foreign sources, much of it from the Middle East. This growing dependence on Middle Eastern oil was dramatized in October 1973 when oil-producing nations in that region decided to retaliate against the United States because of its continuing support for Israel. Together they formed the Organization of Petroleum Exporting Countries (OPEC) and in October 1973 declared an embargo on oil shipments to the United States. By early 1974 motorists had to wait in long lines outside the few gasoline stations that were able to obtain supplies. Gasoline prices also rose steeply from about 35 cents per gallon in 1973 to 50 cents per gallon less than two years later. The rising price of gasoline and other fuels derived from petroleum could only reinforce inflationary trends.

Nixon responded to the growing energy crisis by lowering the speed limit on interstate highways from 70 to 55 miles per hour. The reduced speeds saved some fuel, and resulted in fewer traffic fatalities, too, and Congress made the new speed limit permanent in 1975. Nixon also supported legislation that permitted an oil pipeline from newly opened Alaskan oil fields to the western states. Finally, he created a new Federal Energy Administration. Unfortunately, most Americans refused to believe that conservation was necessary. They were slow to turn down thermostats in winter and equally resistant to suggestions that they form car pools or refrain from unnecessary driving. At the same time, automobile manufacturers failed to build smaller and more fuel-efficient models, supposing that the consumers' love affair with large ''gas guzzlers'' would continue indefinitely.

Nixon also had to face a growing environmental problem. For decades Americans had polluted lakes, rivers, and oceans, along with the air around them. Assuming that the land contained inexhaustible resources, they had plundered the forests and mines as if there were no tomorrow. Various citizens groups like the Sierra Club, in addition to numerous scientists, had begun to call for greater conservation, combined with massive programs to clean up the natural environment and to safeguard it in the future. In 1970 the president created the Environmental Protection Agency to administer the government's various antipollution programs, but Nixon did not call for new environmental legislation.

Working for Détente   Nixon's foreign policies likewise turned out to be quite pragmatic. Indeed, Nixon had long believed that his greatest abilities lay in the management of foreign affairs, and he was determined to make a lasting mark in this area. Here he enlisted the aid of Henry Kissinger, a Harvard professor and foreign policy advisor to Nelson Rockefeller, who had written several works on nuclear strategy and national defense. When he took office, Nixon named Kissinger his assistant for national security affairs, and in September 1973 Kissinger became secretary of state.

Nixon astounded many on both the right and left when he announced plans for a trip to the People's Republic of China in February 1972. Over the years he had been a leading anti-Communist and had vehemently opposed any move to recognize Communist China, but Nixon and Kissinger believed that the time had come to normalize relations. They also hoped to use better relations with China, then feuding with the Soviets, as a diplomatic lever against Moscow. In addition, Nixon wanted the trip to increase his political standing at home, and the event was carefully orchestrated to take full advantage of television coverage. His talks with Communist Party Chairman Mao Tse-tung and Foreign Minister Chou En-lai did not lead immediately to diplomatic recognition; however, the United States promised to withdraw its forces from Taiwan and to accept, in principle, that Taiwan was part of China. The talks led to further dialogue between the two countries, and in 1978 the United States extended full diplomatic recognition to the People's Republic of China.

There were fears that the Soviets would take the Chinese trip as a calculated slight. Partly in order to neutralize such speculations, Nixon made another well-publicized trip, this time to Moscow, in May 1972. The president held long private talks with Communist Party chief Leonid Brezhnev and before leaving signed a Strategic Arms Limitation Treaty (SALT) that governed the deployment of antiballistic missiles. The two leaders further agreed to recognize the status quo in Berlin, while the East and West German governments subsequently signed treaties recognizing each other and assenting to the division of Germany. One of the most explosive issues of the postwar world was thus defused to the relief of both sides. The diplomatic establishment as well as the press used the word *détente* to label these better relations between East and West. Nixon made a continuing détente one of his top priorities.

Nightmare in Vietnam   Nixon was not so successful when it came to Vietnam. During the 1968 campaign he claimed to have a secret plan for ending the war in an honorable fashion. His plan turned out to be ''Vietnamization,'' a program to build up the South Vietnamese army while gradually withdrawing American troops from Southeast Asia. Meanwhile Nixon hoped for progress at the peace talks that had been established in Paris just before Lyndon Johnson left office, but the North Vietnamese demanded a unilateral withdrawal of American troops and the destruction of the Thieu regime in South Vietnam as a precondition for serious negotiations.

Nixon refused these demands, and in March 1969 he ordered the bombing of Communist supply lines in neighboring Cambodia. Knowing that these air raids would provoke a new wave of antiwar demonstrations, Nixon directed that the operations take place in secret. In April 1970 the president again ordered attacks on Communist forces in Cambodia—this time with American and South Vietnamese ground forces, but now he announced his decision over nationwide television, unleashing a torrent of protests. From one end of the country to the other the college campuses exploded. At Kent State University in Ohio, panicky National Guard troops fired their rifles into a group of rock-throwing students, killing four and seriously wounding nine others. Several days later

Panic and death in Saigon.

two more students were shot and killed at Mississippi's Jackson State University. Students across the nation reacted in fury, occupying administration buildings, boycotting classes, and demonstrating wherever they could. Many colleges simply closed for the balance of the semester in order to avoid further violence.

There was also widespread opposition in Congress. Legislators responded by requiring American troops to withdraw from Cambodia within 30 days, the first formal and effective move by Congress to limit the war in Southeast Asia. In spite of Congress's clear opposition to widening the conflict, Nixon ordered American air support for a South Vietnamese invasion of Laos in February 1971. American bombers similarly pounded North Vietnam daily in an effort to force the Communists to soften their demands at the peace table. The removal of American troops from Vietnam continued, however, and by May 1972 only 69,000 remained.

The withdrawal of American troops greatly demoralized the South Vietnamese, who proved unable to stop Communist advances. In the spring of 1972 an angry but determined Nixon ordered the mining of Haiphong harbor, North Vietnam's principal port, and directed American B-52 bombers to hit heavily populated areas in the North. Then in October 1972 the North Vietnamese, acting under pressure from the Soviets, signaled their willingness to resume serious talks and Nixon called off the bombers. Negotiators in Paris agreed that remaining American troops would leave Vietnam, with Communist forces maintaining their current positions in the field. South Vietnamese president Thieu would stay in power for the time being. Thieu rejected the peace plan

CHAPTER 15: REVOLT AND REACTION

and Nixon resumed heavy bombing over Christmas 1972. In January 1973 both sides finally accepted an agreement that was little different from the one proposed the preceding October, and American participation in the Vietnam War finally came to an end. Over 56,000 Americans had died and more than 300,000 were wounded in the nation's longest war. About a million Vietnamese were killed and millions remained homeless.

It was only a matter of time until the Communists triumphed in South Vietnam. In April 1974 Saigon fell to North Vietnamese and Vietcong forces. The United States had clearly lost the war, but few citizens wanted to admit it; only an entirely new generation could assess the tragic conflict with greater objectivity. Yet it was clear that sending military forces to Southeast Asia had been a costly and sad mistake. Nixon admitted as much in July 1969 during an address on the island of Guam in the Pacific. In what has been labeled the Nixon Doctrine, the president announced that the United States would limit its assistance to Asian and Pacific peoples to economic and military aid, while actual troops would have to come from recipient governments. Vietnam had already proven a bitter lesson, and in his own way, Nixon was willing to accept the limits of American power.

THE IMPERIAL PRESIDENCY

Opposition to the war throughout Nixon's first term angered and frustrated him, and he was increasingly convinced that the nation faced dangerous internal forces. His zeal in combating them, along with attempts to amass more and more power for the executive branch of government, led the country another step closer to what historian Arthur M. Schlesinger, Jr., has called the Imperial Presidency. This exaltation of executive power also led to a series of illegal acts that ended in the president's forced resignation in August 1974. Nixon's campaign for a second term in 1972 figured importantly in his demise.

Nixon Wins Again   In the midst of the final peace negotiations Nixon stood for reelection against Democratic Senator George McGovern of South Dakota. McGovern had chaired a committee of the Democratic party that drew up new rules for the selection of delegates to the national convention, rules that required greater participation for blacks, women, and other minorities. As a result nearly 40 percent of the delegates to the 1972 national convention were female and 14 percent were black, while 3 percent of the delegates were also under 25 years of age. By appealing to these newly ''enfranchised'' groups, McGovern easily won the party's presidential nomination. His most serious contender had been George Wallace, who had decided to seek the Democratic endorsement for his second presidential bid, but Wallace was shot at a suburban shopping mall near Washington, D.C., and had to drop out of the race.

Nixon's nomination proceeded smoothly at a Republican convention that was orchestrated completely by the White House. Spiro Agnew once again took second place on the ticket. In the ensuing campaign Nixon denounced the protesters and critics of American life, but generally remained aloof from the fray and tried to look presidential. McGovern came out as an avowed antiwar candidate and called for an immediate end to the Vietnam conflict. He also promised to continue and extend the liberal programs

THE IMPERIAL PRESIDENCY

371

initiated under Lyndon Johnson. His call for strict limitations on personal income and inheritance alienated many, including far from wealthy blue-collar workers who continued to believe that they or their children might someday strike it rich. McGovern's choice of Senator Thomas Eagleton of Missouri as his running mate also hurt him after it was revealed that Eagleton had been hospitalized several times for severe depression. McGovern said that he backed Eagleton ''a thousand percent,'' but shortly thereafter changed his mind and replaced him with Sargent Shriver. McGovern's initial failure to examine Eagleton's background more thoroughly and then his rapid change of heart made him look incompetent as well as irresolute.

Nixon won the 1972 election with a landslide victory of 47,167,000 popular votes to McGovern's 29,168,000, taking 49 of the 50 states. In historical terms, Nixon's 60.7 percent of the popular vote nearly equaled Roosevelt's 1936 sweep and was higher than Lyndon Johnson's nearly record vote in 1964. The electoral count was an overwhelming 521–17.

Several factors accounted for Nixon's spectacular success at the polls. The highly productive and much publicized trips to China and the Soviet Union elevated the president to the status of a great statesman. Continuing troop withdrawals from Vietnam, along with the resumption of peace talks in October 1972, went a long way toward undermining McGovern's peace platform. Nixon's southern strategy had likewise paid off, giving him all 11 states of the former Confederacy, once a bastion of Democratic strength. Catholics, blue-collar workers, and European ethnics—all formerly mainstays of the Democratic party—also voted Republican in larger numbers than ever before. To some extent this switch reflected their continuing movement into the middle class, but many of them saw Nixon as a patriotic, law-and-order president who would stand up to the protesters and draft dodgers. Nixon's campaign organizers also collected a record $55 million and spent lavishly on television advertising. Later evidence would show that part of this money went to finance unparalleled acts of political sabotage against McGovern forces. These advantages, combined with McGovern's unfortunate image of an indecisive radical, spelled overwhelming victory for Richard Nixon.

Surprisingly, the Nixon sweep did not translate into large Republican gains on Capitol Hill. The party won 12 additional seats in the House but lost two in the Senate. The new House would contain 243 Democrats to 192 Republicans, the Senate 57 Democrats to 43 Republicans. Voters may not have wanted the reforms proposed by George McGovern, but they clearly did not want a Republican Congress to repeal the programs already in place.

Yet another incongruity of the election was the small voter turnout, only 55.7 percent of voting-age citizens bothering to show up at the polls, the lowest percentage since 1948. For many of them, the electoral process had lost its significance, for no matter how they voted it seemed that the nation remained the same.

Exalting the Presidency   If some citizens were alienated or ambivalent, Richard Nixon most certainly was not. He took his landslide election as a personal mandate and set about to achieve certain goals that had gone unrealized during his first term. Among them was a plan to elevate the presidency to new heights by concentrating more authority than ever before in the White House. Nixon, of course, was not alone in seeking to increase the power of the presidency. Since the beginning of the twentieth century, wars, economic emergencies, and the centralizing forces of modern life had led to greater executive authority. Both Truman and Johnson had taken the country into war without congressional consent and the legislators had not done anything to stop them. The Congress had also given the president wide discretion in administering domestic programs. Legislatures are ill-equipped to administer policy, and thus have had no alternative but to give additional duties to the presidential office. Finally, the modern media have given tremendous advantages to the president. The president can command free air time merely by requesting it, while even the most powerful legislators cannot. And when the latter do appear on television, few know who they are or bother to watch.

Some of Nixon's plans fell into the category of executive reorganization. Like several presidents before him, he wanted to streamline the executive branch and make it work more efficiently. Accordingly, he sought to apply modern management techniques to the cabinet and White House staff. Instead of working through his various cabinet secretaries and department heads, Nixon wanted to create four ''general management groups,'' each organized along functional lines. These were Human Resources, Natural Resources, Community Development, and Economic Affairs. Department and agency chiefs would report to the heads of these supradepartments, which functioned somewhat like corporate vice-presidents, and not to the president himself. In one sense, the plan was not unreasonable. The executive branch had grown large and unwieldy, and some kind of supraorganization seemed in order. But such a plan could isolate the president from his constituencies, while concentrating potentially dangerous amounts of power in the hands of men who were loyal only to the president. Although Nixon failed to obtain formal legislative approval for such a reorganization, he did delegate extraordinary authority to his White House chief of staff, H. R. (Bob) Haldeman, and several of his lieutenants. During the second term the White House would also create its own intelligence agency and seek to override congressional appropriations through the illegal impoundment of funds.

Other presidents had impounded funds, but only temporarily in order to expend them in a more orderly or appropriate fashion. Nixon, however, sought to use impoundment as a way to nullify congressional overrides of his own vetoes. In 1972, for example, Congress voted to override the president's veto of a $1 billion water pollution bill. Nixon withheld more than half the money, claiming that he wanted to curb federal spending and thereby reduce inflation, but his action thwarted the unmistakable will of Congress and was clearly unconstitutional. The legislators brought the president's action before the Supreme Court, the justices eventually ordering him to release the funds.

With the election behind him, Nixon was also determined to control the flow of information from the administration to the press. The problem of unauthorized news leaks had plagued a number of presidents, but his methods to combat them led to something of a chain reaction that ended only with the president's resignation from office.

Nixon's first actions against press leaks occurred well before his reelection, when the *New York Times* published stories about the secret bombing of Cambodia in early 1969. Nixon then ordered the FBI to install wiretaps on the telephones of 4 newspeople and 13 administrative aids. The wiretaps clearly violated the Fourth Amendment protection against illegal searches and seizures, but the White House justified them in the name of national security. In any case, the wiretaps failed to turn up any evidence of consequence.

THE IMPERIAL PRESIDENCY

Then in July 1971, the *New York Times* began publishing the so-called Pentagon Papers, a collection of documents that revealed a calculated scheme during the Johnson administration to mislead press and public alike about the war in Vietnam. Nixon feared that the publication of these papers would make the government appear lax and irresponsible in Soviet eyes and thus damage future negotiations. He directed the Justice Department to file suit, asking the courts to enjoin the continuing publication of the Pentagon Papers. Meanwhile he authorized a special White House unit to investigate this and other leaks of classified information. Nicknamed the "plumbers," this wholly illegal group sought to discredit Daniel Ellsberg, a former Defense Department employee who was now accused of having passed the controversial documents to the *New York Times*. Among other activities, they broke into the office of Ellsberg's psychiatrist in hopes of finding evidence with which to discredit the defendant.

In addition to plugging leaks, Nixon tried to bring the press more in line with administrative thinking. He believed that the media were controlled by liberals and that their coverage of the White House was unfairly negative. Vice-President Agnew, who was fond of alliterative phrases, took to the hustings for the administration, denouncing the press as an "elite corps of impudent snobs," and on another occasion calling them "nattering nabobs of negativity." The White House also prepared an "enemies list" that contained the names of 280 individuals who were critical of the administration. In addition to journalists, the list included prominent Democrats and labor leaders. The White House then ordered the IRS to launch special tax audits of these detractors, and the IRS rightly refused. Finally, Nixon asked the Federal Communications Commission (FCC) to review the license of television stations that were allegedly guilty of slanting the news against the administration. Happily, the FCC did not comply.

Watergate   If nothing else, the White House enemies list suggests that Richard Nixon lived in a state of emotional siege, believing that he and his administration were beset on all sides by dangerous foes. In such a mood he authorized Chief of Staff Haldeman to form a Committee to Re-Elect the President (CREEP), an organization that completely bypassed the Republican National Committee. Attorney General John Mitchell resigned his cabinet post in order to head the independent group.

With the $55 million that they raised from private individuals, as well as from various interest groups, CREEP set out to battle the Democrats. With some of these funds they launched a campaign of "dirty tricks" against opposition candidates. Paid operatives mailed out false or misleading campaign literature under the signatures of Democratic contenders, and an espionage team, much like the "plumbers" unit, was formed to investigate press leaks. Under orders from Mitchell, they broke into the offices of the Democratic National Headquarters, housed in Washington's Watergate complex. There they installed bugging devices. When one of their wiretaps failed, they staged a second break-in on June 17, 1972, but were caught by a security guard who promptly summoned the police. What would be called the Watergate affair had thus begun.

From the very first Nixon directed a conspiracy to cover up the Watergate crime. Above all, he did not want courts and public to trace the break-in to CREEP and from there to the White House, for he doubtless feared that exposés of the Watergate operation would lead to revelations of other illegal activities within the administration.

All seemed to go well at first. Nixon authorized bribes to keep the seven Watergate burglars from admitting their connections to CREEP, but defendant James McCord testified that "higher-ups" in the administration were implicated in the break-in, as well as in attempts to cover it up. Meanwhile there were demands for a special prosecutor in the Justice Department to investigate the whole Watergate affair. Nixon acquiesced and Attorney General Elliot Richardson named Archibald Cox of Harvard Law School. In May the Senate convened a televised investigation of the scandal, chaired by Democrat Sam Ervin of North Carolina.

At this point the whole case began to unravel. Former presidential counsel John Dean testified that Nixon had been involved in the cover-up from the start. The Ervin Committee also discovered that the president was in the habit of making secret tape recordings of conversations in the oval office. (An electronic device, it appeared, automatically activated a concealed tape recorder whenever anyone spoke.) The committee then subpoenaed several tapes that they thought might confirm the president's role in the cover-up, and so did Special Prosecutor Cox.

Nixon countered with a proposal to allow conservative Senator John Stennis of Mississippi to review the requested tapes and submit synopses to Cox and the Ervin committee. When Cox refused to accept the compromise, Nixon ordered Attorney General Richardson to dismiss the special prosecutor. Richardson himself resigned, as did his deputy William Ruckelhaus, rather than fire Cox. Finally, the third in command at Justice, Solicitor General Robert Bork, issued the dismissal order. Public reaction to this so-called Saturday night massacre was overwhelmingly against the president. To compound the matter, the White House denied that nine of the tapes existed at all and said that three other tapes contained blank spots that ran for a total of $18\frac{1}{2}$ minutes. Experts later testified that the tapes had been erased.

If this were not enough, Vice-President Agnew was charged with income tax evasion and with accepting kickbacks from contractors while governor of Maryland. He resigned from office, and through a special arrangement with the Justice Department, he pleaded no contest to the tax evasion charges. In accordance with the recently ratified Twenty-fifth Amendment, Nixon appointed Representative Gerald R. Ford of Michigan to replace Agnew, and the Senate quickly concurred.

Nixon, too, ran afoul of the IRS when it was discovered that he had illegally backdated the donation of his vice-presidential papers to the National Archives in order to receive a tax deduction that was no longer permissible. Other revelations showed that the government had spent tens of thousands of dollars improving the president's private home at San Clemente, California. Some of the work could be considered essential for security, but much of it was purely cosmetic.

By early 1974 the Republican press as well as influential Republicans on Capitol Hill began to desert the president. In February the House of Representatives voted overwhelmingly to authorize the Judiciary Committee to hold impeachment hearings on Nixon, and in July the Supreme Court ordered the president to surrender all the tapes that had been subpoenaed. In August the released tapes proved without question that Nixon had helped to engineer the cover-up from start to finish. They also showed him to be intemperate in his language. Almost simultaneously the House Judiciary Committee drew up three counts of impeachment, charging Nixon with obstruction of justice, abuse of power, and unconstitutional defiance of congressional subpoenas. Impeachment in the

House as well as conviction in the Senate were almost certain. On August 8 Nixon resigned from office and flew off to his home in San Clemente. At noon Vice-President Ford took the oath of office and became the thirty-seventh president of the United States.

The Watergate affair and the president's forced resignation shook the nation to the core. Some took comfort from the fact that the "system had worked," that justice had prevailed in the end, but the nation had had a close brush with political disaster. The recent defeat in Vietnam, the widespread domestic violence over the past decade, and Nixon's forced resignation would leave a bitter taste for years to come. Public demonstration and mistrust of government in general would linger for the rest of the decade and affect American politics profoundly.

BIOGRAPHICAL SKETCH

JOAN BAEZ · *born 1941*

More than any other musician during the 1960s Joan Baez represents the powerful link between folk music and social protest. Born in Staten Island, New York, Joan was of mixed ethnic roots, with a Mexican father and a mother of Scots-Irish background. Joan grew up in several communities around the country, as her physicist father moved to a variety of teaching and research institutions.

Joan experienced racial prejudice firsthand when neighbors shunned her because of her dark complexion. "As far as they knew," she wrote, "we were niggers." She was later rejected by the Mexican-American community because she could not speak Spanish.

Joan rebelled against parental wishes that she go to college, dropping out of Boston University after only one month of classes. She was equally untutored in music. A gifted soprano voice, combined with techniques picked up from other folksingers, gave her a sincere and natural sound that appealed to youthful audiences.

Baez began performing in coffeehouses around Harvard Square in the late 1950s, but it was her "surprise" appearance at the Newport Folk Festival in the summer of 1959 that

won her national attention and led to her initial record album in 1960. Soon thereafter she gave the first of many successful college tours.

Students and others were attracted by the pure, liquid tones that seemed to spill out effortlessly as Baez sang one selection after another. Her unaffected manner and casual dress were also compelling to a generation that prided itself on sincerity. They also applauded the social criticism inherent in so many of her songs.

376 CHAPTER 15: REVOLT AND REACTION

Offstage Baez became increasingly active in the civil rights movement. She performed with Bob Dylan during the March on Washington in August 1963 and the following year led about a thousand Berkeley students in a 15-hour occupation of the university's administration building.

By the mid-1960s Baez was in the vanguard of protests against the war in Vietnam. She helped picket the White House and encouraged young men to resist the draft. She also refused to pay the 60 percent of her federal income taxes that went for military purposes. In March 1968 she pointedly married a draft resister, David Harris, who was shortly sentenced to three years in prison. Baez herself was arrested and jailed several times for her protests. And in December 1972 she went to Hanoi to denounce American participation in the war.

Despite the emergence of the black power and other militant movements in the late 1960s, Baez remained faithful to her belief in nonviolence, claiming Mahatma Gandhi as her inspiration and guide. Her California-based Institute for the Study of Non-Violence, which she founded in 1965, continued to teach a pacifist philosophy, and in the early 1970s it also began to take up energy and environmental questions.

Among Baez's most popular recordings were "We Shall Overcome," which became something of an anthem for peaceful protesters. Also important were "What Happened to the Rain," a song about nuclear fallout, and "All the Weary Mothers of the World," whose words looked forward to the day when mothers, farmers, laborers, and other benign groups would come together to forge a peaceful world.

Baez has not been without her critics. Some on the right have denounced her as a dangerous radical or Communist. Others have called her a hypocrite for lashing out at capitalist society while reaping hundreds of thousands of dollars from concerts and recordings. Although Baez has made a great deal of money from her singing, she has often refused lucrative offers, insisting that her music must remain a vehicle of social protest. Now in her mid-forties, Baez remains committed to the causes of peace, social justice, and environmental integrity.

SUGGESTED READINGS

For an overview of this period, see Judith and Stewart Albert, eds., *The Sixties Papers: Documents of a Rebellious Decade* (1984); Ronald Berman, *America in the Sixties* (1968); Peter N. Carroll, *It Seemed Like Nothing Happened: The Tragedy and Promise of American Life in the 1970's* (1982); William L. O'Neill, *Coming Apart: An Informal History of America in the 1960's* (1971); and Sohnya Sayers et al., eds., *The Sixties Without Apology* (1984).

There is a growing body of literature on the various liberation movements during the late 1960s and early 1970s. More general works include Edward D. Baccionocco, Jr., *The New Left in America: Reform to Revolution, 1956 to 1970* (1974), and Irwin Unger, *The Movement: A History of the American New Left, 1959–1972* (1974). On the black power movement in particular, see Benjamin Muse, *The American Negro Revolution: From Violence to Black Power* (1968); Raymond L. Hall, *Black Separatism in the United States* (1978); and Alphonso Pickney, *Red, Black, and Green* (1976). The Chicano movement is treated in Alfredo Mirandé, *The Chicano Experience* (1985); Joan W. Moore, *Mexican Americans* (1970); and Ellwyn R. Stoddard, *Mexican Americans* (1973). On Native Americans there are Vine Deloria, Jr., *God is Red* (1973) and *Custer Died for Your Sins* (1969); Helen Hertzberg, *The Search for an American Indian Identity* (1971); Andrew F. Rolle, *The American Indians: Their History and Culture* (1972); and Stan Steiner, *The*

SUGGESTED READINGS

New Indians (1968). For the women's liberation movement, see Barbara Deckard, *The Women's Movement* (1975); Sara Evans, *Personal Politics: The Roots of Women's Liberation in the Civil Rights Movement and the New Left* (1979); Sarah S. Schramm, *Plow Women Rather than Reapers: An Intellectual History of Feminism in the United States* (1980); Gayle and Graham Yates, *What Women Want: The Ideas of the Movement* (1975).

On the sexual revolution and the changing nature of the American family there are John D'Emilio, *Sexual Politics, Sexual Communities, 1940–1970* (1983); Betty Gorburg, *The Changing Family* (1973); Christopher Lasch, *Heaven in a Heartless World: The Family Besieged* (1977); Salvatore J. Liata and Robert D. Peterson, *Historical Perspectives on Homosexuality* (1981); and Paul Robinson, *The Modernization of Sex* (1976). A revealing statistical study of changing sexual attitudes is Daniel Yankelovich, *The New Morality: A Profile of American Youth in the 70's* (1974).

There are a number of excellent studies on the youth movements and countercultures: Morris Dickstein, *Gates of Eden* (1977); Kenneth Keniston, *Youth and Dissent* (1971); and Theodore Roszak, *The Making of a Counter Culture* (1969). Studies of higher education during this period are Robert S. Morrison, ed., *The Contemporary University: U.S.A.* (1966), and Joel Spring, *The Sorting Machine: National Educational Policy Since 1945* (1976). An anthropological overview of the counterculture and other changes in national life is Marvin Harris, *America Now: The Anthropology of a Changing Culture* (1981).

Insights into popular music in the 1960s and 1970s may be found in Julian Messner, *The Super Stars of Rock: Their Lives and Their Music* (1980); Terence J. O'Grady, *The Beatles: A Musical Revolution* (1983); and John Orman, *The Politics of Rock* (1984). On art there are Amaya Mario, *Pop Art and After* (1965), and Lucy R. Lippard, *Pop Art* (1966). On social themes in American movies see Peter Roffman and Jim Purdy, *The Hollywood Social Problem Film* (1981).

Several works take up the subject of white ethnic groups and their reactions against the counterculture and the various power movements. Among them are Nathan Glazer and Daniel P. Moynihan, *Beyond the Melting Pot* (1970); Richard Krickus, *Pursuing the American Dream: White Ethnics and the New Populism* (1976); and Michael Novak, *The Rise of Unmeltable Ethnics* (1972). On blue-collar discontent in particular there is Stanley Aronowitz, *False Promises: The Shaping of American Working Class Consciousness* (1974). Concentrating on Italians are Richard D. Alba, *Italian Americans: The Twilight of Ethnicity* (1985), and Luciano J. Iorizzo and Salvatore Mondello, *The Italian Americans* (1980).

General studies of politics during the Nixon years are Kirkpatrick Sale, *Power Shift: The Rise of the Southern Rim and Its Challenge to the Eastern Establishment* (1975); Richard M. Scammon and Benjamin J. Wattenberg, *The Real Majority* (1970); and Arthur M. Schlesinger, Jr., *The Imperial Presidency* (1973).

On the Nixon administration per se are Rowland Evans, Jr. and Robert D. Novak, *Nixon in the White House* (1971); Richard Nixon, *RN: The Memoirs of Richard Nixon* (1978); and Jonathan Schell, *The Time of Illusion: An Historical and Reflective Account of the Nixon Era* (1975). Perspective on the growth of presidential authority under Nixon may be found in Otis L. Graham, Jr., *Toward a Planned Society: From Roosevelt to Nixon* (1976). Nixon's environmental policies should be considered in the light of such works as Barry Commoner's *The Closing Circle* (1971), and Victor Ferkiss, The *Future of Technology* (1974). A particularly dismal view of the environmental and economic crises of the 1970s is Robert L. Heilbroner, *An Inquiry into the Human Prospect* (1974).

The most thorough accounts of the Watergate affair are by investigative reporters Carl Bernstein and Bob Woodward: *All the President's Men* (1974) and *The Final Days* (1976). Books on the affair by Nixon staffers include John Dean's *Blind Ambition: The White House Years* (1976) and H. R. Haldeman's *The Ends of Power* (1978). There is also Theodore H. White's *Breach of Faith: The Fall of Richard Nixon* (1975). Several other studies try to use psychological insights to explain Nixon's behavior as president. Among these are Fawn Brodie, *Richard Nixon: The*

Shaping of His Character (1983), and Gary Wills, *Nixon Agonistes* (1971). On Agnew's fall from power is Richard M. Cohen and Jules Witcover, *A Heartbeat Away: The Investigation and Resignation of Spiro T. Agnew* (1974).

Overviews of Nixon's foreign policies are Henry Brandon, *The Retreat of American Power* (1972); Seyom Brown, *The Crisis of Power: An Interpretation of U.S. Policy During the Kissinger Years* (1979); and Tad Szulc, *The Illusion of Peace: Foreign Policy in the Nixon Years* (1978). These should be read beside Henry Kissinger's *Years of Upheaval* (1982). On Vietnam in particular there is Weldon Brown, *The Last Chopper: The Denouement of the American Role in Vietnam, 1963–1975* (1976); Lew Y. Guenter, *America in Vietnam* (1978); Alexander Kendrick, *The Wound Within: America in the Vietnam Years, 1945–1974* (1974); and the pertinent chapters in George C. Herring, *America's Longest War: The United States and Vietnam, 1950–1975* (1979).

16

Crisis of Confidence

The six years following Richard Nixon's resignation proved a difficult and frustrating time for the American people. Memories of Watergate remained fresh as Gerald Ford pardoned his predecessor for all crimes he may have committed, thereby saving Nixon from an agonizing trial and possible jail sentence. In the process Ford lost the trust of many citizens and convinced others that government was essentially corrupt. A seeming inability to cope with major domestic problems also shook voter confidence. Neither Ford nor Carter could tame skyrocketing inflation, harness unemployment, or find acceptable solutions for the continuing energy crisis.

In foreign affairs there were a few encouraging signs. Ford and Carter worked out a second SALT agreement with the Soviets, and in the Middle East Carter scored a significant breakthrough when he convinced Egypt and Israel to settle their most serious differences. But in Iran Carter's vacillation helped lead to the capture of the American embassy in Teheran and the seizure of more than 50 American citizens. The resulting hostage crisis was yet another blow to the American ego, forcing the nation to realize that it was no longer omnipotent in world affairs.

Under the circumstances it seemed hardly the time to celebrate 200 years of independence, yet the bicentennial arrived and millions enjoyed the colorful and varied festivities. For some, the observances served as a reminder that the republic had survived numerous difficulties in the past and had often emerged stronger and more confident than before.

THE TRIALS OF GERALD FORD

The man who succeeded Richard Nixon in August 1974 was the first chief executive in the country's history who had assumed the office without being elected president or vice-

President Gerald R. Ford

president—Ford claiming only the electoral support of several hundred thousand Michigan constitutents who had sent him to Congress. Born in 1913, Ford had grown up in the politically conservative community of Grand Rapids, Michigan. He played football during his four years at the University of Michigan, earned a law degree at Yale, and saw combat as a naval officer in World War II. After the war he returned to Grand Rapids to practice law, and in 1948 won a seat in the U.S. House of Representatives. For the next 23 years he represented Michigan's Fifth District on Capitol Hill. As a loyal party member from a safe constituency, Ford eventually became House Minority Leader, with hopes of someday moving into the Speaker's chair. Nixon selected him as vice-president because of his conservative record and his reputation for party loyalty. He also knew that Ford could win quick confirmation in the Senate, thus sparing the embattled White House further criticism from an already hostile legislature.

Ford took the presidential oath following Nixon's resignation, confident that he could handle the job after nearly a quarter century in public life. He was well liked in Congress, where he was known as an honest and hardworking legislator. His mature and conventional appearance, combined with his calm manner of speaking and upper midwestern accent, added to the new president's image of decency and dependability.

THE TRIALS OF GERALD FORD

Ford Pardons Nixon   In the first weeks of his presidency Ford received high marks from press and public alike. He presided over a smooth transition, keeping the Nixon cabinet for the time being and assuring foreign leaders that there would be no abrupt changes in direction. Yet the question of Nixon's legal status threatened to undermine the administration from the beginning. Ford found himself spending an inordinate amount of time on the question, as the Justice Department, the press, and even Nixon's attorneys looked to the new president for answers. At his first press conference on August 28, 1974, reporters deluged him with questions about Nixon's fate. If this were not enough, Ford learned a week later in a private communication from Special Prosecutor Leon Jaworski, who had been appointed following Cox's dismissal, that a trial date for Nixon was at least a year away, and that subsequent appeals could drag the case out for several years more. Ford found the situation untenable, and sometime in early September he decided to pardon Richard Nixon; only then, he reasoned, could the people put Watergate behind them.

The most important obstacles to a quick solution were the Nixon papers and tapes. Presidents had traditionally taken such materials when they left office and Nixon clearly wanted them for his defense as well as for writing his memoirs, but the Justice Department also needed them for its continuing investigations. Administration lawyers worked out a compromise that gave both Nixon and the government access to the materials. They also hoped to exact some admission of guilt from Nixon, but he refused to make such a confession. In a written statement he would only go so far as to "regret" the "pain and anguish my mistakes over Watergate have caused the nation. . . ." In the end a Ford emissary did get a weak verbal assent from Nixon that accepting a pardon "constituted an admission of guilt."

On Sunday September 8, President Ford went before television cameras to announce that he was pardoning Richard Nixon. In a firm yet apologetic tone he told viewers that he could no longer "prolong the bad dreams that continue to reopen a chapter that is closed. . . . My conscience tells me it is my duty not merely to proclaim domestic tranquility but to use every means that I have to ensure it. . . ."

The announcement unleashed a torrent of criticism. Just before the telecast Ford's press secretary Gerald terHorst resigned in protest. To pardon Nixon while continuing to prosecute his subordinates struck terHorst as contradictory and unjust, as did Ford's refusal to pardon Vietnam draft resisters. Others spoke of a double standard of justice. Common offenders, they observed, must suffer the full penalty of the law, while influential people received special treatment. Still others suspected a secret deal between the two presidents just before Nixon left office. Ford strenuously denied it, but the rumors persisted. Finally, critics argued that many details of the Watergate scandal would have been revealed in court; now they would remain buried forever. Hoping to rid himself of a debilitating issue and spare everyone the shame of watching a former president stand trial, Ford would be haunted by the pardon for the rest of his term.

Vice-President Rockefeller   Another major decision early in the Ford administration also stirred up a hornet's nest of controversy—the selection of a new vice-president. Ford considered several names, but the choice narrowed to two: George Bush, then chairman of the Republican National Committee, and the immensely rich former governor of New York, Nelson Rockefeller. After weighing their credentials, Ford chose Rockefeller. He had had extensive experience as a public servant and possessed wide knowledge of foreign and domestic affairs. Besides, Rockefeller's reputation as a liberal Republican might add balance to the party ticket if Ford decided to run for president in 1976.

Yet the choice of Nelson Rockefeller may have hurt Ford in the end, for the Rockefeller name was still synonymous in many minds with the bloated Standard Oil trust and tainted wealth. Meanwhile Senate confirmation hearings revealed that Rockefeller had given large monetary gifts to former employees like Henry Kissinger, that he had forgiven equally generous loans to other friends and associates, and that he himself had underpaid his federal income taxes. Since Kissinger was still secretary of state, Rockefeller's previous gifts raised questions over a possible conflict of interest between the two former associates; nor did Rockefeller's controversial divorce and quick remarriage sit well with some. Rockefeller finally admitted to having a number of faults and his candor helped to win confirmation, but the Senate revelations did little to boost Ford's image. Over the next two years Rockefeller would also incur the increasing ire of party conservatives. Nevertheless, Ford made extensive use of Rockefeller, placing him in charge of several investigations and policy committees. In addition, Rockefeller and his wife became the first couple to occupy an official residence for the vice-president, located on the grounds of the Naval Observatory. Formerly vice-presidents had provided their own housing in the capital.

Voter Disgust   The Nixon pardon and continuing anger over the whole Watergate fiasco did not bode well for the Republicans in the 1974 congressional elections. Ford did his best to campaign for Republican candidates, but to no avail. Only 38 percent of the electorate bothered to go to the polls, the lowest turnout for an off-year election since World War II, a sure sign of voter apathy and disgust. The Democrats added 49 more seats to their House majority and picked up 5 seats in the Senate. When the new Congress convened in January 1975, there were 291 Democrats to 144 Republicans in the House, and 61 Democrats to 38 Republicans in the Senate, with one vacancy. Voter registrations were more than two to one in favor of the Democrats, and there was widespread talk about the death of the Republican party. The efforts of Richard Nixon and others to create a new Republican majority of moderate-to-conservative voters now seemed utterly hopeless; nor did the huge Democratic majorities on Capitol Hill offer much encouragement for Ford's legislative programs.

Economic Woes   Beyond his party's dismal showings, Ford had to face serious economic problems from the moment he took office. The inflation rate was higher than at any time since the end of World War II. In the past inflation had generally been associated with low unemployment, but contrary to conventional wisdom, this episode of rising prices was accompanied by a high rate of joblessness, causing some economists to dub the phenomenon "stagflation." Whatever one called it, the statistics were grim. In September 1974 annual inflation was running at 11.5 percent, while unemployment reached 7.1 percent by year's end.

Nixon had largely ignored the economic situation during his last troubled months in office and now there were loud cries for action. But the conservative Ford rejected wage and price controls and instead asked Congress to enact a 5 percent surcharge on

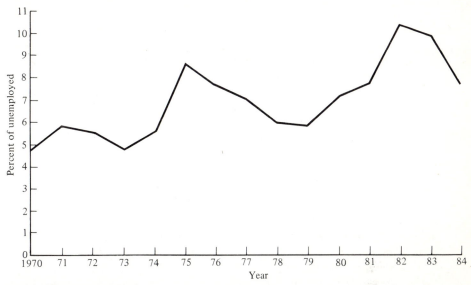

Unemployment, 1970–1984.

income taxes and to cut spending. Beyond that he urged voluntary actions to fight inflation: Businesses should hold the line on prices; labor should refrain from making large wage demands; and consumers should limit their purchases and conserve energy. Wearing a lapel button with the motto WIN (short for Whip Inflation Now), Ford implored Americans to cooperate. Then to combat unemployment he proposed investment tax credits for business and enlarged unemployment benefits for the jobless. Democrats countered with a measure to create thousands of public service jobs and proposed mandatory price controls in certain markets. The result was something of a compromise. Congress passed an emergency jobs bill and extended unemployment benefits, while rejecting the president's surcharge and scaling down his investment tax credits. But the Democrats' price control measure also failed to pass. At the same time Ford's WIN campaign aroused considerable ridicule, and an administration plan to distribute millions of WIN buttons died before it really began. Administration spending cuts did help to curb inflation; by July 1975 the annual inflation rate was around 7 percent. But unemployment rose to over 9 percent, signaling the worst recession since the 1930s.

The Energy Debate The Ford administration recognized that increasing energy costs were responsible for many recent price rises. The president endorsed Nixon's proposal to make the United States independent of foreign energy sources and advocated greater use of coal, nuclear power, and synthetic fuels. He also urged larger import fees for foreign oil, increased conservation, and decontrol of petroleum prices to bring them more in line with market realities and discourage waste. Congressional Democrats countered with an elaborate scheme of higher gasoline taxes, mandatory rationing, and tax incentives for energy conservation. But fearing adverse public reactions, they failed to enact their program into law. They did vote to continue price controls on oil and natural gas for the next three years, after which prices would be permitted to rise gradually.

Ford's own reluctance to intervene boldly in the economy was heightened in the summer of 1975 when New York City could no longer sell bonds and found itself on the verge of bankruptcy. A number of factors had contributed to the crisis, including financial mismanagement, increasing welfare costs, wage demands from municipal unions, and a declining tax base brought about by the continuing flight of individuals and businesses into the suburbs, a scenario that many other large cities confronted. Desperate, New York authorities appealed to the federal government for aid. At first Ford refused but then compromised with Congress and signed a $2.3 billion loan bill.

THE NATION'S BICENTENNIAL

The nation's economic woes and fresh memories of the Watergate scandal unfortunately coincided with the two-hundredth anniversary of national independence; nor was there any focus for the bicentennial celebration, as there had been a hundred years before when the country had feted its centennial with a world's fair in Philadelphia. Instead, many cities decided to reclaim historic neighborhoods or otherwise spruce up their communities for the bicentennial year. In Philadelphia, for instance, city fathers banned automobile traffic on a segment of Chestnut Street near Independence Hall, transforming it into a tree-lined pedestrian walkway. And in Philadelphia, as elsewhere, there were historical pageants, street-corner skits, and roving musicians. In Boston the high point

Youthful fife and drum corps celebrates the nation's bicentennial, July 4, 1976.

of the Indepencence Day celebration was a Boston Pops concert along the Charles River, accompanied by a spectacular fireworks display, while New Yorkers thrilled to a parade of tall sailing ships on the Hudson River. And in smaller communities throughout the land there were parades, picnics, athletic contests, and the best fireworks anyone could remember.

Nevertheless, there was an unmistakable nostalgia that bicentennial summer, a longing for simpler, better, more honest days that existed more in memory than in reality. The America of 1876 or even 1776 seemed preferable to many whose faith in the nation and themselves had been shaken by Vietnam, Watergate, and the violent upheavals at home during the late 1960s and early 1970s. But beside these romantic longings there was also a more sophisticated historical consciousness, a realization in more citizens than ever before that the present had flowed out of the past, that the past had quite literally given birth to the present and pointed the way to the future. Placing the country's present dilemmas in a broad historical context could only help the American people to know themselves better and to profit from their individual and collective experiences.

THE BICENTENNIAL ELECTION

In addition, 1976 was an election year. Ford had announced shortly after assuming office that he would stand for election in his own right. Not to do so, he reasoned, would make him a lame duck president lacking the power to threaten and encourage through the promise of patronage in a second administration. But Ford confronted a formidable Republican opponent in former California Governor Ronald Reagan. As spokesman for the most conservative wing of the party, Reagan criticized détente as a dangerous and unwarranted surrender to the Communists. He called for a hard line against the Soviets, a buildup of American arms, and a reassertion of national pride and self-assurance.

Reagan and Ford went on to battle it out in the primaries, with the nomination in doubt even as the Republicans assembled for their convention. Then Reagan blundered by announcing Senator Richard Schweiker of Pennsylvania as his choice for vice-president. Schweiker was an outspoken liberal and his selection angered conservatives, while other Republicans denounced the move as an opportunistic bid to attract more moderate Republicans to the Reagan cause. For both reasons the plan backfired and Ford won the nomination. Ford took Senator Robert Dole of Kansas as his running mate, having jettisoned the controversial Rockefeller.

The "Amateur" from Georgia Former Georgia Governor Jimmy Carter surprised political experts by breaking through his personal and regional obscurity to defeat all the leading contenders for the nomination. Several more prominent Democrats had battled him in the early primaries—Indiana's Senator Birch Bayh, Kennedy in-law Sargent Shriver, and Alaska's Representative Morris Udall among them. But their campaigns all stalled before the superb planning of the Carter campaign. Late entries by Idaho's Senator Frank Church and California's Governor Jerry Brown also failed to stop the Carter bandwagon.

Born in 1924 near Plains, Georgia, James Earl Carter descended from a long line of successful farmers. Although not of the wealthy planter class, the Carters had done well through farming, land speculation, and small business ventures, and in Carter's childhood they were the most influential family in the area. Jimmy, as he insisted upon being called in politics as well as in private life, turned out to be a bright and ambitious child. He won an appointment to the U.S. Naval Academy shortly after Pearl Harbor and spent seven years in the Navy following graduation, the last year as an officer in the nuclear submarine program. His father's death in 1953 took him back to Plains, and for the next decade Carter threw himself into the family enterprises, cultivating several thousand acres of land and building up a peanut warehouse. He won a seat in the Georgia senate in 1962 and launched an unsuccessful bid for the Georgia governorship in 1966. He tried again four years later and won. During both campaigns he posed as the innocent outsider who would bring honesty and businesslike efficiency to the job.

As governor of Georgia and later during the presidential campaign, Carter made no secret of his strong Baptist faith. Some critics dismissed him as some kind of rural fundamentalist, but he had read deeply into Christian theology and was particularly fond of Reinhold Niebuhr. Like Niebuhr, Carter held that the Christian must do his best to establish justice in a sinful world.

In addition to his religious faith, Carter believed that the good politician should try to accommodate various points of view. He almost always saw both sides of any question and frequently addressed two or more perspectives himself in an attempt to sort out the options for his listeners. This approach helped him win support from otherwise conflicting segments of the population, but it would later confuse a public that wanted its officials to present simple issues and even simpler solutions.

The contest between Ford and Carter was marked by its general lack of excitement. Ford decided to stay in the White House most of the time and look presidential, and because he frequently appeared amidst the roses outside his office, the press soon labeled his efforts the ''rose garden'' campaign. Ford as well as Carter tried to portray themselves as wholly honest men who would bring greater economy and efficiency to government, but Carter, who had never held federal office, had a distinct advantage. He did not have to run on a previous presidential record and could play the political novice, castigating the Ford administration for not disciplining the bureaucracy or cutting back sufficiently on government expenditures.

If there was an exciting moment in the campaign, it came when *Playboy* magazine released a recent interview with candidate Carter. The ''born again'' Georgian admitted that he had ''looked on a lot of women with lust [and] committed adultery in my heart many times.'' But he was sure that God had forgiven him for it. Extreme moralists were appalled, while some urban sophisticates mocked his many years of marital fidelity and pious assumptions of forgiveness.

Shortly thereafter it was Ford's turn to blunder. During his second televised debate with Carter, the president exclaimed that there was ''no Soviet domination of Eastern Europe, and there never will be under a Ford administration.'' More alert viewers wondered whether Ford needed a lesson in geography or if he had been utterly asleep during the 30 years since the end of World War II. Such a misstatement, combined with Ford's tendency to trip over objects in his path or even to stumble over his own feet, completed the image of a well-meaning but bumbling president. Then Secretary of Agriculture Earl Butz greatly embarrassed the administration by telling a joke that contained obscene remarks about blacks. He had told the story in private, but an alert reporter turned it into his editor, who then published it.

In the end the candidates' blunders probably cancelled each other out and the election results were quite close. Carter led in the popular count 40,827,000 to 39,145,000; the electoral college tally was 297 to 240. Ford took 27 states to Carter's 23 (plus the District of Columbia), but Carter won more of the larger states. Ford ran best among whites, and won every state west of the Mississippi. Carter's strength lay in the South, in the large cities of the North, and among blacks, Hispanics, and other minorities. The Carter victory made him the first president from the Deep South since the Civil War, an indication that lingering sectional hostility was largely dead.

CHALLENGES AT HOME

Common Man in the White House Jimmy Carter, the self-proclaimed outsider, was determined to lend a new personal tone to the presidency. Spurning tradition, he wore a plain business suit to the inauguration instead of the usual black tails and gray morning trousers. And in a surprise departure from custom he and wife Rosalynn walked from Capitol Hill to the White House following the swearing-in. In the early years of his administration he forbade the Marine band to play "Hail to the Chief" at ceremonial functions, delivered television addresses while attired in a sweater and slacks, and sold the presidential yacht. He also directed subordinates not to drive around Washington in chauffeured limousines. Jimmy Carter of Plains, Georgia, would have nothing to do with the Imperial Presidency, and he believed that most Americans would applaud his bid for

President Jimmy Carter in his favorite casual attire.

simplicity. Yet every president since George Washington had known that the public craved a bit of pomp and circumstance. Deep down, most men and women did not want to believe that the president was merely an ordinary citizen, but a person of special qualities who could provide a reassuring presence and lead the country through times of stress. By striking a common note, Carter lost the respect of numerous voters.

The administration's amateur stance was reinforced by the many Georgians Carter brought to Washington as his assistants. These included Chief of Staff Hamilton Jordan, Attorney General Griffin Bell, and Budget Director Bert Lance. This "Georgia Mafia," as some called them, could be counted on for loyalty, but they were woefully short on Washington experience. And this inexperience proved most telling in the administration's initial dealings with Congress. Carter operatives failed to consult key legislators on important bills, ignored customary rules of senatorial courtesy, and frequently invited contempt for their downright ignorance of how things were supposed to be done.

The Continuing Energy Crisis   Such strained relations with Congress were unfortunate, given the need for action on energy. In this area Carter inherited numerous headaches from the last two administrations. He was frequently more courageous in addressing these issues than his predecessors, having great faith in the power of moral persuasion. If he explained the situation frankly and called upon the public to do the right thing, then surely the people and the Congress would respond with appropriate action. Carter was to be badly disappointed.

The energy question in particular seemed to elude him at every turn. An unusually harsh winter in 1977, with record snowfalls and subzero temperatures throughout the North, appeared to give Carter an excellent opportunity to address the energy issue. Fuel shortages forced schools and manufacturing plants to close, throwing 1.6 million workers off the job. In response Carter delivered a series of televised speeches in which he asked the nation to declare a "moral equivalent of war" on the energy crisis. He asked citizens to conserve energy as never before and Congress to enact a tax package that penalized energy waste and encouraged conservation. He also advocated a federal Department of Energy. Entrenched interests sabotaged all but a new Department of Energy. But the president did not give up, and early in 1978 he again pressed hard for passage of his energy package. By year's end Congress had passed the essential legislation, though much diluted from what Carter had wanted in most instances. The so-called conversion scheme used both penalties and inducements to get electrical utilities to burn more coal and less oil or natural gas. Another bill provided fines for auto manufacturers who did not meet federal mileage requirements. Natural gas prices were to be deregulated gradually, and tax credits were offered to individuals and businesses that installed solar collectors, insulation, and other energy-saving devices.

The difficulty of providing sufficient energy took on a new dimension on March 30, 1979, when a nuclear reactor at Three Mile Island near Harrisburg, Pennsylvania, overheated and almost resulted in a "melt down" of the reactor core, an event that would have sent deadly radiation into the surrounding countryside. Fearing such an outcome, 100,000 residents evacuated the area until the reactor was brought under control almost two weeks later. The near disaster at Three Mile Island undermined an already dubious public confidence in nuclear power and cast grave doubts on the future of nuclear energy.

CHALLENGES AT HOME 389

Aerial view of nuclear reactors at Three Mile Island near Harrisburg, Pennsylvania.

While still reeling in horror over the Three Mile Island disaster, the country was beset with a massive gasoline shortage as the summer began and OPEC announced another round of oil price increases. Motorists panicked and flocked to service stations just to "top off" partly filled tanks. Tempers flared in the long lines that led to the gasoline pumps. More intemperate customers used fists, knives, and even guns to contend for dwindling supplies. In Levittown, Pennsylvania, where residents were virtually imprisoned in their bedroom suburb without the use of a car, angry drivers went on a rampage, attacking and burning several service stations. Meanwhile the nation's independent truckers struck to protest the high price of diesel fuel. Despite the panic, Congress refused to give Carter the authority to ration gasoline. Several states took the matter into their own hands with "odd-even" plans that required motorists to purchase gasoline on alternate days, depending on whether their license tags ended with odd or even numbers.

Escalating energy costs were bound to fuel inflation, and by the end of 1979 the annual inflation rate was at 13.3 percent. Unemployment also remained high. Carter initially planned to combat joblessness with a tax rebate to individuals, along with an

390 CHAPTER 16: CRISIS OF CONFIDENCE

increase in government spending, but he backed away from both when Federal Reserve Chairman Arthur Burns warned that such actions would only make inflation worse. Carter then proposed voluntary wage guidelines, urging labor to demand no more than a 6.5 percent raise in wages and business to keep price increases below 7 percent. Such exhortations did no more good than Ford's WIN buttons, and his failure to control inflation would prove a growing political handicap.

Billygate and Other Scandals   While President Carter was trying to deal with energy and the economy, a series of minor scandals further marred the administration's credibility. Particularly embarrassing were the antics of Carter's younger brother Billy. The press had found a new folk hero in Billy during the campaign, and all the attention proved too much for the younger Carter. For reporters as well as tourists, Billy played the easygoing ''red-neck,'' guzzling beer outside his gas station in Plains and telling deprecating jokes on himself and his family. He soon became a popular speaker who commanded high fees, at the same time lending his name to a new brew called Billy Beer. Then Billy became a paid agent for Libyan oil companies, and Congress began to investigate a possible conflict of interest. By then the Carter brother had become an alcoholic. He went into a hospital to break his drinking habit and cooperated fully with the investigators. The president himself gave voluntary testimony, and the committee concluded that Billy had not tried to influence the president in any way on behalf of the Libyans.

The accusations against Budget Director Bert Lance were even more damaging. Bank examiners charged that Lance, an Atlanta bank president before joining the Carter administration, had permitted members of his family to overdraw their checking accounts by large amounts. He had also allegedly made a number of dubious loans to friends and political associates. Carter supported his friend throughout the grueling investigation, and although Lance was eventually cleared of any criminal charges, the whole affair tarnished Carter's image as a moral leader.

Several other scandals, though not involving members of Carter's family or administration, added to the growing belief that government was always corrupt. Just before Carter's election the *Washington Post* claimed that over 100 Congressmen had taken bribes from a South Korean lobbyist named Tongsun Park in exchange for favorable legislation. The subsequent ''Koreagate'' investigation led to the disciplining of three legislators and the jailing of another. During Carter's last year in office, the FBI revealed that Congressmen had taken bribes from several Arab millionaries. The press called this latest scandal ABSCAM (short for Arab Scam). Six members of the House were indicted for bribery and conspiracy, and four were eventually convicted.

THE BURGER COURT

Meanwhile, the Supreme Court continued to work in its own deliberate way on a number of difficult questions. By this time the conservatives who had taken their place on the bench were beginning to make an impact on decisions. Yet this Court, led by Chief Justice Warren Burger, did not wholly repudiate the work of its immediate predecessors.

THE BURGER COURT

In some areas it actively continued along lines set down during the Warren years, while in others it altered rulings somewhat—but without overturning them altogether.

The case of *Roe* v. *Wade* (1973), which forbade the states to interfere with a woman's decision to have an abortion, along with several related cases, provide good examples of continuity between the Warren and Burger Courts. In *Griswold* v. *Connecticut* (1965), for instance, the Warren Court had outlawed state statutes that prohibited the sale and use of contraceptives, arguing that the citizens' inherent right to privacy protected them from such intrusive legislation. *Roe* v. *Wade* extended the privacy argument to cover abortion, contending that the question should be left to the pregnant woman and her physician. And in response to arguments that unborn fetuses had a right to life under the Fifth and Fourteenth Amendments, the court explained that unborn children had never been recognized under the law as ''persons,'' and were therefore not covered by ''due process'' protections. The Court thereby held that abortions could be performed for any reason during the first trimester of pregnancy. This decision outraged many religious people who contended that abortion was outright murder. Supporters of the decision countered that the legality of abortion stemmed from a woman's right to control her own body. They also observed that antiabortion laws did not deter women from seeking abortions, but instead forced many to undergo dangerous procedures outside the medical profession.

In the area of due process, however, the Burger Court backed away somewhat from the more advanced positions of its predecessor. The decision in *United States* v. *Robinson* (1973), for example, permitted police to search an automobile following a traffic arrest without a warrant. And in *United States* v. *Calandra* (1974) the Court allowed illegally seized evidence to be presented before a grand jury, though not at the trial itself. Several other cases made exceptions to the *Miranda* rule, which had directed arresting officers to read defendants their rights. On school prayer, however, the justices did not alter the strong stand taken by the Warren Court against religious exercises in public schools. But on the pornography issue, Burger and his more conservative associates did try to give local authorities greater range. In *Miller* v. *California* (1973) the Court upheld a California law that prohibited the knowing sale of pornographic material. Here Chief Justice Burger specifically rejected the earlier *Roth* rule, which had declared that the work in question must be ''utterly without redeeming social value.'' In the long run such decisions did little to stop the proliferation of hard-core pornography.

On the question of race relations the Burger Court tried to revise its predecessor's decisions in a more conservative direction. The majority in *Keyes* v. *Denver School District* (1973) held that only *de jure* (or legally mandated) segregation was unconstitutional and that school boards were not obliged to alter systems that had not been intentionally segregated by law or other public action, a decision that gave comfort to those who opposed busing as a remedy to de facto segregation. In another case, *Regents of the University of California* v. *Bakke* (1978) the Court considered the equally controversial question of affirmative action programs. The case concerned one Alan Bakke, a white student who applied for admission to the University of California Medical School at Davis, which had reserved 16 of its 100 places for minority applicants. Bakke failed to gain admission, although his grades and test scores would have clearly won him a place had there been no affirmative-action program. Claiming reverse discrimination,

Bakke charged that his exclusion from medical school violated Title IV of the Civil Rights Act of 1964, which forbade exclusion from any program receiving federal assistance on account of ''race, color, or national origin.'' He won his suit, but, in an ambiguous decision that did not fully please either side, the principle of affirmative action seemingly remained intact.

Although a number of decisions by the Burger Court have reflected its more conservative tenor, there has been no wholesale repudiation of the Warren Court. The main body of its work remains intact and is unlikely to be dismantled in the foreseeable future. All in all, the Supreme Court remains committed to racial equality, to due process of law, to separation of church and state, and to a wide berth for freedom of expression.

FORD AND CARTER FOREIGN POLICY

As with the Supreme Court, there was both continuity and departure in foreign affairs under Presidents Ford and Carter. But in the conduct of foreign relations there was much less drama than under Nixon, and there were none of the spectacular summits that had marked his handling of international affairs. Instead, there was an exaggerated sense that the United States had lost much of its power in the world and that the country's most glorious days were somehow over.

This relative erosion of American global power was to some extent real and should have been anticipated, for to a large degree American predominance had been grounded in the unusual circumstances that followed World War II. At the end of 1945 most of Europe was devastated and demoralized, Japan had been crushed as an international power, and China was embroiled in civil war. Meanwhile, the United States had a monopoly on atomic weapons, and for a number of years after the Soviets exploded their first atomic device Americans continued to enjoy a vast nuclear superiority.

But 30 years had done much to alter the international balance, and by 1975 conditions that had favored overwhelming American predominance were fading or nonexistent. But there was also a brighter side to the equation. Massive aid to Western Europe and Japan had brought about their economic recovery in a startlingly brief period. Now, of course, American products had to compete with the newer and often more efficient industries of its Japanese and European rivals. Yet even this competition might prove beneficial in the long run, forcing American companies to become as productive as the best foreign competition.

In the Third World former colonial peoples had obtained independence from their European masters and were determined to follow an independent course. Despite American fears that they would fall under Soviet domination, these new nations generally refused to follow the wishes of either Moscow or Washington, but too many Americans continued to believe that their willingness to take aid from the Soviets put them solidly in the enemy camp. At the same time Americans resented the refusal of third world countries to accept aid from the United States in exchange for strict obedience to American wishes, concluding wrongly that rubles somehow purchased more influence than dollars.

It should have also been evident in 1975 that the rigid cold war policies of the 1950s and 1960s were now inappropriate. In particular, the idea that all Communist nations followed Kremlin wishes had been disproved by the historical record. In Yugoslavia Marshal Tito had pursued his own road to socialism, refusing to join the Warsaw Pact or to become a puppet of Moscow. Nor did the triumph of Chinese Communists lead to close friendship and collaboration between China and the Soviets. On the contrary, age-old animosities between the two countries grew more pronounced with time. And likewise, a North Vietnamese victory did not make Indochina into a satellite of either China or the Soviet Union. It was obvious, too, that a Communist Vietnam did not threaten American interests in any important way. (By the mid-1980s it was not inconceivable that the United States would someday recognize a Communist Vietnam, carry on normal trade relations with it, and even extend foreign aid to this former enemy.)

But few citizens were willing to admit the realities of an altered world, and instead many demanded a full restoration of national power and prestige. And for them such a restoration was merely a matter of will. The United States must flex its collective muscles, spend more on defense, and demand agreement from its allies. All too many politicians shared these naive assumptions, or at least were willing to pander to the sentiments that underlay them.

Congress Reasserts Itself In addition to coping with the changed international situation, both Ford and Carter had to confront a suspicious Congress, intent on reasserting some of its authority over foreign affairs. To a large extent, of course, Ford and Carter were paying for the sins of their predecessors. First Truman and then Kennedy and Johnson had committed the country to major foreign conflicts without a declaration of war from Congress. Legislators had grumbled about such actions, but they did nothing substantial about it until 1973, when they passed the War Powers Act. Recognizing that presidents may not have the time to obtain approval from Congress in every instance, the act permitted a chief executive to commit American troops for only 60 days, after which Congress would have to authorize continued deployments.

Congress also found other ways to assert its weight in foreign affairs. A good example was the dispute between Ford and Congress over Cyprus in the autumn of 1974. Congress had responded to a Turkish invasion of the island by cutting off all military aid to Turkey, but Ford believed the action would alienate the Turks unnecessarily and weaken the NATO alliance. He vetoed two attempts to cut off aid, only to compromise with legislators in the end. The law would remain on the books but not go into effect for another two months. In December, however, the legislators voted to continue the ban. Congress also would try to place restrictions on Ford's negotiations with the Soviet Union.

Ford and the Soviets In dealing with the Soviets, Ford and Secretary of State Henry Kissinger continued Nixon's policy of détente. Accordingly, August 1975 found the president in Helsinki, Finland, where Ford and European heads of state formally accepted the Continent's postwar boundaries. In effect the United States and its allies were recognizing the Soviet-imposed settlement in Eastern Europe. For their own part the Soviets agreed not to interfere with purely domestic matters in the satellite countries and to respect human rights there. Many conservative Republicans, including Ronald Reagan, denounced the Helsinki agreements, seeing them as a sellout to the Soviet Union. But this official recognition of an accomplished fact in Eastern Europe could only clear the air and promote better relations between the superpowers.

Ford also continued to work with the Soviets on nuclear arms control. In November 1974 he met with Soviet Premier Brezhnev at the Siberian port of Vladivostok, where they discussed the possibilities of a second SALT treaty. They agreed to accept equivalent nuclear capabilities, but left the details for future negotiations. Still, the Ford administration hailed the meeting as an important breakthrough, vastly exaggerating the progress that had been made toward a SALT II agreement.

Other approaches to détente ran into congressional roadblocks. Ford, like Nixon, wanted to give the Soviets "most favored nation" trade status, meaning that they would receive the same low tariff rates that the United States extended to any third nation. But Democratic Senator Henry ("Scoop") Jackson of Washington kept such a trade bill bottled up in committee, hoping to use the proposal as a lever to make the Soviets let more Jews out of the country. Jackson promised not to relent until the Kremlin signed a statement promising to let 50,000 Jews leave the Soviet Union annually. Ford believed that quiet diplomacy would lead to a more lenient immigration policy, but Jackson would not give in and the trade bill languished. Later the Soviets themselves repudiated the trade agreement.

Vietnam Aftermath   Jackson and the other hardliners were in part reflecting a sense of national humiliation that had followed the final defeat of South Vietnam in April 1975. Saigon fell with unanticipated swiftness and American forces had to scramble to evacuate their remaining nationals, along with 55,000 loyal Vietnamese. Unfortunately, the United States could not rescue everyone who feared reprisal at the hands of the Communist victors. Back home television audiences saw desperate South Vietnamese throwing themselves at American helicopters and ships while military personnel held them back at gunpoint. In some cases, Vietnamese clung to the struts of departing helicopters only to fall to their deaths as they lost their precarious grip.

President Ford urged his fellow citizens to put Vietnam behind them, but warned potential enemies that present difficulties should not be seen as a "slackening of national will." And as if to prove the point, he reacted quickly and forcefully when overzealous Cambodian patrol boats captured an American merchant ship, the S.S. *Mayaguez*. He ordered the bombing of Cambodian port facilities and sent several hundred Marines in by helicopter to rescue the crew. By this time Cambodian officials had already decided to release the men. The mission cost 40 American lives in all, and in retrospect appears quite unnecessary, but press and public alike applauded Ford for his swift reassertion of American will.

The enthusiasm was short-lived, however, as an investigation chaired by Idaho's Senator Frank Church revealed gross abuses within the CIA. Besides its illegal operations against domestic dissidents, the agency had been involved in assassination plots aimed at foreign leaders, including Fidel Castro, Rafael Trujillo, and Ngo Dinh Diem. Ford issued an executive order that laid down strict guidelines for future operations, but only time would show if they were effective.

Carter's Crusade for Human Rights   Such abuses disgusted Jimmy Carter, whose genuine religious faith called for a more moral approach to foreign affairs. Many members of Congress and their constituents had also grown critical of Henry Kissinger's *realpolitik,* with its primary emphasis on national interest. As president, Carter called for a more ethical approach to foreign affairs that would pay particular attention to human rights around the globe.

This was by no means a novel idea. Thomas Jefferson and many of the other founders saw the American revolution as an example to all mankind, and hoped that their words and deeds would loose the bonds of tyranny everywhere. In the twentieth century Woodrow Wilson made proper behavior by new governments a prime condition for recognition by the United States. Later he billed American participation in World War I as a moral crusade to save the world for peace and democracy. Franklin Roosevelt's Four Freedoms, the United Nations Declaration of Human Rights, and portions of the Helsinki agreement also reflected a continuing American interest in furthering basic rights and obtaining better treatment for the downtrodden and abused. As Carter himself put it: "Ours was the first nation to dedicate itself to basic moral and philosophical principles[,] a singular act of wisdom and courage[,] . . . a revolutionary development that captured the imagination of mankind."

In practice such ideals proved difficult to implement on a global scale. In the first place, international law long held that purely internal affairs were beyond the legitimate concern of other nations. Americans might not like the way a given government treated its citizens, but the United States simply lacked jurisdiction to interfere—practically as well as legally. Verbal and even economic sanctions often proved futile and made the United States look both foolish and weak. In the last analysis, only war could force an obstinate government to change its ways. Others pointed out that strict adherence to a human rights policy might endanger détente, as the United States tried to pressure the Soviets into better treatment for dissidents and oppressed minorities. Devoted anti-Communists, on the other hand, worried that the new policy would force the United States to abandon right-wing dictatorships, whose only recommendation had been their opposition to communism.

In actual practice, Carter's human rights policy produced mixed results. His attempts to persuade the Shah of Iran to allow more dissent met with a polite but firm refusal. Nor was he successful in inducing the Israelis to give West Bank Palestinians the right to vote, to assemble, or to own property. Economic and moral pressures against the Soviets following their invasion of Afghanistan in late 1979 also proved futile. Carter suspended grain sales to the Soviet Union and persuaded American Olympic officials to boycott the 1980 games in Moscow, but the Kremlin proceeded undeterred with its Afghan campaign. Carter contends, however, that subtle pressure on the Soviets through 1979 induced them to release more Jewish immigrants than ever before. And there is evidence to suggest that the human rights policy helped win friends in the third world, as did Carter's appointment of Andrew Young, a black Georgian, as ambassador to the United Nations. Black Africans in particular applauded the increasing American criticism of racial oppression (apartheid) in South Africa.

Treaty Making: SALT II and Panama   Fortunately, friction over human rights did not keep Carter from pursuing nuclear disarmament with the Soviet Union, and in June 1979 he signed a second SALT agreement with the Soviets. As planned, it provided for nuclear parity between the two superpowers. Each side was permitted a total of 2,250 missile launchers, 1,320 of which could carry multiple warheads. The two sides also worked out electronic verification systems. From the start there was opposition from right-wing spokesmen, who charged that the SALT II agreement would keep the United States from improving its nuclear arsenal. The treaty failed to win clearance in the Senate, in part because of the president's ineptitude in dealing with Capitol Hill. But the administration decided to proceed as if it had been approved, a policy that Ronald Reagan adopted after his inauguration in 1981, but later repudiated.

Carter was more successful with his Panama Canal treaty. Panamanian opposition to continued American control of the Canal Zone had grown over the years, and by the time Carter took office, there was a real danger that local extremists might attack the waterway itself. American intransigence over the canal was also helping to alienate other Latin American nations. By August 1977 the United States and Panama had worked out an agreement that returned the Canal Zone to Panama and permitted joint operation and maintenance of the canal itself. The United States could protect the canal until the year 2000, after which American forces would leave. However, the United States reserved the right to protect the waterway from external threats.

At first there was great opposition to the canal treaty. Some critics associated American control of the Canal Zone with its rise to world power early in the century and saw the agreement as another sign of national decline. Nevertheless, Carter used all the power at his disposal to push the treaty through the Senate. In the long run, the treaty may do much to improve hemispheric feelings.

Success and Failure in the Middle East   Carter also met with surprising success in his efforts to negotiate a settlement between Israel and Egypt. Since 1948, when Israel became a nation, the United States had remained its staunchest friend, viewing the fledgling state as its most dependable ally in the Middle East. American arms and American economic aid, to say nothing of the vast financial assistance of the American Jewish community, had helped to keep Israel afloat in a hostile Arab sea. The United States had supported Israel during its 1967 war with Egypt and Syria and again during the 1973 war with its Arab neighbors. But growing American dependence on Middle Eastern oil indicated a more balanced policy in that region. And clearly some sort of accommodation between Israel and its Arab opponents would help the United States to maintain good relations with both sides.

A moderating stance by Egypt's Anwar Sadat made rapprochement between Egypt and Israel more possible than in the past. Carter invited Sadat to join him and Israel's Prime Minister Menachem Begin for a meeting at his Camp David retreat in September 1978. After 13 days of difficult negotiations, the three leaders announced a tentative ''framework for peace.'' Implementing the agreement proved more difficult than Carter expected, but Egypt did extend diplomatic recognition to Israel and Israel withdrew its troops from Egypt's Sinai Desert, occupied by the Israelis since the 1973 war. Other Arab nations did not immediately follow Egypt's example and several Middle Eastern leaders openly denounced Sadat for his perfidy.

Unfortunately, Carter was unable to repeat his success in Iran, where the situation turned largely on internal struggles. Since 1953, when it helped to overthrow Mossadegh, the United States had been intimately involved with Iran. It had supported a return of the Iranian monarchy under Shah Mohammed Reza Pahlevi, whose outspoken anti-communism seemed a guarantee against Soviet adventurism in the oil-rich Persian Gulf.

Under the Shah, Iran had also undergone much modernization and realized a genuine improvement in its standard of living. But his regime was ruthlessly oppressive, critics being savagely tortured or executed. When a revolution against the Shah broke out in 1978, Carter continued to support Pahlevi, while gradually losing faith in his ability to govern Iran. In January 1979 the administration persuaded him to abdicate, and for a brief period Iran's government rested in the hands of moderate politicians. Then on February 1 the Ayatollah Khomeini, a religious mystic who had led radical Moslem revolutionaries from exile in Paris, returned to Iran and took control.

The Ayatollah's return ended the reign of the moderates. It also signaled the be-

Defiant Iranian revolutionaries burning an American flag in Teheran.

ginning of fierce anti-American demonstrations in Iran, caused in large part by pent-up resentment against a quarter century of American support for the hated Shah. While mobs demonstrated in the streets, the revolutionary government revoked American oil concessions in Iran and also forced the United States to give up listening posts used for monitoring Soviet activities just across the border.

Carter then made matters worse when he admitted the deposed Shah to the United States for medical treatment. He assured the Iranians that the Shah would stay no longer than necessary, but revolutionary terrorists retaliated by storming the American embassy in Teheran on November 4 and capturing some 50 hostages in the process. In exchange for their prisoners they demanded the return of the Shah and his considerable fortune, making no secret of their desire to try and execute the former leader. Carter refused their demands, terminated oil purchases from Iran, and in mid-November ordered all Iranian assets in the United States to be frozen. At the same time he explored every diplomatic channel to obtain the hostages' freedom. His efforts were compounded by the political chaos in Iran and the resultant confusion over who was really running the country. At times it appeared that the radicals who held the American embassy were making all the decisions on the hostages; at others it seemed that the Ayatollah Khomeini was completely in charge. Yet the United States was forced to deal indirectly through Iranian Prime Minister Bani-Sadr, whose authority was quite uncertain.

With diplomacy at an impasse, Carter authorized a daring military raid to rescue the hostages. The mission got under way on April 24, 1980, but was aborted when two of the six helicopters needed for the rescue broke down in the desert outside Teheran. News of the cancelled action infuriated the Iranians, who removed the hostages from the embassy and dispersed them to various sites. Carter came off looking quite incompetent and the United States more impotent than ever.

ENTER RONALD REAGAN

The continuing hostage crisis turned out to be a major blow to the already unpopular Carter. Despite his successes with the Panama Canal treaty and the Israeli-Egyptian negotiations, wide segments of the population believed that the president was totally inept. The fact that he had had the courage to tackle the energy question head-on also hurt him. Few wanted to hear that they must cut back on energy use, and Carter's long battle with Congress over energy only served to underline his weakness on Capitol Hill. Even an attempt to explain the country's difficulties backfired on him. In July 1979 he announced that the country faced a "national malaise," a "crisis of the American spirit." The people had lost faith in the future, according to Carter, and were reluctant to challenge present problems. Critics immediately charged that it was the president in whom the people had lost confidence. Following the televised address Carter's approval rating fell to 26 percent in the polls; clearly, he would face a hard time winning reelection in 1980.

For a while it even looked as if Carter would be denied the Democratic nomination. His most serious challenger was Senator Edward Kennedy, who announced in the fall of 1979 that he intended to seek the nomination. The Iranian crisis resulted in a temporary

ENTER RONALD REAGAN

groundswell of support for the president. Questions also arose about an automobile accident at Chappaquiddick, Massachusetts, in the summer of 1969. Kennedy had driven his car off a bridge late one evening, causing the death by drowning of a young woman who was in the car with him. An inquest had cleared Kennedy of any criminal responsibility, but many believed that his acquittal owed more to his wealth and family name than to the facts of the case. Others wondered if Kennedy had been drunk at the time or if there had been any romantic attachment between Kennedy and the drowned woman. The incident was likely to plague Kennedy for the rest of his political career. In any case, Carter went on to win most of the primaries and a majority of the delegates to the Democratic convention.

A number of Republicans entered the field, including former Texas Governor John Connally, George Bush, and Senator Howard Baker of Tennessee, but conservative Ronald Reagan was the front-runner from the beginning. The only handicap was his age, for if he won the election, Reagan would become the oldest man ever to sit in the White House. Vigorous campaigning in the early primaries soon allayed any fears about Reagan's health, and he easily won the party's nomination.

Reagan's success baffled many political observers who at first had refused to take his candidacy seriously. Barry Goldwater had turned out to be such a disaster for the Republicans in 1964 that conventional wisdom held little promise for another "true believer." It soon became evident that Reagan was striking a kindred note for many Americans in this time of hesitation and doubt.

Born in 1911 in Tampico, Illinois, Reagan grew up amidst the uncomplicated verities of small-town America. Never an outstanding student, he excelled in high school sports and social activities. His college days were spent at Eureka College, a small sectarian institution run by the Disciples of Christ. He then worked for several years as a radio announcer in Des Moines, Iowa. From there he went to Hollywood, took a screen test, and began to play minor parts in movies. In 1939 he married actress Jane Wyman, whom he later divorced.

Although Reagan never became a big star, his performances in several movies were quite professional, and he received moderate critical acclaim. His film career began to decline after World War II, however, and he made a successful switch to television, hosting the "General Electric Theater" for several years and then becoming announcer for the popular "Death Valley Days" program. Meanwhile, he had his first taste of leadership as president of the Screen Actors Guild, leading fellow members in a successful strike to obtain a percentage of profits from televised movies.

In politics, Reagan began as a partisan Democrat and was a great admirer of Franklin Roosevelt. He grew more conservative with time, perhaps returning to the political beliefs of his childhood. His marriage in 1952 to Nancy Davis, whose parents were staunch Republican conservatives, doubtless speeded his conversion. While with the "General Electric Theater," he began touring his sponsor's plants, giving conservative pep talks to management.

During the 1980 campaign Reagan was outspoken in his criticism of the Carter administration, denouncing the Panama Canal treaty and Helsinki agreements and calling for a tougher line with the Soviets. Above all, he castigated greater federal control over the economy. He promised to "take government off the backs of the great people of this country, and turn you loose again to do the things you can do so well because you did them and made this country great.'' Reagan also called for a crackdown against criminals and welfare cheats, along with a restoration of traditional values. In this way he attracted the support of law-and-order advocates and those who saw a general decay of moral standards. But Reagan was never quite as blunt as Goldwater had been, and he moderated his stance on Panama and other issues as the November election drew near. His rugged good looks and unfailing geniality also kept him from seeming like an extremist.

Carter tried to counter Reagan with an uncharacteristic barrage of cold war rhetoric, castigating the Soviets for their invasion of Afghanistan and their general record on human rights. But on the domestic front the president continued to insist that the country must learn to accept limits on its economic growth and particularly on its energy use. Reagan countered these gloomy warnings by denying that there was a real energy shortage or that the country had to dampen its expectations, a message that most voters far preferred to hear. Nor did Carter succeed in beating Reagan at debate. Here Reagan's skills as an actor paid off handsomely, as the television audience watched a well-spoken and self-assured Reagan appear just as presidential as his opponent.

Voters who liked neither Reagan nor Carter had another choice in Illinois Representative John Anderson, who ran as an independent candidate. He proved a skillful speaker and effective campaigner, offering moderate solutions for most of the country's problems. However attractive voters found him, many believed that their vote would be wasted on a third-party candidate. But others decided to vote for Anderson, if only to demonstrate their displeasure with both the major candidates.

And if voter participation meant anything, much of the electorate was disenchanted with all three choices. Only 52.3 percent of eligible voters bothered to go to the polls, an even worse showing than four years earlier. Despite poor participation, Reagan won an impressive victory with 43,889,000 popular votes to Carter's 35,481,000. The electoral tally was even more lopsided at 489–49. As expected, Anderson came in third, accumulating 5,719,000 votes and no electoral votes. Carter ran well among blacks and Hispanics, but lost votes to Reagan in every other traditionally Democratic group: organized labor, Catholics, Jews, and southerners. The Republicans also took control of the Senate for the first time in over 25 years. At the same time they won 33 additional seats in the House, making the new balance 242 Democrats to 192 Republicans. Republicans took great satisfaction in the results and hoped that they represented a realignment in American politics, with the Republican party emerging once again in the majority.

Only time would tell if the Republicans were correct. The nation had clearly been through a time of disappointment and frustration. If the new Reagan administration could begin managing a host of difficult problems and give the American people a sense of national renewal, then the Republicans stood to gain substantially.

BIOGRAPHICAL SKETCH

NELSON A. ROCKEFELLER · *1908–1979*

A grandson of John D. Rockefeller, Sr., Nelson Rockefeller was born into one of the richest, most influential, and hated families in America. His father, John D. Rockefeller, Jr., spent much of his adult life trying to salvage the family name. He kept a low profile, spent millions on philanthropy, and worked constantly to make his four sons and one daughter into public-spirited citizens. Nelson was also the grandson of Nelson Aldrich, the wealthy and very powerful U.S. senator from Rhode Island during the late nineteenth and early twentieth centuries.

Rockefeller did badly in school, in part because of dyslexia, yet he managed to make it through Dartmouth and soon thereafter wed Mary Todhunter Clark of Philadelphia. Like many sons of wealthy and successful fathers, Nelson was anxious to make his own mark as quickly as possible, and a job managing family properties in New York soon disappointed him. A junior directorship at New York's Museum of Modern Art helped to relieve the tedium and intensified a lifelong interest in the arts. Another welcome opportunity came in 1935 when he became a director of the Creole Petroleum Corporation, a Standard Oil of New Jersey affiliate that owned vast oil fields in Venezuela. Rockefeller soon grew concerned over Latin American animosities toward the United States, as well as over German attempts to gain a larger economic and cultural foothold south of the border. Rockefeller shared his alarm with President Roosevelt, who created an Office of Inter-American Affairs in August 1940, with Nelson as its coordinator.

Over the next four years Rockefeller

launched an ambitious program of loans, trade agreements, and cultural exchanges that helped maintain good relations during World War II between Washington and the Latin American republics. Then in 1944 Rockefeller became assistant secretary of state for Latin American affairs and was instrumental in laying the groundwork for the Organization of American States (OSA), founded at Bogotá, Colombia, in 1948. After the war he continued his interests in Latin America, establishing two private investment groups that sought to use American capital to raise standards of living in South America and thereby thwart Communist efforts to exploit poverty and discontent. Such efforts brought him to the attention of President Truman, who in 1950 named Rockefeller chairman of a committee to oversee the Point Four Progam. Three years later President Eisenhower made him under secretary of health, education, and welfare.

Dissatisfied with these minor federal appointments, Rockefeller ran for governor of New York in 1958, winning an upset victory over incumbent Averell Harriman. During his four terms as governor he launched massive projects in higher education, highway construction, and urban renewal. He also sponsored generous scholarship programs, expanded welfare benefits, and enlarged other public services. In the process he became one of the most liberal governors in the country and leader of the liberal wing of the Republican party.

Rockefeller clearly wanted to use the governorship as a stepping-stone to the White House, and in 1960 he made his first bid for the presidency. But Richard Nixon had accumulated too many political favors while vice-president, and he easily won the nomination. Rockefeller also failed to win the 1964 nomination, in part because of his controversial divorce and quick remarriage to Margaretta ''Happy'' Murphy. His slashing attacks on candidate Barry Goldwater and subsequent refusal to campaign for him made permanent enemies among party members. And in 1968 Rockefeller was once again defeated by Nixon's years of hard work at the grass-roots level.

By the mid-1970s Rockefeller's public life seemed in shambles. He had made numerous enemies in the Republican fold and revelations about personal finances during his confirmation hearings for the vice-presidency reminded the public of his great wealth and potential for abusing it. It appeared that all his father's efforts to redeem the family's reputation were threatened by his son's unquenchable thirst for high office.

Even after Ford dropped him from the ticket in 1976, Rockefeller did not give up altogether on his presidential dreams and held out some hope for 1980. Meanwhile he concentrated on his vast art collections, writing several books about them and other artistic matters. He died of a heart attack on January 29, 1979.

SUGGESTED READINGS

For a critical overview of the period, again see Peter N. Carroll, *It Seemed Like Nothing Happened: The Tragedy and Promise of America in the 1970's* (1982). On the Ford administration there are the president's own memoirs, *A Time to Heal* (1979). Ford's chief speech writer, Robert Hartmann, gives a sympathetic look at the administration in *Palace Politics: An Inside Account* (1980). More objective but still sympathetic is John Osborne's *White House Watch: The Ford Years* (1977). Highly critical is Clark Mollenhoff, *The Man Who Pardoned Nixon* (1976). Leon Jaworski's *The Right and the Power* (1976) offers insight into the denouement of Watergate. Ford's extensive use of Vice-President Rockefeller is examined in Michael Turner, *The Vice-President as Policy Maker* (1982).

On the election of 1976 there is Jules Witcover's *Marathon* (1977). The increasing importance of the South in presidential politics is delineated in Kirkpatrick Sale, *Power Shift: The Rise of the Southern Rim and Its Challenge to the Eastern Establishment* (1975). Students of the Carter years might begin with Jimmy Carter's *Why Not the Best?* (1975), a unique sort of campaign autobiography, and *Keeping Faith: Memoirs of a President* (1982). An excellent personal biography is Bruce Mazlish and Edwin Diamond, *Jimmy Carter: An Interpretive Biography* (1979). Very critical of the administration is Clark Mollenhoff, *The President Who Failed: Carter Out of Control* (1980). For a perspective on Carter's energy policies, see Richard Victor, *Energy Policy in America since 1945* (1984).

Concerning the election of 1980 is Elizabeth Drew, *Portrait of an Election* (1981). Studies on the decay of the New Deal coalition and the resurgence of the political right are John R.

SUGGESTED READINGS

403

Petrocik, *Realignment and the Decline of the New Deal Party System* (1981), and David W. Reinhard, *The Republican Right Since 1945* (1983).

For an overview of foreign policy under Ford and Carter, see Stanley Hoffman, *Primacy and World Order* (1978). Then there are the relevant portions of Henry Kissinger's somewhat self-serving *White House Years* (1979). Again, this should be read along with Seyom Brown, *The Crisis of Power: Foreign Policy in the Kissinger Years* (1979). CIA excesses are treated in Victor Marchetti and John D. Marks, *The CIA and the Cult of Intelligence* (1974), and John Stockwell, *In Search of Enemies: A CIA Story* (1979).

A cogent analysis of American diplomacy toward Jews and Arabs is W. B. Quandt, *Decade of Decision: American Foreign Policy Toward the Arab-Israeli Conflict, 1967–1976* (1978). Works on the final episodes of the Vietnam War are, again, Weldon Brown, *The Last Chopper: The Denouement of the American Role in Vietnam, 1963–1975* (1976), and A. E. Goodman, *The Lost Peace: America's Search for a Negotiated Settlement of the Vietnam War* (1978). Perspective on the Iranian hostage crisis may be found in Benson L. Grayson, *United States-Iranian Relations* (1981), and Barry Rubin, *Paved with Good Intentions: The American Experience in Iran* (1981).

17

A Changing Society

American society continued to experience rapid change in the years after Watergate and Vietnam. Many changes were the result of scientific and technological innovation, ranging from basic research in genetics to the widespread introduction of computers. Other transformations grew out of demographic shifts, as the birthrate fell and longevity increased. Meanwhile the American economy underwent major alterations. Service industries expanded, while jobs in manufacturing declined at an alarming rate. Various economic difficulties in the Northeast and Midwest also sent thousands of families to the South and Southwest in search of new opportunities.

Massive immigration, much of it illegal, further shaped the contours of American society during this period and touched off the hottest debates over immigration since the 1930s. Many of these new arrivals found themselves trapped in a cycle of poverty and discrimination, as did millions of native-born Americans. Yet the political climate was much less receptive to the needs of disadvantaged persons than a decade or two earlier. Indeed, many employed citizens complained that no one appreciated their hard work and steady patriotism. And most Americans opposed any extension of the social welfare system and the tax increases that would be required to finance it.

At the same time, a sense of moral outrage captured public attention. Protestant fundamentalists and Roman Catholics joined hands to protest legalized abortion and to denounce what they deemed other evils of modern life. Their demonstrations, in turn, touched off a major controversy over the proper role of religion in politics and in American society at large.

SCIENCE AND TECHNOLOGY

Scientific and technological innovation were, of course, nothing new to the American people by the mid-1970s. Their unparalleled prosperity and economic might had resulted in large part from a willingness to develop and use the latest machinery and techniques. And although some had grown alarmed in recent years over the negative effects of science and its applications, most citizens continued to believe that science and technology were the keys to even greater happiness and prosperity.

The Computer Chief among the new technologies was the computer. Developed during the darkest days of World War II, its initial task was deciphering enemy codes and plotting bomb trajectories. These early computers, like the one developed at the University of Pennsylvania, were large and cumbersome affairs that were greatly limited in the operations they could perform and in the amount of data they could store. The machines required thousands of vacuum tubes which overheated and burnt out with alarming frequency, leading to frustrating breakdowns of the entire system. The invention of the transistor in 1947 and the silicone chip somewhat later resulted in smaller, more efficient, and greatly more sophisticated computers that were able to store millions of pieces of data and to perform thousands of different functions.

By the mid-1980s it was obvious that the computer had become a permanent fixture

The large "Eniac" computer at the University of Pennsylvania, 1946.

of American life, yet its impact was harder to assess. Undoubtedly, it saved millions of hours of labor, releasing employees from tedious manual calculations and storing information far more efficiently than the filing cabinet or index card. Banks used computers to keep track of customer accounts, to transfer funds from one institution to another, to maintain current information on loans and other investments, or to prepare employee paychecks—all more quickly and accurately than before. In medicine the applications were even more impressive. Here computers stored patient histories, gave statistics on diseases, called up the latest research and treatment procedures, offered information on prescription drugs, helped locate organ donors, and provided ways of viewing the body's interior without dangerous X rays or exploratory surgery.

Without the computer, many human ventures of the past two decades would have been clearly impossible. Space travel, which requires myriads of mathematical calculations, would have proved beyond the capacity of traditional methods. But the social implications of computers may be even more far-reaching. The computer, for instance, may give greater flexibility on the job. With a small, desk-top unit many employees could conceivably do the bulk of their work at home, saving them an unnerving and expensive trek to the office downtown. Such a practice, if widespread, could produce further dispersion of the population throughout the countryside.

Computers have also proven a major vehicle for crime. White-collar thieves have used them to steal classified information from the government and the military, and to obtain information about impending business ventures. Others have used the computer to embezzle money from bank accounts or to obtain confidential files on taxpayers, employees, or medical patients. Here the judicial system found it difficult to catch up with the new technology.

Satellites, VCRs, and Lasers   Other advances in communication likewise changed the way people lived and thought. One was the increasing use of orbiting satellites. From hundreds of miles above the earth, communication satellites received telephone, television, and radio signals from special transmitters and beamed them back over wide areas of terrain. Most international telephone calls were sent in this manner, at much greater speed and at lower cost. Global television broadcasts have also been made possible by this means.

Closer to home, the video-cassette recorder (VCR) enabled television fans to record their favorite shows for later viewing or to rent and purchase a wide variety of programming to be enjoyed whenever convenient or desired. Video games, learning aids, and old movies, as well as the most blatant pornography were to be had at the local video store. VCRs thus have given television consumers an independence and flexibility undreamed of in the early days of the industry and have threatened the near monopoly of the major networks over program content.

Yet another boon to communications was the laser, a powerful and finely focused beam of light or radio waves. Developed by a number of researchers in the late 1950s and early 1960s, the laser has permitted quick and reliable communications with space vehicles and will undoubtedly play an important role in future space missions. The laser may also be used as a weapon in space warfare, its powerful beams used to destroy enemy missiles and satellites.

To date, however, the laser has proved a benign instrument in many areas besides

SCIENCE AND TECHNOLOGY

communications. Its straight and narrow beams have been used to measure distances to an accuracy of 40 millionths of an inch, making it a valuable instrument for surgeons, physicians, and the assembly of microscopic circuitry. By bouncing a laser beam off the moon, for example, scientists were able to measure its distance from the earth to a fraction of an inch. But the most amazing applications have come in medicine. There it has been used to perform delicate eye surgery, cutting optical tissues and welding them back together again.

Medicine   Lasers, of course, have been only one among many new approaches to medicine and public health. Most startling has been the upsurge of organ transplants, including the heart. By using drugs to block the immune system's rejection of a donated organ, cardiac surgeons have successfully transplanted human hearts from deceased individuals to men and women suffering from incurable heart disease. Dr. Michael De Bakey of Houston, Texas, pioneered in this technique during the late 1960s and early 1970s. Less successful and far more controversial was an attempt in 1984 to transplant a baboon heart to an infant. Even more spectacular was the invention of a mechanical heart, which was first implanted in a human chest late in 1982. The procedure remains very risky, and the mechanical heart needs a cumbersome array of mechanical equipment to keep it pumping, but the device holds much promise for future refinements and may play a role in the fight against heart disease.

In addition to such spectacular feats, which were applicable to only a limited number of patients, artificial hips and other joints, along with microscopic surgery and new diagnostic tools such as the CAT-scan, promised longer and more comfortable lives for thousands. New vaccines over the past two generations had also made important inroads against childhood diseases like measles and polio. Before the development of a polio innoculation in the mid-1950s by Dr. Jonas Salk, this disease crippled or killed thousands of children and young adults every year.

At the same time, important advances were made against cancer. A combination of surgery, radiation, and chemotherapy resulted in complete cures for several kinds of cancer. Meanwhile, researchers continued to explore the causes of cancer, thus far isolating genetic, environmental, immunological, and viral sources of the disease.

Probes into the genetic causes of cancer, as well as into the nature of life itself, have been vastly assisted by new insights into the genetic system. The most exciting breakthrough in this area was the discovery of DNA, short for deoxyribonucleic acid. DNA, as James D. Watson and Francis Crick learned in the mid-1950s, contained an intricate chemical code that served as a kind of brain center in each body cell. It also transmitted genetic information to offspring and thereby determined inherited traits.

The discovery of DNA and the accompanying insights into organic reproduction have already had a great impact in science and medicine, and promise vast implications for the future. Some believe that cracking the genetic code may lead to an all-encompassing cure for cancer, while others hope to eliminate inherited diseases by altering those segments of the genetic system that have caused them. Plant researchers have already manipulated vegetable genes so as to produce better strains. Such genetic engineering, as it is called, has understandably provoked a number of ethical questions. The manipulation of human genes, critics point out, could inadvertently change human behavior and even threaten the extinction of the entire human species.

CHAPTER 17: A CHANGING SOCIETY

ECONOMIC AND DEMOGRAPHIC SHIFTS

Few would deny that new scientific discoveries and their technological applications have had and will continue to have a great impact on the American economy. The development, manufacture, and sale of computers, VCRs, and advanced medical equipment, for instance, have opened up whole new markets. And those farsighted enough to take advantage of these new technologies will continue to enjoy an advantage over those who do not.

A Changing Labor Market   In a very real sense, then, the new technology has created a host of opportunities for some. At the same time it has destroyed or seriously undermined thousands of jobs in other areas of the economy. Industrial robots, programmed by powerful computers, have displaced thousands of workers on auto assembly lines and will continue to do so in this and other manufacturing areas. Robotics, combined with stiff foreign competition in steel, textiles, and automobiles, have predictably led to massive unemployment among blue-collar workers in particular, many of them living in the so-called Rust Belt of western Pennsylvania and the near Midwest. Inhabitants of these areas have demanded protective tariffs and import quotas, hoping that less foreign competition will restore blue-collar jobs. But even with fewer imports, jobs in the nation's ''smokestack'' industries are unlikely to rebound altogether, for the United States is clearly a postindustrial nation. The country has solved the age-old problem of physical production through greater and greater mechanization.

Not surprisingly, the greatest growth in employment opportunities has been in service industries such as banking, insurance, fast-food restaurants, communication companies, and enterprises that cater to leisure activities. By 1982 service workers amounted to 53.7 percent of the work force, up from 48.3 percent in 1970. At the same time, blue-collar workers declined from 35.3 percent to 29.7 percent of all workers. Unfortunately, many blue-collar workers did not have the skills necessary to obtain jobs in the higher-paying service sector, most of which required either a college education or some kind of specialized training. Less skilled service jobs seldom paid as well as those in manufacturing, were usually nonunionized, and offered few fringe benefits.

Rise of the Sunbelt   Besides forcing some men and women into lower-paying service jobs, the decline of smokestack industries in the Northeast and Midwest also sent many to other parts of the country in search of jobs, primarily to the South and Southwest, an area that journalists and others dubbed the ''sunbelt.'' Some manufacturers, lured by lower energy costs and the relative absence of labor unions, had moved south and west in the decades after World War II, causing a portion of the labor supply to follow. Other workers were attracted to the sunbelt by aerospace, computer, and related industries that flourished there. And with increasing populations, the sunbelt provided a growing pool of service jobs. Whatever the reasons for moving south and west, this migration represented a major shift in population. Between 1970 and 1980, for example, the number of people in the northeastern states declined by nearly 2 million and the north central states lost almost a million and a half over the same period. Meanwhile the South increased its population by over 7.5 million, and the West by slightly more than 5 million. Politicians were not slow to recognize or exploit these realities; in 1976 and again in 1980, American voters chose presidents from these fast-growing regions.

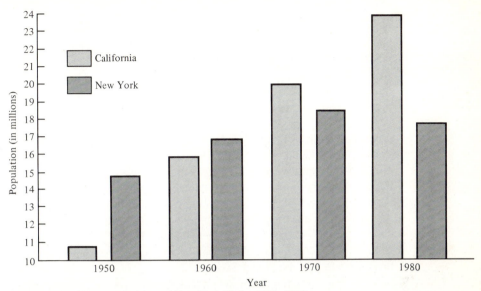

Population growth in California and New York State, 1950–1980.

Falling Birthrates and the Aging of America Still other demographic shifts resulted from changes in the birthrate and increases in longevity. Together, the two phenomena have produced an aging population, with manifold implications for both present and future.

This change came as a surprise to some who had grown used to a constantly falling median age during the 20 years after World War II. But the baby boom came to an end in the mid-1960s as birthrates fell lower and lower. Statistically, the birthrate declined from a postwar high of 26.6 live births per thousand in 1947 to a low of 14.6 in 1975. By 1980 it had rebounded slightly to 15.9, but even at that point adult Americans were not producing enough children to replace themselves, prompting many demographers to predict that the nation's population would begin to decline sometime during the first half of the twenty-first century. Recent large increases in immigration, however, may offset these predictions.

Falling birthrates stemmed from several sources, the most important of which were probably the introduction of the birth control pill in the early 1960s, the wider acceptance of surgical sterilization, and the legalization of abortions. Women's liberation also took its toll, as many young women came to believe that jobs and careers were as important as—if not more important than—rearing children. Consequently, many young women decided to bear fewer children or to have none at all. Finally, a more generalized emphasis upon self-gratification and personal fulfillment left less room for children among young adults. Whatever the reasons, this precipitous fall in the birthrate further accentuated the force of the earlier boom, as that generation failed to reproduce in as large numbers as their parents. Standing between two relatively smaller generations, the baby boomers would remain a demographic bulge in the nation's population for the rest of the twentieth century and beyond.

Lower birthrates after 1965 and the aging of the baby boom generation itself would have been sufficient to produce an older population. But advances in medicine, nutrition, and general health care added to these effects. Major inroads against degenerative illnesses like heart disease, cancer, and even some forms of senility all promised longer lives for most Americans. Most important of all, there has been a great decline in infant mortality and death from childbirth. As a result, average life expectancy has risen dramatically since the beginning of the century. In 1900 average life expectancy was 47.3 years; by 1982 it was 74.5—70.8 for men and 78.2 for women. Even more revealing, a person who lives to age 65 can expect to live nearly two decades more. The fastest-growing age category was, in fact, those over 85, with their numbers expected to increase around 80 percent by the end of the century. Some experts on aging were claiming that the life span (the outward limit of human longevity) was 120 years or more, and that a surprising number of Americans would reach such an age within several decades.

Whatever the figures or the reasons behind them, the American population was clearly aging. By 2025 the average age in the United States is projected to be 37.6, up from 27.9 in 1970. Such a shift would have a large effect on society and public policy—most obviously in the Social Security system.

Passed in the middle of the Great Depression, the Social Security Act of 1935 had been written with a far different population in mind. The age at which workers could receive Social Security benefits, for example, was set at age 65. Yet in 1935 average

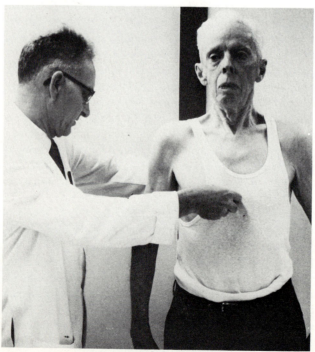

One of an increasing number of elderly Americans receiving a medical checkup.

ECONOMIC AND DEMOGRAPHIC SHIFTS

life expectancy was 61.7—59.9 for men and 63.9 for women. This meant that the majority of those covered by the act would not live long enough, at least in theory, to collect even one payment under the system. And at first there were 13 persons paying into the Social Security fund for every one receiving benefits.

By the 1980s demographic changes posed a grave threat to Social Security. Most workers would now live long enough to collect benefits for a decade or more, and in the early 1960s the government allowed both men and women to retire at 62 with only slightly lower benefits. Inflation, too, ravaged the system, as Congress voted annual cost-of-living increases for recipients. Finally, the bulge of baby boomers, who would begin to retire around 2011, posed a long-term threat to the system. The program clearly faced bankruptcy unless something were done. After much debate, some of it quite heated, Congress acted in 1983 to repair the program. The legislators increased payroll taxes, taxed part of the benefits going to wealthier recipients, and authorized a plan to raise the age of eligibility by gradual increments. By 2027 that age would rise to 67, a plan that obviously reflected the increase in average life expectancy.

Congress had already raised the age of mandatory retirement from 65 to 70, the law taking effect in January 1979, and at present there are attempts to outlaw compulsory retirement at any age. Indeed, age discrimination has become a controversial topic, as the question has found itself into several high court cases.

The escalating cost of medical and health care for the elderly likewise posed difficult questions. Older Americans required more frequent treatments and longer hospitalizations than younger citizens, and the new procedures for dealing with degenerative diseases were quite expensive. Yet many retirees were unable to meet their medical expenses. After 1965 Medicare covered much of the cost, but by no means all of it, and even the Medicare Trust Fund was threatened by constantly rising costs. Prolonged stays in convalescent centers and nursing homes, however, were not covered by Medicare, and many elderly patients were forced to spend their entire life savings before Medicaid and other public assistance programs would take over such expenses.

Indisposed and elderly patients also strained the emotional and financial resources of their adult children. It was not unusual for a retiring child to be faced with caring for an even older parent. The ''young old,'' looking forward to a few years of leisure after a lifetime of work, instead found themselves taking care of an even older generation. It is these adult children, too, who often have to make painful choices about prolonging a parent's life through artificial means. The invention of these devices, including mechanical breathing systems and greatly improved intravenous feeding devices, has also forced legislators and the courts to come up with new definitions of death, as mechanical devices keep both heart and lungs working long after the brain is officially dead.

These realities made it easy to overlook the more positive benefits of an aging population. Older citizens have a wealth of knowledge and experience to share and have the leisure hours to spend with youngsters that working parents simply cannot afford. An aging population may also result in a lower crime rate, since the majority of violent crimes are committed by people under 30. Older citizens vote in greater numbers, too, than the young and middle-aged, and thus an aging population will presumably take a more active role in the political process. Finally, the prospect of a longer, healthier, and more productive life should be good news for everyone.

New Patterns in Immigration   Still another demographic shift involved continued immigration into the United States, and from a greater variety of sources than ever before. The pluralistic nature of this immigration owed in large part to legislation in the 1960s which abolished the old national quota system that had hitherto favored Europeans. This meant that new arrivals were as likely to come from Asia or Africa as from Britain or Italy, and by the mid-1980s over 80 percent were coming from non-European nations. The largest single source, however, was the Latin American countries, and much of the immigration was illegal. Virtually every night hundreds of illegals simply walked across the lightly patrolled border between the United States and Mexico or landed along secluded portions of Florida's extensive coastline. Immigration officials estimated that there were between 3.5 and 6 million illegal aliens in the United States by 1978, the vast majority of them from Spanish-speaking countries of the New World. All in all, immigration was higher than at any time since the restriction acts of the 1920s.

Some of the new arrivals were fleeing political or religious persecution in their homelands. This was certainly true of Russian Jews or of Nicaraguan, Salvadoran, and Cuban dissidents, and equally true of thousands of Vietnamese refugees who came after the fall of Saigon. But the great bulk of them came for the same reasons as earlier immigrants—to realize a higher standard of living. And despite low pay, substandard housing, and ethnic and racial discrimination, most have realized better lives for themselves and their families.

However they fared, these newest immigrants confronted a native population that was increasingly alarmed by the higher rates of entry and particularly over the flood of new illegal entrants. Workers repeated the old complaint that immigrants deprived them of jobs or accepted low pay, thus driving down wages for the entire population. But it is doubtful that most native-born labor would take the low-paying, menial jobs occupied by immigrants and especially by the illegals. Others pounced on the fact that a handful of aliens smuggled drugs or turned to other forms of crime. In fact, most aliens, whatever their legal status, were hardworking, law-abiding residents who wanted nothing more than to be left alone to make a decent living.

As might be expected, the assimilation question has also reemerged as a controversial topic, with a growing Spanish-speaking population as its principal target. Hispanic communities have, in fact, created their own churches, newspapers, businesses, and clubs. And unless they venture outside the *barrio,* residents can get along quite well without speaking a word of English. Some of these communities also want their children to be taught in Spanish-speaking or bilingual schools.

Critics have charged that separate linguistic communities would ultimately divide the nation, making it impossible for all segments to communicate with one another, or for non-English-speaking groups to participate fully and effectively in the political process. Others emphasize the economic handicaps to be encountered by young men and women who grow up without learning much English. For them, jobs would be limited to their own communities, without much chance of advancing to more lucrative positions in the nation at large. Parents have responded that it is their right to educate and train their children as they see fit, a claim that has echoed throughout the land since the advent of compulsory education. And as residents of non-English-speaking communities have pointed out, the right to be different in language, custom, or religion is one of the most precious guarantees of the American constitutional system. The debate is thus a difficult

ORAL HISTORY
Growing Up in the Twentieth Century

MERI JIMÉNEZ · *born 1961*

My father had always wanted to come to the United States. He heard about the United States since he was very young. He learned from other people who had been there how it was. Also, some Americans would come to Colombia. They knew Spanish and they would tell my father how nice it was in America.

My father was in the army in Colombia and they taught him to be a mechanic, to fix heavy equipment. He then got a job as a mechanic with an American company in Colombia and they asked him if he would like to work in the United States. So he left and worked there two years before he finally sent for the rest of us to come.

I was ten years old then and was very scared. I didn't want to go to a strange country. Things were familiar to me in Colombia and I didn't know how to speak English. I didn't want to be in a strange place; I didn't know how I would handle it.

Before leaving we had to sell all the furniture. We had to leave almost everything behind. My father told us not to take so many clothes, because here in America everything was different. We weren't to bring any of our school things—nor pictures or anything.

We flew from Bogotá to New York. My impression of the New York airport was awful. I thought that being in the United States would be fantastic, that everything would be nice and clean and bright and that all the people would be nice and tall with blond hair and blue eyes. That's the kind of Americans you would see in Colombia and the people I saw in New York were not very tall or very blond.

My mother and my brothers and I all held hands. The customs people searched everything, everything they could get their hands on. We had to get a green card; we had to get our pictures taken. It was just awful because I didn't expect it at all. They told us we always had to be with that card and to show it to whoever wanted to see it.

I saw so many cars at the airport. I have never seen so many cars in my life. I was shocked. It was around 5:30 in the afternoon already and it was still so bright out. In Colombia it was always dark around 6:00. We didn't know that the days were longer in the United States in the summer. We only knew that there would be four seasons. It didn't get dark that night till about 9:30 and I was sleepy. Then we went to a restaurant and I hated the food. We had pizza and I had never tasted pizza before.

The neighborhood we moved into was an Italian neighborhood and they did not want to have anything to do with Spanish-speaking people. Behind us was a black neighborhood and they didn't want to deal with us either. The neighbors completely ignored us. They didn't know we were Colombians. They thought that because we spoke Spanish we were Puerto Rican. They would say, "P.R., P.R., Puerto Rican, Puerto Rican!"

I didn't know a word of English when I started to school. The students were not used to someone not speaking their language and they wouldn't play with me at first. I used to write down every English word I saw and at night I would look it up to see what it meant. I read and read and watched TV and that's how I learned English. I told myself that I didn't want to learn street language, but that I wanted to learn it properly from the books.

I decided to become a citizen of the United States when I was 18. I did not ever want to go back to Colombia to live there permanently. And I knew that by becoming a citizen I would never have to go back.

Here in America I had found so much freedom. I had found a way to be myself and to show myself. I could be a person here in the United States, whereas Colombia is still a male-oriented society and women are not taken seriously enough. American men are not so much that way. A child has more liberties here than in Colombia. This is good; a child can develop more of a sense of self and is able to cope with the world better.

I like the fact that there is more opportunity here, that a person can develop to her own potential. In Colombia you could not and cannot do this. If I had stayed there I would never have been able to go to college and would always have been poor.

one, involving some of the basic tenets of national life. Yet the arguments are older than the country itself and alarmists should take heart from knowing that the descendants of nearly all immigrants have learned the English language quite effectively and have fit comfortably into the nation's mainstream.

The matter of illegal immigration likewise raises difficult issues. Congress as well as the White House have been under increasing pressure to seal off the southern borders and expel illegal aliens; other proposals would tighten the borders but give amnesty to the illegals already here. Whatever is done, the debate will continue for some time.

RELIGIOUS TRENDS

Accompanying these demographic shifts, though by no means a direct result of them, there was much ferment in the area of religion. Some churchgoers tried to accommodate themselves better to rapid social changes, while others resisted the tide with all their might and sought to restore more traditional patterns.

Among the liberal accommodators were members of the older, more established Protestant denominations—Episcopalians, Presbyterians, and Methodists—along with the various branches of reformed Judaism. They generally rejected a literal interpretation of scripture, became increasingly lenient about divorce and remarriage, took a permissive stance on birth control, and elevated women to the clergy. These groups also tended to place great emphasis on the social gospel, urging their congregations to work for a juster society.

American Catholics and Vatican II During the early 1960s the Roman Catholic Church also began to take a more moderate stance on several issues. At the invitation of Pope John XXIII, about 2,500 delegates, representing some 135 nations, met in Rome's Vatican City from 1962 to 1965 to discuss ways of bringing the church more in line with the realities of modern life. Known as Vatican II, the council eventually issued 16 documents that would alter both the worship and beliefs of Roman Catholics and touch off a storm of controversy.

In order to make the liturgy more understandable and ultimately more familiar, the council ordered that it be given in the various national languages rather than in the traditional Latin. Altars were turned around so that the priest faced the congregation, lay parishioners were allowed to distribute communion and to form advisory bodies within each church. Furthermore, the laity were invited to sing hymns during services, much as Protestants had done since the Reformation. Other council directives gave greater voice to the bishops in each country, permitted more latitude in biblical scholarship and interpretation, and encouraged an ecumenical dialogue with other Christians. At the same time the council recognized the legitimacy of non-Catholic religious beliefs and specifically condemned anti-Semitism. In perhaps the most far-reaching of its pronouncements,

Pope John XXIII, who presided over the "revolutionary" Vatican II Council.

Vatican II embraced the social gospel, encouraging the laity and clergy alike to practice their beliefs in the world at large.

For many American Catholics, living as they did in a country that extolled open discussion and religious pluralism, Vatican II came as a welcome release from increasingly troublesome restraints. The more liberal among them hoped that the council was only the beginning of more massive reforms. They frequently spoke about the "spirit of Vatican II," rather than about the documents themselves, and urged American clergy to interpret the new directives as loosely as possible. In the 1960s particularly, such Catholic liberals called for a more permissive stand on birth control and divorce, and went so far as to propose a married priesthood. The Vatican, of course, had no intention of permitting any of these practices, and over the next several years the Holy See reiterated its traditional positions in these matters.

Even so, conservative American Catholics often felt betrayed or threatened by changes in their church. They missed the Latin mass, refused to join in congregational singing, and found it difficult to regard other Christian denominations as legitimate. And they were appalled by the attitudes of more liberal Catholics on social issues. By the mid-1980s conservative lay Catholics had banned together to support the church's teachings on sex, birth control, and other issues.

Despite their differences, Catholics have in fact been much more vocal on social questions than before Vatican II. In 1983 the Council of American Bishops issued a controversial letter concerning world peace that condemned nuclear war and urged disarmament on the superpowers. In another much debated letter, issued in 1985, the bishops criticized the country's capitalist economy for not meeting the needs of the poor and disadvantaged. Many lay Catholics have also become active in the peace movement, while others have become vigorous opponents of the Supreme Court decision *Roe* v. *Wade* (1973), which legalized abortions.

Such activism undoubtedly reflected new directions in the Catholic Church since Vatican II, but it also demonstrated that American Catholics were fully assimilated into the mainstream of national life. Previously, most American Catholics were recent immigrants, or their immediate descendants, who hesitated to join in any sort of protest lest they draw attention to themselves and invite even more hostility. But, on another level, Catholics in the United States were only following the nationwide trend to organize and press particular points of view in the public arena.

The Moral Majority   Joining Catholics in their social activism were numerous Protestants, including various fundamentalist groups. Indeed, the fundamentalist churches were experiencing much greater growth than the more established denominations. Episcopalians, Methodists, and certain Lutheran congregations reported only negligible increases in membership over the past decade or two, while the Presbyterians suffered a slight decline. On the other hand, the Assemblies of God, Latter-Day Saints (or Mormons), and Southern Baptists reported large increases.

These rapidly growing fundamentalist groups were likely to insist on the literal and inerrant truth of scripture, to oppose modern biblical criticism, and to emphasize the need for a spiritual rebirth. Most also opposed the teaching of evolution in the schools, rejected sex education outside the home, and demanded the removal of "immoral" literature from school libraries. On sexual matters, they commonly upheld nineteenth-century moral standards, condemning premarital sex, homosexuality, and all forms of pornography. And on legalized abortion they joined ranks with Roman Catholics and Orthodox Jews to oppose it.

Although these positions were echoed from the pulpit, spokespersons from the Protestant right sought a larger forum through television. By 1984 their programs were viewed regularly by more than 13 million men and women. The television preachers were more sophisticated in their appeals than hometown clergy, but their message was essentially the same: The country had fallen into moral decay and the faithful must join hands to redeem it. Among the more powerful of the television preachers was the Reverend Jerry Falwell, who created the Moral Majority in 1979. A coalition of conservative Protestants from different denominations and sects, Falwell's organization contended that the majority of Americans were disgruntled with post-1960s morality. Falwell called on the faithful to share their displeasure with the public at large and thereby rescue the country's moral fiber.

A Plethora of Cults   Then there were those who went beyond the boundaries of Judeo-Christian religion altogether. Since the 1960s non-Western sects have found a larger audience in the United States than ever before. The most visible of these are the various Krishna groups, whose adherents dressed in flowing saffron robes and chanted through the streets of major cities. Sung Myung Moon, a charismatic missionary from Korea, has also gathered thousands of Americans into his Unification Church. Members of one cult made world headlines when their leader Jim Jones led them from California to Guyana and there convinced more than 700 members to commit ritual suicide. Opponents of the cults, often relatives of those who have entered them, claim that converts are brainwashed, drugged, and held against their will. Some parents have gone so far as to ''kidnap'' their young adult children and force them to undergo a painful ''deprogramming.'' Whatever the full truth may be about these more extreme cults, all of them promised a comprehensive spiritual rebirth to those who entered. If nothing else, they demonstrated that some Americans could find little meaning in contemporary society or in standard religious offerings.

THE NEW CONSERVATISM

Although it would be incorrect as well as unfair to compare the Moral Majority with these non-Western cults, both of them emphasize a personal kind of salvation and have very little to say about the social gospel. And in this sense they have much in common with political conservatives who disparage attempts to reform society through more government programs.

Neoconservatism and the New Right   The new thinkers of the right have been called neoconservatives and include such writers as Irving Kristol and Michael Novak. They and others have sought to defend what they call democratic capitalism against the advocates of a large welfare state. They generally decry the growth of federal control over the economy and the increasing bureaucratization of American life. They also lament that government programs have singled out women, particular races, and ethnic groups for special treatment. At the same time, they applaud the rise of ethnic consciousness as a buffer against the growing power of central government.

Sharing most of the ideas of the neoconservatives is the New Right, but its adherents are more interested in political action than they are in theory. And although the New Right generally feels more comfortable with the Republican party, it has often been critical of the existing two-party system, charging that major candidates are more interested in expediency than they are in a legitimate conservative program. Leaders of the New Right have accordingly made direct appeals through their own organizations such as Howard Phillip's Conservative Caucus or Terry Dolan's National Conservative Action Committee. These and other groups have been very successful with direct-mail campaigns and have raised large sums in this way for conservative candidates and causes. This energetic canvasing underlines the New Right's determination to succeed and to overcome their image as a ''thankless persuasion,'' as Clinton Rossiter has defined conservatism.

Like neoconservatives and earlier spokespersons for the conservative cause, the New Right frequently condemns communism and appeals for a stronger national defense. They also continue to extol the free enterprise system while damning the growth of social welfare progams. But they are far more likely than conservatives of the previous generation to concentrate on moral and social issues. The New Right generally advocates a more traditional morality that prohibits abortion, homosexuality, and recreational sex. They also point with distress to rising divorce rates and the accompanying breakdown of the two-parent household. Some, like Phyllis Schlafly, link this disintegration to women's liberation and have been vocal opponents of the Equal Rights Amendment and of women's rights initiatives in general. As for their own legislative agenda, the New Right has rallied around an antiabortion amendment to the U.S. Constitution as well as an amendment to permit prayer in the public schools. Finally, the New Right has cried loudly for a crusade against crime, striking a responsive chord in many Americans.

Figures show that violent crime has declined a bit overall, but the United States continues to have the highest homicide rate of any nation in the Western, industrialized world. And in some metropolitan areas like New York, violent crime has become epidemic. Liberals continue to talk about the social causes of crime—poverty, unemployment, lack of education, and racial discrimination—and there is little doubt that all of these are among the most serious underlying causes of criminal behavior. Nevertheless, many Americans believe that the time has come to wage an all-out war against crime and violence. There have been calls for stiffer jail sentences, a reinstatement of the death penalty, and less stringent guidelines for gathering and using evidence. An increasing number have gone further and bought guns to defend themselves from criminal attack. When New Yorker Bernhard Goetz shot four youths who accosted him in a subway in 1984, most fellow Gothamites applauded him, as did millions of others across the country who had grown tired of fearing for their lives. Yet such approval signaled an alarming lack of faith in official law enforcement, combined with a growing belief that individuals must protect themselves with guns and other dangerous weapons.

Drug and Alcohol Abuse   In addition to increasing concern over violent crime, many Americans remained alarmed over drug and alcohol abuse. Like the overall crime rate, certain kinds of drug usage had actually declined during the past decade or so. Adolescents in particular had turned away from marijuana, as surveys showed that its use among high school seniors had declined from 37 percent in 1979 to 29 percent in 1982. At the same time, however, cocaine usage among adults increased at an appalling rate, some estimating its rise at 10 percent each year. Even more disturbing, the use of cocaine and other drugs was gaining wide acceptance among the middle classes. Public concern has thus begun to shift away from the proverbial skid-row addict to the increasingly common sight of drug addiction among prosperous and respectable suburbanites. Of course, middle-class drug abuse did not minimize the rash of crimes committed by impoverished addicts who turned to theft to pay for their habits.

The federal government reacted to the drug problem with a crackdown on the drug trade. Greater funding was provided for customs surveillance, the State Department sought agreements largely with Latin American governments to eliminate production and shipment at the source, and President Reagan endorsed testing for drug abuse in wide segments of the work force. But such policies produced few results by the mid-1980s.

The problem of alcohol abuse was, of course, more widespread than drug addiction. Unlike drugs, alcohol consumption was considered highly respectable among large segments of the population. Drinking had long been associated with sophisticated living, warm companionship, manly behavior, and a variety of positive images—all of them reinforced by appealing liquor advertisements. Whatever their reasons for drinking, most imbibers did not become alcoholics, but for the estimated 14 million victims and their families alcohol addiction was an unremitting nightmare.

The response to excessive drinking took several directions. On one level there were new approaches to treatment, ranging from the psychological to the medical. Medical researchers, for instance, discovered that many alcoholics do not metabolize alcohol properly, resulting in a progressive poisoning of the body, along with an increasing dependency on drink. There were also renewed efforts on the legal front. Alarmed at the deaths and injuries resulting from drunken driving, many states imposed stiff fines and even jail sentences for driving while intoxicated. In most instances, legislatures were responding to intense pressure from citizen lobbies like Mothers Against Drunken Drivers (MADD). State authorities also increased the legal drinking age, and there were indications that all the states were moving toward a uniform drinking age of 21, particularly in the face of threats to withdraw federal highway funds to states that failed to raise the drinking age. College authorities, too, began to adopt more restrictive policies toward drinking on campus. Indications were that these diverse actions were paying off. In New Jersey, for instance, highway deaths related to drinking declined by over 40 percent between 1981 and 1985. There was also evidence that younger citizens were more aware of the dangers of hard liquor. As a result the consumption of distilled spirits has actually declined in comparison to the use of beer and wine, and drunkenness at social functions has not been as acceptable as it was in prior generations.

LIFE STYLES

Yuppies Although concern over crime and various forms of addiction loomed large in the public consciousness, it did not keep millions of more affluent Americans from reveling in their material success. Better-educated baby boomers, for instance, were now trading their skills for handsome incomes, and with fewer children than their parents' generation, it was not unusual for both husband and wife to hold down well-paying jobs. Journalists dubbed this group ''yuppies,'' short for young and upwardly mobile. Statistically, they were between 30 and 45 years of age and earned over $35,000 per annum.

Merchandisers became acutely aware of their large disposable incomes and taste for well-made, attractive items, ranging from sports cars to Gucci shoes to the latest fashions in jogging attire and camping equipment. They were also very house conscious and often were in the forefront of movements to renovate decayed but architecturally significant areas of the city. Some critics deplored their flagrant materialism and seeming lack of social conscience, while others congratulated them for their hard work and success.

Although yuppies shared some of the conservative emphasis on the work ethic, there were few indications that they accepted the Moral Majority's attitude toward sex — nor did the rest of the country. Most Americans continued to approve of legalized abortion, and the number of couples living out of wedlock rose to over two million by 1985, a threefold increase since 1970. The practice became so familiar that hardly anyone noticed or complained.

But there were other signs that the sexual revolution had run its course. The divorce rate leveled off by the mid-1980s and showed few signs of increasing further. Toleration of extramarital sex declined as well, with the percentage of disapproval rising from 65 percent in 1978 to 72 percent in 1985. Meanwhile an epidemic of venereal diseases had a dampening effect on sexual promiscuity of all sorts. Especially hard hit was the homosexual community, the principal sufferers of a devastating new disease called AIDS (acquired immune deficiency syndrome). Caused by a virus, the disease was communicated primarily through sexual contact, destroying the immune system of its victims and invariably leading to death. In some cases the disease was contracted through blood transfusions from AIDS carriers or from hypodermic needles used by drug addicts. There were fears that AIDS would spread from the homosexual community to the general population and be transmitted widely through heterosexual contact. Understandably, many adults were more discriminating about their sexual partners, while the steady, longer-term relationship was likely to regain some of its popularity.

Poverty and Child Abuse   The continuing problem of poverty did not attract nearly the attention that the AIDS epidemic did, but far more Americans suffered from poverty than from AIDS — or from any single disease. For despite the War on Poverty and other federal programs to aid the indigent, the number of Americans living below the poverty line rose to over 15 percent in 1983, higher than at any time since 1965, but endemic poverty showed no signs of disappearing in the near future. Especially hard hit were children. Indeed, the number of children living in poverty rose from around 16 percent of the total in the late 1970s to almost 20 percent by 1983.

Analysts blamed the upsurge in poverty rates on many causes. Some castigated the Reagan administration for cuts in social welfare, while others pointed to the recessions of the early 1980s or to structural unemployment. Still others emphasized the high divorce rate and the parallel rise of households headed by women who continued to receive lower pay than men. Whatever the causes of poverty, there were still two Americas, one relatively prosperous and secure, the other mired in devastating poverty.

Besides being the principal victims of poverty, children were also the targets of serious physical and mental abuse. Child abuse had always existed to some degree, and there was much debate over whether it had increased in recent years. But there was definitely a new awareness of the problem, as social workers, physicians, neighbors, and local governments were willing to report incidents of abuse. In 1983 the number of known episodes reached the one-million mark, with perhaps 75 to 90 percent of cases

EDUCATION **421**

going unreported. The principal abusers were parents themselves, but there were sensational revelations of sexual and other forms of physical abuse in the nation's burgeoning day-care centers. Perhaps worst of all, some 50,000 children disappeared every year, the majority of them abducted by divorced parents, but all too many by total strangers.

EDUCATION

The College Scene It was still too early to tell if the sexual revolution had run its course on the college campus. Certainly, there was no reason to believe that students were ready to return to the sexual mores of the 1950s. In other respects, however, students more resembled their counterparts of 30 years before than they did those of the late 1960s and early 1970s. It was clear, for instance, that students in the 1980s were much more interested in preparing for well-paying jobs than they were in social and political issues. Professors who had once wearied of campus demonstrations now missed the crackling debates that had spilled from the picket line into the classroom.

The decline of campus demonstrations may have owed something to economic conditions. In the 1960s the economy was booming and fewer students were worried about making a living after graduation. Time spent in protests may have been hard on the grade point average, but employers were less concerned over scholastic achievement than they were a few years later when the competition for jobs was greater. The number of demonstrations declined, too, because many of the issues that had inspired them were absent in the 1980s. The Vietnam War was over, and the civil rights and women's movements had achieved most of their immediate goals. Yet certain issues could still stir the student conscience. Thousands marched against nuclear armaments, and a number of campuses witnessed demonstrations against apartheid in South Africa. In the spring of 1985 over 100 students at New York's Cornell University staged a sit-in to demand that the institution sell its investments in South Africa, and in the spring of 1986 several dozen campuses reported similar demonstrations against South Africa. Despite such incidents, there was no reason to anticipate a series of nationwide campus protests like those of the 1960s.

In addition to the relative quietude of the nation's campuses, authorities observed that students were much less interested in the humanities and social sciences than they had been 20 years before. The liberal arts accordingly suffered substantial declines in enrollments, as students flocked to business, engineering, computer science, and other so-called practical majors. The reasons for the shift were not entirely evident, but the inflation and unemployment of the previous 15 years or so may account for much of the move to vocation-oriented departments. One unfortunate consequence was a continuing decline in verbal skills. By the mid-1980s reports on higher education urged more required courses in the liberal arts, along with increased attention to writing skills.

The Schools There was also much concern over the quality of education below the college and university level. As verbal scores fell on standard college entrance exams, and professors found that students could not read and write as effectively as in the past, attention began to focus on secondary and elementary schools. A number of culprits were blamed for poor preparation. Some pointed to the rising tide of violence in urban schools; others singled out the curriculum for not placing enough emphasis on basic skills such as reading, writing, and mathematics. Then there was television, which kept children

BIOGRAPHICAL SKETCH

LEE IACOCCA · *born 1921*

There is perhaps no one else today who better represents both the spirit and reality of the American dream than Lee Iacocca. The son of Italian immigrant parents, he has become the nation's most celebrated industrialist and has even been mentioned as a presidential candidate. For millions of citizens, he is living proof that native ability and hard work can indeed lead to great success.

Iacocca was born in Allentown, Pennsylvania, and attended the public schools there. A straight-A student at nearby Lehigh University, he earned a bachelor's degree in industrial engineering in only three years. After graduating in 1945 he entered an executive training course at Ford Motor Company in Dearborn, Michigan, interrupting his program there to earn a master's degree in mechanical engineering at Princeton University. Complications from rheumatic fever during childhood kept him out of World War II.

Iacocca served briefly as a Ford engineer but quickly realized that he preferred a career in sales, and for nearly a decade he worked at various marketing and sales jobs at Ford's Eastern District office in Chester, Pennsylvania. In 1956 he launched a brilliantly successful sales campaign and caught the attention of top Ford executives, who called him back to the company's main office in Dearborn. There he became a protégé of Robert McNamara, soon to be president of Ford. Over the next 20 years, Iacocca developed a number of spectacular new models. His most famous was the Ford Mustang, which set an all-time record for first year sales after it was unveiled at the New York World's Fair in 1964. Understandably impressed,

Henry Ford II made Iacocca the company's president in 1970.

Unfortunately, Iacocca and his boss did not always get along. Iacocca claims that Henry Ford became increasingly jealous of his success and for that reason fired him in 1978. Iacocca has been outspokenly critical of Ford since then and because of it, has won a number of enemies, many of whom have been offended by Iacocca's aggressive personality.

Iacocca's firing left him emotionally devastated, but he bounced back quickly, becoming head of the already ailing Chrysler Corporation. Through incredibly hard work and imagination Iacocca saved Chrysler from bankruptcy, persuading Congress to vote the company nearly $2 billion in loan guarantees and convincing management as well as the United Auto Workers to take cuts in pay and benefits. Meanwhile he christened a new fleet of compacts called K-Cars. By 1984 Chrysler was turning a healthy profit and was able to repay its loans seven years ahead of schedule. Iacocca had undoubtedly saved the country's third largest automotive producer, along with hundreds of thousands of jobs.

Iacocca clearly does not give up easily. He remains confident that American manufacturers can compete successfully with the Japanese and that the nation as a whole faces a bright future. It is this optimism, coupled with his proven ability as a leader, that has caused some to propose him for high elective office. So far Iacocca has dismissed such talk, but has indicated his willingness to serve as a top presidential advisor and has gone so far as to offer ways of dramatically reducing the federal deficit. For the present he has confined his public energies to writing a best-selling autobiography and to organizing a campaign to restore the Statue of Liberty and Ellis Island. Iacocca sees the statue as an important symbol of the millions of immigrants who have come to the United States and made a better life through opportunity and hard work.

from reading as many books as in the past and made the classroom seem far less exciting by comparison.

It was also evident that many teachers were poorly equipped for their tasks. Most teacher training programs lacked special entrance requirements, made no effort to discourage poor prospects once they arrived, and required no minimum performance levels for certification by the state. Nearly all these programs emphasized courses on how to teach at the expense of content subjects. As a result young teachers were often quite ignorant about the material they were supposed to impart. In addition, the brightest and most promising members of the college population were not likely to consider a career in teaching. The pay was low and the profession commanded little respect among the public at large. Average salaries for public school teachers, for instance, were only $18,000 in 1981. For all these reasons, there was a shortage of 12,000 teachers as the 1985 school year began, and some experts predicted a shortfall of over a million teachers by 1990. Clearly, governments as well as educators had to work quickly and thoughtfully to cope with a very real crisis in American education.

The crisis in education was just one example of how American society had changed since the beginning of the century. Then teachers had enjoyed great popular esteem, and there were high hopes among progressive educators that schools could solve many of the country's problems. Now the schools themselves were an immense social problem. With little more than a decade to the century's end, it was too early to predict what would be happening in education—or in any other area of national life. But it was safe to say that American society had changed almost beyond recognition from the beginning of the twentieth century.

SUGGESTED READINGS

For further information on the most recent social and cultural trends, students would do well to rely on newspapers, magazines, and other periodical literature. Nevertheless, there are already a number of studies on contemporary American life.

On the implications of science and technology there are Loren R. Graham, *Between Science and Values* (1981); Larry Laudan, *Progress and Its Problems: Toward a Theory of Scientific Growth* (1977); Charles E. Rosenberg, *No Other Gods: On Science and American Social Thought* (1976); and Frank Coppa and Richard Harmond, eds., *Technology in the Twentieth Century* (1983). On computers per se, see Michael L. Dertouzos and Joel Moses, eds., *The Computer Age: A Twenty Year View* (1979); Tom Forester, ed., *The Microelectronics Revolution* (1981); and Tracy Kidder, *The Soul of a New Machine* (1981). Studies on medicine and society include Howard Brody, *Placebos and the Philosophy of Medicine: Clinical, Conceptual, and Ethical Issues* (1980); Richard Shryock, *The Development of Modern Medicine* (1979); and V. S. Yanovsky, *Medicine, Science, and Modern Life* (1978).

There are a number of critical works on industry and American life. Among these are Thomas C. Cochran, *Challenges to American Values: Society, Business, and Religion* (1985); William A. Faunce, *Problems of an Industrial Society* (1981); and Robert Heilbroner's very pessimistic *Business Civilization in Decline* (1976). Much more optimistic is Lee Iacocca's *Iacocca: An Autobiography* (1984).

For insights into population shifts, see Richard M. Bernard and Bradley R. Rice, eds., *Sunbelt Cities: Politics and Growth since World War II* (1983), and Joseph J. Spengler, *Population and America's Future* (1975). Students should also look at relevant portions of Landon Y. Jones, *Great Expectations: America and the Baby Boom Generation* (1980). Focusing on the phenomenon of aging are Richard B. Calhoun, *In Search of the New Old: Redefining Old Age in America, 1945–1970* (1978); Ronald Gross et al., *The New Old: Struggling for Decent Aging* (1978); and Henry J. Pratt, *The Gray Lobby* (1979), a work that investigates the political implications of an aging population. Recent analyses of immigration and ethnicity are Thomas Kessner and Betty Caroli, *Today's Immigrants: Their Stories* (1981); Jack Kinton, ed., *Ethnic Revivalism: Group Pluralism Entering America's Third Century* (1978); and Milton D. Morris, *The Administration of Immigration Policy* (1974).

Examining changes in American Catholicism are Judith Dwyer, ed., *The Catholic Bishops and Nuclear War* (1984) and *The Church and the Modern World: Two Decades after Vatican II* (1985). And on the activism of fundamentalist Protestants there is Robert Fowler's, *A New Engagement: Evangelical Political Thought, 1966–1976* (1982). Valuable information on conservative thought and action can be found in Lewis A. Coser, *The New Conservatives: A Critique from the Left* (1975); Jonathan M. Kolkey, *The New Right, 1960–1968* (1983); Gillian Peele, *Revival and Reaction: The Right in Contemporary America* (1984), which contains insights into the Moral Majority and other groups on the religious right; and Peter Steinfels, *The Neoconservatives* (1979).

Current educational problems and trends are treated in Erwin Johanningmeier, *Americans and Their Schools* (1980); Diane Ravitch, *The Troubled Crusade: American Education, 1945–1980* (1983); and Sanford W. Reitman, *Education, Society, and Change* (1981). Students might also want to look at recent reports on American education. Two of these are *A Nation at Risk: The Imperative for Educational Reform* (1983), issued by the U.S. Commission on Excellence in Education, and *Involvement in Learning: Realizing the Potential of American Higher Education* (1984), written for the National Institute of Education.

18

The Reagan Years

Challenger Ronald Reagan had capitalized on intense voter dissatisfaction with incumbent Jimmy Carter to score a stunning triumph in the 1980 presidential election. Rightly or wrongly, the victor interpreted his win as a mandate for sweeping changes along conservative lines. Attacking the effects of big government, he spoke of a renewed commitment to limited government and individual initiative, as well as a return to the more traditional mores and morality that predominated in American life before the social upheavals of the 1960s. Similarly, he pledged a foreign policy that would revert back to the pre-Vietnam era, when the United States reigned indisputably as the most powerful nation on the planet. His goals, if implemented, promised major changes for the nation.

DOMESTIC AFFAIRS

Reaganomics Soon after his inauguration President Reagan moved to fulfill his campaign promise to revitalize the nation's economy. He envisioned sharp cuts in both domestic spending and taxes, but also strong increases in military spending. The results, he assured, would both curb inflation and reduce the serious budget deficit. Dubbed ''Reaganomics,'' his plan appealed to many because of its simplicity. Others pointed to its contradictions or argued that it would produce largely negative results. Vice-President George Bush, as a contender for the GOP presidential nomination, had earlier derided the Reagan proposals as ''voodoo economics.''

Supply-side economics provided the basis for the president's economic program. Hailed by some conservative economists and members of Congress, as well as by newly appointed Budget Director David Stockman and Secretary of the Treasury Donald Regan, it proposed a tax cut for business and upper-income groups. It was expected that both

425

segments would use these tax savings for capital investments. This "trickle-down" approach, which was reminiscent of the policies of the Coolidge and early Hoover administrations, presumably would reinvigorate a sluggish economy. It was hoped that such fiscal cuts, along with a diminished role for government throughout the economy, would realize Reagan's promise of a "new beginning" for the American people.

Severe budget reductions seemed essential to the success of the president's supply-side scheme. Anticipating huge losses of federal revenue because of diminished taxes, Reagan called for deep slashes in government spending to avoid spiraling deficits and increased interest rates that would result from massive government borrowing. He flatly promised a balanced budget by 1985—the first since 1969. Toward that end he asked Congress to approve cuts of more than $40 billion in federal spending. Liberals complained that many of the proposed reductions involved expenditures for such social welfare programs as food stamps and training for the unemployed.

By June Congress passed the Reagan budget without major alterations, thanks to a coalition of Republicans and "boll weevils," a group of conservative Democrats from the South and Southwest. Passage also reflected the president's exceptional ability to recruit public support. The "great communicator," as he was called, had been able to mold public opinion more effectively than any president since Franklin D. Roosevelt. Sympathy for the president following an assassination attempt also helped the budget get through Congress. On March 6, 1981, a mentally unstable young man shot the president as well as his press secretary, a Secret Service agent, and a policeman. Despite his age, Reagan recovered quickly from serious wounds amid an outflow of great popular concern.

The president's call for sharp tax reductions met stiffer opposition than did his budget proposals. Both liberals and orthodox economists balked. But in August, thanks again to a coalition of Republicans and conservative Democrats, Congress enacted a series of tax reductions on individual incomes that amounted to 25 percent over a three-year period. It also lowered the tax on estates and provided for Individual Retirement Accounts (IRAs). The latter permitted individuals to save part of their yearly income for retirement while deducting this amount from current taxable income. Many hoped that this plan would encourage savings, diminish consumer spending, and bring down inflation.

Reaganomics achieved mixed results. Inflation, which had climbed to more than 10 percent during the Carter presidency, fell to roughly 7 percent by summer 1981. Significant decreases in the costs of various goods, particularly oil, helped to produce these results, as did continuing high interest rates. On the negative side, the costs of entitlement programs like Social Security, Medicare, and Medicaid mounted. These, coupled with the increases in military spending and decreased tax revenues, forced the government to borrow at alarming interest rates. By 1982 the budget deficit had reached $110 billion, nearly double the $57 billion deficit recorded the previous year.

The budget deficit and high interest rates helped bring on an economic recession that began in the summer of 1981 and worsened the following year. The difficulty of borrowing made businesses wary of new capital investment, despite the tax cuts that Congress had legislated. Production lagged, especially in bellwether industries such as steel and automobiles. Foreign competition, particularly from Japan, added to domestic industrial woes, as did outmoded technology in older heavy industries. By late 1982 the unemployment rate had risen to higher than 10 percent, or more than 11 million workers.

DOMESTIC AFFAIRS   **427**

Hardest hit were those living in the North and Midwest, areas some had dubbed America's "Rust Belt." By any account, the United States was experiencing its worst recession since the Great Depression.

President Reagan pleaded that his policies needed more time to work. Meanwhile criticism intensified from different quarters when in August 1982 he called for further cuts in social welfare programs but yielded to demands for various tax increases that would amount to nearly $100 billion over a three-year period. Reflecting growing discontent, the November off-year elections saw Democrats gain 26 seats in the House. The Senate, however, remained in Republican control. The president had lost some popularity—but only some.

Economic conditions improved markedly during the next two years. The overall unemployment rate fell and remained below the 10 percent level, although lack of jobs remained a cruel fact of life for minorities and young people. The nation's poorest also continued to suffer from the cutbacks in federal programs affecting general welfare. The deficit, which by the end of 1983 had reached nearly $200 billion, caused added concern. Yet the administration seemed to be winning at least a temporary victory over inflation, which by 1984 had dropped below the four percent level, less than one-third of what it had been only a few years earlier. This resulted from the Reagan-supported persistent tight-money policy of the Federal Reserve Board and its chairman, Paul A. Volcker, and the consequent maintenance of high interest rates, as well as from a glut in the world oil supply and a subsequent lowering of oil prices. By 1984, moreover, interest rates were declining dramatically. This made it possible for Americans to increase their purchases of large consumer items such as homes and cars. The stock market provided a further barometer of growing confidence in the economy. On election day 1984 the Dow-Jones Average stood at 1229.24, nearly 300 points higher than on the day voters first elected Reagan to the presidency.

Reagan and Deregulation   From the New Deal onwards the size of the federal bureaucracy had ballooned, as had the scope of government intervention in the lives of citizens. Ronald Reagan promised to reverse this trend. Declaring that "government is the problem," he resolved to "curb the size and influence of the federal establishment." Upon assuming office he announced his intention to cut 37,000 federal jobs. And in August he fired 13,000 federal air traffic controllers who had gone on strike, despite their previous pledge not to do so. He also instituted a freeze on new regulatory programs and staffed existing ones with members whose backgrounds or points of view frequently reflected the interests of the industries that they were supposed to regulate. The administration claimed that such vital components of the nation's economy as banking, airlines, and telephones would thrive as a result of deregulation. Not everyone agreed. Public opinion polls further indicated a deep-seated concern that deregulation could—and would—lead to an erosion of important health and safety standards.

No area of deregulation evoked more controversy than that pertaining to the environment, as attested to by the resignation of Anne Burford as director of the Environmental Protection Agency (EPA) in March 1983. Burford, who enjoyed close political ties to the president, left office in the midst of a scandal involving toxic waste. Critics accused her agency of having failed to clean up waste materials, of having misused funds, and of having coddled businesses that exacerbated toxic waste concerns. In De-

Ronald Reagan

cember, Rita M. Lavelle, another high official in the EPA, was found guilty of perjury. Equally insensitive to environmental problems was Secretary of the Interior James Watt. The outspoken Watt was part of the "Sagebrush Rebellion," a movement among largely western business leaders who wished to reverse the longstanding tradition of strong federal protection of the nation's public lands and natural resources, and to turn over their development to private entrepreneurs. Among other controversial actions, Watt attempted to sell 35 million acres of the public domain. He also rationalized such harmful measures as strip-mining. Environment-conscious individuals and groups like the Sierra Club fought Watt's efforts doggedly, as did a number of members of Congress. In 1983 the embattled secretary, although still enjoying the confidence of the president, tendered his resignation.

The president also envisioned turning over various federal programs to the individual states. Like President Nixon before him, he believed that this "new federalism" would result in increased efficiency. Widespread fears that it might effect a nightmare of confusion and increased costs dampened enthusiasm for the venture.

The Moral Majority and Minorities Despite the dubious achievements of deregulation and the failure to advance the "new federalism," enthusiasm for Reagan remained high among most of his conservative supporters. This was especially true for the Moral Ma-

FOREIGN POLICY

429

jority, one of whom described the president as ''the real champion of those values and rights that Christian Fundamentalists believe in.'' As a group that claimed a membership of more than 6 million, and with strong congressional supporters like North Carolina Senator Jesse Helms, the Moral Majority nursed hopes of obtaining favorable political action to achieve their goals.

Certainly President Reagan shared most of the views of the Moral Majority. He had indicated his support for prayer in the public schools, as well as his opposition to abortion, the ERA Amendment, and efforts to achieve racially integrated schools through busing. He had also struck a responsive chord with religious fundamentalists by denouncing pornography and calling for a return to traditional values.

But the president, for all his firm convictions, remained a practical politician. Wishing to maintain ties with those who disagreed with the Moral Majority, he failed to give his unstinting support to the campaigns for school prayer and against abortion. In March 1981 he also disappointed his Moral Majority backers by naming Sandra Day O'Connor, who defended legalized abortion, as the first female justice of the U.S. Supreme Court.

The O'Connor appointment was highly ironic. Feminists had strongly attacked Reagan for his stand on abortion and the ERA Amendment, which had failed to win ratification by the prescribed 1982 deadline. They also denounced his cuts in funding for day-care centers and school lunches. His opposition to the concept of equal pay for equal work, which feminists believed would lead to more equitable salaries and wages for women, added to their disappointment. Yet the president had placed more women in high-ranking federal positions than had any previous chief executive. In addition to the selection of O'Connor, he named Elizabeth Dole as secretary of transportation, Margaret Heckler as secretary of health and human resources, and Jeane Kirkpatrick as U.S. ambassador to the United Nations.

Minorities also complained that they had received short shrift from the Reagan administration. Budget cutbacks adversely affected the poor, many of whom were from minority groups. The president's opposition to school busing also earned denunciations from minority spokespersons, though not necessarily from all minority members. Although Congress voted in 1982 to extend the Voting Rights Act of 1965, many feared that the president would try to undo or limit other gains in civil rights achieved since the 1960s. His commitment in this area seemed increasingly suspect when he took advantage of a restructuring of the Civil Rights Commission to add three conservative appointees.

FOREIGN POLICY

Controversy also characterized the Reagan administration's foreign policy. The key elements of that policy flowed from the president's determination to restore the United States to a position of world primacy, combined with a desire to stop the spread of communism. To achieve these goals he pursued a course that blended frequently strong rhetoric with the more occasional use of force.

United States-Soviet Relations President Reagan adopted a generally tough stance against the Soviet Union. Ironically, he did lift the grain embargo imposed against the Soviets by former President Carter, but this move resulted more from a promise to aid the embattled American farmer than from any softening of his resolve to combat communism. Hearkening back to the days of harsh cold war rhetoric, the president denounced the Soviet Union as an ''evil empire'' that would commit ''any crime'' to achieve its goal of world dominance. He insisted on interpreting world politics in simple terms: communism versus anticommunism. The United States, he stressed, must be prepared to thwart the Soviets and their client states from spreading their revolutionary ideology to other nations, particularly those of the third world. The ''thaw'' in the cold war of the 1950s and the détente of the 1970s now seemed memories of the past, as verbal hostility increased on both sides and the politics of confrontation loomed increasingly large.

The Soviet Union contributed generously to deteriorating relations with the United States. The war against Afghan rebels that had begun during the Carter administration continued unabated during Reagan's first term in office. The Soviets poured more men and materiel into that fray with little to show except greater casualties on both sides. Persistent charges that they were using chemical warfare in a desperate effort to subdue the stubborn rebels and end the quagmire served to augment anti-Soviet sentiment. That sentiment intensified when the Moscow-controlled Polish government reacted against the dissident Solidarity movement that had been demanding political and economic reforms. A military coup in December 1981 resulted in the proclamation of martial law and further arrests of Polish protesters. The United States responded with economic sanctions against both the Soviet Union and Poland. Denunciations of Soviet behavior reached new heights in September 1983 when the Soviets shot down a Korean commercial airliner that had strayed into their territory. Forty-four Americans were among the 269 passengers killed. Few were willing to believe Soviet allegations that the airliner was on a spying mission for the United States or that the CIA had duped it into veering off course in order to test Soviet reactions. For their part, the Soviets may have acted more from a lack of precise information than from sheer ruthlessness. Indeed, critical misunderstandings on the part of all parties concerned, including the United States, may have been primarily responsible for the tragedy.

During these years the Soviet Union experienced changes in leadership that left relations with the United States further unsettled. Ailing Communist party leader Leonid Brezhnev died in 1982. Yuri Andropov, his successor, spoke of improving relations between the two countries, but his background as director of the dreaded KGB, or secret police, did not inspire confidence. Andropov himself died the following year. Power then passed to Constantin Chernenko, a representative of the old guard whose advanced years and questionable health kept Kremlinologists guessing about what would happen when he, too, departed. Their conjecturing was brief. Chernenko died in 1985 and was replaced by the younger, more dynamic Mikhail Gorbachev. Again, no one could predict what policies Moscow would follow.

In dealing with the perceived Soviet threat, Reagan broke with his immediate predecessors in at least one important way. Since the 1960s American presidents had been willing to accept general military parity with the Soviet Union. Reagan, however, was determined to restore American superiority. Upon entering office he announced a military buildup that would cost $1.5 trillion over a five-year period. One hundred costly B-1 bombers, soon to become obsolete when the more advanced Stealth bombers came into operation at the end of the decade, were included in his budget. So, too, were funds

FOREIGN POLICY

for the controversial MX missiles, which critics claimed were vulnerable to enemy attack and unnecessary in light of the capacity to launch missiles from strategic bombers and submarines.

The Reagan administration underscored its commitment to military strength by deploying Pershing II missiles in Europe beginning in 1983. The administration argued that this countered the deployment of Soviet missiles that were aimed at Western European nations. Far from feeling protected, many Europeans protested that the Pershing missiles enhanced the likelihood of their lands becoming the site for a future nuclear holocaust. Many Americans concurred and expressed their concern that the administration was needlessly fueling the nuclear arms race. In 1982 private citizens as well as more than 100 members of Congress asked for a nuclear arms freeze on both sides.

The president tried to reassure critics that he also favored an abatement of the arms race. In 1982 he called for Strategic Arms Reduction Talks (START) to replace the unratified Salt II accords. The following year he proposed the startling Strategic Defense Initiative (SDI), soon dubbed ''Star Wars,'' that would create an American antiballistic missile system in space. By destroying offensive missiles, the system, he reasoned, would reduce prospects for war. Critics denounced the proposal as infeasible and incredibly costly. They argued further that building such a system would invite a first strike by a potential enemy before the system was completed. By the end of Reagan's first term in office arms control remained at an impasse. The Soviets had angrily terminated discussions once the United States began deploying Pershing II missiles. Nonetheless, both nations continued to abide by the provisions of the still unapproved Salt II agreement.

Problems in the Middle East   Tensions also remained high in the Middle East, due primarily to continued Arab-Israeli enmity. The Camp David accords had brightened hopes that peace might yet come to this troubled region, but a variety of events during the Reagan years dimmed such prospects. First, Egyptian zealots assassinated their president, Anwar Sadat, in October 1981. It remained to be seen whether Hosni Mubarak, Sadat's successor, would continue the policy of accommodation with Israel or whether Egypt would return to its pre-Camp David position of hostility. Meanwhile Israeli Prime Minister Menachem Begin, as promised, gave back the Sinai to Egypt in April 1982. But contrary to the expectations of many, he expanded Israeli settlements on the west bank of the Jordan River, an area some thought would be a homeland for Palestinian refugees.

Washington's displeasure with these settlements formed only part of the growing friction between the United States and Israel. In 1981 Reagan had pushed through Congress the sale of $8.5 billion in military equipment to Saudi Arabia, including Airborne Warning and Command System aircraft (AWACS). Israel, which had worked feverishly to block the sale, denounced the president's action as a threat to its security. The administration countered that the sale did not jeopardize Israel's safety, but would improve the security of the Saudis against Arab extremists. Israel's annexation of the Golan Heights and bombing of Iraq's nuclear reactor in 1981 intensified difficulties.

The situation in Lebanon brought further strains to the ''special relationship'' between the United States and Israel, and aggravated threats to the fragile stability of the Middle East. Two avowed foes of Israel, the Palestine Liberation Organization (PLO) and Syria, were entrenched in Lebanon, from which they could originate attacks against

A Marine standing guard in front of the U.S. embassy in Beirut that was destroyed by a terrorist bomb attack.

Israel. The latter had invaded Lebanon in 1978 and over the next several years had struck at PLO camps in retaliation for PLO raids. In June 1982 Israel launched a successful all-out attack on Lebanon, immobilizing the Syrian air force and defeating PLO forces. The United States sent Marines to the war-torn country and arranged for the evacuation of defeated PLO forces. In September the Lebanese Christian Phalangists, unrestrained by Israeli troops, massacred a large number of Palestinian civilians, including women and children. American Marines, along with troops from other nations, then returned to Lebanon to act as peacekeepers. The following month a Moslem extremist drove his explosive-filled truck into the ill-guarded Marine compound, killing 241. (Several months earlier a similar mission had destroyed the U.S. embassy in Beirut.) Although he pledged that the United States would not be swayed by acts of terrorism, President Reagan withdrew American military forces from Lebanon in early 1984.

The United States also experienced difficulty with Libya, whose leader, Muammar al-Qaddafi, supported acts of international terrorism. In August 1981 Qaddafi, a vehement foe of both the United States and Israel, lost two jets in dogfights with American naval planes conducting maneuvers in the Mediterranean. A few months later reports surfaced that Libyan agents in the United States were plotting to assassinate the president and other prominent figures. Nothing happened, but Washington responded by banning travel to Libya and the importation of Libyan oil.

Intervention in Central America and the Caribbean Neighbors to the south, particularly Nicaragua and El Salvador, also provided great worry for the United States. Alexander M. Haig, Jr., who served as secretary of state until his abrupt resignation in

June 1982, warned the president that the Soviet Union and Cuba were actively aiding the spread of communism in Central America. The president, who needed little persuading, reacted by taking a variety of measures that he hoped would thwart leftists and stabilize the region.

Concern for Nicaragua dated from 1979 and the overthrow of the pro-American dictatorship of Anastasio Somoza Debayle. The rebels had enjoyed broadly based support in their struggle against the unpopular ruler, and President Carter, whose concern for human rights had convinced him not to protect the Somoza regime, hoped that nonradicals would dominate the new government. Instead, pro-Marxist Sandinistas took control, denouncing the United States as an imperial power.

In addition to their rhetoric, the Reagan administration claimed, the Sandinistas were welcoming Cuban military and civilian advisors, and were suppressing the native anti-Marxist opposition. Further, they were allegedly supplying aid to rebels in El Salvador. The subversion of the latter, it was feared, could destabilize the entire region. Although the Sandinistas denied the charges, the United States cut off economic assistance to Nicaragua in 1981.

Many hoped that problems between the United States and Nicaragua could be resolved amicably. The Contadora group—Mexico, Panama, Colombia, and Venezuela—urged negotiations. And in 1983 President Reagan appointed Henry Kissinger to head a bipartisan commission to study the situation in Central America. The following year the commission reported that misery and degradation lay at the root of that region's problems, and that an infusion of massive economic aid was desperately needed. It urged that the United States provide $24 billion by 1990. The president lauded the report and asked Congress to appropriate the necessary funds.

Reagan, however, did not commit himself solely to the pacific approach to hemispheric problems advocated by the Kissinger Commission. The CIA as well as private American citizens contributed arms and funds to the *contras,* a group of anti-Sandinistas who plotted to overthrow the regime. The contras received training in both the United States and Honduras, from where they launched raids into Nicaragua. The CIA at one point also mined Nicaraguan ports and provided the rebels with information on how to subvert governments. In 1984 the Sandinistas claimed that the United States was preparing to launch an invasion of their country by year's end. President Reagan denied the charge. Fearful of growing American involvement, Congress, which two years earlier had prohibited the use of secret funds to aid the contras, now banned all federal funds for them.

Problems in El Salvador seemed as intractable as those in Nicaragua. President Carter had vacillated in his support for the military junta that in 1979 had seized power from a government dominated by an oligarchy of wealthy landowners. The junta proposed land reforms and placed a civilian, José Napoleon Duarte, at the head of the government. Duarte soon lost control of the situation as left-wing rebels and right-wing ''death squads'' vied for dominance in a bloody civil war. The 1982 elections gave victory to the right-wing forces led by Colonel Robert D'Aubisson.

Convinced that the rebels must be defeated, President Reagan and his advisors backed increased military and economic aid for El Salvador, despite repeated outcries from members of Congress and others that a government that tolerated and perhaps abetted death squads did not deserve support. The president denounced terrorism but

CHAPTER 18: THE REAGAN YEARS

continued to differentiate between friendly "authoritarian" governments and unfriendly "totalitarian" ones. In 1983 the contingent of American military advisors to El Salvador, who now numbered more than 50, sustained their first death. The following year saw Duarte win the presidency from D'Aubisson during an election in which many citizens courageously voted in the face of threats from rebels. The moderate Duarte promised to uproot the death squads, continue land reform, and seek an end to the civil war.

The tiny Caribbean island of Grenada also caused Americans concern. A coup by radicals in 1983 resulted in the death of Prime Minister Maurice Bishop, who ironically was a Marxist. Mindful of the recent hostage crisis in Iran, the United States feared for the fate of more than 100 Americans at a Grenadian medical school. On October 25, about 6,000 American troops invaded the island, quickly defeating the small Grenadian forces and their Cuban allies. This easy victory helped relieve some of the frustrations experienced in Nicaragua and El Salvador. The fact that most Grenadians and their island neighbors welcomed the American invasion made the triumph all the more satisfying.

THE ELECTION OF 1984

President Reagan also hoped to win a triumphant reelection. The 1984 Republican convention renominated him and Vice-President Bush without opposition and enthusiastically praised the administration's record. Looking back upon four years of Reaganism, delegates applauded the decline in inflation and interest rates, as well as the upturn in various economic indicators. They also endorsed the president's strong stand against communism and for traditional values.

Democrats did not have such an easy time selecting their ticket. Ohio senator and former astronaut John Glenn appeared the front-runner at first but quickly lost momentum and dropped out of the race. Both Walter Mondale, the former Minnesota senator and vice-president under Carter, and Colorado's Senator Gary Hart possessed solid liberal credentials. Hart made a special appeal to younger voters with his claim to "new ideas," which he never spelled out. South Carolina's Senator Ernest Hollings trailed both men. So did the party's most exciting and controversial aspirant, the Reverend Jesse Jackson.

Long active in the civil rights movement, Jackson was a superb orator and became the first black presidential contender to command widespread support. Immensely appealing to blacks, he called for a "Rainbow Coalition" of minorities and others to back him as an advocate of social justice and an opponent of Reaganomics. His chances of actually winning the nomination were nil, although blacks registered to vote in large numbers. But he hoped to use his candidacy to force the party to take more seriously the needs and aspirations of minorities. Some ethnic slurs against Jews—he referred to New York City as "Hymietown"—hurt his credibility and diminished his luster among liberals, however.

Despite some difficulties in the primaries, Mondale captured his party's presidential nomination on the first ballot. Then, confounding critics who thought him safely predictable, he handpicked Congresswoman Geraldine Ferraro of New York as his vice-presidential running mate. A three-time member of the House, Ferraro was a liberal, a Catholic, and an Italian-American. More striking, she was the first woman from either party to receive the vice-presidential nomination.

Geraldine Ferraro

During the course of the campaign Mondale attacked Reagan for having amassed huge federal budget deficits and for having failed to bring down interest rates further. He also denounced his economic policies as aiding the rich at the expense of the poor. The Democratic candidate bravely promised to raise taxes—both to shrink the deficits and to promote needed social programs. He also attacked the massive outlays for military spending, as well as the administration's foreign policy that seemed to scorn détente with the Soviets.

But Mondale faced an uphill battle. He did well in the first of two nationally televised debates with his opponent, only to have Reagan recover in the second debate. Ferraro proved an able campaigner, but her refusal to disclose information concerning her husband's financial assets hurt her. More important was President Reagan's personal appeal and seeming immunity to attack. He was the "Teflon president," joked some: derogatory charges failed to stick, and calamitous events such as the deaths of the Marines in Lebanon failed to affect his popularity. Finally, as former President Nixon privately noted during the campaign: "You cannot beat an incumbent President in peacetime if the nation is prosperous."

CHAPTER 18: THE REAGAN YEARS

The election results proved Nixon right. Reagan's popular plurality of nearly 17 million votes was exceeded only by Nixon's in 1972; his electoral victory (525–13) was greater than any except Franklin D. Roosevelt's in 1936. Mondale captured the electoral votes of only his home state and the District of Columbia. Among definable groups of voters he won only the black vote. Yet the Democrats maintained control of the House, losing but 14 seats. The new House would contain 252 Democrats to 182 Republicans. They also reduced Republican control of the Senate by two seats to a margin of 53–47. The election had confirmed Ronald Reagan's popularity. It had not offered indisputable proof of any major shift in party strength or any "conservative revolution." Such proof would have to wait for the events of the president's second term of office.

SECOND TERM

Buoyed by his powerful election victory, Ronald Reagan entered the second term of his presidency determined to pursue the general policies and directions that had marked his first term as chief executive. In his State of the Union Address of February 6, 1985, he called for no less than a "second American Revolution." He would work for tax revision, sustained economic growth, and an end to fears of nuclear holocaust.

Tax Revision   Numerous critics had spelled out the shortcomings of the nation's tax system, some agreeing with former President Carter that it represented a "disgrace to the human race." But few believed that sweeping reform was likely. Nonetheless, bipartisan congressional support for lower rates and tax simplification had emerged by 1985. In May the president himself proposed a new law that would eliminate a number of deductions and loopholes, and transform the system from one that was "un-American" to one that was "clear, simple and fair for all." After much struggle the Tax Reform Act became law the following year.

The new tax measure produced the most fundamental changes in federal income tax policy since World War II. First, it simplified the tax code by eliminating scores of deductions and exclusions and by reducing the number of tax rates on individuals from 15 to 2. Under this system an estimated six million Americans at or below the poverty level would pay no taxes at all, and by some estimates, 80 percent of all taxpayers would gain some relief. The law also shifted more of the tax burden to businesses. While the maximum rate on business was actually reduced, the elimination of various special benefits and loopholes promised to affect enterprises that previously had paid little if any tax.

The Tax Reform Act seemed to represent a triumph for supply-side economics. The president believed that lower taxes would translate into greater consumer spending, business prosperity, and future economic growth. Others were skeptical. Some feared that the new law would discourage business investment and further injure the smokestack industries. They also worried that the measure would diminish general economic expansion and bring on a recession. Other doubters questioned just how far-reaching the law was. The actual tax saving for most people, they argued, would be quite small. But most could agree that no one really knew for certain what the long-range effects would be.

Budget and Trade Deficits   Whatever the effects of tax reform, the Reagan administration pointed with pride to several economic developments that occurred during the two years after his election. Unemployment fell to around the 7 percent level; inflation reached below 4 percent, its lowest level since the early post-World War II years; interest rates dropped sharply; and the Dow-Jones Average posted extraordinary gains of more than 500 points. Even so, huge deficits in the federal budget and in the nation's international trade loomed menacingly.

The budget deficit, which had reached an alarming $110 billion in 1982, was nearly twice that size by 1986. Sharp disagreements over where to make cuts exacerbated the problem. Democrats generally pushed for greater reductions in military spending, while their Republican counterparts, with the backing of the president, called for increased slashes in domestic appropriations. In December 1985 the controversial Gramm-Rudman law proposed a drastic solution. If the president and Congress failed to agree on cuts, the law mandated automatic yearly reductions, evenly divided between military and domestic allocations. These reductions would eliminate all deficits by 1991. In February 1986, however, a federal court invalidated the automatic reduction provision. This clouded the outlook for Gramm-Rudman itself and for an end to the spiraling budget deficits.

Trade deficits represented yet another serious and seemingly intractable problem. So staggering was the imbalance that in 1985 the United States became a debtor nation for the first time since 1914. Between 1980 and 1985 imports increased by 41 percent as exports decreased by three percent. Trade with Latin American nations alone went from a surplus of $1.9 billion in 1981 to a sprawling $17.2 billion deficit five years later. By mid-1986 the adverse balance of trade promised to reach at least $170 billion, more than a 10 percent increase over the preceding year's record shortfall.

A decline in the value of the dollar did give some hope for making American goods more competitive in foreign markets, but the recovery of a healthy foreign trade remained elusive. Angry business leaders and their equally angry workers demanded protection, as did many members of Congress. The president resisted. In August 1986 he vetoed a protectionist bill, noting that it would bring increased prices to consumers and invite retaliation from foreign countries. Instead, he called upon other nations to lower their trade barriers voluntarily. Japan, the principal worry, agreed to open its market to American semiconductors. Yet competition from abroad continued to beleaguer such industries as shoemaking and machine tools, and in summer 1986 LTV, the nation's second largest manufacturer of steel, filed for bankruptcy due, in large part, to foreign competitors.

The Judiciary   Controversy also surrounded the nation's courts. During his second term President Reagan continued his efforts to reshape the federal judiciary along more conservative lines. Some estimated that by the end of his presidency he would have the opportunity to appoint more than one-half of the nearly 800 federal judges. These appointees presumably would hold views akin to his on such substantial issues as abortion, affirmative action, pornography, women's rights, school prayer, government regulation of business, the death penalty, and criminal due process. Both his supporters and detractors agreed that any remolding of the judiciary along conservative lines would constitute one of his most enduring achievements.

438 CHAPTER 18: THE REAGAN YEARS

A major opportunity for reshaping the Supreme Court presented itself in 1986 when Chief Justice Warren Burger announced his resignation. Moving quickly, the president nominated Associate Justice William Rehnquist to fill the vacancy. Since his appointment to the Court in 1972, Rehnquist had proven himself the most conservative member of that judicial body. To take Rehnquist's place the president chose Antonin Scalia, a justice of the U.S. Court of Appeals for Washington, D.C., and the first Italian-American to sit on the high bench. Like Rehnquist, Scalia held staunchly conservative views. Both men won confirmation by the Senate, although Rehnquist met with stiff opposition from many who deemed him insufficiently sensitive to minorities.

Yet the Supreme Court gave no indication of abandoning its generally moderate position. In June 1986 it reaffirmed the right of women to procure abortions. The following month it upheld the principle of affirmative action. Despite this continued approval from the high court, Attorney General Edwin Meese announced that the Justice Department would not press for affirmative action unless discrimination was clearly present; otherwise, he argued, the government would be sponsoring ''reverse discrimination.''

Arms Control   In terms of foreign policy, reducing the threat of nuclear war between the United States and the Soviet Union remained a high priority during the president's second term in office. He and Soviet leader Gorbachev met in Geneva in January 1985 and agreed that their countries would hold arms control talks in the same city a year later. In the late summer of 1986 the Soviets announced that they were continuing their moratorium on nuclear weapons testing and invited the United States to follow suit, suggesting that a treaty banning all tests might ensue. Citing the need to check the reliability of its weapons, combined with the difficulty of verifying any moratorium, the Reagan administration declined the proposal.

But the chief obstacle to any arms control accord remained SDI (Star Wars), which the Soviets denounced. Three years after its inception in 1983 SDI had already cost $4.7 billion and had not erased serious doubts as to whether it could produce a fool-proof system of defense against missile attacks or could serve as a bargaining chip for Soviet arms reductions. The debate over the Star Wars program continued as the January 1, 1987 expiration date for the Salt II treaty limits drew nearer. Pointing to certain advantages the treaty offered the Soviets, the administration announced that the United States would have to exceed the imposed limits by year's end.

Contrary to expectations, the two superpowers almost achieved a major breakthrough at an October summit in Iceland. There Reagan and Gorbachev met to arrange for a larger conference later in the United States. The Soviet leader offered a variety of disarmament proposals, most notably one that would drastically reduce and then eliminate long-range nuclear missiles stockpiled by both sides. In return the United States would promise not to develop, test, or deploy SDI for 10 years. Reagan refused to accept the package, arguing that it would leave the United States and its allies open to Soviet cheating. Gorbachev then rejected the president's counterproposals. The arms impasse continued, although the door to future negotiations remained open.

Continued Tensions: The Middle East and Latin America   Meanwhile tensions in the Middle East persisted. Continued fighting between Christians and Moslems left Lebanon in a state of undeclared war; the problems of Palestinian refugees, of Israel, and

SECOND TERM 439

of its hostile Arab neighbors defied solution. Equally intransigent was the question of terrorism. Shiite Moslems skyjacked a plane in June 1985 and seized 153 hostages, 104 of them Americans. They freed their captives after 17 days, but not before executing an American navy diver and getting Israel to release a number of imprisoned Shiites. In October four Palestinians seized the Italian cruise ship *Achille Lauro* as it approached Egypt. The terrorists demanded freedom for 50 Palestinians held by Israel. Before fleeing the ship, the hijackers killed a crippled, elderly American citizen and threw his body overboard. The terrorists fled aboard an Egyptian airliner that was soon intercepted by American navy fighters and forced to land in Italy, where the highjackers were arrested by Italian authorities.

American officials believed that this most recent terrorist attack, like many before it, had been sponsored by Libyan leader Muammar al-Qaddafi. In late March 1986 the two nations exchanged missiles during American naval maneuvers in disputed Mediterranean waters. But the terrorism continued. The bombing of a Berlin nightclub killed an American serviceman, and an explosion aboard a commercial airliner en route from Rome to Athens took the lives of four passengers.

In retaliation the United States launched a nighttime air strike on April 14 against Libyan military targets and a suspected training school for terrorists. The strike caused substantial damage and underscored the administration's vow to combat terrorism. Most Americans approved of the strike, but allies throughout the world feared that it would only incite Colonel Qaddafi and others to further desperate acts. And within a few days three Westerners who had been held hostage in Lebanon were executed. Then in September four Palestinian terrorists seized an American plane in Karachi. Before Pakistani troops recaptured the plane the terrorists had killed 21 and injured 150.

Closer to home, the United States continued to experience frustration in its dealings with Nicaragua. The administration maintained its support for the contras, asking Congress for $100 million in aid. The policy had many critics in Congress and the press, and in the public at large. They pointed to the reported corruption of some contra leaders and, more important, echoed earlier fears of an ultimate deployment of American troops. Supporters of the administration countered by arguing that military pressure by the contras might force the Sandinistas to negotiate and hold free elections. American support of the contras, they insisted, would preclude direct American intervention. As the debate in the United States wore on, the Sandinista regime remained entrenched and was less tolerant than ever of internal dissent.

Trouble of another sort was also brewing in Latin America. International drug trafficking in various nations of the hemisphere became a prominent concern as the use of drugs, particularly cocaine, by Americans reached epidemic proportions. In an attempt to combat the problem President Reagan announced in 1986 that he would use the armed forces if necessary. In August he ordered a small contingent of American troops to Bolivia, where they joined officials of that country in a mission to destroy drug crops. Though a dramatic symbol, the measure in itself did little to effect a long-range solution. Hoping for more substantial results, Congress appropriated $1.7 billion in October to fight the drug problem.

On a more positive note, the situation in El Salvador, while still serious, had not deteriorated further. President Duarte continued to enjoy popular support, as his rebel opponents remained at bay. Right-wing death squads had also become silent. Nonethe-

CHAPTER 18: THE REAGAN YEARS

less, the problem of extensive poverty remained as grim as ever and portended continuing difficulties.

New Tensions: The Philippines and South Africa   As the second Reagan administration began the United States also found itself in a thorny situation with one of its most faithful allies, the Philippines. For several years Philippine President Ferdinand Marcos had been losing support among the Filipinos, due largely to growing economic difficulties and charges of government corruption and repression. Reports that Marcos and his wife had plundered the Philippine treasury of millions of dollars provoked indignation at home and abroad. Communist rebels, though a distinct minority, were gaining strength in portions of the archipelago. Further trouble arose when Benigno Aquino, a leader of the non-Communist opposition to Marcos, was assassinated on August 21, 1983, as he returned to the Philippines after several years of exile in the United States. The assassin was caught and immediately killed, but even a government investigation failed to convince many that high officials were not involved in a conspiracy to slay the popular anti-Marcos figure.

Corazon (Cory) Aquino, the victim's widow, returned to her homeland to lead the opposition and she ran against Marcos in the presidential election of February 1986. With both sides claiming victory, the United States sent observers, who reported that the election had been marked with widespread fraud. As fighting in the streets of Manila and elsewhere intensified, the Reagan administration faced the hard choice of whether to persist in backing an increasingly unpopular but proven ally or take its chances with his opponent. Much was at stake, including the strategic naval and air bases that would come up for renewal in several years. In March, President Marcos fled the country after the United States began pressuring him to resign and two key Philippine leaders announced their support for Aquino. Aquino then became president, vowing to restore the nation's pillaged economy, maintain friendship with the United States, and negotiate with the rebels to lay down their arms. Despite the serious and ongoing problems facing the Philippines, the United States felt relieved that a violent revolution had been narrowly averted.

Fears arose during this same period that South Africa, another staunch ally, could not escape a bloodbath of its own. For decades the minority white South African government had imposed a system of apartheid that denied basic political and civil rights to the nation's nonwhite inhabitants. The violence became more frequent by 1985, as blacks demanded greater rights and the release of African National Congress leader Willie Mandela, who had been a political prisoner since 1962. The government promised to release Mandela if he would refrain from political activity, a bargain that he refused. Meanwhile the authorities lifted the ban on interracial marriage. These concessions failed to quiet the unrest, which the government rigorously suppressed by force. Between early fall 1984 and April 1986 more than 1,300 persons died as a result of racial violence.

Americans were divided over how to respond to the grave situation in South Africa. Earlier administrations had deplored the policy of apartheid and Congress had passed a law requiring American firms to treat all South African employees equally. But both presidents and Congress tempered their repugnance for apartheid with realistic considerations: South Africa was a firmly anti-Communist nation that controlled vital sea lanes and possessed such invaluable resources as gold and platinum.

A student sit-in held at the University of Pennsylvania on January 17, 1986, to protest the university's investments in South Africa.

As the situation worsened, an increasing number of Americans demanded stronger measures. College students demonstrated and held sit-ins, while others picketed the South African embassy. Various public institutions and private firms withdrew their funds from South Africa in an attempt to apply financial pressure. In 1985 and 1986 more than 60 American companies left South Africa. Congress called for limited trade and financial sanctions in 1985, but was preempted by President Reagan, who ordered lighter sanctions through executive order. Reagan was reluctant to impose stronger sanctions, which he felt would hurt South African blacks as well as neighboring black African nations. Calling for "constructive engagement" and denouncing the "Soviet-armed guerillas of the African National Congress," he tried to convince the South African government to dismantle apartheid voluntarily. Congress forced his hand the following year when it banned new American investments and bank loans to South Africa, and prohibited the importation of South African coal, uranium, steel, iron, and agricultural goods. The president vetoed the measure but in early October Congress overrode the veto, presenting Reagan with a rare but sharp defeat in his dealings with the legislative branch.

Midterm Elections The midterm congressional elections brought the president more bad news. Despite his vigorous efforts on behalf of party candidates, Republicans lost a total of eight Senate seats and control of the upper house. Democrats extended their victory by adding several seats to their existing majority in the House of Representatives. Public opinion polls confirmed the president's continuing personal popularity, but he had not been able to transfer this approval to the candidates he backed. There were, in fact, indications that his highly partisan campaigning backfired.

In public the president remained optimistic as he vowed "to complete the revolution that we have so well begun." He noted that most of the Senate races were closely contested, and that Republicans had gained eight governorships. Nonetheless, Democrats, who showed increased strength in the South and West, had gained control of the One-hundredth Congress. It now seemed virtually certain that several of Reagan's major policies and positions, including aid to the contras, the SDI program, and the reshaping of the federal judiciary, would meet with intensified opposition from a revitalized Democratic party.

BIOGRAPHICAL SKETCH

JEANE J. KIRKPATRICK · *born 1926*

Born in Duncan, Oklahoma, the daughter of an oil prospector, Jeane Kirkpatrick graduated from Barnard College in 1948 and received a master's degree from Columbia University two years later. After subsequent study in Paris she returned to the United States and for the next several years worked for the State Department and as a research assistant at Georgetown University. In 1967 she obtained her doctorate in political science from Columbia, writing her dissertation on Juan Perón and Argentine politics. The degree completed, she returned to full-time teaching at Georgetown.

Dr. Kirkpatrick's interest in politics went well beyond the classroom. Married to a prominent political scientist (Evron Kirkpatrick), she shared her husband's Democratic party allegiance as well as his enthsiasm for Hubert H. Humphrey. The bitter anti-Humphrey protests during the 1968 Democratic convention in Chicago and the failure of numerous Democrats to support the Minnesota senator against Richard Nixon chilled Kirkpatrick's faith in her party. In 1972 she helped to organize the Coalition for a Democratic Majority, a group opposed to the radical counterculture that had emerged from the 1960s.

By decade's end, disillusionment with American foreign policy had transformed her into a neoconservative.

Kirkpatrick came to the attention of Ronald Reagan as a result of an article she published in 1980. In it she criticized President Carter for having pursued a soft line toward the Soviet Union. After much deliberation, Kirkpatrick decided to campaign for the Republican presidential candidate. Once elected, Reagan rewarded her with the post of U.S. ambassador to the United Nations. At confirmation hearings she told senators that she would serve notice on those groups hostile to the United States "that the patience of the American people has very nearly run out."

True to her word, Kirkpatrick vigorously defended the nation's interests during her four years (1981–1985) at the U.N. Complaining that the United States was "ignored, despised, and reviled," she railed at both Communist and nonaligned countries for their condemnation of American policies. Yet for all her acerbity, she could be adept in the use of diplomatic persuasion. When in 1981 the U.N. threatened an arms embargo against Israel, Kirkpatrick convinced delegates to settle for a verbal condemnation. Many Americans

warmly applauded her strong enunciation of national interests. Others demurred, as when she drew the controversial distinction between the need to support friendly repressive governments while denouncing hostile ones.

Persistent rumors that President Reagan would appoint Kirkpatrick to a higher administration position failed to materialize. In early 1985 Kirkpatrick formally resigned and announced that she would return to Georgetown and teaching. Referring to her difficulties with other Reagan appointees, she noted that "I was a woman in a man's world," as well as "a Democrat among Republicans." Shortly afterward she formally became a Republican amid speculation that her new party would someday again select her for an important post.

SUGGESTED READINGS

Much of the reading on the Reagan years reflects the passion and rush of current events rather than the greater detachment and reflection associated with history. Nonetheless, a number of fine studies already exist. Lou Cannon's *Reagan* (1982) is a solid biography. Other useful works on Reagan include: Hedrick Smith et al., *Reagan the Man, the President* (1981); Robert Dallek, *Ronald Reagan: The Politics of Symbolism* (1984); Ronnie Dugger, *On Reagan: The Man and the Presidency* (1983); and L. I. Barrett, *Gambling with History: Reagan in the White House* (1984).

For domestic economic issues, see both George Gilder, *Wealth and Poverty* (1981), which presents conservative arguments that became essential parts of Reaganomics, and P. C. Roberts, *The Supply-Side Revolution* (1984). T. B. Edsall, *The New Politics of Inequality* (1984), strongly dissents from Reaganomics, as do Lester C. Thurow, *The Zero-Sum Society* (1980) and *The Zero-Sum Solution* (1985). Further disapproval can be found in David Stockman, *Triumph of Politics: How the Reagan Revolution Failed* (1986), the memoirs of Reagan's original budget director and a one-time advocate of Reaganomics. S. J. Tolchin and Martin Tolchin, *Dismantling America: The Rush to Deregulate* (1983) is highly critical of the Reagan administration's approach to regulatory activities. Barry Bluestone and Bennett Harrison, *The Disindustrialization of America* (1983), offers important insights into the severe problems faced by the nation's basic industries.

Arms control, nuclear weapons, and the military have received a good deal of attention. Strobe Talbott's *Endgame* (1979) and *Deadly Gambit* (1984) are detailed analyses of the complexities of arms control. Paul B. Stares, *The Militarization of Space: U.S. Policy, 1945–1984* (1985) is comprehensive and balanced, as is Walter A. McDougall, *The Heavens and Earth: A Political History of the Space Age* (1986). Robert Scheer, *With Enough Shovels: Reagan, Bush and Nuclear War* (1982), argues that the administration is intent on winning any possible nuclear war. Less shrill is George Kennan, *The Nuclear Delusion: Soviet-American Relations in the Atomic Age* (1982). Edward N. Luttwak's *Making the Military Work* (1985) is a most provocative and challenging study. The most persuasive analysis of the downing of the Korean commercial airliner to date is Seymour M. Hersh, *"The Target Is Destroyed." What Really Happened to Flight 007 and What America Knew About It* (1986).

Seth P. Tillman's *The United States in the Middle East: Interests and Obstacles* (1982) is a balanced analysis of U.S. foreign policy in one of the world's most troubled regions. More biased but still important is Noam Chomsky, *The Fateful Triangle: The U.S., Israel, and the Palestinians* (1983). See also Edward P. Haley, *Qaddafi and the United States Since 1969* (1984).

Few detailed studies of contemporary United States involvement in Central America exist. Alexander M. Haig, Jr.'s *Caveat: Realism, Reagan and Foreign Policy* (1984) covers, among other matters, the former secretary of state's concerns for Communist subversion. R. S. Leikin, ed., *Central America: Anatomy of Conflict* (1984) is quite useful. Highly informative in supplying background is Walter LaFeber, *Inevitable Revolutions: The United States in Central America* (1983). Joan Didion, *Salvador* (1983) is a firsthand account by a contemporary fictionist.

William A. Henry III, *Visions of America* (1985), is a highly readable account of the 1984 presidential election. For a behind-the-scenes look at the 1984 campaign, see Peter Goodman and Tony Fuller, *The Quest for the Presidency 1984* (1985).

Epilogue: Coming of Age

Although the twentieth century was yet unfinished, the decades since 1900 had marked out new contours for the American nation. Socially, the country remained as pluralistic as ever. The melting pot had not melted as experts and popular writers had predicted early in the century, while millions of immigrants from Asia, Africa, and Latin America had added several more elements to the ethnic mix. These newcomers, like those before them, confronted considerable hostility, but the civil rights laws of the 1960s and 1970s made it considerably more difficult to practice the most blatant forms of discrimination. Native women and blacks meanwhile had made great strides since World War II. The black middle class had grown enormously, and thousands of women were moving into occupations that were hitherto reserved for men. Despite progress in these areas, the nation still had a long way to go before complete sexual and racial equality had been achieved.

If there had been progress in minority rights, a weakening of the American family over the decades gave much cause for alarm and represented the nation's greatest social threat by the 1980s. The epidemic of divorce was blamed for escalating suicide rates, drug use, and illegitimacy among teenagers, while numerous single-parent households meant that more and more children fell below the poverty line. And even in homes where father and mother remained together, it was not unusual for children to come home to an empty house after school to await the return of working parents.

In politics the United States was clearly more democratic than it had been a century before. Direct election of senators, primary elections, women's suffrage, black civil rights, and the enfranchisement of 18-year-olds had all opened the political process to greater participation. Yet the emergence of television in the post-World War II period threatened to undermine these reforms by favoring candidates with the most money and the best media personalities.

Economically, Americans had experienced unparalleled growth and prosperity during the century, as the middle class swelled to include the majority of citizens. But along with prosperity had come environmental pollution and the depletion of natural resources. Nor did everyone share in the horn of plenty. For in spite of several reform movements, including the much heralded war on poverty during the 1960s, 15 to 20 percent of the population still lived in poverty.

But the most astonishing feature of the economy was the shift to service industries as the century came to a close. Since the beginning of human history the production of physical goods had been the chief economic preoccupation. Technology had now assured a superabundance of material goods, combined with decreasing demands for unskilled labor. The result was crippling unemployment among blue-collar workers and ever greater educational requirements for the more desirable jobs. Americans were clearly living in a postindustrial age.

The twentieth century also saw the United States emerge from its cultural dependence on Europe and claim global recognition in the arts and sciences. New York became one of the leading intellectual and artistic centers of the world. American jazz and later American rock set the tone for modern music everywhere, and writers like Ernest Hemingway and William Faulkner achieved international stature. In science and medicine, too, Americans had no reason to apologize. J. Robert Oppenheimer, Jonas Salk, and Michael DeBakey were only a few of the country's pioneers in these areas.

It was in foreign affairs, however, that the most marked changes had occurred. In the 1890s the United States was not yet considered a great power. Half a century and two world wars later the country was a global colossus whose armies and navies encircled the earth. The old isolationism died as citizens finally concluded that events nearly anywhere in the world might have a bearing on their own well-being. By mid-century Americans were proud of their predominance and were determined to stay at the top, even if it meant opposing revolution abroad in an effort to maintain the status quo. Pursuing such a course was not without its risks, as wars in Korea and Vietnam and the nuclear arms race clearly showed. In the process many Americans learned the hard way that being a world power was not so much glorious as it was fraught with constant dangers and frustrations.

Americans had thus reached a sort of plateau by the end of the twentieth century. They had filled out the boundaries of their vast territorial domain, had solved the problems of physical production, and had used their economic and political resources to become the most powerful nation on earth. At the same time there was a sense that the country had gone about as far as it wanted or needed to go. This was not to say that no new challenges remained. The continued existence of poverty at home and abroad, not to speak of the ever-present threat of nuclear annihilation, provided abundant challenges to the rising generation. Nor was there any doubt that medical researchers would find new cures or that scientists would extend the frontiers of human knowledge and provide even greater human comforts. Even so, the country's years of unprecedented growth and boundless optimism had been tempered by its own success. In a very real way America had passed through its most formative period and had truly come of age.

Index

Abington v. *Schempp,* 340
Abortion, 391, 404, 416, 429
ABSCAM scandal, 390
Acheson, Dean, 252, 253, 262
Acquired immune deficiency syndrome (AIDS), 420
Adams, Henry, 2, 14
Adams, James Truslow, 187
Adams, Sherman, 294
Adamson Act of 1916, 68
Addams, Jane, 40, 41, 44, 64
Advertising industry, 122
Affirmative action, 391–392, 438
Agee, James, 188
Agnew, Spiro T., 345, 364, 370, 373, 374
Agrarian writers, 140
Agricultural Adjustment Act (AAA), 166–167, 176
Agriculture. *See* Farmers
Aguinaldo, Emilio, 72–73
Aid to Families with Dependent Children (AFDC), 336
Aiken, Conrad, 177
Airborne Warning and Command System (AWACS), 431
Airline industry, 122
Alcohol abuse, 419
Aldrich, Nelson W., 59, 62, 67, 401

Aldrich, Thomas Bailey, 13
Algeciras Conference of 1906, 83
Alger, Russell A., 76
Alianza de Las Mercedes, 351
Alliance for Progress, 322–323
All in the Family, 364
Alperovitz, Gar, 246
Ambrose, Stephen, 292
America First Committee, 206
American Civil Liberties Union, 130
American Federation of Labor (AFL), 37–38, 105, 123, 150, 179
American Indian Movement (AIM), 351–352
American Liberty League, 173–174
American Protective League, 108
Amusement parks, 20
Anderson, John, 400
Anderson, Marian, 181
Anderson, Sherwood, 139
Andropov, Yuri, 430
Anthony, Susan B., 45
Anticommunism, 264, 299
  and espionage cases, 273–275
  McCarthyism, 275–277, 284
  as political issue, 273
Anti-Saloon League (ASL), 41

Apollo 11, 325–326
Appalachian Regional Development Act of 1965, 336
Aquino, Benigno, 440
Aquino, Corazon ''Cory,'' 440
Arbenz, Jacobo, 287
Arbuckle, Roscoe ''Fatty,'' 134
Architecture
  in 1920s, 137–138
  postwar, 313–315
  at turn of century, 27, 29
Armory Show, 27
Arms control
  of atomic energy, 252–253, 263, 288
  SALT agreement, 368, 394, 395–396, 431, 438
  Strategic Arms Reduction Talks (START), 431
  and Strategic Defense Initiative (SDI), 431, 438
  test ban, 326, 438
  Washington Naval Conference, 193–194
Armstrong, Neil A., 325
Army
  -McCarthy hearings, 284
  Root's reform of, 76
  in World War I, 100–103
  in World War II, 217–222

447

448

INDEX

Army War College, 76
Art
  of Depression, 188
  in 1920s, 137
  in 1960s, 363
  postwar, 312–313
  at turn of century, 26–27
Ash Can School, 26–27, 137
Atlantic Charter, 209–210
Atlee, Clement, 229
Atomic bomb
  development of, 225, 263
  on Hiroshima/Nagasaki, 225,
    226–227
  and international control,
    252–253, 263, 288
  in Rosenberg spy case, 275
Atomic Energy Commission
  (AEC), 263–264
Automobile, 18–19, 120
Automobile industry, 120, 267,
  337

Babbitt (Lewis), 139–140
Baby boom(ers), 297, 299–300,
  409, 419
Baer, George, 56
Baez, Joan, 375–376
Bailey, Thomas A., 114–115
Baker, Howard, 399
Baker v. *Carr,* 339
Bakke, Alan, 391–392
Ballinger, Richard A., 63
Ballinger-Pinchot controversy, 63,
  69
Banking Act of 1935, 169
Banks
  computer use in, 406
  and New Deal legislation, 166,
    169
Barkley, Alben, 270
Barton, Bruce, 122
Baruch, Bernard, 104, 253
Baseball, 19, 135–136, 310
Basketball, 310
Battista, Fulgencio, 291
Bauhaus School, 314
Bayh, Birch, 385
Bay of Pigs invasion, 323
Beard, Charles, 35, 187

Beard, Mary, 187
Beatles, 358, 361, 362
Beat writers, 311–312
Beer-Wine Revenue Act of 1933,
  166
Begin, Menachem, 396, 431
Bell, Griffin, 388
Bellows, George, 137
Bendix, Reinhard, 304
Benton, Thomas Hart, 188, 312
Berger, Victor, 38, 108–109
Berkeley, Busby, 188
Berle, Adolf A., Jr., 165
Berlin
  access routes to, 290, 324
  blockade of, 255–256
  Wall, 324
  zones of occupation, 228
Berlin, Irving, 21
Bethune, Mary McLeod, 181
Bicentennial celebration, 384–385
Bicycle, 18
Birth control, 45, 46, 391, 409
Birth of a Nation, 21–22
Birthrate, 17, 133, 297, 299–300,
  409–410
Blackmun, Harry, 366
Black Muslims, 350
Black Panthers, 350–351, 359
Blacks. *See also* Civil rights laws;
  Civil rights movement
  and affirmative action, 391–392
  in armed services, 106, 234, 269
  in baseball, 136, 310
  Black Power movement,
    350–351
  Booker T. Washington and, 16
  Harlem Renaissance, 140, 142
  and job discrimination, 107, 234
  nationalism, 128, 129
  and New Deal, 180
  progressive reformers, 42–44
  in race riots, 106, 107, 234,
    344, 351
  school desegregation, 283–284,
    330, 391
  segregation of, 15, 269,
    282–283, 304
  urban migration of, 44, 107
  and voting rights, 336, 341

Blum, John Morton, 99
Bolshevik Revolution, 101, 111,
  123–124
Bond, Mary W., 6–7
Bonnie and Clyde, 363
Bonus Army, 159–160
Booth, Albie, 135
Borah, William Edgar, 113
Bork, Robert, 374
Bow, Clara, 134
Bowles, Chester, 328
Boxing, 20, 135
Boyce, Fran, 358–359
Brains Trust, 165
Brandeis, Louis D., 54, 65, 68,
  69, 110, 179
Bretton Woods Conference of
  1944, 241
Brezhnev, Leonid, 368, 430
Briand, Aristide, 194, 195
Bricker, John W., 238
Broadway musicals, 310
Brooklyn Dodgers, 310
Brooks, Van Wyck, 187
Browder, Earl, 178, 239
Brown, H. Rap, 351
Brown, Jerry, 385
Brown v. *Board of Education,*
  282–283, 304, 338
Bryan, William Jennings, 58, 61,
  65, 67, 79, 85, 93–94, 95,
  130
Bryan-Chamorro treaty, 86
Bryce, Lord James, 49
Buck, Pearl, 187
Budget and Accounting Act of
  1921, 145–146
Bulganin, Nikolai, 288
Bulge, Battle of, 222
Bull Moose party, 64
Bunau-Varilla, Philippe, 79
Burchfield, Charles, 137
Burford, Anne, 427
Burger, Warren, 366, 390–392,
  438
Burleson, Albert S., 108
Burnham, Daniel H., 27
Burns, Arthur, 390
Burns, James McGregor, 179
Bush, George, 399, 425

INDEX **449**

Bush, Vannevar, 229
Business. *See* Industry
Butz, Earl, 386
Byrnes, James F., 253

Cable, George Washington, 15
Cahensly, Peter, 14
Caldwell, Erskine, 186
Calles, Plutarco Elias, 197
Cambodia, U.S. relations with, 368, 394
Camp, Walter, 20
Canada, U.S. relations with, 84–85
Cancer research, 407
Cannon, Joe "Uncle Joe," 62–63, 65
Capone, Al "Scarface," 131
Carmichael, Stokely, 351
Carnegie, Andrew, 11, 23
Carnegie, Dale, 187
Carnegie Endowment for International Peace, 194
Carranza, Venustiano, 87
Carswell, G. Harrold, 366
Carter, Billy, 390
Carter, Jimmy, 436
 background and career of, 385–386
 economic program of, 389–390
 election of 1976, 385, 386–387
 election of 1980, 400
 and energy crisis, 388–389, 398
 foreign policy of, 395–398
 and hostage crisis, 398
 human rights policy of, 394–395
 presidential style of, 387–388
 public confidence in, 398
 scandals of administration, 390
Carver, George Washington, 22
Casablanca Conference of 1943, 227
Castillo Armas, Carlos, 287
Castro, Cipriano, 79
Castro, Fidel, 291, 323, 324, 331
Cather, Willa, 26
Catholic Church. *See also* Religion
 immigrants in, 13–14
 social activism in, 416
 and Vatican II, 415–416

Catt, Carrie Chapman, 45
Central Intelligence Agency (CIA), 286–287, 291, 323, 364, 394, 433
Chamberlain, Neville, 203–204, 205
Chambers, Whittaker, 273–274
Chamoun, Camille, 287
Chautauqua lectures, 23
Chavez, César, 351
Cheever, John, 177
Chemical industry, 121
Chernenko, Constantin, 430
Chiang Kai-shek, 198, 211, 212, 227, 258, 286
Children
 abuse of, 420–421
 labor laws, 38, 54, 68
 rearing practices, 17, 133
 and sexual revolution, 355, 356, 445
China
 Communist takeover in, 257, 258
 Japanese invasion of, 202–203
 in Korean War, 262, 264, 280
 Manchurian crisis in, 198
 and Quemoy-Matsu crisis, 286
 U.S. relations with, 75–76, 83, 84, 85, 193, 198, 257, 258, 286, 368
Chinese-Americans, 16
Chrysler Corporation, 422
Church, Frank, 385, 394
Churchill, Winston, 205, 208, 209–210, 216–217, 220, 227, 228, 229, 248, 252
Churchill, Winston (writer), 24
Cities
 bicentennial celebrations in, 384–385
 boss rule in, 49–50
 decay of, 302–303
 federal loans to, 384
 Great Society programs for, 337
 population in 1900, 51
 progressive reform in, 50–52
Civilian Conservation Corps (CCC), 170
Civil Rights Act of 1964, 332

Civil rights laws, 234, 269, 332, 338, 365–366, 429
Civil rights movement
 freedom riders, 330
 march on Washington, 346, 376
 and Martin Luther King, Jr., 346–347
 Montgomery bus boycott, 304–305
 voter registration campaign, 330–331
 and white backlash, 363–364
Civil Works Administration (CWA), 171
Clark, Champ, 65, 84
Clark, J. Reuben, 197
Clark Memorandum of 1930, 197
Class
 mobility, 11, 304
 in 1900, 5–10
 resentments, 364
 in wartime, 236
Clayton Act of 1914, 68
Clayton-Bulwer Treaty of 1850, 78
Cleaver, Eldridge, 358
Clemenceau, Georges, 110, 111
Cohan, George M., 20, 101, 237
Coit, Stanton, 40
Cold War, origins of, 246, 247
Colleges and universities. *See also* Education
 affirmative-action programs in, 391–392
 desegregation of, 330
 elective system in, 23
 and federal student loans, 336, 338
 shift from liberal arts, 421
 sports in, 310
 student protest in, 360, 368–369, 421, 441
Collier, John, 181
Colombia, U.S. relations with, 78–79
Columbia Broadcasting System (CBS), 134
Congress of Industrial Organizations (CIO), 180
Committee on Public Information (CPI), 107–108

450

INDEX

Committee to Re-Elect the President (CREEP), 373, 374
Commons, John R., 33, 41
Communist Party, 124, 173, 239
Computers, 405–406
Congress. *See also* Elections, congressional
    Cannonism in, 62–63
    Carter and, 388
    civil rights legislation in, 234, 269, 332, 338
    conservative coalition in, 240, 328–329
    Eisenhower and, 284
    failure to ratify Versailles Treaty, 111, 112–114
    Ford and, 383, 393, 394
    and foreign affairs, 204, 209, 341, 342, 369, 393, 433, 439
    Great Society legislation in, 336–338
    and Hiss case, 274
    Kennedy and, 329
    McCarthy investigations in, 275–277, 284
    neutrality laws in, 202
    New Deal legislation in, 166–171, 175–179, 271–272
    Nixon and, 372
    opposition to New Deal, 183, 240
    Reagan and, 426, 433, 439, 441–442
    tariff bills in, 62, 66–67
    Truman and, 268, 269, 271, 272
    Watergate investigations in, 374
Conkin, Paul, 185
Connally, John, 331, 399
Conroy, Jack, 186
Conservation policy
    antipollution programs, 367
    Ballinger-Pinchot controversy, 63, 69
    Great Society program, 337–338
    New Deal program, 169–170
    and Reagan's deregulation, 427–428
    of Theodore Roosevelt, 59–60
Conservatism, 417–418, 429

Constitution, amendments to, 45, 62, 277, 341
Consumer Protection Act of 1968, 337
Containment policy, 252
Contras, in Nicaragua, 433, 439
Coolidge, Calvin, 123, 140, 193
    election of 1924, 148–149
    personality of, 147–148
    probusiness policy of, 149–150
Coral Sea, Battle of, 222–223
Coué, Emil, 134
Coughlin, Charles E., 175, 178, 189–190
Council for Mutual Economic Assistance (COMECON), 255
Council of Economic Advisors, 268
Counterculture, 356–363
Cox, Archibald, 374, 381
Cox, George B., 50
Cox, James M., 115
Cramer, Charles F., 147
Crane, Stephen, 25
Creel, George, 107–108
Crick, Francis, 407
Crime
    and due process, 340, 391
    in 1980s, 418
    Prohibition gangsters, 130–131
Croly, Herbert, 65
Cromwell, William Nelson, 78
Crosby, Harry, 138
Cuba
    American protectorate in, 74, 80
    Bay of Pigs invasion of, 323
    Central Intelligence Agency (CIA) in, 291
    missile crisis in, 324
    rise of Castro, 291
Culbertson, Ely, 187
Culture. *See* Popular culture
Curry, John Steuart, 188
Cyprus, 393
Czechoslovakia, Munich agreement on, 204
Czolgosz, Leon, 55

Daladier, Edouard, 203–204
Darlan, Jean, 219

Darrow, Clarence, 130, 168
Darwinism, and Scopes trial, 129–130
D'Aubisson, Robert, 433, 434
Daugherty, Harry, 145, 147
Davies, Joseph, 237–238
Davis, John W., 149, 174
Dawes, Charles G., 146, 148, 195
Dawes Plan of 1924, 195
Dawes Severalty Act of 1887, 181
Dean, James, 309, 311
De Bakey, Michael, 407
Debs, Eugene Victor, 38–39, 64, 66, 108, 146
Defense, Department of, 269
de Kooning, Willem, 312
De Lesseps, Ferdinand, 78
Dell, Floyd, 119
Democratic party. *See also* Congress; Presidential elections
    in conservative coalition, 328–329
    -Dixiecrat split, 270
    period of dominance, 266
Dempsey, Jack, 135
Demuth, Charles, 137
Denby, Edwin, 145, 147
Deoxyribonucleic acid (DNA), 407
Depression. *See* Great Depression
Dewey, John, 2, 23, 34–35, 44
Dewey, Thomas E., 207, 238, 239, 270–271, 272
Dialectic of Sex (Firestone), 353–354
Díaz, Adolfo, 84, 86
Díaz, Porfirio, 87
Diem, Ngo Dinh, 328
Dillon, Douglas, 321
Divorce rate, 17, 44–45, 133, 232, 355–356, 420
Dixon, Thomas, Jr., 24
Dixon-Yates affair, 281
Dobrynin, Anatoly, 324
Doheny, Edward L., 147
Dolan, Terry, 418
Dole, Elizabeth, 429
Dole, Robert, 385
Dollar diplomacy, 83–84
Dominican Republic, U.S. relations with, 80–81, 86, 197

INDEX   **451**

Dos Passos, John, 186, 187
Douglas, Lewis, 165, 166
Douglas, William O., 238
Douglass, Frederick, 16
Dreiser, Theodore, 15, 25
Drug(s)
    abuse, 418–419
    cult, 359, 362
    traffic, 439
Duarte, José Napoleon, 433, 434,
    439
Dubinsky, David, 206
DuBois, W. E. B., 42–43, 66,
    106, 129
Dulles, John Foster, 289, 291,
    293–294
Dunne, Finley Peter, 59
Dylan, Bob, 362, 376

Eagleton, Thomas, 371
Eakins, Thomas, 2, 26
Eastern Europe
    Soviet Union and, 250, 255,
        289, 290, 293, 324, 393
    uprisings in, 289
    in Yalta agreement, 228, 248
East Germany, recognition of, 290
Eccles, Marriner, 183
Economy
    in Great Depression, 155–156,
        164, 183, 184
    inflation of 1970s, 366–367,
        382–383, 389–390
    in 1920s, 119–120, 149–150,
        153–154
    in 1980s, 426–427, 437
    postwar, 297
    stock market crash, 154–155
    wartime inflation, 231
Edison, Thomas Alva, 21
Edmunds, Walter D., 187
Education. See also Colleges and
    universities; School(s)
    bilingual, 412, 414
    and federal aid, 329–330, 336
    in G.I. Bill, 240
    medical, 22
    in 1900, 22–23
    professional, 23
    quality of, 421, 423

science, 289
    and teacher shortage, 423
Eggleston, Edward, 24
Egypt
    Camp David accords, 396, 431
    Suez crisis, 287
Einstein, Albert, 225
Eisenhower, David, 292
Eisenhower, Dwight D., 270,
    298–299, 318
    assessment of, 292, 294
    atoms for peace program, 288
    and civil rights, 282–284, 304
    and Congress, 284
    election of 1952, 277–279
    election of 1956, 284–285
    farm program of, 281
    fight for balanced budget,
        280–282
    on German rearmament, 288
    and highway bill, 282
    and Korean War settlement, 280
    and Khrushchev, 290–291
    and McCarthy hearings, 284
    and Middle East, 287
    on military-industrial complex,
        294
    and Nationalist China, 286
    and public power, 281
    in SEATO agreement, 286
    social program of, 281
    space program of, 289
    at summit meeting, 288–289,
        291
    and Vietnam, 285–286
    in World War II, 214, 219,
        221–222
Eisenhower Doctrine, 287
Elderly
    medical care for, 336, 411
    population of, 410–411
Elections. See also Presidential
    elections
    congressional, 63–64, 160, 183,
        240, 269, 279, 328, 336, 345,
        371, 382, 400, 436, 441
    reforms, 52–53
Electric power. See Power utilities
Elementary and Secondary School
    Act of 1965, 336

Eliot, Charles W., 22, 23
Eliot, T. S., 142
Elkins Act of 1903, 58
Ellison, Ralph, 177
Ellsberg, Daniel, 373
El Salvador, U.S. relations with,
    433–434, 439–440
Ely, Richard T., 33
Emergency Banking Relief Act of
    1933, 166, 169
Employment. See also Unemploy-
    ment
    discrimination, 15, 44, 107,
        132, 234, 305, 353
    full, 268
    of immigrants, 10, 412
    legal protection in, 54, 176,
        181
    in service industry, 408, 446
Employment Act of 1946, 268
Energy
    alternate sources of, 383
    crisis, 367, 388–389, 398
    nuclear, 388
Engle v. Vitale, 340
Environment. See Conservation
    policy
Environmental Protection Agency
    (EPA), 367, 427–428
EPIC (End Poverty in California),
    171
Equal Rights Amendment (ERA),
    45, 305, 353, 429
Ervin, Sam, 374
Espionage
    Hiss case, 273–274
    Rosenberg case, 275
Espionage Act of 1917, 108, 109,
    110
Ethiopia, Mussolini's invasion of,
    201, 202
Evans, Hiram W., 127
Evans, Walker, 188
Evers, Medgar, 331
Export-Import Bank, 200

Fads, 134–135
Fair Deal, 272
Fair Employment Practices Com-
    mittee (FEPC), 234, 239

INDEX

Fair Labor Standards Act of 1938, 181
Fall, Albert, 145, 147
Falwell, Jerry, 417
Family
  and baby boom, 299–300
  in 1900, 17
  and sexual revolution, 355, 356, 360
  wartime strains on, 232
  weakening of, 445
Farewell to Arms, A (Hemingway), 138
Farm Credit Act of 1933, 167
Farmers
  in Dust Bowl, 157, 167
  and farm bloc, 150–151
  in Great Depression, 157
  and New Deal, 166–167, 176, 281
  population decline, 303
  in social order, 10
  soil bank program for, 281
Farm Security Administration (FSA), 176
Farrell, James T., 186
Faubus, Orval, 284
Faulkner, William, 140, 311
Federal Communications Commission (FCC), 373
Federal Deposit Insurance Corporation (FDIC), 169
Federal Emergency Relief Act (FERA), 171
Federal Employee Loyalty Program, 270
Federal Farm Board, 158
Federal Home Loan Bank Act of 1932, 158
Federal Housing Administration (FHA), 171, 301
Federal Reserve Act of 1913, 67
Federal Reserve system, 67–68, 166, 169
Federal Securities Act of 1933, 169
Federal Trade Commission (FTC), 68
Feis, Herbert, 246
Ferraro, Geraldine, 434, 435

Ferlinghetti, Lawrence, 311
Filene, Edward, 174
Filene, Peter, 32
Firestone, Shulamith, 353
Fitzgerald, F. Scott, 119, 138, 139
Five-Power Treaty, 193
Flynn, John T., 185
Football, 20, 135, 309–310
Foraker, Joseph B., 42
Foraker Act of 1900, 74
Forbes, Charles R., 146–147
Ford, Gerald R., 374, 402
  background and career of, 379–380
  economic policy of, 382–383, 384
  election of 1976, 385, 386, 387
  foreign policy of, 393–394
  and Nixon pardon, 381
  selection of Rockefeller, 381–382
Ford, Henry, 19, 96, 120–121, 125, 150, 196, 214
Ford, Henry, II, 422
Ford, John, 237
Fordney-McCumber Tariff, 146, 151
Foreign policy, U.S. *See also* World War I; World War II
  Cambodia, 368, 394
  Canada, 84–85
  China
    détente, 368
    Nationalist China, 258, 286
    Open Door, 75–76, 83, 84, 85, 193, 257
    Stimson Doctrine, 198
  Colombia, 78–79, 85
  colonialism, 72–76, 80
  Congress and, 341, 393
    Contra aid, 433, 439
    Gulf of Tonkin Resolution, 342
    isolationist bloc, 204, 209
    opposition to Vietnam War, 369
  covert activities in, 286–287, 291, 293, 394
  Cuba, 74, 80, 291, 323, 324

Dominican Republic, 80–81, 86, 197
Egypt, 287, 396
El Salvador, 433–434, 439–440
France, 83, 193, 194–195, 285
Great Britain, 90, 193
  and Panama Canal, 78, 86, 87
  violation of neutral rights, 95–96
  wartime assistance, 93–94, 208–210
Greece, 253
Grenada, 434
Guatemala, 287
Haiti, 86, 197
Honduras, 84, 197
international cooperation, 194–195
  United Nations, 241, 249–250, 443
Iran, 286–287, 396–398
isolationist, 192, 200–202, 204–206
Israel, 257, 396, 431–432
Japan, 81–83, 85, 193, 202–203, 210, 211–212
Korean War, 259–262, 264
Laos, 326
Latin America. *See also specific country*
  Alliance for Progress, 322–323
  colonialism, 72–74
  dollar diplomacy, 83–84
  drug traffic and, 439
  economic aid, 255, 323, 433
  Good Neighbor, 197, 200
  military intervention, 196–197
  and Panama Canal, 78–79, 396
  Roosevelt Corollary, 79–80, 197
  and security zone, 205
Lebanon, 287, 431–432, 438
Libya, 432, 439
Marshall Plan, 254–255
Mexico, 87–89, 197, 200
Middle East, 287, 431–432, 438
Nicaragua, 83–84, 86, 197, 433, 439

INDEX **453**

North Atlantic Treaty Organization (NATO), 256
Panama, 396
Philippines, 440
South Africa, 440–441
Soviet Union
  arms control, 252–253, 326, 368, 394, 395–396, 431, 438
  arms race, 253, 288, 289, 290
  containment policy, 252
  Cuban missile crisis, 324
  détente, 368, 393–394
  John Foster Dulles in, 293–294
  in 1920s, 196, 199–200
  NSC-68 report on, 258–259
  under Reagan, 429–430, 438
  roots of Cold War, 246, 247
  summit meetings, 288–289, 291, 323–324, 438
  Truman Doctrine, 254
  U-2 incident, 291
  wartime alliance, 247–248, 251
Vietnam, 285–286, 328, 341-344
Forest Reserve Act of 1891, 60
Formosa (Taiwan), 286, 368
Forrestal, James V., 252, 269
Four-Power Treaty, 193
Fourteen Points, 110, 111
France
  Allied invasion of, 221–222
  in Suez crisis, 287
  U.S. relations, 83, 193, 194–195, 285
  Vichy, 205, 206, 219
  in Vietnam, 285
Frankfurter, Felix, 165
Frazier-Lemke Farm Bankruptcy Act, 167
Freedom riders, 330
Freeman, Douglas Southall, 187
Freudianism, 133
Friedan, Betty, 353
Fuchs, Klaus, 275
Fulbright, J. William, 343
Full employment, 268

Gagarin, Yuri, 325
Galante, Joseph, 126–127
Galbraith, John Kenneth, 321
Garfield, Harry A., 104
Garland, Hamlin, 25
Garner, John Nance, 160
Garvey, Marcus, 128, 129
Gary, Elbert H., 123
Gay Rights movement, 354
Genetic engineering, 407
George, Alexander L., 99
George, Juliette L., 99
German-Americans, 93, 108, 236
Germany. *See also* Berlin; East Germany; West Germany
  Nazi regime, 198, 201, 203–204
  in World War I, 92, 93, 94–95, 100, 101, 102, 111–112, 195–196
  in World War II, 204–205, 209, 217, 219, 222, 250–251
Gershwin, George, 137
Giannini, A. P., 174
Gibbons, James Cardinal, 14
Gibbs, Josiah Willard, 22
G.I. Bill of Rights, 240, 297
Gibson, Charles Dana, 18
Gibson, Josh, 136
Gideon v. *Wainwright,* 341
Gilbert, Cass, 29
Gilman, Charlotte Perkins, 44
Ginsberg, Allen, 311
Gladden, Washington, 36
Glasgow, Ellen, 24, 26
Glass-Steagall Act of 1932, 158, 169
Glavis, Louis, 63, 69
Glenn, John, 325
Goetz, Bernhard, 418
Going My Way, 237
Goldfine, Bernard, 294
Goldman, Emma, 45, 124
Gold Reserve Act of 1934, 169
Gold standard, 158, 169, 199
Goldwater, Barry, 334–335, 336, 399
Gompers, Samuel, 37–38, 68, 105, 150
Gomulka, Wladyslaw, 289
Goodman, Paul, 356

Good Neighbor Policy, 197, 200
Gorbachev, Mikhail, 430, 438
Gorgas, William, 22
Gorky, Arshile, 312
Graduate, The, 363
Graham, Billy, 307
Grange, Red, 135
Grant, Madison, 42, 125
Great Britain
  appeasement policy of, 204
  in Suez crisis, 287
  U.S. relations with, 78, 86, 87, 90, 93–94, 95–96, 193, 208–210
  in World War II, 204–205, 208–210, 216–222, 227–228, 250–251
Great Depression. *See also* New Deal
  foreign policy during, 198–210
  Hoover program in, 157–159, 164
  human misery in, 155–157, 172–173
  photography of, 188
  roots of, 153–154
  stock market crash, 154–155
Great Gatsby, The (Fitzgerald), 138
Greece, U.S. relations with, 253
Green, William, 150
Greening of America (Reich), 356–357
Green v. *County Board of Education,* 338
Grenada, invasion of, 434
Grey, Sir Edward, 96, 114
Griffes, Charles Tomlinson, 20
Griswold v. *Connecticut,* 391
Growing Up Absurd (Goodman), 356
Guatemala, U.S. relations with, 287
Guggenheim (Solomon R.) Museum, New York City, 315
Gulf of Tonkin Resolution, 342
Guthrie, Woodrow Wilson "Woody," 187

Haiti, U.S. relations with, 84, 86, 197

454 INDEX

Haldeman, H. R. "Bob," 372, 373
Hall, G. Stanley, 22
Hammerstein II, Oscar, 310
Hammer v. *Dagenhart,* 68
Handy, W. C., 137
Hanna, Mark, 55, 58
Hanson, Ole, 123, 124
Harding, Warren Gamaliel, 193, 194
  election of 1920, 115
  normalcy program of, 144–146
  scandals of administration, 146–147
Harlem Renaissance, 140, 142
Harriman, E. H., 57
Harriman, W. Averell, 328
Harrington, Michael, 333
Harris, Joel Chandler, 24
Hart, Gary, 434
Harvey, George, 65
Hauptmann, Bruno Richard, 214
Hawaii, 74, 212
Hawley-Smoot tariff, 158
Hawthorne, Nathaniel, 25
Hay, John, 75, 78, 85
Hay-Herrán treaty, 79
Haynsworth, Clement, 366
Hay-Pauncefote treaty of 1900, 78, 86
Hays, Will H., 134, 188
Haywood, William "Big Bill," 38, 109
Hazelton, Philip, 298–299
Head Start, 333
Health, Education, and Welfare (HEW), Department of, 281
Hearst, William Randolph, 24, 168, 178
Heckler, Margaret, 429
Helms, Jesse, 429
Helsinki agreement, 393
Hemingway, Ernest, 138, 311
Hepburn Act of 1906, 58–59
Herberg, Will, 302
Herbert, Victor, 20
Herrán, Thomas, 79
Hersey, John, 238
Herter, Christian, 291
Hicks, Granville, 187

Higher Education Act of 1965, 336
Highway Safety Act of 1966, 337
Highway system, interstate, 282
Hill, James J., 57
Hillquit, Morris, 38
Hippies, 358, 360–361
Hiroshima, bombing of, 225, 226–227
Hiss, Alger, 273–274
Historians, progressive, 35
Hitler, Adolf, 198, 201, 203–204, 205, 222
Hobby, Oveta Culp, 281
Ho Chi Minh, 285
Hoffman, Abbie, 358
Hollings, Ernest, 434
Holmes, Oliver Wendell, Jr., 34, 110, 124, 273
Holocaust, 243
Home Owners' Loan Corporation (HOLC), 171, 173
Homosexuals
  and AIDS epidemic, 420
  Gay Rights movement, 354
Honduras, U.S. relations with, 84, 197
Hoopes, Townsend, 292
Hoover, Herbert Clark, 115, 131
  clash with Bonus Army, 159–160
  Depression program of, 157–159, 164
  election of 1928, 151–152
  election of 1932, 160, 162
  foreign policy of, 197, 198
  personality of, 151
  Secretary of Commerce, 145, 146, 196
  voluntarism of, 157
  as wartime administrator, 105
Hoover, J. Edgar, 124
Hopkins, Harry L., 165, 171, 177, 181
Hopper, Edward, 137
House, Edward M., 95, 96, 114
House Committee on Un-American Activities (HUAC)
  and Hiss case, 274
  and movie industry, 276–277, 309

Housing
  in 1900, 8
  suburban development, 301–302
  tenement, 40
Housing and Urban Development, Department of, 337
How the Other Half Lives (Riis), 12
Howells, William Dean, 25, 44
Huerta, Victoriano, 87, 88
Hughes, Charles Evans, 53, 97, 145, 178, 179, 193
Hughes, Emmet J., 292
Hull, Cordell, 200, 202, 203, 205, 206, 211
Human rights policy, 394–395
Humphrey, Hubert, 319, 334, 335, 344–345, 442
Hungary, 1956 uprising in, 289
Hunt, Richard Morris, 9, 27
Hunter, Robert, 40–41
Hutcheson, Bill, 180

Iacocca, Lee, 422–423
I Am Curious Yellow, 363
Ickes, Harold L., 165, 168, 181, 268–269
Illegal aliens, 412
Immigrants. *See also specific groups*
  domestic servants, 10
  family, 17
  hostility toward, 13, 16, 41–42, 108, 124–125, 234–236
  and melting-pot solution, 12–13
  newest, 412–414, 445
  quotas for, 125, 127, 412
  and religion, 13–14
  unskilled workers, 10
Indian Reorganization Act of 1934, 181–182
Industrial Workers of the World (IWW), 38–39, 109
Industry
  government regulation of, 36, 57–58, 68, 427–428
  growth in 1920s, 120, 121–122, 149
  mergers, 36–37, 57, 58

INDEX **455**

and New Deal legislation, 167–168
and organization man, 306
safety codes for, 54
service, 408, 446
wartime production, 104–105, 230, 231
Inflation, 231, 267, 366–367, 382–383, 389–390, 411, 426
Inland Waterways Commission, 60
Insull, Samuel, 154, 169
International Monetary Fund, 241
Interstate Commerce Commission (ICC), 2, 58, 59, 62
Iran
  hostage crisis in, 398
  Mossadegh coup in, 286–287
  U.S. relations with, 286–287, 396–398
Irish-Americans, 14, 93
Iron Curtain, 252
Israel
  Camp David accords, 396, 431
  invasion of Lebanon, 432
  U.S. relations with, 257, 396, 431–432
Italian-Americans, 125, 126–127, 236, 364
Italy
  Fascist regime in, 201, 202
  in World War II, 219–221, 242
Ives, Charles, 20

Jackson, Henry "Scoop," 394
Jackson, Jesse, 434
Jackson, Joe, 135
Jackson, Robert H., 243
Jacobellis v. *Ohio,* 340
Jagger, Mick, 362
James, Henry, 25
James, William, 2, 22, 34
Japan
  annexation of Korea, 259
  attack on Pearl Harbor, 210–211, 212
  invasion of China, 202
  Manchurian crisis, 198
  in Tripartite Pact, 206

U.S. relations with, 81–83, 85, 193, 202–203, 210, 211–212
in World War II, 222–227, 228
Japanese-Americans, 82, 235–236
Jaworski, Leon, 381
Jazz, 28, 136–137, 142, 310
Jazz Singer, The, 134
Jewett, Sarah Orne, 24
Jews. *See also* Religion
  anti-Semitism, 125
  and Holocaust, 243
  immigrants, 14
  Reform Judaism, 14
  Russian, 394, 395
Jiménez, Meri, 413–414
Job Corps, 333–334
John XXIII, Pope, 415
Johnson, Hiram, 64, 113, 115
Johnson, Hugh S., 168
Johnson, Jack, 20, 135
Johnson, Lyndon B., 292, 319, 325, 371
  background and career of, 332
  election of 1964, 334–336
  Great Society program of, 332–334, 336–338
  and Vietnam War, 341–344
Johnson, Tom L., 36, 51
Johnson Debt Default Act of 1934, 199
Jolson, Al, 134
Jones, James, 311
Jones, Jesse, 174
Jones, Jim, 417
Jones, Samuel M. "Golden Rule," 36, 51
Jones Act of 1916, 73–74, 85
Joplin, Scott, 21, 28
Jordan, Hamilton, 388
Journalism
  mass-market, 24
  muckraking, 32–33, 53

Kantor, MacKinlay, 311
Keating-Owen Child Labor Act, 68
Kefauver, Estes, 278, 285
Kelley, Florence, 44
Kellogg, Frank B., 195, 197
Kellogg-Briand Pact of 1928, 194–195

Kelly, Gene, 309
Kennan, George F., 99, 252, 254
Kennedy, Edward, 398–399
Kennedy, Jacqueline, 320–321
Kennedy, John F., 269, 292
  and Alliance for Progress, 322–323
  assassination of, 331
  background and career of, 319–320
  and Bay of Pigs disaster, 323
  and Berlin crisis, 323–324
  cabinet and staff of, 321–322
  and civil rights, 330–331
  and Congress, 328–329
  and Cuban missile crisis, 324
  election of 1960, 319, 320
  and Laos, 326
  on New Frontier, 322, 328
  and Peace Corps, 323
  social program of, 329–330
  and space program, 325–326
  in trade agreements, 326
  and Vietnam, 326–328
Kennedy, Joseph P., 169, 174, 319–320
Kennedy, Robert F., 321–322, 324, 330, 344
Kent State University, student protest at, 368–369
Kerouac, Jack, 311–312
Kerr, Clark, 360
Kessner, Thomas, 13
Keyes v. *Denver School District,* 391
Keynes, John Maynard, 183, 241
Khanh, Nguyen, 341
Khomeini, Ayatollah, 397–398
Khrushchev, Nikita, 288, 290–291, 323–324
King, Martin Luther, Jr., 304, 344, 346–347
Kinsey, Alfred C., 45
Kirkpatrick, Jeane J., 429, 442–443
Kissinger, Henry, 368
Knowland, William, 286
Knox, Philander C., 57, 83–84
Kolko, Gabriel, 246
Kolko, Joyce, 246
"Koreagate," 390

456 INDEX

Korean War, 259–262, 264, 280
Kristol, Irving, 417
Ku Klux Klan, 127–129
Kurusu, Saburo, 211

Labor. *See* Employment
Labor unions. *See also* Strikes
  decline in 1920s, 150
  Gompers's leadership of, 37–38
  growth of, 181, 230
  legislative controls on, 268
  and New Deal, 176
  in 1900, 37
  and Theodore Roosevelt, 56–57
  for unskilled workers, 179–180
  in World War I, 105
La Follette, Robert M., 53–54, 59,
  60, 64, 66, 98, 113, 149
Lance, Bert, 388, 390
Landis, Kenesaw Mountain, 58,
  135
Landon, Alfred M., 172–178
Lansing, Robert, 93, 293
Laos, U.S. relations with, 326
Laser, 406–407
Latin America. *See also specific*
  countries
  immigrants from, 412–414
  Nelson Rockefeller and, 401
  U.S. relations with
    Alliance for Progress,
     322–323
    colonialism, 72–74
    dollar diplomacy, 83–84
    drug traffic and, 439
    economic aid, 255, 323, 433
    Good Neighbor, 197, 200
    military intervention, 196–197
    and Panama Canal, 78–79,
     396
    Roosevelt Corollary, 79–80,
     197
    and security zone, 205
Lavelle, Rita M., 427–428
League of Nations, 110, 111,
  114–115, 192, 194, 198, 201
League of Women Voters, 305
Leary, Timothy, 359
Lebanon, U.S. relations with, 287,
  431–432, 438

Ledbetter, Huddie, 187
Lemke, William, 178
Lend-lease program, 208–209
Leuchtenburg, William E., 185
Levin, N. Gordon, Jr., 99
Levitt, William, 302
Levittowns, 302
Lewis, John L., 179–180, 230,
  267–268
Lewis, Sinclair, 139–140
Libraries, 23
Libya, U.S. relations with, 432,
  439
Life expectancy, 14–15, 410–411
Lilienthal, David, 252, 253
Lindbergh, Anne Morrow, 214
Lindbergh, Charles A., 122, 206,
  213–214
Lindsey, Ben, 41
Link, Arthur S., 99
Lippmann, Walter, 70, 99
Lipsit, Seymour, 304
Literature
  in Depression, 186–187
  in 1920s, 138–140, 142
  post–World War II, 311–312
  at turn of century, 24–26
  in World War II, 238
Litvinov, Maxim, 200
Lloyd, Henry Demarest, 38
Lochner v. *New York,* 34, 54
Lodge, Henry Cabot, 76, 111,
  113–114, 319, 320
Loeb, Jacques, 22
London, Jack, 25, 42
London Economic Conference of
  1933, 199
Lonely Crowd, The (Riesman),
  306
Long, Huey P. "Kingfish," 175,
  178
Lopez Tijerina, Reies, 351
Low, Seth, 51
Lowden, Frank O., 115
Loyalty program, federal, 270
Ludlow, Louis, 203
Ludlow Massacre, 38
Lukacs, John, 246
Lunderstad, Geir, 246
Lusitania, 95, 96

McAdoo, William G., 104, 149,
  151
MacArthur, Arthur, 73, 75
MacArthur, Douglas, 160, 259,
  260, 262, 264
McCarthy, Eugene, 344
McCarthy, Joseph, 275–276, 284
McClure's magazine, 32
McCutcheon, George Barr, 24
MacDowell, Edward, 20
Macfadden, Bernarr, 18
McGovern, George, 370–371
Machine politics, 49–50
McKim, Mead and White, 27
McKinley, William, 2, 55, 73, 76
McNamara, Robert, 321
McNamee, Graham, 134
McPherson, Aimee Semple, 130
Madero, Francesco I., 87
Mahan, Alfred Thayer, 76
Mailer, Norman, 311
Malenkov, Georgi, 288
Manchuria, Japanese invasion of,
  198
Manhattan Project, 225, 263, 275
Mann-Elkins Act of 1910, 62
Mao Tse-tung, 258, 286, 368
Mapp v. *Ohio,* 340
March on Washington, 346, 376
Marcos, Ferdinand, 440
Marin, John, 137
Marshall, George C., 210, 255,
  258, 275, 284
Marshall, Thurgood, 282
Marshall Plan, 254–255
Masaryk, Jan, 255
Mauldin, Bill, 238
May, Ernest K., 99
Meat Inspection Act of 1906, 59
Medicaid, 336, 338, 411
Medicare, 336, 338, 411
Medicine
  advances in, 407
  computer use in, 406
  education, 22
  and elderly, 411
Meese, Edwin, 438
Mellon, Andrew, 145, 146, 150,
  154, 159, 161–162
Mencken, H. L., 129, 140, 173

INDEX

Meredith, James, 330
Mexican-Americans, 16, 182, 235, 351
Mexico, U.S. relations with, 87–89, 197, 200
Michelson, Albert A., 22
Midway, battle of, 222, 223
Mies van der Rohe, 314
Miller, Thomas W., 147
Miller, William E., 334
Miller v. *California,* 391
Millett, Kate, 354
Millis, Walter, 99, 201
Mining industry, strikes in, 56–57, 230, 267–268
Minorities. *See* Blacks; Immigrants; *specific groups*
Miranda v. *Arizona,* 340, 391
Mission to Moscow, 238, 276
Mitchel, John Purroy, 51
Mitchell, John, 364, 373
Mitchell, Margaret, 187
Model Cities Act of 1966, 337
Mohammed Riza Pahlevi, shah of Iran, 286–287, 395, 396–397, 398
Moley, Raymond, 165, 178, 185
Molotov, Vyacheslav, 249
Mondale, Walter, 334–335, 436
Monroe Doctrine, Roosevelt Corollary to, 80, 197, 200
Montessori, Maria, 23
Montevideo Inter-American Conference of 1933, 200
Montgomery bus boycott, 304–305
Moody Bible Institute of Chicago, 14, 129
Moon, Sung Myung, 417
Moral Majority, 416–417, 428–429
Morgan, J. P., 36, 57, 60, 67, 93, 206
Morgan, Thomas Hunt, 22
Morgenthau, Henry, Jr., 165
Moroccan crisis of 1905–1906, 83
Morrow, Dwight W., 197, 214
Moskowitz, Belle, 132
Mossadegh, Mohammed, 286–287

Movies
  and congressional investigation, 276–277
  in Depression, 188
  in 1900, 21–22
  in 1920s, 134, 141
  in 1960s, 363
  in World War II, 237
  post–World War II, 309
Moynihan, Daniel Patrick, 366
Mrs. Miniver, 237
Mubarak, Hosni, 431
Muckrakers, 32–33, 53
Muhammad, Elijah, 350
Muir, John, 60
Muller, Hermann J., 22
Muller v. *Oregon,* 54, 69
Munich agreement, 204
Munsey, Frank, 64
Murphy, Charles F., 52
Murphy, Frank, 180
Murray, Bill "Alfalfa," 53
Murray-Patman Act of 1942, 231
Music
  in Depression, 187
  of 1920s, 136–137
  of 1960s, 361–363, 375–376
  post–World War II, 310–311
  at turn of century, 20–21, 28
Muskie, Edmund, 345
Mussolini, Benito, 198, 201, 220–221

Nagasaki, bombing of, 225, 226–227
Nagy, Imre, 289
National Aeronautics and Space Administration (NASA), 289
National American Woman Suffrage Association (NAWSA), 45
National Association for the Advancement of Colored People (NAACP), 44, 282–283, 304
National Broadcasting Company (NBC), 134
National Guard, 76
National Housing Act of 1934, 171
National Industrial Recovery Act (NIRA), 167–168, 175

National Labor Relations Act (Wagner Act), 176, 179
National Labor Relations Board (NLRB), 176
National Organization for Women (NOW), 353
National Origins Act of 1924, 125
National Recovery Administration (NRA), 167, 168
National Security Act of 1947, 269
National Velvet, 237
National Women's Party, 45
Native Americans, 16, 181–182, 351–352
Nativists, 41–42, 125–126
Naval War College, 76, 77
Navy
  disarmament, 192–194
  expansion of, 76–77
  in wartime, 100, 222–223
Nelson, Donald, 229
Neoconservatism, 417
Neustadt, Richard, 292
Neutrality Acts of 1935–1937, 202
Newberry, William, 23
New Deal
  assessment of, 183–185
  and banking crisis, 166, 169
  and Blacks, 181
  end of, 182–183
  farm program of, 166–167, 176
  financial reforms of, 169, 176
  First, 165–175
  industrial program of, 167–168
  and labor, 176, 179, 181
  and minorities, 181–182
  newness of, 164
  opposition to, 171, 173–175, 183, 189–190, 240
  and public power, 169–170, 176
  relief measures of, 170–171, 177
  Second, 175–177
  Supreme Court decisions on, 168, 175, 176, 178, 179
New Federalism, 365–366, 428
Newlands Act of 1902, 60
New Left, 350
New Nationalism, 63, 65–66
New Right, 418

458   INDEX

New York City, federal loans to, 384
Nicaragua, U.S. relations with, 78, 83–84, 86, 197, 433, 439
Nickelodeon, 21
Niebuhr, Reinhold, 306–307
Nine-Power Treaty, 193, 198
Nixon, Richard M., 269, 299, 435
  background and career of, 319
  Checkers speech of, 278–279
  crusade against dissidents, 364
  economic policy of, 366–367
  election of 1960, 318–319, 320, 402
  election of 1968, 344–345
  election of 1972, 370–371
  Ford's pardon of, 381
  foreign policy of, 367–368
  and Hiss case, 274
  New Federalism of, 365–366
  and presidential powers, 371–372
  and press, 372–373, 374
  and Vietnam War, 368–370
  and Watergate affair, 373–375
Nock, Albert Jay, 173
Nomura, Kichisaburo, 211
Norris, Frank, 25
Norris, George W., 63, 98, 150, 169
North Africa, Allied invasion of, 219
North Atlantic Treaty Organization (NATO), 256, 288
Northern Securities Co. v. *United States,* 57–58
Novak, Michael, 417
NSC-68 report, 258–259
Nuclear energy, and Three Mile Island disaster, 388
Nuremberg trials, 243
Nye, Gerald P., 201

O'Connor, Carroll, 364
O'Connor, Sandra Day, 429
Odets, Clifford, 186
Office of Economic Opportunity (OEO), 333
Office of Price Administration (OPA), 231, 267

Oil. *See* Petroleum
O'Keeffe, Georgia, 137
Oldenburg, Claes, 363
Older, Fremont, 51
Olson, Floyd, 171
O'Neill, William L., 292
Open Door policy, 75–76, 83, 84, 193, 257
Oppenheimer, J. Robert, 263–264
Organic Act of 1902, 73
Organization Man, The (Whyte), 306
Organization of Petroleum Exporting Countries (OPEC), 367, 389
Organ transplants, 407
Osgood, Robert E., 99
Oswald, Lee Harvey, 331

Paige, Satchell, 136
Palestine Liberation Organization (PLO), 431–432
Palmer, A. Mitchell, 124
Panama
  canal treaty with, 396
  independence of, 79
Panama Canal, 78–79, 86, 396
Park, Tongsun, 390
Parker, Alton B., 58
Parks, Rosa, 304
Patton, George S., 242–243
Paul, Alice, 45
Pauley, Edwin, 268
Pauncefote, Sir Julian, 78
Payne-Aldrich tariff, 62, 84
Peace Corps, 323
Peale, Norman Vincent, 307, 315–316
Pearl Harbor, Japanese attack on, 210–211, 212
Penal reform, 41
Pendergast, James, 49
Pentagon Papers, 373
Perkins, Frances, 165
Perkins, George W., 64
Permanent Court of Arbitration, 85
Pershing, John J., 88, 101, 116–117, 242

Pétain, Henri Philippe, 205
Petroleum
  glut, 427
  rising price of, 367
  shortage of, 389
Philippines
  independence of, 72–74
  opposition to Marcos, 440
  in World War II, 223–225
Phillips, David Graham, 53
Pickford, Mary, 134
Pinchot, Gifford, 60, 63, 64, 69
Planned Parenthood Federation of America, 46
Platt Amendment of 1901, 74, 81
Plessy v. *Ferguson,* 15, 283
Plunkitt, George Washington, 49
Poetry in 1920s, 142
Poland
  Nazi invasion of, 204
  1956 uprising in, 289
  and postwar settlement, 228, 250
  Solidarity movement in, 430
  Soviet invasion of, 205
Pollock, Jackson, 312
Pop art, 363
Popular culture
  movies, 21–22, 134, 141, 188, 237, 276–277, 309
  music, 20–21, 28, 136–137, 310–311
  radio, 134, 187–188, 307
  recreation and amusements, 18–22, 133–136, 187–188, 237
  sports, 19–20, 135–136, 237, 309–310
  television, 307–309
Population
  aging of, 410–411
  birthrate, 17, 133, 297, 299–300, 409–410
  divorce rate, 17, 44–45, 133, 232, 355–356, 420
  geographic shifts in, 408
  life expectancy, 14–15, 410–411
Pornography, 340, 363, 391
Porter, Katherine Anne, 107

INDEX **459**

Potsdam Conference, 228, 250–251
Poverty, 420, 446
Powers, Gary Francis, 291
Power utilities, 121, 150, 169–170, 176, 281
Prange, Gordon W., 211
Pratt, Enoch, 23
Presidential elections
  1904, 58
  1908, 61, 62
  1912, 65–66
  1916, 96–97
  1920, 115
  1924, 148–149
  1928, 151–152
  1932, 160, 162
  1936, 177–178
  1940, 208–209
  1944, 238–239
  1948, 270–272
  1952, 277–279
  1956, 284–285
  1960, 319, 320
  1964, 334–336
  1968, 344–345
  1972, 370–371
  1976, 385, 386–387
  1980, 398–400
  1984, 434–436
  party affiliation and, 266
  religion issue in, 151–152, 319
  voting age in, 341
Presley, Elvis, 311
Price control, 267, 366, 383
Princip, Gavrilo, 92
Progressive party, 149
Progressivism
  achievements of, 70
  black leaders, 42–44
  and business regulation, 36–37, 57–59, 68
  in city government, 49–52
  defined, 31–32
  and humanitarian reform, 39–41
  and intellectuals, 33–35
  and labor, 37–38, 56–57
  and muckrakers, 32–33, 53
  and social control, 41–42

and Social Gospel movement, 35–36
  and socialism, 37–38
  in state government, 52–54
  of Theodore Roosevelt, 56–61
  and women, 44–47
  of Woodrow Wilson, 66–68, 70
Prohibition, 130–132
Protestantism. *See also* Religion
  Fundamentalists, 129, 130, 416–417, 428–429
  rifts in, 14
  and Scopes trial, 129–130
  Social Gospel movement, 35–36
Psychology in 1920s, 133
Public Utility Holding Company Act of 1935, 176
Public Works Administration (PWA), 168, 171, 183
Public Works and Economic Development Act of 1965, 336
Puerto Rico, 74, 85
Pujo, Arsène, 67
Pulitzer, Joseph, 24
Pure Food and Drug Act, 59
Pyle, Ernie, 238

Qaddafi, Muammar al, 432, 439
Quemoy-Matsu crisis, 286

Race. *See* Blacks; Civil rights laws; Civil rights movement
Radio, 134, 187–188, 307
Ragtime, 21, 28
Railroads
  regulation of, 58–59
  strikes, 267, 268
Randolph, A. Philip, 234
Rankin, Jeanette, 98
Rauschenbusch, Walter, 36
Rayburn, Sam, 238, 329
Reagan, Ronald, 385, 393, 396, 442, 443
  and arms control, 431, 438
  background and career of, 399
  and civil rights, 429
  deregulation by, 427–428
  economic policy of, 425–427, 437
  election of 1980, 399–400

election of 1984, 434–436
  invasion of Grenada, 434
  judicial appointments of, 437–438
  and Latin America, 432–434, 439–440
  and Middle East, 431–432, 438–439
  military buildup by, 430–431, 438
  and Moral Majority, 428–429
  and Philippines, 440
  popularity of, 426, 441
  and South Africa, 440–441
  and Soviet Union, 430–431, 438
  and tax reform, 436
Reaganomics, 425–427
Rebel Without a Cause, 309, 311
Reconstruction Finance Corporation (RFC), 158–159
Recreation and amusements
  in 1900, 18–22
  in 1920s, 120, 133–137
  postwar, 307–311
  in World War II, 237
Red Scare, 123–125
Reed, Walter, 22
Regan, Donald, 425
Regents of the University of California v. *Bakke,* 391–392
Regional Trade Agreements Act of 1934, 200
Rehnquist, William, 438
Reich, Charles, 356–357
Religion. *See also* Catholic Church; Jews; Protestantism
  and abortion protest, 404, 416, 417
  cults, 417
  and immigrants, 13–14
  in postwar period, 307, 315–316
  as presidential campaign issue, 151–152, 319
  school prayer issue, 340–341, 391
  and social activism, 414
Republican party. *See also* Congress; Elections, congressional; Presidential elections

460　　INDEX

Republican party (*Continued*)
  in conservative coalition,
    328–329
  and Eisenhower, 284
  post-Watergate, 382
  and Taft-Progressive split,
    63–64
Resettlement Administration (RA),
  176
Revenue acts
  1921, 146
  1926, 150
  1928, 150
  1935, 176
Rhee, Syngman, 259, 262
Richardson, Eliot, 374
Richardson, Elmo, 292
Riesman, David, 306
Riis, Jacob, 12, 13
Rinehart, Ruth H., 172–173
Roberts, Owen J., 178
Robinson, Jackie, 136, 310
Robinson, James Harvey, 35
Robinson, Joel, 151
Rockefeller, John D., 41, 58, 124,
  149, 401
Rockefeller, Nelson, 318,
  381–382, 401–402
Rock music, 310–311, 361–363
Rockne, Knute, 135
Roe v. *Wade,* 391
Rodgers, Richard, 310
Rolling Stones, 362
Rome-Berlin Axis of 1936, 198,
  201, 205
Roosevelt, Eleanor, 181, 182, 184
Roosevelt, Franklin D., 115, 232,
  234, 236, 241, 371, 395. *See
  also* New Deal
  background and career of, 160
  Brains Trust of, 165
  court-packing plan of, 178–179
  declaration of war, 213
  election of 1932, 160, 162
  election of 1936, 177–178
  election of 1940, 206–208
  election of 1944, 238–239
  fireside chats of, 166
  foreign policy of, 199, 200,
    202, 206, 208–210, 247, 248
  and Manhattan Project, 225

  at wartime conferences, 227,
    228, 248
Roosevelt, Theodore, 18, 27, 32,
  36, 41, 42, 73, 90, 96, 97,
  115, 116–117
  achievements of, 60–61
  and business trusts, 57–58
  career of, 55
  conservation policy of, 59–60
  election of 1904, 58
  election of 1908, 60–61
  election of 1912, 64, 65–66
  food/drug regulation by, 59
  foreign policy of, 77–83, 117
  and labor unions, 56–57
  and naval expansion, 76–77
  New Nationalism of, 63, 65–66
  and Panama Canal, 78–79
  personality of, 55–56
  railroad regulation by, 58–59
  Square Deal of, 56
Roosevelt Corollary, to Monroe
  Doctrine, 80, 197, 200
Root, Elihu, 74, 76, 85, 89–90
Root, John W., 27
Root-Takahira Agreement of 1908,
  83, 84
Rosenberg, Ethel, 275
Rosenberg, Julius, 275
Ross, Edward A., 41
Ross, Nellie, 132
Rossiter, Clinton, 418
Rostow, Walt, 321
Roth v. *United States,* 340, 391
Ruby, Jack, 331
Ruckelshaus, William, 374
Ruef, Abe, 51
Rural Electrification Administration
  (REA), 176
Rusk, Dean, 321
Russo-Japanese War, 75, 78, 81,
  117
Ruth, George Herman "Babe,"
  19, 135–136

Sacco, Nicola, 124–125
Sadat, Anwar, 396, 431
St. Valentine's Day Massacre,
  131
Salinger, J. D., 311
Salk, Jonas, 407

SALT agreements, 368, 394,
  395–396, 431, 438
Sandinistas, 433, 439
Sandino, Augusto, 197
Sanger, Margaret, 45, 46
Satellites, communication, 406
Saudi Arabia, arms sales to, 431
Scalia, Antonin, 438
Schechter v. *United States,* 168
Schlafly, Phyllis, 418
Schlesinger, Arthur M., Jr., 184–
  185, 246, 292, 321, 328, 370
School(s). *See also* Education
  busing, 338, 429
  desegregation, 282–284, 391
  prayer, 340–341, 391
Schweiker, Richard, 385
Science and technology, 22,
  405–407
Scopes, John Thomas, 130
Seagram Building, New York City,
  314
Securities Exchange Act of 1934,
  169
Securities Exchange Commission
  (SEC), 169
Sedition Act of 1918, 108
Seidel, Emil, 51
Selective Service Act of 1918,
  100–101
Settlement houses, 39–40
Sexual Politics (Millett), 354
Sexual revolution
  end of, 420
  in 1920s, 132–133
  in 1960s, 354–356, 359–360
Share Our Wealth Society, 175
Shaw, Anna Howard, 45
Sheeler, Charles, 137
Sherman Antitrust Act, 2, 57, 68,
  168
Shirer, William L., 237
Shotwell, James T., 194–195
Shriver, Sargent, 323, 333, 371,
  385
Shuping, Ralph, 224–225
Simmons, William J., 127
Sims, William S., 100
Sinclair, Harry F., 147
Sinclair, Upton, 59, 171
Sister Carrie (Dreiser), 15

INDEX

461

Skidmore, Owings, and Merrill, 314

Smith, Alfred E. "Al," 129, 132, 149, 151–152, 160, 174, 178

Smith, Gerald L. K., 178

Smith, Hoke, 53

Smith, Howard, 329

Smith, Jesse, 147

Smith Act of 1940, 206

Social class. *See* Class

Social Gospel movement, 36

Socialist party, 38–39, 171, 173

Social Security, 177, 271, 281, 336, 410–411

Somoza, Anastasio, 197, 433

Sound and the Fury, The (Faulkner), 140

Sousa, John Philip, 20

South Africa, U.S. relations with, 440–441

Southeast Asian Treaty Organization (SEATO), 286

Soviet Union
  Berlin blockade by, 255–256
  and Eastern Europe, 250, 255, 289, 290, 293, 324, 393
  German invasion of, 209
  leadership changes in, 430
  pact with Hitler, 204, 205
  at Potsdam Conference, 250–251
  space program of, 289, 325
  in United Nations, 241, 249–250
  U.S. relations with
    arms control, 252–253, 326, 368, 394, 395–396, 431, 438
    arms race, 253, 288, 289, 290
    containment policy, 252
    Cuban missile crisis, 324
    détente, 368, 393–394
    John Foster Dulles in, 293–294
    in 1920s, 196, 199–200
    NSC-68 report on, 258–259
    under Reagan, 429–430, 438
    roots of Cold War, 246, 247
    summit meetings, 288–289, 291, 323–324, 438
    Truman Doctrine, 254
    U-2 incident, 291

wartime alliance, 247–248, 251
  at Yalta Conference, 228, 248

Space
  Apollo 11, 325–326
  Sputnik, 289
  Strategic Defense Initiative (SDI), 431, 438

Spanish Civil War, 201, 202

· Sparkman, John J., 278

Sports
  in 1900, 19–20
  in 1920s, 135–136
  postwar, 309–310
  in World War II, 237

Spreckels, Rudolph, 51

Sputnik, 289

Square Deal, 56

Stalin, Joseph, 227, 228, 247, 250, 251, 252, 288

Standard Oil, 58

Stanton, Elizabeth Cady, 45

"Star Wars" (Strategic Defense Initiative), 431, 438

States
  legislative reapportionment in, 339
  and New Federalism, 365–366, 428
  progressive reform in, 52–54

Steel industry
  Kennedy and, 329
  strikes in, 123, 180, 273
  trusts, 36–37
  unionization of, 180

Steffens, Lincoln, 50, 51

Stein, Gertrude, 138

Steinbeck, John, 157, 186, 238, 311

Stella, Joseph, 137

Stennis, John, 374

Stephenson, David, 128

Stevenson, Adlai, 278, 279, 285

Stimson, Henry L., 198

Stimson Doctrine, 198

Stockman, David, 425

Stock market crash, 154–155

Stoddard, Lothrop, 42, 125

Strategic Arms Limitation Treaty (SALT) agreements, 368, 394, 395–396, 431, 438

Strategic Arms Reduction Talks (START), 431

Strategic Defense Initiative (SDI) "Star Wars," 431, 438

Strikes
  Ludlow Massacre, 38
  mine workers, 56–57, 267–268
  in 1919, 123
  in 1946, 267–268
  sit-down, 180
  steel workers, 123, 180, 273
  wartime arbitration of, 105

Strong, Josiah, 36

Student Non-violent Coordinating Committee (SNCC), 351

Student protest, 360, 368–369, 421, 441

Students for a Democratic Society (SDS), 360

Suburbs, development of, 8, 301–302

Suez crisis, 287

Sullivan, Louis H., 2, 27, 29, 137

Sumner, William Graham, 33

Sunbelt, rise of, 408

Sunday, Billy, 14, 130

Supply-side economics, 425–426

Supreme Court
  Brandeis on, 68, 69
  Burger Court, 390–392
  decisions
    on abortion, 391
    on business trusts, 57–58
    on due process, 340, 391
    on espionage/sedition acts, 110
    on First Amendment rights, 340–341
    on labor issues, 34, 38, 54, 150, 273
    on New Deal legislation, 168, 175, 176, 178, 179
    on race relations, 15, 282–283, 3304–305, 338, 391–392
    on reapportionment, 339
  Nixon appointments to, 366
  -packing plan, 178–179
  Reagan appointments to, 438
  Warren Court, 338–341, 391

Symington, Stuart, 319

462　　　　　　　　　　　　　　　　　　　　　　　　　　　　　　　　　　INDEX

Taft, Robert A., 207, 255, 277
Taft, William Howard, 42, 66, 73, 77, 90, 114
  career of, 61–62
  conservatism of, 62
  dollar diplomacy of, 83–84
  election of 1908, 61–62
  election of 1912, 64–66
  and Progressive split, 62–64
  treaties of, 84–85
Taft-Pⁱⁱey Act of 1947, 268, 272
Taft-Katsura Agreement of 1905, 81
Taiwan (Formosa), 286, 368
Tansill, Charles C., 210
Tarbell, Ida, 32
Tariffs
  Fordney-McCumber, 146, 151
  Hawley-Smoot, 158
  most-favored-nation clause in, 200
  Payne-Aldrich, 62, 84
  Underwood-Simmons, 66
Tax
  reduction, 425–426
  reform, 436
Tax Reform Act of 1986, 436
Taylor, Frederick Winslow, 34
Taylor, Maxwell D., 328
Teapot Dome scandal, 147
Teheran Conference of 1943, 227
Television, 307–310, 445–446
Teller Amendment of 1898, 74
Tenement house reform, 40
Tennessee Valley Authority (TVA), 169–170, 281
terHorst, Gerald, 381
Test ban treaty, 326
Thayer, Webster, 125
Theater, 142
Thieu, Nguyen Van, 342, 369–370
Third World, 392
Thomas, Norman, 171, 178
Three Mile Island disaster, 388
Thurmond, Strom, 270
Tillman, Ben, 42
Tojo, Hideki, 211
Toland, John, 210
Townsend, Francis E., 174–175, 178

Trade. *See also* Tariffs
  agreements, 326
  deficits, 437
Trefousse, Hans L., 211
Trade Expansion Act of 1962, 326
Traffic Safety Act of 1966, 337
Tregaskis, Richard, 238
Triangle Shirtwaist Company, 54
Trujillo, Rafael Leonidas, 197
Truman, Harry S, 209, 230, 238, 293, 298, 401
  and Berlin airlift, 256
  and cabinet opposition, 268–269
  career of, 248–249
  and civil rights, 269
  and Congress, 268, 269, 271, 272
  decision to bomb Japan, 226–227
  election of 1948, 270–272
  Fair Deal program of, 272
  federal loyalty program of, 270
  and Korean War, 260–262, 264
  and labor unions, 267–268, 273
  and McCarthy investigations, 275–276
  and Marshall Plan, 254–255
  personality of, 270
  at Potsdam conference, 250–251
  recognition of Israel, 257
  scandals of administration, 272
  and Soviet Union, 249, 250, 251, 252, 254, 259
  support for Chiang Kai-shek, 257–258
  Truman Doctrine, 254
  and wage/price controls, 267
Tugwell, Rexford Guy, 164, 165, 176
Tunney, Gene, 135
Tuskegee Institute, 16, 22
Twain, Mark, 24

U-boats, 94–95, 100, 209, 210
Udall, Morris, 385
Underwood, Oscar W., 65
Underwood-Simmons tariff, 66
Unemployment
  in Great Depression, 155–156

  New Deal program for, 170–171, 177
  in Rust Belt, 408, 426–427
United Auto Workers (UAW), 180
United Mine Workers (UMW), 56–57, 179, 230, 267
United Nations, 241, 249–250, 443
United States Steel, 36–37, 60, 64, 179, 329
United States v. *Butler,* 176
United States v. *Calandra,* 391
United States v. *Robinson,* 391
Universal Negro Improvement Association (UNIA), 129
Urban Development Act of 1966, 337
U-2 incident, 291

Valentino, Rudolph, 134, 141
Vallee, Rudy, 134
Vandenberg, Arthur H., 207, 254
Vanderbilt, William K., 9
Van Devanter, Willis, 179
Vanzetti, Bartolomeo, 124–125
Vatican II, 415–416
Vaudeville, 20
Vaughn, Harry, 272
Veblen, Thorstein, 33–34
Veiller, Lawrence, 40
Venezuela, U.S. relations with, 79
Videocassette recorder (VCR), 406
Vietnam
  American evacuation from, 394
  Communist movement of, 326–327
  Vietminh uprising in, 285
Vietnam War
  American involvement in, 328, 341–344
  American withdrawal from, 369–370
  opposition to, 343, 344, 347, 360, 364, 368–369, 376
  Vietnamization program in, 368
Villa, Francisco "Pancho," 88
Villard, Oswald Garrison, 44
Volcker, Paul A., 427
Volunteers in Service to America (VISTA), 334

INDEX

Voting rights
  act of 1965, 366, 429
  constitutional amendments, 341

Wagner, Robert F., 176, 179
Wagner Act, 176, 179
Wald, Lillian, 40
Wallace, George, 345, 370
Wallace, Henry A., 165, 166, 207, 238, 254, 255, 269
Wallace, Henry C., 145
Walsh, Thomas J., 147
Ward, Lester Frank, 34
War Food Administration, 229
Warhol, Andy, 363
War Manpower Commission, 229
War on Poverty, 333–334, 336
War Powers Act of 1973, 393
War Production Board (WPB), 229
Warren, Earl, 283, 331, 338–341, 366
Washington, Booker T., 16, 42, 44
Washington Naval Conference, 193
Wasteland, The (Eliot), 142
Watergate affair, 373–375
Watson, James D., 407
Watson, John B., 133
Watson, Thomas A., 174
Watt, James, 428
Weather Underground, 359
Weinstein, Edwin A., 99–100
Welles, Orson, 188
Wells, H. G., 188
West Germany, in NATO alliance, 288. *See also* Berlin
Westmoreland, William, 342
Wharton, Edith, 15, 25–26
Wheeler, Burton K., 149, 209
White, William Allen, 66, 205–206
White-Anglo-Saxon-Protestant (WASP) establishment, 14, 236
Whiteman, Paul, 137
Whyte, William H., Jr., 306
Wickersham, George C., 63
Wiley, Harvey, 59
Wilhelm II, kaiser, 83
Willard, Frances, 41

Willard, Jess, 135
Williams, William Appleman, 99, 246
Williams v. *Mississippi,* 15
Willkie, Wendell, 207, 238–239
Wilson, Henry Lane, 87
Wilson, Sloan, 311
Wilson, Woodrow, 45, 53, 77, 140, 247, 293, 395
  background and career of, 65
  banking/currency reforms of, 67–68
  and business trusts, 68
  election of 1912, 65, 66
  election of 1916, 96–97
  foreign policy ideals of, 86–87
  and League of Nations, 111, 112, 114, 115
  and Mexico, 87–89
  New Freedom of, 65–66
  personality of, 66
  and tariff revision, 66–67
  and World War I, 93–96, 97–100, 110–115
WIN campaign, 383
Wisconsin, La Follette reforms in, 53–54
Wise, Isaac Mayer, 14
Wister, Owen, 24
Wobblies, 38–39, 109. *See also* Industrial Workers of the World (IWW)
Wohlstetter, Roberta, 211
Wolfe, Thomas, 140
Women
  Equal Rights Amendment (ERA), 45, 305, 353, 429
  job discrimination, 15, 44, 132, 305, 353
  legal rights of, 15
  liberation movement, 305, 352–354, 355, 409
  ''new woman'' of 1920s, 132–133
  in 1900, 14–15
  and progressive reform, 44–47
  Reagan appointments of, 429, 442–443
  and sexual revolution, 133, 355
  suffrage for, 45, 68, 97

  in wartime, 105–106, 233
  and work hazards, 54
Women's Christian Temperance Union (WCTU), 41
Women's International Feminist Conspiracy from Hell (WITCH), 353
Wood, Grant, 188
Wood, Leonard, 74, 115
Wood, Robert E., 206
Woodrow Wilson Foundation, 194
Woods, Robert, 40
Works Progress Administration (WPA), 177
World Bank, 241
World Court, 194
World's Columbian Exposition, 20, 28
World War I
  American entry into, 97–100
  American neutrality in, 93, 94–96
  civil liberties in, 108–109
  costs of, 92–93, 103, 115–116
  financing, 107
  land war, 100–103, 117
  loans to allies, 93–94
  outbreak of, 92
  peace treaty in, 110–115
  public opinion in, 107–108
  reparations and war debts in, 195–196
  sea war, 94–95, 100
  veterans of, 159–160
  war effort in, 104–105
World War II
  American entry into, 213
  American neutrality in, 204–206, 208–210
  attack on Pearl Harbor, 210–211, 212
  economic mobilization in, 229–230
  European theater, 217–222
  financing, 230
  Holocaust in, 243
  inflation control during, 231
  outbreak of, 203–204
  Pacific theater, 220–221, 222–227

World War II (*Continued*)
  recreation and amusements during, 237–238
  shortages during, 230–231
  summit meetings, 227–229, 250–251
  treatment of minorities during, 234–236
  veterans' benefits, 240
  war effort in, 231–232
Wright, Frank Lloyd, 29, 137, 315

Wright, Orville, 18, 122
Wright, Richard, 177, 186, 238
Wright, Wilbur, 18, 122
Wyeth, Andrew, 312–313

Yalta Conference, 228, 248
Yankee Doodle Dandy, 237
Yates v. *United States,* 340
Yerkes, Charles T., 51
Young, Andrew, 395
Young, Owen D., 195

Youth
  counterculture of 1960s, 349, 356–360
  cult of 1920s, 132
Yugoslavia, 220, 392–393
Yuppies, 419–420

Zangwill, Israel, 12
Zanuck, Darryl, 237
Zapata, Emiliano, 88
Ziegfeld, Florenz, 20
Zimmermann Telegram, 97, 98